MW01099043

Resolving Conflicts in the Law

Resolving Conflicts in the Law

Essays in Honour of Lea Brilmayer

Edited by

Chiara Giorgetti
Natalie Klein

BRILL
NIJHOFF

LEIDEN | BOSTON

Library of Congress Cataloging-in-Publication Data

Names: Brilmayer, Lea, honouree. | Giorgetti, Chiara, editor. |
    Klein, Natalie (Natalie S.), editor.
Title: Resolving conflicts in the law : essays in honour of Lea Brilmayer /
    edited by Chiara Giorgetti, Richmond Law School; Natalie Klein, UNSW
    Sydney Faculty of Law.
Description: Leiden ; Boston : Brill/Nijhoff, 2019. |
    Includes bibliographical references.
Identifiers: LCCN 2018053300 (print) | LCCN 2018056071 (ebook) |
    ISBN 9789004316539 (ebook) | ISBN 9789004316522 (hardback : alk. paper)
Subjects: LCSH: Conflict of laws. | Dispute resolution (Law) | Brilmayer, Lea.
Classification: LCC K7040 (ebook) | LCC K7040 .R47 2019 (print) |
    DDC 340.9—dc23
LC record available at https://lccn.loc.gov/2018053300

Typeface for the Latin, Greek, and Cyrillic scripts: "Brill". See and download: brill.com/brill-typeface.

ISBN 978-90-04-31652-2 (hardback)
ISBN 978-90-04-31653-9 (e-book)

Copyright 2019 by Koninklijke Brill NV, Leiden, The Netherlands.
Koninklijke Brill NV incorporates the imprints Brill, Brill Hes & De Graaf, Brill Nijhoff, Brill Rodopi,
Brill Sense, Hotei Publishing, mentis Verlag, Verlag Ferdinand Schöningh and Wilhelm Fink Verlag.
All rights reserved. No part of this publication may be reproduced, translated, stored in a retrieval system,
or transmitted in any form or by any means, electronic, mechanical, photocopying, recording or otherwise,
without prior written permission from the publisher.
Authorization to photocopy items for internal or personal use is granted by Koninklijke Brill NV provided
that the appropriate fees are paid directly to The Copyright Clearance Center, 222 Rosewood Drive,
Suite 910, Danvers, MA 01923, USA. Fees are subject to change.

This book is printed on acid-free paper and produced in a sustainable manner.

Contents

Acknowledgements

It was a great pleasure to work on this book, for many reasons. Most of all we are happy to have had the opportunity to celebrate our wonderful friend and mentor, Lea—even if this book may not have been the way she wanted us to show our respect and admiration for her! Ultimately, it reflects only one dimension of our relationship and sits with many rich and wonderful memories. We are also very grateful for the efforts of the many contributors to this book: it was an honor and privilege to work with you all.

For us, and we imagine for many of those who know Lea, it is impossible to celebrate her many achievements without also acknowledging the enduring support of Bill Horne, throughout her entire career and for over 40 years. We are also particularly grateful for his insights and advice in the preparation of this book for Lea.

Our thanks to all who helped with the process of bringing this volume to fruition. We have benefitted from the editorial assistance of several people, including Jason Zarin, masterful librarian at Richmond Law School, and the Richmond Law students who helped us finalize the manuscript: Andrew Abraham, Phillip Grubbs, Abigail Parsons, Paula Roberts, Rebecca Schultz, and Yanie Yuan, as well as UNSW law student, Jessie Zhang. At Yale Law School, we are grateful to Barbara Mianzo. Our publisher, Brill, embodied in this case by Marie Sheldon, has been as helpful and supportive as can be.

Natalie and Chiara

A keen word of thanks to Natalie, for making this project an enjoyable and thoroughly rewarding one, she is amazingly responsive, smart and always good-humored. She really is one of a kind. I remember that sixteen years ago, I took over her apartment in New Haven, as she left Yale and I arrived. It has been just wonderful to reconnect and work together on this project. As always, my deepest love and gratitude to Andre, and to Charlotte and Alexander, for being there.

CG

And my sincere thanks to Chiara, who made sure that this idea actually came to fruition—many of us are better off because of her efforts and generous nature. I would also like to acknowledge the University of Edinburgh, which provided a wonderful environment for working on this book during my time as a MacCormick Fellow. My thanks as always to Matthew, Dulcie, Tessa and Joshua for their ongoing love, support and (most days) understanding.

NK

Professor Lea Brilmayer: Biographical Note

Lea Brilmayer is the Howard Holtzmann Professor of International Law at Yale Law School. She has also taught as a visiting professor or full time faculty at the law schools at Chicago, Texas, Harvard, Columbia, and New York University. Her main teaching interests are conflict of laws, international law, civil procedure, contracts, and African legal affairs. She has written dozens of articles on those subjects, and several books about international jurisprudence (including *Justifying International Acts* and *American Hegemony: Political Morality in a One Superpower World*). Her books on jurisdiction include *Conflict of Laws: Cases and Materials* (2d through 8th editions, co-authored, 2015); *An Introduction to Jurisdiction in the American Federal System; Conflict of Laws: Foundations and Future Directions* (1991); and *Conflict of Laws* (*Introduction to Law Series*) (co-author, 1995). Her most recent book is a path-breaking survey of international claims commissions, *International Claims Commissions: Righting Wrongs after Conflict*, with Chiara Giorgetti and Lorraine Charlton. Other edited collections and co-authored works include: *Global Justice* (co-editor, 1999); *Rethinking Food Systems: Structural Challenges, New Strategies and the Law* (co-editor, 2014).

Professor Brilmayer has had extensive experience as a consultant in conflict of laws and private international law. She has also served as lead attorney in several important public international law arbitrations dealing with boundary issues (Eritrea v. Yemen and Ethiopia v. Eritrea); maritime delimitation (Eritrea v. Yemen) and civil compensation for violations of the laws of war (Eritrea v. Ethiopia). Her current research interests center around the use of international litigation as a tool for the pursuit of international justice.

Lea Brilmayer
Courtesy of Yale Law School

Professor Lea Brilmayer: Selected Publications

1 Books

International Law/Relations

Justifying International Acts (1989, Cornell University Press)

American Hegemony: Political Morality in a One-Superpower World (1996, Yale Univ. Press)

Global Justice (co-editor) (1999, New York Univ. Press)

Rethinking Food Systems: Structural Challenges, New Strategies and the Law (co-editor) (2014, Springer)

International Claims Commissions Righting Wrongs After Conflict (co-author) (2017, Elgar Publishing)

Conflict of Laws/Civil Procedure

An Introduction to Jurisdiction in the American Federal System (co-author) (1986)

Conflict of Laws: Foundations and Future Directions (2d ed. 1991)

Conflict of Laws (*Introduction to Law Series*) (1995)

Conflicts of Laws: Cases and Materials (co-author) (3rd–7th editions, Aspen) (2015)

2 Articles

International Law/Relations

Res Judicata and Multi-State Integration, 80 MICHIGAN LAW REVIEW 892 (1983)

International Remedies, 14 YALE JOURNAL OF INTERNATIONAL LAW 579 (1989)

Secession and Self-Determination: A Territorial Interpretation, 16 YALE JOURNAL OF INTERNATIONAL LAW 177 (1991)

International Law in American Courts: A Modest Proposal, 100 YALE LAW JOURNAL 2277 (1991)

The Odd Advantage of Reliable Enemies, 32 HARVARD INTERNATIONAL LAW JOURNAL 331 (1991)

Groups, Histories, and the International Law, 25 CORNELL INTERNATIONAL LAW JOURNAL 555 (1992)

Trade Policy: The Normative Dimension, 25 NEW YORK UNIVERSITY JOURNAL OF INTERNATIONAL LAW AND POLITICS 211 (1993)

Federalism, State Authority, and the Preemptive Power of International Law, 1994 SUPREME COURT REVIEW 295

What's the Matter with Selective Intervention?, 37 ARIZONA LAW REVIEW 955 (1995)

Transforming International Politics: An American Role for the Post Cold War World, 64 UNIVERSITY OF CINCINNATI LAW REVIEW 119 (1995)

The Moral Significance of Nationalism, 71 NOTRE DAME LAW REVIEW 7 (1995)

International Justice and International Law, 98 WEST VIRGINIA LAW REVIEW 611 (1996)

Altruism and the International Environment (60th Cleveland-Marshall Fund Lecture), 44 CLEVELAND STATE LAW REVIEW 1 (1996)

The Institutional and Instrumental Value of Nationalism, in INTERNATIONAL LAW AND ETHNIC CONFLICT (David Wippman ed. 1998, Cornell University Press)

Realism Revisited: The Morality of Means and Ends in Anarchy, in GLOBAL JUSTICE (Ian Shapiro & Lea Brilmayer eds.1999, New York University Press)

Commentaries on Lea Brilmayer, Secession and Self-Determination: A Territorial Interpretation: One Decade Later (Twenty-Fifth Anniversary Commemoration), 25 YALE JOURNAL OF INTERNATIONAL LAW 283 (Summer 2000)

America: The World's Mediator? (1999 Daniel J. Meador Lecture), 51 ALABAMA LAW REVIEW 715 (Winter 2000)

What Use Is John Rawls' Theory of Justice to Public International Law?, 6 INTER-NATIONAL LEGAL THEORY 36 (2000)

Land and Sea: Two Sovereignty Regimes In Search of a Common Denominator (with Natalie Klein), 33 NEW YORK UNIVERSITY JOURNAL OF INTERNATIONAL LAW AND POLITICS 703 (2001)

Family Separation as a Violation of International Law (Stefan A. Riesenfeld Symposium 2002) (with Sonja Starr), 21 BERKELEY JOURNAL OF INTERNATIONAL LAW 213 (2003)

From 'Contract' to 'Pledge': The Structure of International Human Rights Agreements, 2006 BRITISH YEARBOOK OF INTERNATIONAL LAW 163

Ownership or Use? Civilian Property Interests in International Humanitarian Law (with Geoffrey Chepiga), 49 HARVARD JOURNAL OF INTERNATIONAL LAW 413 (2008)

Treaty Denunciation and "Withdrawal" from Customary International Law: An Erroneous Analogy with Dangerous Consequences, Comment. (with Isaias Yemane Tesfalidet) 120 YALE LAW JOURNAL ONLINE (2010)

Third State Obligations and the Enforcement of International Law, 44 NEW YORK UNIVERSITY JOURNAL OF INTERNATIONAL LAW AND POLITICS 1 (2011)

Initiating Territorial Adjudication: The Who, How, When, and Why of Litigating Contested Sovereignty (with Adele Faure), in LITIGATING INTERNATIONAL LAW DISPUTES: WEIGHING THE OPTIONS (Natalie Klein ed. 2014, Cambridge University Press)

Regulating Land Grabs: Third Party States, Social Activism, and International Law (co-author), in RETHINKING FOOD SYSTEMS: STRUCTURAL CHALLENGES, NEW STRATEGIES AND THE LAW (co-editor 2014, Springer)

The Illogic of Cultural Relativism in Global Human Rights Debate (with Tian Huang), in THE GLOBAL COMMUNITY YEARBOOK OF INTERNATIONAL LAW AND JURISPRUDENCE (Giuliana Ziccardi Capaldo ed. 2014)

Notes on Contributors

Eyal Benvenisti

is Whewell Professor of International Law at the University of Cambridge, CC Ng Fellow of Jesus College, Cambridge, and the Director of the Lauterpacht Centre for International Law. He is also Professor of Law at Tel Aviv University and Global Visiting Professor at New York University School of Law, a Member of the Institut de Droit International and of the Israeli Academy of Sciences and Humanities. He is a Co-Editor of the British Yearbook of International Law, and was on the Editorial Board of the *American Journal of International Law* (2009–18).

Kathleen Claussen

is Associate Professor at the University of Miami School of Law. Immediately prior to joining the Miami Law faculty, Professor Claussen was Associate General Counsel at the Office of the U.S. Trade Representative. Earlier in her career, she served as Legal Counsel at the Permanent Court of Arbitration in The Hague. She received her J.D. from the Yale Law School where she was Editor-in-Chief of the *Yale Journal of International Law*. At Yale, she was also awarded the Jerome Sayles Hess Fund Prize for excellence in international law and the Howard M. Holtzmann Fellowship in international dispute resolution.

John R. Crook

teaches international arbitration at GW Law School, frequently acts as an arbitrator in international proceedings, and served on the Eritrea-Ethiopia Claims Commission. During three decades in the U.S. State Department's Office of the Legal Adviser, he was U.S. Agent at the Iran-United States Claims Tribunal and was deeply involved in creating the UN Compensation Commission. He later was General Counsel of the Multinational Force and Observers, which operates peacekeepers in the Sinai Desert. Crook is past vice-president of the American Society of International Law and on the Board of Editors of the *American Journal of International Law*.

Rebecca Crootof

is the Executive Director of the Information Society Project and a Research Scholar and Lecturer in Law at Yale Law School. Her work explores questions stemming from the iterative relationship between law and technology, often in light of social changes sparked by increasingly autonomous systems, artificial intelligence, cyberspace, and robotics. Her dissertation, *Keeping Pace: New Technology and the Evolution of International Law*, discusses how technology fosters change in the international legal order, both by creating a need for new regulations and by altering how sources of international governance develop and interact. She enjoys reading science fiction "for work."

Chiara Giorgetti

is Professor of Law at Richmond Law School, where she teaches courses in international law and international dispute resolution. Prior to joining the Richmond faculty, she practiced international arbitration in Washington D.C. and Geneva. She served as Counsel for Eritrea in two territorial disputes and in the Eritrea-Ethiopia Claims Commission, worked for the United Nations in New York and Nairobi, and clerked at the International Court of Justice. She received an LL.M. and J.S.D. from Yale Law School, a M.Sc. from the London School of Economics and a Laurea in Giurisprudenza (J.D.-equivalent) from Bologna University. Her latest monograph, *International Claims Commissions: Righting Wrongs after Conflict*, is co-authored with Lea Brilmayer and Lorraine Charlton.

Harold Hongju Koh

is Sterling Professor of International Law and former Dean at Yale Law School (2004–09), where he has taught since 1985. He has served as Legal Adviser, U.S. Department of State (2009–13), U.S. Assistant Secretary of State, Democracy, Human Rights and Labor (1998–2001) and Attorney-Adviser, Office of Legal Counsel, U.S. Department of Justice (1983–85). He has been Honorary Fellow of Magdalen College, Clarendon Law Lecturer and Visiting Fellow, All Souls College, Oxford, Goodhart Visiting Professor of Legal Science and Visiting Fellow, Trinity College and Christ's College, Cambridge, and a Fellow of the American Philosophical Society and the American Academy of Arts and Sciences.

Natalie Klein

is a Professor at UNSW Sydney's Faculty of Law, Australia. She was previously at Macquarie University where she served as Dean of Macquarie Law School between 2011 and 2017, as well as Acting Head of the Department for Policing, Intelligence and Counter-Terrorism at Macquarie in 2014–2015. Professor Klein teaches and researches in different areas of international law, with a focus on law of the sea and international dispute settlement. Prior to joining Macquarie, Professor Klein worked in the international litigation and arbitration practice of Debevoise & Plimpton LLP, served as counsel to the Government of Eritrea (1998–2002) and was a consultant in the Office of Legal Affairs at the United Nations. Her masters and doctorate in law were earned at Yale Law School and she is a Fellow of the Australian Academy of Law.

William J. Moon

is an Assistant Professor of Law at the University of Maryland. His research focuses on domestic and transnational law governing cross-border commercial transactions. His scholarship has been published or is forthcoming in student-edited law reviews—including the *Michigan Law Review* and the *Vanderbilt Law Review*—and in peer-reviewed journals, including the *European Journal of Law and Economics* and the *Journal of International Economic Law*. Will served as a research assistant to Professor Lea Brilmayer while attending Yale Law School, and subsequently co-authored a book chapter with Professor Brilmayer entitled *Regulating Land Grabs*.

Erin O'Hara O'Connor

is Dean of Florida State University College of Law. Dean O'Hara O'Connor is a noted scholar in several areas, including conflict of laws, arbitration and the law market. Prior to joining Florida State in 2016, Dean O'Hara O'Connor taught at Vanderbilt Law School, where she served as director of the Law and Human Behavior program from 2007 to 2010, associate dean for academic affairs from 2008 to 2010, and director of graduate studies for the Ph.D. Program in Law and Economics from 2011 to 2016. Dean O'Hara O'Connor received her juris doctor, magna cum laude, from Georgetown University Law Center, where she was a senior articles selection editor on the *Georgetown Law Journal*. Upon graduating from law school, she clerked for Chief Judge Dolores K. Sloviter, of the U.S. Court of Appeals for the Third Circuit. Dean O'Hara O'Connor began her career in academia at the University of Chicago Law School and has taught at several other schools.

W. Michael Reisman

is Myres S. McDougal Professor of International Law at the Yale Law School where he has been on the Faculty since 1965. He has been a visiting professor in Tokyo, Hong Kong, Berlin, Basel, Paris and Geneva. He is a Fellow of the World Academy of Art and Science, President of the Arbitration Tribunal of the Bank for International Settlements, a member of the Board of The Foreign Policy Association and a member of the *Institut de Droit International*. In 2018, he was elected Honorary President of the American Society of International Law.

Kermit Roosevelt III

is a professor of law at the University of Pennsylvania Law School, where he teaches Conflict of Laws and Constitutional Law. After graduating from Harvard University and Yale Law School, he clerked for Judge Stephen F. Williams and Justice David H. Souter before joining the Penn faculty. In 2014, he was selected by the American Law Institute as the Reporter for the Third Restatement of Conflict of Laws.

Stephen M. Schwebel

was a judge of the International Court of Justice 1981–2000 and its president 1997–2000. He sat in a number of international arbitral proceedings, including two in which Professor Brilmayer was lead counsel for Eritrea.

Laura S. Underkuffler

is J. DuPratt White Professor of Law at Cornell University. She has also taught at Duke University, Harvard University, the University of Pennsylvania, Georgetown University, and the University of Maine. She has published widely in the United States and abroad in the fields of constitutional law, group rights, property theory, and the problem of corruption and democratic governance. Before entering the academy, Underkuffler practiced litigation law for six years, and was appointed to the Advisory Committee for the United States Eighth Circuit Court of Appeals. She also served as special counsel to the United States Senate and has been a Fellow at the Woodrow Wilson International Center for Scholars.

Carlos M. Vázquez

is a Professor of Law at the Georgetown University Law Center in Washington, DC, and he currently co-directs the Center for Transnational Legal Studies in London. From 2012 to 2016, he was a member of the UN Committee for the Elimination of Racial Discrimination. From 2000 to 2003, he was a member of the Inter-American Juridical Committee of the Organization of American States. He has served on the Board of Editors of the *American Journal of International Law* and on the Executive Council of the American Society of International Law. He is a member of the American Law Institute, where he has advised on the RESTATEMENT (FOURTH) OF FOREIGN RELATIONS LAW OF THE UNITED STATES and the RESTATEMENT (THIRD) OF CONFLICT OF LAWS. He served as a law clerk to the Honorable Stephen R. Reinhardt. He has written extensively in the areas of public and private international law, foreign relations law, and constitutional law.

Robert G. Volterra
is recognised in the global legal directories as one of the world's top public
international law practitioners. He advises and represents governments, international organisations and private clients on a wide range of contentious and
non-contentious public international law issues. He is a visiting professor of
law at University College London and a visiting senior lecturer at King's College
London, where he has taught a variety of public international law topics for
more than 20 years. He regularly acts as co-agent, counsel and advocate before
the International Court of Justice and ad hoc international arbitration tribunals. Under Professor Brilmayer's leadership, he was counsel and advocate for
Eritrea in Phase II (maritime delimitation) of the Eritrea/Yemen arbitration
and before the Eritrea/Ethiopia Compensation Commission.

Philippa Webb
is Reader (Associate Professor) in Public International Law at King's College
London. She is also a barrister at 20 Essex Street Chambers specializing in
international law. Philippa previously served as the Special Assistant and Legal
Officer to President Higgins of the International Court of Justice. Her books
include *Oppenheim's International Law: The United Nations* (OUP, 2017, with
Dame Rosalyn Higgins, Dapo Akande, Sandy Sivakumaran and James Sloan)
and *The Law of State Immunity* (OUP 2015, with Lady Hazel Fox QC). She has a
J.S.D. from Yale Law School supervised by Professor Lea Brilmayer.

CHAPTER 1

"This Is Your Wake-up Call": Lea Brilmayer's Impact as a Scholar and Teacher

Chiara Giorgetti and Natalie Klein

1   Introduction

Our intention in initiating this book as a celebration of the life-long achieve-ments of Professor Lea Brilmayer was two-fold: to honor Lea's contributions as an outstanding scholar in conflict of laws, international relations and public international law, and to reflect the profound appreciation of many students and colleagues who have benefitted from her teaching, mentoring and advice. The legacy of a great intellect is derived both from the original ideas and think-ing that have shaped the world and from those who have enhanced their own development and understanding through interacting with that intellect. Lea's influence in both regards is manifest. In this Introduction, we endeavor to demonstrate these dimensions in Lea's life.

The co-editors, Chiara Giorgetti and Natalie Klein, came to know Lea as recent graduates from our respective law schools in Italy and Australia. Natalie first met Lea as a Masters student at Yale Law School. When Lea issued the rally cry to "ditch those nerds in New York, and come work in Africa!", Natalie turned down a job offer at a New York law firm and worked full time with Lea on the second phase of the *Eritrea Yemen* arbitration.[1] A particularly strong memory of working for Lea at this time arose when Natalie was sent to London to help oversee the final production of the Memorial. After returning to the hotel at 1am, and dutifully setting the hotel wake-up call function for 4am, the phone started ringing at 3am. Picking up the receiver in the dark and expecting some automated voice to kick in, instead that American drawl came through:

> "Natalie? Natalie? Are you there?"
> "Oh, Lea, it's you. I thought it was my wake-up call."
> "Natalie, this IS your wake-up call."

---

[1] Eritrea / Yemen, Award on Territorial Sovereignty and Scope of the Dispute, (1998) XXII RIAA 211, (1999) 119 ILR 1, (2001) 40 ILM 900, ICGJ 379 (PCA 1998), 9th October 1998, Permanent Court of Arbitration [PCA]; Eritrea / Yemen, Award on Maritime Delimitation, 40 ILM 983 (2001).

© KONINKLIJKE BRILL NV, LEIDEN, 2019 | DOI:10.1163/9789004316539_002

While literally true in this context, many of us who know Lea will attest to the fact that she has been a "wake up call" in so many ways: foremost as a teacher, bringing to life diverse areas of law from civil procedure and contract to international dispute settlement. She opens students' minds to new ways of thinking and always encourages them to see where their own ideas and research might take them. As a scholar, she has been a "wake up call" in bringing to light new ways of thinking about complex and multifaceted problems; sometimes with such logic and clarity that the reader would be inexorably drawn to the conclusions she reached and wonder why something now seemingly so obvious because of Lea's discussion had not been evident all along. Sometimes her views provoked other scholars either to defend a challenged orthodoxy,[2] or to elaborate on further nuances or consequences from the points she raised.[3] The stimulation provided by Lea's "wake up calls" seems boundless.

Yet for the purposes of this Introductory Chapter, we will endeavor to create some bounds to highlight the extraordinary life and influence of Lea Brilmayer thus far. Part 2 outlines her career trajectory, including her passage through some of the top law schools in the United States, her development work in Namibia and Eritrea, sharing her expertise with the US Supreme Court, lower and intermediate appellate jurisdictions, and appearing before international tribunals. Part 3 discusses some of her intellectual influence across different fields of law, but most notably in conflict of laws, international relations and public international law, especially international dispute settlement. Her research in these areas has not been linear, progressing from one discipline to another, but her deep understanding in one area has undoubtedly shaped her analysis of other areas. Part 4 situates the contributions in this volume in relation to Lea's life and influences as scholar and teacher. We note that there were many other scholars, practitioners, colleagues and former students who would have liked to add their contribution but, given the nature of these collections and its timing, were unable to do so.

---

2 See, e.g., Herma Hill Kay, *"The Entrails of a Goat": Reflections on Reading Lea Brilmayer's Hague Lectures* 48 MERCER L. REV. 891, 915 (1996–1997) ("She deserves much credit for having forced those of us who continue to work within the framework Currie provided to re-examine our assumptions and to defend our methods."); Robert A. Sedler, *Interest Analysis as the Preferred Approach to Choice of Law: A Response to Professor Brilmayer's "Foundational Attack"*, 46 OHIO ST. L.J. 483 (1985).

3 See, e.g., Michael Steven Green, *Choice of Law as General Common Law: A Reply to Professor Brilmayer*, in DONALD EARL CHILDRESS III (ed.), *The Role of Ethics in International Law* 125 (2012); James A. Martin, *The Constitution and Legislative Jurisdiction*, 10 HOFSTRA L. REV. 133 (1981) (elaborating Brilmayer's proposal to require contacts that would be legally relevant to a wholly domestic case).

2   A Career as a Scholar, Teacher and Advocate

After growing up on the east coast of the United States, Roberta Brilmayer moved to California and started her college studies at Berkeley in 1967, during "the summer of love" as Lea liked to describe it. She chose the name Lea at this time, which appealed to her because of its meaning of meadow. Lea graduated with a BA in Mathematics from Berkeley in 1970. After starting graduate studies in that discipline, Lea said she "dropped out of college to join an Irish folk band, The All-Oakland Ceilidh Band, travelling along the West Coast. I played the concertina, a little ragtime piano. I was busy being a hippy, living communally, playing on the streets of San Francisco."[4] She did, however, find her way back to Berkeley where she graduated from Boalt Hall School of Law with her JD in 1976 and decided to pursue her interests in questions of jurisdiction. From Lea's perspective, "after you've done mathematical logic, nothing can seem boring".[5] She completed her LLM at Columbia Law School in 1978.

After a stint at the University of Texas, Lea was one of the first women tenured at the University of Chicago Law School and subsequently broke the same barrier at Yale Law School, becoming tenured there as the Nathan Baker Professor of Law. She visited at Harvard Law School, and also visited at Columbia University in the late 1980s, as well as teaching summer sessions at the University of Michigan and the University of Amsterdam. In 1988, the *New York Times* described Lea as typifying "today's perambulatory pedagogue".[6] Lea ultimately left Yale for NYU Law School in 1991 where she was the Benjamin F. Butler Professor of Law, returning to Yale in 1998. She was the first holder of the Howard M. Holtzmann Chair of International Law at Yale Law School. At the time when Lea was the only woman tenured at Yale Law School, she appreciated the importance of role models and set about creating a project to assist women students who wanted to become law professors.[7] Lea was concerned, and at times pessimistic, about the gender inequality she saw at Yale Law School throughout her two periods of tenure.[8]

---

4   Michela Wrong, *Lunch with the FT: Court in the Crossfire*, FINANCIAL TIMES, 2 April 2005, https://www.ft.com/content/5752cefa-a0e3-11d9-95e5-00000e2511c8.

5   *Ibid.*

6   David Margolick, *The Law; At the Bar*, NEW YORK TIMES, Mar. 25, 1988, https://www.nytimes.com/1988/03/25/us/the-law-at-the-bar.html.

7   Howard LaFranchi, *Women in the law: Do they change the legal perspectives?*, CHRISTIAN SCIENCE MONITOR, Oct. 26, 1984, https://www.csmonitor.com/1984/1026/102657.html/(page)/2.

8   Saundra Torry, *At Yale Law, A Gender Gap in who gets Clerkships Sparks Debate*, WASHINGTON POST, May 31, 1991, https://www.washingtonpost.com/archive/business/1991/05/13/at-yale-law-a-gender-gap-in-who-gets-clerkships-sparks-debate/fc6756af-428d-4333-9714-9ed222fed25c/?noredirect=on&utm_term=.fe44bd6b9a29; Aleksandra Gjorgievska, *After*

She personally considered that gender dynamics at the School had improved after she returned.[9]

Throughout her career, Lea has been invited to give numerous endowed lectures at other American law schools,[10] and has also taught twice at the summer session of the Hague Academy of International Law. Her standing as an academic has been evidenced in a variety of ways—from her inclusion in HeinOnline's Top Ranked Women by citation,[11] to her election to the American Academy of Arts and Sciences in 1994, among the first female law professors joining this prestigious group.[12]

Lea has always been a devoted and loved teacher. At Yale, she has long taught Contracts to first-year students and Conflict of Laws, as well as International Courts and Tribunals, Public Order of the World Community (with Michael Reisman) and seminars on the laws of war and on African current affairs. At NYU, she also led a weekly seminar on International Jurisprudence. Many alumni will remember the barbecues she hosted at her home for her students each year. Her interest and insights into the doctoral theses she supervised were critical for their success.

Lea's expertise in conflict of laws prompted her engagement as consultant or expert in diverse cases before courts in the United States, including the Supreme Court.[13] Her clients have ranged from Larry Flynt (though she resigned from this role when Mr. Flynt sent an obscene letter to the only female justice on the Supreme Court at the time) to Paul McCartney. She has contributed to amicus briefs before the US Supreme Court,[14] and appeared

Report, Yale Law School Improves Gender Balance, YALE DAILY NEWS, Feb. 21, 2013, https://yaledailynews.com/blog/2013/02/21/after-report-law-school-improves-gender-balance/.

9   Daniel Sisgoreo, Law School Battles Gender Imbalance, YALE DAILY NEWS, Apr. 20, 2012, https://yaledailynews.com/blog/2012/04/20/law-school-battles-gender-imbalance/.

10   See, e.g., The William B Lockhart Lecture: Consent, Contract and Territory, 74 MINN. L. REV. 1 (1989–1990).

11   Kaylyn Zurawski, Celebrate Women's History Month with HeinOnline's Top Ranked Women in ScholarRank!, HEIN BLOG, Mar. 5. 1995, https://www.wshein.com/blog/2015/03/05/celebrate-womens-history-month-with-heinonlines-top-ranked-women-in-scholarrank/ (Lea was ranked third after Judith Resnik and Ruth Bader Ginsburg).

12   Members of the American Academy Listed by election year, 1950–1999, https://www.amacad.org/multimedia/pdfs/publications/bookofmembers/electionIndex1950-1999.pdf (Lea was elected only five years after her teacher from Berkeley, Professor Herma Hill Kay).

13   See, e.g, Daimler Chrysler v Bauman, Brief of Amica Curiae Professor Lea Brilmayer Supporting Petitioner, No. 11–965, https://www.americanbar.org/content/dam/aba/publications/supreme_court_preview/briefs-v2/11-965_pet_amcu_prof-lb.authcheckdam.pdf.

14   Ibid.

before congressional hearings, including on questions of gay marriage.[15] She is a member of the Texas and Supreme Court bars.

Lea's interest in international development issues first led her and a group of students to Namibia. She subsequently visited Eritrea and was impressed by the efforts of a young nation seeking to establish itself in the international community after a thirty-year struggle. Lea provided advice on diverse issues, ranging from rights of pensions for returning soldiers through to constitutional law matters. When Yemen occupied islands in the middle of the Red Sea, the Office of the President of Eritrea turned to Lea for advice on resolving this dispute. Partnering with different law firms, Lea and her team of NYU and then of Yale researchers (or her "bunch of teenagers" as she called us) investigated and advised the Eritrean Government through the territorial sovereignty and maritime boundary phases of the *Eritrea / Yemen* arbitration.[16]

On the eve of the territorial sovereignty decision, military hostilities broke out between Eritrea and Ethiopia over the location of their land boundary. During the two-year conflict,[17] Lea worked tirelessly gathering evidence and leading research into the border dispute and the violations of international law, particularly international humanitarian law, that were perpetrated during this time. Following the conclusion of the Algiers Agreement on 12 December 2000, Lea had the primary role in presenting Eritrea's case before the Eritrea Ethiopia Boundary Commission,[18] and the Eritrea Ethiopia Claims Commission.[19] She undertook this work on a pro bono basis, although she was not fond of the term "pro bono". Lea considered: "People shouldn't have to have money to get justice. And in my own case, everyone should do something at least once in their life just because they think it's right."[20]

3   Intellectual Contributions

During Lea's initial years as an academic, her writing interests mainly concerned conflict of laws (in particular, personal jurisdiction and choice of law);

---

15   Lolita C. Baldor, *Congress Set to Debate Gay Marriage*, THE WASHINGTON POST, Mar. 3, 2004, http://www.washingtonpost.com/wp-dyn/articles/A25853-2004Mar3.html?noredirect=on.
16   Eritrea / Yemen arbitration, *supra* note 1.
17   A conflict that Lea described in 2000 as a "fraud". See Thomas Keneally, *The Kosovo of Africa*, THE GUARDIAN, 29 July 2000.
18   Eritrea-Ethiopia Boundary Commission, documents available at http://www.pca-cpa.org.
19   Eritrea-Ethiopia Claims Commission, documents available at http://www.pca-cpa.org.
20   Wrong, *supra* note 4.

federal jurisdiction; and jurisprudence. Her conflict of laws writings have included one theoretical book on the subject, *Conflict of Laws: Foundations and Future Directions*,[21] and a leading casebook (co-authored more recently with Jack Goldsmith and Erin O'Hara O'Connor and currently in its seventh edition).[22] Together with a group of Yale student contributors, she published *An Introduction to Jurisdiction in the American Federal System*.[23] Her publications now span over eighty journal articles and book chapters, as well as including a total of nine authored, co-authored or edited volumes, including two further monographs in the area of international relations and political theory. In 1996, as her interest in public international law became more evident, she published *American Hegemony—Political Morality in a One-Superpower World*.[24] Lea's recent monograph, co-authored with Chiara Giorgetti and Lorraine Charlton, *International Claims Commissions: Righting Wrongs after Conflict*,[25] draws on Lea's expertise and experience working on the Eritrea Ethiopia Claims Commission.[26]

In looking at her scholarship, one cannot but notice how often Lea has co-authored with her students, an experience at once intellectually and personally pivotal to many academic careers. Indeed, both editors and many contributors of this book co-authored pieces with Lea somewhere along their and her careers.

Crossing into contemporary media more recently, Lea was asked by the United Nations to prepare a series of lectures for the United Nations International Law Audiovisual Library. She delivered two lectures on "The Problem of Secession in International Law",[27] and "Cultural Relativism: The Basic Problem

---

21   Lea Brilmayer, Conflict of Laws: Foundations and Future Directions (1990).

22   R. Lea Brilmayer, Jack L. Goldsmith, Erin O'Hara O'Connor, Conflict of Laws: Cases and Materials (7th ed. 2015).

23   Lea Brilmayer et al., An Introduction to Jurisdiction in the American Federal System (1986).

24   Lea Brilmayer, American Hegemony—Political Morality in a One-Superpower World (1996).

25   Lea Brilmayer, Chiara Giorgetti, Lorraine Charlton, International Claims Commissions: Righting Wrongs after Conflict (2017).

26   Lea's further reflections on the roles of claim commissions have been published in Lea Brilmayer, *Understanding "IMCCs": Compensation and Closure in the Formation and Function of International Mass Claims Commissions*, 43 Yale J. Int'l L. (2018).

27   Lea Brilmayer, *The Problem of Secession in International Law*, UN Audiovisual Library of International Law, 2015, http://legal.un.org/avl/ls/Brilmayer_S.html.

and Some Complexities".[28] Lea has also provided commentary on contemporary issues to the media.[29]

We have highlighted some aspects of Lea's scholarship below, and further reflected on this scholarship in the context of the contributions to this volume in Part 4 of this Chapter.

3.1   Conflict of Laws

In commenting to us on Lea's scholarship in this area,[30] Professor Jack Goldsmith (a former student and co-author of Lea's) wrote:

> Lea's scholarly career took root in the topics of federal jurisdiction, personal jurisdiction, and choice of law but expanded outward, so to speak, to all of the jurisdictional puzzles in conflict of laws, to federal extraterritoriality, and to international law and justice.
>
> Lea wrote with extraordinary insight and influence on all of these topics. But she never was more devastating than in her early critique of Brainerd Currie's interest analysis, and especially in her famous article, *Interest Analysis and the Myth of Legislative Intent*.[31] To paraphrase what Currie said about Walter Wheeler Cook's debunking of Joseph Beale, Lea discredited the intellectual foundations of Currie's interest analysis as thoroughly as the intellect of one scholar can ever discredit the intellectual product of another.[32]

Lea demonstrated the intrinsically vague and often self-contradictory nature of policy-based analysis embedded in the interest analysis approach.[33] In doing so, Lea "place[d] interest analysis exactly where it belongs, in the ashbin of conflicts history, right beside the vested rights doctrine".[34] Her 1991

---

28   Lea Brilmayer, *Cultural Relativism: The Basic Problem and Some Complexities*, UN Audiovisual Library of International Law, 2017, http://legal.un.org/avl/ls/Brilmayer_IL.html.

29   See, e.g., Lea Brilmayer, "Why the Crimea Referendum is Illegal", Mar. 14 2014, THE GUARDIAN, https://www.theguardian.com/.../2014/.../crimean-referendum-illegal-international-law.

30   Cited with the permission of Professor Goldsmith.

31   Lea Brilmayer, *Interest Analysis and the Myth of Legislative Intent*, 78 MICH. L. REV. 392 (1980).

32   Cf. CURRIE, SELECTED ESSAYS ON THE CONFLICT OF LAWS 6 (1963) (Cook's work "discredited the vested-rights theory as thoroughly as the intellect of one man can ever discredit the intellectual product of another").

33   See, e.g., Lea Brilmayer, *Governmental Interest Analysis: A House without Foundations*, 46 OHIO ST. L.J. 459 (1985).

34   Patrick J. Borcher, *Professor Brilmayer and the Holy Grail*, 1991 WIS. L. REV 465, 474 (1991).

book *Conflict of Laws: Foundations and Future Directions* systematically demonstrated the weaknesses in governmental interest analysis and posited the rights-based analysis, which drew from game theory models of cooperation and political rights. One reviewer considered this analysis 'an important break with current theories and deserves the careful attention of conflicts scholars and judges'.[35] Her novel perspectives in the area meant that she frequently engaged with other conflict of laws scholars in her writing.[36]

During her time as Visiting Scholar at the Hague Academy of International Law in 1995, her research and lecture on *The Substantive and Choice of Law Policies in the Formation and Application of Choice of Law Rules* was published in the prestigious *Recueil des Cours*.[37] To this day, and as noted in Roosevelt's chapter in this volume, Lea continues to contribute to the development of conflict of laws, including in the work on the Third Restatement.[38]

3.2   *International Relations Theory*

As someone who sought to understand the rationale and the explanatory paradigms for the operation of law, Lea was drawn to topics concerning political theory, jurisprudence and international relations.

In *Justifying International Acts*, Lea explored the "horizontal" and "vertical" relationships between states, and between states and foreign nationals, respectively, as a means of assessing the legitimacy of their actions.[39] In this book, Lea demonstrated how political theory justifies the exercise of domestic authority by the state concerned and proposed; as one reviewer described, "a state's actions outside its borders must be evaluated in terms of the justification that grants the state the right to operate domestically".[40] As Lea herself put it: "The vertical thesis holds that whether a state has authority to act in some particular interstate or international context must be analyzed by some reference to the constituting political theory that grants it authority to act

35   Craig Y. Allison, *Conflict of Laws: Foundations and Future Directions by Lea Brilmayer*, 90 *Michigan L. Rev.* 1682 (1992).

36   See, e.g., Lea Brilmayer, *Related Contacts and Personal Jurisdiction*, 101 HARVARD L. REV. 1444 (1987–1988) (responding to work by Professor Mary Twitchell).

37   Lea Brilmayer, *The Substantive and Choice of Law Policies in the Formation and Application of Choice of Law Rules*, RECUEIL DES COURS (1995).

38   See, e.g., Lea Brilmayer, *What I Like Most about the Restatement (Second) of Conflicts, and Why It Should Not Be Thrown Out with the Bathwater*, 110 AJIL UNBOUND 144 (2016).

39   LEA BRILMAYER, JUSTIFYING INTERNATIONAL ACTS (1989).

40   Andrew J. Pierre, *Lea Brilmayer: Justifying International Acts*, FOREIGN AFFAIRS, Winter 1989–1990, https://www.foreignaffairs.com/reviews/capsule-review/1989-12-01/justifying-international-acts.

domestically."[41] Although Lea's thesis was not endorsed by all,[42] she still provoked her readers to think about jurisdictional boundaries and the interaction
of actors within and across those boundaries in different ways.[43] It reached
out beyond international lawyers to "those concerned with the international
applications of political philosophy and ethics".[44]

In *International Law in American Courts: A Modest Proposal*,[45] published in
the *Yale Law Journal*, Lea reprised the distinction between "horizontal" and
"vertical" relationships to argue that there are ways of "understanding international law that fit it squarely into traditional forms of domestic adjudication"[46]
because both are also about the relations between states and individuals, as
courts have implicitly recognized by adjudicating vertical cases with no res-
ervation. She therefore argues that there is no reason to categorically exclude
international clams from domestic courts since "even a restrained notion of
judicial function has room for international adjudication."[47]

In her second monograph reflecting on international relations, *American
Hegemony: Political Morality in a One-Superpower World*,[48] Lea was compli-
mented for "display[ing] real virtuosity as an analytical philosopher".[49] A
reviewer noted that "[t]he task Brilmayer sets for herself is to seek a measure
of morality in the international scene as it is structured today ... She does not
withdraw to thought experiments but instead she examines a much more
concrete ... question: what sort of arrangements between unequal parties,
if any, do we have reason to respect?".[50] Shortly after this publication, Lea

---

41   BRILMAYER, JUSTIFYING INTERNATIONAL ACTS, at 22.
42   See, e.g., Martti Koskenniemi, *Justifying International Acts. By Lea Brilmayer. Ithaca
      and London: Cornell University Press, 1989. Pp. 161.*, 85 AM. J. INT'L L 385 (1991); Stanley
      Hoffman, *Review: Applying Political Theory to International Law*, 99 YALE L.J. 1707 (1990).
43   See, e.g., J.H. Bogart, *Reviewed Work: Justifying International Acts. by Lea Brilmayer*, 101
      ETHICS 880 (1991) (describing the book as "provocative and intriguing").
44   Alan James, *Justifying International Acts. By Lea Brilmayer*, 67 INT'L AFF. 568, 569 (1991).
45   Lea Brilmayer, *International Law in American Courts: A Modest Proposal*, 100 YALE L.J.
      2277 (June 1991).
46   Ibid., at 2314.
47   Ibid.
48   LEA BRILMAYER, AMERICAN HEGEMONY—POLITICAL MORALITY IN A ONE-
      SUPERPOWER WORLD (1996).
49   David C. Hendrickson, *American Hegemony: Political Morality in a One-Superpower
      World by Lea Brilmayer*, FOREIGN AFFAIRS, March/April 1995, https://www.foreign
      affairs.com/reviews/capsule-review/1995-03-01/american-hegemony-political
      -morality-one-superpower-world.
50   Yael Tamir, *American Hegemony: Political Morality in a One-Superpower World. by Lea
      Brilmayer*, 107 ETHICS 155 (1996).

reflected, in *The Moral Significance of Nationalism*,[51] on the increasingly important issue of nationalism, examining the essential question of what constitutes
a nation, and the relationship between nationalism and the state. Though this
article was published in 1995, its arguments are as topical now are as they
were then.

Given her increasing interest in the role and action of states, venturing into
public international law issues could be well understood as the next logical
step for Lea.

3.3   *Public International Law*

In the nineties, Lea became gradually more and more interested in public international law, and specifically on issues related to independence,
self-determination, cultural relativism and other issues analyzing relations
between different actors and bodies of law.

Lea's 1991 essay, *Secession and Self-Determination: A Territorial Interpretation*,[52]
in the *Yale Journal of International Law* reinterpreted secessionist movements.
She argued, contrary to popular assumptions at the time, that difficult normative issues arising out of secessionist claims do not involve an incompatibility
between the principles of territorial integrity and the right of peoples to self-
determination, but they can work in tandem.[53] She argues that "the normative
force behind secessionist arguments derives ... from ... the right to territory
that many ethnic groups claim to possess."[54] This article became one of the
most cited publications for the *Yale Journal of International Law*.[55]

This article was subsequently revisited by Lea in 2000.[56] Against the
backdrop of the collapse of the Iron Curtain in Europe and the subsequent
breakdown of the Soviet Union and the Federation of Yugoslavia, which led to
the secessionist movements in the Baltic States and the Yugoslav countries, and
an example from the Pacific (the independence of East Timor from Indonesia), she analyzed the new wave of secessions. She argued that the "erroneous

---

51   Lea Brilmayer, *The Moral Significance of Nationalism*, 71 NOTRE DAME L. REV. 7 (1995).
     See also Lea Brilmayer, *Institutional and instrumental value of nationalism*, in DAVID
     WIPPMAN (ED.) INTERNATIONAL LAW AND ETHNIC CONFLICT (1998).
52   Lea Brilmayer, *Secession and Self-Determination: A Territorial Interpretation*, 16 YALE J.
     INT'L L. 176 (1991).
53   Ibid., at 177.
54   Ibid., at 179.
55   Fred R. Shapiro, *The Ten Most-Cited Works from* The Yale Journal of International Law *and
     Its Predecessors*, Yale Studies in World Public Order *and* The Yale Journal of World Public
     Order, 25 YALE J. INT'L L. 271, 271 (2000) (this article was ranked equal first).
56   Lea Brilmayer, *Secession and Self-Determination: One Decade Later*, 25 YALE J. INT'L L. 283
     (2000).

interpretation of nationalist claims as being all of the sort 'my nation, right or wrong' has two consequences. First, this misunderstanding obscures whatever real justification might exist (or be thought to exist by the national group) for the claim in question. The outside observer has no reason, or need, to take seriously the moral or legal argument. Second, this misunderstanding gives nationalistic claims a pervasively negative connotation."[57] In a further piece in 2014–2015,[58] Lea was able to reflect more on direct territorial claims as the basis of secessionist movements. In *Secession and the Two Types of Territorial Claims*, she distinguished between a territorial claim based on past injustice, called "remedial",[59] and a territorial claim based on assertions that the current group of inhabitants are the legitimate owners, also called "directly territorial."[60] She concluded that a successful secessionist claim should be based on a direct territorial claim as "it is the direct territorial model which conforms to the current intuitions of the secessionists themselves about what ought to matter."[61]

As her practice in international tribunals built up, Lea also increasingly wrote about issues she encountered in her practice as counsel.

In *Land and Sea: Two Sovereignty Regimes in Search of a Common Denominator*,[62] written with Natalie Klein, the authors noted the difference between land and sea regimes in international law, and explored why the two regimes were different and what they had in common, highlighting the different histories proper to each regime and observing that, while maritime space had more often been allocated by operation of law, land was more commonly acquired through physical manifestations of authority. Working with Adele Faure, Lea also examined why states would refer territorial sovereignty disputes to international litigation.[63] Their research into territorial sovereignty cases dispelled assumptions that states would only adjudicate these cases

---

57   Ibid., at 285.
58   Lea Brilmayer, *Secession and the Two Types of Territorial Claims*, 21 ILSA J. INT'L & COMP. L 325 (2014–2015).
59   Ibid., at 327 ("The grant of territory upon which to found a new state, constitutes a remedy for past injustices, as well as providing the means to allow the secessionist group better to defend itself.").
60   Ibid., at 328 ("the proponent of secession argues that his or her group is entitled to a particular territory on its own merits, as a consequence of international law concerning rightful acquisition.").
61   Ibid., at 330.
62   Lea Brilmayer & Natalie Klein, *Land and Sea: Two Sovereignty Regimes in Search of a Common Denominator*, 33 N.Y.U. J. INT'L L. & POL. 703–768 (2000–2001).
63   Lea Brilmayer & Adele Faure, *Initiating territorial adjudication: the who, how, when, and why of litigating contested sovereignty*, in LITIGATING INTERNATIONAL LAW DISPUTES: WEIGHING THE OPTIONS (Natalie Klein (ed), 2014) 193.

when there was an existing consent to jurisdiction allowing proceedings to commence at the instigation of one of the parties.[64] They developed explanations that appreciated the complexity and nuances in explaining why states would turn to adjudication of territorial disputes.

International Claims Commissions: Righting Wrongs after Conflict[65] draws on Lea's extensive practice at the Eritrea Ethiopia Claims Commission and assesses International Mass Claims Commissions (IMCCS) as possible special dispute resolution mechanisms in post-traumatic situations. The book, which has been seen as an "important addition to the literature," offers "recommendations to ensure that an interstate arrangement that is supposed to provide post-conflict justice for the 'collateral' victims does not degenerate into a continuation of war by other means."[66]

At the time of writing this Chapter, we know that Lea is busy, among many other things, updating her *Conflict of Laws* text, writing several articles, including for example on the responsibility of the international community to enforce boundary decisions and acting as counsel in several cases.

4   Contributions to This Volume in Honour of Lea Brilmayer

This volume opens with a personal tribute to Lea from a long-time colleague at Yale Law School, Harold Hongju Koh. Koh perfectly captures her "legendary" status as a scholar across conflict of laws, international law and international relations, and further shows her much-admired standing as an academic colleague, mentor, teacher and friend. Koh's description of his relationship with Lea would resonate with many people who have encountered Lea and admired her accomplishments, as well as providing an insight into Lea's many strengths for those who have not yet had such an opportunity.

The contributions that immediately follow Koh's piece focus on Lea's first and enduring scholarly passion: conflict of laws.

Kermit Roosevelt III, also a leading conflict of laws scholar, has considered how Lea's scholarship has shaped the field and currently influences the development of the Third Restatement of Conflict of Laws, for which Roosevelt

---

64   Ibid., at 211.
65   LEA BRILMAYER, CHIARA GIORGETTI, LORRAINE CHARLTON, INTERNATIONAL CLAIMS COMMISSIONS: RIGHTING WRONGS AFTER CONFLICT (2017).
66   Michael Reisman, *Editorial Review of International Claims Commissions: Righting Wrongs after Conflict.* For other work related to her practice, see for example, Lea Brilmayer & Isaias Yemene Tesfalidet, *Third State Obligations and the Enforcement of International Law,* 44 N.Y.U. J. INT'L L. & POL. 1–53 (2011).

serves as the Reporter.[67] Consistent with Lea's scholarship, Roosevelt agrees on the importance of theoretical foundations and he describes a two-step model that involves identifying the relevant states and choosing the law of one of the states. Roosevelt advocates the use of ordinary language and a simple process of identifying a law as relevant if it gives a right to one of the parties.[68] Determining whether a right is granted could be a process of interpretation, though Roosevelt takes on board Lea's criticisms of Brainerd Currie's interest analysis and approach to interpretation. Instead, "state specifications of scope are binding, but that in the absence of such specification, courts should presume that state laws grant rights to all persons within the state and to domiciliaries outside, when doing so would advance their purposes".[69] In the next step of deciding on priority of rights, Roosevelt reflects on Lea's recent scholarship in this area and her advocacy for a "multi-factor balancing, or the center-of-gravity approach",[70] rather than a single-factor trigger. While Lea might not agree with all aspects of the final formulation of the Third Restatement, her insights in the field have clearly had a profound influence.

Carlos M. Vázquez also engages with issues of conflict of laws. In his contribution, *Choice of Law As Geographic Scope Limitation*, he questions the mainstream doctrinal approach that distinguishes between the problems of the application of U.S. federal law to international disputes and the problems of domestic conflict of laws. Inspired by Lea's own comments, Professor Vázquez argues that the questions are conceptually identical. In his piece, he posits that from the perspective of a U.S. state that has enacted a given law, the question whether that law should be applied to a case having contacts with other states or nations is conceptually identical to the question whether federal law should be applied to a dispute having contacts with other nations.

Philippa Webb, a former doctoral student of Lea's, has focused on the private international law doctrine of *forum non conveniens* in her contribution to this volume. In doing so, she draws out the way Lea herself has moved between areas of public and private international law by observing the public

---

67   Roosevelt notes that the views expressed in the chapter are his own and do not necessarily reflect those of the American Law Institute or the Associate Reporters, Laura Little and Chris Whytock.

68   Lea wrote about rights theory in *Rights, Fairness, and Choice of Law* 98 YALE L.J. 1277 (1989). Roosevelt also notes Larry Kramer's influence in this area. See, e.g., Larry Kramer, *Return of the Renvoi*, 66 N.Y.U. L. REV. 979, 990–991 (1991).

69   See Roosevelt chapter in this volume, p. 24.

70   See Lea R. Brilmayer, *What I Like Most About the Restatement (Second) of Conflicts, and Why It Should Not Be Thrown Out With the Bathwater*, 110 AJIL UNBOUND 144, 146–147 (2017).

international law dimensions in the application of this doctrine before national courts. Webb's analysis thus draws inspiration from Lea's *International Law in American Courts: A Modest Proposal*.[71] Webb explores whether there is a possibility of establishing a common approach to *forum non conveniens*, despite it being applied in different stages of proceedings in different states and despite the way it is applied also varying across jurisdictions. She further observes how the doctrine has been used as an avoidance device by multinational corporations, as well as the counter-steps taken by national courts and legislatures to prevent cases being sent to an alternative forum to ensure resolution in the defendant's domicile. Webb supports Lea's argument that there is an important role for domestic courts to play in this form of international adjudication and considers how Lea's analysis could equally apply in the context of claims of *forum non conveniens*. Webb therefore highlights the importance of understanding and critiquing issues that sit at the intersection of private and public international law.

As manifest in this volume, Lea's scholarship is distinguished by her ability to move between private international law and public international law. Harold Koh noted their shared fascination with jurisdiction and it is perhaps this interest in how relationships between people and spatial areas operate that connects Lea's work in both fields.

Michael Reisman starts the contributions addressing public international law by highlighting how Lea's scholarship crossed boundaries, and builds on this observation by contributing a chapter that explores boundaries of non-intervention in a world without boundaries. He focuses on how the cardinal principle of non-intervention in the internal affairs of other States should be applied in cases where external but disguised efforts are targeted at influencing procedures and outcomes of elections. Professor Reisman notes that the external "ideological" mode of influencing has thus far been something of a juridical outlier. He argues that the new technology of social media and the shifting of political forces make thinking about addressing election intervention and the dissemination of disinformation with an inter-state agreement more urgent. In the short term, this could be done through a Security Council Chapter VII Resolution, or even without that, with a "Gentleman's Agreement". In the long-run, a treaty concluded under the auspices of the United Nations and establishing a common international policy, committing States to refrain from disinformation and election meddling and possibly creating a standing fact-finding commission could be the right approach.

---

71   Lea Brilmayer, *International Law in American Courts: A Modest Proposal*, 100 YALE L.J. 2277 (1990–1991).

Rebecca Crootof's contribution also relates to a novel issue of public international law. She takes on the problem of "jurisprudential space junk"—defined as treaties that have been modified by subsequently developed customary international law, and which result in laws on the books that only clutter and confuse the relevant legal regime. This problem is particularly important in technological treaties that can become swiftly outdated. Crootof argues that there are two approaches to deal with the problem of jurisprudential space junk: states need to avoid creating treaties that will quickly be rendered irrelevant by adopting flexible treaty formats, and by finding alternative options for international technological governance; moreover when a provision becomes irrelevant, states should acknowledge and remedy the provisions that clutter the international legal space.

One critical area of public international law that Lea has hugely influenced is in relation to secession and self-determination. As noted above, her 1991 piece in the *Yale Journal of International Law* on this topic, *Secession and Self-Determination: A Territorial Interpretation*, has become "required reading for anyone interested in secession and self-determination."[72]

In light of this contribution, Will Moon, also one of Lea's former students and co-authors, writes on the issue of international recognition, which is so often inextricably linked to secession. His analysis assesses how and why the rules governing international recognition and statehood matter today, formulating recognition as a threshold condition to receive "rewards". Those rewards entail legal title to a defined area of territory as well as varied financial benefits from the international community. Moon adopts a constructivist approach to examine the issue of recognition distinctively from the traditional debates between constitutive and declaratory theories of statehood. This approach enables theorizing of how the institutional norms governing recognition create expectations and shape the behaviors of both "states" and "rebel groups." Importantly, Moon highlights how rewards influence the power structure of various groups within the juridical state. Moon concludes: "It is for this reason that the law of recognition ought to be taken seriously as a causal variable in the vicious cycle of civil wars, corruption, and the collapse of state institutions."[73]

Kathleen Claussen, another of Lea's former students, touches on the same overall issue and focuses her contribution on the problem of rights and obligations of entities that are not recognized as States, but aspire to become States. She points out how Lea's work has drawn attention to issues faced by quasi-states

---

72   David Wippman, *Secession, Territorial Claims, and the Indeterminacy of Self-determination*, 25 YALE J. INT'L L. 287, 289 (2000).

73   Moon chapter in this volume, p. 129.

for over 20 years. Studying non-recognized States like Kosovo, Hong Kong, Palestine, Taiwan and others, she argues that international economic law can serve as a gatekeeping function and allow them to make meaningful contributions to international law despite not being generally recognized as States. This is particularly true, she notes, in international economic institutions through their dispute settlement mechanisms. She concludes by arguing that, increasingly, sovereignty is situated in the eye of the beholder, and specifically in the practice of any given actor, and that the historical bilateral exchange of the legal exercise of State recognition now includes new interactions with international economic institutions.

Along a similar vein, Laura Underkuffler addresses the related issue of rights of sub-state groups. Building on Lea's "territorial thesis" for separatist claims, she focuses on what circumstances should lead to the recognition of sub-state groups and their demands. She concludes that the identification of abstract criteria or characteristics for sub-state group qualification is of limited usefulness. Indeed, although it is tempting to try to establish a set of universally applicable and abstract threshold criteria, the qualification of the group for international recognition and the merits of the group's claims cannot be separated. She argues that, as Lea had implicitly recognized, the first is derivative of the second, so that the recognition of a sub-state group as a rights-bearing entity is necessarily a function of what international legal recognition seeks to achieve in any given case.

Eyal Benvenisti's contribution also explores an issue relevant to recognition and the rights of non-state actors. He explores the issue of accountability to individuals of international organizations. In his contribution, greatly influenced by Lea's own writing,[74] Benvenisti seeks to identify a legal basis for accountability of international organizations towards individuals who are affected by their policies. After exploring and rejecting the rule of law and human rights as possible bases for accountability, Benvenisti offers trusteeship as a concept that can serve as the normative foundation for the emergence of global administrative law.

Within the field of public international law, Lea's contributions are especially notable in the area of international dispute settlement because of her many years working as the Legal Advisor to the President of Eritrea and her lead role representing that state in the *Eritrea / Yemen* arbitration, as well as the Eritrea Ethiopia Boundary Commission and Eritrea Ethiopia Claims Commission.

Chiara Giorgetti began working with Lea in the *Eritrea / Yemen* arbitration, and was also part of the teams that represented Eritrea below the Eritrea-Ethiopia

---

74   LEA BRILMAYER, JUSTIFYING INTERNATIONAL ACTS (1989).

Boundary Commission and the Eritrea-Ethiopia Claims Commission. In her contribution, she delves into one important aspect of her work with Lea: access by individuals to international fora. She builds on the book she co-authored with Lea to address the specific issue of the paucity of international forums that are directly available to individuals to address their grievances arising out of international law and posits whether international claims commissions might be the right instruments to fill the vacuum. Specifically, she asserts that the flexibility that is inherent to such instruments, together with the approach to nationality requirements embedded in their constitutive instruments and resulting from their decisions, have made claims commissions a viable—yet not perfect—alternative for individual remedies.

Natalie Klein, who worked with Lea on the maritime boundary phase of *Eritrea / Yemen* and on the Eritrea Ethiopia boundary dispute, contributes a piece that endeavors to reflect on Lea's profound understanding of the role of territory in international law as well as on her expertise in international dispute settlement. Klein's chapter revisits themes from an article she co-authored with Lea, *Land and Sea: Two Sovereignty Regimes in Search of a Common Denominator*,[75] which explored how and why the legal regimes for the acquisition of land territory and maritime space had developed differently. A dichotomy could largely be drawn between land disputes that were predominantly resolved only with the consent of the States concerned and maritime disputes that could be referred to an international court or tribunal based on compulsory jurisdiction under the UN Convention on the Law of the Sea (UNCLOS). Klein's contribution examines how this dichotomy is being tested in the cases that have been referred for resolution under the dispute settlement procedures of UNCLOS. She explores how legal processes available under UNCLOS are being prevailed upon, or could be prevailed upon, not only to quiet maritime title, but also to resolve territorial sovereignty conflicts persisting over islands. Klein's chapter further examines the use of UNCLOS norms and procedures where the interface between land and sea is (literally) blurring: first, where land is lost to rising sea levels and, second, the human-made constructions of "land" and consequent implications for maritime allocations. The resolution of these issues necessitates reliance on norms to secure the rights of small, less powerful States. Yet, Klein questions whether the conditions exist now that had previously supported the normative demands of these actors in the international legal system.

---

75   Lea Brilmayer & Natalie Klein, *Land and Sea: Two Sovereignty Regimes in Search of a Common Denominator*, 33 N.Y.U. J. INT'L L. & POL. 703–768 (2000–2001).

John Crook served as a commissioner on the Eritrea Ethiopia Claims Commission and became familiar with Lea's "insight and determination" in her role as Eritrea's agent. His contribution to this volume assesses the use of evidence that is obtained from satellites, which was part of Eritrea's submissions to the Eritrea Ethiopia Claims Commission. Crook describes how raw "earth observation data" is processed into usable material and has been of assistance in establishing the factual bases of claims before international tribunals. He traces how different international courts and tribunals have grappled with this evidence and how it may be effectively used. To do so, Crook outlines what procedures might be needed to enhance its probative value.

Robert Volterra undertakes a critical examination of the Eritrea Ethiopia Claims Commission's decisions on diplomatic inviolability. Through an examination of the core rules of diplomatic privileges and immunities, as have been recognized in international treaties, State practice, and domestic court decisions, Volterra is able to contrast the approach of the Eritrea Ethiopia Claims Commission in assessing each State's liability for violations of diplomatic inviolability during armed conflict. He observes the limited legal analysis afforded by the Commission on important questions of international law relating to diplomatic inviolability and questions the emphasis placed on reciprocity when dealing with absolute and unqualified standards. As such, any precedential value that might have otherwise been ascribed to these decisions has arguably been undermined.

Judge Schwebel, who also met Lea in the context of her work in international dispute settlement, offers insightful remarks on the application of the Minimum Standard of Treatment (MST) in international investment arbitration within the North Atlantic Free Trade Agreement (NAFTA). Assessing an impressive set of prime materials, Judge Schwebel points out how parties to NAFTA have misinterpreted the principle of the MST in such a way as to lessen their exposure to suits against them. He concludes that the readings of the MST principle in several recent NAFTA cases are unconvincing, and argues that the reading suggested by other cases, such as *Mondev, ADF, Waste Management II, Merrill & Ring*, and *Bilcon*—that accept and espouse a more modern and enlightened perspective on MST—is to be preferred.

Final reflections to conclude the volume are offered by Professor Erin O'Hara O'Connor, who has collaborated with Lea in the highly-regarded *Conflict of Laws* textbook. In addition to her remarks, we make a last observation that many of the contributions have been influenced by Lea's exploration of theories of international relations in assessing international law. Moon draws on a constructivist approach to highlight the inadequacies of the more positive-oriented theories of statehood and is thus able to better explain the political dynamics that are at play in a "rewards" approach to international recognition. Klein revisits realist and norms-based explanations of title to land and sea. She questions whether the current use of UNCLOS dispute settlement procedures show norms-reliance in the ascendancy and whether this shift is a cause for celebration. To draw on what might be described as "theoretical zing" is a chance to emulate Lea's own deep appreciation of the different explanatory paradigms that could be used to understand and resolve conflicts in the law.

5   Conclusion

This collection of essays is intended to honor Lea Brilmayer as a scholar and to highlight the profound impact her writings have had on such diverse issues as conflict of laws, international relations and public international law. At the same time, this collection also seeks to honor Lea as a colleague and friend and to show the long-lasting significance that her teaching, mentoring and advice has had not only on the contributors of this book, but on many others.

The editors of this book can think of many a conversation that would profoundly impact on their thinking on a specific issue, be it self-determination, nationality, law of the sea or boundary issues. At times, the discussions would linger in one's mind for days and the true impact would hit as a revelation days after the discussion. And these profound discussions often occurred in conjunction with a glass of wine and a good meal. Lea has always been so generous with both her intellect and friendship, and it is a true privilege now for us to honor her accomplishments through this book.

CHAPTER 2

Lea Brilmayer: How Contacts Count

*Harold Hongju Koh**

Lea Brilmayer was one of my very first friends in legal academia, and one of my very first friends at Yale Law School. When I came to New Haven for my job interview in 1984, she was already legendary, for her meteoric rise from a street musician/mathematician, who famously sold her blood on the streets of Berkeley to pay for her schoolbooks, to become a legendary teacher, mentor and academic pioneer, moving from Columbia to Texas to Chicago to Yale and writing article after article about personal jurisdiction and conflict of laws.

On the day I met her, she happened to be serving as a member of the Dean's Search committee at Yale Law School that eventually picked Guido Calabresi as our Dean. That choice sparked a watershed in Yale's institutional trajectory that carries our school to this day. I will never forget the moment when my office interview with Lea was interrupted by a knock on the door; she opened it only to find the great Guido standing there. But instead of treating him with the deference that I would have expected from a young faculty member to the next Dean, Lea instead demanded that Guido apologize for not returning her phone calls about some matter. To my amazement, an embarrassed Guido dropped to his knees in apology. Lea had quite literally brought the Dean to his knees! I remember thinking to myself, "That Lea Brilmayer is one formidable person!" And in the years since, my view on that has never changed.

Over the next few years, Lea and her wonderfully kind and gentle husband, Bill Horne, became valued friends to my wife Christy and me. During my first year, they invited us often to their beachfront house to celebrate our arrival to New Haven and Yale. Lea regaled me with stories of the Yale Law School I was entering, and all the ways it could be better. I listened carefully and learned, and years later, as Dean, tried to implement many of her suggestions.

As I started teaching Procedure and she started teaching international law, our worlds gradually started to overlap and merge. Along with a number of talented students, she authored *An Introduction to Jurisdiction in the American Federal System*, an admirably clear exposition that she analogized in the Preface to a "perfectly baked chicken," satisfying to consume because while

---

* Sterling Professor of International Law, Yale Law School; Dean, Yale Law School, 2004–09.

© KONINKLIJKE BRILL NV, LEIDEN, 2019 | DOI:10.1163/9789004316539_003

relatively modest in aspiration, it was so perfect in execution. Helped by Lea's writings, I finally started to learn about Conflict of Laws, a topic on which Lea was the acknowledged master.[1] With Alex Wendt and David Lumsdaine, then two young international relations scholars on the Yale political science faculty, we taught a seminar together for a number of years that educated us both about two scholarly disciplines divided by a common language: international law and international relations. That seminar and the thoughts that grew out of it eventually led Lea to write two provocative books on international jurisprudence that combined philosophy, international relations, and international law: *Justifying International Acts* and *American Hegemony: Political Morality in a One-Superpower World.*

In the early 1990s, we engaged in a lengthy debate in the *Yale Law Journal* that set us both on the scholarly paths that we are still on. She wrote about "international law in American courts"[2] and I wrote about transnational public law litigation,[3] an element of the broader phenomenon of transnational legal process that consumes me still.[4] A few years later, I had actually become enmeshed in an exhausting, brass-knuckles version of transnational public law litigation, fighting over the human rights of Haitian refugees on the high seas and on Guantanamo. For nearly two years, that litigation consumed every bit of my time and energy.[5] Overwhelmed with work, I called Lea and begged off a prior academic commitment I had made to her. She had every right to be angry, but I will never forget what she said instead: "Harold, I envy you. You've found a deep passion in the law. Something you're really ready to fight for. I hope someday to find a similar passion in my own life. So of course, you have to pursue it. Forget your promise to me; of course, you will make it up to me someday. But good luck and follow your heart." I hung up the phone realizing that I had made a real and true friend.

By the mid-1990s, Lea had in fact found her own passion in the law: the struggles of the newly minted nation of Eritrea for global recognition and human rights respect. During those years, Lea moved part-time to Asmara and

---

1   See generally LEA BRILMAYER & ERIN O'HARA O'CONNOR, CONFLICTS OF LAWS: CASES AND MATERIALS (2015); LEA BRILMAYER, CONFLICT OF LAWS (1995); LEA BRILMAYER, CONFLICT OF LAWS: FOUNDATIONS AND FUTURE DIRECTIONS (1990).

2   Lea Brilmayer, *International Law in American Courts: A Modest Proposal*, 100 YALE L.J. 2277 (1991).

3   Harold Hongju Koh, *Transnational Public Law Litigation*, 100 YALE L.J. 2347 (1991).

4   See generally HAROLD HONGJU KOH, THE TRUMP ADMINISTRATION AND INTERNATIONAL LAW (2018), Harold Hongju Koh, *Why Do Nations Obey International Law?*, 106 YALE L.J. 2599 (1997); Harold Hongju Koh, *Transnational Legal Process*, 75 NEB. L. REV. 181 (1996).

5   See Harold Hongju Koh, *Enduring Legacies of the Haitian Refugee Litigation*, 61 NYLS L. REV. 31 (2016–17).

litigated multiple huge arbitrations and international dispute settlements on behalf of a fledgling government of which she became a de facto citizen. Along the way, she left Yale and moved to New York, and I thought my days of colleagueship with her had passed.

But happily, I was wrong. In the late 1990s, Lea returned to Yale a different, happier person. She engaged less in academic battles, and focused more on the kind of international dispute settlement that we had in common. Between stints in the U.S. government, and as Yale Law School's Dean, I taught a class with her on international and transnational dispute resolution. Lea's fascination with international claims led her, along with Chiara Giorgetti and Lorraine Charlton, to assemble what is now probably the definitive work on the role and function of post-conflict international claims commissions.[6] Along the way, she did thoughtful work on nationalism and state secession on which I have relied in my own work, academic and governmental.

During my time as Dean, and since I returned from my last stint in the U.S. government, we have happily taught many of the same first-term students. They love Lea because of her good humor and deep devotion to their well-being. Every year, she and Bill invite the new students to their seaside home for an "adult sleepover," where the students sit with each other in a hot tub, or sail in kayaks out to the islands of Branford. Lea's and Bill's simple act of hospitality teaches these new lawyers to learn about law at the same time as they learn about building a community of friends, perhaps the essential skill in leading a happy life as a lawyer.

These past few years have been happy times in our friendship, as we have enjoyed letting other people battle over the kinds of issues of academic politics that we once cared so much about earlier in our careers. I love telling Lea's Contracts students that she really should be teaching them Procedure. And she never fails to be surprised when one of her students finally comes to understand the subject of personal jurisdiction not from my lectures, but from reading Lea's landmark article on "How Contacts Count."[7]

Over time, contacts count by building the shared experiences among colleagues that make the heart grow fonder. I like to think of Lea now as an inspired gardener—a nurturing soul who, as she yearly does in her own garden, plants bulbs that give rise to many different, but always beautiful kinds of flowers and bouquets. As time has unfolded, I have realized that our shared

---

6 Lea Brilmayer, Chiara Giorgetti & Lorraine Charlton, International Claims Commissions: Righting Wrongs After Conflict (2017).

7 Lea Brilmayer, *How Contacts Count: Due Process Limitations on State Court Jurisdiction*, 1980 S. Ct. Review 77.

fascination with jurisdiction has grown out of our common interest in studying how transactions become relationships: how repeated contacts give
rise to collaborations and partnerships that in time create abiding bonds of
mutual loyalty and obligation. In 1991, as part of our debate about international law in American courts, I thanked Lea for her "enduring friendship and
colleagueship."[8] Thirty-four years into our friendship, I thank her again, this
time only double underscoring the word "enduring."

I close on this note: You did it, Lea! After 34 years, you have brought another
Dean to his knees! There is no one else quite like you! Brava, my dear and cou-
rageous friend! Long may we teach together!

---

8   Koh, supra note 3, at 2347 n.*.

CHAPTER 3

Professor Brilmayer and the Third Restatement

*Kermit Roosevelt III**

It is an honor to contribute to a volume recognizing Lea Brilmayer. Given the significance of Lea's legal scholarship, such a volume would have been appropriate at virtually any time in the past few decades, but it comes at a particularly propitious moment now. The American Law Institute is at work on a Third Restatement of Conflict of Laws, for which I am the Reporter. This essay thus affords an opportunity to look over Lea's many years of scholarship on the conflict of laws and to see what guidance can be gleaned for the project. In what follows, I attempt to articulate, as best I can, what that guidance is: what Lea's body of work suggests a Third Restatement should look like.[1] It will show, I hope, just how much influence her work has exerted over the design thus far.

1   With or without Foundations?

A first question for the drafters of a Restatement is what the balance should be between purely descriptive statements of law, ("a court will do thus and so," or "the law governing a claim of X sort is the law of Y"), and explanations of why or how a particular law has been selected. Should there be an attempt to describe the choice-of-law process in more general, theoretical terms—to explain the goals and methods of reasoning that have been used to generate the specific black letter provisions?

Lea suggests that there should be. Certainly some sort of foundation is necessary for the intelligent drafting of a choice-of-law system; as Lea puts it, "the

---

*   Professor of Law, University of Pennsylvania Law School. I am the Reporter for the Third Restatement of Conflict of Laws. The views expressed here are my own and do not necessarily reflect those of the American Law Institute or the Associate Reporters, Laura Little and Chris Whytock.

1   There are, of course, other ways of finding out Lea's views on the proper content of a Third Restatement: since she is, happily, an Adviser to the project, we receive her comments on drafts. The point of this essay is to document the influence of her scholarship: to show just how much we are already in her debt.

idea that foundations are unnecessary is demonstrably wrong."[2] When hard or unusual cases arise, theory guides: "there is a *need* for a theoretical foundation in novel or controversial cases if one is to think intelligently about what one wishes to do."[3] And the foundation is necessary not just for the producers of the system but also for the consumers. "It just does not seem that one can really apply a choice of law analysis sensibly without knowing the underlying reasoning."[4]

How we understand what goes on in choice of law will affect how the Restatement is drafted and used. Setting out a conceptual framework will achieve two main goals. For users of the Restatement, it will let them know how particular rules have been derived, what they are intended to achieve, and—in consequence—when following a rule in a particular case would lead to unanticipated results and should be avoided. For professors, teaching the next generation of lawyers, judges, and law professors, it will facilitate presentation of the Restatement as a coherent approach rather than a congeries of ad hoc rules. And for drafters of the Restatement, it will provide some analytical structure. Once we select a particular theoretical framework, a particular understanding of what goes on in a choice of law decision, we will find that we have answered some questions about which results are appropriate and which are impermissible according to our premises.

2   What Foundations?

What should our conceptual framework be? At the most general level, I will suggest, all approaches to choice of law share the same structure: what I call the two-step model. The Third Restatement should of course do the same, and perhaps there is some value in making the two-step model explicit. But since all approaches share this structure, the general two-step model does not take us very far. The important question will be how we understand the two steps. Here, I will suggest, Lea's scholarship provides a host of valuable suggestions. First, though, it is necessary to explain the model.

2   Lea R. Brilmayer, *Governmental Interest Analysis: A House Without Foundations*, 46 Ohio St. L.J. 459, 460 (1985).
3   *Id.* at 461.
4   *Id.*

2.1   *The Two-Step Model*

At a high level of generality, every approach to choice of law shares the same basic structure. First, they identify the relevant states—the states whose law might ultimately be chosen to govern an issue. Second, they choose the law of one of those states. Different approaches perform these two steps in different ways, and they place different degrees of reliance on the two steps. First Restatement analysis, the territorialism of Joseph Beale, relies entirely on the first step.[5] Only one state is relevant, according to Beale: the state where rights vest. And since according to Beale's premises there can be only one such state, once we determine where rights come into being, we have identified the governing law.

At the other extreme, the Second Restatement places very little emphasis on the first step. It does not explicitly tell its users anything about how to identify relevant states. Any state suggested by the section 6 factors[6] would seem to be a candidate; judges, it seems, must find them on their own. (This need not mean that anything goes, however. Some of the section 6 factors refer specifically to "interested" states,[7] which would seem to exclude states without an interest, and other sections specify the contacts to be taken into account in applying the section 6 factors.[8] These contacts are probably best understood as pointers identifying states that are likely to be interested. While uninterested states

---

5   *See* Kermit Roosevelt III, *The Myth of Choice of Law: Rethinking Conflicts*, 97 MICH. L. REV. 2448, 2455–2458 (1997) (describing Beale's system).

6   The section 6 factors (Restatement, Second, of Conflict of Laws, § 6(a)-(g)) are (a) the needs of the interstate and international systems, (b) the relevant policies of the forum, (c) the relevant policies of other interested states and the relative interests of those states in the determination of the particular issue, (d) the protection of justified expectations, (e) the basic policies underlying the particular field of law, (f) certainty, predictability and uniformity of result, and (g) ease in the determination and application of the law to be applied.

7   *See* RESTATEMENT, SECOND, OF CONFLICT OF LAWS § 6(b), (c). It is not entirely clear what the Second Restatement means by an interest, or whether it is the same as what Brainerd Currie meant. *See generally* KERMIT ROOSEVELT, CONFLICT OF LAWS 43–90 (2d ed. 2015) (discussing interest analysis and the Second Restatement). I will suggest and endorse an understanding that Currie also endorsed: asking whether a state has an interest is just the same thing as asking whether its law reaches the facts of the case—that is, asking whether its law creates rights or obligations based on those facts, or asking whether the facts fall within the scope of its law. Though Currie did endorse this understanding, he then proceeded to do his analysis in a way that fits very awkwardly with his premises. *See, e.g.*, Larry Kramer, *Interest Analysis and the Presumption of Forum Law*, 56 U. CHI. L. REV. 1301 (1989) (arguing that Currie's presumption of forum law contradicts his premises); Larry Kramer, *The Myth of the Unprovided-for Case*, 75 VA. L. REV. 1045 (1989) (arguing that Currie's solution to unprovided-for cases contradicts his premises). I will try to suggest a more sensible way to do it.

8   See RESTATEMENT, SECOND, OF CONFLICT OF LAWS §§ 145 (torts), 188 (contracts).

might come into the analysis through factors such as the protection of justified expectations (§ 6(d)) or ease in the determination and application of the
law to be applied (§ 6(e)), the comments to § 6 suggest that generally the law
selected by § 6 analysis will be the law of an interested state—in fact, the state
with the dominant interest. "In general, it is fitting that the state whose interests are most deeply affected should have its local law applied. Which is the
state of dominant interest may depend upon the issue involved."[9]) Brainerd
Currie's interest analysis occupies an intermediate position: the relevant states
are the interested ones, with the forum coming in to fill any gaps—at least in
early versions of the theory.[10]

So deciding that the Third Restatement will work in terms of the two-step
model commits us to nothing—approaches as disparate as territorialism and
the Second Restatement do so as well. What separates the approaches are how
they perform the two steps. The first important theoretical question the Third
Restatement faces, then, is how to identify the relevant states.

2.2   Thinking in Terms of Rights

What might be a good approach to identifying relevant states? It would be
nice if choice-of-law analysis resembled ordinary legal analysis, the sort used
to resolve analogous problems in purely domestic cases. This would be nice
for two reasons. First, there are some principles that guide the resolution of
analogous problems in purely domestic cases. Some of these principles, particularly those that allocate interpretive authority among different actors,
are considered binding limits in the ordinary legal context.[11] If choice of law
uses a similar conceptual framework, we will be able to see if it honors those

---

9   *Id.* § 6, cmt. f.
10   Currie believed that forum law should be used to decide unprovided-for cases, where no
     state had an interest, and also that there should be a presumption in favor of forum law.
     Larry Kramer has suggested, and I agree, that neither of these rules is consistent with
     Currie's underlying premises. See *supra* note 6.
11   It is generally accepted, for instance, that, (within constitutional limits), states are author-
     itative as to the scope and meaning of their law. A state gets to decide to whom, and under
     what circumstances, its law grants rights. *See, e.g., Erie Railroad v. Tompkins*, 304 U.S. 64,
     78 ("The authority and only authority [with respect to state law] is the State, and if that
     be so, the voice adopted by the State as its own (whether it be of its Legislature or of
     its Supreme Court) should utter the last word."") (quoting *Black and White Taxicab Co. v.
     Brown and Yellow Taxicab Co.*, 276 U.S. 518 (1928) (Holmes, J., dissenting). It is also gener-
     ally accepted that state court interpretations of their own law are authoritative. *See, e.g.,
     Johnson v. Fankell*, 520 U.S. 911, 916 ("Neither this Court nor any other federal tribunal has
     any authority to place a construction on a state statute different from the one rendered by
     the highest court of the State.").

principles or not. In my view, we should not depart from those principles without a justification that thus far has not been provided.

Second, an approach that resembles ordinary legal analysis will be intelligible to non-specialists. Generalist judges and lawyers are often mystified by
the esoteric vocabulary of conflicts, its talk of interests, depecage, renvoi, and
unprovided-for cases. If we can explain these concepts in ordinary legal language, (or perhaps even do without them), it will help users of the Restatement.

So how would it look if we tried to describe choice of law from the perspective of ordinary legal analysis? Perhaps the biggest difference between choice
of law and ordinary legal analysis is one of vocabulary. Choice of law has its
own specialized jargon, as noted above, but perhaps more important it largely
lacks one of the most fundamental concepts of ordinary legal analysis: the idea
of a right. The reasons for this are largely historical. The Realists ridiculed Beale
and his reliance on vested rights, and they attacked the idea of "rights" more
broadly.[12] Sophisticated scholars, not wishing to be accused of hoary metaphysics, began to talk instead of policies, or interests, or functional approaches.

In 1989, Lea published Rights, Fairness, and Choice of Law.[13] It recommended that choice of law scholars not be afraid of using the concept of
rights.[14] As Lea, and later Larry Kramer pointed out, the Realist revolution
that swept the concept from choice of law had the effect of separating choice
of law from ordinary legal discourse, which pervasively relies on the concept of
a right.[15] Does the plaintiff have a claim under a particular statute? Does the
defendant have an immunity to invoke? In ordinary legal analysis, these questions are discussed in terms of rights created by law and given to individuals.
We do not think that rights are physical objects, but we do generally engage
in much the sort of reification that the Realists scorned. Legal rights—claims
and defenses—exist in a very substantial sense. They often accrue at a particular moment, and we have rules about how to determine when they accrue,

---

12   See, e.g., WALTER WHEELER COOK, THE LOGICAL AND LEGAL BASES OF THE
      CONFLICT OF LAWS, 30–33 (1942); Felix S. Cohen, Transcendental Nonsense and the
      Functional Approach, 35 COLUM. L. REV. 809 (1935).
13   98 YALE L.J. 1277 (1989).
14   Admittedly, the rights that Lea argued for in that article were not the ordinary positive-
      law rights discussed in this section—the claims and defenses created by state law. They
      were, rather, political rights that she suggested should prevent unfair exercises of state
      authority. Those rights will come into play when we start trying to give more content to
      the two steps of the two-step model: determining the scope of state law and granting
      priority to one law over another when laws conflict. See infra §§ 4, 5.
15   See 98 YALE L.J. at 1278 ("in other areas of law, many of us continue ... to discuss legal
      problems in terms of the parties' rights."); Larry Kramer, Return of the Renvoi, 66 N.Y.U.
      L. REV. 979, 990–991 (1991).

(though we tend not to care as much as Beale did about where). They may expire after a certain period of time. They can be raised, or waived, or forfeited; they can even be bought and sold through settlement, assignment, or champerty. There is perhaps a debate to be had about the ontological status of these things, but that our ordinary legal analysis uses the concept of rights is hardly open to question.[16]

Interestingly, our ordinary legal analysis uses the concept of rights in a manner very similar to the two-step model described above.[17] In deciding whether plaintiff or defendant should prevail in a purely domestic case, a judge will first identify the relevant legal rules. Is there a common law rule that gives the plaintiff a cause of action? Is there a statute that immunizes the defendant? Might some state law be preempted by federal law, or invalidated by the state or federal constitution? Having identified the relevant legal rules, the judge then decides which one will be given effect if they conflict.[18] Statutes prevail over common law; state constitutions over state statutes; federal statutes over state law in all its forms; and the federal constitution over all else. Identify the sources of rights and, when there is more than one, decide which takes priority. That is what happens in ordinary cases.

Might it be fruitful to describe choice of law from this perspective? Certainly, such a description is possible. What happens in a multistate case, we might say, is that the parties invoke rights—claims and defenses—not just from one state's law, or from state law and federal law, but from the laws of multiple states. This complicates matters, of course, because while we do have a clear hierarchy of laws within a single state—common law, state statutes, state constitution, federal statutes, federal constitution—we have no such ranking of the laws of the several states. Instead, we will have to create rules that tell us which state law should be given priority. But the two steps are the same: we identify the relevant laws and then (somehow) select one.

Thinking in ordinary legal terms tells us something else, at least if we follow the analogy. It tells us which states' laws are relevant. In the ordinary domestic case, a law will be relevant if it gives a right—a claim or a defense—to one of the parties. That is what makes it a candidate for selection at the second step. A plaintiff cannot recover under a law that does not give him or her a claim; a defendant cannot avoid liability based on a law that does not give him or her

---

16   See Larry Kramer, *Return of the Renvoi*, 66 N.Y.U. L. Rev. 979, 990–991 (1991) ("Our entire legal system rests on the concept of vested rights.").

17   The discussion that follows is inspired in large part by the work of Larry Kramer, perhaps most notably *Rethinking Choice of Law*, 90 COLUM. L. REV. 277 (1990).

18   See *Id.* at 280.

a defense. Analogously, we might say, the relevant state laws in the multistate context are those that grant the parties rights (claims or defenses), or those that attach legal consequences to the facts of the case, or those that include the facts of the case within their scope.

Now we have a description of the choice of law process. A judge must first decide which states' laws grant rights to the parties, and second, if more than one law grants rights and those rights conflict, decide which rights will be given effect. Suppose we think this is a plausible way to conceptualize choice of law. It has the virtue of resembling ordinary legal analysis. This will be good for non-specialists—generalist lawyers and judges will be able to understand it without wading into the esoterica of choice of law theory. What remains to be done in terms of designing a Restatement, and what are the implications of this conceptual model? And—a question not without importance for a Restatement—is there support in the cases for such a characterization?

3   The Source of Rights: Interest Analysis and Statutory Interpretation

As it turns out, the idea that choice of law can in part be assimilated to ordinary legal analysis has a very prominent place in choice of law scholarship. It is what has been called Brainerd Currie's basic insight, and it has been developed further by Larry Kramer.[19]

Attributing this model to Brainerd Currie carries some danger. For one, Currie's exegesis is an industry of its own, and one risks getting bogged down in debates about precisely what he said and meant—and how consistent his applications of his theory are with its underlying premises.[20] For another, Currie and his version of interest analysis were the target of sustained and forceful criticism by none other than Lea Brilmayer, so someone following her scholarship might be wary of getting too close to Currie.[21] What I will suggest, though, is that we can profitably retain Currie's basic insight—that the first

---

19   *See* Kramer, *Return of the Renvoi*, 66 N.Y.U. L. Rev. at 998 ("Currie's basic insight ... was that choosing the applicable law is a process of interpreting the relevant laws."); Rethinking Choice of Law at 292 ("My understanding—though the matter is not free from doubt—is that when Currie says a state is 'interested,' he means that the state's law confers a right in a particular case.") (footnote omitted).

20   For Currie's own statement of his views, see generally BRAINERD CURRIE, SELECTED ESSAYS ON THE CONFLICT OF LAWS (1963).

21   *See, e.g.*, Lea R. Brilmayer, *Governmental Interest Analysis: A House Without Foundations*, 46 OHIO ST. L.J. 459 (1985); Lea R. Brilmayer, *Methods and Objectives in the Conflict of Laws: A Challenge*, 35 MERCER L. REV. 555 (1984).

step of choice of law is determining what rights the parties can invoke under positive law and the second is resolving any clashes between those rights—if we go on to develop it while keeping Lea's criticisms in mind. What follows is an attempt to do just that.

What does retaining Currie's basic insight as a starting point tell us? It tells us that, as Currie often claimed, our first step—deciding whether the laws grant rights to the parties—is a matter of interpreting the law.[22] This is more or less definitionally true: figuring out whether a law gives rights to an individual under certain circumstances is what interpretation is, or does. If we are trying to figure out who can claim rights under the law based on a particular set of facts, we are interpreting it. The argument runs in the other direction as well: when Currie said that we should ask whether application of a law would promote the policies behind it, he was identifying the same question that interpreters of the law ask in a purely domestic case. What they find out by asking that question is whether the law attaches legal consequences to certain events: whether it creates rights or obligations based on those events, or, in other words, whether the facts of the case fall within the scope of the law. It makes sense, then, to suppose that this is also what we find out by asking that question in the multistate case.

The payoff isn't just definitional, though. Understanding that the first step of choice of law amounts to interpreting the states' laws tells some other things. It tells us something about how power is allocated in this venture. We know that states are authoritative as to the scope of their laws. Subject of course to some constitutional limits, state legislatures get to decide to whom their laws give rights: they are the authoritative lawmakers. State courts, similarly, are the authoritative interpreters of their own laws: when they interpret a state law to tell us to whom it grants rights, courts of other states must follow those interpretations.[23]

Insofar as choice of law is concerned, this allocation of power has several immediate consequences. It tells us that when a state law specifies its scope, that specification must be honored. If a case falls outside the scope of a state's law, its law creates no rights or obligations pertaining to that case. It cannot be used as a rule of decision to govern issues in the case—or if it, does the outcome of deciding the case under it must be that the plaintiff fails to state a claim. If a statute provides a cause of action for wrongful deaths caused in the state, for instance, it cannot be used by the courts of any state to give a remedy for a death caused outside the state. Whether a state law grants rights

---

22   See *supra* note 18.

23   *See supra* note 10.

to certain people under certain circumstances is a question of the content and meaning of that law, and the courts and legislature of that state are authoritative on that question.

It should be immediately evident that this approach to choice of law coheres with ordinary legal analysis and the ordinary allocation of authority with respect to the making and interpretation of state law: ordinarily, state courts and legislatures have the last word as to the content and meaning of that state's law. A look at the caselaw gives some reason to think that it is also on the right track in terms of restating choice of law, too, for the rule that a statutory specification of scope binds all courts is accepted at least widely and perhaps universally.[24] And it is, moreover, consistent with Lea's admonition that states know their own interests: it is perhaps the best way to operationalize that insight. Identifying the relevant laws as those that grant the parties rights places authority exactly where Lea says it should go. "Choice-of-law theory recognizes that judges accept the other state's definition of its own substantive law,"[25] Lea wrote. And, she continues, "[c]hoice of law divergence is no

---

24   See, e.g., Budget Rent-A-Car System v. Chappell, 304 F. Supp. 2d 639 (E.D. Pa. 2004) (Pennsylvania choice of law), rev'd on other grounds, 407 F.3d 166 (3d Cir. 2005); Budget Rent-A-Car System v. Chappell, 407 F.3d 166, 172 (3d Cir. 2005) (Pennsylvania choice of law); Garcia v. Plaza Oldsmobile Ltd., 421 F.3d 216, 220–221 (3d Cir. 2005) (Pennsylvania choice of law). In the slightly different context of contractual choice of law, the rule seems even more strongly established. See, e.g., Gravquick A/S v. Trimble Navigation Int'l Ltd., 323 F.3d 1219 (9th Cir. 2003) (California choice of law); Cotter v. Lyft, Inc., 60 F.Supp.3d 1059 (N.D. Cal. 2014) (California choice of law); Shaver v. Soo Line R.R. Co., 284 F. Supp. 701, 702 (E.D. Wis. 1968) (Wisconsin choice of law); Cromeens, Holloman, Sibert, Inc. v. AB Volvo, 349 F.3d 376, 385 (7th Cir. 2003) (Arkansas choice of law); Peugeot Motors of America, Inc. v. Eastern Auto Distributors, Inc., 892 F.2d 355 (4th Cir. 1989) (New York choice of law); Sawyer v. Mkt. Am., Inc., 661 S.E.2d 750 (N.C. Ct. App. 2008). It is also worth noting the U.S. Supreme Court's decisions about the extraterritorial application of U.S. law. In a number of cases, the Supreme Court has made it quite clear that determining whether a U.S. federal statute gives a cause of action for events occurring outside the territory of the U.S. is a matter of statutory interpretation, and a matter of the substance of the law and the merits of the case, so that if a plaintiff seeks to recover for events outside the scope of the statute, the correct outcome is a merits dismissal. See, e.g., Morrison v. Nat'l Australia Bank Ltd., 561 U.S. 247, 254 (2010) ("But to ask what conduct [a statute] reaches is to ask what conduct [it] prohibits, which is a merits question."). What is perhaps more problematic is the Court's unwillingness to consider a second step—to consider the possibility that a case could fall within the scope of U.S. law but that foreign law might nonetheless be given controlling force. See Lea R. Brilmayer, Extraterritorial Application of American Law, 50 Law & Contemp. Probs. 11, 20–23 (1987).

25   Lea R. Brilmayer, The Other State's Interests, 24 CORNELL INT'L L.J. 233, 235 (1991).

different from substantive law divergence."[26] Exactly so: choice of law, at the first step, is no different from substantive law. The first question is which laws grant the parties rights, and that is a question that is within the authority of each state's lawmakers and judges.[27]

So, it is not at all clear that Lea's attacks on Currie imply or amount to a rejection of this first conceptual point.[28] Currie's problem, we could say, was not that he thought the first step of choice of law was statutory interpretation, but rather that he did the statutory interpretation badly and sometimes asserted an authority that he didn't have. That he, "had his own beliefs about how far statutes ought to reach,"[29] in multistate cases and that he, "sought to camouflage his preferences as effectuation of *legislative* policy goals."[30] The obvious task for the Third Restatement is to come up with more plausible interpretations—interpretations that can be used as a presumption and set aside in the face of legislative direction to the contrary.[31]

---

26   *Id.* at 236. Elsewhere, Lea quotes, (though perhaps not with full approval), Russell Weintraub's suggestion that choice-of-law's alienation from ordinary legal analysis is a problem. See Brilmayer, 35 MERCER L. REV. at 630 ("I ... share Professor Currie's belief that the evils that had beset conflicts methodology were the result of separating the conflict of laws from the mainstream of legal reasoning; that good conflicts analysis is good legal analysis and—this is crucial—vice versa.").

27   *See Id.* at 241, ("If we take seriously the idea that conflict of laws is really an extension of substantive law, then it would seem that the forum ought to treat the other state's determination regarding the territorial scope of its statutes with the same deference as it treats the other state's determination of what substantive rule to apply. Each of these determinations should be taken as a given....") To put the point in the terms Lea used, she is correct that interests are subjective. This is an issue on which interest analysts split— which is one reason it might be good to avoid the vocabulary of interests in favor of the vocabulary of rights—and on which Currie waffled, which is a reason to avoid getting bogged down in Currie exegesis.

28   As Larry Kramer put it, Lea's objection "is not an objection to a choice of law method alone, or even primarily: it is an objection to a conventional method of statutory construction." 90 COLUM. L. REV. at 300.

29   Lea R. Brilmayer, *Methods and Objectives in the Conflict of Laws: A Challenge*, 35 MERCER L. REV. 555, 555 (1984).

30   *Id.*

31   The draft Restatement describes the presumptions used to determine the scope of state law and then accommodates contrary legislative specification of scope by noting that such specification may justify the use of a different state's law than the one selected by the Restatement's rules. See Restatement, Third, of Conflict of Laws, Council Draft 2, § 5.02 Cmt. *c.* (September 17, 2017).

4   Presuming Scope

How should a court determine the scope of a state law in a multistate case, if the legislature has not specified it?[32] Currently, there are two main answers. Neither is satisfactory, and Lea has shown the deficiency of both. One is Brainerd Currie's infamous selfish state hypothesis: the scope of state law should be whatever will advantage locals.[33] This approach to determining scope is unpleasantly parochial. In some contexts, it may run afoul of constitutional antidiscrimination norms—if, for instance, it suggests that rights under a state's law are not available to visiting out-of-staters.[34] And it does not seem consistent with the evidence we have of actual legislative intent.[35]

So, the selfish-state approach is a nonstarter, for reasons Lea has demonstrated. The other major approach that exists in the caselaw is the presumption against extraterritoriality used by the Supreme Court to determine the scope of federal statutes. In a number of cases, the Supreme Court has confronted the question of whether a federal statute gives rights in cases involving foreign elements. The Court's ultimate conclusion has been that federal statutes are presumed to have a territorial scope; unless that presumption is overcome, they do not create rights or obligations with respect to events occurring outside the United States.

This is a well-developed approach that certainly merits consideration as a way to determine the scope of state law. But federal extraterritoriality jurisprudence has a bit more to teach us before we get to the question of its suitability for that purpose. It shows us—and Lea seems to agree with it to this extent—that determining the scope of a statute is indeed a matter of statutory interpretation, as Currie claimed. Over and over the Supreme Court has

---

32   It is important to understand precisely what this question means. It is not equivalent to the question "when should a state's law be used to govern an issue?" Which state's law should govern an issue is the ultimate question in choice of law analysis. The determination of scope tells us which state laws are relevant—that is, which should be considered as available to govern an issue. If an issue falls within the scope of more than one state's law, we will have to choose one to govern. That is the second step, what I call the determination of priority.

33   See CURRIE, MARRIED WOMEN'S CONTRACTS: A STUDY IN CONFLICT-OF-LAWS METHOD, IN SELECTED ESSAYS ON CONFLICT OF LAWS at 77, 89 (1963). Currie was explicit there that he put this hypothetical forward as an oversimplified example to show how the analysis worked. He failed, however, to move much beyond it.

34   See, e.g., John Hart Ely, Choice of Law and the State's Interest in Protecting Its Own, 23 WM. & MARY L. REV. 173, 180–191 (1981); Lea R. Brilmayer, Interest Analysis and the Myth of Legislative Intent, 78 MICH. L. REV. 392, 408 (1980).

35   See Brilmayer, 78 MICH. L. REV. at 424–429.

described its task in such cases as one of interpretation. And it has made clear that in deciding whether a statute reaches certain conduct or not it is deciding a merits question—it is not deciding whether the law "applies" in some abstract, procedural, or jurisdictional sense; it is deciding whether the plaintiff has a claim or not.[36]

So, if asked whether we believe that determination of scope is statutory interpretation, we can respond along the lines of the joke about infant baptism: "Believe in it? Why, I've seen it done!"[37] But what about the appropriateness of the presumption against extraterritoriality as a method of determining the scope of state law?

Like the selfish state hypothesis, the presumption against extraterritoriality turns out to be a bad idea. It does a slightly better job of capturing actual practice: some states do in fact have a presumption against extraterritoriality as part of their statutory interpretation.[38] But to adopt a presumption against extraterritoriality would be a step backwards for choice of law theory—few people suggest that the field would advance by a general retreat to territorialism.[39] We can do better in determining scope.

The problem, we could say, is that the selfish state version of interest analysis made the analysis all about domicile, while the presumption against extraterritoriality gave no weight to domicile. A better approach would understand that domicile matters sometimes, but not always. That's true enough, and it's a diagnosis that Lea offered, but there's another point, which Lea also made. Courts determining the scope of federal statutes face a problem. If they seek to promote the purposes behind the statute, they are likely to presume a broad scope. But once they have done so, they find it difficult to limit that scope out of deference to the interests of other states. As Lea put it, "since congressional intent has already been declared to require application, [courts think that] there is no principled basis for later limitation."[40] And yet, as Lea points out,

---

36   Failing to have the required events occur in the U.S. is the failure to satisfy an element of the claim just as the failure to satisfy the numerosity requirement of Title VII. See Morrison, 561 U.S. at 254.

37   See, e.g., Frank H. Easterbrook, *Alternatives to Originalism?*, 19 HARV. J.L. &PUB. POL'Y 479, 479 (1996).

38   See, e.g., *Sullivan v. Oracle Corp.*, 254 P.3d 237 (Cal. 2011).

39   For a discussion of the history of choice of law and suggestions for the future, see, e.g., LEA R. BRILMAYER, CONFLICT OF LAWS: FOUNDATIONS AND FUTURE DIRECTIONS (2d ed. 1995).

40   Lea R. Brilmayer, *The Extraterritorial Application of American Law: A Methodological and Constitutional Appraisal*, 50 L. & Contemp. Probs 11, 20 (1987).

"the interests of foreign states or nations might very well be thought important by the legislature itself."[41]

Fortunately, there is a way out of this problem, though the U.S. Supreme Court does not seem to see it as a possibility. The fact that other states' laws and policies might matter means that a second step in the analysis is required: after deciding that a state's law reaches some set of facts, a court should also consider whether some other state's law reaches those facts, and if so, which law should be given priority. That, of course, is the second step of the two-step model, and the subject of the following section. It is one of the great contributions of Lea's "Extraterritorial Application of American Law" to make the case that the Supreme Court's approach—which decides, or assumes, that U.S. law must be used to govern every case within its scope—is missing something.[42]

Returning to the question of scope: neither the selfish-state hypothesis nor the presumption against extraterritoriality gives a sensible answer as to the scope of state law in a multistate case. The sensible answer, which takes both domicile and geography into account, is that a state's law should be presumptively available to everyone within its borders and, under certain circumstances, for cases involving its domiciliaries outside its borders. This answer is in large part directed by the Constitution: the Privileges and Immunities Clause of Article IV renders it at best problematic to deny rights under local law to visiting out-of-staters,[43] while the Due Process Clause usually prevents states from prescribing that their law reaches out-of-state cases not involving their domiciliaries.[44] The category of out-of-state cases involving domiciliaries is subject to less regulation, so the main remaining question is which such cases should be presumed to fall within the scope of state law?

The category of out-of-state cases involving domiciliaries can be divided into three subcategories: those in which both parties are domiciliaries, those in which one party is and that party is favored by the state's law, and those in which one party is and that party is disfavored by the state's law. Extending

---

41   *Id.* at 22.

42   One might think that the Court cannot use the two-step approach because it might not have jurisdiction to decide cases under foreign law: if it does not use U.S. law as the rule of decision, the case does not arise under federal law. But this confuses jurisdiction and merits. If there is a claim under U.S. law that should be subordinated to rights under foreign law, the case still arises under U.S. law. In fact, in the antitrust context the Court has considered the possibility of case-by-case balancing, but rejected it. See *F. Hoffman-La Roche Ltd v. Empagran S.A.*, 542 U.S. 155, 168 (2004) ("In our view, however, this approach is too complex to prove workable."). It has settled instead on a statute-by-statute balancing. *See id.*

43   *See* Ely, *supra* note 32.

44   *See, e.g., Home Insurance Co. v. Dick*, 281 U.S. 397 (1930).

the scope of a state's law to the first subcategory is relatively uncontroversial.[45] So too for the second one—it would, we shall see, be more controversial to assert that the state's law should *govern* the case or issue, (that is, that it should be given priority over another conflicting law), but the idea that domiciliaries may claim the protection of their own law if no other law intervenes is fairly straightforward and plausible. The third category is more problematic, and cases tend to reject it—they hold that a state's law should not be, as Chief Judge Fuld put it (quoting Second Restatement Reporter Willis Reese), "manna for the entire world."[46] Thus it seems sensible to exclude it—subject as always to legislative correction.

5 Deciding Priority

Thus far, following Lea's suggestions to think in terms of rights and to understand that states control to whom their laws grant rights, we have achieved the following. We have decided that a law is relevant—that it is a candidate for selection as the law governing an issue—if it actually grants rights to the parties, or, in other words, if the facts of the case bring it within the scope of that law. We have decided that state specifications of scope are binding, but that in the absence of such specification, courts should presume that state laws grant rights to all persons within the state and to domiciliaries outside, when doing so would advance their purposes. The task that remains is deciding how to resolve the conflicts that this presumptive scope generates. What happens, for instance, when a married couple from a state that lacks interspousal tort immunity get into a car accident in a state that has it? According to the scope we have presumed, both states' laws grant rights based on that accident, and those rights conflict. We must now decide which law gets priority.

There are, of course, already several ways to do this. We could tell courts to choose the law of the state with the dominant interest, or the one whose policies will be more impaired if its law is not chosen, or we could tell them to identify the state with the most significant relationship to the issue. Each of these is a reasonable way to get what you could call the right answer to a particular choice of law problem—to give priority to the law of the state

45 It is this extension that makes it possible to say, for instance, that interspousal tort immunity in a car accident case should be governed by the law of marital domicile rather than the law of the place of the accident, which is a widely-accepted resolution. *See, e.g., Haumschild v. Continental Cas. Co.*, 95 N.W.2d 814 (Wisc. 1959).

46 *Neumeier v. Kuhner*, 286 N.E.2d 454, 458–459 (N.Y. 1972) (quoting Willis Reese, *Chief Judge Fuld and Choice of Law*, 71 COLUM. L. REV. 548, 563 (1971).

that has the best claim to regulatory authority in some normative sense. (The
best way to describe the right answer is probably the one that, over time,
maximizes aggregate state policy satisfaction. This is the explicit goal of comparative impairment, and a plausible understanding of interest balancing and
the Second Restatement.)

But Lea has more to teach us here. One of her greatest contributions to the
analysis of choice-of-law problems has been to suggest that getting the right
answer is not the only goal. "Right answer" considerations might guide us in
deciding a single case but are not the only ones to think about in designing a
choice of law system. Instead, "scholars and courts can and should heed some
of the values that interest analysts condemned as metaphysical, such as even-
handedness and predictability. In doing so, a court would not disregard its duty
to follow the commands of its legislature. Legislatures, like conflicts theorists,
have frequently concerned themselves with systems values."[47] What we want,
then, is a set of rules that courts can follow, rules that will get most cases right
while remaining simple enough to do so cheaply and easily.

What should these rules look like? Lea's most recent work has spent a fair
amount of time criticizing what she calls single-factor triggers.[48] Approaches
that give decisive significance to one connecting factor—the place of injury,
for instance, or one party's domicile—predictably generate results that look
perverse because they predictably confront cases in which every other connecting factor points to a different state. These cases are the ones that casebooks
tend to use to illustrate the operation and the limitations of the traditional
approach, choice-of-law chestnuts like *Carroll*.[49] They are the ones that show
us creative judges using escape devices to avoid those results, cases like *Levy*[50]
and *Grant*.[51] And, Lea shows, they are the cases that prompt judges to take the
more radical step of abandoning the single-factor trigger.

Lea is certainly correct that single-factor triggers are problematic and
should be avoided. In their place, she recommends something like multi-factor

47   Brilmayer, 78 MICH. L. REV. at 430. *See generally* Lea R. Brilmayer, *The Role of Substantive
      and Choice of Law Policies in the Formation and Application of Choice of Law Rules*, 252
      Recueil des cours 9 (1995).
48   *See, e.g.*, Lea R. Brilmayer, *What I Like Most About the Restatement (Second) of Conflicts,
      and Why It Should Not Be Thrown Out With the Bathwater*, 110 AJIL UNBOUND 144 (2017);
      Lea R. Brilmayer, *Hard Cases, Single Factor Theories, and a Second Look at the Restatement
      2D of Conflicts*, 2015 U. ILL. L. REV. 1969; Lea R. Brilmayer & Raechel Anglin, *Choice of Law
      Theory and the Metaphysics of the Stand-Alone Trigger*, 95 IOWA L. REV. 1125 (2010).
49   *Alabama Great Southern R.R. Co. v. Carroll*, 11 So. 803 (Al. 1892).
50   *Levy v. Daniels U-Drive Auto Renting Co.*, 143 A. 163 (1928) (using characterization to avoid
      territorialist result).
51   *Grant v. McAuliffe*, 264 P.2d 944 (1953) (using characterization to avoid territorialist result).

balancing, or the center-of-gravity approach.[52] But this prescription is not the only possibility. And if we want to write rules that will give courts meaningful guidance, it is perhaps not the best one. It may in fact be possible to write rules that direct specific outcomes without falling prey to the weakness of the single-factor trigger.

The first step in creating such a rule is to recognize that the cases Lea identifies as demonstrating the weakness of the single-factor trigger tend to feature something more than a fact-pattern where all the factors but the triggering one point away from the chosen state. They also feature a kind of rule or issue that fits poorly with the triggering contact. Territoriality looks bad not just when the injury is the only contact with a state but when the issue being considered is about allocation of loss rather than wrongfulness of conduct. This is true of *Carroll* and *Levy*, which are about vicarious liability; it is true of *Haumschild*, which is about interspousal tort immunity; it is true of *Grant v. McAuliffe*, which is about abatement of a tort claim upon the death of the tortfeasor. The issue in all of those cases was not whether certain conduct was wrongful but how the loss caused by wrongful conduct should be distributed. Because it is generally presumed that states have a greater interest in the allocation of loss among their domiciliaries than among the domiciliaries of some other state, the use of a single *territorial* connecting factor makes the decision seem even more perverse. Likewise, in a case where a person from a state whose law does recognize a particular claim is injured in another state whose law does not recognize the claim, the decision to consider only the plaintiff's domicile in granting relief (as some crude versions of interest analysis might), the result is perverse because a single *domiciliary* contact is given decisive effect, when the issue is whether the conduct is wrongful or not.

So, a single factor trigger might not be terrible if the factor is chosen with a little more attention to the kind of issue involved. But we might also be able to do a bit better. We might, for instance, provide rules based on multiple contacts. For tort claims involving issues of conduct regulation, for instance, if conduct and injury occur in the same state, it is probably safe to pick that state's law. For loss allocation issues, if both parties are domiciled in the same state, it is safe to pick that state's law. Split domicile cases are harder, but we can at least avoid single-factor triggering by using territoriality to break the tie.[53] Cross-border torts with conduct-regulation issues raise perhaps the most difficult problems. But here the use of a single factor may be more defensible. Since we are talking about conduct regulation, the territorial connecting factor

---

52   *See* Brilmayer, 110 AJIL UNBOUND at 146–147.
53   *See* Brilmayer, 98 YALE L.J. at 1303.

of conduct will not appear as arbitrary as it does in *Carroll* or *Levy*: people generally know where they are and can reasonably be asked to conform their acts to the law of that place.[54]

Sometimes then, a single factor may be the best we can do.[55] Usually it is to be avoided, and other Restatement rules also use multiple contacts. The proposed choice of law for products liability, for instance, looks for groupings of contacts. So do the presumptions for contracts not governed by a choice of law clause. The rule for punitive damages attempts to avoid perverse results by authorizing them only if they are available under the law of states providing at least two of three relevant connecting factors.

I hope then, that the specific rules of the Restatement will avoid the perverse results generated by the single-factor trigger. In crafting them, I have been heavily influenced by Lea's admonitions. Lea offers another way to test choice-of-law rules, too. They should not favor locals, as the crude version of interest analysis does. This is so for two reasons: first, doing so violates principles of fairness that Lea identifies;[56] second, it produces nonuniformity, which is undesirable from a systemic perspective. "Territoriality," she observes, "would seem to be an obvious candidate for dealing with the hard cases."[57] As noted above, the Restatement draft uses territoriality pervasively—as a dispositive factor for conduct-regulation issues and as a tiebreaker for loss-allocation ones.

6   Conclusion

Lea Brilmayer has taught us much about choice of law. She has taught us that we should not be afraid to frame our analysis in terms of rights. That when we ask what rights a state has given to parties, we must remember that this is a question within the authority of that state. That it is not reasonable to suppose that states dispense rights in the narrowly parochial manner described by

---

54   The current restatement draft actually allows for the law of the place of injury in cross-border torts if it is foreseeable and the injury party requests it—which will be the case, presumably, if it favors the victim. See Restatement, Third, of Conflict of Laws, Preliminary Draft 3, § 6.05. This rule reflects a judgment that in cross-border torts, the state with the more restrictive law has the dominant interest.

55   The alternative with a cross-border tort is presumably to turn to domiciliary connecting factors as a tiebreaker. This is possible, but because domiciliary connections have less relevance to conduct regulation and cross-border torts are often split-domicile cases anyway (with tortfeasors acting in their home states and victims receiving injury in theirs), the gain would be slight and probably not worth the added complexity.

56   *See* Brilmayer, 98 YALE L.J. at 1308–09.

57   *Id.* at 1303.

crude versions of interest analysis. That when we try to construct a choice-of-law system to resolve conflicts between rights created by the laws of different states we should think about systemic values rather than simply getting the right answer in a single case—that there is a strong argument to be made for simple rules that can be applied easily and uniformly. And that when crafting such rules we should avoid single-factor triggers and try to use considerations that are fair to parties and generate uniform results regardless of forum.

In my drafting work on the Third Restatement, I have taken each of these admonitions to heart.[58] In this essay I have sought to show how Lea's insights inform and support both the general approach of the Restatement and some of its specific rules. I must admit, of course, that as of the publication date Lea herself does not entirely agree. We have had some spirited and useful exchanges on these points, and I look forward to our future conversations. A point on which I will brook no disagreement, though, is the extent to which I have benefited from and been inspired by her work throughout my career. For that work I offer my thanks and my applause.

---

[58] Since this is a personal tribute, I do not attempt to speak for the other Reporters in that regard, but I think it is fair to say that we all view Lea as a giant in the field.

CHAPTER 4

Choice-of-Law as Geographic Scope Limitation

Carlos M. Vázquez[*]

Among Lea Brilmayer's many seminal and lasting contributions to Conflict of Laws scholarship has been her work calling attention to "the interesting pattern of similarities and differences between the problems of the application of American law to international disputes and the problems of domestic 'conflict of laws.'"[1] Professor Brilmayer is undoubtedly correct in observing that the doctrines have been approached by courts and scholars as "methodologically distinct."[2] My thesis in this chapter is that these questions are conceptually identical. The question whether state law should be applied to a case having contacts with other states or nations is conceptually identical to the question whether federal law should be applied to a dispute having contacts with other nations. Federal extraterritoriality doctrine is well understood to address the question whether federal law, properly interpreted, applies to a given dispute having links to other nations. In other words, federal extraterritoriality doctrine purports to address the geographic scope of federal law. Inter-state choice-of-law doctrine has long been understood to address the same question.[3] I argue here that a state's choice-of-law rules operate no less (and no more) as implicit geographic scope limitations as do the rules on federal extraterritoriality. If the latter determine the forum's law's substantive applicability to disputes having links to other states or nations, so do the former.

---

[*] Professor of Law, Georgetown University Law Center. I am grateful for very helpful comments from Lea Brilmayer, Ralf Michaels, Horatia Muir Watt, Kermit Roosevelt III, and Celia Wasserstein Fassberg. These reflections were inspired by Lea Brilmayer's pathbreaking work on the relationship between state choice of law and federal extraterritoriality, which is just one of the many issues, both within and outside the field of Conflict of Laws, on which her work has profoundly influenced my thinking. For another example, *compare* Lea Brilmayer, *International Law in American Courts: A Modest Proposal*, 100 YALE L.J. 2277 (1991), *with* Carlos M. Vazquez, *Customary International Law as U.S. Law: A Critique of the Revisionist and Intermediate Positions and a Defense of the Modern Position*, 86 NOTRE DAME L. REV. 1495 (2011).

1 Lea Brilmayer, *The Extraterritorial Application of American Law: A Methodological and Constitutional Appraisal*, 50 L. & CONTEMP. PROBS. 11, 11 (1987).

2 *Id.*

3 By using the term "geographic scope," I do not mean to suggest that the applicability of a law to disputes having connections with other states necessarily turns on the place where certain events occurred. The law's applicability may turn instead on other sorts of connections with other states or nations, such as the place of habitual residence of some of the parties.

My claim is conceptual. I do not argue for any particular approach to answer the choice of law question. Indeed, my claim is that the choice of law issue is properly conceived as identical to the extraterritoriality issue no matter which approach to answering the question is adopted. Though conceptual, my claim also has practical doctrinal implications. These implications are best appreciated by examining the thesis of an influential group of scholars who have articulated a "two-step" approach to choice of law.[4] The claims of the two-step theorists are of particular current interest because this theory supplies the theoretical foundation for the current draft of the American Law Institute's Third Restatement of Conflict of Laws.[5] According to the two-step theory, choice-of-law rules that function as geographic scope limitations are binding on the courts of other states. Thus, if a state has enacted a law but limits its scope to cases having a specified connection to the state—such as cases in which the injured party is a state resident or the conduct that gave rise to the injury occurred in the state—the state's law, properly interpreted, does not extend to cases beyond the specified scope. It follows that another state purporting to apply that state's law commits an error when it applies the law beyond its geographic scope.[6] This is true whether the scope limitation is contained in express statutory language or is inferred through its choice-of-law rules. In other words, according to the two-step theory, the forum's courts, in deciding whether to apply the local law of another state,[7] must engage in *renvoi*, at least for the purpose of determining whether the law of the other state extends to the case at hand.[8]

But, according to the two-step theorists, not all choice-of-law rules function as geographic scope limitations. Some function instead as "rules of priority." The forum's rules of priority tell the courts which state's law should be applied when more than one state's laws extend to the case. The two-step theorists

---

4   The principal texts are Kermit Roosevelt III, *Resolving Renvoi, The Bewitchment of Our Intelligence By Means of Language*, 80 Notre Dame L. Rev. 1821 (2005); Larry Kramer, *The Return of the Renvoi*, 66 N.Y.U. L. Rev. 979 (1991).

5   Professor Roosevelt is the chief reporter of the Third Restatement of Conflict of Laws.

6   *See* Larry Kramer, *The Myth of the Unprovided-For Case*, 75 Va. L. Rev. 1045, 1052 (1989) ("Rights that can be enforced in court do not exist in the abstract. Courts only enforce rights that are conferred by positive law.").

7   A state's "local law" is the law that a state would apply to a case lacking foreign elements— that is, a case in which all of the parties are from the state and all events occurred within the state. *See* Restatement (Second) of Conflict of Laws § 8, cmt. d (Am Law Inst. 1971), especially the accompanying illustration: "If the X court decides that the reference is to Y local law, it will decide the case in the same way as a Y court would have decided if A had been a Y national and if all other relevant contacts had been located in Y...." *Id.* Thus, the term "local law" refers to a state's law shorn of its geographic scope limitations.

8   On whether this constitutes *renvoi, see infra* note 29.

maintain that rules of priority do not operate as scope limitations, even when they instruct the forum's courts to apply a law other than its own. Because rules of priority do not function as scope limitations, they do not bind the courts of other states.

This Chapter argues that *all* choice-of-law rules—even the rules that the two-step theorists denominate rules of priority—operate equally as geographic scope limitations when they lead to non-application of the enacting state's law.[9] Thus, if we accept the two-step theorists' claim that some choice of law rules operate as geographic scope limitations, and if we also accept their claim that choice of law rules that operate as geographic scope limitations are binding on the courts of other states, then (I argue here) the courts must apply *all* of the choice-of-law rules of the other relevant states in order to determine whether the other state's laws extend to the case at hand. If the enacting state's choice of law rules—even its rules of priority—would lead that state's courts not to apply its own law, then sister states would be prohibited from applying that law as well.

On the other hand, I question the two-step theorists' claim that "rules of scope" should be binding on the courts of other states. This claim rests on an unsound analogy between rules of scope (as two-step theorists understand the concept) and what I call "internal" scope limitations. Unlike internal scope limitations, what the two-step theorists call rules of scope do not necessarily reflect the enacting state's preference that its law *not* be applied beyond its specified scope. Rather, such rules, even if framed as geographic scope limitations, are ordinarily based on the enacting state's deference to the legislative authority of other states. To the extent the enacting state has limited the scope of its law out of deference to the legislative authority of other states, other states should be free to decline such deference if, under their own choice-of-law rules, the local law of the enacting state should be applied.

The latter conclusion, in turn, leads me to question whether choice of law rules—whether they be "rules of scope" (in the parlance of the two-step theorists) or "rules of priority"—function as scope limitations at all. If a state's choice of law rules tells us that the enacting state's local law does not extend to a particular case having foreign elements, then it does seem to follow that the courts of another state commit an error when they resolve the dispute

---

9   To the extent a given state's choice-of-law rules identify which other state's law should be applied, when more than two are in contention, they do more than specify the geographic scope of that state's law. This is concededly one respect in which state's choice of law rules differ from federal extraterritoriality doctrine. But, if the state's choice of law rules identify another state's law as applicable, these rules simultaneously tell us that that state's law does not extend to the case.

by applying that state's local law. If other states are free to resolve disputes by using such law, then it would seem to follow that the enacting state's choice of law rules do not in fact limit the scope of that law—they do not tell us that such law simply does not extend to this case. My claim about the nature of "geographic scope limitations" thus calls into question whether choice of law rules—including the rules of federal extraterritoriality doctrine and, indeed, statutory provisions expressly framed as geographic scope limitations— should be understood as scope limitations at all.

This Chapter begins by examining how the Supreme Court ("the Court") conceptualizes federal extraterritoriality doctrine. It then shows that a state's choice-of-law rules have long been conceptualized in the same way: as implicit limits on the territorial reach of the state's laws. I then discuss the two-step theory's rationale for regarding only some choice-of-law rules as geographic scope limitations and show that the rules that the two-step theorists call "rules of priority" function as geographic scope limitations just as much as do the rules that the two-step theorists call "rules of scope" (at least when they lead the enacting state's courts to apply a law other than its own). I then argue, however, that, unlike internal scope limitations, rules of (geographic) scope (as the two-step theorists understand the term) should not always bind the courts of sister states.[10] The final section of the Chapter considers whether a restriction that is binding on the enacting state's courts but not the courts of sister states can properly be understood as a substantive limitation on the reach of the enacting state's law—that is, as a scope limitation.

1 Federal Extraterritoriality Doctrine

Today the Supreme Court clearly understands federal extraterritoriality doctrine as determining the proper interpretation of federal law with respect to its geographic scope. The Court's clearest recent articulation of this view came in *Morrison v. National Australia Bank, Ltd.*[11] The plaintiffs in *Morrison* asserted a claim for relief under section 10(b) of the Securities Exchange Act of 1934 based on conduct that occurred in part outside the territory of the

---

10   To be clear, I am not arguing that state should be prohibited from considering another
      state's geographic scope limitation. For example, a state that employs governmental
      interest analysis may reasonably regard another state's geographic scope limitation as
      indicative of the strength of its interest in having its law applied to particular cases having
      foreign elements. I am merely arguing that states need not regard other states' geographic
      scope limitations as binding.
11   Morrison v. Nat'l Australia Bank Ltd., 561 U.S. 247 (2010).

United States. The Court clearly viewed the question whether the Act should be applied by the court as a question about "what conduct § 10(b) reaches," which, the Court made clear, "is a merits question."[12] The Court thus rejected the lower court's conceptualization of the issue as one of jurisdiction. Before *Morrison*, the Court had sometimes treated the issue differently. In *Hartford Fire Insurance Co. v. California*, for example, the Court treated the question as whether the court should refrain from applying a concededly applicable law out of deference to the interests of other nations.[13] Justice Scalia, the author of *Morrison*, had dissented in *Hartford Fire*, chiding the majority for misconceiving the issue.[14] Since *Morrison*, the court has consistently understood the extraterritoriality question as determining whether the federal law involved, properly construed, extends to the case at hand.[15]

The Court's conceptualization of this issue as involving the proper construction of the statute with respect to its geographic scope was not a new one (although *Hartford Fire* illustrates that the Court sometimes strayed from this understanding). The Court has long conceived of the extraterritoriality issue as requiring a determination of a statute's geographic scope. As the Court noted in *Lauritzen v. Larsen*, Congress typically writes statutes in broad, all-encompassing terms. Read literally, such general laws would be applicable no matter where the conduct occurred or where the parties were from. Unless some limitation were read into them, generally-worded laws would apply to the conduct of every person in the world anywhere in the world—"a hand on a Chinese junk, never outside Chinese waters, would not be beyond [the law's] literal wording."[16]

The Court's extraterritoriality doctrine instructs that generally-worded statutes are not to be read literally. This does not mean that the courts are defying Congress' wishes. To the contrary, as stated by Judge Hand in the oft-cited *Alcoa* decision, "the only question open is whether Congress intended to impose liability and whether our own Constitution permitted it to do so: as a court of the United States we cannot look beyond our own law."[17] Thus, if Congress has clearly addressed the question of geographic scope, the courts are obligated to enforce the statute as written (subject to constitutional constraints). But, in the absence of express language addressing the question of geographic scope, the courts assume that Congress legislated with only the purely domestic

---

12   *Id.* at 254.
13   *See* Hartford Fire Ins. Co. v. California, 509 U.S. 764, 797–98 (1993).
14   *See id.* at 813–820 (Scalia, J., dissenting).
15   *See, e.g.,* RJR Nabisco, Inc. v. European Cmty., 136 S. Ct. 2090, 2099–100 (2016); Kiobel v. Royal Dutch Petrol. Co., 569 U.S. 108, 115 (2013).
16   Lauritzen v. Larsen, 345 U.S. 571, 577 (1953).
17   United States v. Aluminum Co. of Am. (*Alcoa*), 148 F.2d 416, 443 (2d Cir. 1945).

case in mind, leaving the question of territorial scope to the courts. The Court has, in turn, developed a general rule to address this question. This rule operates as a "canon of construction ... whereby unexpressed congressional intent may be ascertained,"[18]—that is, as "a presumption about a statute's meaning."[19] The purpose of this rule is "to protect against unintended clashes between our laws and those of other nations which could result in international discord."[20] It reflects the assumption that, unless it clearly stated otherwise, Congress did not intend to "rule the world."[21]

In *Morrison*, the Court adopted the presumption against extraterritoriality as the rule the courts should ordinarily apply in determining the geographic scope of federal statutes. But the Court's conceptualization of the issue as one of geographic scope is entirely independent of the particular approach the Court employs to answer the question. Thus, in *Lauritzen v. Larsen*, the Court applied a very different approach to determine the geographic scope of the Jones Act, yet it conceptualized the issue, as it did in *Morrison*, as "a question of statutory construction rather commonplace in a federal system."[22]

Thus, as understood by the Court, the rules the Court applies to determine federal extraterritoriality function as implicit geographic scope limitations. Today, the Court favors the presumption against extraterritoriality, but with respect to some statutes the Court has employed, and continues to employ, quite different approaches.[23] Regardless of the particular approach used, the relevant rules are understood to function as implicit limits on the scope of federal statutes, to be employed unless Congress has expressly addressed the issue.

2   State Choice-of-Law Rules as Geographic Scope Limitations

State choice-of-law rules have also long been understood as implicitly delineating the geographic scope of forum law. As with federal extraterritoriality doctrine, the province of choice-of-law rules has long been understood to be to define the territorial scope of a state's law in the absence of explicit legislative guidance on the question. Judge Hand in *Alcoa* explicitly recognized the conceptual similarity when he noted, in a federal extraterritoriality case, that "we are not to read general words [in a federal statute] without regard to

---

18   E.E.O.C. v. Arabian Am. Oil Co. (*Aramco*), 499 U.S. 244, 248 (1991) (quoting Foley Bros. v. Filardo, 336 U.S. 281, 285 (1949)).

19   *Morrison*, 561 U.S. at 255.

20   *Aramco*, 336 U.S. at 248.

21   *Kiobel*, 569 U.S. at 115 (quoting Microsoft Corp. v. AT&T Corp., 550 U.S. 437, 454 (2007)).

22   *Lauritzen*, 345 U.S. at 578.

23   *See, e.g.*, F. Hoffmann-La Roche Ltd. v. Empagran S.A., 542 U.S. 155 (2004).

the limitations ... which generally correspond to those fixed by the 'Conflict of Laws.'"[24] Unless the legislature specifically addresses the statute's geographic scope, the courts assume that the legislature intended the law to extend only to those cases to which the law would extend under prevailing choice-of-law rules.

The famous decision of the Alabama Supreme Court in *Alabama Great Southern Railroad v. Carroll* well illustrates how the courts understood the function of choice-of-law rules under the traditional approach to choice of law reflected in the First Restatement of Conflict of Laws.[25] *Carroll* involved an injury suffered by an employee of a railroad as a result of the negligence of another employee. Under the common-law fellow servant rule, an employer was not liable for injuries suffered by one employee as a result of the negligence of another employee. The Alabama legislature had repealed that rule by statute, but the legislature had not specified the territorial scope of the statute. The court held that the statute should be understood to incorporate the traditional *lex loci delicti* choice-of-law rule, under which tort cases are governed by the law of the state in which the injury occurred. As the court wrote, "Section 2590 of the Code ... is to be interpreted in the light of universally recognized principles of private international or interstate law, as if its operation had been expressly limited to this State and as if its first line read as follows: 'When a personal injury is received in Alabama by a servant or employee,' etc."[26]

Alabama's choice of law rule—*lex loci delicti*—thus functioned as an implicit limitation on the geographic scope of the Alabama statute. At the same time, the *lex loci delicti* rule instructed the Alabama courts to apply the law of the place of injury, which in this case was Mississippi. Because Mississippi's substantive law was the fellow-servant rule, the court ruled against the plaintiff. If the Alabama legislature had instead specified that its statute repealing the fellow-servant rule applied whenever the employer-employee relationship was centered in Alabama, or when the conduct causing the injury occurred in Alabama, the court would presumably have concluded that the statute extended to the case and would have ruled the other way.[27] As the *Carroll*

---

24   *Alcoa*, 148 F.2d at 443. *See also* Justice Holmes' opinion in American Banana Co. v. United Fruit Co., 213 U.S. 347 (1909), a federal extraterritoriality case that relies on such Conflict of Laws chestnuts as Milliken v. Pratt, 125 Mass. 374 (1878).

25   Alabama Great Southern Railroad v. Carroll, 97 Ala. 126 (1892).

26   *Id.* at 134.

27   I say "presumably" because the U.S. Supreme Court during that era appeared in some cases to regard the traditional choice-of-law rules reflected in the First Restatement of Conflict of Laws to be constitutionally required. *See, e.g.*, New York Life Ins. v. Dodge, 246 U.S. 357 (1918). The Court today emphatically does not. *See, e.g.*, Allstate Ins. Co. v. Hague, 449 U.S. 302 (1981).

opinion appeared to recognize, the courts of a state will follow the directives of the state's legislature regarding the territorial scope of the state's statutes (and other laws). In the absence of such directives, however, the court will assume that the legislature did not address the statute's territorial scope when enacting a statute. Instead, the court assumes that the statute reflects the legislature's preferences with respect to the purely domestic case—in which all of the parties and all of the events occurred within the state—and meant to leave the question of extraterritorial scope to be governed by prevailing choice-of-law rules. The court accordingly applies the prevailing choice-of-law rules as reflecting the legislature's (implicit) preferences regarding the territorial reach of the statutes it enacts (as well as of substantive common law rules).[28]

3 The Two-Step Theory

Although the proposition that choice-of-law rules implicitly limit the geographic scope of forum law has a long pedigree, this conceptualization of choice-of-law rules has only been partially embraced by scholars. Nor has the proposition that conceptualizing choice-of-law rules as scope limitations requires the courts to engage in *renvoi* been widely embraced. But the latter proposition has been forcefully advanced recently by scholars who have developed a "two-step" approach to choice of law. The draft Third Restatement operationalizes this theory by providing that, when the forum court applies the law of another state, it must give effect to the law's geographic scope restrictions.[29] Indeed, according to the draft Third Restatement, a court would be violating the Full Faith and Credit Clause of the U.S. Constitution if it

---

28   Mississippi at the time also adhered to the *lex loci delicti* rule, so according to Mississippi's implicit geographic scope limitation, its law applied to the case. Under the First Restatement's approach to renvoi, whether Mississippi would also apply its own law would not have mattered. Under the two-step theory, discussed below, the Alabama court would not apply Mississippi law if Mississippi had engrafted a geographic scope limitation rendering it inapplicable. Whether the Alabama courts should treat Mississippi's geographic scope limitation as binding in this context is discussed in Part 3.2, below.

29   The Third Restatement achieves this result indirectly by, first, defining "internal law" as including geographic scope limitations, *see* RESTATEMENT (THIRD) OF CONFLICT OF LAWS § 1.03 cmt. a (AM. LAW. INST., Council Draft No. 2, 2017) and then providing in § 5.05(1) that, "[w]hen directed by its own choice-of-law rule to apply the law of any state, the forum applies the internal law of that state ..." Section 5.05(2) permits the forum under limited circumstances to apply a sister state's choice-of-law rules (defined to exclude geographic scope limitations, *see infra* note 31), but § 5.05(1) requires the forum to apply its sister states' geographic scope limitations whenever it applies the state's substantive law.

applied the law of a sister state without giving effect to its geographic scope limitations.[30] These same scholars, however, maintain that only *some* choice-of-law rules function as geographic scope limitations.

In this Part, I examine the two foregoing claims of the two-step theorists. First, I examine the claim that "rules of scope" function as geographic scope limitations but "rules of priority" do not. I argue that the better view is that the latter rules function no less as geographic scope limitations than do the former. Second, I examine the two-step theorists' claim that choice-of-law rules that function as geographic scope limitations must be applied by sister states—in other words, that conceptualizing choice of law rules as scope limitations means that the courts of one state must engage in *renvoi* in order to determine that the laws of their sister states purport to apply to the case at hand.[31] I argue that, because of the nature of these limitations, the courts of one state should

---

30   *See* RESTATEMENT (THIRD) OF CONFLICT OF LAWS § 5.02 Reporters' note (AM. LAW. INST., Council Draft No. 2, 2017) ("A state court applying another State's statute to a set of facts outside its specified scope would violate the Full Faith and Credit Clause, if the scope restriction is clear and brought to the court's attention."). Although this report-ers' note refers only to statutory scope restrictions, the Third Restatement's reasoning appears to require the same conclusion for the scope restrictions read into a statute by the enacting states' courts as well as for geographic scope limitations read into a sister state's non-statutory law by the sister state's courts. *See* § 5.01 cmt. c ("The scope of foreign internal law is a question of foreign law.... It is determined in light of how the foreign law is understood and applied in the foreign jurisdiction ... The forum accepts authoritative statements from foreign states as to the scope of their law.").

31   The draft Third Restatement distinguishes between geographic scope limitations and choice-of-law rules, and reserves and latter term for what its chief reporter has called "rules of priority." *See* RESTATEMENT (THIRD) OF CONFLICT OF LAWS § 1.03 (AM. LAW. INST., Council Draft No. 2, 2017) (defining "internal law" as "a state's law exclusive of its rules of choice of law"); *id.* cmt. a (stating that "[i]nternal law, as defined here, includes restrictions the law places on the persons who may assert rights under the law or the geographic scope of the law"). Professor Kramer, for his part, understands the term "choice-of-law rule" to embrace both geographic scope limitations and rules of priority. *See* Kramer, *supra* note 2, at 1005 ("[B]ecause choice of law is a process of interpreting laws to determine their applicability on the facts of a particular case, the forum can never ignore other states' choice of law systems—whether these consist of ad hoc decisions, functional rules, or jurisdiction-selecting rules of the First Restatement variety. On the contrary, the applicability of another state's law must be determined in light of its choice-of-law system. Hence, a proper understanding of choice of law means the return of the renvoi."); *id.* at 1011 ("A state's approach to choice of law *by definition* establishes the state's rules of interpretation for questions of extraterritorial scope." (emphasis in original)); *id.* at 1012 ("Like it or not, and however foolish they may seem, traditional choice-of-law rules are intended to limit the scope and meaning of substative law ... [T]hey reflect state's decisions about how far to extend local law in multistate cases."). In my view, Professor Kramer's usage is the more conventional one and I employ it here. See also SYMEON C. SYMEONIDES, CHOICE OF LAW: THE OXFORD COMMENTARIES ON AMERICAN LAW 494 (2016) ("Despite their location in substantive statutes (and despite their variations

be regarded as free to apply a sister state's substantive law even if that state's courts would not apply that law because of the geographic scope limitation.

3.1   Which Choice-of-Law Rules Function as Geographic Scope Limitations?

The two-step theory distinguishes between choice-of-law rules that function as geographic scope limitations and choice-of-law rules that function as rules of priority. According to the two-step theory, a choice-of-law rule that functions as a geographic scope limitation defines the territorial scope of a law and must be treated by the courts of other states as a binding interpretation of the reach of the underlying substantive law. Rules of priority, however, are not geographic scope limitations and sister states are not bound to give them effect. I examine the claim that geographic scope limitations must be given effect by sister state courts in section B. First, in this section, I question the two-step theorists' claim that rules of scope function as geographic scope limitations but rules of priority do not.

3.1.1   The Distinction between Rules of Scope and Rules of Priority

The two-step theory is a refinement of governmental interest analysis. To understand the two-step theory's distinction between rules of scope and rules of priority, it is useful to begin by explaining the basic analytical approach of governmental interest analysis and certain concepts introduced by Brainerd

---

in content and wording), all of these localizing provisions qualify as *choice-of-law* rules, albeit of the *unilateral* type.").

The draft Third Restatement purports to be rejecting *renvoi* to the same extent as the Second Restatement (which rejected *renvoi* in most circumstances). The former provides that, when directed by their choice-of-law rules to apply the law of a given state, courts are ordinarily to apply the "internal law" of that state, whereas the latter provides that, in such circumstances, the courts are ordinarily to apply "local law" of that state. *Compare* RESTATEMENT (THIRD) OF CONFLICT OF LAWS § 5.05(a) (AM. LAW. INST., Council Draft No. 2, 2017) *with* RESTATEMENT (SECOND) OF CONFLICT OF LAWS § 8(a) (1977). However, the Third Restatement's definition of "internal law" differs fundamentally from the Second Restatement's definition of "local law". The current draft of the Third Restatement defines the term "internal law" as a state's substantive law as limited by the state's geographic scope limitations. *See* RESTATEMENT (THIRD) OF CONFLICT OF LAWS § 1.03 cmt. a (AM. LAW. INST., Council Draft No. 2, 2017). Thus, the Third Restatement contemplates that the forum will apply the geographic scope limitation of the other state's law, while the Second Restatement contemplates that the forum will ordinarily apply the law a state would apply in a case having no foreign elements. See *supra* note 7 under the Second Restatement's conception of what counts as a "conflict of laws rule," applying another state's geographic scope limitation would count as *renvoi*. Professor Kramer appears to agree with the Second Restatement, and to diverge from the draft Third Restatement on this terminological point, as he argues that the two-step theory requires the courts to "accept the renvoi." See Kramer, *supra* note 4, at 983, 1030.

Currie. Professor Currie's fundamental insight was that not all disputes that involve states having different substantive laws pose true conflicts.[32] It may be that only one of the states has an interest in having its law applied to the dispute. If so, the dispute presents a "false conflict," and the law of the only interested state should be applied. If both states have an interest in having their law applied, the dispute presents a true conflict. For such cases, Currie initially advocated that the forum should apply its own law, on the theory that weighing the conflicting state policies to determine which state had a greater interest is not an appropriate role for courts. Currie's approach to resolving true conflicts found less favor among courts and commentators than his identification of false conflicts. As discussed below, he later modified his approach to true conflicts, and other scholars have proposed alternative approaches for resolving true conflicts.

Of greater significance to the present discussion is Currie's approach to determining whether a state has an interest in having its law applied. Currie argued that this question should be approached as a question of statutory interpretation. In the purely domestic case, the court must interpret the statute to determine whether it applies to certain marginal domestic circumstances (for example, does a statute prohibiting vehicles in the park apply to bicycles?). Currie argued that determining whether the state has an interest in having its law applied to a case having foreign elements is basically the same problem, and it should be approached in the same way—by applying ordinary rules of statutory interpretation.[33] The court should "try[] to decide [the question of whether the state has an interest in having its law applied to a particular case] as it believes [the legislature] would have decided had it foreseen the problem."[34] Thus, he argued, the courts should seek to determine the purpose of the statute and should conclude that the state has an interest in having its law applied to a case if the statute's purposes would be advanced by applying

---

32   See LEA BRILMAYER, CONFLICT OF LAWS: FOUNDATIONS AND FUTURE DIRECTIONS 70 (1990) ("It has often been remarked that the biggest success of Currie's scheme was the identification of false conflicts."). Professor Brilmayer, I should add, does not agree with this assessment.

33   See Brainerd Currie, Comments on Babcock v. Jackson—A Recent Development in Conflicts of Laws, 63 COLUM. L. REV. 1233, 1242 (1963).

34   Brainerd Currie, The Verdict of the Quiescent Years: Mr. Hill and the Conflict of Laws, 28 U. CHI L. REV. 258, 277 (1961). The appropriate approach to interpreting statutes is of course contestable. Currie's purposivist approach to statutory interpretation has fallen out of favor in certain circles, and the Supreme Court expressly rejected it in the federal extraterritoriality context. See Morrison, 561 U.S. at 261 (rejecting an approach that seeks to "divin[e] what Congress would have wanted if it had thought of the situation before the court" as "judicial-speculation-made-law" and adopting instead the presumption against extraterritoriality).

it to the case. For present purposes, Currie's purposive approach to statutory interpretation is less important than his idea that this aspect of the choice-of-law process should be approached as a matter of statutory interpretation aimed at determining the reach of each state's law.

As noted, Currie's solution to true conflicts has not been widely embraced by courts and commentators.[35] Other scholars have accepted Currie's basic insights but rejected his conclusion that the forum state should always apply its own law if the law's purposes would be advanced. Professor William Baxter, for example, argued that, in true conflict cases, courts should apply the law of the state whose policies would be most impaired if not applied.[36] Professor Joseph Singer has proposed that, in cases presenting real conflicts, forum law should be displaced when applying it would "significantly interfere with the ability of another state to constitute itself as a normative and political community and the relationship between the forum and the dispute is such that the forum should defer to the internal norms of the foreign normative community."[37] The Second Restatement adopted a different rule: application of the law of the state with the "most significant relationship" to the dispute.[38]

The two-step theory builds upon Currie's insights. The first step of the two-step analysis corresponds to the initial determination of whether the purposes of a state's law would be advanced if applied to the case at hand. Like Currie, the two-step theorists conceptualize this step as a determination of the geographic scope of the state's law, properly treated as a matter of statutory interpretation. The second step of the two-step analysis consists of the analyses the courts employ to determine which law to apply if, in the first step, the court determines that more than one states' laws extend to the case. In the parlance of the two-step theory, the rules that courts apply in this second step are "rules of priority."[39] A given state's rule of priority might be "always apply forum

---

35   Currie himself later modified his view, proposing that, "[i]f the court finds an apparent conflict between the interest of the two states," it should consider whether the conflict might be avoided through a "more moderate and restrained interpretation of the policy of interest of one state or the other." Currie, *supra* note 33, at 1242.

36   William Baxter, *Choice of Law and the Federal System*, 16 STAN. L. REV. 1, 9 (1963).

37   Joseph Singer, *Real Conflicts*, 69 B.U. L. REV. 1, 70 (1989). Professor Singer's concept of a "real conflict" differs somewhat from Currie's concept of a "true conflict."

38   The Second Restatement does not explicitly set forth the "most significant relationship" test as a mechanism for resolving true conflicts. Nevertheless, there is some basis in the Second Restatement for approaching the test in this manner, and some courts have done so. *See, e.g.*, Phillips v. Gen. Motors Corp., 995 P.2d 1002, 1004 (Mont. 2000). *See also* RESTATEMENT (THIRD) OF CONFLICT OF LAWS, ch. 5, topic 1, intro., at 110 (AM. LAW. INST., Council Draft No. 2, 2017) ("Pennsylvania, and until recently New Jersey, use the Restatement Second's 'most significant relationship' [test] to resolve [true] conflicts.").

39   *See* Roosevelt, *supra* note 3, at 1874–87.

law" (Currie's initial approach) or "apply the law whose purposes would be most impaired if not applied (Baxter's approach) or "apply the law of the state with the most significant relation to the dispute" (the Second Restatement's approach).

Scholars have criticized Currie's approach to both the first and the second steps.[40] Two-step theorists are agnostic as to the particular approach a court should use at both the first and the second steps.[41] But they insist that the choice-of-law process consists of these two steps. And, most importantly for present purposes, they insist that the point of the first step—and *only* the first step—is to determine the geographic scope of the relevant laws. The court in the first step is interpreting the reach of its state's law to a case having foreign elements. A state court's interpretation of its own law's geographic scope is the equivalent of its interpretation of the law's applicability to certain marginal domestic situations. Indeed, a state court's determination in the first step that the law extends to cases having particular connections to the state is the equivalent of *the state legislature's* specification that the law applies in marginal domestic cases.[42]

According to two-step theorists, the second step—which is governed by "rules of priority"—is very different. The key difference between the rules applied in the two steps is reflected in the very different effect the enacting state's courts' resolution of the two steps has for the courts of other states. Because, in the first step, a state's court determines the geographic scope of its own law, the court's decision is binding on sister state courts to the extent the decision is that the law does not extend to the case.[43] But, when a state's courts apply that state's rules of priority and conclude that another state's law

---

40   With respect to the first step, scholars have questioned, among other things, Currie's assumption that a state would deem its law applicable only if it would operate in favor of a state resident or domiciliary. *See, e.g.,* John Hart Ely, *Choice of Law and the State's Interest in Protecting Its Own,* 23 WM. & MARY L. REV. 173 (1981). Indeed, scholars have questioned whether the spatial scope of statutes can be deduced by reference to their underlying policies. *See* T. DE BOER, BEYOND LEX LOCI DELICTI: CONFLICTS METHODOLOGY AND MULTISTATE TORTS IN AMERICAN CASE LAW 426, 439 (1987); Brilmayer, *supra* note 32, at 54.

41   *See* Kermit Roosevelt III & Bethan Jones, *What a Third Restatement of Conflict of Laws Can Do,* 110 AM. J. INT'L L. UNBOUND 139, 143 n. 19 (2016) ("[W]hile we agree with Currie that determining scope is a matter of interpreting law, we do not necessarily agree with the interpretations he suggested ... The Restatement draft does not follow Currie's assumptions about state interests or his conclusions as to the scope of state laws, much less his views on how to resolve conflicts between them.").

42   *See* Roosevelt, *supra* note 4, at 1860.

43   To the extent the state's geographic scope limitations establish that the state's law does extend to the case at hand, these rules authoritatively determine the reach of the other

should be applied instead of its own, they are not, in the view of the two-step theorists, determining the geographic scope of their own law. Because a rule of priority does not determine geographic scope, a state court's application of such a rule is not binding on other states.

3.1.2   Rules of Priority as Rules of Scope
My claim is that, properly understood, a state's step-two rules operate no less as geographic scope limitations than do its step-one rules. The first step of Currie's choice-of-law inquiry asks whether the policy underlying a state's law would be advanced if applied to the case; if it would not be, the underlying law does not extend to the case. Professor Currie took the position that, if the policies underlying the state's law would be advanced, the state's law does extend to the case. He was of the view that a state's courts should always apply forum law when the state's policies would be advanced by doing so. For courts and scholars who reject Professor Currie's (initial) solution for true conflicts, however, the inquiry did not end there. These scholars have articulated a variety of alternative approaches for determining which law to apply in true conflict situations. As put forward by these scholars, these rules, too, function no less as geographic scope limitations. When these rules yield the conclusion that another states' law should be applied to the case, they are telling us that, despite the state's apparent interest in having its law applied to the dispute, the state's law does not *actually* extend to the dispute.

The alternative view treating only the rules applied at the first step as scope limitations would regard a state court's decision at the second step not to apply forum law as a decision to decline to enforce a law of its own state that, properly interpreted, extends to the case at hand. This conceptualization raises questions about the proper role of courts in a legal system. Professor Currie believed that it was the role of courts in a legal system to apply that system's positive law whenever it applied; the only proper basis for declining to apply that law is that the law does not purport to apply. His views on this point have a venerable pedigree. It is widely understood that the courts of a state have an obligation to enforce legislation enacted by the state's legislature (to the extent it is valid) in cases within their jurisdiction. "There is one rule or policy which, wherever applicable, takes precedence over others ... That controlling policy, obvious as it may be, is that a court must follow the dictates of its own

state's law, but other states are free to apply their own law (or the law of a third state) pursuant to its rules of priority.

legislature to the extent these are constitutional."[44] The two-step theorists' claim that a court's step-two decision to apply another state's law is a decision not to enforce its own state's concededly applicable statute violates that "obvious" "controlling policy."

As noted, legislatures typically write laws in general terms; if read literally the laws would extend to conduct performed anywhere in the world by anyone in the world. Of course, forum courts do not apply these laws as written; they apply the forum's choice-of-law rules and, pursuant to such rules, they sometimes apply the substantive law of a different state instead. But, when they do so, they do not purport to be defying the will of their own legislature. Rather, as the analysis in the *Carroll* case shows, they assume that the legislature did not focus on the statute's geographic scope, and they treat the issue as subject to judicial interpretation. The First Restatement states, the courts assume that the legislature intended the statute to be consistent with traditional rules of conflict of laws. Thus, as the court stated in *Carroll*, statutes addressing tort cases should be construed to apply when the injury occurred in the state's territory. States that have rejected the First Restatement approach have adopted alternative ways of construing the statutes' geographic scope in the face of legislative silence. But, in both situations, the relevant choice-of-law rules are understood to function, for forum courts, as implicit limitations on the geographic reach of forum law. When a court determines that the forum's choice-of-law rule requires application of another state's law, either at the first or the second step, it does not refuse to apply forum law that extends to the case; rather, it decides that forum law does not extend to the case.

The analyses of Professor Currie and subsequent governmental interest analysts are consistent with this conceptualization. As discussed above, Professor Currie's initial view was that, if the policies underlying the forum state's law would be advanced if applied to the case, the forum state's courts should always apply forum law (subject to constitutional limitations). This conclusion followed from a combination of two distinct propositions embraced by Professor Currie. First, he insisted that, if the forum state's law extends to the case, it is the duty of the state's courts to apply that law (subject to constitutional limitations). There is no legitimate basis (other than constitutional limits) for a state's courts to decline to apply a law that the state's legislature has enacted and that, correctly interpreted, applies to the case. But that leaves open the second question: whether the law extends to the case.

---

44   *Lauritzen*, 345 U.S. at n. 7 (1953) (quoting Elliott E. Cheatham & Willis L.M. Reese, *Choice of the Applicable Law*, 52 COLUM. L. REV. 959, 961 (1952)). Judge Hand expressed a similar view in *Alcoa*; *see* text accompanying note 15.

To answer this question, Professor Currie argued that, if the legislature has not addressed it, courts should ask if the substantive purposes underlying the forum state's law would be advanced if applied to the case. An affirmative answer, in his view, means that the law, properly interpreted, extends to the case. This is the question the courts address in Step One. Professor Currie concluded that Step One fully answers the question of geographic scope because he did not believe that courts could legitimately weigh the forum state's interest in advancing its policies through application of forum law against another state's interest in advancing its policies through application of its law. Thus, the forum court's determination that the policies underlying the forum's law would be advanced if the law were applied to the case ended the choice-of-law analysis because he believed *both* that (a) a state's courts must apply forum law if forum law extends to the case, *and* (b) whether forum law extends to the case depends *entirely* on whether the policies underlying that law would be advanced if the law were applied to the case.

The scholars who disagreed with Professor Currie's approach to resolving true conflicts did not dispute his premise that a state's courts are obligated to apply forum law if forum law, properly interpreted, extends to the case. Instead, they disagreed with Currie's conclusion that the forum's law extends to the case as long as its purposes would be advanced if applied to the case. Professor Baxter's analysis is instructive. He entirely agreed with Currie's analysis except for his conclusion that a law should be deemed applicable as long as any of its purposes would be advanced to any extent if applied to the case.[45] He even agreed with Currie's view that courts should not weigh the governmental interests reflected in the contending local laws.[46] But he argued that courts *could* legitimately assess the extent to which each state's law would be impaired if not applied. In his view, the interests of all states would be maximized if all states applied the law whose policies would be most impaired if not applied to a given case.[47]

Most importantly for present purposes, Professor Baxter argued that, in true conflict situations, each state's *legislature* should be presumed to have wanted its law to be applied only if the policies underlying its law would be more impaired if not applied.[48] Thus, Professor Baxter proposed "comparative

---

45   Baxter, *supra* note 36, at 8–10.
46   *Id.* at 18–19.
47   *Id.* at 21–22.
48   *Id.* at 7–9. Professor Baxter regarded comparative impairment analysis as an extension of Currie's approach to identifying false conflicts, and he defended it on the same grounds. "The same analysis by which Currie distinguishes real from false conflicts can resolve real conflicts cases. The question 'Will the social objective underlying the X rule be furthered

impairment" analysis as an alternative way to determine the geographic scope
of forum law in true conflict situations.

Two-step theorists regard the comparative impairment analysis as
a rule of priority and not a rule of scope. But, as Baxter's analysis shows, a
comparative-impairment state's true rule of scope is more complex than the
two-step theorists recognize. The rules that state courts employ at the first
and the second steps are *both* just parts of the courts' approach to determining
the geographic scope of forum law. For a state that adheres to Baxter's comparative impairment approach, the state's complete rule of scope should be
understood by the state's courts to be as follows: "Our law applies if the purpose of our law would be advanced if applied to this case *and* if the purpose
of our law would be more impaired if not applied than would the purposes of
another state's law." Similarly, for a state that uses the Second Restatement's
"more significant relationship" test to resolve true conflicts, the state's rule of
scope should be understood as follows: "Our law applies if the purposes of our
law would be advanced if applied to this case *and* if no other state has a more
significant relation to the dispute."

According to Professor Kramer, the difference between step-one rules and
step-two rules is that the former are "unilateral" rules while the latter are
"multilateral."[49] The former are unilateral in that they focus only on forum
law and the forum state's interests.[50] Multilateral rules, by contrast, require

---

by application of the rule in cases like the present one?' need not necessarily be answered
'Yes' or 'No'; the answer will often be, 'Yes, to some extent.' The extent to which the purpose underlying a rule will be furthered by application or impaired by nonapplication to
cases of a particular category may be regarded as the measure of the rule's pertinence and
of the state's interest in the rule's application to cases within that category." Baxter argued
that "if the lawmakers of [two states] assembled for interstate negotiations on the scope
of application of [their] inconsistent rules," they would agree on application of the law of
the state whose law would be most impaired if not applied. Although Baxter regarded a
negotiated agreement adopting comparative impairment to be the preferred solution, *see
id.* at 10, he also believed that states should adopt the comparative impairment approach
even without such an agreement (presumably in the hope that other states would follow
suit). *See id.* at 42. *See also id.* at 10 n. 22. Indeed, he employed the thought experiment
positing an imaginary assembly of lawmakers to explain the *first* step of Currie's governmental interest analysis. *See id.* at 7–8. He proposed his second step—the comparative
impairment analysis—as the result the hypothetical assembly of lawmakers would favor
to resolve true conflicts. Baxter thus conceptualized both steps of the analysis he was
proposing as aimed at delineating the geographic scope of the relevant state laws.

49   *See* Kramer, *supra* note 4, at 1033. Some rules of priority are not multilateral, however.
Currie's rule of priority (always apply forum law) is an example of a unilateral rule of
priority.

50   Even the first step is not purely unilateral, however. As discussed in the next section, all
choice-of-law rules are multilateral insofar as they reflect deference to the potentially

the courts to consider the content of other states' laws and those states' possible interests in having their law applied. Professor Kramer is (largely) correct in distinguishing step-one from step-two rules in this respect. But the multilateral rules address the question of the scope of the forum state's law no less than the unilateral rules applied in the first step. Baxter did not challenge Currie's claim that a state's courts had no legitimate basis for declining to apply forum law when applicable. He merely advocated a more complex approach to determining the scope of forum law in the absence of an express legislative resolution of that question. Thus, when a court applying the "comparative impairment" approach concludes that the purposes of the forum state's law would be advanced if the law were applied to the case but nevertheless decides to apply another state's law because the policies underlying that state's law would be more impaired if not applied, the court has determined that, despite the forum state's apparent interest in having its law applied, the forum state's law does not extend to *this* case.

That multilateral choice of law rules, no less than unilateral ones, can function as geographic scope limitations is shown further by the case-law concerning federal extraterritoriality. As discussed in Part I, there is no question that the Court conceives of federal extraterritoriality doctrine as addressing the geographic scope of federal law. The Court today favors a simple, (seemingly) unilateral rule—the presumption against extraterritoriality.[51] But, with

_____

superior legislative authority of other states. Additionally, as the first step is usually applied, a state's "interest" in having its law applied depends on the content of the laws of the other states connected to the dispute. As noted, the first step in Currie's analysis is to determine if the forum and other potentially interested states have an interest in applying their laws. If only one state has an interest, then we have a false conflict and the choice of law analysis ends. In determining whether the relevant states have an interest, forum courts do not usually look at their laws in isolation. Rather, they focus on how their laws differ from the laws of the other relevant states. Thus, in *Babcock*, the court determined that New York had an interest in applying its law to the case only because the other potentially relevant law—that of Ontario—would, if applied, operate in a way that would disfavor the injured New York resident. Assume that Vermont had a guest statute providing that guests can recover against their hosts only if the host was reckless. If the injured party was from Vermont and the host was from Ontario, Vermont would have an interest in applying its law because the other option—Ontario law—would deny the injured Vermont resident any compensation. If the driver was from New York, on the other hand, Vermont would not have an interest in applying its law because the other option—New York law—would be even more favorable to the injured Vermont resident.

51 The presumption against extraterritoriality is unilateral in that it does not require courts to take into account the interests of other states in the particular case. But, as noted in Part I, the presumption against extraterritoriality can be said to be multilateral in the sense that it is based on the desire to "protect against unintended clashes between our laws and those of other nations which could result in international discord." *Aramco*, 499

respect to some statutes, the Court has employed a multilateral approach. For example, in *Lauritzen v. Larsen*, the Court adopted a multilateral approach to determining the geographic scope of the Jones Act. The Court was very clear in conceptualizing the issue as one of geographic scope; as noted above, the Court stated that "we are simply dealing here with a question of statutory construction rather commonplace in a federal system."[52] Yet the approach it adopted to decide that question of statutory construction was a distinctly multilateral one, taking into account "considerations of comity, reciprocity, and long range interest" in order to "define the domain that each nation will claim as its own."[53] As described in *Romero v. International Terminal Operating Co.*, the *Lauritzen* approach is based on "due recognition of our self-regarding respect for the relevant interests of foreign nations," with "the controlling consideration [being] the interacting interests of the United States and foreign countries."[54]

The courts' shifting approaches to the extraterritorial scope of the U.S. antitrust laws over the years further illustrate the point. In *American Banana Co. v. United Fruit Co.*, the Supreme Court interpreted the Sherman Act to apply only when the conduct on which the suit was based took place on U.S. territory.[55] In the *Alcoa* case, the U.S. Court of Appeals for the Second Circuit later interpreted the statute to apply to conduct having an actual and intended effect on U.S. commerce.[56] Because *Alcoa*'s unilateral approach to the scope of the antitrust laws generated significant international friction, the U.S. Court of Appeals for the Ninth Circuit, in the influential *Timberlane* decision, adopted a multilateral approach (which it called the "jurisdictional rule of reason"), asking "whether the interests of, and links to, the United States—including the magnitude of the effects on American foreign commerce—are sufficiently strong vis-à-vis those of other nations, to justify an assertion of extraterritorial authority."[57] The Supreme Court later shifted to a hybrid approach,[58] but the important point for present purposes is that each of these approaches— the multilateral approach of *Timberlane* no less than the unilateral approaches

---

U.S. at 248. As discussed in the next section, all geographic scope limitations are multilateral in the sense that they are based on deference to the legislative authority of other states or nations.

52   *Lauritzen*, 345 U.S. at 578.
53   *Id.* at 582.
54   Romero v. International Terminal Operating Co., 358 U.S. 354, 383–84 (1958).
55   *American Banana*, 213 U.S. at 357.
56   United States v. Aluminum Co. of Am., 148 F.2d 416, 444 (2d Cir. 1945) (en banc).
57   Timberlane Lumber Co. v. Bank of Am. Nat'l Trust & Savs., 549 F.2d 597, 613 (9th Cir. 1976).
58   *See Empagran*, 542 U.S. at 164.

of *American Banana* and *Alcoa*—purported to address the geographic scope of the U.S. antitrust laws.[59] Thus, even though he emphatically understood that the issue before him was the geographic scope of the antitrust laws, Justice Scalia (the author of *Morrison*) had no trouble in *Hartford Fire* adopting the multilateral approach of the Third Restatement of Foreign Relations Law as the applicable rule.[60] Justice Scalia was writing in dissent, but the majority in *Hartford Fire*, and later in *Empagran*, rejected the *Timberlane* approach not because it believed that geographic scope limitations must, by their nature, be governed by unilateral rules, but because it concluded that the *Timberlane* approach was too complex to be administrable.[61]

Professor Kramer has recognized that the Court has at times adopted multilateral approaches to federal extraterritoriality. In a forceful critique of the Court's revival of the presumption against extraterritoriality, he described the earlier approaches in *Lauritzen* and *Romero* with approval.[62] Even in the inter-state context, Professor Kramer has argued forcefully and persuasively that choice of law rules should be understood as geographic scope limitations. "[B]ecause choice of law is a process of interpreting laws to determine their applicability on the facts of a particular case, the forum can never ignore other states' choice of law systems—whether these consist of ad hoc decisions, functional rules, or jurisdiction-selecting rules of the First Restatement variety. On the contrary, the applicability of another state's law must be determined in light of its choice of law system."[63] In Professor Kramer's words "[a] state's choice of law *by definition* establishes the state's rules of interpretation for questions of extraterritorial scope."[64]

Indeed, the very term that Professor Kramer coined to describe the conclusion a court reaches at step one when it determines that the state has an interest in having its law applied supports the idea that step-two choice-of-law rules operate as geographic scope limitations. He describes the step-one inquiry as aimed at determining whether the state's law is "prima facie applicable."[65] To say that a law is prima facie applicable is not to say that it is *actually*

---

59 The point was expressed forcefully by Justice Scalia in *Hartford Fire*, 509 U.S. at 800–821 (Scalia, J., dissenting) (endorsing a multilateral approach).

60 *Hartford Fire*, 509 U.S. at 818–19 (Scalia, J., dissenting).

61 *Empagran*, 542 U.S. at 168.

62 Larry Kramer, *Vestiges of Beale: Extraterritorial Application of American Law*, 1991 S. CT. REV. 179, 195–96 (1991). He also discussed the multilateral approach of *Timberlane* without suggesting that this approach did not operate as a rule of scope. *See id.* at 193.

63 Kramer, *supra* note 4, at 1005.

64 *Id.* at 1011 (emphasis added).

65 *See id.* at 1014.

applicable.[66] Rather, the term describes a *tentative* conclusion concerning the law's applicablility. Professor Kramer's terminology suggests that step one leads to a tentative conclusion that a state's law extends to the case, but, if another state's law is also tentatively applicable, the determination that a state's law is *actually* applicable is determined by the rules the state applies at step two to resolve the true conflict. Only if the step two inquiry results in the state's law being applied instead of the law of other states whose laws are also prima facie applicable does the court reach the conclusion that the state's law is *actually* applicable.

When he directly addresses the nature of the choice of law rules applicable at step two, however, Professor Kramer concludes that they are not geographic scope limitations, but instead determine whether the state's courts should decline to enforce a law of that state that is admittedly applicable to the case. This conceptualization is, of course, in conflict with the view expressed above regarding the role of a state's courts in the legal system. As Professor Kramer himself notes, "[j]udges are, after all, agents of the states' citizenry and law-makers, and their paramount responsibility must be the implementation of the state's own law."[67] To be sure, Professor Kramer criticized Professor Currie's reliance on this idea in concluding that the forum should always apply forum law in true conflict situations, but his criticism of Currie echoes Baxter's and does not contradict the proposition that a state's courts paramount responsi-bility is to resolve disputes in accordance with applicable forum law. Indeed, his critique of Professor Currie supports the conclusion that even step-two choice of law rules operate as geographic scope limitations. Thus, Professor Kramer notes that "the fact that another state's law is also prima facie appli-cable (i.e., that there is a true conflict) is itself relevant *in interpreting the law*."[68] Indeed, "it hardly makes sense to presume that forum lawmakers want forum law enforced in every true conflict. Accordingly, absent a clear directive never to defer to other states, courts should not *interpret forum law* that way."[69] Here, Kramer appears to be acknowledging that a state's approach to resolving true conflicts is itself a matter of interpretation of that state's law.

Notwithstanding these passages, Professor Kramer ultimately concludes that step-two choice of law rules are not geographic scope limitations even

---

66   "Prima facie" means "based on the first impression; accepted as correct until proved otherwise." *See Prima facie*, GOOGLE DICTIONARY, https://www.google.com/search?q= prima+facie+definition&oq=prima+facie&aqs=chrome.4.69i57j0l5.6047j0j1&sourceid= chrome&ie=UTF-8.

67   Kramer, *supra* note 4, at 1015.

68   *Id.* at 1016 (emphasis added).

69   *Id.* at 1017.

when they tell us that the relevant state's courts would not apply its law in the particular case.[70] This conclusion appears to be based on his firm conviction that sister states should be free to apply another state's law, so long as it is "prima facie" applicable, even if the other state's courts would not apply its own law when faced with a true conflict. The two-step theorists maintain that sister states are required to respect sister states' geographic scope limitations. If a state's law is subject to a geographic scope limitation, then the law simply does not confer a right as a substantive matter in cases falling outside its scope. Sister states would be misinterpreting that state's law if they applied it to cases to which it is not applicable. Professor Kramer argues persuasively that the courts of one state should not be required to apply the rules another state's courts apply at step two to resolve true conflicts, even if they would lead that state's courts not to apply their own law. Having reached that conclusion, Professor Kramer considers whether this conclusion is consistent with the view he had earlier defended that choice-of-law rules function as geographic scope limitations, and he finds no inconsistency because, whereas "most rules of interpretation are unilateral," "[t]he rules for true conflicts are ... multilateral in the sense that they look to the interests of other states as well."[71] They "purport to reflect an accommodation that, over the run of cases, is best for all states given their differing unilateral interests." Thus, when a state decides not to apply its prima facie applicable law, "rather than saying that [it] has

---

70   When another state's step-two rules lead to the conclusion that the state *would* apply its
      law to the particular case, the forum's step-two rules function as rules of scope as well.
      If the forum's step-two rules instruct the courts to apply forum law notwithstanding the
      fact that the other state's law also extends to the case, it is deciding that forum law does
      extend to the case, and, pursuant to the principle that a state's courts are agents of that
      state and are required to apply its law if applicable, the forum will apply forum law. One
      might argue that the forum would not be defying forum law if it entertains a cause of
      action under a sister state's law under circumstances in which forum law would deny
      a cause of action. There is not necessarily a conflict between the absence of a cause of
      action under forum law and the existence of a cause of action under another state's law.
      By analogy, when a plaintiff presents claims under both state and federal law, these are
      generally regarded as alternative causes of action, and the plaintiff is free to rely on both
      laws as alternative bases for relief. If a state were to take such an approach to sister state
      causes of action, however, it would be systematically favoring pro-recovery policies and
      systematically thwarting non-recovery policies. For this reason, a state may well deter-
      mine that its non-recovery law should prevail over another state's pro-recovery law. At
      bottom, this too is a matter of interpretation of forum law. Just as a federal law denying a
      cause of action might be interpreted to preempt state laws conferring a cause of action,
      a state might interpret its law denying a cause of action as "preempting" causes of action
      under the laws of other states. The forum court's treatment of this issue can be regarded
      as part of the forum's step-two analysis.
71   Kramer, *supra* note 4, at 1033.

conferred no rights in this case, it is more accurate to say that [it] is willing to forego enforcing these rights and apply [the other state's] law because [it] assumes that this is what [the other state] prefers."[72]

As discussed above, however, the fact that a rule is multilateral and takes into account the potential interests of other states in having their law applied to a particular case does not mean that the rule is any less a geographic scope limitation. The federal extraterritoriality cases demonstrate as much, as does Professor Baxter's analysis and, indeed, Professor Kramer's own critique of Professor Currie's forum preference. I agree entirely that states should be free to apply a sister state's local law even if the sister state's own courts, pursuant to a step-two analysis, would not apply their own law, and I agree that this is because of the nature of these choice-of-law rules—in particular that they reflect the state's attempt to accommodate the interests of other states. But I draw a different conclusion from Professor Kramer's analysis; rather than showing that step-two choice-of-law rules operate any less as geographic scope restrictions than do step-one rules, Professor Kramer's analysis shows why other states should not be bound by *either* step-one or step-two rules. Step-two rules are not "unique." As I argue in the next section, a state's courts should not even be bound by sister states' *step one* determinations that their laws are not "prima facie applicable." The features of step-two rules that lead Professor Kramer to conclude that step-two determinations of non-applicability are not binding on sister states apply equally to step-one determinations, and, indeed, to all choice-of-law rules, even geographic scope limitations expressly incorporated into substantive statutes.

The next section explains why step-one rules should not be binding on sister state courts any more than step two rules. The final Part of this Chapter considers whether it follows from this argument, as Professor Kramer appears to believe, that neither set of rules actually functions as geographic scope limitations.

3.2 *Are Step-One Limitations Binding on Other States?*

If I am right in concluding that all choice of law rules function equally as geographic scope limitations, then the two-step theory would require courts to engage in *renvoi* much more broadly than the two-step theorists recognize. The forum would have to apply the other states' step-two rules, as well as any hybrid rules, to ensure that the other states' local laws extend to the case. If the laws do not extend to the case, the two-step theory insists that the courts of other states are not free to apply them to the case. The two-step theorists argue

---

72   *Id.* at 1034.

that only the step-one rules are binding on other states. According to Professor Kramer, step-two rules (and hybrid rules such as those of the First and Second Restatements) are not binding on other states because of "the unique nature of the second-order rules for solving true conflicts," by which he means that these rules are multilateral rather than unilateral and that they "purport to reflect an accommodation that, over the run of cases, is best for all states given their differing unilateral interests."[73] In this section, I argue that even step-one rules are "multilateral" in the relevant sense, and that both step-one and step-two rules differ from internal scope limitations in a way that warrants the conclusion that, unlike internal scope restrictions, neither rules are binding on the courts of other states.

According to the two-step theory, determining the geographic scope of a statute is no different from determining the statute's internal scope.[74] Both scope questions are a matter of statutory interpretation. A court interpreting a statute to determine its applicability to cases having connections to other states is engaged in the same enterprise as a court interpreting a statute to determine its applicability to certain marginal domestic situations. Just as a court must interpret a statute to determine whether it applies to persons under 18 years of age, a court must interpret a statute to determine if it applies to a case in which some of the relevant conduct took place in another state. Most importantly for present purposes, two-step theorists maintain that a court's determination that a statute does not apply to a dispute having certain foreign elements is an authoritative interpretation of the statute, binding on the courts of other states. It is no less of an error for the courts of a sister state to apply another state's local law to an inter-state dispute to which it does not extend than it is to apply a statute that applies only to persons over 18 years of age to a person under 18 years of age.

This analysis misses an important difference between geographic scope limitations and internal scope limitations. Internal scope limitations reflect the law-maker's determination that a particular substantive rule is appropriate for persons or conduct within the statute's scope but inappropriate for persons or conduct outside its scope. If a legislature enacts a substantive rule but limits its applicability to persons who are over 18 years of age, the scope limitation reflects the judgment that the rule is not appropriate for persons

---

73   *Id.* at 1033.

74   I use the term "geographic scope limitation" to include limits a state places on the persons
      to which its law extends when those limits are based on the persons' lack of ties to the
      state. On the other hand, a provision limiting the scope of the law to certain categories of
      persons domiciled in the state (such as those under 18 years of age) is an internal scope
      limitation.

under 18. Persons under 18 years of age remain subject to a different rule or
regulatory regime *of that same state*. Similarly, if a legislature enacts a substantive rule and specifies that it is applicable to conduct occurring in parks, the
scope limitation reflects a judgment that the rule is inappropriate for conduct
occurring in spaces that are not parks. Conduct outside parks is governed by
different rules of that state. If another state's courts purport to be applying the
enacting state's law but do not give effect to an internal scope limitation, they
are misapplying the enacting state's law.

Geographic scope limitations, by contrast, do not necessarily reflect a determination that the substantive rule is inappropriate for persons or situations
that fall outside the law's scope.[75] Geographic scope limitations ordinarily
reflect the state's forbearance from applying its substantive rule to disputes that
other states might have a stronger claim to regulate. Geographic scope limitations, in other words, ordinarily reflect comity concerns. The scope limitation
may reflect the state's willingness to entertain the possibility that its local
law may not be well-suited for disputes having closer connections to states
having different values, traditions, social structures, levels of development,
topographic characteristics, etc. Or the state may regard its substantive rule
to be substantively superior and appropriate for persons or situations having
substantial connections to other states but be willing to defer to another state's
potentially stronger claim to legislate with respect to the particular matter.[76]
In either case, the geographic scope limitation reflects, at most, agnosticism
about whether its law should be applied beyond the specified scope. In the
case of internal scope limitations, on the other hand, the legislature has ple-
nary, uncontested legislative authority, yet it chooses to limit the statute's
scope to certain types of persons or spaces or situations, leaving disputes
involving other persons, places, or situations to be governed by a *different* law
of that state. A geographic scope limitation does not necessarily reflect the
view that cases falling outside the law's geographic scope should be governed

---

75   In this section, I will assume that the rules we are discussing are geographic scope limi-
      tations. (Indeed, my analysis here applies to statutory provisions expressly framed as
      geographic scope limitations, as well as choice of law rules that have long been thought
      to function as implicit geographic scope limitations.) In the next section, I will consider
      whether a limitation that is binding on the enacting state's courts but not the courts of
      other states can properly be considered a scope limitation at all.

76   To say that the scope limitations reflected in choice-of-law rules are based on comity con-
      cerns does not mean that states necessarily adopt them out of a sense of altruism. It is
      possible that states adhere to these limits in the self-interested hope that sister states will
      adhere to similar limitations when the shoe is on the other foot. *See Romero, supra* text
      accompanying note 54. My argument does not depend on the claim that states adhere to
      these limitations out of a sense of altruism.

by a *different* rule. Indeed, the enacting state does not provide another rule to govern such cases.

If State A enacts a substantive rule and engrafts geographic scope limitations to it for reasons of comity, it is not expressing an affirmative preference that the rule not be applied to disputes falling outside the rule's scope. It may indeed prefer that the rule also be applied to disputes falling outside the rule's scope. Thus, if the limitation was enacted for reasons of deference, State A would not be offended or in any way disrespected by State B if State B's courts decided that deference was not necessary and went ahead and applied State A's local law.

Professor Kramer maintains that, unlike step-two rules, step-one rules do not reflect the enacting state's accommodation of the competing interests of other states or nations. If a step-one analysis reveals that the enacting state has no interest in applying its law to the case in the first place, there is no need to accommodate its own interests to those of other states. But this argument reflects a too-narrow understanding of a state's possible interest in having its law applied. A state's local law reflects that state's lawmakers' views of the optimal substantive standards for resolving disputes of the relevant type. It is for that reason that the state has adopted the substantive rule to resolve disputes having no out-of-state contacts. In cases pending before its courts, the enacting state therefore may have a residual interest in having its law applied to cases having out-of-state elements: its interest, as a justice-administering state, in resolving the dispute according to the rule that its lawmakers have determined is the "best" rule for the type of case involved.[77] Applying forum law can also be expected to ease the burden on its courts, as forum law will be more familiar to forum courts than another state's law.[78]

Of course, that interest might be overcome in a particular case having foreign elements. To recognize that a state always has a residual interest in having the dispute resolved according to what its lawmakers regard as the "best" local law does not dictate what weight this interest should have in the choice-of-law

---

[77] Professor Singer relies on this interest in urging a presumption of forum law. *See* Singer, *supra* note 37, at 83. This interest is also recognized by Professor Leflar's "better law" approach. Professor Brilmayer advances a version of this argument in her critique of interest analysis. She posits a legislature controlled by consumer advocates that enacts a consumer-protective law in order to benefit consumers worldwide. *See* BRILMAYER, *supra* note 32.

[78] *See* Elliott E. Cheatham and Willis L.M. Reese, *Choice of the Applicable Law*, 52 COLUM. L. REV. 959, 964 (1952) ("Obviously, a court is most familiar with its own local law. It should not assume the burden of ascertaining and applying that of another state without good reason. And the greater the burden involved, the more compelling must be reason for assuming it. This policy is basic to choice of law.").

analysis. Because all states may be said to have this interest, the enacting state's interest in having its law applied will (arguably) always be cancelled out by the interest of other states connected to the dispute in having *their* laws applied, if the other state has a different substantive law. Thus, taking this interest into account in the choice-of-law process may in the end not be very helpful in resolving a choice-of-law problem.[79] For this reason, a state may well adopt a choice-of-law approach under which this sort of interest is always trumped by the sort of interest that two-step theorists would find in step one. Recognizing this interest therefore may not produce a different outcome for two-step theorists (apart from the *renvoi* question). Nevertheless, it remains true that, for a state that adopts the two-step approach and finds in the particular case that only one state has an interest in applying its law (as the two-step theorists define such interests), the step-one analysis is actually functioning as a "rule of priority" because the court is implicitly holding that the sort of interest the two-step theorists find determinative should prevail over another state's residual interest in having the dispute resolved according to the local law with which its courts are most familiar and its lawmakers regard as best.

If we take into account that states have these residual interests, then every decision not to extend that law to an inter-state or international case reflects the state's subordination of these residual interests. If the state's geographic scope limitations reflect a subordination of the state's interest in resolving the dispute according to the best or most familiar law (as well as other interests the state may have) out of deference to the potential interest of other states in regulating the matter, then the scope limitation does not reflect an affirmative preference that other states *not* apply its substantive law. The situation thus fits Professor Kramer's description of the type of case in which he thinks it is not necessary for a state's courts to follow a sister state's decision not apply its own law: As he describes it, the step-two analysis calls to mind

> Dean Griswold's image of Alphonse and Gaston politely deferring to each other and never getting through the door. Like the two comic characters, [the two states] defer to each other not because neither wants to enter (i.e., not because they have no interest), but because each believes the other would or should prefer to go first. Once Alphonse makes sure that

---

79   Some scholars would give this interest considerable weight, however. *See* Singer, *supra* note 37; Robert A. Leflar, *Conflicts Law: More on Choice-Influencing Considerations*, 54 CALIF. L. REV. 1584, 1585 (1966).

> Gaston is wrong and that he (Alphonse) genuinely prefers to see Gaston
> go first, he should escort Gaston through the door.[80]

Similarly, if the forum state is convinced that, under the preferable choice of law rule, its sister state's law should be applied, it should not be deterred from applying it out of deference to its sister state's deference-based scope limitation.

I have so far been assuming that a state's geographic scope limitations are based on comity. It is, of course, possible that a given state's scope limitation is not based on comity. A state might instead choose to limit the scope of its law in order to restrict the benefit of its better law to domiciliaries, or to externalize the costs of its law to out-of-staters. (We might call these "protectionist" interests.) If the geographic scope limitation reflects these sorts of interests, the enacting state may well prefer that its law not be applied beyond its specified scope.[81] But geographic scope limitations motivated by such aims are not ones that other states or nations should feel obligated to respect. Ordinarily, another country would simply decide to apply its own law instead or would decline to entertain a cause of action designed to disadvantage its own nationals. In the inter-state context, scope limitations of this sort would in many cases be unconstitutional. As Professor Kramer has recognized, if a state has limited the benefits of its own law to state residents or domiciliaries, the restriction is valid when it serves a "substantial nonprotectionist objective."[82] In his view, scope restrictions that limit the benefit of state laws to residents are generally permissible when "the justification for limiting the scope of [such] laws ... is comity."[83] In such cases, the scope limitation "is a means of accommodating the interests of other states,"[84] which is permissible because "reducing interstate friction is the central purpose of the privileges and immunities clause."[85] Thus, "[a] state may withhold the benefits of its law [from nonresidents] in order to

---

80   Kramer, *supra* note 4, at 1034 (footnote omitted).
81   Even this is questionable, however, as the enacting state does not purport to be enacting a
      different rule for disputes beyond the local law's specified scope. Instead, it leaves disputes
      beyond the law's geographic scope to be addressed under the laws of other states, which
      might indeed adopt the same substantive law for the case at hand. Presumably, the enact-
      ing state does not provide a different law to govern disputes beyond its local law's scope
      because it doubts its legislative authority over such cases. Thus, even here, the geographic
      scope limitation may be said to reflect comity concerns.
82   Kramer, *supra* note 6, at 1067.
83   *Id.*
84   *Id.*
85   *Id.* at 1067–68.

apply the law of another interested state, but not otherwise."[86] If comity is the only legitimate reason for limiting the geographic reach of a state's local law, states would be warranted in presuming that a sister state's geographic scope limitations do not reflect a preference that the enacting state's local law not be applied beyond the specified scope.[87]

It is also possible that a state's geographic scope limitation is not entirely based on comity or entirely based on protectionism or discrimination against out-of-staters or other illegitimate purposes. For example, a state might decide to limit the scope of its law *primarily* for reasons of deference to other states, but its selection of a particular scope limitation might reflect other legitimate purposes as well. If a state's sole purpose in limiting the scope of its law is deference to other states' superior legislative authority, one might expect it to adopt a scope limitation along the lines of the Second Restatement's "more significant relationship" test or *Timberlane*'s jurisdictional rule of reason. In other words, the state's choice-of-law rule might provide in open-ended terms that its substantive law applies to cases having foreign elements unless, in light of the facts of the case and other relevant considerations, another state has a stronger claim to having its law applied. But the state might also be concerned that such an approach is too complex for judicial administration, and for this reason it might choose a more streamlined rule. (This was, indeed, the reason

---

86   *Id.* at 1068. This analysis leads Professor Kramer to conclude that scope limitations that limit the benefits of a state's law to residents are constitutional in true and false conflict situations. In both of those contexts, if the forum decides not to apply its law to benefit nonresidents, it is doing so in order to defer to another state's interest in applying its own law to its residents. *See id.* at 1068–72. In unprovided-for cases, however, such a scope limitation would violate the Privileges and Immunities Clause because the comity-based justification for denying the nonresident the benefit of the law would be inapplicable. As Professor Kramer argues, "[t]o the extent that the reason for treating nonresidents differently is comity, there must be another state that wants to treat the nonresident differently." *Id.* at 1068. In unprovided-for cases, by hypothesis, the other interested states do not have an interest in having their law applied.

87   My analysis in this essay suggests that Professor Kramer's view of when another state has an interest in having its law applied may be too narrow. If, as I argued above, a state always has a residual interest in resolving the dispute according to the law its lawmakers have determined is best, then a state having a different substantive law than the forum's will always be an interested state. But the point here is that, to the extent such a state declines nevertheless to extend its law to cases having foreign elements, its only *legitimate* reason for doing so is deference to the legislative authority of another state. If deference is the reason for the limitation, then the limitation does not reflect an affirmative preference that the law not be applied. Other states should not feel constrained to accept the other state's deference to it.

the Court gave in *Empagran* for rejecting the *Timberlane* approach.)[88] If so, then the state's reasons for selecting the particular scope limitation it selected would reflect a combination of its desire to defer to other states' lawmaking authorities in appropriate cases and a desire to simplify the judicial task.

If a state's scope limitation reflects this combination of interests, however, it is unlikely to reflect an affirmative desire that *other states* apply the scope limitation. A state that adopts such a scope limitation (even if it expressly incorporates it into the substantive statute) would likely have preferred to apply its substantive law more broadly, but it declined to do so for comity reasons. It could have accomplished its comity goals by adopting an all-things-considered balancing test, but it declined to do so in order to ease the administrative burden on the courts. This ease-of-administration goal would appear to be implicated only when the dispute is being adjudicated in *that state's* courts. If another state is not similarly concerned about burdening its courts with a complex, all-things-considered balancing process and consequently adopts a Second Restatement-type approach, it may well conclude that the enacting state has the most significant relationship to the dispute and that its law should therefore be applied even if the enacting state's courts would not apply it. It seems to follow that, if the forum were to apply its sister state's local law but disregard its hybrid geographic scope limitation, it would *not* be disrespecting the enacting state's preferences. We can assume that the enacting state's preference was that its local law be applied whenever it had the superior claim to regulate the matter, but that it subordinated that preference to a desire to simplify the job of its own courts.[89]

A geographic scope limitation might also reflect a combination of comity concerns and a desire to provide regulated parties with a greater degree of certainty and predictability about the applicable law than would be provided by an all-things-considered approach such as that of the Second Restatement. (This appears to be the aim of the draft Third Restatement.) Whether a sister state would be disrespecting such a state's preferences were it to apply its substantive law to disputes falling outside the scope of the law, as determined

---

88 The Court said the *Timberlane* approach was "too complex to prove workable." *Empagran*, 542 U.S. at 168. As the Court explained, "[t]he legally and economically technical nature of that enterprise means lengthier proceedings, appeals, and more proceedings to the point where procedural costs and delays could themselves threaten interference with a foreign nations' ability to maintain the integrity of its own antitrust enforcement system." *Id.* at 168–69.

89 The judicial administration concern underlying the scope limitation is thus akin to a procedural concern. Like other procedural rules, it should apply only if the adjudication is pending in the enacting state's courts.

by the terms of the scope limitation, presents a more complex question—
one beyond the scope of this Chapter.[90] My analysis so far should suffice to
establish that a geographic scope limitation (even an express geographic scope
limitation incorporated into the text of a statute) should not *always* bind
the courts of sister states. Some such limitations will be unconstitutional (in the
inter-state context) or in any event undeserving of the respect of sister states
or foreign nations because they are discriminatory or protectionist. If based on
comity, scope limitations do not express a preference that other states adhere
to them. If they reflect a combination of deference to other states and another
valid concern, the other valid concern may not extend to cases being litigated
in the courts of other states.

4   Choice-of-Law Rules as Geographic Scope Limitations Redux

Does the conclusion that a choice-of-law rule is not binding on the courts of
other states mean that the rule is not *really* a geographic scope limitation?
Professor Kramer concluded that step-two rules were not geographic scope
limitations *because* they are not binding on the courts of other states. In his
view, to say that a given state's law does not extend to this case because of
a geographic scope limitation means that the law "confer[s] no rights in this
case."[91] If a law confers no rights, then it cannot be the basis for a judicial
decision in favor of the plaintiff. Thus, if another state has determined that
the enacting state's law governs the case, it would be required to dismiss on the
ground that the law does not confer a right on the plaintiff. If sister states are
free to apply the underlying local law without regard to step-two rules (and,

---

90   My tentative view is that this sort of hybrid scope limitation should also not be binding on
      sister state courts. The interest in certainty and predictability may, of course, be relevant
      to the constitutional analysis. Thus, to apply a criminal statute beyond its geographic
      scope as reflected in an express statutory scope limitation is likely unconstitutional. Even
      in civil cases, constitutional doctrine requires consideration of whether application of a
      state's law would be "arbitrary [or] fundamentally unfair," *see Allstate Ins. Co.*, 449 U.S. at
      312, which in turn makes relevant whether the parties could have anticipated application
      of that state's law. *See id.* at 317 (noting that defendant "can hardly claim unfamiliarity
      with the laws of the host jurisdiction and surprise that the state courts might apply forum
      law …") Within these constitutional limits, however, a state should be free to weigh the
      interest in certainty and predictability differently than do their sister states and accord-
      ingly to apply their sister states' laws beyond their geographic scope as specified in a
      scope limitation or inferred from the enacting states' choice of law rules.
91   Kramer, *supra* note 4, at 1033.

if my argument in section 3 is right, at least some step-one limitations), then such rules do not in fact operate as geographic scope limitations.

There is some appeal to that view. To say that these rules limit the geographic scope of a law does seem to mean that the law simply does not extend to disputes beyond its scope, which in turn seems to mean that, regardless of the forum, the law does not confer substantive rights to the parties or otherwise apply to such cases. If so, then my claim that sister states may properly apply that law to disputes beyond its scope seems tantamount to a conclusion that these provisions do not really function as geographic scope limitations. If my analysis is correct, then even express statutory language purporting to limit the geographic reach of a statute does not actually operate to limit the reach of the statute (to the extent the provision is based on comity). The statutory text binds the enacting state's courts, but it does not purport to bind other states, which remain free to apply the substantive law more broadly.

Admittedly, the idea of a limitation on the substantive scope of a law that varies depending on the forum is elusive. There would appear to be (at least) two other possible conceptualizations compatible with my thesis that the courts of other states are free to apply such laws even when the courts of the enacting state would not. First, one can understand a state's local law as conferring a right even when that state's courts would not apply it because of step-one or step-two rules, or, indeed, because of express statutory restrictions on the scope of a state's law. On this view, the step-one and step-two rules, as well as express statutory scope limitations, would operate as instructions to the local courts to forego application of otherwise applicable law in order to accommodate the interests of other states. These rules would still be binding on the enacting state's courts, but they would not operate as substantive limits on the scope of the state's law. They would operate instead as a sort of procedural instruction to the courts of the enacting states, but would not purport to bind the courts of other states. So conceptualized, the rules would not function as scope limitations at all.

This would appear to be a natural way to conceptualize choice of law rules enacted by the legislature in a general choice-of-law statute. Such statutes are rare in the United States, but are common in the rest of the world, where choice of law rules form part of the Civil Code.[92] Such rules do not purport to

---

92   *See, e.g.,* Constituição Federal [C.F.] [Constitution] art. 105(I) (Braz.); Zhonghua Renmin Gongheguo Minshi Shusong Fa (中华人民共和国民事诉讼法) [Civil Procedure Law of the People's Republic of China] (promulgated by Order of the President Aug. 31, 2012, effective Jan. 1, 2013) NPCSC Official Gazette May 2012, at 525, 525–560 (China); Zhonghua Renmin Gongheguo Shewai Mishi Guanxi Falv Shiyoung Fa (中华人民共和国涉外民事关系法律适用法) [Law of the People's Republic of

be limitations on the substantive scope of the enacting state's laws, and can easily be understood as instructions from the state's legislature to the state's courts regarding the circumstances in which it is proper for forum courts to refrain from applying forum law. This conceptualization is also more consistent with another aspect of such statutes: they not only instruct the state's courts not to apply forum law in some cases, but they also instruct the court to apply the local law of another state or nation. For example, the Rome II regulations of the European Union instructs member states to apply the law of the place of injury to tort cases (subject to certain exceptions) and expressly prohibit *renvoi*.[93] By requiring application of another state's law without regard to whether the other state's law would be applicable under its choice of law rules, the regulations appear to conceptualize choice-of-law rules as something other than limitations on the law's substantive scope.

To be sure, this conceptualization is in tension with how choice-of-law rules have been thought to operate in common law systems lacking general choice-of-law statutes. As the *Carroll* case illustrates, the courts have generally reconciled the application of such rules with the judicial obligation to apply statutes enacted by the legislature by conceptualizing such rules as implicit limitations on geographic scope. Federal extraterritoriality doctrine is similarly well understood to be "a matter of statutory construction" regarding the territorial reach of federal law. As discussed, this conceptualization has been the basis for reconciling such rules with the court's obligation to resolve disputes in accordance with applicable forum state law. The court assumes that the legislature did not mean to resolve the geographic scope question.

But the latter problem can be addressed through a slight reconceptualization of the issue. The courts can assume instead that the legislature meant to leave open a slightly different question: not whether the law extends to cases having foreign elements, but whether the forum's courts should apply it to such

---

China on Choice of Law for Foreign-related Civil Relations] (promulgated by Order of the President Oct. 28, 2010, effective Apr. 1, 2011) NPCSC Official Gazette July 2010, at 640, 640–643 (China); CODE CIVIL [C. CIV.] [CIVIL CODE] art. 311–14–311–17, 370-3–370–5 (Fr.), CODE DE LA CONSOMMATION [C. CONSOM.] [CONSUMER CODE] art. L135–1 (Fr.); Einführungsgesetz sum Bürgerlichen Gesetzbuche [EGBGB] [Civil Code Introduction Act], Sep. 21, 1994, BGBl 1 at 2494 (Ger.); Legge 31 maggio 1995, n. 218, G.U. Jun 3, 1995, Suppl. Ordinario n. 68 (It.); Hō no tekiyō ni kansuru tsūsokuhō [Act on the general rules for application of laws], Act no. 78 of 2006 (Japan); Constitución política de los Estados Unidos Mexicanos [CP], Tit. III, chap. IV art. 104, Tit. IV art. 121, Diario Oficial de la Federación [DOF] 01-31-1917, últimas reformas DOF 10-02-2014 (Mex.).

93 Commission Regulation 864/2007, of the European Parliament and of the Council of 11 July 2007 on the Law Applicable to Non-Contractual Obligations (Rome II), 2007 O.J. (L 199) 40, arts. 4, 24 (EC).

cases. Choice-of-law rules can be understood as a presumptive caveat *to the forum courts* about their obligation to apply forum law to cases having foreign elements. The reasons that have been thought to justify the court's articulation and application of these "background rules of interpretation" to determine the statute's geographic scope equally justify their articulation and application as presumptive instructions to forum courts not to apply otherwise applicable law to cases having foreign elements.

The proposed reconceptualization of choice of law rules as merely instructions to the forum courts to refrain from applying laws that are in principle universally applicable is perhaps most difficult to accept with respect to statutory provisions expressly written as geographic scope limitations.[94] If my analysis in Part 3 is sound, these limitations too should be no more binding on the courts of other states than are other choice-of-law rules (at least to the extent they are based on comity concerns). The reconceptualization is justified because, to the extent the limitations are based on comity, they do not reflect the enacting state's affirmative desire that other states not apply its law. The reconceptualization would admittedly be in tension with the text of these laws, but if the courts are justified in reading a scope limitation into a law that is written in universal terms, then they would seem to be justified in reading a clause that is written as a geographic limit as instead an instruction to forum courts to decline to enforce the substance of the law to the specified cases.[95] Admittedly, however, asking the courts to treat an express geographic scope limitation as something other than a geographic scope limitation may be a bridge too far.

---

94   As discussed above, such statutory provisions are themselves a type of choice of law rule.
      See Symeonides, *supra* note 31.

95   There is another possible problem with State B applying a State A statute containing
      an express geographic scope limitation beyond its specified scope: it could result in
      the application of the law to persons who may have reasonably assumed (based on the
      text) that the statute did not reach their conduct. In the penal context, doing so could
      be in violation of constitutional due process principles or even of international human
      rights norms. This problem may also apply where the "geographic scope" issue has been
      authoritatively determined through judicial decisions, even in the absence of an express
      statutory provision. This is not a reason to reject the proposed reconceptualization of
      geographic scope limitations as instructions to the forum courts to refrain from applying
      laws that are in principle of universal reach. State B's courts are of course constrained
      by State B constitutional principles and applicable international law. Beyond that, State
      B can, and should, take the protection of justified expectations into account pursuant
      to its own non-constitutional choice of law rules. *Cf.* Second Restatement of Conflict of
      Laws, § 6(2)(c). State B's courts thus can and should consider the role of statutory provisions (and judicial decisions) written as geographic scope limitations in giving rise to
      justified expectations in appropriate cases as part of its own choice-of-law analysis.

The other possible conceptualization would treat all of these rules as geographic scope limitations but reconceptualize what the courts *of other states* are doing when they apply the local law of another state to cases beyond that law's geographic scope. On this view, the enacting state's law does not apply *ex proprio vigore* to cases beyond its geographic scope as specified in an express statutory scope limitation as or inferred from step-one or step-two rules, but other states would be free to resolve cases according to the local law of the enacting state even when the law does not reach the dispute of its own force. When it does this, we might say that the court is incorporating the substantive rule of another state's local law as its own for purposes of deciding the case. This conceptualization resembles the once fashionable but now much derided "local law" theory of choice of law, under which a state that decides to resolve a dispute under the law of another state is understood to have incorporated that law as its own law for purposes of that case.[96] But the conceptualization being considered here does not go that far. The "local law" theory posits that the forum is *always* incorporating another state's law as its own. The reconceptualization being considered here would require this understanding of what a court is doing when it applies another state's law only when the enacting state's law does not purport to apply. If the enacting state's courts would apply its own law, then a sister state that decides to resolve the case according to the enacting state's law could be said to be applying that law *qua* sister state law.

In the inter-state context, a constitutional issue might arise if the forum does not have enough contacts to the dispute to permit it to apply its own law. By hypothesis, the enacting state's law does not reach the case because of the geographic scope limitation. If the forum does not have enough contacts to apply its own law, can it apply its sister state's (by hypothesis inapplicable) local law *qua* its own law? A full analysis of this issue is beyond the scope of this Chapter, but the analysis in Part 3 suggests that doing so should not be deemed a violation of the Full Faith and Credit Clause. If I am right that geographic scope limitations do not reflect the enacting state's affirmative desire that the dispute not be resolved according to its local law, then the forum would not be disrespecting the enacting state's wishes if it resolve the case according to its local law even if the enacting state's courts would not. But perhaps it would be a violation of the Due Process Clause, which imposes similar limits on a state's ability to extend its own law extraterritorially.

As between these two alternative conceptualizations, the first would involve a greater departure from current understandings of the choice-of-law process and federal extraterritoriality doctrine, and it would require a radical

---

96   *See, e.g.,* Grant v. McAuliffe, 41 Cal. 2d 859, 862 (Cal. 1953).

departure from the text of comity-based statutory scope limitations. But it would accord with the rationale for these limitations (which would no longer be understood as scope limitations). It would also bring the U.S. conceptualization of the choice of law rules closer to how these rules are understood in the civil law world. And it would more elegantly avoid the constitutional issues just discussed.

In any event, whether we regard these provisions as a special type of scope limitation or as not geographic scope limitations at all, this Chapter's analysis, if correct, establishes that the characterization applies to all choice-of-law rules, not just those that are applied to resolve true conflicts. Indeed, the characterization also applies to express statutory provisions purporting to limit the applicability of the enacting state's substantive law to cases having certain connections to the enacting state (to the extent that they reflect comity concerns). Insofar as these provisions call for non-application of the enacting state's substantive law, they are binding on the enacting state's courts, but they are not binding on the courts of other states. The two-step theorists, and the current draft of the Third Restatement, are right to conclude that step-two rules are not binding on the courts of other states, but they are wrong to insist that step-one rules are binding on other states. Even express statutory limitations on a statute's geographic scope may be disregarded by the courts of sister states to the extent they are based on deference to other states (or if they reflect protectionist or discriminatory purposes).

CHAPTER 5

Forum non conveniens: Recent Developments at the Intersection of Public and Private International Law

Philippa Webb*

1   Introduction

A distinctive feature of Lea Brilmayer's career is her ability to move masterfully between the connected realms of private international law and public international law. Her writings and practice have shaped the development of the law in both fields and helped to bridge the perceived gaps between them.

My topic of *forum non conveniens* is one that also traverses different realms: it is a doctrine of private international law that is raised in domestic cases that have an international element, which may well involve an alleged breach of public international law or require analysis according to international legal standards. The doctrine allows a court that has jurisdiction over a case to order a stay or dismissal if the court determines that the case may be heard more appropriately in another court, usually in another country.[1]

Lea Brilmayer has written on *forum non conveniens* in her work on conflict of laws.[2] She has also published seminal articles on the overarching concept of a state's right to exercise general jurisdiction.[3] In this chapter, I have been inspired by her influential article at the intersection of public and private international law: *International Law in American Courts: A Modest Proposal.*[4]

---

* I am grateful to Matthew Nelson for excellent research assistance.
1 As set out in Part 2 below, the "more appropriate" test has variations in different jurisdictions. The alternative court is usually in another country but may be in another state in federal systems like the United States.
2 E.g. Brilmayer & Underhill, *Congressional Obligation to Provide a Forum for Constitutional Claims: Discriminatory Jurisdictional Rules and the Conflict of Laws*, 69 VA. L. REV. 819, 836 (1983).
3 E.g. Brilmayer, *How Contacts Count: Due Process Limitations on State Court Jurisdiction*, 1980 SUP. CT. REV. 77; Brilmayer, Haverkamp, Logan, Lynch, Neuwirth & O'Brien, *A General Look at General Jurisdiction*, 66 TEX. L. REV. 721 (1988); Brilmayer, *Related Contacts and Personal Jurisdiction*, 101 HARV. L. REV. 1444 (1988).
4 Brilmayer, *International Law in American Courts: A Modest Proposal*, 100 YALE L.J. 2277 (1990–1991).

© KONINKLIJKE BRILL NV, LEIDEN, 2019 | DOI:10.1163/9789004316539_006

International Law in American Courts does not expressly refer to *forum non conveniens*. It takes as its framework the choice between judicial and political resolution of disputes, or between domestic courts and international mechanisms, whereas *forum non conveniens* is usually—but not always—concerned with the choice between a domestic court and a foreign court. Nonetheless, several aspects of the article are relevant to contemporary developments in *forum non conveniens*.

First, *forum non conveniens* can be used as an "avoidance technique," in a similar way to how Brilmayer explains that the requirements of standing, private cause of action, and having a self-executing treaty are used to screen out certain cases.[5]

Second, Brilmayer's analysis of the "horizontal model" (where the proper subjects of international law are the states themselves) and the "vertical model" (where both states and individuals have rights)[6] is relevant to understanding the challenge of holding multinational corporations (MNCs) accountable for violations against states or individuals. It is cases involving claims against MNCs that have been driving the development of *forum non conveniens*.

Third, in certain jurisdictions the judicial analysis required in *forum non conveniens* challenges has come to focus heavily on the extent to which a foreign legal system or international mechanism meets standards of due process. Brilmayer's article engages with the role of the American judge in deciding delicate foreign policy issues and proposes ways of understanding international law that "fit it squarely into traditional forms of domestic adjudication."[7]

It is also serendipitous that two important and recent cases on *forum non conveniens* concern Eritrea,[8] a state for which Lea Brilmayer previously served as lead counsel in several international inter-state arbitrations concerning maritime delimitation, land boundaries, and mass claims for violations of the laws of war.

This chapter proceeds as follows. Part 2 will examine the definition of the doctrine and the different tests used in several jurisdictions. It will also address attempts at harmonization such as regulations in the EU and the resolution of the *Institut de droit international*. Part 3 will consider how *forum non conveniens*, like some of the other legal concepts that Brilmayer has written about, may be used as an avoidance device by defendants. The focus is on MNCs,

---

5   *Id.* at 2302–2304.

6   *Id.* at 2297.

7   *Id.* at 2314.

8   *Nemariam v. Federal Democratic Republic of Ethiopia*, 315 F.3d 390 (D.C. Cir. 2003) and *Araya v. Nevsun Resources Ltd.*, BCSC 1856 (2016); 2017 BCCA 401.

which traverse the "horizontal" and "vertical" models identified by Brilmayer. Part 4 draws on Brilmayer's work on the judicial function in the light of *forum non conveniens* cases where judges evaluate a foreign legal system or an international mechanism as the potentially alternative forum for the dispute.

2 In Search of a Common Approach to *forum non conveniens*

A famous judicial statement on the variability of *forum non conveniens* made more than two decades ago, remains relevant today: "The discretionary nature of the doctrine, combined with the multifariousness of the factors relevant to its application ... make uniformity and predictability of outcome almost impossible."[9]

The application of the doctrine varies along two axes. First, some states include the *forum non conveniens* analysis as part of the determination on whether jurisdiction exists in the first place.[10] In other states, the analysis is conducted only after jurisdiction has been established. Second, and more importantly, states vary as to the test for *forum non conveniens* and the factors to be taken into account.

2.1 *The Tests in Different Jurisdictions*
In the United States, the Supreme Court has stated the test as follows:

> A plaintiff's choice of forum should rarely be disturbed. However, when an alternative forum has jurisdiction to hear the case, and when the trial in the chosen forum would 'establish ... oppressiveness and vexation to a defendant ... out of all proportion to a plaintiff's convenience,' or when 'the chosen forum [is] inappropriate because of considerations affecting the court's own administrative and legal problems,' the court may, in the exercise of its sound discretion, dismiss the case.[11]

---

9   *American Dredging Co. v Miller*, 510 U.S. 443, 455 (1994).
10   Ronald A. Brand, *Forum non Conveniens*, MAX PLANCK ENCYCLOPEDIA OF PUBLIC INTERNATIONAL LAW (2013), para. 2.
11   *Piper Aircraft Co. v. Reyno*, 454 US 235, 241 (1981) *quoting Koster v. (Am,) Lumbermans Mut, Cas, Co.*, 330 US 518, 524 (1947); *See also Sinochem International Co. Ltd. v. Malaysia Interna'l Shipping Corp.*, 549 US 422, 429 (2007) and Am. Dredging Co. v. Miller, 510 US 443, 447–8 (1994).

The US courts will consider a range of public and private interests—and not just the interests of the plaintiff—in deciding whether to decline to exercise jurisdiction:

> An interest to be considered, and the one likely to be most pressed, is the private interest of the litigant. Important considerations are the relative ease of access to sources of proof; availability of compulsory process for attendance of unwilling, and the cost of obtaining attendance of willing witnesses; possibility of view of premises, if view would be appropriate to the action; and all other practical problems that make trial of a case easy, expeditious and inexpensive. There may also be questions as to the enforceability of a judgment if one is obtained. The court will weigh relative advantages and obstacles to fair trial. It is often said that the plaintiff may not, by choice of an inconvenient forum, 'vex,' 'harass,' or 'oppress' the defendant by inflicting upon him expense or trouble not necessary to his own right to pursue his remedy. But unless the balance is strongly in favour of the defendant, the plaintiff's choice of forum should rarely be disturbed.
>
> Factors of public interest also have place in applying the doctrine. Administrative difficulties follow for courts when litigation is piled up in congested centres instead of being handled at its origin. Jury duty is a burden that ought not to be imposed upon the people of a community which has no relation to the litigation. In cases which touch the affairs of many persons, there is reason for holding the trial in their view and reach rather than in remote parts of the country where they can learn of it by report only. There is a local interest in having localized controversies decided at home. There is an appropriateness, too, in having the trial of a diversity case in a forum that is at home with the state law that must govern the case, rather than having a court in some other forum untangle problems in conflict of laws, and in law foreign to itself.[12]

This multi-factor analysis bears some resemblance to Lea Brilmayer's writing in a choice of law context. She divides the standard into (1) contacts with the forum; (2) interests arising from these contacts; and (3) fairness to the defendant. Contacts include events leading to the litigation or the state residence of the litigants. These contacts create interests, but "courts have

---

12   *Gulf Oil Corp v. Gilbert*, 330 US 501, 508–9 (1947).

offered no satisfactory formulation for what kinds of interests suffice."[13] Indeed, in the *forum non conveniens* context, the test has been estimated to include up to 25 different variables.[14]

Whereas the US test for *forum non conveniens* may be bluntly termed "the chosen forum is inappropriate," the test in the United Kingdom (UK)[15] may be summarised as "the alternative forum is more appropriate," reflecting a different emphasis and a different process of reasoning.

The English doctrine is stated in *Spiliada Maritime Corp v. Cansulex Ltd.*:[16]

> The basic principle is that a stay will only be granted on the ground of *forum non conveniens* where the court is satisfied that there is some other available forum, having competent jurisdiction, which is the appropriate forum for the trial of the action, i.e., in which the case may be tried more suitably for the interests of all the parties and the ends of justice.[17]

As with the US approach, the English courts look at the interests of all the parties, not just the plaintiff. The English courts look at a range of factors, including the availability of witnesses, multiplicity of proceedings, the governing law, and the places where the parties reside or carry on business.[18] The burden of proving these factors in favour of the alternative forum lies with the defendant. If the alternative forum appears to be more appropriate, the burden of proof shifts to the plaintiff to show that "circumstances by reason of which justice requires that a stay should nevertheless not be granted."[19] The English court will not be deterred from granting a stay simply because that plaintiff would be deprived of "a legitimate personal or juridical advantage," such as more generous damages, a more complete discovery procedure, a power to award interest,

---

13   Lea Brilmayer and Charles Norchi, *Federal Extraterritoriality and Fifth Amendment Due Process*, 105 HARV. L. REV. 1217, 1242–43 (1992); *See also* Lea Brilmayer, *The Other State's Interests*, 24 CORNELL INT'L L.J. 233 (1991).

14   David Robertson, *The Federal Doctrine of Forum non Conveniens: An Object Lesson in Uncontrolled Discretion*, 29 TEXAS INT. L.J. 353, 359 (1994).

15   Scottish courts are credited with developing the doctrine over four centuries ago in cases where the courts declined to a hear a case in "the interest of justice": Vernor v Elvies (6 Dict of Dec 4788 [1610] [Scot]). The UK House of Lords acknowledged and defined the Scottish doctrine in La Societe du Gaz de Paris v La SA de Navigation 'Les Armateurs Francais' [1926] Session Cases 13: Brand, *supra* note 10, at para. 4.

16   [1987] AC 460 (House of Lords).

17   [1987] AC 460, 476 (House of Lords).

18   [1987] AC 460, 469 (House of Lords).

19   [1987] AC 460, 482 (House of Lords).

or a more generous limitation period.[20] The court must nonetheless be "satisfied that substantial justice will be done in the available appropriate forum," which may take it into an examination of the quality of the other state's legal system (see Part 4 below).

The *Spiliada* approach has had a mixed reception in Commonwealth countries. It has been followed in New Zealand,[21] Singapore, and Malaysia.[22] It has deliberately not been followed in Australia, as it is seen as not giving sufficient weight to the plaintiff's choice of forum. Australian courts require defendants to show that "the chosen forum is clearly inappropriate," keeping the focus on the factors linking the dispute to Australia rather than evaluating alternative fora.[23] It has been criticised as "unnecessarily parochial."[24] Others, however, have said that the UK-Australia differences are overstated and the conceptual space between the approaches "is so narrow as to be practically non-existent."[25]

The Canadian test is that "the alternative forum is clearly more appropriate."[26] It departs from *Spiliada* in two ways: first, Canadian courts treat the potential loss of a plaintiff's juridical advantage as one of the factors to be weighed, not a separate stage of inquiry; second, Canadian courts conduct the *forum non conveniens* analysis at the time jurisdiction is determined (in the context of service *ex juris*), as well as in consideration of whether to exercise an existing jurisdiction.[27]

20   [1987] AC 460, 482 (House of Lords).

21   *Club Mediterranee v. Wendell*, 1 NZLR 216, 219 (1989).

22   *Brinkerhoff Maritime Drilling Corp. v. PT Airfast Services Indonesia (Brinkerhoff)*, 2 LSR 776 (1992); *American Express Bank Ltd v Mohamed Toufic Al-Ozeir*, 1 Malaysian Law Journal 160 (1995); *See also* the similar approach in Hong Kong: *S. Megga Telecommunications Ltd. v. Etowaru Co. Ltd.*, HKC 761 (1995).

23   *Oceanic Sun Line Special Shipping Company Inc. v. Fay*, 165 CLR 197, 247–55 (1988); *Voth v. Manildra Flour*, 171 CLR 538 (1990); *Regie National des Usines Renault SA v. Zhang*, 210 CLR 491 (2002).

24   Anthony Gray, *Forum non Conveniens in Australia: A Comparative Analysis*, 38 COMMON LAW WORLD REVIEW 207 (2009); *See also* Richard Garnett, *Stay of Proceedings in Australia: A Clearly Inappropriate Test?*, 23 MELB. UNIV. L. REV. 30 (1999). For a positive take on the Australian approach, see Alan Reed, *Venue Resolution and Forum non Conveniens: Four Models of Jurisdictional Propriety*, 22 JOURNAL OF TRANSNATIONAL LAW AND CONTEMPORARY PROBLEMS 369 (2013).

25   Ardavan Arzandeh, *Reconsidering the Australian Forum (non) Conveniens Doctrine*, 65 INT. & COMP. L.Q. 475, 476 (2016).

26   *Workers' Compensation Board v. Amchem Products Inc.*, 1 SCR 897, 931 (1993).

27   Brand, *supra* note 10, paras. 13–14. However, in Quebec, which is a civil law jurisdiction, Art. 3135 of the Civil Code provides that the court must first decide on whether it has jurisdiction before entertaining a motion to dismiss on the grounds of *forum non conveniens*.

It is true that "theoretical differences in wording may not have very much practical impact on the way cases are actually decided," and that "the same acts would very often lead to the same decision."[28] But litigation and advocacy are often built on the parsing of words and the differences in language also reflect variations in emphasis, the stages of the reasoning process and, therefore, the exercise of discretion.

The *Institut de droit international* has noted that "[N]ational court systems have developed differing solutions with questions of transnational jurisdiction and independence," including *forum non conveniens*.[29] The *Institut* proposed the following formulation of the test in its 2003 Resolution:

1. When the jurisdiction of the court seised is not founded upon an exclusive choice of court agreement, and where its law enables the court to do so, a court may refuse to assume or exercise jurisdiction in relation to the substance of the claim on the ground that the courts of another country, which have jurisdiction under their law, are clearly more appropriate to determine the issues in question.

2. In deciding whether the courts of another country are clearly more appropriate, the court seised may take into account (in particular): (a) the adequacy of the alternative forum; (b) the residence of the parties; (c) the location of the evidence; (d) the law applicable to the issues; (e) the effect of applicable limitation or prescription periods; (f) the effectiveness and enforceability of any resulting judgment.

The Rapporteur, Sir Lawrence Collins (now Lord Collins), was a Justice of the UK Supreme Court and has been the general editor of the seminal UK text on conflict of laws, *Dicey, Morris and Collins*, since 1987. Nonetheless, the *Institut* formulation is not identical to *Spiliada* and actually seems closer to the Canadian test.

2.2   *The Evisceration of the English Approach in* Spiliada?

Whereas the *Institut*'s attempt at harmonization was to propose the above formulation for the doctrine of *forum non conveniens*, the European approach to harmonization has been to reject the doctrine.[30]

---

28   Ben Juratowitch, *Fora non Conveniens for Enforcement of Arbitral Awards against State*, 63 INT. & COMP. L.Q. 477, 479 (2014).

29   *Resolution on the Principles for Determining when the Use of the Doctrine of Forum non Conveniens and Anti-Suit Injunctions is Appropriate* (Bruges 2003) (Second Commission, Rapporteur Sir Lawrence Collins) at (b).

30   On harmonization, *see* Simona Gross, *The US Supreme Court and the Modern Common Law Approach*, Chapter 4 PERSONAL JURISDICTION AND FORUM NON CONVENIENS IN A TRANSNATIONAL CONTEXT, 104–180 (2014).

The doctrine has long been considered to be incompatible with the Brussels Convention on Jurisdiction and the Enforcement of Judgments in Civil and Commercial Matters 1968.[31] The Schlosser Report (1979) stated:

> The Contracting States are not only entitled to exercise jurisdiction in accordance with the provisions laid down in Title 2: they are obliged to do so. A plaintiff must be sure which court has jurisdiction. He should not have to waste his time and money risking that the court concerned may consider itself less competent than another ... the plaintiff has deliberately been given a choice, which should not be weakened by the application of the doctrine of *forum non conveniens*.[32]

Arguably, the Schlosser Report did not consider[33] whether the doctrine of *forum non conveniens* is available where the alternative forum is in a non-Contracting State to the Brussels Convention, now the Brussels 1 Regulation Recast.[34] But the 2005 *Owusu* Judgment of the European Court of Justice (ECJ) confirmed that *forum non conveniens* does apply in such a scenario, thus appearing to eviscerate the applicability of the *Spiliada* approach.

Mr. Owusu, a British national and resident, had suffered a serious accident while on holiday in Jamaica rendering him tetraplegic. He brought proceedings against Jackson, the anchor defendant, from whom he had rented his holiday villa. The defendant was domiciled in England, but the other defendants were all Jamaican companies.[35] The English Court of Appeal referred the following question to the ECJ:

> 1. Is it inconsistent with the Brussels Convention on Jurisdiction and Enforcement of Judgments 1968, where a claimant contends that jurisdiction is founded on Article 2, for a court of a Contracting State to exercise discretionary power, available under its national laws, to decline to hear proceeding brought against a person domiciled in that State in favour of the courts of a non-Contracting State: (a) if the jurisdiction of

---

31 Official Journal L 299, 31/12/1972, pp. 0032–0042.

32 Schlosser Report, OJ C 59/66 at 97–8 (1979). This was an explanatory report on the Convention on the accession of Denmark, Ireland and the United Kingdom.

33 Barry J. Rodger, *Forum non Conveniens Post-Owusu*, 2 JOURNAL OF PRIVATE INTERNATIONAL LAW 71, 73–4 (2006).

34 Regulation (EU) No 1215/2012 of the European Parliament and of the Council of 12 December 2012 on jurisdiction and the recognition and enforcement of judgments in civil and commercial matters.

35 Rodger, *supra* note 33, 78.

no other Contracting State under the 1968 Convention is in issue; (b) if the proceedings have no other connecting factors to any other Contracting State? 2. If the answer to question 1(a) or 1(b) is yes, is it consistent in all the circumstances or only in some and if so in which?[36]

According to the ECJ, it is inconsistent with the Brussels Convention (and Brussels I Regulation Recast) for a UK court to exercise its discretion to decline to hear proceedings brought against a natural or legal person domiciled in the UK in favour of the courts of a non-Contracting State, even where the jurisdiction of no other Contracting State is in issue and the proceedings have no connection to any other Contracting State.[37] The doctrine does not apply even when the plaintiff is not domiciled in a European Union Member State and when the more appropriate forum would be outside the EU.[38] The ECJ emphasised that one of the primary objectives of this approach was to achieve certainty, which would allow a well-informed defendant reasonably to foresee in which courts he or she may be sued.[39] The Court, somewhat oddly, said that allowing the plea of *forum non conveniens* would undermine the legal protection of the defendant, despite the fact that the plea is invoked by the defendant.[40]

The contours of *Owusu* have been litigated in the English courts. In cases where the alternative fora proposed by the defendants were, for example, Zambia[41] and Kenya,[42] the English courts held that the "upshot" of *Owusu* was that, the defendant being domiciled in England and Wales, "the claim had to be brought here."[43] *Forum non conveniens* was held to be available, however, where the claimants, domiciled in Scotland, brought claims against defendants domiciled in England and Wales: the claims were "wholly internal to one member state" and thus did not have the international element required for the application of the Brussels Regulation (Recast).[44]

There is one other way in which *forum non conveniens* may survive *Owusu* in the English courts: the scenario of parallel proceedings. The adoption

---

36   *Owusu v. Jackson*, [2002] EWCA Civ 877, (2002) OJ C233/16 EU. The second question was found to be inadmissible by the Advocate General.
37   *Owusu v. Jackson*, Case C-281/02 [2005] ECR I-1383. Brand, note 10 *supra*, para. 7.
38   *Owusu v. Jackson*, Case C-281/02 [2005] ECR I-1383.
39   Para. 38.
40   Rodger, *supra* note 33, 87. Jonathan Harris, *Stays of Proceedings and the Brussels Convention*, 54 INT. & COMP. L.Q. 933, 937 (2005).
41   *Lungowe v. Vedanta Resources PLC* [2017] EWCA Civ 1528.
42   *AAA v. Unilever PLC*, [2017] EWHC 371 (QB).
43   AAA para. 66, Vedanta, paras. 54–6.
44   *Cook v. Virgin Media Ltd.*, [2015] EWCA Civ 1287.

of new Articles 33 and 34 in the Brussels I Regulation Recast deal with the stay of proceedings brought in the courts of a Member State based on certain jurisdictional rules of the Regulation when there are prior proceedings pending in a non-Member State.[45] The Regulation has introduced the possibility of staying the Member State proceedings on a discretionary basis that resemble the doctrine of *forum non conveniens*, which in the English courts would lead to the application of the *Spiliada* approach.[46]

In sum, even in a mechanical instrument like the Brussels Regulation, and even with European resistance to the doctrine of *forum non conveniens*, there may be a need to introduce discretionary stays in some cases. The exercise of discretion is dependent not on judicial misgivings about the prospects of justice in another forum,[47] but on whether parallel proceedings exist in a non-Member State.

3 *Forum non conveniens* as an Avoidance Device

3.1 MNCs *and the Avoidance of Litigation*

Forum non conveniens is an avoidance technique in litigation, with similarities to how defendants invoke deficiencies in standing, the existence of a private cause of action, or the absence of a self-executing treaty, as Lea Brilmayer has explained.[48] Defendants work hard to obtain *forum non conveniens* dismissals,

---

45   Article 33 provides that where a member state court has jurisdiction over a pending action on the basis of Article 4 (domicile of the defendant) or Articles 7 to 9 (special jurisdiction, based for example on the place of performance of a contractual obligation or the domicile of a co-defendant), and an action involving the same cause of action and parties is already pending before a non-member state court, the EU court has a discretion to stay its proceedings if the non-member state court is expected to give a judgment capable of recognition and enforcement in that member state *and* the member state court considers a stay is necessary for the proper administration of justice. Article 34 provides that in the same scenario as set out in Art. 33, the EU court has a discretion to stay its proceedings if it is expedient to hear and determine the related actions together to avoid the risk of irreconcilable judgments, the non-member state court is expected to give a judgment capable of recognition and enforcement in that member state, and the member state court considers a stay is necessary for the proper administration of justice. *See, e.g., Blomqvist v. Zavarco Plc*, [2015] EWHC 1898 (Ch) (considering pending proceedings in Malaysia).

46   P Rogerson, "Lis Pendens and Third States: The Commission's Proposed Changes to the Brussels I Regulation", in E Lein (ed), *The Brussels I Review Proposal Uncovered* (2012), 103; P Franzina, *Lis Pendens Involving a Third Country under the Brussels I-bis Regulation: An Overview, Rivista di diritto internazionale privato e processuale* 23 (2014).

47   *See* Part 4 below.

48   *Id.* at 2302–2304.

not necessarily because they prefer the alternative forum, but because this will often represent the last they will see of the litigation.[49] Plaintiffs usually face significant obstacles in bringing their claims in the alternative forum, especially if restrictions on damages awards, contingency fee arrangements, or class action possibilities make such proceedings prohibitively expensive.[50]

Some of the most active users of *forum non conveniens* as a legal tool have been MNCs involved in litigation arising from their operations in developing countries. Making a motion to dismiss on the grounds of *forum non conveniens* "is practically a knee-jerk reaction."[51] MNCs fall somewhere between Brilmayer's "horizontal model" (inter-state relations) and the "vertical model" (state-individual relations).[52] In the transverse plane, MNCs are said to owe obligations to both states in which they operate and individuals affected by those operations, including employees and local communities.[53]

Private parties have been pursuing claims relating to environmental damage, human rights abuses, and labour code violations in the form of domestic tort claims against MNCs. Theoretically it is preferable to bring a claim in the jurisdiction in which the underlying events occurred, but in many cases the domestic legal system is unwilling (due to corruption or a lack of independence), or unable (due to the resources, expertise or the availability of legal aid and class action mechanisms), to provide an avenue for redress. Plaintiffs have thus been seeking to bring claims in the home state of the MNC.

In *Jesner et al v. Arab Bank Plc*, the U.S. Supreme Court held (5-4) that foreign corporations could not be defendants in claims brought under the Alien Tort Statute.[54] However, recent practices in The Netherlands, Canada, and the UK indicate domestic courts are increasingly reluctant to let MNCs 'off the hook' on the basis of *forum non conveniens*.

---

49   Jacqueline Duval-Major, *One-way Ticket Home: The Federal Doctrine of Forum non Conveniens and the International Plaintiff*, 77 CORNELL L. REV. 650, 672 (1992). A successful *forum non conveniens* plea will usually represent the "death knell" of the litigation in question: Simona *Grossi, THE US SUPREME COURT AND THE MODERN COMMON LAW APPROACH* (2014), 72.

50   Philippa Webb, *The Inconvenience of Liability: The Doctrine of Forum non Conveniens in International Environmental Litigation*, 6 ASIA PACIFIC J. ENV. LAW 377 (2001).

51   Howard M. Erichson, *The Chevron-Ecuador Dispute, Forum non Conveniens, and the Problem of Ex Ante Adequacy*, 1 STAN. J. COMPLEX LITIG. 417, 420 (2013).

52   *Id.* at 2297.

53   See generally Webb, *supra* note 50 (considering litigation in Australia, the UK, Hong Kong, Singapore, Malaysia and the US).

54   No. 16–499 (2017).

In *Akpan v. Royal Dutch Shell PLC*,[55] the Shell parent company domiciled in The Netherlands and its Nigerian subsidiary were alleged to be responsible for oil pollution in the Niger Delta. The Dutch court held that *forum non conveniens* no longer played a role under the Dutch code and that even if the claims were dismissed against the Dutch parent company, there would still be jurisdiction in the matter against the Nigerian subsidiary "not even if subsequently, in fact, no connection or hardly any connection would remain with Dutch jurisdiction."[56]

In *Araya v. Nevsun Resources Ltd.*,[57] Eritrean plaintiffs are refugees living in Canada, who claimed they were conscripted into the Eritrean National Service Program, which forced them to provide unpaid labour to the companies constructing a gold mine. They claimed that Nevsun and its Eritrean subsidiary, Bisha Mine Share Company, entered into contracts with two Eritrean companies, to develop the gold mine. The plaintiffs brought proceedings against Nevsun in British Columbia, Canada, seeking damages for the use of forced labour, torture, slavery, cruel, inhuman or degrading treatment, and crimes against humanity.[58]

Nevsun asked the Supreme Court of British Columbia to stay the proceedings because the courts of Eritrea were a more appropriate forum. Conscious of the multi-factorial approach to *forum non conveniens*, the defendant gave the reasons based on procedural and cost factors for having the proceedings in Eritrea:[59] the comparative convenience and expense for the parties and their witnesses "overwhelmingly favours proceeding in Eritrea," including the fact that the "vast majority of the witnesses—hundreds, if not thousands—are in Eritrea;" Eritrean law applied to the dispute; staying the proceeding ensured that the plaintiffs were not able to circumvent Eritrean law's allocation of subject matter competence over labour claims to specialized labour tribunals; proceeding in Eritrea would avoid the jurisdictional problems posed by the class being composed entirely of persons outside British Columbia; proceeding in Eritrea would avoid the jurisdictional limitation imposed by the act of state doctrine; and "the overall mandates of order and fairness" pointed to Eritrean courts as the most appropriate fora. The plaintiffs emphasized a real risk that justice will not be obtained in Eritrea, pointing to: severe barriers to justice given their status as traitors who could not return to Eritrea; the

---

55   Arrondissementsrechtbank Den Haag, 30 January 2013 Case No. C/09/337050/HA ZA 09–1580.
56   *Id.* at para. 4.6.
57   2016 BCSC 1856, upheld on appeal in 2017 BCCA 401.
58   2016 BCSC 1856, para. 43.
59   *Id.* at para. 234.

Eritrean judiciary was "not independent and subject to extensive interference by the executive, the military and the Special Courts;" Eritrea did not have a constitution or functioning legislature; Eritrea did not recognize customary international law, the basis of the claims; the Eritrean legal system was "not fully developed and ha[d] significant gaps in the areas of evidence, jurisdiction and choice of law;" there were fewer than 10 lawyers who are licensed to practice in the High Court of Eritrea; the practice by contingency fees arrangements was unknown; and "the state operate[d] an extensive surveillance and spy network within Eritrea."[60]

The Supreme Court of British Columbia concluded that Nevsun had not established Eritrea was the more appropriate forum.[61] In particular, it was persuaded that there was a "real risk of an unfair trial" in Eritrea.[62] Drawing from expert witness testimony and documentary evidence, the Court highlighted the fact it would defy common sense for it not to find a real risk of an unfair trial where the plaintiff, as a pre-condition to returning to Eritrea, would have to "(a) pay a tax or fine as punishment for having left the country illegally; (b) render a written apology for their conduct; and (c) possibly attend a six week course designed to enforce their patriotic feelings."[63] This was particularly so where the plaintiffs were making "the most unpatriotic allegations against the State and its military, and call[ing] into question the actions of a commercial enterprise which is the primary economic generator in one of the poorest countries in the world."[64] In November 2017, the Court of Appeal of British Columbia dismissed the appeal brought by Nevsun, holding that the lower court had correctly rejected the plea of *forum non conveniens*.[65]

The impact of the Brussels I Regulation Recast and *Owusu* is apparent in claims brought against MNCs in the English courts. In *Lungowe v. Vedanta Resources Plc*[66] a claim was brought by a group of Zambian villagers alleging that harmful effluent from Vedanta's Zambian subsidiary's copper mining

60   *Id.* at para. 236.
61   *Id.* at para. 338.
62   *Id.* at para. 251.
63   *Id.* at para. 286.
64   *Id.*
65   2017 BCCA 401, para. 122. *See also* Choc v. Hudbay Minerals Inc., [2013] ONSC 1414. A group of 11 Guatemalan women filed a lawsuit against an MNC and its subsidiary, alleging that the companies were complicit in gang rapes committed by security personnel hired by the companies. They claimed the rapes occurred in the context of forced evictions of the Mayan Q'eqchi' community from land used by the companies for nickel mining operations. The MNC lodged a mission to dismiss that included *forum non conveniens*, but dropped the argument shortly before the hearing.
66   [2017] EWCA Civ 1528.

operations had been discharged into waterways. Vedanta invoked *forum non conveniens*, arguing that *Owusu* should be distinguished because it was a unitary claim arising from one incident whereas the current case was a group action arising from multiple events. The Court of Appeal found that the ECJ in *Owusu* did intend a "one size fits all" solution.[67] Vedanta also pointed out that *Owusu* was wrongly decided in that it justified the principle of making *forum non conveniens* unavailable on the basis of certainty for a defendant, but the defendant is the party seeking to invoke *forum non conveniens*. The Judge at first instance agreed that such reasoning was "capable of sustained criticism," but that did not make the result in *Owusu* less binding.[68]

In *AAA v. Unilever PLC*,[69] the claimants were the victims of ethnic violence carried out by armed criminals on a tea plantation after the Presidential election in Kenya in 2007. They sued Unilever and its Kenyan subsidiary for failing to protect them from the risks of such violence. Unilever invoked *forum non conveniens*, arguing the case should be tried in Kenya. Once again, the first instance judge found *Owusu* applied and was binding.[70] Interestingly, however, Unilever succeeded in having the case dismissed on a different ground: that as the parent company, it did not owe a duty of care to the claimants.[71] In *Vedanta*, by contrast, the Court of Appeal held that a duty was owed by the parent company to those affected by acts of subsidiaries, potentially even beyond employees.[72]

In sum, *forum non conveniens* has not proven to be an effective avoidance technique in recent practice. We may see a shift to MNCs using arguments based on the absence of a duty of care instead of—or alongside—challenges to the forum.

---

67   [2016] EWHC 975 (TCC), para. 67.
68   [2016] EWHC 975 (TCC), paras. 70–1.
69   [2017] EWHC 371.
70   *Id.* at para. 68.
71   *Id.* at para. 173; upheld on appeal, [2018] EWCA Civ 1532".
72   Simon LJ in *Vedanta* held, "A duty may be owed by a parent company to the employee of a subsidiary, or a party directly affected by the operations of that subsidiary, in certain circumstances" (para. 83). The fact that no such duty to parties other than employees had been found in the jurisprudence to date "does not render such a claim unarguable. If it were otherwise the law would never change" (para 88). For more on parent company liability, *see Chandler v. Cape Plc.*, [2012] EWCA Civ 525 and *Thompson v. The Renwick Group Plc*, [2014] EWCA Civ 635.

3.2 *Challenges to the Use of* forum non conveniens *as an Avoidance Technique*

Challenges to the use of *forum non conveniens* as an avoidance technique have come not just from judges who are willing to hear the case in the forum chosen by the plaintiff, but also from national legislatures. Latin American states have enacted blocking statutes to make their local courts unavailable for cases filed overseas and then dismissed on the basis of *forum non conveniens*.[73] Such legislation favours litigation in the court of the defendant's domicile and prevents referral to another court, even if it is considered to be the more appropriate forum.

Latin American courts have also engaged in "boomerang litigation" in which they take up the litigation dismissed by US courts and issue a large judgment, resulting in the defendant filing actions to prevent recognition of the judgment.[74] The extensive litigation by Ecuadorian plaintiffs against Texaco seeking damages for oil contamination in the Amazon is an example. The suit was dismissed in US courts on the basis of *forum non conveniens*. The Ecuador court then awarded US$27.3 billion against Chevron (which had merged with Texaco), later reduced to US$18 billion.[75]

Dissatisfaction with *forum non conveniens* has also manifested itself in an arbitral context, where an award creditor attempts to confirm an award rendered in a foreign state and the motion is denied on the grounds that the case would be better decided in the courts of that foreign state. In *Figuieredo Ferraz v. Peru*, a Brazilian company sought to enforce a Peruvian arbitral award against a Peruvian governmental agency in a US court.[76] The U.S. court declined to confirm the arbitral award and proceed to its enforcement against Peru's assets in the jurisdiction on the basis that the US was not the appropriate forum. It held that jurisdiction should be exercised in Peru because there was a "principal public interest factor": a Peruvian statute capping the amount of damages payable annually at 3 per cent.[77] The deployment of the *forum non conveniens* doctrine in this context has been criticized as circumventing the New York Convention on the Recognition and Enforcement of Foreign Arbitral Awards

73   Brand, *Challenges to Forum non Conveniens*, 45 N.Y.U. J. INT'L L. & POL. 1003, 1017–1021 (2012–13). *See also* Dante Figueroa, *Are there ways out of the Current Forum non Conveniens Impasse between the United States and Latin America?*, BUS. L. REV. (AM.U.) 42, 44 (2005).
74   Brand, *supra* note 73, 1023. Christopher A. Whytock and Cassandra Burke Robertson, *Forum non conveniens and the Enforcement of Foreign Judgments*, 111 COLUM. L. REV. 1444, 1448 (2011).
75   Erichson, *supra* note 51; Whytock and Robertson, *supra* note 74.
76   665 F 3d 384 (2nd Cir 2011).
77   *Id.* at 386.

1958.[78] The *Figuieredo Ferraz* decision may also have implications beyond the arbitral context, such as actions to recognise foreign judgments.[79] Engaging in a fresh *forum non conveniens* analysis at the enforcement stage may allow the defendant to find an "enforcement loophole" to escape accountability for harm it was found to have committed.[80]

4 The Judicial Function in *forum non conveniens* Cases

Lea Brilmayer has argued for what she calls a modest and restricted role for the domestic judge in the enforcement of international law. In short, "[c]ases between states [horizontal model] do not belong in our courts; cases between a state and an individual [vertical model] typically do."[81] She was not writing on *forum non conveniens* cases. Such cases usually lie somewhere between the vertical model and the horizontal model in that the parties may be an individual, group, state, company or MNC and violations of domestic or international law may be alleged. But each *forum non conveniens* case will require a judge in a domestic court to evaluate, to some extent, the appropriateness of a foreign state's legal system, for which an understanding of international law and standards will be important. Lea Brilmayer's observation is relevant to this exercise:

> There are ways of understanding international law that fit squarely into traditional forms of domestic adjudication. There is no reason categorically to exclude international claims from our courts. Even a restrained notion of judicial function has room for international adjudication.[82]

---

78 Juratowitch, *supra* note 28. He explains persuasively that such a "public interest factor" is not envisaged in the Convention. The Convention's provision on declining to recognise or enforce an award for "public policy" reasons did not apply because it is the public policy of the enforcement forum state that matters, not the public policy of the alternative forum (at 478).

79 Brand, *supra* note 73, 1028–30.

80 Mark E. Gray, *Don't Leave us Just Yet: Forum Non Conveniens and the Federal Court's Power to Stay and Monitor Actions in the "Interest of Justice"*, 46 LOY. L.A. L. REV. 293, 312 (2012); Josh Burke, *When Forum non Conveniens Fails: the Enforcement of Judgments in Foreign Courts obtained after Forum non Conveniens Dismissal in the United States*, 36 REV. LITIG. 247, 284 (2017).

81 Brilmayer, *International Law in American Courts*, *supra* note 4, 2306.

82 *Id.* 2314.

4.1   *Evaluating a Foreign Legal System*

Two controversies arise when a judge evaluates a foreign legal system. First, there is the question of ability: is a national judge, often sitting at first instance, capable of this task? Second, there is the question of whether it is appropriate for a national court to pronounce on the integrity of another legal system, potentially causing diplomatic tensions and foreign policy embarrassment.

Regarding ability, a leading U.S. commentator has expressed doubt as to whether district courts are capable of appraising "the competence and character of a foreign tribunal".[83] The view of Lea Brilmayer is to be preferred: "While it is sometimes said that international law falls outside the scope of the judicial function or expertise, this depends on how one conceives of international law."[84] She rightly observes that "[a] court that feels comfortable adjudicating domestic cases involving individual political rights is unlikely to feel completely at sea when asked to adjudicate the vertical elements of an international dispute."[85]

Similarly, a judge in a well-functioning legal system is unlikely to feel completely at sea when asked to evaluate another legal system. Indeed, in the context of the act of state doctrine, Lord Justice Rix held that the rule against passing judgment on the acts of a foreign state does not apply to *judicial* acts. The act of state doctrine:

> does not prevent an investigation of or adjudication upon the conduct of judiciary of a foreign state.... The judicial acts of a foreign state are judged by judicial standards, including international standards regarding jurisdiction, in accordance with doctrines separate from the act of state doctrine, even if the dictates of comity still have an important role to play.[86]

Regarding appropriateness, the *Institut de droit international* endorses the role of the judge in taking into account, "the adequacy of the alternative forum," and, "the effectiveness and enforceability of any resulting judgment."[87] In cases mentioned above, such as *Nevsun*, the courts engaged in detailed analysis of expert testimony and lengthy pleadings in order to assess whether "there is a real risk that justice will not be obtained in the foreign court by reason

---

83   CHARLES ALAN WRIGHT ET AL., 14D FEDERAL PRACTICE AND PROCEDURE, § 3828.3 (3d 2013), quoted in Grossi, *supra* note 49, 94.
84   *Id.* at 2308.
85   *Id.* at 2306.
86   *Yukos Capital SARL v. OJSC Rosneft Oil Company* [2012] EWCA Civ 855, paras. 73, 86–7.
87   *Institut, supra* note 29, Art. 2.

of incompetence or lack of independence or corruption."[88] As the Supreme Court of British Columbia pointed out, the focus is "not on whether Canada's legal system is fairer and more efficient than the foreign forum, but whether the foreign legal system is capable of providing justice to the parties in the proceeding."[89]

In the *AAA v Unilever* case, the judge observed that she was engaged in a risk assessment, not a definitive fact-finding exercise:

> I cannot make a factual assessment, on the balance of probabilities, about whether or not [claimants] will get substantial justice in Kenya ... What I can do, rather, is to assess the risk that they will not get substantial justice.[90]

She concluded that there was a real risk that the claimants would not get substantial justice in Kenya because they were victims of terrible violence in 2007 based on a combination of their ethnicity and perceived political affiliation, and that "[t]heir case is not seen in Kenya as a claim ... against their employer or against a foreign multi-national. It is seen as a case brought by Kisii against Kalenjin."[91] She was also persuaded of the problem with judicial corruption in Kenya.[92] On a very practical note, she noted the evidence about funding litigation in Kenya. Although the claimants were not entitled to "a Rolls Royce presentation" of their case, the lack of legal aid system militated against their ability to bring and prosecute the claims, "even as far as a trial on liability of a small number of test cases."[93] Such judicial analysis comes across as thoughtful, not politicized nor paternalistic.[94]

4.2   *Evaluating an International Mechanism*
In most *forum non conveniens* cases, the court will be assessing the adequacy of a foreign court. But there are occasional cases where an international mechanism is evaluated.

---

88   *Nevsun, supra* note 8, para. 253.

89   *Id.* para. 255.

90   *AAA, supra* note 69, para. 166, citing Cherney v Deripaska [2009] EWCA Civ 849 paras. 27–29.

91   *Id.* at para. 167.

92   *Id.* at para. 168.

93   *Id.* at para. 170.

94   Cf Erichson's criticism of US jurisprudence, *supra* note 51.

Nemeriam v. Ethiopia[95] is an important decision that addresses whether an international tribunal may be an adequate alternative forum in the context of *forum non conveniens*. The question was whether the Eritrea-Ethiopia Claims Commission was a more appropriate forum than the U.S. courts for a claim brought regarding confiscated property belonging to individuals of Eritrean descent during the 1998–2000 war between Eritrea and Ethiopia.

The district court had held that the Claims Commission was an adequate alternative forum for the case based on six factors: the composition and competencies of the Commission; the claims brought could be espoused by Eritrea; the mass claims process was well underway; Eritrea had stated its intention to pursue the claims in issue and had no incentive not to espouse as many meritorious claims as possible; there was nothing to indicate that Eritrea's successful claims would be set off by successful claims brought by Ethiopia; and Eritrea was represented by "a Yale Law School professor, Lea Brilmayer, and her deputy on claims procedure."[96] The district court thus dismissed the claim on the grounds of *forum non conveniens*. The D.C. Circuit Court of Appeal, however, disagreed. It focused on, "the Commission's inability to make an award directly to Nemariam, and the possibility that Eritrea could set off Nemariam's claim or even an award in her favour against claims made ... in favour of Ethiopia."[97] The circuit court refused to rely on Eritrea's pledge that it would disburse funds to individual claimants.[98] Brilmayer has written, in a different and more general context, on the importance of claims commissions having a mechanism that ensures and oversees payment of claims to the victims as well as actually having funds available.[99] There were awards made in favour of Nemariam by the Claims Commission,[100] but none of the final awards have been paid.[101]

The circuit court's decision in *Nemeriam* means that "diplomatic espousal claims before international tribunals can never afford claimants an adequate forum justifying dismissal based on *forum non conveniens*," unless they meet domestic requirements of standing and execution of judgment.[102] As Alford

---

95   315 F. 3d 390 (D.C. Cir), cert denied 124 S. Ct. 278 (2003).

96   Roger Alford, *Introductory Note to US Court of Appeals for the District of Columbia Circuit: Nemariam et al v. Ethiopia*, 42 ILM 420 (2003).

97   Id. 421.

98   315 F. 3d 390, 394 (D.C. Cir),

99   Lea Brilmayer, *Chapter 8: Conclusions*, in Brilmayer, Giorgetti and Charlton, INTERNATIONAL CLAIMS COMMISSIONS: RIGHTING WRONGS AFTER CONFLICT (2017).

100   Final Award, Eritrea's Damages Claims, 17 August 2009, Claims 27 and 28, para. 407 (awarding US$319,615).

101   Brilmayer, *supra* note 99.

102   Alford, note 96 *supra* at 421.

observes, this view is in tension with the U.S. practice of resolving state-to-state claims through diplomatic channels and in other instances setting up international mechanisms for the adjudication of claims.[103] Bergsieker persuasively argues that the U.S. decision is an overly formalistic approach that emphasises party structure over interest representation.[104] The U.S. court could have determined that that the *Nemariam* case fit within an exception to the treaty between Eritrea and Ethiopia because it was filed in another forum six months prior to the effective date of the treaty.[105] This would have avoided creating a troubling precedent for the relationship between U.S. courts and international mechanisms.

5   Conclusion

In 2001, I wrote an article (my first publication) calling for the abolition of *forum non conveniens*.[106] Seventeen years later, and with the benefit of teachers like Lea and time spent in legal practice and academia, I find myself taking a less absolutist position. I believe the doctrine has a role to play, albeit a modest one, in helping national courts resolve questions of transnational jurisdiction. Its benefit is apparent when parallel proceedings are underway, but it has potential value even prior to that stage by seeking to find a judicial—and peaceful—resolution to a dispute in an appropriate forum.

The doctrine is undermined by the range of tests in different jurisdictions, its exploitation by certain MNCs, and its invocation to circumvent treaties on enforcement. Nonetheless, I am hopeful that domestic judges are generally capable of engaging in cogent analysis of foreign legal systems as and when required. Ultimately, I share the optimism in Lea Brilmayer's *International Law in American Courts* that there is a proper and important role for domestic judges in international and transnational adjudication. The understanding of that role will be enhanced by more scholarship like Lea Brilmayer's work at the intersection of public and private international law.

---

103   *Id.*
104   Ryan Bergsieker, *International Tribunals and Forum Non Conveniens Analysis*, 114 YALE L.J. 443, 444 (2004).
105   Bergsieker, *supra* note [], 448 citing the Peace Agreement, 2138 UNTS at 98.
106   Webb, *supra* note 50.

CHAPTER 6

Meddling in Internal Affairs: Establishing the Boundaries of Non-Intervention in a World without Boundaries

W. Michael Reisman

For Lea Brilmayer whose scholarship knows no boundaries.

∴

1

It is characteristic of periods of change that they often require adapting procedures and policies embodied in venerable legal arrangements to new and different contexts. In well-organized and efficient legal systems, that task is principally—and properly—assigned to the legislature. In our global civilization of science and technology in which "radical impermanence [is] an enduring tradition",[1] the formal international law-making process is notoriously cumbersome. The task of analyzing and proposing the necessary adjustments often falls, on a case-by-case basis, to courts, tribunals and, with the luxury of time for more searching deliberation, on private juridical bodies, dedicated to promoting the progressive development of international law. In the interim, there is often anomie.

One issue in which new technologies of social communication and shifting political forces are challenging inherited legal arrangements is how the principle of non-intervention in the internal affairs of other states should be applied to the external but disguised influencing of the procedures and outcomes of elections there. This type of interference may seem to pale in comparison to the more overt and material forms of intervention but because it can profoundly

---

1 Philip Roth on the US, in a Speech to PEN www.newyorker.com/magazine/2017/06/.../i-have
   -fallen-in-love-with-american-name ... Jun 5, 2017.

© KONINKLIJKE BRILL NV, LEIDEN, 2019 | DOI:10.1163/9789004316539_007

affect sovereignty, indeed, governmental legitimacy itself, it is generating acute inter-state conflict.

2

A foundational international legal principle is respect for the political independence and socio-economic and cultural integrity of every State. The principle of non-interference in the internal affairs of other states and its corollary that international politics should be confined to the international arena is easily stated. The problem with implementing it is that the so-called "international arena", in which international politics is supposed to play out, is a metaphysical abstraction. There is no such thing as the international arena; because there are only other States, to interact with them is, to an inescapable extent, to interfere in them. In actuality, much of what we call "international politics" is the effort of one state to influence policy-formation and specific decisions *within* other States.

Alongside, the diplomatic, military and economic modes of influencing the behavior of others is what has been called the "ideologic" mode or propaganda. While the diplomatic instrument involves direct inter-elite communications by one government to another, ideologic communications, comprised of signs and symbols, by-pass the other state's government and are directed to popular audiences *within* the other State. And in contrast to the diplomatic mode whose objective is to secure inter-state agreement, the objective of the ideologic strategy—far from achieving agreement but more like the effect sought by the military and economic instruments—is to *compel* the target state's government to change certain policies and/or personnel. This is accomplished by undermining or strengthening popular support for those policies or simply weakening that other government by eroding the relationship between its elite and rank-and-file and fostering division within the body-politic; and the more democratic a State, the more vulnerable it is to external ideologic influencing. If the method is not physically coercive, its objective is.

To varying degrees, international law tries to regulate the different modes of influence in ways compatible with its basic principles: for example, the lawfulness of the resort to *military* force, the jus ad bellum, is regulated by the Charter; the actual use of military force by the *jus in bello*. The use of the economic instrument in peace time, while regulated by the OAS Charter, is not mentioned in the UN Charter. The law for the diplomatic mode is codified in the Vienna Convention on Diplomatic Relations. But the ideologic mode, which was often referred to as "propaganda", is something of a juridical outlier.

3

As long as the technology of mass communication was relatively primitive and literacy among the rank-and-file was a scarce resource, the use of the ideologic strategy and its limited effectiveness made it a marginal political issue and, accordingly, a minor focus of international legal scholarship. In the 15th century, the technological innovation of Guttenberg's movable type created new ideologic possibilities, but the transnational use of the ideological strategy was most profoundly affected by the French Revolution; Robespierre's program and doctrines were designed to export the Revolution, by taking advantage of the contemporary technology.

The early efforts to enlist the then burgeoning social sciences in the use of propaganda occurred in the First World War. The USSR continued to use the ideological instrument as a major strategy in the inter-war period. Attempts to regulate the use of propaganda were the subject of a few bilateral treaties and discussions in the League.

The invention and diffusion of radio afforded opportunities which were brilliantly exploited by Goebbels in the Second World War. But the utility and potentiality of that technology and its successors seem simply primitive in comparison to the possibilities opened by the Internet. In a world of widely accessible electronic simultaneity, the ideologic instrument has come to be used almost routinely by many governments as well as by myriad non-official actors; methods range from overt direct exhortation, to methods that conceal the identity of the actual agent, including for the diffusion of apparently "neutral news", the use of trolls and bots, of hacking, the strategic release of hacked material and so forth. These techniques have come to be used to influence, among other things, voting in other States. Indeed, democratic elections, with their free-for-all market place of ideas have proved to be especially attractive and vulnerable targets for ideologic intervention. Even when they do not change an election's outcome, they can undermine confidence in the fairness of the elections themselves and, thus, erode the intangible yet vital legitimacy of an elected government.

While these techniques do not seem to be as brutal as an explicit regime-change, they may well be comparable in effect. Yet it would be a stretch to cabin such an action under U.N. Charter Article 51's "armed attack", a characterization that would import the possibility of far-reaching unilateral responses.

4

Although the UN Charter makes no express mention of the use of the ideologic instrument, its lawful use has been discussed in the United Nations and some draft conventions have been framed. Lawyers, in search of "evidence," will seize onto almost anything written to support a legal position but stillborn treaties that failed of acceptance are actually negative evidence, showing that their formulations are not law. More credible normative guidance might be found in accepted and analogous normative arrangements in other areas of international law. Parallel to the concept of perfidy in the law of armed conflict, some international legal policies would seem to prohibit the peacetime inter-state use of the ideologic instrument to affect elections. The Declaration on Friendly Relations affirms, for example, that "Every State has an inalienable right to choose its political, economic, social and cultural systems, without interference **in any form** by another State." That would certainly cover an externally managed regime change, but can it be interpreted to go so far as to prohibit, in terms, efforts to influence, by the use of the ideologic instrument, the outcome of elections in other States?

Even assuming that the Declaration on Friendly Relations does prohibit it, there are also policies that may run counter to Friendly Relations. For example, Article 19 of the Universal Declaration of Human Rights states in relevant part that "Everyone has the right [...] to receive and impart information and ideas **through any media and regardless of frontiers.**" Article 25 of the Covenant on Civil and Political Rights is to similar effect.[2]

In fact, the program of the international protection of human rights is particularly relevant to this discussion, for international law's venture into installing universal human rights has ineluctably undermined the wall theretofore protecting the internal affairs of States. Kofi Annan, from the perspective of United Nations Secretary General, went so far as to say in one Annual Report, that

> State sovereignty, in its most basic sense, is being redefined by the forces of globalization and international cooperation.
>
> ...

---

2 "Every citizen shall have the right and the opportunity [] without unreasonable restrictions:
   ...
   (b) to vote and to be elected at genuine periodic elections which shall be by universal and equal suffrage and shall be held by secret ballot, **guaranteeing the free expression of the will of the electors.**"

He added, with admirable understatement:

> These parallel developments—remarkable and, in many ways, wel-
> come—do not lend themselves to easy interpretations or simple
> conclusions.[3]

The developments to which Kofi Annan referred could be said to act to legitimate direct actions by one State—or its citizens—in response to and with a
view to influencing the internal arrangements and popular political choices
in other States, *if this is done for the avowed purpose of advancing the international protection of human rights there.* NGOs, with or without the blessing
and financing of governments, assist and even finance, in whole or part, local
NGOs, while latter-day electoral "freebooters" or electoral mercenaries—individuals from one State who are adept in the use of social media techniques for
the purpose of influencing electoral outcomes—can now export those skills in
support of parties or factions in other States which they favor or which are able
to purchase their services. These activities, conducted openly, may be viewed
in the target States as less concerned with the integrity and enhancement of
the local democratic and electoral processes and more concerned with favor-
ing a particular group, often one ranged against the incumbent government. In
other words, the government and groups within the target States may see the
actions as a violation of what they understand the non-intervention principle
in the Friendly Relations Declaration to require.

5

Antinomies—inconsistent norms—are not unknown in international law and
some scholars believe that their very complementarity functions to enable
decision-makers to fashion, case-by-case, a contextually appropriate remedy.
But the normative ambiguity which complementary norms generate can also
lead to actions that exacerbate inter-state relations and provoke conflict. To
cite a current and notorious example: The United States Congress has already
imposed economic sanctions against Russia for what American intelligence
agencies have unanimously identified as Russian interference in the 2016 presidential election.

Crafting a relevant and practicable international legal arrangement that lays
down what should and may not be done should, on the one hand, allow for

---

3 Press Release SG/SM/7136 GA/9596 SECRETARY-GENERAL PRESENTS HIS ANNUAL
   REPORT TO GENERAL ASSEMBLY.

transnational promotion of meaningful democratic process within States yet, on the other hand, protect the integrity of free and fair elections and their outcomes. This is a task, to recall Kofi Annan's words, for which there are neither easy interpretations nor simple conclusions. To the contrary, difficult questions abound.

– Should international law distinguish between substance and procedure: outsiders, whether they are State or non-State actors, who are intervening to support or enhance the integrity of democratic processes, on the one hand, and outsiders who are intervening to support a particular candidate, on the other?
– Should the **content** of a cross-border ideological instrument affect the lawfulness of the action?
– For a cross-border ideological communication to be lawful, other things being equal, should the ultimate actor's identity accompany the message and be public or may the communicator use an alias or "cut-out" and impose the burden of identification and attribution on others?
– Does the variable of peace or war affect the assessment of lawfulness of the use of an ideologic strategy and are the Laws of Armed Conflict's distinctions of permissible ruses and misinformation ("psychwar") or "perfidious" actions adaptable or relevant in non-belligerent situations?
– Should only information that is factually correct be used to influence electoral outcomes in another country while only false statements violate international law?

This last question touches a central and sensitive issue that has bedeviled efforts at securing international agreement. Long ago, in the United Nations Sub-Commission on Freedom of Information and the Press, the then Yugoslav member stated, "I join the words 'information' and 'propaganda'. [...] Today there is no neutral news and no neutral information." One might have thought that the end of the Cold War had finally awarded victory to "information". Alas, even in the United States, at the moment, the political system is wrestling with the epistemological neologism of "alternate facts" in what threatens to augur a "post-truth society".[4] A century ago, Franz Kafka anticipated such a dystopia, in which he wrote, "Die Lüge wird zur Weltordnung gemacht". "The lie becomes the organizing principle of reality." The assumption that civil, rational discourse with more information and more speech will ensure that the truth will prevail presupposes that there are some shared common truths, affording community members the ability to differentiate between information and disinformation, between propaganda and intelligence, between lies and.... In the multi-cultured world in which international law perforce operates, the absence of common truths will exacerbate an already fraught situation.

---

4   Stacie Strong, Alternate Faces and the Post-Truth Society, 165, U. Pa. L. Rev. 137 (2017).

6

For all the difficulties these questions pose, principles of substance and procedures to remedy them must be sought. Until now the U.S. reaction has been
unilaterally punitive and, on the domestic front, focused on technological
fixes, in a word, defensive. It is just a matter of time until increasingly more
severe counter-measures are mounted to deter election meddling. While they
may ultimately arrest meddling, they will exacerbate international relations.

An effort to arrive at an international agreement on conduct and responsibility does not appear to have been essayed. As remote as its likelihood seems
at the moment, it should not be excluded. Galdorisi and Kaufman write of
a seemingly intractable dispute at the height of the Cold War "between the
United States and the former Soviet Union over the right of warships to conduct innocent passage in territorial seas without providing prior notice or
seeking consent."

> That dispute began with the famous "Black Sea Bumping" incident ... and
> ended with a "Joint Statement by the United States of America and the
> Union of Soviet Socialist Republics". The Joint Statement included a "Uni-
> form Interpretation of Rules of International Law Governing Innocent
> Passage," in which the United States and the Soviet Union agreed that
> "All ships, including warships, regardless of cargo, armament or means of
> propulsion, enjoy the right of innocent passage through the territorial sea
> in accordance with international law, for which neither prior notification
> nor authorization is required".[5]

An effort to agree on comparable principles now, this time on election-
meddling, may *not* be quixotic. In a study in the American Political Science
Review, Johannes Bubeck and Nikolay Marinov, scholars at the University of
Mannheim, conclude that

> investing in the elections of others is not necessarily utility enhancing for
> the outside powers. In elections wars against powers that do not value—
> or even oppose—democracy, a liberal hegemon's utility is generally low.
> In fact, both intervening states may be better off jointly committing not
> to intervene than expending resources against each other.[6]

---

5 Galdorisi & Kaufman, *Military Activities in the EEZ: Preventing Uncertainty and Defusing Conflict*, 32 CAL. WESTERN INT'L L. REV. 253, 295 (2001).
6 Johannes Bubeck & Nikolay Marinov, *Process or Candidate: The International Community and Demand for Electoral Integrity*, 111 AM. POL. SCI. REV., 535, 554 at 548 (2017).

This analysis suggests that there may yet be space for inter-state agreement.

Assuming that there is, several possible and practicable modes of implementation recommend themselves: A treaty, concluded under the auspices of the United Nations and establishing a common international policy, committing the States' parties to refrain from disinformation and election meddling, with, perhaps, a standing fact-finding commission to investigate allegations and attributions and establish a jurisprudence, would take time to negotiate and agree. In the interim, a Security Council Chapter Seven Resolution could offer a short-term solution. Even without that, a Gentleman's Agreement between the relevant actors could clarify the normative regime and secure commitment to it. At some point and with or without agreement, a transnational normative code will emerge. Hopefully, it will be one which supports the free flow of accurate information and meaningful democratic elections in every state.

CHAPTER 7

Jurisprudential Space Junk: Treaties and New Technologies

*Rebecca Crootof**

1   Introduction

The first semester I was able to select my own law school classes, I elected for an ambitiously-entitled seminar: "Public Order in the World Community," co-taught by W. Michael Reisman and the one and only Lea Brilmayer. It is not an exaggeration to say that this course—and these professors—changed my life.

I came to law school intent on continuing my career as a domestic civil rights advocate with an interest in strategic litigation. I had trudged through the usual 1L classes, volunteered in the human rights student organization, and attended any civil rights or human rights lecture I could fit into my schedule.

Then I took Public Order, where Michael opened my eyes to the long history and admirable aims of international law, and Lea—well, Lea made it real, and Lea made it fun. Her insights into human nature pervaded her assessments of how and why law evolved as it did, and her cutting, sarcastic humor never masked her deep empathy and generous heart. That semester marked a sea of change in my life, as I saw how one could be both a scholar who thought deeply about the law's purposes and impacts and a practitioner who applied those insights to promote the rule of law and human rights aims.

Given this, it was with no small amount of gratitude that, years later, I gave a guest lecture in the same course in which I had once been an awed student. This chapter draws on that day's discussion, which focused on how new technologies have fundamentally altered the ways in which international law develops, evolves, and sometimes inappropriately persists.

• • •

*   Executive Director, Information Society Project; Research Scholar and Lecturer in Law, Yale Law School. Portions of this chapter are drawn from ideas developed more fully in Rebecca Crootof, *Change Without Consent: How Customary International Law Modifies Treaties*, 41 YALE J. INT'L L. 237 (2016). Thanks to Asaf Lubin for helpful suggestions and to Chiara Giorgetti and Natalie Klein for midwifing this celebratory collection.

It is an understatement to note that new technologies—particularly new travel and communications technologies—have dramatically sped up the development of international law.[1] Treaty negotiation is faster and easier, in part because state representatives can meet more frequently and because negotiators can receive guidance and approval more quickly.[2] Customary international law, which once slowly developed over decades, can now form over the space of a few years, as the increased number of state interactions and the ease of disseminating information make it far easier to identify relevant state practice and *opinio juris*.[3] General principles, judicial decisions, soft law, scholarship, and other formal and subsidiary means of determining states' international legal rights and obligations have mushroomed.

This facilitated legal creation is accompanied by an increase in legal fragmentation, conflict, and desuetude.[4] Multilateral treaties regulating new technologies are particularly susceptible to early obsolescence, both because of the pace of technological change and because of the difficulty of amending them to address those changes. As a result, these treaties are more likely to be modified by subsequently developed customary international law, resulting in laws on the books that are theoretically in force but actually simply clutter and confuse the relevant legal regime.[5] Or, as Lea put it, in her characteristic way of cutting through jargon and adding a dash of humor: "It's jurisprudential space junk."

As with actual space junk,[6] the scope of the jurisprudential space junk problem is widely underestimated. Treaty provisions that have been significantly

---

1   Colin Picker, *A View from 40,000 Feet: International Law and the Invisible Hand of Technology*, 23 CARDOZO L. REV. 149, 197–201 (2001).

2   This shift was noted at least half a century ago: "Now information can be transmitted quickly in both directions, and the process of final approval can be expedited.... Thus new application of technology and science lead not only to new rules but also to new methods of creating rules." Louis B. Sohn, *The Impact of Technological Changes on International Law*, 30 WASH. & LEE L. REV. 1, 10 (1973).

3   Of course, the converse is true as well: it is now also easier to identify conduct or statements that diverge from and thereby undermine a developing or existing norm.

4   *Cf.* Int'l Law Comm'n, *Fragmentation of International Law: Difficulties Arising from the Diversification and Expansion of International Law*, U.N. Doc. A/CN.4/L.682 (Apr. 13, 2006).

5   Crootof, *Change Without Consent, supra* note 1.

6   Millions upon millions of pieces of "space junk"—spent rockets, old satellites, and other debris—surround the Earth, cluttering useful orbital tracks. Not only does this floating garbage pose a threat to future manned and unmanned missions, space shuttle trips, and the International Space Station, they threaten the thousands of orbiting communications, navigation, meteorological, and commercial satellites that facilitate our daily life. If these satellites were to go silent, Internet and phone communication would be limited to fiber-optic and undersea cables; GPS—upon which air travel, the financial sectors, and the electrical

modified by subsequently developed customary international law are dis-
persed throughout the international legal firmament. In some cases, state
parties' obligations under a treaty have been substantially reduced;[7] in others,
they have been dramatically expanded.[8] And, as new customary international
law develops at an increased rate in the shadow of relatively stable multilateral
treaties, jurisprudential space junk will proliferate.

Additionally, jurisprudential space junk is far from harmless. International
law has long had to defend its status *as law*, particularly in American legal
academia. It has been critiqued on the grounds that it is often violated (as if
there is perfect compliance with domestic law) and that it has no physically
coercive enforcement mechanisms (while ignoring its physically coercive[9] and
non-physically coercive enforcement mechanisms[10]). The law of armed conflict in particular is mocked by those quick to recite that there are no rules in
love or war—in spite of evidence of state compliance with those rules.[11] But

---

power grid depends—would disappear. A U.K. security study predicted that if we were
to go three days without the services provided by these satellites, modern society would
devolve into chaos. *See* John Sheldon, Visiting Professor, Air University at Maxwell
Air Force Base, Address Before the Space Enterprise Council of the U.S. Chamber of
Commerce and the George C. Marshall Institute (Oct. 16, 2008), *in* A DAY WITHOUT
SPACE: ECONOMIC AND NATIONAL SECURITY RAMIFICATIONS 40 ("[I]n 'a day without space,' the world would not end, but life as we know it would.").

    Space junk also sometimes re-enters Earth's atmosphere, raising a different set of
problems. Small items will burn up during re-entry, but in the process they might be read
as missiles by radar, triggering false missile-attack warning alarms. Larger items might
survive re-entry to crash or disintegrate and spread debris over wide swaths of land. In
2017, a piece of a rocket used to launch a Chinese GPS satellite in 2007 landed in Indonesia;
in 2016, at least two SpaceX rocket tanks fell on Indonesian islands. No one was hurt in
either case, though there was some property damage. The most famous unintended reentry occurred in 1978, when a Soviet satellite re-entered Earth's atmosphere, disintegrated
and spread its wreckage over three Canadian provinces. Settlement of Claim Between
Canada and the Union of Soviet Socialist Republics for Damage Caused by "Cosmos 954",
Canada-U.S.S.R., Apr. 2, 1981. All but two of the recovered fragments were radioactive,
some lethally so. *Id.*

7   *See infra* Part 2.2 (discussing the London Protocol).

8   Crootof, *Change Without Consent*, *supra* note 1, at 274 (discussing examples).

9   The U.N. Charter's prohibition on the threat or use of force, U.N. Charter art. 2(4),
famously has two exceptions. States may use force pursuant to a Security Council resolution, *id.* art. 42, or in self-defense, *id.* art. 51.

10   *See, e.g.*, Oona A. Hathaway & Scott J. Shapiro, *Outcasting: Enforcement in Domestic and
International Law*, 121 YALE L.J. 252 (2011).

11   *See, e.g.*, *IHL in Action: Respect for the Law on the Battlefield*, INT'L COMMITTEE RED
CROSS, https://ihl-in-action.icrc.org/ (providing "a collection of real case-studies docu-
menting compliance with international humanitarian law (IHL) in modern warfare");
see also Oona Hathaway & Scott J. Shapiro, *What Realists Don't Understand About Law*,

notwithstanding the fact that "almost all nations observe almost all principles of international law and almost all of their obligations almost all of the time,"[12] the idea that international law somehow *isn't really law* persists. And jurisprudential space junk—law on the books that is widely ignored because it is no longer the most relevant rule—bolsters this misconception.

In the interest of minimizing future jurisprudential space junk, this chapter questions the common assumption that a multilateral treaty regime is the ideal means of regulating new technologies at the international level. Instead, after reviewing problems associated with such treaties, it suggests that other, more flexible forms of international lawmaking—namely, soft law and customary international law—will sometimes be far better suited to international technological governance.

2   Swiftly Outdated Technological Treaties

Once, customary international law was the static backdrop against which states enacted relatively flexible bilateral treaties.[13] The situation today is far more complicated. Customary international law still provides background default rules, and most treaties are still bilateral.[14] But the rise of "constitutive" multilateral treaties, swiftly-developing customary international law, and a host of new kinds of regulatory devices has expanded the menu of international law-making options.[15]

Still, treaties are generally viewed as the gold standard, the ideal—if sometimes unattainable—expression of a state's international legal obligations.[16] However, multilateral treaties regulating new technologies are particularly susceptible to early obsolescence. Not only are multilateral treaties far more difficult to amend than their bilateral cousins, inflexible written law is ill-suited to regulating fast-paced technological innovation. This section first reviews issues with modifying multilateral treaties generally, then discusses how treaties attempting to regulate new technology are especially likely to become jurisprudential space junk.

FOREIGN POL'Y, (Oct. 9, 2017) (discussing how, "[w]hen it is most effective, the law doesn't induce states to act contrary to incentives; it changes those incentives themselves").

12   LOUIS HENKIN, HOW NATIONS BEHAVE 47 (2d ed. 1979) (emphasis omitted).

13   Crootof, *Change Without Consent, supra* note 1, at 242–43.

14   *Id.* at 243.

15   *Id.* at 243–47.

16   *See infra* Part 2.2.

2.1   *The Difficulty of Modifying Multilateral Treaties*

Treaties are written agreements between two or more states.[17] They have the clarity and practical utility associated with the written word, the legitimacy that accompanies explicit state consent, and the stability to warrant state investment in the treaty-making process.[18] In stating conditions and consequences upon which all parties can agree, they represent considered compromises. They can be tailored to address a specific issue, or they can codify aspirational principles.[19]

As a formal matter, treaties can be modified or terminated in various ways: with the consent of all state parties,[20] by the denunciation of one party after a material breach by another,[21] or in light of a fundamental change in circumstances or other supervening event that would make the performance of a legal promise impossible.[22] Treaties may also be modified by other, later-in-time agreements: they may be invalidated by a superseding treaty or augmented by an additional protocol.[23]

While the default rules apply equally to bilateral and multilateral treaties, it is far easier to modify a bilateral treaty.[24] As the number of state parties to an agreement increases, so does the difficulty of substantively altering its text by mutual consent. Additionally, many of the strategies states employ to pressure a reluctant treaty partner to agree to a modification in the bilateral context lose force in a multilateral regime. For example, one state promoting

---

17   Vienna Convention on the Law of Treaties art. 2, May 23, 1969, 1155 U.N.T.S. 331 [hereinafter VCLT].

18   Accordingly, "for a host of functional reasons, practitioners and judges tend to favor the *lex scripta*." Crootof, *Change Without Consent, supra* note 1, at 240.

19   *See* Lea Brilmayer, *From 'Contract' to 'Pledge': The Structure of International Human Rights Agreements*, 77 BRIT. Y.B. INT'L L. 163 (2006).

20   VCLT, *supra* note 18, arts. 39, 53. Additionally, certain types of treaties are assumed to permit unilateral denunciation. *See, e.g.*, G. Fitzmaurice (Special Rapporteur), *Special Report on the Law of Treaties*, Int'l Law Comm'n 16, 22, U.N. Doc. A/CN.4/107 (Mar. 15, 1957). Whether there is a customary right permitting states to unilaterally withdraw from or denounce all treaties is a subject of heated debate. *Compare* Curtis A. Bradley & Mitu Gulati, *Withdrawing from International Custom*, 120 YALE L.J. 202, 204 (2010), *with* Lea Brilmayer & Isaias Yemane Tesfalidet, *Treaty Denunciation and "Withdrawal" from Customary International Law: An Erroneous Analogy with Dangerous Consequences*, 120 YALE L.J. FORUM 217 (2011), http://www.yalelawjournal.org/forum/treaty-denunciation-and-qwithdrawalq-from-customary-international-law-an-erroneous-analogy-with-dangerous-consequences.

21   VCLT, *supra* note 18, art. 60.

22   *Id.* arts. 61, 62.

23   *See* Crootof, *Change Without Consent, supra* note 1, at 250–52.

24   Careful drafting may lessen this problem. *See infra* Part 3.1.

a proposed modification to a provision could threaten to breach the treaty if the modification is not accepted—in a bilateral setting, this could terminate the treaty, which might spur a treaty partner to bargain; in the multilateral context, it would likely have little effect on the treaty regime and treaty partners.[25] Additionally, when some but not all state parties agree to a modification of a multilateral treaty, this results in a partial amendment that fractures the treaty regime. As this fragmentation risks "the stability, clarity, and gravitational pull of the regime," some states might avoid clearly-needed improvements when there is not complete consensus to avoid undermining the treaty regime's overall force.[26] Multilateral treaty modification through supersession or additional protocols faces similar challenges.

Because modification by mutual consent is so difficult in multilateral treaty regimes, states often employ adaptive interpretations to reconcile outdated text with state action. As a matter of doctrine, these interpretations are legitimate to the extent all state parties to the treaty explicitly or implicitly consent to the new understanding and to the extent the new understanding interprets—but does not modify—the treaty provisions.[27] As a matter of practice, however, adaptive interpretations rarely enjoy widespread agreement,[28] often cross the line between interpretation and modification,[29] and risk permitting problematic state action based on unilateral, self-interested interpretations.[30]

2.2   *Problems with Treaties Regulating New Technologies*
New technologies expand human capabilities—and in doing so, they sometimes enable entirely new kinds of problematic human conduct or create new negative externalities.[31] When these developments have an international

---

25   *But see* Laurence R. Helfer, *Terminating Treaties, in* THE OXFORD GUIDE TO TREATIES 634, 635 & n. 7 (Duncan B. Hollis ed., 2012) (discussing exceptions to this general rule, including the situation where a multilateral agreement specifies that it will not remain in force if the number of member states drops below a specific number).

26   Brian Israel, *Treaty Stasis*, AJIL UNBOUND (May 8, 2014, 2:40 PM), https://www.asil.org/blogs/treaty-stasis-agora-end-treaties.

27   Crootof, *Change Without Consent, supra* note 1, at 252. State acceptance might take a variety of forms: it might be noted in a written instrument, evidenced through subsequent state practice, or inferred in certain circumstances from state silence. *Id.*

28   This is largely due to the difficulty in determining when state silence is intended to signal agreement. *Id.* at 256–59.

29   *Id.* at 259–64.

30   *Id.* at 293.

31   For the purposes of this piece, I define "technology" as any combination of tools, skills, processes, and techniques by which human capability is extended. *Cf.* Lyria Bennett Moses, *Why Have a Theory of Law and Technological Change?*, 8 MINN. J.L. SCI. & TECH. 589, 591–92 (2007).

component, someone will inevitably suggest that the new technology be regulated by a new multilateral international treaty.[32] In the wake of proliferating malicious cyberoperations, cybercrimes, and ransomware, the President and Chief Legal Officer of Microsoft proposed a new "Digital Geneva Convention" that would "commit governments to protecting civilians from nation-state attacks in times of peace."[33] There have been similar calls by academics, international organizations, and advocacy groups for treaties to regulate drones,[34] autonomous weapon systems,[35] anti-satellite weapons,[36] self-assembling nanomaterials,[37] human cloning and gene-editing technologies,[38] and artificial intelligence.[39] In legal articles, these proposals follow a similar pattern: a discussion about why a treaty would be ideal is followed by the grudging acknowledgement that it is politically infeasible and an assessment of how international law should best limp along until a treaty becomes a more viable possibility.[40]

But even if these constitutive, multilateral treaty regimes were easily created, the pace of technological change and difficulties of formal amendment means that multilateral treaties regulating specific technologies are likely to become quickly outdated. They are susceptible to an alternative kind of treaty

---

32   I admittedly have taken this approach in my own writing on new technologies. Rebecca Crootof, *The Killer Robots Are Here: Legal and Policy Implications*, 36 CARDOZO L. REV. 1837 (2015); Oona A. Hathaway, Rebecca Crootof, Philip Levitz, Haley Nix, Aileen Nowlan, William Perdue & Julia Spiegel, *The Law of Cyber-Attack*, 100 CALIF. L. REV. 817 (2012).

33   Brad Smith, *The Need for a Digital Geneva Convention*, MICROSOFT (Feb. 14, 2017), https://blogs.microsoft.com/on-the-issues/2017/02/14/need-digital-geneva-convention/; *see also* Duncan B. Hollis, *An E-SOS for Cyberspace*, 52 HARV. INT'L L.J. 373, 425 (2011).

34   *See, e.g.*, Michael Shank & Elizabeth Beavers, *Sign a Drone Treaty before Everyone Does as We Do*, U.S. NEWS, Feb. 4, 2014, https://www.usnews.com/opinion/blogs/world-report/2014/02/04/us-must-support-an-international-drone-treaty.

35   *See, e.g.*, *About Us*, THE CAMPAIGN TO STOP KILLER ROBOTS, https://www.stopkillerrobots.org/about-us/ (last visited Sep. 4, 2017) (calling for an international ban on autonomous weapon systems).

36   David A. Koplow, *An Inference About Interference: A Surprising Application of Existing International Law to Inhibit Anti-Satellite Weapons*, 35 U. PA. J. INT'L L. 737, 819 (2014).

37   *See, e.g.*, *Nanotechnology*, ETC GROUP, http://www.etcgroup.org/issues/nanotechnology (last visited Sep. 5, 2017).

38   *See, e.g.*, Int'l Bioethics Comm., *Report of the IBC on Updating Its Reflection on the Human Genome and Human Rights*, U.N. Doc. SHS/YES/IBC-22/15/2 Rev. 2 (Oct. 2, 2015).

39   *See, e.g.*, John Frank Weaver, *Asimov's Three Laws Are Not an International Treaty*, SLATE (Dec. 1, 2014), http://www.slate.com/articles/technology/future_tense/2014/12/autonomous_weapons_and_international_law_we_need_these_three_treaties_to.html.

40   *See, e.g.*, Crootof, *Killer Robots, supra* note 33, at 1897; Hollis, *supra* note 34, at 425; Koplow, *supra* note 37, at 739.

amendment, one not grounded in state consent: modification by subsequently developed customary international law.

Treaties and customary international law are coequal sources of states' international legal obligations.[41] Given this, under the *lex posterior* principle, subsequently-developed customary international law may displace existing treaty law.[42] Thus, the actual international law regulating the technology evolves, while the treaty text remains unaltered—becoming just another piece of jurisprudential space junk.

Consider the laws governing the use of submarines. The 1930 London Naval Treaty and 1936 London Protocol equated submarines with surface warships, requiring them to comply with the prohibition against neutralizing enemy merchant vessels without first ensuring the safety of their passengers and crew.[43] This could be accomplished in one of two ways: the warship was supposed to accompany a captured vessel to port for a prize hearing; if that was not possible, it could take the crew and passengers onboard before sinking the ship.[44] But submarines' safety depends on stealth and they have limited space, making it impossible for them to either accompany captured vessels to port or take on additional passengers. During World War II, after some initial attempts at compliance, these rules were widely ignored. Eventually, all naval powers (excepting Japan) engaged in some form of unrestricted submarine warfare, in clear violation of their treaty obligations.[45]

Some argue that states party to the London Protocol are still bound by its text, as it "continues to be a valid and subsisting part of the law of war at sea."[46] A more accurate assessment would acknowledge that a subsequently-developed customary international law of submarine warfare has displaced the treaty text, reducing state parties' obligations and expanding their rights with regard

---

41   Crootof, *Change Without Consent, supra* note 1, at 285 n. 274 (citing sources).

42   *Id.* at 284–88.

43   Treaty for the Limitation and Reduction of Naval Armament, Apr. 22, 1930, 46 Stat. 2858, 112 L.N.T.S. 65 [hereinafter London Treaty]; Procès-verbal Relating to the Rules of Submarine Warfare Set Forth in Part IV of the Treaty of London of 22 April 1930, Nov. 6, 1936, 173 L.N.T.S. 353 [hereinafter London Protocol].

44   London Treaty, *supra* note 44, art. 22; London Protocol, *supra* note 44, at 357; *see also* Declaration of London Concerning the Law of Naval War arts. 48–50 Feb. 26, 1909, 208 Consol. T.S. 338 (clarifying the law of armed conflict governing surface warships).

45   Jane Gilliland, Note, *Submarines and Targets: Suggestions for New Codified Rules of Submarine Warfare*, 73 GEO. L.J. 975, 985 (1985).

46   Howard S. Levie, *Submarine Warfare: With Emphasis on the 1936 London Protocol, in* THE LAW OF NAVAL WARFARE: TARGETING ENEMY MERCHANT SHIPPING 28, 59 (Richard J. Grunawalt ed., 1993).

to the lawful use of submarines.[47] Confusingly, however, the London Treaty and Protocol remain the final written word on the matter, apparently binding on all state parties notwithstanding the extensive contradictory subsequent state practice and acknowledged customary "exceptions."[48]

This is not a tech-determinist tale: certainly, it might have been possible for states to forego using submarines entirely or to negotiate new rules to govern this new kind of tech-enabled conduct (as eventually occurred).[49] Rather, it is a story about an attempt to apply extant rules to new technologies, without considering how the new technological architecture might alter their application. The rules governing surface warships simply did not make sense for submarines, and attempting to import them whole-cloth rendered them dead letter. All multilateral treaties that suggest that states can simply apply existing rules to new technologies, without evaluating how new technological design features might alter assumptions upon which the older rules are grounded, also risk early obsolescence and displacement by subsequently developed customary international law.

2.3   The Special Case of Bans

Somewhat counterintuitively, the most extreme form of multilateral treaty regulation of a technology—a complete ban on its creation or use—may be most likely to stand the test of time. This is largely due to the fact that the aim of a ban is not to accommodate shifting state party needs or new technological developments. Rather, it draws a line in the sand and marks a certain technology permanently off limits. However, a ban will only evade becoming jurisprudential space junk if it is successful in the first place and if later technological developments do not alter its foundational assumptions.

A technological ban is successful if it is effective at controlling the creation or use of the banned technology, which in turn will depend on the technology's

---

47   Crootof, *Change Without Consent, supra* note 1, at 271–72 (reviewing customary "exceptions" to the treaty law and arguing that they "have essentially swallowed the rule").

48   *See, e.g.,* J. Ashley Roach, *Submarine Warfare*, MAX PLANCK ENCYCLOPEDIA OF PUB. INT'L L., http://opil.ouplaw.com/view/10.1093/law:epil/9780199231690/law9780199923169 oe412?rskey=ugUuAj&result-2&prd=OPIL (Aug. 2009) (describing six customary 'exceptions' to the London Protocol, including situations where the enemy merchant vessel "is armed" or the ship has been integrated into the enemy's war-fighting effort and compliance with the Protocol would "subject the submarine to imminent danger or would otherwise preclude mission accomplishment").

49   The San Remo Manual—and its creation of the concept of delineating "military objectives" from unlawful targets—was drafted in part to address the lack of clear law regarding the use of submarines. *See* Louise Doswald-Beck, *San Remo Manual on International Law Applicable to Armed Conflicts at Sea*, INT'L REV. RED CROSS, Nov.–Dec. 1995, at 583, 590.

architecture, what human conduct it enables, and the greater social context. To create the needed momentum, the negative impacts of a new technology must significantly outweigh the positives. So, while there are periodic movements to ban various new technologies, such as certain pesticides,[50] human cloning,[51] and the use of fossil fuels,[52] only rarely is the international community sufficiently galvanized to enact a technological ban.

Because they deal with intentionally destructive technologies where the benefits/drawbacks calculus is more stark, weapons bans are the most common kind of international technological ban. After conducting an analysis of weapons bans with varying degrees of success, I have identified eight characteristics common to successful weapons bans.[53] In a separate but similar analysis, Sean Watts found seven factors relevant to whether a weapon was "regulation-tolerant" (as opposed to "regulation-resistant").[54] Unsurprisingly, many of these factors overlapped: when combined, our studies suggest that a weapons ban is most likely to be successful when:

– The weapon is ineffective
– Other means exist for accomplishing a similar military objective
– The weapon is not novel: it is easily analogized to other weapons, and its usages and effects are well understood
– The weapon or similar weapons have been previously regulated
– The weapon is unlikely to cause social or military disruption
– The weapon has not already been integrated into a state's armed forces
– The weapon causes superfluous injury or suffering in relation to prevailing standards of medical care[55]
– The weapon is inherently indiscriminate[56]

---

50   Stockholm Convention on Persistent Organic Pollutants, May 22, 2001, U.N. Doc. UNEP/Pops/CONF/4, 40 I.L.M. 532–34.

51   United Nations Declaration on Human Cloning, G.A. Res. 59/280, U.N. Doc. A/RES/59/280 (Mar. 23, 2005).

52   *See* Michael Slezak, *Pacific Islands Nations Consider World's First Treaty to Ban Fossil Fuels*, THE GUARDIAN, July 14, 2016, https://www.theguardian.com/world/2016/jul/14/pacific-islands-nations-consider-worlds-first-treaty-to-ban-fossil-fuels.

53   Crootof, *Killer Robots, supra* note 33, at 1884.

54   Sean Watts, *Regulation-Tolerant Weapons, Regulation Resistant Weapons and the Law of War*, 91 INT'L L. STUD. 540 (2015).

55   Weapons that cause superfluous injury or unnecessary suffering are prohibited under customary international humanitarian law. In practice, states regularly disagree about which weapons cause such superfluous harms. Crootof, *Killer Robots, supra* note 33, at 1884.

56   As indiscriminate attacks are prohibited by customary international humanitarian law, inherently indiscriminate weapons—weapons that cannot be directed at a specific military objective and weapons whose effects cannot be controlled—are per se unlawful.

- The weapon is or is perceived to be sufficiently notorious to galvanize public concern and spur civil society activism
- There is sufficient state commitment to enacting regulations
- The scope of the ban is clear and narrowly tailored (in other words, states understand precisely what technology and associated capabilities they are voluntarily relinquishing)
- Violations can be identified[57]

While all these factors are relevant, most failed bans either attempt to prohibit the use of extremely effective weapons or ban weapons which, at least at that point in time, were unique in their ability to cause a certain kind of destruction or accomplish certain military aims.[58]

Granted, none of these factors are determinative. A particularly problematic usage of a weapon might spur states to ban something they might otherwise have regulated; a lack of such incidents may lessen momentum towards a treaty.[59] In short, "every weapon ban success story is the product of a unique combination of factors, including the weapon's inherent traits, its recent usage, prevailing moral and ethical concerns, and the status and interests of concerned states," rendering each one somewhat "*sui generis*, the product of hard work and happy coincidence."[60] That being acknowledged, the more of these traits that are present, the easier it will be to generate momentum for a ban.

But even if a ban is negotiated, ratified, and serves its original aim of reducing the use of a certain kind of weapon, the line in the sand drawn by its drafters may not seem reasonable decades later, especially in light of new social and technological developments. The ban on permanently blinding

---

Again, however, there can be good faith disagreement among states about whether a given weapon is inherently indiscriminate. *Id.* at 1885–86. Sometimes weapons that are not universally recognized as inherently indiscriminate at the time a ban is concluded are later recognized as such, and the ban is often credited with the increased stigmatization. *Id.* at 1886.

57   This list is based off of a prior attempt to compile Watts and my combined factors. Rebecca Crootof, *Why the Prohibition on Permanently Blinding Lasers is Poor Precedent for a Ban on Autonomous Weapon Systems*, LAWFARE (Nov. 24, 2015, 7:00 AM), https://www .lawfareblog.com/why-prohibition-permanently-blinding-lasers-poor-precedent-ban -autonomous-weapon-systems.

58   Crootof, *Killer Robots, supra* note 33, at 1887, 1888.

59   *See* Michael C. Horowitz & Julia M. Macdonald, *Will Killer Robots Be Banned? Less from Past Civil Society Campaigns*, LAWFARE (Nov. 5, 2017, 10:00 AM), https://www.lawfareblog. com/will-killer-robots-be-banned-lessons-past-civil-society-campaigns (comparing the campaigns to ban landmines and autonomous weapon systems).

60   Crootof, *Killer Robots, supra* note 33, at 1884.

laser weapons, for example, allows the use of laser weapons intended to kill,[61] a morally bizarre distinction that has prompted some to question the law's priorities.[62] Meanwhile, the Chemical Weapons Convention permits the use of riot control agents for domestic law enforcement purposes while prohibiting their use as a method of warfare.[63] This distinction—the product of a drafting compromise[64]—becomes even more problematic as the lines between military, peacekeeping, and police actions are blurred and as better nonlethal crowd control weapons are developed. Charles Dunlap recounts a particularly harrowing anecdote of how a ban intended to minimize suffering might inadvertently have become the cause of more death:

> In 1991, when US forces were confronted by Iraqi troops who chose to stay in their trenches or behind obstacles and fight during the breaching operations, American tanks were fitted with plows that—in a technique permissible under international humanitarian law (IHL)—were used to bury Iraqi infantrymen alive in their trenches. The result was a ghastly scene of a bunch of buried trenches with people's arms and legs sticking out of them.
>
> Is being buried alive somehow less horrific than being subjected to *temporary incapacitation* via chemical means? Existing law implies "yes," though common sense loudly says "no."[65]

---

61   Protocol on Blinding Laser Weapons (Protocol IV) art. 1, Oct. 13, 1995, S. Treaty Doc. No. 105–1, 2024 U.N.T.S. 167 (prohibiting the employment of "laser weapons specifically designed, as their sole combat function or as one of their combat functions, to cause permanent blindness to unenhanced vision, that is to the naked eye or to the eye with corrective eyesight devices").

62   Charles J. Dunlap, Jr., *Is It Really Better To Be Dead Than Blind?*, JUST SECURITY (Jan. 13, 2015; 9:10 AM), https://www.justsecurity.org/19078/dead-blind/.

63   Convention on the Prohibition of the Development, Production, Stockpiling and Use of Chemical Weapons and on Their Destruction art. 1(1), Jan. 13, 1993, S. Treaty Doc. No. 103–21, 1974 U.N.T.S. 45 (prohibiting the development, production, acquisition, stockpiling, retention, transfer, and use of chemical weapons); *id.* art. 2(9) (excluding chemicals used for "[l]aw enforcement including domestic riot control purposes" from that prohibition); *id.* art. 1(5) ("Each State Party undertakes not to use riot control agents as a method of warfare."); *id.* art. 2(7) (defining a riot control agent as "any chemical not listed in a Schedule, which can produce rapidly in humans sensory irritation or disabling physical effects which disappear within a short time following termination of exposure").

64   *Riot Control Agents*, ORGANISATION FOR THE PROHIBITION OF CHEMICAL WEAPONS, https://www.opcw.org/about-chemical-weapons/types-of-chemical-agent/riot-control -agents/ (last visited Aug. 25, 2017).

65   Charles J. Dunlap, Jr., *Guest Post: To Ban New Weapons or Regulate Their Use?*, JUST SECURITY (Apr. 3, 2015; 12:24 PM), https://www.justsecurity.org/21766/guest-post-ban -weapons-regulate-use/ (emphasis in original) (quotation marks omitted).

Regardless of whether this technique was lawful in this situation,[66] laws that tracked morality would certainly prioritize the use of temporary, nonlethal chemical agents over the use of lethal physical force.

Bans can be useful in stigmatizing and minimizing the use of some weapons,[67] but they also can also become yet another piece of jurisprudential space junk. Even though they are not intended to be modified, they may become outdated as technological and social developments upend built-in assumptions and render once-sensible prohibitions empty or absurd.

•••

There are two approaches to the actual space junk problem. First, we should ensure that what is sent up will come back down (and burn up on reentry).[68] Second, there is the possibility of remediation. Scientists have proposed a variety of ways of destroying physical space junk, ranging from focusing the sun's rays to vaporize it[69] to grabbing it with a net or robotic arm and deorbiting it into Earth's atmosphere.[70]

---

66   There are reasons to question the lawfulness of this action, especially given that "between 80 and 250 Iraqis had been buried alive" and that neither one of the U.S. commanders nor a Pentagon spokesman could confirm that "wounded Iraqi soldiers had been able to get out of the trenches in time." Eric Schmitt, *U.S. Army Buried Iraqi Soldiers Alive in Gulf War*, N.Y. Times, Sep. 15, 1991. Lawful attacks must distinguish between active combatants and wounded or surrendering combatants. *See, e.g., Rule 47. Attacks against Persons Hors de Combat*, Int'l Committee Red Cross Customary Int'l Humanitarian L. Database, https://ihl-databases.icrc.org/customary-ihl/eng/docs/v1_rul_rule47 (last visited Aug. 25, 2017) (citing supporting treaty provisions and examples of state practice).

67   *See* Crootof, *Killer Robots, supra* note 33, at 1911–12 (discussing the reduction in the use of anti-personnel landmines subsequent to the general adoption of the 1997 Mine Ban Convention).

68   An international standard provides that satellites should be designed to burn up in the atmosphere within 25 years after the end of their operational life, and SpaceX and OneWeb have announced that they intend to lower the orbits of their unused satellites so that they will decay in less than five years. Sarah Scholes, *The Space Junk Problem is About to Get a Whole Lot Gnarlier*, Wired (Jul. 31, 2017), https://www.wired.com/story/the-space-junk-problem-is-about-to-get-a-whole-lot-gnarlier/.

69   *Solar Flux Concentration for Orbital Debris Remediation*, Johns Hopkins Applied Physics Laboratory, http://www.jhuapl.edu/ott/technologies/technology/articles/P02955.asp (last viewed Aug. 25, 2017).

70   *See CleanSpace One*, Space Engineering Center ESPACE, http://espace.epfl.ch/CleanSpaceOne_1 (noting that a cone-shaped net for capturing space junk is being funded and could launch as early as 2018); Hao Jiang et al., *A Robotic Device Using Gecko-Inspired Adhesives Can Grasp and Manipulate Large Objects in Microgravity*, 2 Sci. Robotics (2017).

We need to think similarly about jurisprudential space junk. On the front end, states need to avoid creating treaties that will quickly be rendered irrelevant; on the back end, states should acknowledge and 'vaporize' the provisions that now clutter the international legal atmosphere. The remainder of this chapter focuses on the front-end problem of how to mitigate the creation of future jurisprudential space junk, both by introducing flexibility into multilateral treaty regimes and by rethinking the assumption that treaties are the ideal means of regulating new technologies.

3   More Flexible Treaty Options

Multilateral treaties are valued in part because they are stable, relatively inflexible written documents. That very stability, however, renders them ill-suited to regulating new and evolving technologies. Treaty drafters aware of the risk of obsolescence can incorporate flexibility into a treaty regime by creating treaties with more easily modified formats and by employing relatively tech-neutral language.

3.1   *Treaties with Flexible Formats*
A multilateral treaty regime can be made more flexible at the outset, if its drafters build in procedures by which it can be easily updated without risking its overall structure.[71] For example, a treaty might have a built-in revision schedule or procedure. The International Whaling Convention creates an International Whaling Commission with the power to amend treaty provisions.[72] While state parties still have the opportunity to object to and exempt themselves from such amendments, having an independent body recommend changes may minimize the fragmentation that usually attends unilateral attempts at modification. Alternatively, the agreement establishing the World Trade Organization provides that state parties "have the exclusive authority to adopt interpretations" by "a three-fourths majority,"[73] which will be easier to achieve than the Vienna Convention's default consensus requirement.[74]

---

71   OSCAR SCHACHTER, INTERNATIONAL LAW IN THEORY AND PRACTICE 76–77 (1991) (discussing specific strategies); Israel, *supra* note 27.

72   International Convention for the Regulation of Whaling art. V, Dec. 2, 1946, 161 U.N.T.S. 72 (entered into force Nov. 10, 1948).

73   Marrakesh Agreement Establishing the World Trade Organization art. IX(2), Apr. 15, 1994, 1867 U.N.T.S. 154, 159.

74   VCLT, *supra* note 18, arts. 39, 53.

Treaty drafters can also introduce reasoned flexibility into a treaty regime without losing cohesion by designating an authoritative interpreter, charged with resolving disputes over the text's meaning in light of future developments. In most domestic legal regimes, there are various authoritative interpreters who evaluate the appropriate scope and implementation of old laws in new circumstances. There is often no similar entity at the international level. Instead, "the legitimacy of a new interpretation depends on whether the audience—the other treaty partners, which in multilateral conventions can include the entire international community—accepts it."[75] Unfortunately, the decisions of the court of international public opinion are often confused and inconsistent, making it difficult to determine whether a new interpretation is generally accepted by state parties.[76] Establishing an interpreter at the outset can help clarify which interpretations are authoritative.[77]

Furthermore, a treaty need not be a single document. Some framework treaties are designed to be augmented by additional protocols, which allow for tinkering and correction without risking the overarching legal regime.[78] The Convention on Certain Conventional Weapons, for example, was always intended to be supplemented by additional protocols.[79] Alternatively, rather than aspiring to a broad multilateral treaty, advocates of treaty regulation could focus on developing a network of relatively flexible bilateral treaties. Finally, a governance regime could be comprised of a mixture of multilateral and bilateral agreements, as has occurred in international trade law.

---

75   Crootof, *Change Without Consent, supra* note 1, at 255. State parties to a treaty may also always issue an interpretive statement, which constitutes subsequent state practice for the purposes of interpreting the treaty. *See* VCLT, *supra* note 18, art. 31(3)(a).

76   Crootof, *Change Without Consent, supra* note 1, at 293, n. 314.

77   Sometimes this occurs intentionally; other times it arises inadvertently through state practice. As noted above, the WTO agreement establishes a group of state party representatives as the authoritative interpreters of the treaty, while panels and the Appellate Body can only decide disputes before them. In practice, decisions of the panels and Appellate Body have taken on "a kind of *de facto* finality as interpretations of law, even if they lack *de jure* finality." Robert Howse, *The Most Dangerous Branch? WTO Appellate Body Jurisprudence on the Nature and Limits of the Judicial Power, in* THE ROLE OF THE JUDGE IN INTERNATIONAL TRADE REGULATION—EXPERIENCE AND LESSONS FOR THE WTO, WORLD TRADE FORUM 11, 15 (T. Cottier and P.C. Mavroidis eds., 2003).

78   *See* Crootof, *Killer Robots, supra* note 33, at 1897–99 (discussing the relative benefits and drawbacks associated with comprehensive treaties, piecemeal treaty regulation, and framework conventions).

79   Convention on Prohibitions or Restrictions on the Use of Certain Conventional Weapons Which May Be Deemed to Be Excessively Injurious or to Have Indiscriminate Effects art. 4(3), Oct. 10, 1980, 1342 U.N.T.S. 137.

What these treaty regimes gain in flexibility, they lose in cohesion. With a framework treaty, different states may ratify some but not all additional protocols, subject to differing reservations. Bilateral treaties will be well-tailored to the two state parties' needs, but the legal obligations they create might vary dramatically. Finally, these fragmented regimes are ill-suited to addressing "tragedy of the commons" problems enabled by new technology, like overfishing or pollution.

3.2   Tech-Neutral Rules

General John Alexander, former Commander of the Joint Non-lethal Weapons Directorate, argues that many tech-specific weapons treaties are inherently flawed because they regulate specific technologies rather than undesired behavior.[80] In contrast, much of customary international humanitarian law remains relevant precisely because it is relatively tech-neutral. The requirement that an attack discriminate between lawful and unlawful targets applies equally to swords and laser beams.

By regulating problematic behavior rather than specific technologies, tech-neutral rules are less likely to be underinclusive and are more likely to avoid arbitrary distinctions. Tech-neutral rules also help avoid a new and otherwise unregulated technology being used in problematic ways before new regulations emerge. This is particularly important in environments like the international legal order, where it can be difficult to create new regulations quickly. Thanks to the relatively tech-neutral nature of most international humanitarian law, "*most* law-of-war rules apply *most* of the time to *most* new technologies."[81]

While this flexibility is useful, the more tech-neutral the rule, the less it constrains later interpreters. Take the seemingly tech-neutral requirement that a state "take all feasible precautions in the choice of means and methods of attack with a view to avoiding, and in any event to minimizing, incidental loss of civilian life, injury to civilians and damage to civilian objects."[82] What is "feasible" is a context-driven analysis, which will encompass "the environment in which the attack is to be carried out" as well as "a range of factors including time, terrain, weather, capabilities, available troops and resources, enemy

---

80   JOHN B. ALEXANDER, FUTURE WAR: NON-LETHAL WEAPONS IN TWENTY-FIRST-CENTURY WARFARE 198–99 (1999).

81   Kristen E. Eichensehr, *Cyberwar and International Law Step Zero*, 50 TEX. INT'L L.J. 357, 359 (2015).

82   Protocol Additional to the Geneva Conventions of 12 August 1949, and Relating to the Protection of Victims of International Armed Conflicts (Protocol I), art. 57(a)(ii), adopted June 8, 1977, 1125 U.N.T.S. 3.

activity and civilian considerations."[83] The tech-neutral "feasibility" criterion could thus easily be read to vary from state to state, depending on their respective technological capabilities.[84] Of course, tech-neutral language that will necessarily be interpreted in tech-specific contexts is hardly limited to international humanitarian law treaties. The U.N. Convention on the Law of the Sea requires states parties to "protect and preserve the marine environment" and take "all measures ... that are necessary to prevent, reduce, and control pollution of the marine environment from any source";[85] the Convention on the Rights of Persons with Disabilities provides that state parties "shall take all appropriate steps to ensure that reasonable accommodation is provided";[86] and the International Covenant on Economic, Social and Cultural Rights recognizes "the right of everyone to the enjoyment of the highest attainable standard of physical and mental health."[87]

Because they delegate regulatory power to later-in-time interpreters, tech-neutral laws can be construed to apply in ways that seem completely at odds with their apparent intent. Consider the customary prohibition on weapons whose effects cannot be controlled or do not adequately distinguish between lawful and unlawful targets. Despite the fact that it is nearly impossible to imagine a scenario where then-available nuclear weapons could satisfy this requirement, seven of the fourteen ICJ judges in the 1996 *Nuclear Weapons Advisory Opinion* did not hold that the use of nuclear weapons would always be unlawful.[88] In effect, when asked to evaluate the legality of the use of

---

83   Int'l L. Ass'n Study Group on the Conduct of Hostilities in the 21st Century, *The Conduct of Hostilities and International Humanitarian Law: Challenges of 21st Century Warfare*, 93 INT'L L. STUD. 322, 373 (2017) (citing sources).

84   This idea has sparked a whole subset of literature on whether or not states might have a duty to use a new weapon. *See, e.g.*, Oren Gross, *The New Way of War: Is There a Duty to Use Drones?*, 67 FL. L. REV. 1 (2015) (considering this question in the context of drone warfare); Duncan Hollis, *Re-Thinking the Boundaries of Law in Cyberspace: A Duty to Hack?*, *in* CYBERWAR: LAW AND ETHICS FOR VIRTUAL CONFLICTS (J. Ohlin et al., eds., 2015) (same, with regards to cyberoperations); Christopher B. Puckett, *In This Era of "Smart Weapons," Is a State Under an International Legal Obligation to Use Precision-Guided Technology in Armed Conflict?*, 18 EMORY INT'L L. REV. 645 (2004) (same, with regard to precision-guided missiles).

85   United Nations Convention on the Law of the Sea arts. 192, 194, Dec. 10, 1982, 1833 U.N.T.S. 397.

86   Convention on the Rights of Persons with Disabilities art.5(3), opened for signature Dec. 13, 2006, 2515 U.N.T.S. 3 (entered into force May 3, 2008).

87   International Covenant on Economic, Social and Cultural Rights art. 12(1), Dec. 16, 1966, S. Treaty Doc. No. 95–19, 993 U.N.T.S. 3.

88   Legality of Threat or Use of Nuclear Weapons, Advisory Opinion, 1996 I.C.J. Rep. 226, 266 (July 8).

nuclear weapons under well-established, apparently tech-neutral law, the ICJ created a tech-specific exception.

Given this, it is worth acknowledging the benefits of more tech-specific rules. First, they are less likely to be overinclusive. The 1899 ban on aerial bombardment was not renewed in 1907 in part because it prohibited "the launching of projectiles and explosives from balloons, *or by other new methods of a similar nature.*"[89] Had the prohibition been limited to balloons, it might well have been renewed after the 1903 invention of the airplane.[90] Second, tech-specific rules minimize ambiguity, which in turn makes compliance and enforcement easier: states understand what they are foregoing at the time of treaty ratification, countries and companies are less likely to invest in developing related technology, and enforcers can identify violations.[91] The Chemical Weapons Convention has been effective in part because of its extensive annexes, which describe what specific chemical agents are prohibited.[92] Finally, in contrast to tech-neutral rules, tech-specific rules vest the power of governance with the rule-maker, rather than the rule-interpreter.

The relative benefits of a tech-neutral and tech-specific text will ultimately depend on a host of factors. Is it more important to create a long-standing rule? Or one that will address a particular and reasonably well-understood problem? Is it more important that the rule be overinclusive to avoid arbitrary distinctions or underinclusive to avoid inappropriate restrictions? How much interpretative flexibility should be built into the regime? Does the rule maker or rule interpreter have more institutional competence to determine how regulations should apply? Unfortunately, it will not always be possible to answer these questions ex ante.

•••

As noted above, treaties are often considered the gold standard of international law. But many of the traits that make multilateral treaties so valued—their written nature, their stability, and their grounding in state consent—also makes them difficult to modify. As a result, multilateral treaties regulating new

---

89 Declaration (IV, 1), to Prohibit, for the Term of Five Years, the Launching of Projectiles and Explosives from Balloons, and Other Methods of a Similar Nature, July 29, 1899, 32 Stat. 1839, 1 Bevans 270 (emphasis added).

90 *See* Arthur K. Kuhn, *The Beginnings of an Aërial Law*, 4 AM. J. INT'L L. 109, 119–20 (1910) (suggesting that the invention of the airplane impeded the renewal of the prohibition).

91 Crootof, *Killer Robots, supra* note 33, at 1888.

92 *Id.*

technologies are particularly likely to become jurisprudential space junk.[93] While careful drafting and structuring might alleviate this problem, it will not eliminate it. Instead, other, more flexible forms of international rulemaking may be preferable.

4   Alternative Options for International Technological Governance

4.1   *Soft Law*

Soft law consists of "nonbinding rules or instruments that interpret or inform our understanding of binding legal rules or represent promises that in turn create expectations about future conduct."[94] It might include state resolutions, state declarations, and what former U.S. Legal Advisor Harold Koh has called "twenty-first-century international lawmaking," a combination of "nonlegal understandings," "layered cooperation," and "diplomatic law talk."[95] Other quasi-legal commitments, such as publicized domestic policies and non-precedential decisions of international tribunals, might also qualify. Arguably, "private standards, guidelines, codes of conduct, and principles" might also be considered kinds of soft law governance.[96] These private means of self-regulation are useful, insofar as they are formed by those with the most immediate knowledge of the capabilities and limitations of a new technology. However, they are necessarily more limited in perspective than state-made law, necessitating care before they are promoted to the level of soft law, customary international law, or treaty provisions.[97]

---

93   Picker, *supra* note 2, at 185 ("[T]he very speed with which technology changes may suggest that binding treaties are … not the ideal mechanism for impounding technological change into international law. No sooner is the ink dry … than the technology changes again and forces a reevaluation of the treaty.").

94   Andrew T. Guzman & Timothy L. Meyer, *International Soft Law*, 2 J. LEGAL ANALYSIS 171, 174 (2010).

95   Harold Honju Koh, *Address: Twenty-First-Century International Lawmaking*, 101 GEO. L.J. ONLINE 1, 13–16 (2012).

96   Gary E. Marchant & Brad Allenby, *Soft Law: New Tools for Governing Emerging Technologies*, 73 BULL. ATOMIC SCIENTISTS 108, 112 (2017).

97   *Cf.* Kenneth W. Abbott, Douglas S. Sylvester & Gary E. Marchant, *Transnational Regulation of Nanotechnology: Reality or Romanticism?, in* INTERNATIONAL HANDBOOK ON REGULATING NANOTECHNOLOGIES 525, 538 (Graeme A. Hodge, Diana M. Bowman, Andrew D. Maynard, eds., 2010) (noting that, "once a polity has gained experience with … private norms, public authorities can ratify, modify or override them as appropriate").

Soft law has many of the benefits associated with treaties. It is "almost always negotiated, written, and rarely universal either in formation or application."[98] It often represents compromises upon which all parties can agree, it has the clarity and precision of the written word, and it can be tailored to address a specific issue.

When compared with treaties, soft law is relatively easy to create and modify, allowing it to evolve in real time and making it particularly attractive for regulating technologies with social, political, environmental, or other impacts that are not yet well understood.[99] Soft law also can be created by a wider array of actors: in addition to states, international tribunals, non-profit organizations, multilateral companies, groups of like-minded entities, and even individuals can contribute to the development of soft law.

Of course, soft law is not formally legally binding. That being said, it often serves as a signaling device by which states or relevant communities identify what they will or will not do—and this signal may be equivalently important for both soft and hard law.[100] As Andrew Guzman has argued, if international law is conceived as "any promise that material alters state incentives," then "soft law" is merely one point on "a spectrum of commitment along which states choose to locate their promises."[101] Furthermore, because it can be incorporated in other documents, soft law can be enforced indirectly in international contracts or by insurers who require compliance with applicable standards.[102] For example, the International Society of Stem Cell Research "has produced guidelines on stem cell research that restrict certain types of research and

---

98   Lawrence R. Helfer & Ingrid B. Wuerth, *Customary International Law: An Instrument Choice Perspective*, 37 MICH. J. INT'L L. 563, 567 (2016).

99   Andrew Guzman and Timothy Meyer have identified four reasons for why states employ soft law: (1) "states may use soft law to solve straightforward coordination games in which the existence of a focal point is enough to generate compliance"; (2) "moving from soft law to hard law generates higher sanctions that both deter more violations and ... increase the net loss to the parties"; (3) "states choose soft law when they are uncertain about whether the rules they adopt today will be desirable tomorrow and when it is advantageous to allow a particular state or group of states to adjust expectations in the event of changed circumstances"; and (4) soft law may serve as "a nonbinding gloss that international institutions, such as international tribunals, put on binding legal rules." Guzman & Meyer, *supra* note 95, at 171.

100 Many modern human rights and international humanitarian law treaties, for example, are more akin to pledges than contracts. Brilmayer, *supra* note 20.

101 Andrew T. Guzman, *A Compliance-Based Theory of International Law*, 90 CALIF. L. REV. 1823, 1823, 1828 (2002).

102 Marchant & Allenby, *supra* note 97, at 112.

provide ethical safeguards for other types" which "can be indirectly enforced by research institutions, funding agencies, and scientific journals."[103]

4.2   *Customary International Law*

Customary international law is recognized as existing when states generally engage in specific actions (the "state practice" element) on the grounds that those actions are legally obligatory or permitted (the *"opinio juris sive necessitatis"* element). In other words, "a rule of customary international law is authoritative because states generally abide by it in the belief that it is law."[104] Importantly, customary international law has no formal temporal requirement;[105] as evidenced by the swiftly-developing customary rules regarding a state's territorial sea, new customary international law can form over just a few years.[106] Unlike domestic custom, which derives much of its legal authority from being a longstanding rule, customary international law derives its legitimacy from the fact that states comport with it in the belief that it is law.[107]

Customary international law has been dismissed by some as increasingly unimportant in the modern world of proliferating treaties.[108] But states might

---

103   *Id.* at 113.

104   Crootof, *Change Without Consent, supra* note 1, at 242.

105   *See, e.g.,* Ian Brownlie, Principles of Public International Law 7 (7th ed. 2008). Some have gone so far as to argue that customary international law can be formed instantaneously. Bin Cheng, *United Nations Resolutions on Outer Space: "Instant" International Customary Law?,* 5 Indian J. Int'l L. 23, 45 (*1965*) ("International customary law requires only one single constitutive element, namely, the *opinio juris* of States."), *reprinted in* International Law: Teaching and Practice 237, 260 (Bin Cheng ed., 1982).

106   Crootof, *Change Without Consent, supra* note 1, at 250 (describing the swift evolution of the customary rules regarding coastal states' rights in adjacent waters).

107   *Cf. id.* at 242 n. 19 ("This necessarily circular reasoning has long plagued international law scholars, especially as it will be exceedingly difficult to demonstrate that a state acted in a specific manner out of a sense of legal obligation—both because the state [is comprised of] different components and because customary international law [often] arises out of convenient cooperative practices. However, states do abide by customary rules, even when it is against their own immediate self-interest.").

108   *See, e.g.,* Andrew Guzman, *Saving Customary International Law,* 27 Mich. J. Int'l L. 115, 119 (2005) (observing that "modern international relations have made the treaty a more important tool, relative to [customary international law], than it has been in the past"); Timothy Meyer, *Codifying Custom,* 160 U. Pa. L. Rev. 995, 1000 (2012) (noting that codifying custom in treaties "allows states to specify more precisely what customary international law requires, thereby facilitating deeper cooperation and avoiding costly disputes over vague legal rules"); Joel P. Trachtman, *The Growing Obsolescence of Customary International Law, in* Custom's Future: International Law in a Changing World 172, 172 (Curtis A. Bradley ed., 2016) (arguing that customary international law cannot effectively address either longstanding or modern challenges to the international legal order).

sometimes prefer that new technological regulations develop as customary international law, as this form might offer certain relative advantages.[109] For example, customary international law is universally applicable, which allows states to solve the potential holdout problem associated with any system grounded on consent.[110] Relatedly, there is little risk of fragmentation. As opposed to treaty law's opt-in approach, customary international law has a limited opt-out option: at least theoretically, a state may avoid being bound by a developing customary international law rule by consistently contesting the rule's existence or applicability. In practice, there are few such examples of this occurring.[111] Additionally, customary international law is not negotiated, and so "its norms are not subject to the bargains that undercut the original aims of treaty provisions, domestic legislation, and written soft law."[112] Given these traits, customary international law may be particularly well-suited to addressing "tragedy of the commons" problems.[113]

To be sure, there are drawbacks to grounding regulations of new technologies entirely in customary international law, precisely because it is universally binding, nonnegotiated, and unwritten. It can be difficult to identify new customary international law, permitting advocates of a new norm to read *opinio juris* into a few events and encouraging the selective parsing of state practice (usually by a limited number of states in the global north). A piece on drone law that cites only recent state practice by, say, the United States and Israel, hardly provides evidence of new customary international law. Customary international law may also be an inappropriate form of international technological regulation when state practice is largely hidden, as with state action in cyberspace.[114]

• • •

---

109   Helfer & Wuerth, *supra* note 99.

110   Crootof, *Change Without Consent, supra* note 1, at 297.

111   David A. Colson, *How Persistent Must the Persistent Objector Be?*, 61 WASH. L. REV. 957 (1986).

112   Crootof, *Change Without Consent, supra* note 1, at 297 (citing Helfer & Wuerth, *supra* note 99, at 568).

113   *See* Helfer & Wuerth, *supra* note 99, at 600 (discussing how the 1958 Geneva Convention on the High Seas, which recognized the right of states "to unilaterally exploit non-living resources on the deep seabed," was displaced by the customary concept that such resources were "the 'common heritage of mankind'" and could only be exploited by states "acting as an agent of the international community as a whole.").

114   Rebecca Crootof, *International Cybertorts: Expanding State Accountability in Cyberspace*, 103 CORNELL L. REV. 565, 643 (2018) ("There simply aren't enough examples [of state practice in cyberspace] to establish that states reliably act in a certain way in the belief that those actions are permitted or required by law.").

As is often the case in technological regulation, there will be no one-size-fits-all solution. In some situations, a multilateral treaty may well be the best option for regulating a new technology; in others, soft law or customary international law may be better able to address new tech-enabled conduct. Determining which means of regulation will be preferable will depend on answering scores of questions that this chapter cannot begin to address.[115] Instead, the aim of this chapter has been to question the common default assumption that multilateral treaties are inherently superior to other forms of international technological regulation—not least because they are far more likely to become jurisprudential space junk.

5   Conclusion

Why care about jurisprudential space junk? Because rules matter. Jurisprudential space junk is not just outdated law that makes it difficult to identify the most relevant regulations. Seemingly ineffectual law on the books creates the perception that international rules have little power, thereby weakening the entire international legal system.[116] By diminishing the power of international rules, jurisprudential space junk simultaneously erodes their ability to accomplish their underlying cooperative and humanitarian aims.

Now, Lea is not one to blindly believe in the power of rules. Indeed, the first article by Lea Brilmayer I ever read began by questioning "whether anything is gained by taking a moral norm and embedding it in a legal instrument," as she found it "entirely unclear whether human rights conventions achieve any greater level of respect and compliance than the underlying norms on which the conventions are grounded."[117] But while she shares the cynic's concerns that drafting human rights treaties might merely "soothe the consciences of western elites while achieving nothing in the world at large,"[118] Lea also acknowledges the possibility that granting legal recognition to moral norms "changes or solidifies the way we think about human rights."[119]

Lea taught me to think of rules as tools. When crafted or used poorly, rules are at best ineffectual and at worst actively harmful; when crafted and used well,

---

115   *See, e.g.*, Picker, *supra* note 2, at 203–05 (outlining questions for policymakers crafting international regulations for new technologies).

116   Oona A. Hathaway & Scott J. Shapiro, The Internationalists 421 (2017) ("[I]nternational law is a *system* and the rules rise or fall together.").

117   Brilmayer, *supra* note 20, at 166.

118   *Id.* at 195.

119   *Id.* at 199.

rules can prevent deadly conflicts, grant power to the weak, and effect meaningful change. Lea has dedicated much of her life to drafting and implementing
rules as fairly as possible, with the aims of minimizing conflict and elevating
human dignity—and despite her long tenure in the ivory tower, she never for-
gets (or lets her students forget) that rules ultimately affect individuals.

• • •

I could end the chapter there, but I cannot forego this opportunity to note that
Lea Brilmayer is one of Yale Law School's great treasures. In addition to caring
about individuals in the abstract, Lea has a deep and genuine interest in the
people lucky enough to be in her classroom. Her candor, her insights, and her
humor creates a warm environment where students blossom. In short, Lea is
an inspiration: both as a model of how one should think about the potential of
the law, and as a teacher who cares deeply about her students.

CHAPTER 8

Recognition, Rewards, and Regime Change

*William J. Moon**

1 Introduction

A significant part of Professor Lea Brilmayer's many substantial contributions
to legal scholarship revolves around the important and persistent topic of
secession and self-determination under international law. In a majestic work
published in 1991, *Secession and Self-Determination: A Territorial Interpretation*,
Professor Brilmayer advanced a novel idea at the time which argued that viable
secession claims under international law had less to do with any given group's
ethnic or linguistic homogeneity than with the group's historical title to a particular territory.[1] Her work to this day remains a major theoretical breakthrough
in both international law and international relations circles, becoming. "a
required reading for anyone interested in secession and self-determination."[2]

In this contribution, I pay tribute to Professor Brilmayer by exploring a
concept that almost invariably accompanies a group's claim to secession: international recognition. The subject has captured the curiosity of legal scholars
and political philosophers for generations, producing a plethora of academic
commentaries, including those that have served as foundational texts to early
international law. Today, it is also a topic with immensely important practical

---

* Assistant Professor of Law, University of Maryland School of Law. This Essay stems from
numerous conversations I had on the topic with Professor Brilmayer, whose influence is
evident throughout. For helpful comments, I thank Seth Endo, Angela Gius, Jeffrey Javed,
Tal Kastner, Lauren Roth, Eric Ruben, Scott Skinner-Thompson, Naomi Sunshine, and Sarah
Vendzules. I also thank Natalie Klein and Chiara Giorgetti for their tireless efforts in organizing this project and for offering helpful editorial feedback. All errors are mine.

1 Lea Brilmayer, *Secession and Self-Determination: A Territorial Interpretation*, 16 YALE J. INT'L
L. 177, 193 (1991).

2 David Wippman, *Secession, Territorial Claims, and the Indeterminacy of Self-determination*,
25 YALE J. INT'L L. 287, 289 (2000). Professor Brilmayer's work on territoriality as it relates to
American law, needless to say, also maintains a preeminent status to both courts and scholars. *See, e.g.*, Michael Farbiarz, *Extraterritorial Criminal Jurisdiction*, 114 MICH. L. REV. 507,
511 (2016) ("No article in this area is more important than *Extraterritoriality*, published in
1992 in the *Harvard Law Review* by Professors Brilmayer and Norchi.") (citing Lea Brilmayer
& Charles Norchi, *Federal Extraterritoriality and Fifth Amendment Due Process*, 105 HARV. L.
REV. 1217 (1992)).

---

implications, constituting a source of law that purports to decide the fate of disputed territories, secessionist movements, and civil conflicts around the world.

The prevailing academic discussions on the question of international recognition have traditionally split into two camps sharply divided over the legal significance of recognition. Under the constitutive theory, a state is a state when other states recognize it as a state. Statehood is often conceptualized as gaining membership to an exclusive club of states regulated by existing members. The declaratory theory, on the other hand, posits that statehood is tied to meeting several objective criteria—having a permanent population, territory, government, and capacity to enter into relations with other states. Recognition, under this view, is neither a sufficient nor a necessary condition for statehood.

While almost all modern international lawyers subscribe to one of the two theories, the prevailing accounts have only made an incremental contribution to understanding the real stakes at issue. According to Ian Brownlie, the debate has "not only failed to enhance the subject but has created a *tertium quid* which stands, like a bank of fog on a still day, between the observer and the contours of the ground...."[3]

Whereas legal scholars have largely approached the topic by mustering evidence that supports the existence of a particular rule, my goal here is to assess how and why the rules governing international recognition and statehood matter today. Recognition matters, I argue, because it serves as the threshold condition to receive the international community's rationing of what I will refer to as *rewards*: the legal title to a certain territory and the bundle of financial benefits offered by the international community.

Of course, in many parts of the world, legal title recognized by the international community seems (and is) unimportant. For instance, whether North Korea or Cuba decides to recognize the United States as a state is unlikely to have an effect on the United States. Legal title matters, however, when the empirical and juridical claims to a territory do not overlap, as is the case in significant parts of Africa, Latin America, and Asia. Some are locked in struggle with rival entities seeking to replace the central government, while others are in conflict with separatist movements demanding independence.[4] The internationally recognized states in these regions generally lack administrative presence throughout their territorial borders and confront people with

---

3   Ian Brownlie, *Recognition in Theory and Practice, in* THE STRUCTURE AND PROCESS OF INTERNATIONAL LAW: ESSAYS IN LEGAL PHILOSOPHY, DOCTRINE, AND THEORY 627 (R. Macdonald & Douglas Johnston eds., 1983).

4   Lea Brilmayer & William J. Moon, *Regulating Land Grabs: Social Activism, Third Party States, and International Law, in* ACCESS TO FOOD IN A NEW MILLENNIUM, 123, 124–25 (Lea Brilmayer et al., eds., 2014).

weak (if any) allegiance to the idea of a modern Westphalian state.[5] Legal title respected by the international community shifts the power structure of various groups operating in these regions. For instance, since recognized governments are legally entitled to exercise "sovereignty" within their borders,[6] entities that are unrecognized (be it secessionists or insurgencies) are often subject to violent re-absorption by the recognized entity, as was the case for the Biafran secessionist movement in Nigeria that violently ended in 1970.

Recognition also opens the door to financial rewards from international organizations that provide staple sources of income for the ruling elites in weak states that are regarded as "central governments" to outsiders. While recognition does not automatically bestow monopoly over the ability to tax or regulate international commercial transactions, it also provides a competitive advantage for the recognized entity to attract investments from foreign corporations. After all, corporations have an incentive to deal with sovereigns, rather than rebel groups. In geopolitically unstable, underdeveloped regions, these sorts of financial gains make up a significant source of funds that the ruling elites can turn into private gain or deploy to strengthen their grip on rebel groups. In its darkest form, international recognition has turned into a channel through which groups that have little interest in carrying out traditional state-like functions convert public authority into private gain.[7]

Rewards are particularly important in parts of the world where the internationally recognized central government does not have effective control over parts of the territory within the state's juridical boundary. Perhaps with no coincidence, these regions frequently suffer from the collapse of state authority and capacity, with the central government being unable or unwilling to extend security or the rule of law to its population.[8] In these regions,

---

5 Jeffrey Herbst, *Responding to State Failure in Africa*, 21 INT'L SEC. 120, 121–22 (1996).

6 As Professor Reisman reminds us, the term sovereignty "has had a long and varied history during which it has been given different meanings, hues and tones, depending on the context and the objectives of those using the word." W. Michael Reisman, *Sovereignty and Human Rights in Contemporary International Law*, 84 AM. J. INT'L L. 866, 866 (1990). I use the term sovereignty generically in this Essay to refer to the legal authority of the state to monopolize the legitimate use of force within its borders. *See* James A. Caporaso, *The European Union and Forms of State: Westphalian, Regulatory or Post-Modern*, 34 J. COMMON MARKET STUD. 29, 34 (2008).

7 *See infra* Part III; *see also* WILLIAM RENO, WARLORD POLITICS AND AFRICAN STATES (1998).

8 For a related concept of state failure, where a recognized state cannot perform its sovereign functions, see CHIARA GIORGETTI, A PRINCIPLED APPROACH TO STATE FAILURE 6–8 (2009).

recognition is not merely an intellectual exercise. It is a powerful instrument that creates expectations and shapes the behaviors of relevant actors at play.

This account, which is theoretically enriched by drawing on a moderate strand of constructivist thought,[9] presents a new way of thinking about the importance of international recognition under international law. Under the standard account, international law pretends to be descriptive. International lawyers evaluate if entities fit a certain rubric or not.[10] If they are generous, they will also assess if this is fair or not.[11] Both the agents and the rules in the system are taken as exogenous variables. The two variables, in reality, are *not* exogenous. "Facts" are, in many ways, mutually constituted and shaped by the "law." Such changes in the facts, which the declaratory view and the constitutive view take as exogenous from the "law," ought to be taken seriously, for they arise in the form of civil wars, secessionist movements, and warlord politics.

The constructivist approach, it is important to emphasize, does not require one to unsubscribe from the two dominant views on recognition. The constructivist view concurs with the constitutive view to the extent of acknowledging that existing states *do* have discretion to recognize other states. A constructivist, moreover, appreciates recognition's significance, as would a constitutive theorist. Constructivism, nevertheless, fundamentally departs from the constitutive view's *formula* on recognition's significance. Under the constitutive view, statehood is derived from legal fiction. It is viewed as an entity applying for and gaining membership in the exclusive club of states—one that exercises full discretion in reviewing new applications.[12] Under the constitutive view, the importance of recognition rests not on this metaphysical narrative, but on the reality that rewards—which are tied to recognition—endow entities with the gears to potentially establish empirical claims to statehood, or at least extract valuable goods in transit.

The constructivist theory shares a premise with the declaratory theory to the extent that both theories do not view recognition as automatically "creating" a state. The declaratory view famously discounts recognition's significance by

---

9   Constructivism, as elaborated in Part IV teaches that it is through ongoing interactions with social structures—including international legal rules—that the identity and interests of states and state-like actors are shaped. ANTHONY CLARK AREND, LEGAL RULES AND INTERNATIONAL SOCIETY 142 (1999).

10 *See, e.g.,* David A. Ijalaye, *Was "Biafra" at Any Time a State in International Law?*, 65 AM. J. INT'L L. 551 (1971).

11 *See, e.g.,* Alison K. Eggers, *When is a State a State? The Case for Recognition of Somaliland*, 30 B.C. INT'L & COMP. L. REV. 211 (2007).

12 THOMAS D. GRANT, THE RECOGNITION OF STATES: LAW AND PRACTICE IN DEBATE AND EVOLUTION 19 (1999).

reasoning that the international community's opinion on an entity has little or no effect on whether an entity constitutes a state. A constructivist view, similarly, does not necessarily posit that recognition "creates" states. Rather, it treats recognition seriously because it is the time in which an entity receives rewards from the international community. While the declaratory view insists that the elements of sovereignty (e.g., territory, government) *pre-date* recognition, the constructivist view would contend that some elements of sovereignty, in many cases, *derive from* recognition. It is partly for this reason that the constructivist approach offers a theoretical lens to earnestly examine how recognition shapes the identities of various entities at play.

Removing the theoretical constraints inherent to the two dominant views enables us to imagine how institutional norms surrounding recognition induce behavioral changes of relevant actors in the system. Importantly, while there is a tendency to classify civil wars and secessionist movements as rooted in "ancient ethnic hatreds,"[13] this account allows us to better understand that ethnicity and collective group identities are also shaped by greed and conflict, providing the cognitive script to give meaning to the identity and behavior of various groups within the system.[14] While violence premised on ethnic and religious grounds are likely to take place absent international structures, it can be amplified by the presence of how the international community chooses to privilege certain entities with rewards. International law, in some cases, could very well be incentivizing conflict and underdevelopment, rather than ameliorating them.

The remainder of this Essay is organized as follows: Part 2 provides a literature review of the two dominant theories on recognition under international law. Part 3 explains how rewards are tied to recognition in the modern era, and unpacks the source of rewards. I also explain the link between recognition and regime change. Part 4 draws on the constructivist literature to theorize how the institutional norms governing recognition create expectations and shapes the behaviors of both "states" and "rebel groups." Part 5 provides concluding remarks.

---

13   DAVID CAMPBELL, NATIONAL DECONSTRUCTION: VIOLENCE, IDENTITY AND JUSTICE IN BOSNIA (1998).

14   David Keen, *Incentives and Disincentives for Violence, in* GREED AND GRIEVANCE: ECONOMIC AGENDAS IN CIVIL WARS 19, 22 (Mats Berdal & David M. Malone eds., 2000).

2   The Standard Account

The term "recognition" has several distinct meanings and has been used in variety of contexts throughout history. The practice of *state* recognition is said to date back to the early nineteenth century with the rise of formalized diplomatic practices. In 1815, the Final Act of the Congress of Vienna recognized 39 sovereign states (all in Europe) and established the principle that new states would have to be recognized by other states. Each state, at least in theory, was entitled to determine for itself whether an entity qualifies as a state and who qualifies as its government.[15] In the modern era, international recognition is the focal point of the debate on the question of statehood under international law. Two dominant theories offer diametrically opposed prescriptions, as discussed below.

2.1   *Constitutive Theory*

Under the constitutive view, existing states in the system decide which entity constitutes a state. Under this theory, recognition is both the sufficient and the necessary condition to establish a state under international law. Oppenheim, a proponent of the constitutive view, wrote in his famous treatise that "[a] State is, and becomes, an International Person through recognition only and exclusively."[16] This idea has been so pervasive in international law that prominent international jurists take for granted the idea that sovereignty is "rationed and regulated by those who currently enjoy it."[17]

This view owes its intellectual debt to a positivist tradition that dates back to Hegel, who thought that no relations of a legal nature can exist between states without mutual recognition.[18] As pointed out by Martin Wight, states cannot be entirely self-constituted if, "collective judgment of international society [determines] rightful membership of the family of nations[.]"[19] This view seems to mirror reality to a large extent. According to Milena Sterio, "an entity seems to be treated as a state only if the outside world, and specifically, the most powerful states (the Great Powers), wishes to recognize it as such."[20]

---

15   M.J. PETERSON, RECOGNITION OF GOVERNMENTS: LEGAL DOCTRINE AND STATE PRACTICE, 1815–1995, at 2 (1997).

16   1 L. OPPENHEIM, INTERNATIONAL LAW: A TREATISE (8th ed. H. Lauterpacht ed., 1955).

17   GRANT, *supra* note 12, at 19.

18   H. LAUTERPACHT, RECOGNITION IN INTERNATIONAL LAW 38 (1947).

19   Martin Wight, *International Legitimacy*, 4 INT'L RELATIONS 1, 1 (1972).

20   Milena Sterio, *On the Right to External Self-Determination: "Selfistans," Secession, and the Great Powers' Rule*, 19 MINN. J. INT'L L. 137, 149 (2010).

The constitutive view, however, suffers from major shortcomings. First, the constitutive approach ignores the fact that unrecognized entities may perform many state-like functions, while recognized entities may fail to do so. As James Crawford documents in his celebrated work, many unrecognized entities often monopolize the use of force in a territory akin to a state.[21] Second, the constitutive theory's logical prescription that states have unbridled discretion may lead to inconsistent recognition policy by existing states, creating uncertainties about whether a particular entity constitutes a state.[22] In other words, the standard speaks very little as to the *degree* of recognition that would be necessary to gain statehood. Does statehood require a majority of the states? Does statehood require universal acceptance? This limits the universal applicability of the theory to "special cases" like the Republic of China (Taiwan), where only twenty states (as of 2017) formally recognize it as a state.[23]

2.2   *Declaratory Theory*

The declaratory theory is the dominant view subscribed to by modern international jurists.[24] Under this view, an entity that acquires certain factual characteristics constitutes a state regardless of recognition. The often-used criteria under this view is articulated in Article 1 of the Montevideo Convention on Rights and Duties of States, signed in 1933: "(a) a permanent population; (b) a defined territory; (c) government; and (d) capacity to enter into relations with other States."[25] Recognition by foreign nations is simply an acknowledgement of existing status.[26]

The status of statehood is thus based on facts and not recognition. Max Weber's seminal work is embodied in this tradition. In *Politics as a Vocation*, Weber famously conceptualized states as a human community that

---

21   JAMES CRAWFORD, THE CREATION OF STATES IN INTERNATIONAL LAW (2006).

22   *See* Aaron Kreuter, *Self-determination, Sovereignty, and the Failure of States: Somaliland and the Case for Justified Secession*, 19 MINN. J. INT'L L. 363, 366 (2010); *see also* Christopher J. Borgen, *The Language of the Law and the Practice of Politics: Great Powers and the Rhetoric of Self-Determination in the Cases of Kosovo and South Ossetia*, 10 CHI. J. INT'L L. 1, 6–7 (2009).

23   The Republic of China (Taiwan) was replaced by the People's Republic of China in 1971 by the Security Council, at the same point in which majority of the states replaced recognition of the Republic of China with that of the People's Republic of China.

24   Cedric Ryngaert & Sven Sobrie, *Recognition of States: International Law or Realpolitik? The Practice of Recognition in the Wake of Kosovo, South Ossetia, and Abkhazia*, 24 LEIDEN J. INT'L L. 467, 470 (2011).

25   Montevideo Convention on Rights and Duties of States, art. 1, Dec. 26, 1933, 49 Stat. 3097, T.S. 881.

26   IAN BROWNLIE, PRINCIPLES OF PUBLIC INTERNATIONAL LAW 89–90 (2003).

claims, "the monopoly of the legitimate use of physical force within a given territory."[27] More modern writers, such as Alan James, subscribe to the declaratory view but argue that it is the case because states exist ontologically prior to international society.[28]

Normatively attractive arguments are embedded in this view. Since state practice has not accepted a right or a duty of recognition, states have complete autonomy in their recognition practice. They can thus withhold recognition for political reasons. The rule prescribed by the declaratory view minimizes potential abuse and injects a degree of objectivity to the methodology of determining statehood. This view is also supported by an important principle in international law—the right to self-determination, which, at least in theory, is undermined if existing states object to emerging states based on political motives.

Despite its redeeming values, the declaratory theory does not exactly mirror state practice. History is replete with instances when a group is recognized before they meet the Montevideo criteria. Moreover, entities with virtually collapsed governments, like Afghanistan in the 1990s and Somalia since 1991, have retained their status as states. On the flip side, entities who have arguably met the standard—including Somaliland and Northern Cyprus—have not gained recognition. The latter observation speaks to a major weakness of the declaratory theory: the capacity to enter into relations with other states is hard to establish absent recognition. In that sense, even the declaratory theory in international law is quasi-constitutive in that the widely-cited criteria for determining the existence of a state is "the capacity to enter into relations with other states."[29]

If recognition is as an ornamental ritual and immaterial for the purposes of attaining statehood under international law, it is also a descriptively questionable theory. In particular, it begs the question of why states are so nerve-wracked by the recognition practice of other states. The recognition of Republic of Bosnia and Herzegovina by the United States and the European Community in 1992, for example, immediately descended to by far the most serious armed conflict in Europe since World War II.[30] It also cannot explain

---

27   Max Weber, *Politics as a Vocation, reprinted in* MAX WEBER: ESSAYS IN SOCIOLOGY 78 (H.H. Gerth & C. Wright Mills eds., 1958).

28   ALAN JAMES, SOVEREIGN STATEHOOD: THE BASIS OF INTERNATIONAL SOCIETY 152–53 (1986).

29   Montevideo Convention on Rights and Duties of States, art. 1, Dec. 26, 1933, 49 Stat. 3097, T.S. 881.

30   MIKULAS FABRY, RECOGNIZING STATES: INTERNATIONAL SOCIETY & THE ESTABLISHMENT OF NEW STATES SINCE 1776, at 1–2 (2010).

why secession movements and insurgents wage decade-long wars in part to strive for recognition by the international community. More fundamentally, the declaratory view ignores the reality that any standard to statehood must be socially constructed, for no one can actually "see" what a state is.

Although there have been attempts at synthesis, the declaratory and constitutive theories have been assessed to be wholly opposed. As James Crawford explains, a choice has to be made at the fundamental level, for it determines whether the denial of recognition to an entity qualifying as a state entitles other states to act as if it was not a state.[31]

3   Rewards as the Source of Recognition's Significance

The descriptive complexity of the subject at hand, in my view, makes it too limited to analyze the issue of international recognition under either one of the two dominant theories on statehood. One can turn the declaratory view into a constitutive one by merely adding "do states think" to the objective criteria proposed by the declaratory view. The declaratory theory is also quasi-constitutive in a sense that the widely cited element of statehood is "the capacity to enter into relations with other states."[32] The distinction stops being important in understanding the significance of recognition.

Recognition matters in my view not so much because it metaphysically establishes states (as the constitutive theorists would have it) or because it ought to follow when an entity achieves certain objective criterions (as the declaratory theorists would have it). Rather, recognition carries significance today because it has become the precondition for receiving certain "rewards" offered by the international community.[33]

Once an entity is recognized by the international community, it can sign treaties and gain membership in various international organizations, including

---

31   JAMES CRAWFORD, THE CREATION OF STATES IN INTERNATIONAL LAW 27 (2005).

32   Montevideo Convention on Rights and Duties of States, art. 1, Dec. 26, 1933, 49 Stat. 3097, T.S. 881.

33   Of course, I do *not* contend that rewards are invariably tied to recognition. Some entities have benefited from certain rewards without formal recognition. For example, Taiwan is an entity unrecognized by most states, yet maintains membership in the World Trade Organization and benefits from a number of strategic alliances that shield its borders from mainland China's military aggression. The point is that the conflation of recognition and rewards is the dominant phenomenon institutionalized by the rise of international organizations in the aftermath of World War II.

the United Nations. Membership in international organizations is important in it of itself because it gives a voice to "small" states.

But recognition also makes the recognized entity eligible to receive rewards from the international community. I define *rewards* broadly to include the wide range of benefits accrued to an internationally-recognized entity that would have been unavailable absent formal recognition, including legal title to a particular territory and pecuniary goods that flow to an entity as a result of an entity qualifying as a state. Rewards include funds disbursed by international organizations and access to foreign military that may allow the recognized entity to gain competitive advantage over rival rebel groups. Of course, external aid has been a phenomenon ubiquitous throughout recent history, and pervasive in practice throughout the Cold War.[34] But today, the practice is systematized and regulated by the international community based on international recognition. I classify rewards into two categories and elaborate below.

3.1 *Financial Rewards*

To those who study international economic law, the establishment of the Bretton Woods institutions—following the famous conference at the Mount Washington Hotel in Bretton Woods, New Hampshire in 1944—goes down as a critical moment towards an establishment of the modern international financial system. The conference led to the establishment of the International Monetary Fund (IMF) and the International Bank for Reconstruction and Development (the precursor to the World Bank), with a vision to "create stability in currency, to reconstruct the economies of war-ravaged nations, and to establish a regime for international trade and investment."[35]

Today, the World Bank and the IMF are also the two pillars of international organizations that raise the stakes for gaining international recognition. This is so because the two organizations provide financial rewards for recognized *states* in the form of loans, foreign currency, and developmental aid. Under the current rules, resources provided by the two institutions are tied to membership in the organizations, which in turn depends on recognition by foreign nations. Membership applications to the IMF, for one, are determined by

---

34   JEFFRY HERBST, STATES AND POWER IN AFRICA 108 (2000) ("The Cold War had the effect of providing African countries with patrons when their boundaries were challenged internally or externally. The superpowers were concerned with cultivating clients in all parts of the world and therefore were willing to help African nations crush ethnic rebellions or threats from neighbors.").

35   William N. Gianaris, *Weighted Voting in the International Monetary Fund and the World Bank*, 14 FORDHAM INT'L L.J. 910, 912 (1990).

existing members, who cast votes in a "weighted voting system."[36] That IMF membership, in turn, is a prerequisite to join the World Bank.[37]

Once an entity is recognized and gains membership into international organizations, it is able to rely on the international community for a steady flow of financial assistance, regardless of whether it can establish an empirical claim to its territory or whether it can effectively govern the people living within the state's juridical border. As Jeffrey Herbst explains in his seminal work studying African states, the prevailing international norm is that once a state is recognized as one, "it is sovereign forever, no matter what happens within its boundaries."[38]

Consider the World Bank, which is in the business of providing "low-interest loans, zero to low-interest credits, and grants to developing countries."[39] As of 2016, the World Bank's International Development Association (IDA) supports 77 of the world's poorest *countries* (39 of them in Africa), and allocates its resources based relative poverty of the country, defined as GNI per capita below an established threshold and the lack of creditworthiness to borrow on market terms.[40] While some entities have been able to gain membership into the World Bank and the IMF absent full-fledged recognition by the international community (e.g., Kosovo),[41] benefits to these organizations are almost invariably limited to recognized states.

To understand the impact of recognition, take the recent case of South Sudan. In 2011, the secessionist movement gained the recognition of more than a hundred states and was admitted to both the United Nations and the World

---

36   *Id.* at 910.

37   IBRD Articles of Agreement: Article II, at sec. 1(a) ("The original members of the Bank shall be those members of the International Monetary Fund which accept membership in the Bank before the date specified in Article XI, Section 2 (e).").

38   HERBST, *supra* note 34, at 264.

39   The World Bank, What We Do, http://www.worldbank.org/en/about/what-we-do.

40   The World Bank Group, *Borrowing Countries*, http://ida.worldbank.org/about/borrowing -countries ("Eligibility for IDA support depends first and foremost on a country's relative poverty, defined as GNI per capita below an established threshold and updated annually ($1,215 in fiscal year 2016).").

41   Kosovo, for instance, had the support of more than 90 states at the time it was admitted to the World Bank and the IMF in 2009, including some states that did not extend formal recognition at the time. *See* JAMES SUMMERS, KOSOVO: A PRECEDENT? THE DECLARATION OF INDEPENDENCE, THE ADVISORY OPINION AND IMPLICATIONS FOR STATEHOOD, SELF-DETERMINATION AND MINORITY RIGHTS 134 (2011). Kosovo was able to gain membership into the two organizations, despite a significant number of states not recognizing it as such, and its failure to obtain membership in the United Nations largely due to Russia's opposition. *Id.* at 135.

Bank.[42] Within a matter of days, the World Bank cut a check for $75 million in transition trust fund.[43] One observes a similar phenomenon happening in its neighboring state of Somalia. Within the juridical state of Federal Republic of Somalia, there are several competing entities that claim various territories within the internationally-recognized boundary, including self-declared (but unrecognized) states of Puntland and Somaliland. The recognized central government has controlled a small portion of the juridical state in the past several decades (and in 1991 famously collapsed after years of civil wars in the 1980s), yet maintains access to World Bank aid, which has provided funds to the tune of over $500 million since 1962.[44]

In these regions, financial assistance from international organizations make up an important source of funds for the ruling elites to further appropriate an economic benefit or maintain a grip on power.[45] Aid constitutes an important component to international recognition because it is "easy to steal, as it is usually provided directly to governments," rendering the "control over government worth fighting for."[46] By some accounts, President Mobutu Sese Seko in Zaire (now the Democratic Republic of Congo) looted aid of around $5 billion, while President Sani Abacha of Nigeria stole roughly the same amount and placed it in Swiss private banks.[47]

3.2 Legal Title over Territory

Under international law, a recognized state claims ownership over a particular territory. A successful secessionist movement thus seeks to claim legitimate ownership of a part of an existing state's territory (resulting in border re-drawing), while a successful insurgent group aims to claim legitimate

---

42   South Sudan was formally admitted to the IMF on April 18, 2012. See International Monetary Fund, List of Members, https://www.imf.org/external/np/sec/memdir/memdate.htm.

43   The World Bank, World Bank Advances $75 Million for Early Engagement in Upcoming Nation of South Sudan (June 14, 2011), at http://www.worldbank.org/en/news/press-release/2011/06/14/world-bank-advances-75-million-for-early-engagement-in-upcoming-nation-of-south-sudan.

44   The World Bank Group, Country Summary Somalia, https://finances.worldbank.org/en/countries/Somalia.

45   About half of the states in Africa, for instance, receive at least ten percent of GDP in foreign aid, which is "usually their main source of government revenue." PIERRE ENGLEBERT, AFRICA: UNITY, SOVEREIGNTY & SORROW 8 (2009).

46   Niall Ferguson, Forward, in DAMBISA MOYO, DEAD AID: WHY AID IS NOT WORKING AND HOW THERE IS A BETTER WAY FOR AFRICA, at x (2009).

47   DAMBISA MOYO, DEAD AID: WHY AID IS NOT WORKING AND HOW THERE IS A BETTER WAY FOR AFRICA 48 (2009).

ownership over all of an existing state's territory (resulting in no changes to international boundaries). Recognition today is the international community's way of acknowledging legal title to a territory.

International law, of course, lacks a central enforcement mechanism or an authoritative interpreter of the law that will necessarily enforce an entity's juridical title to a particular piece of territory.[48] To some legal scholars, this may raise the question of whether international law is really law. I do not intend to rehash this old debate. In the sphere of recognition, international law largely works through setting international norms that are internalized and enforced by domestic legal regimes.[49] As Harold Koh explains in his seminal work exploring why nations almost always obey international law, "global norms are not just debated and interpreted, but ultimately internalized by domestic legal systems."[50]

Legal title in the international arena denotes territorial integrity that is generally respected by the international community. Under the United Nations Charter Article 2(4), states are instructed to "refrain in their international relations from the threat or use of force against the territorial integrity or political independence of any state[.]"[51] The prohibition against the use of force does not extend to non-recognized groups, meaning that a recognized group is legally entitled to use force within its juridical boundary. That is, the international community tends to look the other way while the "state" fights off its rival "rebel groups."

Non-recognition means that territories controlled by rebel groups— including self-declared but unrecognized secessionist movements—are still *legally* parts of the states they had broken away from, "leaving them permanently exposed to re-absorption by the central government."[52] Consider the case of Chechnya, whose independence movement, the Chechen National Congress, was crushed militarily by Russia, without international observance of its *de facto* independence. The unsuccessful secessionist movement in Biafra

---

48   *See* Jack Goldsmith & Daryl Levinson, *Law for States: International Law, Constitutional Law, Public Law*, 122 HARV. L. REV. 1791 (2009).

49   *See generally* Oona Hathaway & Scott J. Shapiro, *Outcasting*, 121 YALE L.J. 252 (2011).

50   Harold Hongju Koh, *Why Do Nations Obey International Law*, 106 YALE L.J. 2599, 2602 (1997); *see also* ANTHONY CLARK AREND, LEGAL RULES AND INTERNATIONAL SOCIETY 132 (1999) ("Initially, they may accept these legal rules as a short-term convenience. Over a longer period of time, however, state practice that reflects an acceptance of these rules may cause states to have a different sense of identity. They may see themselves as entities that 'simply do not use force' against the territorial integrity or political independence of each other.").

51   U.N. CHARTER Art. 2 para. 4.

52   MIKULAS FABRY, RECOGNITION OF STATES 164 (2010).

during the late 1960s is another example. While Biafra gained the recognition of a few states, the movement did not sufficiently gain traction and the entity was eventually reabsorbed to Nigeria in 1970. Recognition also enables an easier access to foreign military. This is the case because as legitimate agents of states, recognized governments can legally consent to foreign military intervention.

• • •

Legal title and financial rewards are linked, as one might expect. Legal title, for instance, allows the recognized entity to derive competitive advantage over any rival entities to attract foreign direct investments from foreign corporations. For example, recognition has allowed the central governments to sell off or lease large masses of land to foreign corporations in recent years at alarming rates—even in regions where the central governments do not have effective control over the territories.[53] Granting operating licenses to multinational corporations to extract natural resources is another lucrative venture. The extractive industry is particularly attractive from the ruling elite's point of view because it often requires private corporations hiring private security forces to guard their infrastructure. In addition to revenue sharing contracts that generate profits that may go straight into the ruling elite's bank account, private security forces hired by multinational corporations may come with the added benefit of displacing rebel groups or hostile local population.[54] It is no coincidence that the most stable parts of Sierra Leone during the Kabbah regime was found within the archipelago of mineral resources across the country guarded by foreign firms including ArmSec International and Lifeguard.[55]

---

53   Brilmayer & Moon, *supra* note 4, at 124–26.
54   This is not to say that recognition is required to conduct business with multinational companies. Many unrecognized entities control territories replete with natural resources, drawing major multinational companies like Shell and BP to build infrastructure with the consent of the unrecognized government. The unrecognized autonomous governments of Somaliland and Kurdistan, for instance, have awarded lucrative licenses to explore petroleum. There is no international police stopping transnational business enterprises from dealing with rebel groups. However, because of the heightened risk of doing business with rebels (who at least in theory do not have the legal authority to bind the state), there remains significant limits on the ability of unrecognized entities to attract foreign business ventures. Perhaps a prime example is American Mineral Fields (AMF), a rival of De Beers in the former Zaire, who unsuccessfully "rallied around the rebels seeking to overthrow the defunct regime of President Mobutu in the hope of securing lucrative contracts". Musifiky Mwanasali, *The View from Below, in* GREED AND GRIEVANCE: ECONOMIC AGENDAS IN CIVIL WARS 137, 148 (Mats Berdal & David M. Malone eds., 2000).
55   RENO, *supra* note 7, at 139.

3.3   *Rewards at Play: from Warlord Politics to Regime Change*

Rewards are significant in geopolitically unstable regions because income acquired independently of the state's population helps the ruling elite construct an enterprise of what William Reno has classified as *warlords* that operate behind the façade of de jure state sovereignty. As Professor Reno explains, external support for de jure sovereignty with very weak internal administrations relieve rulers of "the need to strengthen institutions to protect productive groups in society, from which regimes could extract income."[56] In some cases, the entity recognized as a state from the international community's standpoint is often no more than private commercial syndicates that turn externally-generated legitimacy and finances into private gain. Warlords in weak states resemble the form of a mafia rather than a government, manipulating "definitions of sovereignty and statehood to protect their personal authority, unhitching it from the dangerous and cumbersome exercise of building effective bureaucracies that could challenge the rulers' private interests."[57]

Recognition of an entity as a legitimate government, in some instances, has the effect of simply privileging one of the many warlords operating within the region. Rewards do not necessarily result in the elimination of competing rival entities. Rather, it can be conceptualized as a subsidy provided to one commercial syndicate over another. Liberia provides an excellent case study. Even as President Taylor made an estimated $400 million to $450 million per year between 1992 and 1996 through extraction of gold, diamond, timber, and rubber,[58] his rival groups based their authority on the territorial control of portions of those and other markets.[59] As observed by Professor Reno, rebel groups in Liberia "tapped into overseas commercial networks without presidential assent ... with foreign firms mak[ing] deals with warlords and not just state leaders."[60]

Rewards, in other contexts, set the stage for full-scale regime change within an existing state. Regime change, a term that has gained currency in both academic studies and even recent American presidential election campaigns,[61]

---

56   William Reno, *Shadow States and the Political Economy of Civil Wars, in* GREED AND GRIEVANCE: ECONOMIC AGENDAS IN CIVIL WARS 43, 45 (Mats Berdal & David M. Malone eds., 2000).

57   RENO, *supra* note 7, at 8–9.

58   Mark Duffield, *Globalization, Transborder Trade, and War Economies, in* GREED AND GRIEVANCE: ECONOMIC AGENDAS IN CIVIL WARS 69, 82 (Mats Berdal & David M. Malone eds., 2000).

59   *Id.* at 79.

60   *Id.* at 106.

61   *See, e.g.*, Jay Butler, *Responsibility for Regime Change*, 114 COLUM. L. REV. 503 (2014); Amber Phillips, *Hillary Clinton: Regime-Changer?*, WASH. POST (Dec. 20, 2015).

powerfully demonstrates the importance of rewards in geo-politically unstable regions. To understand how foreign nations may pull the plug on the sovereign authority of a government, one needs to understand the basic juridical structure of international law.

Under international law, states are international legal persons, and governments are understood to be the agents responsible for "conducting the affairs of states on the international plane."[62] Under this system, "recognition of governments is the legal institution through which the human agents with authority to act on behalf of each state are identified."[63] Similar to recognition of states, recognition of *governments* is typically a result of a decentralized process, whereby each government determines for itself which entities qualify as legitimate governments.[64]

Regime change is intricately linked to the recognition of governments because the recognition of a new entity involves simultaneously the de-recognition of a pre-existing government's claim to being the legitimate agent of the state. This follows the international community's general stance against the re-drawing of existing state borders outside of the de-colonialization process.[65] Regime change is a function of recognition because the legitimate agent of a state can consent to foreign military support, while deriving various financial rewards that can help the recognized entity establish an empirical claim to its territory.

Libya provides an excellent contemporary example. In the wake of civil unrest in Egypt and Tunisia, Libya experienced a civil uprising beginning in February 2011. The movement gained control of Eastern Libya, centered around the city of Benghazi. The anti-Gaddafi rebel group forces organized into a "government" in a matter of weeks, forming the National Transitional Council (NTC).[66] On March 10, 2011, France became the first state to recognize the NTC as the sole representative of Libya. Other states followed soon after, most notably in July 2011, when the U.S. and some 30 other countries officially

---

62   Thomas D. Grant, Book Review, *An Institution Restored? Recognition of Governments: Legal Doctrine and State Practice*, 39 VA. J. INT'L L. 191, 193 (1998).

63   PETERSON, *supra* note 15, at 185; *see also* THE RESTATEMENT (THIRD) OF THE FOREIGN RELATIONS LAW OF THE UNITED STATES § 203, cmt. a (AM. LAW INST. 1987) ("Recognition of a government is formal acknowledgement that a particular regime is the effective government of a state and implies a commitment to treat that regime as the government of that state.").

64   PETERSON, *supra* note 15, at 2.

65   Brilmayer, *supra* note 1, at 193.

66   MARYAM JAMSHIDI, THE FUTURE OF THE ARAB SPRING: CIVIC ENTREPRENEURSHIP IN POLITICS, ART, AND TECHNOLOGY STARTUPS 10–11 (2013).

recognized the NTC as the nation's "legitimate governing authority" at the conclusion of a meeting in Istanbul.

Recognition of the rebel group proved to be more than an intellectual exercise. For one, it allowed billions of dollars in frozen Libyan state assets located
around the world to be released to the country's rebels.[67] Italy led the pack
by opening up a credit line to rebels using Libyan foreign assets as collateral,
transferring $400 million to the rebel group.[68] Then-Secretary of State Hillary
Clinton described the legal significance of U.S. recognition of the rebel group,
publicly stating that "this step on recognition will enable the NTC to access
additional sources of funding[.]"[69] Of course, it was only a few months before
that in February 2011 when then-President Barack Obama signed an executive order freezing a record $30 billion in Libyan assets located in the United
States.[70]

Recognition also aided the rebels in fighting off Gadhafi's army. On March
19, 2011, the United Nations issued a Security Council resolution allowing foreign military intervention, including air strikes by the United States, Britain,
and France.[71] Important for our purpose, foreign recognition of the rebel group
took place while the Gadhafi regime continued to have significant control over
Libyan territory. Indeed, it was not until October 2011 when the empirical control of the Libyan territory actually aligned with the international community's
determination on the legal guardianship of the state.

4   A Constructivist Approach to State Recognition

The story of how rewards configure into the practice of state recognition can
be explained in pure materialistic terms that dominate the liberalist and realist approaches to international relations: states (or state-like entities) act in
strategic ways that maximize their interests, and rewards motivate pleas for
recognition. While insightful in various contexts, the realist and liberalist
approaches offer limited descriptive value in understanding the subject of

---

67   Marc Champion & Joe Parkinson, *U.S. Recognizes Libyan Rebel Group*, WALL ST. J. (July
      16, 2011).
68   Nicole Gaouette & Flavia Krause-Jackson, *Libyan Rebels Get U.S. Recognition Yet Must
      Wait for Cash*, BLOOMBERG (July 15, 2011).
69   Andrew Quinn, *Seeking to Free Funds, U.S. Recognizes Libya rebels*, REUTERS (July 15,
      2011).
70   Helene Cooper, *U.S. Freezes a Record $30 Billion in Libyan Assets*, N.Y. TIMES (Feb. 28,
      2011).
71   JAMSHIDI, *supra* note 66, at 11.

international recognition because both approaches tend to view international actors as inherently pre-social "atomistic egoists" whose interests are formed "prior to social interaction."[72]

Because I am interested in investigating how rules governing international recognition shape the identity and behavior of the relevant actors at play, I approach the subject with a moderate strand of constructivism. While it is beyond the scope of this piece to introduce the theory of constructivism generally or parse out the various permutations of the theory, my goal is to show that a constructivist theoretical approach may augment our understanding of the subject at hand because constructivism treats seriously the idea that the international reality is ideational as well as material.[73]

Constructivism is an ontology emphasizing that "people act toward objects, including other actors, on the basis of the meanings that the objects have for them."[74] This approach does not underplay the reality that actors have needs and interests, but rather focuses on understanding how the needs and interests come to be. Applied to the recognition context, a constructivist approach explains rewards as playing an important role not merely because of its material force but because it influences the social concepts in shaping the identity and behavior of relevant actors. A constructivist does not necessarily obsess over what a state is, but aims to understand the social dynamics and the institutional incentive structures that underlie the behaviors of both "states" and "rebel groups."

Here, it is worth reviewing the general rule—call it international law or not—governing the recognition of states and governments. First, the international community has vigorously stood against border re-drawing outside of the de-colonialization process; and even though there are exceptions, Professor Brilmayer reminds us that viable claims for secession are generally limited to remedy a group's historical title to a particular territory and are unrelated to the ethnic or religious homogeneity of a group.[75] Second, while the

---

72   Christian Reus-Smit, *Constructivism*, in THEORIES OF INTERNATIONAL RELATIONS 193 (Scott Burchill et al., eds., 2005).

73   JOHN GERARD RUGGIE, CONSTRUCTING THE WORLD POLITY: ESSAYS ON INTERNATIONAL INSTITUTIONALISATION 33 (1998).

74   Alexander Wendt, *Anarchy is What States Make of it: The Social Construction of Power Politics*, 46 INT'L ORG. 391, 396–97 (1992).

75   Brilmayer, *supra* note 1; *see also* Lea Brilmayer, *Secession and Self-Determination: One Decade Later*, 25 YALE J. INT'L L. 283, 284 (2000) ("Earlier theorists were incorrect in treating the key determinant to be homogeneity of the conquered people. What matters is not that it is 'a people' who are seeking to be free. What matters is that this group-whether a homogeneous 'people' or not-has a right to a particular parcel of land, a right that was wrongfully taken from them by a powerful neighbor."). More recently, Professor Brilmayer

declaratory theory has had a role in influencing international recognition practice, (or at least been given lip service by states), state practice suggests that the
international community is generally agnostic as to whether the recognized
government actually has empirical claim to an *existing* state.

It is no surprise, then, that various rival entities operating in geopolitically
unstable regions would have an incentive to overthrow existing central governments, who are often no more than groups that control the capital cities,
exercising "only minimal levels of effective domestic sovereignty."[76] In states
like Ethiopia, Zaire (now the Democratic Republic of Congo), and Angola, the
central governments at various times lost control of their territories to rebel
groups, while the international community "always recognized whoever controlled Addis, Kinshasa, and Luanda as the unquestioned leaders of those
territories."[77]

Under this system, rebel group activities also cannot be purely explained
in terms of the desire to form ethnicity-cohesive self-governance structures.
Under the standard account, rebel group identities and interests pre-constitute
the rules laid out by the system. Secessionist movements and insurgents alike
typically narrate their struggle as one of grievance against the central authority
based on ethnic, linguistic, or religious grounds.[78] It is important to recognize, though, that the grievance-based claims may be powerfully shaped by
the motivation of the ruling elite to gain better access to external rewards for
private gain, rather than to provide types of generalized public good typically
associated with functioning states.

Take the case of Africa, where the end of colonialism left the fictional
appearance of states to outsiders in the absence of actual state development
processes experienced elsewhere. In modern Europe, for instance, territorial

---

has articulated multiple ways that groups can frame territorial claims. *See* Lea Brilmayer,
Secession and the Two Types of Territorial Claims, 21 ILSA J. INT'L & COMP. L. 325, 326
(2015) ("First, a territorial claim could take the shape of a generalized right to a territorial
state, as a remedy for past injustices. Theories of this sort have been called 'Remedial
Right Only' theories of secession.... Second, a territorial claim can take the form of an
assertion that the group is currently the correct and legitimate owner of a particular piece
of land.") (internal citation omitted).

76   HERBST, *supra* note 34, at 110.
77   *Id.*
78   This storyline finds political support from the familiar doctrine of the right to self-determination, most famously associated with President Woodrow Wilson: that a group of
people have the right to independently determine "her own political development and
national policy ... under institutions of her own choosing." Woodrow Wilson, President of
the United States of America, President Wilson's Address to Congress, Analyzing German
and Austrian Peace Utterances (Feb. 11, 1918).

conquest was central to the formation of nation states. As Charles Tilly explains, the European state development process was characterized by "a movement toward direct rule that reduced the role of local or regional patrons and places representatives of the nation state in every community, and expansion of popular consultation in the form of elections, plebiscites, and legislatures."[79] Post-colonial Africa, on the other hand, was defined by the decision to retain the boundaries created by the colonialists, even when European colonialism did not actually establish states that "actually sought to rule over all the territories that were indeed said to be theirs."[80] As observed by Professor Herbst, independent Africa thus became a state system with "considerable fictions that were in remarkable contrast to precolonial Africa, where control of almost every square mile of land had to be earned[.]"[81]

In these regions, ethnocentric grievance claims articulated by insurgents are often deeply intertwined with greed-based motives. In the Democratic Republic of Congo, famous for its diamond mines and deadly civil wars, "all the rebellions drew their support predominantly from particular ethnic groups, even if the conflict was resource driven."[82] Ethnicity, in these instances, serves as a sort of "social capital" that rebel group leaders use to increase cohesion and group identity.[83] To a certain extent, this view is backed up by empirical evidence collected by Professor Paul Collier, who famously concluded that "the causes of conflict points to economic factors as the main drivers of conflict."[84]

Of course, we cannot reduce the complexity of group behavior to one of economically-driven causation analysis. A constructivist account should remind us that the narratives deployed by rebel group leaders are often internalized by their followers, while collective group identities are also developed and re-enforced by the devastating ramifications of conflict. As observed by Scott Gates, "[e]ven for the most blatant loot-seeking groups, ethnicity, ideology, and geographical proximity play a direct role in shaping the pattern of compliance and enforcement in a rebel army."[85]

---

79   CHARLES TILLY, COERCION, CAPITAL, AND EUROPEAN STATES 63 (1990).

80   HERBST, *supra* note 34, at 96.

81   *Id.* at 136.

82   PAUL COLLIER ET AL., BREAKING THE CONFLICT TRAP: CIVIL WAR AND DEVELOPMENT POLICY 69 (2003).

83   Scott Gates, *Recruitment and Allegiance: The Microfoundations of Rebellion*, 46 J. CONF. RES. 111, 113 (2002).

84   Paul Collier, *Doing Well out of War: An Economic Perspective, in* GREED AND GRIEVANCE: ECONOMIC AGENDAS IN CIVIL WARS 91, 110 (Mats Berdal & David M. Malone eds., 2000).

85   Gates, *supra* note 83, at 113.

In that sense, there is often a genuine ethnic or religious component to secessionist movements and civil wars. But entirely attributing motives of rebel groups as a struggle to form its own state—with fixation of analyzing civil conflict as a byproduct of intergroup hatred—misses an important piece of the puzzle.[86] Indeed, while civil wars in geopolitically unstable regions are often predicated upon grievance, it can also be driven (at least initially) by an effort for one group to secure rewards that are tied to international recognition, and claim legitimate right "to the full protection offered by the modern understanding of sovereignty."[87]

To be sure, I am not suggesting that there is something inherently pernicious here. The system is in a sense teleological, because the international community must formulate a structure that rations the limited supply of rewards. Achieving statehood serves as a natural guideline. The point is that, while rationing the limited supply of rewards, the international community plays a powerful role in shaping the behaviors of various groups that all too often manifest in the form of corruption, underdevelopment, and violence.

5   Conclusion

Today, statehood is an idea that departs significantly from the conception shared by early political philosophers. States are not always self-constituted, territorially fixed, and mutually exclusive bodies that exist because they perpetuate functioning governments. In certain parts of the world, statehood is legal fiction bestowed upon entities that lack the most basic feature of a sovereign state—physical control over a defined territory.[88] Instead, the international community rations rewards that, to varying degrees, influence the power structure of various groups within the juridical state. It is for this reason that the law of recognition ought to be taken seriously as a causal variable in the vicious cycle of civil wars, corruption, and the collapse of state institutions.

In many regions around the world, rewards are powerful because prolonged poverty, corruption, and underdevelopment have undermined state capacity. This is, of course, no coincidence. The lack of state institutions that can

---

86   It is also worth noting that "[i]f every ethnic, religious or linguistic group claimed statehood, there would be no limit to fragmentation, and peace, security and economic well-being for all would become ever more difficult to achieve." An Agenda for Peace, UN Doc. A/47/277 (1992), para. 17.

87   HERBST, *supra* note 34, at 110.

88   For an excellent commentary of this legal fiction from a state failure perspective, see GIORGETTI, *supra* note 8, at 179.

deliver public goods to the people living within a juridical state sets the stage for ethnic identities to be ideologized. While rebel groups almost always rely on ethnic or religious grievances, economic agenda of rebel group leaders cannot be underestimated. Rewards shape the identity and the narrative on how rebel groups choose to frame their struggles.

A constructivist account of state recognition articulated in this piece fills an inquiry left unanswered by either of the standard accounts to international recognition. This is not to say that the traditional theories have lost their value. The constitutive theory holds descriptive accuracy in diagnosing the importance of recognition in geopolitically unstable regions around the world. But it fails to explain why recognition has such a potent impact, stripped of its metaphysical narrative. Similarly, the declaratory theory shines descriptively in explaining geopolitically stable regions but fails to capture the underlying reality of underdeveloped regions, where the sovereign capacity is partly derived from recognition. More importantly, both theories' agnostic stance on the social construction of group identity tends to underappreciate the institutional incentives manufactured by the system. While conflicts in geopolitically unstable regions are not entirely predicated on rewards, they are powerfully driven by them.

CHAPTER 9

Functional State Recognition and International Economic Law

Kathleen Claussen*

International law does not have a precise vocabulary to talk about the rights and obligations of polities that are not universally recognized as states. The absence is notable when one considers the many entities that fall into this ambiguous and challenging category: "quasi-states". Entities like Taiwan, Kosovo, Transnistria, and others similarly situated all fall into this category: they sometimes act like states, but they are not universally recognized as states, and therefore, they are not afforded privileges reserved for states.

The origin of the term "quasi-state" is not precisely known, but it is the term this chapter will adopt to refer to these complicated entities. Thomas Baty, barrister-at-law, may have been the first to use the term "quasi-states" to refer to partly recognized states in a 1922 article, though he did so with little fanfare and noted the shortcomings of the nomenclature.[1] Seventy years later, Robert Jackson used the term to refer to post-colonial, post-Cold War entities that lacked the "marks and merits of empirical statehood."[2] Quasi-states were not, in Jackson's view, self-standing structures with domestic foundations, but rather territorial jurisdictions "supported from above by international law and material aid—a kind of international safety net."[3]

For more than 20 years, Professor Lea Brilmayer's work has drawn attention to the issues facing quasi-states. Beginning in the early 1990s, Professor Brilmayer provided some of the first analyses in the pre- and post-Yugoslav secession period on the valid bases for secession. In *Secession and Self-Determination:*

---

* Associate Professor, University of Miami School of Law. J.D., Yale Law School. I have benefitted greatly from Professor Brilmayer's work and wise counsel over the last ten years, during which she has held the Howard M. Holtzmann International Law chair at the Yale Law School. It seems fitting that much of the research that led to this project, including personal visits to Transnistria, Kosovo, and South Ossetia, was carried out through the generosity of a Howard M. Holtzmann Dispute Resolution Fellowship I received from the Law School.

1 Thomas Baty, *So-Called "De Facto" Recognition*, 31 YALE L.J. 469, 470 (1922).
2 ROBERT H. JACKSON, QUASI-STATES: SOVEREIGNTY, INTERNATIONAL RELATIONS AND THE THIRD WORLD (Cambridge 1993), 3.
3 JACKSON, 5.

A Territorial Interpretation, she argued that secession is an appropriate remedy for illegal annexation.[4] She anticipated the challenges for the law to accommodating such claims in *International Justice and International Law*.[5] There, she observed that "[b]ecause of its paucity of institutional mechanisms, international law is incapable of recognizing claims of justice and incapable of responding to the needs of history."[6]

Today, quasi-states take on added salience and utility. Quasi-states are not just theoretical constructs as in Baty's article, nor are they merely fledgling polities unable to perform the duties required of states as Jackson may have intended. I use the term "quasi-state" to depict an entity that is not universally considered to be a state, and in some instances, may not be seeking statehood at all, but which operates autonomously or semi-autonomously.[7] These entities typically engage in some foreign relations but not all states consider them to have international legal personality. In the passage of time since the earlier invocations of quasi-states, these entities have become meaningful players on the world stage. One major question about quasi-states has endured: who decides when an entity moves from non-state to quasi-state to state status?

This chapter picks up that story. It argues that the question of "who decides" is evolving most importantly and most noticeably amid the growing industry of international economic law institutions.[8] International economic law serves a gatekeeping function for quasi-states and, in some instances, allows

---

4 Lea Brilmayer, *Secession and Self-Determination: A Territorial Interpretation*, 16 YALE J. INT'L L. 177 (1991).

5 Lea Brilmayer, *International Justice and International Law*, 98 W. VA. L. REV. 611 (1996).

6 *Id.* at 657.

7 Other sources group these differently. Wikipedia, for example, refers to U.N. member states not recognized by at least one U.N. member: Armenia, the People's Republic of China, the Republic of Cyprus, the State of Israel, the Democratic People's Republic of Korea, and the Republic of Korea; Non-U.N. member states recognized by at least one U.N. member: Abkhazia, Taiwan, Kosovo, the Turkish Republic of Northern Cyprus, State of Palestine, Sahrawi Arab Democratic Republic (Western Sahara), and South Ossetia; Non-U.N. member states recognized only by non-U.N. members: Nagorno-Karabakh, and Pridnestrovian Moldavian Republic (Transnistria); Non-U.N. member states not recognized by any state: Somaliland. Wikipedia, *List of states with limited recognition*, https://en.wikipedia.org/wiki/List_of_states_with_limited_recognition.

8 For a discussion of the rise of international economic institutions in the Bretton Woods era, *see* LISA L. MARTIN, INTERNATIONAL ECONOMIC INSTITUTIONS (Oxford 2008). *See also* M.A.G. VAN MEERHAEGHE, A HANDBOOK OF INTERNATIONAL ECONOMIC INSTITUTIONS (Springer 1980); Kyle Bagwell and Robert W. Staiger, *Domestic Policies, National Sovereignty, and International Economic Institutions*, 116 Q.J. OF ECON. 519 (2001); Stephen A. Silard, *International Economic Institutions: The Challenge of Coordination*, 4 AMER. U. INT'L L. REV. 67 (2011).

them to make meaningful contributions to international law despite not being recognized. The chapter examines how quasi-states participate distinctively in international economic institutions and dispute settlement mechanisms— two additional topics on which Professor Brilmayer is expert. In brief, the behavior of these semi-autonomous regions in the international economic regime is influencing the way we think about states—what constitutes a state, what are the contours of entities that call themselves states, *etc.* The chapter considers the intersection of theories on statehood with new and emerging constructs of development and dispute settlement. I ask how international economic law is having an impact on how we conceptualize legal personality[9] and how the participation of these quasi-states has an impact on international economic law and institutions.

The lesson of this study is that sovereignty is increasingly situated in the eye of the beholder, or rather, in the practice of any given actor. The legal exercise of state recognition—historically, a bilateral exchange—now includes new interactions with international economic institutions. The innovations and multiple points of participation of international economic law have, in effect, widened the lens of "subjects" in international law. I reach this conclusion on the basis of a diverse showing among the quasi-states examined here. Although they have distinct historical experiences, these quasi-states *sometimes* gain access to international economic institutions. In other instances they do not, or they may not try. But this capacity to access in itself tells us something about international economic law's unique properties and contributions to the debates on recognition.

For the quasi-state, statehood is no longer a binary qualification (*i.e.*, you have it or you do not), or a judicially confirmed status. Rather, it is a collection of isolated types of engagement. In some instances, the quasi-state is granted access and treated as a state; in other instances, it is not. This mode of access and of recognition does not locate a clear normative foundation. Rather, the law on recognition is evolving. No longer are distinct categories of status required. International law is adapting and becoming more malleable in its accommodation of alternative "lifestyles" as reflected in the activity of international economic institutions.

---

9   Needless to say, there are other developments in the world that are also raising questions about the political dimensions of recognition and statehood. *See, e.g.*, Paul Eden, *Palestinian Statehood: Trapped Between Rhetoric and Realpolitik*, 62 INT'L & COMP. L.Q. 225 (2013). This chapter is not intended to cover the full range of recognition-relevant international legal and political developments.

My purpose in focusing on the international economic sphere is to show that this dynamic area of lawmaking is exceptional in the way it lends itself to making these accommodations more than other areas of law. The multiple entry points of international economic law facilitate the participation of quasi-states and states alike. The plurivalent nature of international economic law dispute settlement and the other access mechanisms created by international economic law have elevated the issue of international organizational membership. Given the diversity in the criteria for statehood, a variety of entities have sought an enhanced status through these channels.

The first Part of this chapter describes the entities under study here. It also explains what is meant by the universe of international economic law and lays out the puzzle: quasi-states are often highly underdeveloped or post-conflict areas in need of foreign investment to strengthen their economic status but the international economic regime is so state-centric—can they benefit?

The second Part turns to the selected case studies and presents the spectrum of activity by quasi-states in the regime. The data show that the status of many quasi-states prohibits them from fully engaging in international law and organizations, prompting some of them to develop creative ways to participate where they can: in international economic institutions. By examining these creative ways, we learn more about these entities, the international community's treatment of them, and the influence and contours of the framework. There is a spectrum of engagement across these entities that purport to operate as states but that are limited by their quasi-state status. Although the international economic law regime offers some flexibility to accommodate non-traditional actors, activities and attempts by quasi-states also indicate the clear limitations on access to and the excludability of the framework.

Finally, I conjecture that the landscape of state recognition is changing as a result of these quasi-states posturing or "impostoring." I outline the connective tissue among the institutions and entities to identify trends in international economic law's contribution to theories on that which constitutes a "state". Driven by a lack of prohibition on their participation, the practice of quasi-states contributes to the evolution of their status. By accommodating quasi-states' state-like behavior, international economic law and its proliferation of institutions blur the lines.

1   Introducing Quasi-States

In 1739, Jacques de Vaucanson created *le Canard Digérateur*, or the Digesting Duck, which was a mechanical duck that looked like it could eat, quack, and

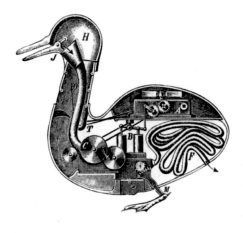

FIGURE 9.1
Vaucanson's Digesting Duck
SOURCE: ALFRED CHAPUIS AND
EDOUARD GELIS, LE MONDE DES
AUTOMATES, 2:151 (1928)

digest kernels of grain.[10] Some sources point to the Digesting Duck as the origin of the phrase "if it looks like a duck, talks like a duck, walks like a duck, it must be a duck."[11] As it turns out, Vaucanson's duck could not walk, talk, or digest—Vaucanson had pre-stored digestive waste inside the machine,[12] so there was likely no doubt that his mechanical novelty was not, in fact, a duck. The idiom outlived the bird.[13]

Today, quasi-states encroach on their own ducks—states. But they remain distinct insofar as they are not seen as states by a significant part of the international community. They are not universally "recognized" as states, despite that, as shown below, they may talk, walk, and look like states to many eyes.

Eight quasi-states make up the focus of this study: Hong Kong, Kosovo, Northern Cyprus, Palestine, Somaliland, South Ossetia, Taiwan, and Transnistria.[14] These eight represent a range of experiences and practices—

---

10   Jacques Vaucanson, "Letter to the Abbé Desfontaines" (1742, *Le Mecanisme du fluteur automate*). *See also* Jessica Riskin, *The Defecating Duck, or, the Ambiguous Origins of Artificial Life*, 29 CRITICAL INQUIRY 599 (2003); VICTORIA DE RIJKE, DUCK (Reaktion Books 2008).

11   Brian Edwards, *Did You Know that the Phrase "If it Looks like a Duck ...,"* THE MIRROR, February 26, 2015, available at http://www.mirror.co.uk/usvsth3m/you-know-phrase-if-looks-5235884. Others point to the period of McCarthyism for the origin of the phrase. DE RIJKE, 124.

12   *See, e.g.*, DE RIJKE, 117; Edwards, 1.

13   Fire destroyed the duck. Edwards, 1.

14   Since this chapter was originally drafted, the Russian involvement in Crimea, Ukraine has also led to significant developments in international economic law as this involvement constituted the basis for a number of disputes, particularly investment disputes at the International Centre for Settlement of Investment Disputes (ICSID) and the Permanent Court of Arbitration (PCA). These cases, like others featured in this chapter, implicate

some with greater success than others in pursuing participation in the international economic regime. Each quasi-state has a distinct history and status on the world stage. Whereas Kosovo, Palestine, Somaliland, and Taiwan seek statehood, Hong Kong does not, and Northern Cyprus, South Ossetia, Transnisitria fall somewhere in between—whether they want independence or to join another state varies, but they share a unique, delicate status and, in some cases, a large percentage of their population is at a minimum seeking an alternative position from the *status quo*. They have different economic statures and varied political histories. Despite these important differences, their common unrecognized status is instructive.

Left out from the focus of this study are other quasi-states that fall close to those named above: Abkhazia, Western Sahara, Nagorno-Karabakh, and Macao, for example. I will refer to several of these in passing.

2   The State of States: a Brief Overview of Recognition Law

The literature on state recognition is vast and exceeds the scope of this chapter.[15] International law draws on a multitude of concepts to speak to the ability of a geopolitical entity to engage in official relations with others, and be recognized as a state. The terms "international legal personality" or "international legal capacity" are frequently employed. Interestingly, the word "personality" is derived from Latin meaning "mask" and was used to refer to masks worn by actors.[16] As this chapter discusses, quasi-states, at the juncture of political and legal, and their behaviour have only imbued the terminology with greater normative value and epitomized the mask concept. Whatever its label, fully recognized statehood is instilled with a deeper meaning than a simple ability to engage in international relations. The dynamic evolution of sovereignty

---

questions of state responsibility and statehood. *See, e.g.*, Alison Ross, *PCA tribunals to split Crimea-related claims*, GLOBAL ARBITRATION REVIEW (Jan. 7, 2016) (describing at least five investment dispute tribunals constituted to hear claims involving Crimea). Thus, this study may shed light on what to expect for Crimea's future and likewise what experiences of other disputed territories may mean for the Crimean economic disputes.

15   *See, e.g.*, JAMES R. CRAWFORD, THE CREATION OF STATES IN INTERNATIONAL LAW, 12–26 (Oxford 2007); SIR HERSCH LAUTERPACHT, RECOGNITION IN INTERNATIONAL LAW (Cambridge 1947); THOMAS D. GRANT, THE RECOGNITION OF STATES: LAW AND PRACTICE IN DEBATE AND EVOLUTION (Greenwood 1999); Stefan Talmon, *The Constitutive Versus the Declaratory Theory of Recognition: Tertium Non Datur?*, 75 BRIT. YB OF INT'L L. 101 (2005); Lea Brilmayer, *Secession and the Two Types of Territorial Claims*, 21 ILSA: J. INT'L AND COMP. L. 325 (2015).

16   Jan Klabbers, *The Concept of Legal Personality*, 11 IUS GENTIUM 35 (2005).

in the post-Cold War era has opened the door to creative grounds for legal personality that expand and contract in different institutional environments.

The international legal community plays a significant role in the dynamism. Academics seeking to explain the developments on the ground by such entities have struggled to keep up. Scholars have made attempts to realign the existing legal conversation about recognition with the reality of the landscape.[17] International courts and tribunals have complicated the state of the law to an even greater degree.[18] No theory of recognition has extinguished its competition because none has gained universal acceptance.[19] Still, states dominate. Membership in the international community of states is important. Thus, although the qualities of statehood may be circumstantial,[20] communities continue to seek recognition. Without any clear legal path, quasi-states have taken advantage of the international economic framework to achieve coveted state status.

Despite the ebbing and flowing of the legal tide on recognition theory, "recognition" still is used to define states as compared to non-states. It carries with it convictions about the rights and obligations on the parts of the grantor and receiver according to a prescribed set of norms that has developed through official statements and through practice. One of those convictions might involve the capacity to become a member of certain organizations, but that is not necessarily assumed.

Operating along the continuum between politics and law, the maintenance of international legal personality and state recognition relates to a process

17   See Patrick Capps, *Lauterpacht's Method*, 2012 BRIT. YB INT'L L. (discussing Lauterpacht's duty of recognition—an attempt to create a stable and predictable structure). *See also* MARTTI KOSKENNIEMI, THE GENTLE CIVILIZER OF NATIONS: THE RISE AND FALL OF INTERNATIONAL LAW (1870–1960) (2002), 363 (discussing the reification of political judgment and state-centered positivism). *See generally* MIKULAS FABRY, RECOGNIZING STATES (Oxford 2010).

18   *E.g.*, Western Sahara, Advisory Opinion, 1975 ICJ Rep. 12 (Oct. 16); Legal Consequences of the Construction of a Wall in the Occupied Palestinian Territory, Advisory Opinion, 2004 ICJ Rep. 136 (July 9); Accordance with International Law of the Unilateral Declaration of Independence in Respect of Kosovo, Advisory Opinion, 2010 ICJ No. 141 (July 22). Legal Consequences for States of the Continued Presence of South Africa in Namibia (South West Africa) Notwithstanding Security Council Resolution 276 (1970), Advisory Opinion, 1971 ICJ Rep. 16 (June 21).

19   William Worster, *Law, Politics, and the Conception of the State in State Recognition Theory*, 27 B.U. INT'L L.J. 115 (2009).

20   James Crawford has written that "special cases" in the field of statehood recognition reflects the principle that "the status of an entity is to be determined not by reference to any overall concept but to the specific circumstances and constituent instruments." CRAWFORD, 197.

of responding to changes within the world community with which legal consequences are associated.[21] In this sense, recognition is not a single event, but rather constantly ongoing, reflective of many types of changes. In many respects, international law has not crystallized on this topic, as is borne out in this study. Put differently, recognition remains political;[22] this chapter does not intend to argue otherwise. Though the state community has developed legal criteria that lend legitimacy to acts of recognition, political overtones largely obscure the application of those criteria. Rather what the chapter seeks to add is that quasi-states are able to game their recognition more today through the international economic law regime than ever before.

At least one state (New Zealand) has announced a policy of no longer making formal declarations about recognition.[23] Another has offered to provide its recognition for a fee: 70 million USD.[24] The commodification of recognition reflects its both political and increasingly economic nature.[25] More states treat recognition less of a status decision and more of a practical form of engagement, perhaps in part to avoid the appearance of being bound to a particular decision in difficult cases. In this context, *practices* such as implied recognition, tacitly permitting membership in international organizations, or engaging in international dispute settlement take on added value.[26]

---

21   See, for related definitions, W. Michael Reisman & Eisuke Suzuki, *Recognition and Social Change in Internatonal Law: A Prologue for Decisionmaking, in* TOWARD WORLD ORDER AND HUMAN DIGNITY: ESSAYS IN HONOR OF MYRES S. MCDOUGAL 403, 424 (W. Michael Reisman & Burns H. Weston eds., 1976).

22   Robert D. Sloane, *The Changing Face of Recognition in International Law: A Case Study of Tibet*, 16 EMORY INT'L L.J. 107 (2002).

23   New Zealand Ministry of Foreign Affairs and Trade, *Post-Election Brief* (November 2008), 22.

24   Ellen Barry, *Abkhazia Is Recognized—by Nauru*, N.Y. TIMES, Dec. 15, 2009; *Nauru agrees to recognise rogue republics for $70m.*, NEW ZEALAND HERALD, December 19, 2009.

25   The commodification effect is a by-product of political competition in some cases. *See* Grant Wyeth, *The Sovereign Recognition Game: Has Nauru Overplayed Its Hand?*, The Diplomat, May 17, 2017 (discussing the truce reached between China and Taiwan in their "attempts to lobby for international recognition" after the foreign minister of Taiwan was forced to resign in 2008 after he "wasted US$30 million in a failed attempt" to get Papua New Guinea to recognize Taiwan). Another economic effect: withholding government funds from support of quasi-states. *See, e.g.*, The Consolidated Appropriations Act, 2017, Pub. L. No. 115-31, May 5, 2017 (prohibiting the United States from providing financial assistance to governments that support the independence of Abkhazia and South Ossetia); Zviad Adzinbaia, *US Congress Conditions Foreign Aid on Georgia*, THE CLARION, May 23, 2017.

26   *See* Stefan Talmon, *New Zealand's Policy of Implied Recognition of States: One Step Ahead or Falling Behind*, 2009 NZ Y.B. INT'L L. 1.

Today, the scope of entities with international legal personality has broadened to include regional organizations, customs and fishing territories, and in some cases sub-state entities especially in international economic law. Sub-state entities that have concluded treaties include: Swiss Cantons, German and Austrian Länder, Hong Kong, Macau, Bermuda, Jersey, The Cook Islands, New Caledonia, Quebec, Puerto Rico, Tatarstan, and Flanders.[27] Their ability to conclude treaties is largely a function of whether they have been authorized to do so. Oliver Lissitzyn explains that international law imposes two prerequisites on sub-state entity treaty-making: (1) the consent of the state responsible for the sub-state actor; and (2) the willingness of the sub-state actor's treaty partners to regard it as capable of entering into treaties.[28] Applied to quasi-states, the first prerequisite is challenging as, in several of these cases, the "mother state" no longer has any practical or functional control of the activities of the quasi-state. The second, then, becomes the critical prerequisite, linked with the acknowledgment of the quasi-state as having treaty-making capacity, if not its recognition as a state.

These developments lend credence to the argument that international legal personality may be a fleeting and outdated concept, especially as entities such as quasi-states tend to act as though they have capacity to enter into international legal relations regardless of whether others believe them to have been endowed with international legal personality. Quasi-states will engage with any institutions or states that will entertain such engagement. Where possible, quasi-states simply act, testing the limits of their capacity.

Thus, it is futile to ask whether a state or entity purporting to be a state has legal personality in the abstract.[29] Instead, one should ask what specific rights,

---

27   For a discussion on the law of treaties, including in respect of sub-state entities, see
      Anthony Aust, Modern Treaty Law and Practice (Cambridge University
      Press 2013). In 1988, Austria amended its constitution to authorize Austrian Länder to
      conclude international treaties with neighboring states and their constituent parts with
      respect to matters falling within the Land's exclusive competence. The same is true under
      the German constitution. Often, however, the authorization will only apply to a single
      agreement like in the cases of Quebec (with the US regarding pensions) and Puerto Rico
      (to join the Caribbean Development Bank).
28   Oliver J. Lissitzyn, Territorial Entities in the Law of Treaties, III Recueil des Cours
      66–71 (1968). See also Report of the International Law Commission on the Work of Its
      Eighteenth Session, (draft) art. 5.2, [1966] 2 Y.B. Int'l L. Comm'n 172, 191, U.N. Doc. A/CN.4/
      ser.A/1966/Add.1 (providing that "States members of a federal union may possess a
      capacity to conclude treaties if such capacity is admitted by the federal constitution and
      within the limits there laid down.").
29   Peter Malanczuk, Akehurst's Modern Introduction to International
      Law (7th Ed., Routledge 1997), 91–108 (speaking of the legal personality of international
      organizations).

duties, and powers it exercises. In what fora does it participate and in what capacity is it viewed in those fora, for example? Those practices continue to highlight the variations in gatekeeping and decision-making in the recognition process. As limited-recognition entities race to accede to those treaties and institutions that do not require affirmation from other states party, who decides which entities are allowed in and which are kept out?

3   The International Economic Law Regime and Its Accessibility

International economic law encompasses a range of activities by states and private actors, and a growing number of institutions to facilitate those activities. In this study, I focus on international investment law and on international trade law. Together with development and finance, investment and trade dominate among both the scholarship and the contributions of states to the development of international law in connection with the world economy. One need not point out that, as a newly formed entity seeks to establish its independence or existence, economic sovereignty and access to scarce resources become critical components to progress. To achieve this, entities often pursue substantial foreign investment. Supporters of the international economic regime applaud what they consider to be a unique balance of power protected by the legal framework for investment, and likewise for trade.[30] According to this view, the instruments and institutions that comprise the regime have evolved to create a level playing field among states. In this often bilateral environment, there is less chance of the system being commandeered or tied to a particular political posture.

These two notions, that the international economic framework is universal in scope and that it has an equalizing effect on power relations, contribute to a third: that the regime is a global public good. Central to our understanding of a global public good is answering the question: who is accessing and using the good? A global public good demands a recipient, a client, a consumer. To conceive of the regime as a global public good requires that the framework be non-excludable, such that one cannot effectively be prevented from consuming it, and non-rival, meaning that consumption of the good by one does not

---

30   *See generally* N.J. Schrijver, *A Multilateral Investment Agreement From a North-South Perspective, in* MULTILATERAL REGULATION OF Investment 17 (E.C. Nieuwenhuys & M.M.T.A. Brus eds., E.M. Meijers Inst. & Kluwer L. Int'l 2001) (observing that BITs have become vehicles for promoting and protecting foreign investment).

reduce the quantity available to others.[31] Access is the keystone of this claim. Contrary to the claim that the international economic law regime is a global public good, the evidence described below makes clear that there are barriers to access. Rather than a global public good, the international economic law framework is more of a limited club good.

Despite the mixed data regarding the economic advantages of participating in the regime,[32] many quasi-states nevertheless seek to engage. Particularly given that risks to an investment are often higher in quasi-states than elsewhere, concluding agreements that protect investors from those risks can further support the quasi-states' economic self-sufficiency, but it is not only economic leverage that many quasi-states seek. The data below show how the battle for recognition is playing out in the international economic regime as quasi-states take advantage of the unique features of the regime.

•••

The international economic law framework, as I refer to it, consists of a network of institutions that are focused on international economic engagement.[33] As noted above, these institutions carry out a wide range of activity in the areas of trade, foreign direct investment, sanctions, economic integration and development, business regulation and taxation, intellectual property, and issues related to the transnational movement and regulation of goods, services, labor, and capital. Some institutions are founded on agreements between states that facilitate cross-border exchange in these areas; others are international organizations with state members. Within this framework, participants have multiple opportunities for states to engage in dialogue, to resolve disputes with other entities, to assume positions of leadership, and to contribute to the development of international law. In so doing, they reify the framework and elaborate its contours.

In light of these interlocking elements, participants in the framework wield considerable authority and potential power. Thus, from the perspective of these limited recognition entities, membership and participation in these

---

31 *See, e.g.*, Bernali Choudhury, *International Investment Law as a Global Public Good*, 17 LEWIS & CLARK L. REV. 481 (2013) (discussing the non-rivalrous and non-excludable nature of a global public good).

32 *See, e.g.*, Jason Yackee, *Do Bilateral Investment Treaties Promote Foreign Direct Investment? Some Hints from Alternative Evidence*, 51 VA. J. INT'L L. 397 (2010).

33 For a detailed analysis regarding the scope of international economic law as a field and term, see Steve Charnovitz, *What Is International Economic Law*, 14 J. INT'L ECON. L. 3 (2011).

institutions is an easy choice. Their rationale relates again to Vaucanson's duck: if an entity looks like a state, acts like a state, and sounds like a state, there comes a point when it may become difficult to think of it as anything other than a state. Indeed, through these mechanisms, economically powerful states are engaging less economically powerful states *and* other entities—and not necessarily to the latter's benefit. Nevertheless, this engagement makes the international economic framework a critical setting for the evolution of international recognition theories.

I turn first to the "how"—the entry points. Two critical points of entry are the subject of this study. The first is state-to-state agreements. Bilateral investment treaties (BITS), free trade agreements (FTAS), and other economic arrangements of that sort remain at the forefront of the sources of international economic law. With respect to quasi-states, they have used BITS as a way to insert themselves into the international economic law realm. BITS enable this participation especially through their bilateralism.[34] Under the Vienna Convention on the Law of Treaties (VCLT) and the Vienna Convention on the Law of Treaties Between States and International Organizations, only states and international organizations can be parties to treaties; however, Article 3 of the VCLT affirms the legal force of other international agreements (non-"treaties") that do not fall within the Convention's scope. The *travaux preparatoires* for the VCLT indicate that the drafters did not intend to reject the concept that other subjects of international law may have the capacity to conclude treaties.[35] Thus, regardless of entity status, treaties act as points of entry. Easily negotiable instruments serve quasi-states well. Moreover, states enter into contracts with non-states as a matter of course.[36]

The second point of entry in this study is the collection of international organizations serving states in the global economy. As for access to these organizations, their founding instruments provide mechanisms for members

---

34   SORNARAJAH, 57.

35   *See* Shabtai Rosenne, *The Temporal Application of the Vienna Convention on the Law of Treaties*, 4 CORNELL J. INT'L L. 8, fn. 25 (1970). Indeed, the U.N. Codification Division's Handbook on Final Clauses sets out the "Vienna formula" according to which participation in a treaty is extended to "Member States of the United Nations, Parties to the Statute of the International Court of Justice and States Members of specialized agencies or, in certain cases,... any other State invited by the General Assembly to become a party." This formula was created to avoid disputes over whether certain entities were to be recognized as states. U.N. Handbook on Final Clauses, https://treaties.un.org/pages/Resource .aspx?path=Publication/FC/Page1_en.xml.

36   Query whether concluding an agreement with a quasi-state poses so much of a problem for universally recognized states; depending on the language or the process for entry into force, the agreement may not even be seen as a treaty.

to join. For example, Article 67 of the International Centre for Settlement of Investment Disputes (ICSID) Convention provides "This Convention shall be open for signature on behalf of states members of the Bank. It shall also be open for signature on behalf of any other state which is a party to the Statute of the International Court of Justice and which the Administrative Council, by a vote of two-thirds of its members, shall have invited to sign the Convention."[37] The Permanent Court of Arbitration (PCA) founding convention speaks of "Powers"—Signatory and non-Signatory.[38] The General Agreement on Tariffs and Trade (GATT) is open to any "government not party to [the GATT] or a government acting on behalf of a separate customs territory possessing full autonomy in the conduct of its external commercial relations and of the other matters provided for in this Agreement."[39] The membership of the European Union (EU) in the World Trade Organization (WTO) makes clear that the WTO is not limited to traditional state members alone. Below, I detail the practices of other organizations in respect of the specific quasi-states under study here. The next Part describes how individual quasi-states have taken up these opportunities to entrench their "de facto statehood."

4   Case Studies

In this Part, I describe the spectrum of quasi-state engagement in the international economic law regime, focusing on the eight selected for this chapter. These quasi-states display a range from high levels of engagement to low levels. Next, I explore the causes of these degrees of engagement. Finally, I turn to their implications. My argument is that these entities, building off a threshold level of recognition, are able to bootstrap their way to higher levels of engagement. There may not be a critical pathway—that is, a single path that a quasi-state must take to achieve success in engaging in the international economic framework, but there is a phenomenon underlying quasi-state activity in this area.

     The spectrum is obvious: some quasi-states such as Kosovo and Hong Kong are wholly or nearly wholly participant in the framework through the signing and ratifying of BITs and entry into force of FTAs, or the enactment of legislation with BIT protection, as well as through the participation in intergovernmental trade and investment bodies and dispute settlement within those bodies.

---

37   *See, e.g.*, 1899 Convention for the Pacific Settlement of International Disputes, Article 59.
38   Convention for the Pacific Settlement of International Disputes, July 29, 1899, 32 Stat. 1779, 187 Consol. TS 410, as amended, Oct. 18, 1907, 36 Stat. 2199, 205 Consol. TS 233.
39   General Agreement on Tariffs and Trade, Article XXXII.

Others have adopted domestic legislation protecting foreign investment, in essence replicating the guarantees found in most BITs, and may have some BITs with limited reach. These middle-of-the-road quasi-states contribute to the development of international economic law nonetheless through their domestic provisions and engage through their presence in organizations. Some provide investors with recourse to international dispute resolution fora. And then there are disengaged quasi-states with very limited legal protections for foreign investments or membership in relevant institutions. These quasi-states are not participating in the transnational framework through legal means though some have made informal contributions by trying to pursue some foreign direct investment.

4.1   *Kosovo*

The most integrated into the international economic law regime of the quasi-states that comprise this study is Kosovo. 110 out of 193 United Nations (UN/U.N.) member states recognize Kosovo as a state.[40] This number puts Kosovo squarely in the quasi-state category—it is not universally recognized as a state, but some, in fact many, states consider it to be one. It also makes Kosovo a prime candidate for study. As a test case, Kosovo demonstrates how quasi-states with some threshold level of baseline international political support or recognition can use international economic law institutions and mechanisms to push up their recognition numbers.

Before any state recognized Kosovo as a state, the Kosovar government established in 2005 a domestic law on foreign investment which provides substantive protections akin to those in a BIT. The principal purpose of the Kosovar law is to promote and encourage foreign investment. The law states that through these guarantees for foreign investors, it will "increase the predictability, stability, and transparency" of Kosovo's legal framework.[41] The fundamental rights and guarantees in the law include the accordance of fair and equitable treatment to foreign investors and their investments; full and constant protection and security; no less favorable treatment than the treatment accorded to any domestic investor; no expropriation of an investment unless certain obligations are fulfilled. The law also allows for arbitration at ICSID, the International Chamber of Commerce (ICC), or under the United Nations Commission on International Trade Law Rules in case of dispute.

The Republic of Kosovo filed an application for admission to membership in the International Monetary Fund (IMF) on July 10, 2008. At that time, only

---

40   Who Recognized Kosova as an Independent State? http://www.kosovothanksyou.com/.
41   Law No. 02/L-33 on Foreign Investment, Article 1.2, available at http://www.assembly
      -kosova.org/common/docs/ligjet/2005_02-L33_en.pdf.

43 U.N. member states recognized Kosovo as a state. In the context of Kosovo's application, the IMF determined that Kosovo had seceded from Serbia as a new independent state and that Serbia is the continuing state. Accordingly, the IMF stated that Serbia continues its membership in the IMF and retains its quota in the Fund, and all assets in, and liabilities to, the IMF. While affirming Serbia's membership, the Fund also accepted Kosovo's application despite the limited international recognition and the fact, that in the eyes of some other Fund members, Kosovo was not a state. The Articles of Agreement of the International Monetary Fund limit membership to "countries".[42] Kosovo became a member on June 29, 2009. By that time, another 17 states recognized Kosovo as a state.

In 2010, Kosovo concluded its first BIT with Austria. Later that year, it concluded a second with Belgium and Luxembourg. Both BITs were signed without prejudice "to positions on status," consistent with U.N. Security Council Resolution 1244.[43] The Ministry of Foreign Affairs of Kosovo reports eight additional bilateral agreements regarding investment promotion and protection: with the United States, Turkey,[44] Albania,[45] Macedonia, Croatia, Montenegro, Kuwait and Qatar.[46] Further, the EU has taken the view that a BIT concluded between the Czech Republic and the former Yugoslavia and a BIT concluded between France and the former Yugoslavia are in effect for Kosovo.[47] Kosovo became a member of ICSID in February 2011. By then, 75 states recognized Kosovo as a state.[48]

---

42   International Monetary Fund, Articles of Agreement, Art. 2, available at https://www.imf
      .org/external/pubs/ft/aa/index.htm#art2.

43   Interestingly, UNCTAD does not track Kosovar BITs, but it does track BITs of certain other
      non-UN members.

44   Republic of Kosovo, Ministry of Trade and Industry, An Agreement on Investment
      Promotion and Protection has been signed between Turkey and Kosovo, http://www
      .mti-ks.org/en-us/Minister's-Diary/An-Agreement-on-Investment-Promotion-and-Protection
      -has-been-signed-between-Turkey-and-Kosovo-2100-2100.

45   Invest in Albania, Trade and Economic Cooperation Agreements, http://invest-in
      -albania.org/trade-agreements/.

46   Ministry of Foreign Affairs, International Agreements, http://www.mfa-ks.net/?page=2,72;
      Kosovo Investment and Enterprise Support Agency, Legislation and Agreements, http://
      www.invest-ks.org/en/Legislation-and-Agreements.

47   List of the bilateral investment agreements referred to in Article 4(1) of Regulation
      (EU) No 1219/2012 of the European Parliament and of the Council of December 12, 2012,
      establishing transitional arrangements for bilateral investment agreements between
      Member States and third countries, available at http://eur-lex.europa.eu/legal-content/
      EN/TXT/?uri=CELEX:52014XC0605(01)#ntr3-C_2014169EN.01000101-E0003.

48   David Lidington, then Minister for Europe in the UK, noted in 2013 that recognition
      by states such as Guyana, Tanzania, and Yemen in 2013 was particularly noteworthy

Although Kosovo is not a member of the WTO, Kosovo participates in the Central European Free Trade Agreement (CEFTA). It joined the CEFTA in 2007, but the party to the Agreement as indicated in its accession instrument is not the government of Kosovo. Rather, it is the United Nations Mission in Kosovo.[49] This accession suggests the evolving views as to which entity—the UN administration or the Kosovar government (or something else still such as Serbia)—has the authority to enter into international agreements that are binding on the territory commonly accepted to be Kosovo.

Already under the few investment arrangements in place, interesting legal battles involving Kosovo have begun in the dispute settlement context where some of these complicated questions may be adjudicated. On June 4, 2015, a German telecom corporation, Axos, filed a notice of arbitration with ICSID against Kosovo. Axos brought its claim under the Germany-Yugoslavia BIT (1989), to which it argues Kosovo is bound by the laws of state succession. The case concerns the privatization of Kosovo's post and telecommunications company, PTK.[50] A consortium including Axos won a tender to buy 75 percent of PTK's shares in 2013 for $382 million. The Axos consortium was due to provide 3G mobile services in Kosovo for the first time as part of the privatisation deal. Media sources reported that the Kosovar government pulled out of the deal at the end of that year, having failed to drum up enough parliamentary support. Instead, in mid-2014, PTK entered into a contract with Alcatel-Lucent and Nokia Siemens Network Services to develop a 4G network.[51] The ICSID tribunal concluded in May 2018 that it did not have jurisdiction over the dispute because the claimants had not made a qualifying investment.[52]

Also in late October 2015, a Serbian state-run skiing company announced that it intends to bring an investment claim against Kosovo for expropriating a

---

to get over half U.N. member states. David Lidington, *Kosovo wins recognition from over half United Nations states*, Foreign and Commonwealth Office blog, June 21, 2013, available at http://blogs.fco.gov.uk/davidlidington/2013/06/21/kosovo-wins-recognition-from-over-half-united-nations-states/.

49   The accession note indicates that UNMIK signed pursuant to Security Council Resolution 1244, but it remains unclear as to what about Resolution 1244 gives UNMIK international legal personality or the capacity to enter international agreements such as CEFTA. See CEFTA Secretariat, http://www.cefta.int/legal-texts. *See also* UN Security Council Resolution 1244, June 10, 1999.

50   Kyriaki Karadelis, *Kosovo faces first ICSID claim*, GLOBAL ARBITRATION REVIEW, June 8, 2015.

51   *Id.*

52   ACP Axos Capital GmbH v. Republic of Kosovo (ICSID Case No. ARB/15/22), Award, May 3, 2018.

popular ski resort.[53] The case is expected to be brought to and administered by
the ICC under the Kosovar investment law. This choice is highly curious given
that Serbia sees Kosovo as a province of Serbia, albeit with some autonomy. By
bringing a claim under a law passed by the Kosovar governing entities, Serbia
may be seen as taking a significant step in its recognition.

Another case commenced against Kosovo in summer 2017. An arbitral
tribunal was constituted on November 20, 2017 at ICSID. The case relates to
the privatization process of the Grand Hotel Pristina, which was sold to a
Serbian entity in 2005 before controversy regarding the sale and subsequent
sales ensued.[54]

Thus, over the course of about 10 years, Kosovo rocketed from having no
state recognize its independence to having 110 U.N. members recognize it as
a state. After it achieved a critical mass of recognitions, it was able to become
a member of the IMF and World Bank, and of the PCA,[55] further enhancing
its presence on the world stage. Although it is difficult to identify any clear
causality between its membership, treaty-making, and its recognition, the
parallel growth pattern is clear. Now, several years after joining ICSID, Kosovo
faces multiple complaints in the international investment arena in which it
will be treated as a state respondent, demonstrating that joining international
economic institutions has its costs, as well as its benefits.

4.2   Hong Kong

A second strong example demonstrating the interconnectedness of
international economic presence and international legal personality is that of
Hong Kong, which, with its own unique history, is challenging as a case study
for identifying a pattern or causality in that interaction.

Hong Kong became the Hong Kong Special Administrative Region (HKSAR)
of the People's Republic of China (PRC) on July 1, 1997. The Basic Law of
the HKSAR, a sort of constitution for the autonomous region, provides that
the HKSAR will "exercise a high degree of autonomy and enjoy executive,

53   Lacey Young, *Ski resort dispute adds frost to Serbia-Kosovo relations*, GLOBAL ARBITRATION
      REVIEW, October 22, 2015.

54   *Mabco Constructions SA v. Republic of Kosovo* (ICSID Case No. ARB/17/25). Zoe Williams,
      *Tribunal for Swiss investor claim against Kosovo is finalized, with George Bermann selected
      to chair the proceedings*, Investment Arbitration Reporter (Nov. 21, 2017). This proceeding
      was stayed in March 2018 for non-payment of the required advances.

55   New PCA Member State: Kosovo (June 14, 2016), https://pca-cpa.org/en/news/
      new-pca-member-state-kosovo/.

legislative and independent judicial power."[56] Moreover, it provides, in Article 151, that the HKSAR "may on its own, using the name 'Hong Kong, China', maintain and develop relations and conclude and implement agreements with foreign states and regions and relevant international organizations in the appropriate fields, including the economic, trade, financial and monetary, shipping, communications, tourism, cultural and sports fields."

Interestingly, in express recognition of the HKSAR's non-state status, Article 152 of the Basic Law indicates that the HKSAR may "participate in international organizations and conferences *not limited to states*."[57] To be sure, no state recognizes Hong Kong as an independent state. Nevertheless, the same Basic Law Article also permits the HKSAR to participate in international organizations (presumably which *are* limited to states) of which the PRC is not a member. Article 153(1) of the Basic Law specifically provides that the views of the HKSAR Government must be sought before international agreements to which China is a party (or becomes a party) are extended to Hong Kong.

With these powers, Hong Kong has cultivated a number of economic and trade relationships through instruments such as BITs. Hong Kong is considered a separate customs territory for purposes of engaging with the WTO. In fact, its participation in the WTO pre-dates its establishment as a Special Administrative Region of China. "Hong Kong, China" became a member of the GATT on April 23, 1986.[58] In addition to regular WTO engagement, "Hong Kong, China" has acted as a complainant in one WTO dispute settlement proceeding (DS29, against Turkey on the issue of restrictions on imports of textile and clothing products), and as a third party in 13 cases.[59]

Hong Kong has 19 BITs registered with the United Nations Conference on Trade and Development (UNCTAD).[60] Hong Kong concluded BITs in the 1990s with major states: the Netherlands, Australia, Denmark, Sweden, Switzerland, New Zealand, Italy, France, Germany, Belgium & Luxembourg, Austria, Japan, South Korea, and the United Kingdom. Since 2000, it has concluded BITs with Thailand, Finland, Kuwait, Canada and Chile. It has also signed free

---

56   Basic Law of the Hong Kong Special Administrative Region of the People's Republic of China, available at http://www.basiclaw.gov.hk/en/basiclawtext/.

57   *Id.* (emphasis added).

58   Hong Kong, China, and the WTO, WTO Secretariat, https://www.wto.org/english/thewto_e/countries_e/hong_kong_china_e.htm.

59   *Id.*

60   UNCTAD IIA Navigator, available at http://unctad.org/en/pages/DIAE/International%20Investment%20Agreements%20(IIA)/IIA-Tools.aspx. Notably, to avoid any doubt, UNCTAD uses the title, "economies," in place of states when allowing a user to search its database.

trade agreements with the European Free Trade Association states (Iceland, Liechtenstein, Norway, and Switzerland), and another with Chile.[61]

The Hong Kong-Australia BIT was implicated in an arbitration hosted by the PCA from 2012 to 2017.[62] Hong Kong was not the respondent, however; rather, a Hong Kong-registered corporation has brought a claim against Australia. Questions as to Hong Kong's status did not arise in the case. There are other similar cases in which Hong Kong-registered corporations have used the international investment law regime, but none, among those publically available, in which Hong Kong was the respondent.[63]

Hong Kong's reputation as a gateway to Asia and a critical business enclave has made it a highly regarded place for international investment arbitration concerning regional claims and even more international claims. The Hong Kong International Arbitration Center handles hundreds of cases each year. In 2016, the HKIAC managed 460 new disputes, including 262 arbitrations related to energy and resources, maritime and shipping matters, consulting and professional services, banking and finance, among other sectors.[64]

By contrast, Macao (or Macau), another Special Administrative Region of China, is not a member of ICSID,[65] but it has concluded two BITs: with Portugal (2000) and with the Netherlands (2008). The BITs accommodate Macao's special status expressly. For example, the Portuguese BIT begins by referencing the parties as Portugal and the Special Administrative Region of Macau "duly authorized by" the PRC Central Government. With respect to trade, "Macau, China" has been a WTO member since January 1, 1995, though it has not been involved in any WTO dispute settlement matters.[66]

4.3   Palestine

The story of Palestine's statehood cannot be addressed by this chapter alone. I note only recent events of interest. According to the Permanent Observer

61   UNCTAD IAA Navigator.
62   Philip Morris Asia Ltd (Hong Kong) v. Commonwealth of Australia (PCA Case No. 2012–12), http://pca-cpa.org/showpage3619.html?pag_id=1494.
63   See, e.g., Standard Chartered Bank (Hong Kong) Limited v. Tanzania Electric Supply Company Limited (ICSID Case No. ARB/10/20).
64   Hong Kong Arbitration Centre, Statistics, http://www.hkiac.org/about-us/statistics.
65   Notably, Macao has been the subject of certain ICSID cases under other BITs. See, e.g., Sebastian Perry and Clemmie Spalton, Macao not covered by Chinese BIT, says Singapore court, GLOBAL ARBITRATION REVIEW, Jan. 26, 2015.
66   CHIEN-HUEI WU, WTO AND THE GREATER CHINA (Martinus Nijhoff 2012), 233–60.

Mission of The State of Palestine to the United Nations, Palestine is recognized as a state by 137 U.N. members.[67]

On October 31, 2011, the United Nations Educational, Scientific and Cultural Organization's (UNESCO) General Conference voted to admit Palestine as a member of the organization. In the flurry of media reports that followed, commentators raised the prospect that Palestine would subsequently join many more international organizations. Some commentators encouraged Palestine to "build on the momentum" it achieved in the UNESCO vote. In other words, be duck-like: build your credibility, your statehood capital, by continuing to act like a state, participating in any regime you can that is thought to be reserved to states. Shortly thereafter, the U.N. General Assembly voted in favour of according Palestine non-member observer state status in the UN, thus bringing Palestine significantly closer to state status.[68]

In the investment and trade realm, however, Palestine has faced several barriers to entry. It is not a member of the World Bank, IMF, or ICSID. It is, however, a member of the PCA as of 2015.[69] Palestine has signed four BITs as "Occupied Palestinian Territory."[70] Two of these are in force: with Egypt (1999) and Germany (2008). One with Jordan was signed in 2012 and another with the Russian Federation in 2016. Palestine also has an FTA with Turkey which came into force in 2005.[71] The Palestinian Authority submitted a request for WTO observer status in October 2009 and again in April 2010, but it has not been granted such status.

As noted at the outset, the barriers to entry in the regime for Palestine are multifaceted and beyond the scope of this article. Still, despite these barriers, Palestine has undertaken efforts to maintain a presence and take advantage of memberships and agreements.

---

67   Permanent Observer Mission of The State of Palestine to the United Nations, Diplomatic Relations, http://palestineun.org/about-palestine/diplomatic-relations/.

68   Dapo Akande, *Palestine as a UN Observer State: Does this Make Palestine a State?*, EJIL: Talk! Blog (Dec. 3, 2012).

69   *New PCA Member State: Palestine* (Mar. 15, 2016), https://pca-cpa.org/en/news/new-pca -member-state-palestine/. ("By a vote of 54 in favour and 25 abstentions, the Council concluded its consideration by taking note that the State of Palestine is a Contracting Party to the 1907 Hague Convention for the Pacific Settlement of International Disputes, and a Member of the Permanent Court of Arbitration, in accordance with the letter of the depositary of the Convention, the Ministry of Foreign Affairs of The Netherlands, dated 13 November 2015.").

70   Occupied Palestinian territory, UNCTAD Investment Policy Hub, http://investmentpolicy hub.unctad.org/IIA/CountryBits/158#iiaInnerMenu.

71   *Id.*

4.4   *Taiwan*

Taiwan (Republic of China), while active in the international economic sphere, suffers from a similar fate to that of Palestine.[72] A fluctuating group of 26 mostly very small states recognize Taiwan as the Republic of China (RoC), an entity that was constitutionally formed in 1912.[73] Despite this low number, Taiwan continues to maintain strong informal and trade relations with roughly sixty other states.

Questions about Taiwan's capacity to sign treaties are not new. Its "proxy organizations" do not conclude treaties in the formal sense of the term.[74] Those organizations do, however, have the authority to conclude transnational agreements. For example, Taiwan and Japan do not formally have an investment agreement, but in 2011, an Agreement for the Mutual Cooperation on the Liberalization, Promotion Protection of Investment was concluded between two entities called the Association of East Asian Relations and the Interchange Association. The two associations commit in the agreement to cooperating with each other to "obtain necessary consent from the relevant authorities" with regard to the protection of investment in their respective home jurisdictions: Japan and Taiwan.[75] The general content of the agreement closely resembles the content of most BITs, as does the form. However, Japan does not recognize Taiwan as a state. Japan has not had an official relationship with Taiwan on a governmental level since 1970 when it signed a Peace Treaty with the People's Republic of China, recognizing the PRC as representing China and accepting the principle of "One China" in which

---

72   The People's Republic of China claims to be the successor of the former Republic of China and claims all the territory of Taiwan, and all that under the Republic's jurisdiction as part of its sovereign territory. *See, e.g.,* Embassy of the People's Republic of China in the United States of America, White Paper—The One-China Principle and the Taiwan Issue, http://www.china-embassy.org/eng/zt/twwt/White%20Papers/t36705.htm (asserting the official position of the People's Republic of China that Taiwan is "an inalienable part of China").

73   For a full list, see CRAWFORD, fn. 27, 201.

74   *See, e.g.,* Chien-Huei Wu, The Many Faces of States in International Investment Law: Supranational Organizations, Unrecognized States and Sub-state Entities (working paper on file with the author) (describing how Taiwan established the Straits Exchange Foundation and other organizations for the purpose of concluding cross-border agreements). *See also* CRAWFORD, 203; AUST, 57–58.

75   Association of East Asian Relations and the Interchange Association signed an Agreement for the Mutual Cooperation on the Liberalization, Promotion Protection of Investment, https://www.koryu.or.jp/taipei/ez3_contents.nsf/04/B943908E522F4EB9492579180005 FEC2/$FILE/%E5%8F%96%E6%B1%BA%E3%82%81%E6%9C%AC%E6%96%87%E F%BC%88%E4%BA%A4%E6%B5%81%E3%83%BB%E4%BA%9C%E6%9D%B1%EF %BC%89.pdf.

Taiwan is considered a part of the PRC.[76] As the Agreement indicates, the two associations are "private" organizations dealing with "working relations on a non-governmental basis" between Japan and Taiwan. Article 17(5) provides that: "Either side shall facilitate that the authorities concerned in the Area of that Side consents to the submission of an investment dispute by a disputing investor to a conciliation or arbitration."

Indeed, Taiwan is most active with its BITs and has a range of BITs in force with the states that recognize it, most of which are not major players on the world stage. In 1946, Taiwan (as RoC) signed a Treaty of Friendship, Commerce, and Navigation with the United States to preserve and promote the "spiritual, cultural, economic and commercial relationship" between the two countries.[77] As early as 1990, Taiwan had a BIT with Singapore. Taiwan made quick work of BITs in the 1990s. In 1992, it concluded BITs with the Philippines, Panama, and Paraguay. Throughout the 1990s, it added Nicaragua (no longer in force), Malaysia, Vietnam, Nigeria, Malawi, Honduras, Thailand, El Salvador, Senegal, Swaziland, Belize, the Marshall Islands, the former Yugoslavia, the Dominican Republic, Guatemala and Costa Rica.[78] Between 2000 and 2010, Taiwan concluded additional BITs with Saudi Arabia, India, St. Vincent and the Grenadines, and the Gambia.[79] In most of these that are publically available, Taiwan is called "Republic of China."

In 2017, Taiwan received its first claim under an international investment agreement: the Agreement between Singapore and the Separate Customs Territory of Taiwan, Penghu, Kinmen, and Matsu on Economic Partnership (ASTEP) over alleged interferences with bank management rights.[80]

Taiwan also participates in certain economic regional and multilateral organizations in some capacity in which investment features prominently. In addition to the WTO, where it participates as the Separate Customs Territory of Taiwan, Penghu, Kinmen, and Matsu or Chinese Taipei,[81] it is a fishing entity under the Convention for the Conservation of Southern Blue-Fin Tuna, the South Pacific Regional Fisheries Management Organization, among other organizations. Taiwan remains a member of the Asian Development Bank

---

76 *See* RYOSEI KOKUBUN, ET AL., JAPAN-CHINA RELATIONS IN THE MODERN ERA, 82–97.
77 Treaty of Friendship, Commerce and Navigation Between the United States of America and the Republic of China, 6 Bevans 761 (1946), 63 Stat. 1299, Preamble.
78 UNCTAD IAA Navigator.
79 *Id.*
80 Notice of Arbitration, Surfeit Harvest Investment Holding Pte Ltd v. Republic of China (Taiwan), June 1, 2017.
81 WU, 128–34.

(called "Taipei, China").[82] The Bank's Charter limits membership to U.N. members, members of specialized U.N. agencies, and members and associate members of the U.N. Economic and Social Commission for Asia and the Pacific, the latter of which includes non-U.N. members, although, surprisingly, Taiwan is not among them.[83] Since 2000, Taiwan also has negotiated six FTAs or agreements that function as FTAs.[84]

Despite its reasonably high number of BITs, its few FTAs, and Taiwan's WTO membership, the ultimate impact of its engagement on its status remains low due to the political factors surrounding its situation. Nevertheless, Taiwan is another good example of quasi-state posturing to look more state-like. It has maximized the opportunities made available to it under the international economic law regime and simultaneously remains excluded from other parts of the regime due to the political views about its status.

4.5   South Ossetia

South Ossetia declared its independence in 1991. It has been recognized by five states: Russia, Nicaragua, Venezuela and Nauru, with Tuvalu recognizing but subsequently withdrawing its recognition.

Both South Ossetia and its sister breakaway region Abkhazia have their own economic agreements with Russia, but that is the extent of their respective engagement with the international economic law framework.[85] These two agreements, in which the parties agree to cooperate in customs affairs and lift trade barriers, are intended as statements of identity and have not precipitated substantial foreign investment into the regions.[86]

---

82   Asian Development Bank, Members, https://www.adb.org/about/members.

83   Agreement Establishing the Asian Development Bank, Art. 3 Membership, https://www.adb.org/sites/default/files/institutional-document/32120/charter.pdf. The history of Taiwan's participation may explain this anomaly. It originally joined as Republic of China representing both the island and the mainland and was permitted to remain, although the issue is subject to some speculation. THOMAS D. GRANT, ADMISSION TO THE UNITED NATIONS: CHARTER ARTICLE 4 AND THE RISE OF UNIVERSAL ORGANIZATION 175 (Brill, 2009).

84   Taiwan Ministry of Economic Affairs, Bureau of Foreign Trade, *FTAs signed with trading partners*, https://www.trade.gov.tw/english/Pages/List.aspx?nodeID=672.

85   These agreements can be found in Russian at http://www.mid.ru/spd_md.nsf/. They are also discussed in Andre W.M. Gerrits & Max Bader, *Russian patronage over Abkhazia and South Ossetia: implications for conflict resolution*, 32 E. EUROPEAN POLITICS 297 (2016).

86   No South Ossetian officials were available to comment on this study during a visit to the region.

4.6   *Northern Cyprus*

The Turkish Republic of Northern Cyprus (TRNC), which has been under Turkish occupation since 1974, declared independence from Cyprus in 1983. Security Council Resolution 550 of May 1, 1984 called on all states not to recognize the TRNC and not to facilitate or assist in any way the secessionist entity.[87] The TRNC has, nevertheless, participated in international conferences and sought to conclude international agreements under the auspices of the UN.[88]

Today, the TRNC is recognized only by Turkey. Cyprus joined the EU in 2004 without the TRNC. In 2010 and 2011, the European Parliament rejected a controversial proposal that would have enabled the TRNC to trade directly with the EU.[89] The Cypriot government at the time had argued that adopting the proposal would have implied recognition of the TRNC as a separate legal entity, a view that had been endorsed by the legal service of the European Council. The Commission's legal service meanwhile noted that the EU trades with other territories that are part of the EU but not inside its customs union, such as Gibraltar.[90]

The TRNC actively encourages foreign investment as part of its development policy and under its Incentive Law.[91] The law gives preferential treatment to export-oriented industries, particularly those industries that facilitate transfers of modern technology and new management techniques. A series of legislative packages provides financing and guarantees for foreign investors including an investment allowance; exemption from custom duties and funds; zero rate value added tax; fund credits; exemption from certain licensing fees; and favorable tax conditions.[92] Cypriot BITs do not clarify how the TRNC territory is to be treated; rather, they exclude it by defining Cypriot territory subject

---

87   U.N. Security Council Resolution 550, May 1, 1984.

88   In 2010, the International Court of Justice stated in an advisory opinion that the Security Council in an exceptional character attached illegality to the Declaration of Independence of TRNC because it was, or would have been connected with the unlawful use of force and "general international law contains no applicable prohibition of declarations of independence." Accordance with International Law of the Unilateral Declaration of Independence in Respect of Kosovo, Advisory Opinion, 2010 ICJ No. 141 (July 22), para. 84.

89   Toby Vogel, *MEPs consider allowing EU trade with northern Cyprus*, POLITICO, May 19, 2010.

90   *Id.*

91   TRNC State Planning Organization website, www.devplan.org.

92   Guide for investors, Invest North Cyprus, http://www.invest-northcyprus.com/guide-for -investors.php.

to the protections of the BITs as only that which constitutes the Republic of Cyprus.[93]

4.7   *Transnistria*

The Pridnestrovian Moldavian Republic, better known as Transnistria, declared its independence in 1990. Moldova claims Transnistria as part of its sovereign territory, but its effective control is highly limited. Sister quasi-states with connections to the Russian Federation recognize Transnistria as sovereign. Although Russia does not officially recognize Transnistria, it is well known that Transnistria benefits from significant Russian support.

Like Northern Cyprus, Transnistria also encourages foreign investment as part of its efforts to gain recognition abroad, led by its very active chamber of commerce. The Moldova Investment and Export Promotion Organization (MIEPO) claims that the Transnistrian chamber of commerce is stronger than the one based in Chisinau, the Moldovan capital.[94] In fact, the Transnistrian Chamber of Commerce serves as a ministry in the Transnistrian governing authority. The chairman has the rank of minister.[95] Relations between the Transnistrian Chamber and MIEPO have been productive for policy implementation purposes, to attract potential investors, and for EU project financing.

Despite these efforts and institutional structure, Transnistria's integration has been limited by the fact that Transnistria lacks international banks and uses its own currency. Transnistria is not a party to any BITs, and does not recognize Moldovan BITs as applying on its territory, although the region also maintains its own laws on investment protection: the Investment Law and Foreign Investment Law, among others.[96]

Still, through trade shows and other business fora in particular, Transnistria has been able to attract investors and joint ventures from Russia, Italy, Hungary,

---

93   *See, e.g.*, India-Cyprus Bilateral Investment Treaty (entered into force Dec. 1, 2004) ("in respect of the Republic of Cyprus:- the territory of the Republic of Cyprus, including the territorial sea and any maritime or submarine area as well as the. exclusive economic zone and the continental shelf that extend outside the limits of the territorial waters over which the Republic of Cyprus exercises or may exercise in accordance with international law, sovereignty, sovereign rights and jurisdiction for the purpose of exploration, exploitation and preservation of the sea-bed, sub soil and natural resources.").

94   Interviews with MIEPO officials. Transnistria, Moldova (March 2011) (meeting notes on file with the author).

95   Interviews with Transnistrian Chamber of Commerce officials. Chisinau, Moldova (March 2011) (meeting notes on file with the author).

96   Investment Law and Foreign Investment Law, available at www.vspmr.org in Russian.

Germany, Belgium, and Austria, particularly in the area of textiles.[97] Most foreign investment in Transnistria is Russian, especially given the challenges of moving goods made in Transnistria to Moldova for onward trade to the west.

Transnistrian business leaders report that certain arrangements with Moldova have facilitated in recent years some limited movement of goods and services.[98] An agreement between Transnistria and Moldova in 2000 committed both sides to protecting foreign investments, for example.[99]

4.8   Somaliland

Somaliland, an autonomous region in Somalia, declared its independence from Somalia in 1991. It maintains a foreign investment protection law as a part of its national legislation[100] but it is not a party to any transnational agreements[101] nor is it a member of any of the relevant multilateral institutions governing investment. Like others disputed territories such as Western Sahara and Nagorno-Karabakh that are not recognized by any state, Somaliland maintains very low engagement with the international economic regime, despite limited efforts to attract investment and some success at that.[102]

• • •

One might expect recently created and recognized states to have followed the same path as the quasi-states above in their movement from UN-administered territories to independent states or in their breakaway from another state. In particular, South Sudan and East Timor (Timor-Leste) recently went through the recognition process. Where do they fall on this messy spectrum, if at all?

South Sudan became a U.N. member state in 2011. On April 18, 2012, South Sudan also joined the IMF, World Bank, and ICSID. South Sudan does not have observer or member status at the WTO. In 2009, the South Sudan Investment

---

97   Interviews with Transnistrian Chamber of Commerce officials. Transnistria, Moldova (March 2011) (meeting notes on file with the author).

98   *Id.*

99   *Id.*

100   Somaliland Foreign Investment Law of 2004, available at http://www.somalilandlaw.com/foreign_investment_law_2004.htm.

101   Aust notes it has entered into some Memoranda of Understanding. See AUST, 60.

102   *See, e.g.*, Sarah A. Topol, *Amid Moroccan Investment in Western Sahara, Tensions Simmer*, BLOOMBERG BUSINESS (May 30, 2013); Vitaly Naumkin, Russia shows interest in Western Sahara, Al-Monitor (April 1, 2015); *Libyan state oil company in Western Sahara meets international protest* (Dec. 20, 2007), WESTERN SAHARA RESEARCH WATCH, available at wsrw.org/a127x622; Kate Parlett, *Trade and Investment Agreements in Disputed Territories: The case of Western Sahara*, KLUWER ARBITRATION BLOG (Apr. 4, 2017).

Promotion Act came into force which provides that any dispute between a
foreign investor and South Sudan in respect of an enterprise may be submitted
to arbitration "within the framework of any bilateral or multilateral agreement
on investment protection to which the Government and the country of ... the
investors ... are parties."[103] South Sudan has concluded no BITs, but it is facing at
least two investment cases: one at ICSID and one at the PCA under a contract.[104]
The ICSID case, *Sudapet Co. Ltd (Sudan) v. South Sudan*, was registered with
ICSID just four months after South Sudan joined ICSID: on August 29, 2012. In
September 2016, the tribunal dismissed the claims against South Sudan.[105] The
PCA case began in November 2012 and concluded in January 2015. In that case,
the tribunal concluded that South Sudan breached its contract obligations to
the claimant.[106]

It is not obvious whether South Sudan has attempted to conclude BITs and
has not been successful in locating willing partners or whether it has not sought
to do so. There is no doubt that South Sudan has tried to attract more investment
and that there have been difficulties. *The Economist* reported in 2011 that Juba
was, at the time, the second most expensive city in the world in which to start
a business, after the Democratic Republic of Congo's capital of Kinshasa.[107] As
the one of the first states to become independent after the height of the BIT
"craze," South Sudan may be one of the first to doubt the strength of these
instruments for that purpose.[108] With IMF, World Bank, and ICSID support,
alongside its almost universal recognition and U.N. membership, South Sudan
may have achieved what it views as necessary thresholds.[109]

Timor-Leste became a U.N. member state on September 27, 2002. Among
all the entities studied here, it has garnered the most recognition. More like
those discussed above, Timor-Leste became a member of the IMF and World

103   South Sudan Investment Promotion Act, available at http://www.wipo.int/wipolex/en/
      details.jsp?id=11414.
104   Sudapet Co. Ltd (Sudan) v. South Sudan (ICSID Case No. ARB/12/26). Active Partners
      Group Limited v. The Republic of South Sudan, PCA Case no. 2013/4.
105   Sudapet Co. Ltd (Sudan) v. South Sudan (ICSID Case No. ARB/12/26). Sudapet is Sudan's
      state-owned oil company.
106   Active Partners Group Limited v. The Republic of South Sudan, PCA Case no. 2013/4,
      Award (Jan. 27, 2015).
107   *Ready, steady, invest*, THE ECONOMIST, July 9, 2011.
108   Governments in Australia, Africa, South America, and Europe have cast doubt on the
      future of their involvement in BITs in particular. *See, e.g.*, Philip Nel, *The Rise and Fall
      of BITs*, Working Paper (Oct. 10, 2014), available at http://www.otago.ac.nz/politics/
      otago061036.pdf.
109   South Sudan is also in the process of acceding to the WTO. WTO, WTO accessions, https://
      www.wto.org/english/thewto_e/acc_e/acc_e.htm.

Bank, as well as of ICSID before it became a U.N. member state. Timor-Leste has concluded only three BITs: with Portugal (2002), with Germany (2005), and with Qatar (2012).[110] Timor-Leste already has won its first case at ICSID under the ICSID Convention. In January 2015, investor Lighthouse Corporation of Australia and Seychelles brought a claim against Timor-Leste in a dispute over a fuel supply agreement.[111] The tribunal was constituted in August 2015 and rendered its final award in December 2017, dismissing the claimants' claims for lack of jurisdiction.[112] Timor-Leste does not have observer or member status at the WTO.

Despite that South Sudan and Timor-Leste do not have more robust international agreement profiles, they are somewhat active in the regime. The newest generation of quasi-states appears less concerned about limiting their exposure as South Sudan and Timor-Leste have done to some degree.

5   Conclusion: Posturing and Impostoring

Quasi-states are pushing the limits of the framework with their activities—which I refer to as posturing (posturing as states), and impostoring (acting as universally recognized states despite their more ambiguous status). Recalling as Professor Brilmayer argued in 2001 that there are no clear principles or practices to restrict their participation in this sphere, quasi-states contribute to the evolution of both international economic law through their substantive contributions, and international law on recognition by making space for themselves.

At the same time that these quasi-states have located places for engagement, others seeking greater autonomy but lacking a minimal level of recognition remain contained by the fundamentally state-based system. The disengaged quasi-states demonstrate the limits on how far the international economic framework will stretch. Hence, while some quasi-states are able to posture and impostor—using this approach to be engaged, others remained constrained by the framework and the universally recognized states that control it. Moreover, that access to the framework is restricted to states further motivates some quasi-states to try to participate, to assume a state posture.

As noted above, there is nothing new to the observation that recognition serves as a ticket to participation in international treaty making. Public

---

110   UNCTAD IAA Navigator.
111   Lighthouse Corporation Pty Ltd and Lighthouse Corporation Ltd, IBC v. Democratic Republic of Timor-Leste (ICSID Case No. ARB/15/2).
112   *Id.*, Award (Dec. 22, 2017).

international law has built-in conditions to entry. In this respect, this study has shown that international economic law remains uniquely positioned. It accommodates alternative "lifestyles," that of the quasi-state, more than other systems of law. In short, categories and labels prove unhelpful. The international law regime needs a framework for recognition based on functional criteria as represented in the international economic law space.

This chapter has described the prevailing approaches to recognition and its legal salience, outlined the contributions of international economic law to transforming the concept, and argued that the activities of quasi-states in the international economic law sphere have signalled a new acceptance of *functional* recognition. The story reflected in quasi-state activity is a story about the changing concept of the state—juridical and empirical—in a diverse, dynamic international framework. International economic law has pushed the limits of that framework and quasi-states have taken advantage accordingly. The more interesting and meaningful issues surrounding the legality of quasi-states' participation in the international economic framework will likely become relevant and problematic in the years ahead in dispute resolution proceedings. There, the quasi-ducks may be challenged on their ability to fly, at cost.

CHAPTER 10

Why Sub-State Groups Are Endowed with Rights

Laura S. Underkuffler

1 Introduction

More than twenty-five years ago, Lea Brilmayer published a seminal article entitled *Secession and Self-Determination: A Territorial Interpretation.*[1] In this article, she examined the factors that are important in the establishment of separatist claims. In such disputes, she wrote, the strength of the separatist claim "does not depend primarily on the degree to which the group in question constitutes a distinct people," in cultural, ethnic, language, or other traditional terms.[2] Rather, the claim—and the recognition of the group by international law as an entity that can assert it—is rooted in the existence of a viable territorial claim. The individuals who make up the group are able to assert the claim in derogation of existing nation-states not because they are a "people," in a cultural, ethnographic, or other communitarian sense, but because their territory was previously taken from them in an act of historical injustice.[3] As a result, "a different set of questions must be addressed in order to evaluate the merits of a separatist movement."[4] How serious was the historical wrong? Was the territory conquered, or was the settlement by the new group a gradual phenomenon? How alive has the wrong been kept in the memories of the dispossessed? Has time created new rights on the part of new settlers?[5]

Brilmayer's position became known as the "territorialist thesis" for separatist claims in international law.[6] Its contribution to thinking about those claims was profound. However, in this chapter I shall explore a broader question that it raises. Under what circumstances should we recognize sub-state groups and, consequently, their demands? Is the separatist context, and its minimalization

---

1 Lea Brilmayer, *Secession and Self-Determination: A Territorial Interpretation*, 16 YALE J. INT'L L. 177 (1991).
2 Ibid., 178.
3 See ibid., 197–201. See also Fernando R. Tesón, "Ethnicity, Human Rights, and Self-Determination," in *International Law and Ethnic Conflict*, ed. David Wippman (Ithaca, N.Y.: Cornell University Press, 1998), 86, 95–96.
4 Brilmayer, "Secession and Self-Determination," 197.
5 See ibid., 199–200; Tesón, "Ethnicity, Human Rights, and Self-Determination," 95.
6 See, e.g., Tesón, "Ethnicity, Human Rights, and Self-Determination," 95–97.

© KONINKLIJKE BRILL NV, LEIDEN, 2019 | DOI:10.1163/9789004316539_011

of the role of cultural, ethnic, language, and other commonly cited factors, unique? How do we decide—how should we decide—which groups are entitled to international legal recognition, and which not?

At its most basic, all law—including international law—is the negotiation and resolution of individual and group conflict. Individuals and groups make claims that affect other individuals and groups, and the resolutions of those conflicts—if recognized and enforced by an authoritative power—are referred to as "law."

Historically, on a conceptual level, international law has been concerned with particular individual and group conflicts: conflicts between nation states, and conflicts between individuals and their own national governments. Recognition and enforcement of other group-identified or group-asserted claims against national governments—particularly, claims involving sub-national groups and their own governments—has long been resisted in international law. Because of the greater threat that recognition of sub-state groups by international law is perceived to present to sovereign nation states—particularly through claimed secessionist rights or other rights to self-determination—there have been attempts both politically and theoretically to minimize international legal recognition of sub-national groups and their claims.

The earliest modern attempts to protect certain groups from the powers of their own state governments were incorporated into treaties among nations in the seventeenth, eighteenth, and nineteenth centuries.[7] Most of these dealt with religious minorities, although non-state nationals living within states were included in some treaties made in the late nineteenth century.[8] Some protection of racial, linguistic, and religious minorities was later evident in treaties concluded during the post-World War I League of Nations era.[9] Rights granted included rights to life and liberty without discrimination; rights to free religious exercise; the preservation of language; the right to maintain educational institutions; and the preservation of citizenship rights.[10]

With the demise of the League of Nations in 1946, and the subsequent establishment of the United Nations, a new regime emerged. The focus in the early United Nations period was more explicitly on the protection of individual rights, although group status was often used in the identification of protected

---

7   *See* Natan Lerner, *Group Rights and Discrimination in International Law*, 2nd ed. (The
     Hague; Martinus Nijhoff Publishers, 2003), 7.
8   These included the Treaty of Berlin, signed in 1878, which attempted to protect Turks,
     Greeks, and Romanians living under Bulgarian rule. See ibid.
9   See ibid., 10–13.
10   See ibid., 12.

individual victims of discrimination. It has been observed that with the establishment of the United Nations, "[t]he emphasis in the protection of human rights ... shifted from *group* protection to the protection of *individual* rights and freedoms, almost exclusively. The new approach was that [rights violations on the basis of a group characteristic]... could be taken care of by protecting the rights of the individual, on a purely individual basis, [through] ... the principle of non-discrimination."[11]

The International Covenant on Civil and Political Rights,[12] adopted by the United Nations General Assembly in 1966, reflected greater recognition of the rights of human groups. However, the change was subtle in nature. At least ostensibly, the Covenant reflects an individual-centric focus when it comes both to rights guarantees and to the mechanism of enforcement. Article 27 of the Covenant states that "[i]n those States in which ethnic, religious or linguistic minorities exist, *persons belonging* to such minorities shall not be denied the right, in community with other members of their group, to enjoy their own culture, to profess and practise their own religion, or to use their own language."[13] Scholars have observed that this guarantee seems to presuppose the protection of the existence of communities and cultures for the benefit of protected individuals; it is impossible to see how individuals can enjoy their own culture, religion, or language "in community with the other members of their group" if the group has been destroyed.[14] However, most concur that the Covenant grants no legal status to groups as such.[15]

In subsequent years, the international community came to recognize that non-discrimination guarantees in an individual-centric system were not enough—alone—to effectively guarantee the rights of those individuals, or

---

11 Ibid., 13 (emphasis in original).
12 See UN General Assembly, *International Covenant on Civil and Political Rights*, 16 December 1966, United Nations, Treaty Series, vol. 999, p. 171, available at http://refworld.org/docid/3ae6b3aao.html (accessed 6 February 2018).
13 Ibid. (emphasis added).
14 *See*, e.g., Yoram Dinstein, "Freedom of Religion and the Protection of Religious Minorities," in *The Protection of Minorities and Human Rights*, eds. Yoram Dinstein & Mala Tabory (Dordrecht, Netherlands: Martinus Nijhoff Publishers, 1992), 145, 157.
15 *See* David Wippman, "Introduction: Ethnic Claims and International Law," in *International Law and Ethnic Conflict*, ed. David Wippman (Ithaca, NY: Cornell University Press, 1998), 1, 14 ("Article 27 affords only very limited protection to minority groups and then only by means of the protection accorded to the individual members of those groups. The collectivity itself has no legal status...."). The language of Article 27 was a compromise, of course, among competing visions of individual and group rights. Attempts to make explicit reference to positive measures to which minority groups would be entitled, such as state-supported schools utilizing minority languages, failed. See Lerner, *Group Rights*, 15.

protect the existence of the groups to which they belonged. In the 1970s and 1980s, the idea of group rights commanded new attention from legal scholars and policymakers as a way to address existing shortcomings in international law.[16] Although there are many declarations and other documents that illustrate this trend,[17] watershed events include the adoption of the Declaration on the Rights of Persons Belonging to National or Ethnic, Religious and Linguistic Minorities by the United Nations General Assembly in 1992.[18] This Declaration represents a conceptual advance in its recognition of the need to protect the existence and identity of sub-state minority groups. Although again couched in terms of "the rights of persons belonging to national or ethnic, religious and linguistic minorities," various provisions elaborate protections and obligations that clearly involve group recognition and empowerment. For instance, under the Declaration, states must protect the national or ethnic, cultural, religious, and linguistic identities of minorities, and must encourage the conditions for the promotion of those identities.[19] As Natan Lerner has argued, "Article 1 does not refer to rights of persons, but to the *identit[ies] of minorities*.... To protect the identity of the minority means recognizing the existence of a collective entity with its own rights, beyond the individual and collective rights of individuals."[20] Articles 2, 3 and 4 further provide that persons belonging to minority groups shall be able to enjoy and develop their culture, language, religion, traditions, and customs—guarantees that, again, assume minority group protection.[21] Group-protection ideas are also a part of the guarantees of Article 2 that such persons must be free "to establish and maintain ... free and peaceful contacts with other members of their group," both nationally and internationally.[22] With the adoption of this Declaration, the idea of sub-national group recognition and participation—of some sort—in the international order was conceptually, if not programmatically, established.

One of the most recent recognitions of sub-state group rights is found in the International Convention on the Elimination of All Forms of Racial

---

16   *See* Corsin Bisaz, *The Concept of Group Rights in International Law: Groups as Contested Right-Holders, Subjects and Legal Persons* (Leiden: Martinus Nijhoff Publishers, 2012), 1.

17   *See* discussion in Lerner, *Group Rights*,16–18; Bisaz, *The Concept of Rights*, 70–127.

18   UN General Assembly, *Declaration of the Rights of Persons Belonging to National or Ethnic, Religious and Linguistic Minorities*, 3 February 1992, A/RES/47/135, available at http://refworld.org/docid/3ae6b38do.html (accessed 6 February 2018).

19   *See* ibid., Article 1.

20   Lerner, *Group Rights*, 19 (emphasis added).

21   *See*, e.g., *Declaration of the Rights of Persons Belonging to National or Ethnic, Religious and Linguistic Minorities*, Article 2 §§ 1,2; Article 3 § 1; and Article 4 § 2.

22   *See* ibid., Article 2 § 5.

Discrimination, adopted by the United Nations General Assembly in 1965.[23] Article 2(2) of the Convention establishes an affirmative obligation on the part of states to take measures to realize the equal treatment of previously disadvantaged racial groups.[24] Commentators have argued that this necessarily creates a protected right to non-discrimination which is held by those racial groups.[25]

Statements of the principle of self-determination—also found in numerous United Nations declarations and other documents[26]—are also assertions of sub-state group rights, although highly controversial. As James Crawford has observed, "[s]elf-determination is plainly a collective rather than an individual right...."[27] In other contexts, the rules of war and other aspects of humanitarian law can be seen as concerned with group rights, as can international law and prohibitions against genocide.[28] "The group dimension of the very term 'war' is obvious; war is a phenomenon between groups...."[29] Similarly, "[b]y genocide

---

23   UN General Assembly, *International Convention on the Elimination of All Forms of Racial Discrimination*, 21 December 1965, United Nations, Treaty Series. Vol. 660, p. 195, available at http://www.refworld.org/docid/3ae6b3940.html (accessed 6 February 2018).

24   See ibid., Article 2 § 2 ("States ... shall, when the circumstances so warrant, take ... special and concrete measures to ensure the adequate development and protection of certain racial groups or individuals belonging to them....").

25   Bisaz, *The Concept of Group Rights*, 74–75.

26   *See*, e.g., U.N. Charter, Article 1 (2) ("The Purposes of the United Nations are ... To develop friendly relations among nations based on respect for the principle of equal rights and self-determination of peoples"); *International Covenant on Civil and Political Rights*, Article 1 § 1 ("All peoples have the right of self-determination. By virtue of that right they freely determine their political status and freely pursue their economic, social, and cultural development.").

27   James Crawford, "The Rights of Peoples: 'Peoples' or 'Governments'?", in *The Rights of Peoples*, ed. James Crawford (Oxford: Clarendon Press, 1988), 54, 59. See also Bisaz, *The Concept of Group Rights*, 8 ("the right to self-government can only be held by a group, and is clearly a group right"); S. James Anaya, "Superpower Attitudes Toward Indigenous Peoples and Group Rights," *American Society of International Law: Proceedings of the Annual Meeting* 93 (1999): 251, 257 (the "right to self-determination ... may be aptly called the mother or all group rights"). "Self-determination" can, of course, have both state-threatening and more limited meaning; it can refer both to national political independence and "the recognition of cultural identity and internal self-government for different groups or peoples within the State." James Crawford, "State Practice and International Law in Relation to Secession," *The British Year Book of International Law 1998* 69 (1999): 85, 114. See also Bisaz, *The Concept of Group Rights*, 54–61 (discussing "external" self-determination or the right of a people to independence and its own state, and "internal" self-determination, or "the right of a people to a certain amount of autonomy short of sovereign independence").

28   *See* Bisaz, *The Concept of Group Rights*, 77–107.

29   Ibid., 79.

we mean the destruction of a nation or of an ethnic group.... It is intended ...
to signify a coordinated plan of different actions aiming at the destruction of
essential foundations of the life of national groups, with the aim of annihilating
the groups themselves." Genocidal actions are directed against individuals—
not in their individual capacities—but as members of the group.[30]

Perhaps the most uncontroverted acceptance of group-rights ideas has
been in conjunction with recognition of the rights of indigenous populations.
For instance, the 1989 Indigenous and Tribal Peoples Convention (No. 169),[31]
adopted by the International Labour Organization, assumes the legitimacy of
group-based rights in broad terms. The Preamble to this Convention recognizes the implicit rights of indigenous peoples "to exercise control over their
own institutions ... and to maintain and develop their identities, languages,
and religions, within the framework of the States in which they live."[32] More
radically, recognition is also extended in the Convention to rights of group
ownership and possession of traditionally occupied lands.[33] Governments are
assigned affirmative responsibilities to protect indigenous peoples' social and
cultural identities, customs, traditions, and institutions, as well as their claims
to traditionally occupied lands.[34]

The United Nations Declaration on the Rights of Indigenous Peoples,
adopted in 2007, is the most recent statement of indigenous peoples' rights
by that international body.[35] This document declares, among other things,
that indigenous peoples shall enjoy "all human rights and fundamental
freedoms" "as a collective or as individuals";[36] that they "have the right to self-
determination";[37] that they "have the collective right to live in freedom ... as

---

30   Raphael Lemkin, *Axis Rule in Occupied Europe: Laws of Occupation: Analysis of Government:
     Proposals for Redress* (Washington, D.C.: Carnegie Endowment for International Peace,
     1944), 79 (footnotes omitted). See also Bisaz, *The Concept of Group Rights*, 86–97.
31   International Labour Organization (ILO), *Indigenous and Tribal Peoples Convention, C169*,
     27 June 1989, C169, available at http://www.refworld.org/docid/3ddb6d514html (accessed
     6 February 2018).
32   Ibid., "Preamble", paragraph 6. See also ibid. Article 8 § 2 ("These peoples shall have the
     right to retain their own customs and institutions, where these are not incompatible with
     fundamental rights defined by the national legal system and with internationally recog-
     nised human rights.").
33   See ibid., Article 14 § 1 ("The rights of ownership and possession of the peoples concerned
     over the lands which they traditionally occupy shall be recognised.").
34   See ibid., passim.
35   UN General Assembly, *United Nations Declaration on the Rights of Indigenous Peoples*:
     resolution adopted by the General Assembly, 2 October 2007, A/RES/61/295, available at
     http://www.refworld.org/docid/471355a82.html (accessed 6 February 2018).
36   Ibid., Article 1.
37   Ibid., Article 3.

distinct peoples";[38] and that they "have the right to participate in decision-making in matters which would affect their rights, through representatives chosen by themselves."[39] Perhaps most notable is the participation of indigenous groups in the Declaration's lengthy negotiation, a powerful—if tacit—admission of the acceptance of sub-state group rights in the international context.

Increased recognition of sub-state group rights as a theoretically and politically viable idea has intensified debate over its limits.[40] Any human population is comprised of a kaleidoscope of overlapping and ever-changing human groups. Race, culture, occupation, religion, gender, physical disabilities, sexual orientation and identity, genetic make-up, history of treatment by nation-states—the list of possible group-identifying characteristics is endless. How do we decide which sub-state groups are entitled to international legal recognition? How should we approach that question?

Surprisingly, in the new and vast literature dealing with the questions of sub-state group rights, there is little discussion of this question. The absence of structural examination of the foundations for group recognition and non-recognition has prompted several scholars to articulate how group-recognition questions should be approached. According to these efforts, it is essentially a two-step process. First, the group's identity must be evaluated under specified neutral criteria. Such criteria include the permanence of group identity for members of the group; the degree of identification of members with the existence of the group; evidence of persecution of group members; the numerical inferiority of the group, as compared with the population of the state; and other factors. Once the group has qualified under these tests for potentially rights-bearing status, then the merits of that group's claims can be addressed.[41]

In this chapter, I will evaluate this approach. Ultimately, I will conclude that the identification of abstract criteria or characteristics for sub-state group qualification is of limited usefulness, and can in fact undermine the underlying, critical values at stake. Although it is tempting to try to establish a set of

---

38   Ibid., Article 7 § 2.
39   Ibid., Article 18.
40   See Danilo Türk, "Introduction: Group Rights and Human Rights," in *The Tensions Between Group Rights and Human Rights: A Multidisciplinary Approach*, eds. Koen De Feyter & George Pavlakos (Oxford: Hart Publishing, 2008), 8 ("The discussion of group rights, while always a part of the human rights discourse, has been gaining importance in the past decade or so. This is [a result]... of the needs felt in increasingly complex societies and ... whether the normative world of human rights can offer meaningful solutions....").
41   *See, e.g.*, Lerner, *Group Rights*, 34–39; Bisaz, *The Concept of Group Rights*, 43–126.

universally applicable and abstract threshold criteria, the two inquiries—the qualification of the group for international recognition, and the merits of the group's claims—cannot be separated. In fact, the first is *derivative* of the second. As Lea Brilmayer implicitly recognized, the recognition of a sub-state group as a rights-bearing entity is *necessarily a function* of what international legal recognition seeks to achieve in any given case. Sets of abstract characteristics of group members are relevant only within that case-specific context; indeed, the use of abstract characteristics that serve international law's function in one case might be quite antithetical to its function in another. In the end, we must hew to what comprises the core of Brilmayer's insight: that the vindication of deeper norms, not superficial group-identity characteristics, must play the determining role in sub-state group recognition in international law.

2   Threshold Tests for Sub-State Groups Endowed with Rights

As noted above, there has been surprisingly little work that explores how we structure questions about the status of sub-state groups in international law. The usual approach is to simply assume that certain groups are rights holders—for instance, cultural, religious, or indigenous groups—without further examination of underlying foundations.

Recently, there have been several notable attempts to address this void by articulating what is essentially a two-step approach. First, a set of abstract characteristics that qualify sub-state groups for international legal recognition is articulated, and the group is evaluated against those requirements. If the group meets those requirements, analysis then turns to the merits of its claims.

There are two particularly good examples of this approach. The first is the well-known—and admirably thorough—account found in Natan Lerner's recent book, *Group Rights and Discrimination in International Law.*[42] In this book, Lerner begins with several group-identifying terms that one finds in international instruments and literature, including "minorities," "communities," and "peoples." Lerner describes how "minorities," particularly religious minorities, were among the earliest groups recognized in international law.[43] The recognition of religious minorities was driven by a perceived need for their protection from discrimination.[44] Later broadening of the concept to others required further delineation of which groups might be protected "minorities,"

---

42   Lerner, *Group Rights.*
43   See ibid., 7.
44   See ibid.

and which not. Lerner identifies various criteria that have been offered for the conferral of recognized numerical "minority" status. These include a numerical ratio between the asserted minority group and the whole population, which establishes the minority group's minority status; the need for a minimum size of the minority group; the need for the group's regional or geographical concentration; the identification of members of the group *with* the group, as a matter of social or political solidarity; and the need for group recognition as a means of group preservation.[45] The existence of the last includes acts such as the non-dominant social and political position of the group, and evidence of discrimination against group members. There must also be identifying characteristics that distinguish the group, such as differences in ethnicity, religion, language, or national origin.[46] Other factors include the origin of the group, and "the group's desires and aspirations as such."[47]

To the extent that evidence of discrimination against group members is pivotal, the prohibited grounds for discrimination obviously become relevant. In international law, Lerner observes, "any distinction, exclusion, restriction, or preference based on race, color, religion or belief, descent, ethnic origin, language, or sex" is potentially prohibited.[48] Distinctions that do not constitute forbidden discrimination include citizen/non-citizen status, occupation, and age.[49]

Literature and international agreements that cite "communities" or "peoples" as the operative sub-state group-rights concept suggest additional elements. Definitions of "communities" generally establish "groups [that are] based upon unifying and spontaneous (as opposed to artificial or planned) factors essentially beyond the control of the members of the group."[50] "This is what makes a 'community' different from a 'society' or 'organization,' terms which refer to bodies established by the deliberate or voluntary action of their members to promote some interests." From this viewpoint, "[f]amilies, tribes, nations, peoples, cultural groups and religious groups are communities. A club, a commercial corporation, [and] a political party are societies."[51]

In recent years, Lerner observes, the term "peoples" has often become pivotal. Although there is no agreed definition of "peoples" in international law,

---

45   See ibid., 8–10.
46   See ibid., 8–9.
47   Ibid., 9.
48   Ibid., 31.
49   See ibid., 33.
50   Ibid., 34 (quoting memorandum of the UN Secretary-General on Definition and Classification of Minorities, UN Doc. E/CN.4/Sub. 2/85 (1949), 4).
51   Ibid.

the idea is generally rooted in the idea of self-determination.[52] One well known scholar takes the view that "peoples" often identifies "the 'national or ethnic subdivisions' in multinational or multiethnic States and dependencies."[53]

Finally, there is the idea of "groups," which is subject to different interpretations in different settings.[54] It is generally considered to be a broader notion than "peoples"; "[g]roups include peoples[, but] not every group can claim the rights of a people."[55] It is most often used in conjunction with identified "communities."[56] The group must regard itself, and be regarded by others, as a distinct community by virtue of certain shared characteristics which are permanent in nature and "are, as a rule, beyond the control of the members of the group."[57] It is assumed that there "'ought to be a sense of belonging together, a we/they sense, a sense of solidarity *vis-a-vis* outsiders, a sense of sharing a common heritage and a common destiny, distinct from the heritage and destiny of others.'"[58]

In the end, Lerner accepts most of these criteria as identifying those groups that are "entitled to enjoy, individually and collectively, certain basic rights that are indispensable to ensure their preservation, development, and effective equality within the general society."[59] "Spontaneity, permanency, identification with the whole, [and] a feeling of belonging ... are characteristics of the groups" that merit international cognizance.[60] Recognition can be "reduced to three basic groups: (1) ethnic or racial groups, which include groups based on color, descent, and national groups (in a sociological and not legal sense); (2) religious groups, difficult to define in ... [cases which involve] groups other than ... well-established, historical religions ...; and (3) linguistic and cultural groups."[61]

Lerner acknowledges that religious groups often "do not fit strictly into the characteristics of spontaneity and permanency. One's religion can be changed by a voluntary act, which is not the case with race, color, language— relatively—and culture."[62] However, the fact that religion is "[f]undamentally ... the outcome of deeply rooted cultural, social, and historical factors" merits

---

52   Ibid., 35.
53   Ibid. (discussing Vernon Van Dyke, *Human Rights, Ethnicity and Discrimination* (Westport, Conn.: 1985)), 12.
54   See ibid.
55   Ibid.
56   See ibid., 34.
57   Ibid., 36, 38.
58   Ibid., 36 (internal quotation marks omitted).
59   Ibid., 38.
60   Ibid., 36.
61   Ibid., 37 (footnotes omitted).
62   Ibid.

its inclusion.[63] Groups defined by and subject to discrimination by reason of "political opinion, social origin, economic condition, [and] birth—in the sense of being born in a certain family or social circle"—are not included "since those categories are more connected with the characteristics of the respective political or social regimes than with those of the affected group."[64] Sex, although frequently a ground for discrimination, does not identify a protected group because it "cannot be categorized ... with discrimination against minorities or other particular non-dominant groups within the population of a State."[65] Homosexuals are also not a cognizable group because the feeling of internal group solidarity that they might share is "not comparable to the link existing among members of an ethnic, religious, or cultural group."[66] The same is true of the "group" of permanently disabled persons.[67] In short, for group-rights status, under traditional accounts, it is critical that the group exists as a collective entity or "unit," and not simply as an aggregation of individuals.[68]

The second prominent work that articulates this approach is the book written by Corsin Bisaz, *The Concept of Group Rights in International Law: Groups as Contested Rights-Holders, Subjects and Legal Persons*.[69] The goal of the book, as articulated by the author, is to "elaborate a more consistent view of [existing group-rights concepts, and]... to provide a more coherent approach" to the identification of potentially rights-bearing sub-state groups in international law.[70] In particular, Bisaz explores whether such groups can be defined in a useful or "reasonably exact" way.[71]

Bisaz first defines a potentially rights-carrying group in this context as a number of individuals larger than one "that is conceived by [the members]... or by others as being in a certain regard connected in a substantive way."[72] Excluded from this definition are groups that "unite willingly," such as companies, political parties, and associations.[73] As in Lerner's account, the emphasis here is on identification by reasons of some intrinsic or immutable characteristic. The "substantive connection" that identifies cognizable groups

---

63   Ibid.
64   Ibid.
65   Ibid.
66   Ibid.
67   See ibid.
68   See ibid., 36; Vernon Van Dyke, "Collective Entities and Moral Rights: Problems in Liberal-Democratic Thought," *Journal of Politics* 44 (1982): 21, 22.
69   Bisaz, *The Concept of Group Rights*.
70   See ibid., 2.
71   See ibid.
72   Ibid., 28 (emphasis deleted).
73   See ibid., 29.

is crucial. "In law and theory," he writes, "substate groups have been classified as ... 'minorities,' 'national minorities,' 'peoples,' 'indigenous peoples,' 'nations,' 'religious communities,' and 'cultures.' The criteria connecting persons belonging to such 'groups' have traditionally been 'race,' 'ethnicity,' 'religion,' culture' and 'language.'"[74] These criteria present the "substantive connections" that create group identity.[75] Until now, "the discussion of group rights is basically restricted to ... 'cultural groups'—groups with common ethnicity/ race, religion, language or lifestyle (culture in a narrower sense)—as opposed to non-cultural groups defined by age, gender, disability, *et al.*"[76] This is because "[i]n general, non-cultural groups are not seen as having [the]... 'substantive connection' [among members] which would justify the provision of rights to the group *as such.*"[77]

There are other commentators who advocate similar approaches. For instance, Francesco Capotorti has defined recognized minority groups as those "which [are]... numerically inferior to the rest of the population of a State and in a non-dominant position, whose members possess ethnic, religious, or linguistic characteristics which differ from those of the rest of the population and who, if only implicitly, maintain a sense of solidarity directed towards preserving their culture, tradition, religion or language."[78]

If we were to distill the common requirements that qualify sub-state groups for international legal recognition under these accounts, we might compile the following list:
– permanency of group identity for members of the group, with identity also being spontaneous, natural, and involuntary;
– identification of members of the group with the existence of the group, and the internalized recognition by members of the need for group preservation;
– numerical inferiority of the members of the group, as compared with the entire state population; and
– evidence of discrimination against or other persecution of group members, in violation of principles of human rights.[79]
The work of Lerner, Bisaz, and other commentators who identify these factors is thorough and exacting; there is little doubt that these factors are those that are commonly cited in international legal accounts. The problem occurs when

---

74   Ibid.
75   See ibid., 28–30.
76   Ibid., 32.
77   Ibid. (emphasis added).
78   Francesco Capotorti, "Minorities," *Encyclopedia of Public International Law*, ed. R. Bernhardt (Amsterdam: Elsevier Science Publishers, 1985), 385, 385.
79   See, e.g., Lerner, *Group Rights*, 8–9, 36–38; Bisaz, *The Concept of Group Rights*, 29, 200.

these distilled factors are used as threshold requirements for the absolute qualification—or disqualification—of sub-state groups.

Upon analysis, the characteristics that these tests establish are quickly
revealed to be highly problematic. Take, for instance, the first requirement:
that the group's identity is permanent, as well as spontaneous, natural, and
involuntary.[80] Undoubtedly, the motivating spirit here is that individuals
should be "unwilling" members of protected groups; that the persecution or
hardship that they suffer should be "involuntary," not something that they
voluntarily assume or embrace. The international legal order, with all of its
costs and complexities, should not be concerned with groups whose members
have the right and ability to simply exit from the group.[81] For this reason, international legal recognition is generally extended to—and limited to—groups
defined by ethnic, cultural, linguistic, or religious characteristics.[82]

In one sense, this is understandable. If members of a group—such as a
social club, corporation, trade union, or political party[83]—can solve their
problems by simply exiting from that group, perhaps the drastic remedy of
international recognition of that group should not be employed to solve their
problems. However, this criterion can become easily perverted. For instance,
the automatic exclusion of social clubs or corporations might seem to be obviously justified on this ground; but the exclusion of groups rooted in marital
status, trade union involvement, and handicaps is not. The inquiry that is missing is why—or how—individuals become or remain members of those groups,
and whether the interests that command membership are important ones in
human life. If married individuals are subject to persecution, can we demand
that they be unmarried in order to avoid their situation? If trade union members are the subject of persecution, can we ignore that group on the ground
that the members can voluntarily give up their attempts to exercise rights to
free speech, assembly, and employment?

Perhaps most difficult to understand is the exclusion of handicaps as identifying characteristics of cognizable group status.[84] Should the persons who
share this group identity be denied recognition because their conditions
are voluntary, or might (through medical or some other intervention) be
cured? For instance, should HIV-infected individuals and groups be excluded
because their medical conditions were often "voluntarily acquired" and might

---

80   See Lerner, *Group Rights*, 36–38.
81   See, e.g., Bisaz, *The Concept of Group Rights*, 202.
82   See, e.g., Lerner, *Group Rights*, 8–9, 36–38; Bisaz, *The Concept of Group Rights*, 200.
83   See Lerner, *Group Rights*, 34; Bisaz, *The Concept of Group Rights*, 29.
84   See, e.g., Lerner, *Group Rights*, 37.

be alleviated through medical intervention? That position seems to assume notions of voluntarism and access to medical interventions that are unrealistic in today's world.

A similar problem arises when one considers sub-state groups identified by birth, caste, or social status.[85] Obviously, if the situation is one that involves a state-enforced or state-sanctioned system of social caste or class, rooted in the circumstances of birth or other indelible characteristics, the requirements of "permanency" and "involuntariness" are met. However, one can readily envision the identification of social groups as "pariahs" or "outcasts" in which that kind of formal and indelible identification is not present, but persecution and oppression of human beings on the basis of their economic or social group identity is a fact nonetheless. There are situations in which group identity— and persecution on the basis of that identity—are real, and recognition of group rights might be justified, even though that identity is not permanent or indelible in the sense of facts of birth or other biological characteristics.[86] Similar concerns surround groups identified by "political or other opinion," or "philosophy and thought," whose members are subject to persecution but whose beliefs fail the "permanent," "natural," and "involuntary" tests.[87]

In sum, although there is something intuitively appealing about limiting protection to identity characteristics that are permanent, spontaneous, natural, and involuntary, those characteristics are at best only surrogates for other, deeper values that must be at work in the identification of includable and excludable groups. Indeed, if involuntary and permanent characteristics are really those that are required for protected sub-state group status, routine inclusion of religious and cultural groups is itself questionable. As Lerner acknowledges, neither religion nor culture is truly involuntary or permanent— religious identity can be chosen, to a large extent, as can cultural affiliation and practices.[88]

---

85   See ibid.
86   Of course, even these "permanent" and "indelible" markers are really less so. As Bulmer and Solomos observe, "[r]ace and ethnic groups, like nations, are imagined communities. People are socially defined as belonging to particular ethnic or racial groups...." Martin Bulmer & John Solomos, "Introduction: Re-thinking Ethnic and Racial Studies," *Ethnic and Racial Studies* 21 (1998): 819, 822. "[G]roup boundaries can be constructed from the outside as well as [from] the inside." Bisaz, *The Concept of Group Rights*, 201–202.
87   See Lerner, *Group Rights*, 37–38.
88   See, e.g., Lerner, *Group Rights*, 37 ("Religiously based groups ... do not fit strictly into the characteristics of spontaneity and permanency. One's religion can be changed by a voluntary act.... Fundamentally, however, religion is also the outcome of deeply rooted cultural, social and historical factors....").

The second requirement—the identification of members of the group with the group, and their dependence upon its existence—is more comprehensively useful, perhaps, but also must be viewed cautiously. What, precisely, do we require in the way of "group identification"? Is it enough that members see themselves as members of the group, as a matter of fact, or must they share a different kind of group identity? If we are to require a sense of dependence by members of the group, or "a sense of solidarity, ... of sharing a common heritage and a common destiny,"[89] in what sense must this be felt or exhibited?

Lerner's discussion of this requirement in conjunction with sexual orientation or gender identity illustrates its hazards. In his view, sexual-orientation or gender-identity groups fail this test. Although these groups are permanent, spontaneous, and non-voluntary (under contemporary understandings), he argues that individuals who are members of groups rooted in sexual orientation or gender identity do not share "the feelings of solidarity ... comparable to the link existing among members of an ethnic, religious, or cultural group."[90] However, how do we know this is true? Members of sexual-orientation or gender-identity groups might not have the formal social structures or institutions that religious or cultural groups might have; however, the requirement of group structures or institutions is not something that is imposed on other groups. In addition, it is difficult—today—to maintain that members of sexual-orientation or gender-identity groups identify less with others who share their community, than do members of (recognized) racial or cultural groups. To be fair, Lerner's book was written fourteen years ago, before gay, lesbian, bisexual, and transgender persons were the powerful and culturally recognized force that they are today. A supposed assessment that members of sexual-orientation or gender-identity groups do not feel the solidarity and group necessity that members of other protected groups feel would seem to be a highly questionable (if not outright erroneous) reason for the exclusion of these groups from group-rights status.

The next two requirements—the numerical inferiority of the group, compared with the population as a whole, and evidence of human rights violations against group members—are attempts to identify the need for group protection through the neutral criteria of numbers and actual persecution. Most often, actually protected groups are those that are numerical minority groups in the states in which they are found, and are the victims of human rights violations. To the extent that these facts are elevated to abstract requirements for sub-state group recognition, they would seem to be at least functionally

---

89   See ibid., 36 (internal quotation marks omitted).
90   Ibid., 37.

coincidental with groups whose claims we might want to protect. If the perse-
cuted group is in fact a numerical majority, so the thinking goes, it can solve its
own problems through the state's political process. As for requiring evidence of
human rights violations, this ensures that the rare remedy of sub-state group
recognition is reserved for the most serious violations of international norms.

However, there are situations in which even these requirements might yield
perverse results. For instance, gender or sex is often brushed aside as a possible
group-right identifier because it does not fit within the idea of numerical-
minority status required for recognition of sub-state groups.[91] If this exclusion
is done because of the theoretical availability of political remedies, it might
or might not be justified depending on the political realities involved. A group
might enjoy majority numerical status, but be barred from political power for
other reasons. Real barriers to political participation by women, members of
particular racial or ethnic groups, or others majority groups must be evaluated
before it can be assumed that a non-minority sub-state group should, as a matter of course, be denied recognition by reason of its non-minority status.

The final requirement—that there be evidence of discrimination against or
other persecution of group members in violation of human rights principles—
will often align with why we feel motivated to recognize particular sub-state
groups as worthy of international protection and recognition. However, the
elevation of this characteristic to an across-the-board, threshold requirement
is also problematic. For instance, the granting of group-rights status to indigenous groups will often be rooted in territorial and other sovereignty claims,
rather than in claims—such as racial, religious, or cultural persecution—that
assert classic deprivations of human rights. One could respond, of course,
that sub-state group claims to sovereignty or other forms of autonomy do
assert "human rights deprivations" in the most abstract sense. For instance,
a territorial claim to ancestral land could be said to involve a deprivation of
property, and self-determination is often said to be—in itself—a human right.
However, such broad interpretations of "persecution" and "human rights violations" are generally not what this threshold requirement for group-rights
status is understood to mean. Indeed, if it is interpreted so broadly, it (arguably) loses its qualifying power. If a desire for autonomous action is all that
this requirement means, it would be met by the simple assertion of freedom of
action involved in any group-rights claim.

We are left, then, with a situation in which the identification of general,
abstract requirements for sub-state group recognition are of limited usefulness. In some cases the requirements seem to identify sub-state groups that
we believe should be entitled to international legal recognition; but in other

---

91   See, e.g., ibid., 37.

cases they do not. Perhaps most troubling, they do not seem to consistently identify *the reasons* for a group's inclusion or exclusion from recognized status. To address these problems, we must take a different approach.

3   An Alternative Approach

To summarize our findings thus far, the quest for a set of abstract requirements that can pre-qualify sub-state groups for international recognition—although an understandable impulse—is very troubled in practice. As described above, even the best and most thoughtful efforts to frame abstract, neutral, and generalizable threshold criteria fail to consistently identify properly included or excluded groups. In addition, as described below, such efforts approach the issue from the wrong direction. Attempts to identify abstract, generalizable requirements for recognition of sub-state groups proceed from the assumption that it is the *nature* of the group, and the *identities* of its members—e.g., as internalizing group membership and identity, having cultural or religious connection, experiencing political powerlessness through minority status, and so on—that drives the determination of international recognition. In fact, those characteristics are merely the administrative or derivative outcomes that implement deeper reasons for group choice. Those deeper reasons involve *the function* that group recognition performs in each case in international law. Recognition of a sub-state group as a rights-bearing entity is necessarily a function of what international legal recognition seeks to achieve in a given case.

To begin, we must ask: *why*, in fact, are sub-state groups recognized in international law? If we reflect upon this question, we realize that they are not recognized because they have a certain internal cohesiveness, or their members share certain commonalities, or because they comprise certain permanent or minority-status societal configurations. Rather, they are recognized because that recognition—in that case—serves a particular function in international law.

The functions that group recognition serves can be grouped into the following clusters:

a. *Sub-state groups are recognized as a function of the international desire to address human rights abuses. Recognition of sub-state groups is a practical way to identify those people who are deserving of international protection because they are part of the targeted or oppressed group.*

When we think of the idea of group rights in international law, this is one of its most prominent functions. In these cases, international law identifies

a particular human right—e.g., freedom from ethnic, religious, or racial discrimination—and the practical task is to identify those individuals who are
experiencing deprivation of that right. Group recognition is important in
determining both 1) whether there is an appellation of human rights denial
that should be used to characterize the experience of the group, and 2) whether
a particular individual is a member of that group, and therefore a beneficiary
of the international effort.

An illustration of this function of the group-rights idea can be found in the
United Nations Declaration on the Rights of Persons Belonging to National or
Ethnic, Religious, and Linguistic Minorities, adopted in 1992.[92] In its Resolution,
the General Assembly stated that its intention was to more effectively implement human rights guarantees regarding "the rights of persons belonging to
national or ethnic, religious and linguistic minorities."[93]

Because the Declaration does not define "minorities" within its text, the
identity of protected minority groups under this (and similar international
instruments) has been a matter of intense debate. As Lerner writes, "[s]cholars
have proposed ... definitions, international treaties have described groups to
which they refer, international tribunals have given their own definition, and
the UN has sponsored studies on the subject."[94] The key concern has been to
choose groups whose members—as definitely as possible—can be identified,
and which are experiencing or at serious risk of experiencing discrimination or
other deprivations of human rights.

In cases of this type, the idea of group rights is used as a way to identify
groups of human beings with characteristics and grievances that deserve
international protection and redress.[95] In that process, there may be a largely
consistent set of characteristics of recognized groups that seems to emerge;
but those characteristics are not the fundamental reason for a group's inclusion. The reason for its inclusion is the actuality or serious potential for the
violation of identified human rights of members. Patterns of group identity,
and the communitarian aspects of that identity, are simply by-products of that
enterprise. To the extent that those characteristics have any independent significance, they function simply as ways to limit the universe of possible groups
(and individuals) who are entitled to recognition and protection on other,
more fundamental, grounds.[96]

---

92   UN General Assembly, *Declaration of the Rights of Persons Belonging to National or Ethnic,*
      Religious and Linguistic Minorities.
93   Ibid., "Preamble," paragraph 10.
94   Lerner, *Group Rights*, 8.
95   See, e.g., ibid., 9–25.
96   Cf. ibid., 34–39 (describing how different understandings of "discrimination" and the
      characteristics of groups (such as their spontaneity, permanence, and members' identifi-
      cation with the whole) function to limit numbers of cognizable groups).

b. *Recognition of a sub-state group as a legal entity is a way to enable the international community to recognize and protect inherently collective interests. In these cases, the group is necessary for the individual members' exercise of protected rights (such as the experience of culture, religious exercise in community, minority language capacity, and others).*

In this set of situations, recognition of groups as legal entities in international law performs a different function. In these cases—as in the cases above—vindication of individual human rights can be said to be a core concern. However, in these cases the group does not simply function as a way to identify individuals who deserve protection. Rather, the group is a necessary construct for the enjoyment or actualization of the protected rights themselves.

Consider, for instance, Article 27 of the International Covenant on Civil and Political Rights.[97] This Article states that "[i]n those States in which ethnic, religious, or linguistic minorities exist, persons belonging to such minorities shall not be denied the right, in community with other members of their group, to enjoy their own culture, to profess and practise their own religion, or to use their own language."[98]

The extent to which this language compels the recognition of groups as rights-bearing entities is contested.[99] Later instruments, in particular, have been cited to bolster the conclusion that international law is engaged in a transition toward guaranteeing "rights inherent to the condition of some specific and well defined groups, together with ... harmonization of the rights of the State, the individual and the group."[100] Whether or not these instruments endow religious, cultural, linguistic, or other communities *qua* communities with recognized and exercisable rights, there is no doubt that the rights involved presuppose the group's existence and protection. The religious, cultural, and language rights that are protected by these instruments can only be exercised in community with others. No individual can exercise and experience the right

---

97   UN General Assembly, *International Covenant on Civil and Political Rights.*
98   Ibid., Article 27.
99   *Compare*, for instance, Wippman, "Introduction," 4 ("Although recognizing the communal aspect of ethnic identity, Article 27 affords only limited protection to minority groups and then only by means of the protection accorded to the individual members of those groups. The collectivity itself has no legal status under the covenant....") *with* Dinstein, "Freedom of Religion," 157 (the purpose of Article 27 is to grant legal recognition and rights to the enumerated groups, as groups).
100 Lerner, *Group Rights*, 16 (emphasis deleted). See also Türk, "Introduction," 8 ("[D]iscussion of group rights, while always a part of the human rights discourse, has been gaining importance in the past decade or so. This is not ... a result of a normative evolution but rather of the needs felt in increasingly complex societies....").

to culture, or the right to linguistic or religious community, by herself alone. In these cases, the idea of group rights functions—at the least[101]—as a way to preserve the conditions that are necessary for the identified individual rights (enjoyment of culture, exercise of religion, use of language) to be actualized.

> c. *Recognition of a sub-state group is an integral part of the group's claims as an entity with independent political existence and status. In these cases, group recognition is necessary for the international community to vindicate the value of self-determination or independent self-government (for example, in the case of a territorial or indigenous self-determination claim).*

In these situations, the ultimate interest that the group wishes to assert is a right to self-government or other form of self-determination. The ultimate goal here is not the preservation of individual rights (such as the exercise of religion or the preservation of language); it is not even the preservation of the group as necessary for the exercise of individual rights (such as the right to language or to experience one's culture). Those interests might be incidentally vindicated by the group-rights claim; but they are *not the essence* of it. Rather, the claim is one of self-government or other form of independent political self-determination. Recognition of groups as legal entities in these cases functions as recognition by the international community of these groups' self-determination or independence claims.

There are many examples of group-rights ideas performing this function in international law. Most notably, group-rights ideas are used to capture the legitimacy of asserted self-determination claims by conquered peoples or those otherwise displaced from ancestral lands. Recognition of group-rights claims of this type can range from the modest—such as enforcing the participatory rights of groups in legislative, administrative, or judicial processes conducted by the nation-state in which the groups are found[102]—to more

---

101   Cf. Lerner, *Group Rights*, 19, 21 (arguing that protection of an individual's rights in community with others implies the "right of the group as such." "To protect [an individual with collective rights]... means recognizing the existence of a collective entity with its own rights, beyond the individual and collective rights of individuals. Some rights can only be exercised collectively, because of their nature." For instance, the guarantee that individuals can "participate effectively in cultural, religious, social, [and] economic ... life" "can be effective [only] if the group as such is [able]... to coordinate and direct [that]... participation.").

102   See, e.g., UN General Assembly, *Declaration of the Rights of Persons Belonging to National or Ethnic, Religious and Linguistic Minorities*, Article 3 (effective participation in decisions at the national or regional level, according to national legislation). See also Lerner, *Group Rights*, 40.

ambitious notions such as the right to self-determination and the recovery of lost territory.[103] The key is that in these cases, group-rights status is conferred because it is a necessary part of international recognition of the validity of the separatist or other self-determination claim.

•••

In summary, under this approach, the idea of a set of neutral, and generalizable requirements for sub-state group recognition is rejected. There is no set of threshold, abstract characteristics that pre-determines the recognition question. Rather, sub-state groups are recognized or not depending on the functions that the group-rights idea, in a particular case, will perform. That function is determined by what international law seeks to achieve in each case. Group identity characteristics do not drive the recognition or non-recognition question; rather, they are simply the practical outcomes that are the result of what international law, on a fundamental level, seeks to achieve.

4   Reprise: Why It Matters

Determining whether a particular group of persons is eligible for international recognition and protection is an obviously important matter. Whether the claim is for the protection of religious institutions, language rights, cultural preservation, or the vindication of territorial and self-government claims, the question whether that group is one that is recognized as the beneficiary of the enforcement of international norms is an obviously crucial one.

The question that this chapter explores is how the inquiry into such a question should be structured—whether it should be made as a threshold matter, using a set of abstract, pre-determined, and "neutral" group-identity criteria; or whether it should be seen, simply, as a function of what (in a particular case) international law seeks to achieve.

There are two reasons why the choice of one approach or the other is of critical importance. The first relates to the serious difficulties inherent in the "threshold requirements" approach itself. As discussed above, the articulated

---

103   See, e.g., Lerner, *Group Rights*, 116 (describing "controversial claims advanced by indigenous groups, such as the right to self-determination; the exclusion of jurisdiction asserted by States over indigenous nations or peoples, except in accordance with their freely expressed wishes; the right to permanent control and enjoyment of historical territories; and the right to restitution of lands"). See also Wippmann, "Introduction," 8–13 (discussing the breadth of self-determination claims in international law).

requirements themselves are highly indeterminate. When do members of a group sufficiently share a "common heritage" or a "common identity"? What is a "permanent" condition that group members must possess, or an "involuntary" one? Perhaps even more disturbing, we are left with no convincing explanations why the particular characteristics—or attitudes—are the critical ones. For instance, is there no articulated reason why race—itself a contested category—is reflexively believed to meet these requirements, but other personal characteristics—such as marital status, gender or social class—are not?

An approach that sees group recognition as a function of what international law is attempting to accomplish in particular cases—rather than as the application of threshold, "neutral" pre-qualification requirements—mitigates the essential arbitrariness that is otherwise involved. In different cases, group recognition serves different functions; and it is those functions that present the determinative questions. In some cases, group recognition is a practical way to identify those people who are suffering human rights abuses, and who are the justified beneficiaries of international actions. In such cases, considerations such as the biological permanency of group identity or internalized belief by members in the need for group preservation might be secondary or unimportant altogether. In other cases, group recognition is required in order to recognize and protect inherently collective interests, or to enable the exercise of rights that require a community of others. In such cases, whether group membership is voluntary will be of little moment. In yet other cases, group recognition is a function of the desire to recognize claims to sovereign or semi-sovereign status. In such cases, issues such as permanency of group identity or belief by members in the need for group preservation might be paramount. The point is that there is simply no adequate universal conception of required group character. To attempt to formulate and to enforce such a conception leads to arbitrary decisions that fail to reflect the true interests involved.

The second reason why the choice of approaches matters is more subtle, but of potentially even greater importance. It is at the heart of Brilmayer's "territorialist thesis," set forth in her seminal article, cited above.

In "Secession and Self-Determination: A Territorial Interpretation," Brilmayer critiqued the way that secessionist claims traditionally have been approached.[104] "The standard account," she wrote, "bases claims to secede upon principles of self-determination of peoples, according to which every nation or people has a right to determine its own destiny."[105] Citing statements found in the United Nations Charter, the United Nations International Covenant on Civil

---

104   Brilmayer, "Secession and Self-Determination."
105   Ibid., 179 (footnote omitted).

and Political Rights, and other foundational documents, secessionist claims focus on self-determination as the right of "peoples," with the only limiting principle supplied by that term. Because democratic principles of consent of the governed and the right to popular sovereignty are bedrock principles in international law, that threshold question—whether the secessionist group is a "people," as claimed—becomes the practically determinative one.[106]

Thus, the critical question in the evaluation of a secessionist claim becomes whether the "would-be secessionists constitute a true nation, especially whether they are racially, linguistically, religiously, or ethnically distinct from the dominant group in the existing state."[107] Put in the terms of the analysis in this chapter, whether a secessionist group meets a threshold set of abstract "identity-constituting" requirements becomes the threshold question for international group recognition, *and* the merits of the secessionist claim.[108] If the secessionist group meets the requirements for a "distinct people," as articulated by threshold tests, democratic principles of consent and popular sovereignty—unassailable principles in international law—"seem to allow the disaffected group the right to opt out of [the] ... existing state."[109]

Brilmayer challenged this familiar account, on the ground that it obscured an important normative basis for secessionist claims. Successful secessionist claims, she wrote, do not turn on racial or ethnic separateness, or other generalizable accounts of "peoples," but on valid claims to territory now governed by others. "[S]ecessionist movements are based upon some sort of historical grievance over territory."[110] "Groups that are ethnically distinct, but possess no independent territorial claims, have very poor chances of convincing anyone of their [claims]."[111] Consider, she wrote, the case of a group of recent immigrants who come to a particular state to engage in commerce or to find employment. "Even if this group is ethnically quite distinct, it cannot establish the requisite claim to territory simply by migrating to an already inhabited area and settling there."[112] Indeed, if the question of the presence of threshold, identity-based characteristics of a "people" is the determinative one, "then Turkish guest workers in Germany have claims on par with black Africans fighting colonial powers." Such a view cannot capture the important, normative grounding of a

---

106   Ibid., 179–84.
107   Ibid., 183 (footnote omitted).
108   See ibid., 179–84.
109   See ibid., 184.
110   Ibid., 190.
111   Id. at 188.
112   Ibid.

successful secessionist demand.[113] The normative dimension of the secessionist claim—its assertion of territorial right—"must be made explicit, and ... its relevance ... recognized under international law."[114]

Brilmayer's vital insight is equally applicable to all claims of group-rights status. The elevation of threshold, group-identification criteria into a qualifying or disqualifying test will almost inevitably obscure or distort the true normative basis on which the case turns. If we are preoccupied with seemingly powerful—but essentially arbitrary—threshold requirements for group recognition, using what are presented as "neutral," universal, and generalizable criteria, consideration of the deep, normative issues that are involved in the claim will be lost. To put it simply, the choice of the approach to be used in the recognition of sub-state groups in international law is not something that affects only the potentially narrow "recognition" question. It can artificially preclude true consideration of the merits of the claim, as well.

---

113   See ibid.
114   Ibid., 189.

CHAPTER 11

Why International Organizations Are Accountable to You

*Eyal Benvenisti**

> If this is true with regard to every species of political dominion, and
> every description of commercial privilege, none of which can be
> original self-derived rights, ... then such rights, or privileges, ..., are
> all in the strictest sense a *trust*; and it is of the very essence of every
> trust to be rendered *accountable*.
>
> EDMUND BURKE, 1783[1]

∵

1   Introduction

I was still a student of Lea Brilmayer's when I read her *Justifying International
Acts* (1989). In this path-breaking book, Brilmayer reminded us that international law until that moment (with *glasnost* and *perestroika*, the Cold War
about to be won) has been focusing on justifying the "horizontal" (inter-state)
obligations. Not enough attention has been paid to the "diagonal" relationship,
namely the relations between states and citizens of other states. Well ahead of
her contemporaries, Brilmayer forcefully argued for the need to develop and
apply a theoretical perspective that would justify the exercise of power by one
state over foreign individuals. One could not think of a more timely theoretical

* Whewell Professor of International Law, University of Cambridge, C C Ng Fellow of Jesus
College, Cambridge, Global Professor of Law, New York University, Professor, Tel Aviv
University Faculty of Law. For many helpful comments, I wish to thank Doreen Lustig, Tamar
Megiddo, and the participants in workshops held at Yale Law School and Tel Aviv University
Faculty of Law. Research for this essay was supported by the ERC Advanced Grant (grant
No. 323323).

1   4 EDMUND BURKE, SELECTED WORKS OF EDMUND BURKE 64 (E.J. Payne ed., 1999),
http://lf-oll.s3.amazonaws.com/titles/659/Burke_0005-04_EBk_v6.0.pdf (last visited Aug. 11,
2018) (Emphasis in original) (Edmund Burke's Speech, Dec. 1, 1783 on the East India Bill).

challenge to international law and politics in a world that was about to be
dominated by a single power. Lea's argument continued to challenge my own
thinking and it was more than twenty years later that I attempted to offer my
theoretical lens for such diagonal relationships.[2] This chapter applies this lens
to international organizations (IOs), as the basis of their obligation to justify
their exercise of power over individuals who are affected by their acts and
omissions.

The law on IOs that emerged after the Second World War was imbued with
irrefutable confidence in their inherent impartiality and competence and
hence reflected an assumption that the subjection of IOs to legal discipline
and judicial review would be unnecessary and even counterproductive.[3] The
law that evolved by a West-dominated International Court of Justice (ICJ)[4]
(and against Soviet opposition on and outside the ICJ bench),[5] exudes faith in

---

2   Eyal Benvenisti, *Sovereigns as Trustees of Humanity: On the Accountability of States to Foreign
     Stakeholders*, 107 AM. J. INT'L L. 295 (2013).
3   Jan Klabbers, *The Life and Times of the Law of International Organizations*, 70 NORDIC J. INT'L
     L. 287, 288 (2001).
4   Hans J. Morgenthau, *The New United Nations and the Revision of the Charter*, 16 REV. POL. 3,
     4, 6–8, 15 (1954) ("While in its relations with its members it is an international government, in
     its relations with the Soviet bloc the new United Nations is a grand alliance opposing another
     grand alliance."). On the UN as a Western actor, see MARK MAZOWER, GOVERNING THE
     WORLD: THE HISTORY OF AN IDEA, 1815 TO THE PRESENT 215 (2012); MARK MAZOWER,
     NO ENCHANTED PALACE: THE END OF EMPIRE AND THE IDEOLOGICAL ORIGINS OF
     THE UNITED NATIONS 77 (2008); PAUL KENNEDY, THE PARLIAMENT OF MAN: THE PAST,
     PRESENT, AND FUTURE OF THE UNITED NATIONS 155 (2006).
5   Kazimierz Grzybowski, *Socialist Judges in the International Court of Justice*, 1964 DUKE L.J.
     536 (Socialist judges do not see the UN as having introduced basic changes in the legal posi-
     tion of the member states, and the latter therefore may continue to question the legality
     of its resolutions). For such views see Judge Milovan Zoricic, of Yugoslavia, in Conditions of
     Admission of a State to the United Nations, Advisory Opinion, 1948 I.CJ. Rep. 57, 106 (May 28);
     Judge Winiarski, of Poland, in Certain Expenses of the United Nations (Article 17, Paragraph 2,
     of the Charter), Advisory Opinion, 1962 I.C.J Rep. 151, 181 (July 20); Judge Winiarski, in Effects
     of Awards of Compensation Made by the United Nations Administrative Tribunal, Advisory
     Opinion, 1954 I.C.J Rep. 47, 63 (July 13); Judge Koretsky, of the Soviet Union, in *Certain
     Expenses*, at 181. On the Soviet attitude toward the law on IOs, see GUY FITI SINCLAIR,
     TO REFORM THE WORLD: INTERNATIONAL ORGANIZATIONS AND THE MAKING OF
     MODERN STATES 140 (2017):
         "International lawyers in the Soviet bloc argued vehemently that member states'
     sovereignty required their explicit consent to any expansion of UN powers. The idea of "con-
     stitutional growth" or "de facto amendment" of the Charter was anathema, not least because
     it served to legitimize what they saw as the unlawful manipulation of Charter rules and pro-
     cedures by the United States and its allies."
         See also GREGORY TUNKIN, INTERNATIONAL LAW IN THE INTERNATIONAL SYSTEM
     169, 173–78 (1975).

international decision-makers as skilful public servants who selflessly toil for the common good.[6] The law insulates these actors from internal and external scrutiny and absolves them of any inherent legal obligations. Despite many examples to the contrary, the international law on IOs continues to do so to this day.

Mistrust in IOs began to trickle through into academic and legal discourse only well after the end of the Cold War and following protests by civil society activists. Gradually, the proliferation of IOs and the growing dependency on them brought home also the understanding that powerful state executives and special interests were, in fact, steering IOs in favour of their own ends and deviating from the common good.[7] Responding to this realization, the academic literature since the early 2000s pressed for more accountable IOs. They did so by borrowing from domestic concepts of the rule of law and sound practices of decision-making by public bodies, implicitly or explicitly regarding IOs as exercising public authority.[8]

But while the operators of certain IOs have adopted and even embraced a 'culture of accountability,'[9] a major impediment continues to undercut the demand for accountability: the law on IOs fails to provide a positive legal basis for grounding the rigorous requirements of public decision-making as understood in well-functioning democracies. In fact, this law stands in sharp contrast to domestic public law doctrines such as *ultra vires* or *détournement de pouvoir* that have inspired the evolution of sound administrative law duties in Western democracies. This law insulates IOs (and their employees) from

---

6   On demands for accountability of the League of Nations through 'publicity' (but also the 'reinvention and rehabilitation of secrecy') in the inter-war period, see Megan Donaldson, *The Survival of the Secret Treaty: Publicity, Secrecy, and Legality in the International Order*, 111 AM. J. INT'L L. 575 (2017).

7   Eyal Benvenisti, *Exit and Voice in the Age of Globalization*, 98 MICH. L. REV. 167 (1999) (arguing that information-based capture at the global level is even more intense than at the domestic level). On selective access to information as empowering special interests see Anthony Downs, *An Economic Theory of Political Action in a Democracy*, 65 J. POL. ECON. 135 (1957); Susanne Lohmann, *An Information Rationale for the Power of Special Interests*, 92 AM. POL. SCI. REV. 809 (1998); GENE M. GROSSMAN & ELHANAN HELPMAN, SPECIAL INTEREST POLITICS (2001).

8   Benedict Kingsbury, Nico Krisch & Richard Stewart, *The Emergence of Global Administrative Law*, 68 LAW & CONTEMP. PROBS. 15 (2005); GLOBAL ADMINISTRATIVE LAW: THE CASEBOOK (Sabino Cassese et al., eds., 3d ed. 2012); ARMIN VON BOGDANDY & INGO VENZKE, IN WHOSE NAME? A PUBLIC LAW THEORY OF INTERNATIONAL ADJUDICATION (2014); *International Public Authority*, MAX PLANCK INSTITUTE, http://www.mpil.de/de/pub/forschung/nach-rechtsgebieten/voelkerrecht/ipa.cfm (last visited Aug. 11, 2018).

9   Michael Zürn & Matthew Stephen, *The View of Old and New Powers on the Legitimacy of International Institutions*, 30 POL. 91, 98–99 (2010).

any external legal discipline or demand for accountability for their acts: IOs have legal personality that is independent of the member states; their powers are broadly defined—even implied—by their constitutive treaty; they are "bound [only] by any obligations *incumbent upon them* under general rules of international law, under their constitutions or under international agreements to which they are parties," (my emphasis);[10] and they enjoy immunity from domestic court review.[11] These are not exactly the building blocks from which one can construct a firm grounding for rigorous rule of law obligations.

This essay seeks to offer such grounding for IO accountability. The admittedly narrow doctrinal opening is provided by the above-mentioned recognition that IOs are bound by "obligations incumbent upon them under general rules of international law."[12] What obligation could generate IO accountability toward people affected by their (or their employee's) acts? To respond to this question, the essay examines the three possible grounds that have informed the evolution of the principle of accountability under major domestic administrative law systems. The first ground is the principle of the rule of law, which stipulates that the executive has only that power granted to it by the legislature and that the exercise of that power is subject to specific demands. The second ground is based on the human rights of those affected by public actors, and the corresponding duty of the public body to respect and protect those rights. The third claim grounds accountability obligations in the idea of a trust between the administrative agency and the trustor, be it the king, the legislator or the citizens, who is therefore entitled to be given account for what is done in its name.[13] After rejecting the first two grounds (Part 2) the essay elaborates on the third ground, promoting the thesis that IOs, just like states, should be

---

10   Interpretation of the Agreement of 25 March 1951 between the WHO and Egypt, Advisory
       Opinion, 1980 I.C.J. Rep. 73, ¶ 37 (Dec. 20). On this statement see JAN KLABBERS, AN
       INTRODUCTION TO INTERNATIONAL LAW 38–39, 46–47 (2d ed. 2009); Eyal Benvenisti,
       *EJIL Foreword: Upholding Democracy Amid the Challenges of New Technology: What Role
       for the Law of Global Governance?*, 29 EUR. J. INT'L L. 9, 22–23 (2018).

11   On the limitations of this law for establishing IO accountability see Benvenisti, *supra*
       note 10, at 16–30.

12   *See* Interpretation of the Agreement, *supra* note 10, *id.*

13   Several political philosophers are satisfied with a grounding that is based simply on
       human interaction, namely positing that individuals owe account to others for the effects
       of their behavior on society. *See, e.g.,* AMARTYA SEN, THE IDEA OF JUSTICE 46 (2009):
            The basic general obligation here must be to consider seriously what one can reason-
            ably do to help the realization of another person's freedom, taking note of its impor-
            tance and influenceability, and of one's own circumstances and likely effectiveness.
            There are, of course, ambiguities here and scope for disagreement, but it does make a
            substantial difference in determining what one should do to acknowledge an obliga-
            tion to consider this argument seriously.

regarded as trustees of humanity and as such they are accountable to those whom they affect by their policies, even if they are foreign nationals.

2   Two False Starts: the Rule of Law and Human Rights

2.1   *The Rule of Law*

When Alfred Venn Dicey contrasted the English administrative law system to the French *droit administratif,* he focused on the principle of the rule of law. This principle stipulated that all—private persons and public officials—are equally subjected to the law.[14] Therefore, when English public officials operated beyond their legal mandate—when they acted *ultra vires*—they lost their official mantle and were transformed into a private person who lacked authority or public status:

> Any official who exceeds the authority given him by the law incurs the common law responsibility for his wrongful act; he is amenable to the authority of the ordinary Courts, and the ordinary Courts have themselves jurisdiction to determine what is the extent of his legal power, and whether the orders under which he has acted were legal and valid.[15]

The agent who oversteps her legal mandate becomes, by that very act, a private individual, just like Cinderella at the stroke of midnight. Her orders are necessarily and promptly null and void. This doctrine has provided an effective judicial check on executive power, because the agent is required to demonstrate the legal source for her exercise of authority. This concept of the rule of law is quite narrow in its source. Synonyms that capture the same approach are

---

See also Ronald Dworkin, *A New Philosophy for International Law,* 41 PHIL. & PUB. AFF. 1 (2013) (states, just like individuals, need to further improve the system they constitute part of). This idea goes back to Vattel (see discussion in Benvenisti, *supra* note 2, at 302, 307–10. But to ground public law obligations, which go beyond what individuals owe each other when interacting in the private sphere, we need a stronger theory that singles out "public action."

14   Dicey's concept of the rule of law consisted of three principles: "that with us no man is above the law, that here every man, whatever be his rank or condition, is subject to the ordinary law of the realm and amenable to the jurisdiction of the ordinary tribunals, [and] that the general principles of the constitution [...] are with us the result of judicial decisions determining the rights of private persons in particular cases brought before the Courts". A.V. DICEY, LECTURES INTRODUCTORY TO THE STUDY OF THE LAW OF THE CONSTITUTION 171–178 (London, MacMillan & Co., 1885).

15   *Id.* at 384-85.

"the principle of legality" or the concept of "the rule *by* law."[16] But with judicial creativity and determination, this rule of law-grounded doctrine was extended beyond the formal authority to act to cover also the manner of action (the procedural aspects, including the right of hearing and due process more generally) and the motivation for action (substantive limitations on the exercise of discretion). The court's authority to review administrative action also derived from the need to ensure the rule of law.[17] As Lord Woolf explained, "[t]here are other principles which are part of the rule of law, for example, that the public are entitled to have resort to the courts; that the courts are for the resolution of their disputes; that it is the courts' responsibility to protect the public against the unlawful activities of others including the executive; and that it is the responsibility of the courts to determine the proper interpretation of the law."[18]

The rule of law approach informed the evolution of domestic administrative law in other legal systems as well. Carol Harlow notes that "[e]very Western administrative law system is founded on the rule of law ... The rule of law ideal forms the central background theory against which the principles of administrative law operate, while at the same time acting as a governing principle."[19] In fact, Neville Brown and John Bell argue that the French principle of *légalité*— "the idea that the administration must be compelled to observe the law [...] is something much more that the English and Scottish doctrines of *ultra vires*" in its procedural and substantive demands from the administration.[20] Augmented by the judicial recourse to the *principes généraux du droit*, the entire edifice of French administrative law is built on this concept.[21]

Like a stalactite that forms in limestone caverns from the slow accumulation of lime from mineral-laden drops of water, administrative law was born from this rule of law concept. Arguably, the strength of Dicey's rule of law approach was in the mandate it gave the courts to deliberate on the meaning of the authorization that the law had granted the public official, thereby incrementally expanding the law's demands from the executive.

---

16   Jeremy Waldron, *The Rule of Law in Public Law* (New York University Pub. Law & Legal Theory Working Papers, Paper No. 481, 2014). *See also* BRIAN TAMANAHA, ON THE RULE OF LAW: HISTORY, POLITICS, THEORY 3 (2004).

17   *See* Carol Harlow, *Global Administrative Law: The Quest for Principles and Values*, 17 EUR. J. INT'L L. 187, 195 (2006); Harry Woolf, *Judicial Review—The Tensions between the Executive and the Judiciary*, 114 LAW Q. REV. 579 (1998).

18   Woolf, *supra* note 17, at 581.

19   Harlow, *supra* note 17, at 190.

20   NEVILLE L. BROWN & JOHN S. BELL, FRENCH ADMINISTRATIVE LAW 202 (4th ed. 1993).

21   *Id.* at 205–23; JEAN RIVERO & JEAN WALINE, DROIT ADMINISTRATIF [ADMINISTRATIVE LAW] 260–64 (20th ed. 2004).

Unfortunately, that first drop of limestone-laden water, that necessary nar-row beginning, is missing in the international legal space. The reason for this is the normative absence in the international legal space of the motivation for the domestic rule of law concept: the agency relationship between the principal who—the king, the voter—and the agent, the public official who is tasked by the former to serve its interests. Dicey emphasized these relation-ships as the key for the rule of law demand when he spoke about "[a]ny official who exceeds the authority *given him by the law.*" But in international law, IOs do not derive their authority to act from states or from international law, and there is no theory that will transform the IO that oversteps its authority into a powerless Cinderella. In fact, the law endorses the opposite approach as the doctrine of implied powers allows IOs to expand their remit beyond the explicit authorizing text. The law reflects the view that like states, IOs remain private actors[22] with the legal capacity to do whatever they wish to *unless lim-ited by the law*. Except the *jus cogens* norms, that are too remote from questions of accountability,[23] the prevailing law on IOs does not support any theory that can accommodate external, public law obligations on IOs. Hence, the rule of law approach is hardly reconcilable with "obligations incumbent [on IOs] under general rules of international law."[24]

2.2   *Human Rights*

Could international human rights law serve as an alternative candidate for accountability obligations of IOs? This is in principle the German approach to administrative law that stipulates that the freedom of action of administra-tive agencies is restricted by the individual's constitutional or statutory rights.[25]

---

22   *See* HERSCH LAUTERPACHT, PRIVATE LAW SOURCES AND ANALOGIES OF
         INTERNATIONAL LAW (1927).

23   The European Court of First Instance in the *Kadi* and *Yusuf and Al Barakaat* judgments
         rejected the claim that procedural guarantees against the freezing of assets by the UN
         Security Council including the right to be heard constituted violation of *jus cogens* norms
         (judgments of the Court of First Instance of the European Communities of Sept. 21, 2005
         in Case T-315/01 Kadi v. Council and Comm'n, 2005 E.C.R. II-3649, and Case T-306/01 Yusuf
         and Al Barakaat International Foundation v. Council and Comm'n, 2005 E.C.R. II-3533).

24   *See* Interpretation of the Agreement, *supra* note 10., *id.*

25   *See* GRUNDGESETZ [GG] [Basic Law], art. 19(4) ("Should any person's rights be violated
         by public authority, he may have recourse to the courts."); VERWALTUNGSGERICHTS-
         ORDNUNG [VwGO] [Code of Administrative Court Procedure], § 42, para. 2 (Unless
         otherwise provided by law, the action shall only be admissible if the plaintiff claims that
         his/her rights have been violated by the administrative act or its refusal or omission). *See*
         also Florian Becker, The Development of German Administrative Law, 24 GEO. MASON L.
         REV. 453, 466–67 (2017).

This approach highlights two types of procedural obligations that derive from human rights to restrict governmental action: first, independent rights such as the right to information, the right to access to judicial remedies, and the right to due process; and second, derivative procedural rights that serve to indirectly protect substantive rights such as the right to life, self-determination, and property, that is, secondary rights that demand compliance with due process obligations in the course of limiting those rights.[26]

The human rights approach to accountability is conceptually weaker from the one based on the rule of law. The human rights perspective is limited to the citizen's human or constitutional rights. It thus does not question the very authority to act, but instead assumes an authority to act and assesses only the effects of the act on the relevant rights. An entire sphere of governmental activity, that which does not affect individual rights, is thus protected from external legal scrutiny. The decision-maker will remain a princess even if she violated the rights of others; the Cinderella-like effects of overstepping authority bounds do not exist under this vision. Conceptually, the scope of review is much limited, since as long as her rights are not violated, the citizen has no standing to demand accountability or involvement in the decision-making process. For those affected by the administrative agency, a preliminary question of entitlement to rights becomes a precondition for the demand for accountability. Those affected by foreign governmental actors would be hard pressed to demonstrate such an entitlement.

This leads to the major impediment for borrowing IO accountability from international human rights law. As is well known, while the Universal Declaration of Human Rights defines the rights as belonging to "all human beings" or "everyone," it conspicuously evades the assignment of the respective obligations and remains silent on the identity of the duty bearers. And when the duties are finally assigned, in the various human rights conventions, the duties to respect, protect, and provide rights are assigned to the state parties each with respect to individuals "subject to [their] jurisdiction."[27] There is no collective, global obligation toward all individuals.

---

26   See, e.g., Article 6(1) of the European Convention on Human Rights (ECHR), "[i]n the determination of his civil rights and obligations…. everyone is entitled to a fair and public hearing within a reasonable time by an independent and impartial tribunal established by law." (Convention for the Protection of Human Rights and Fundamental Freedoms art. 6(1), Nov. 4, 1950, 213 U.N.T.S. 221). See also EYAL BENVENISTI, THE LAW OF GLOBAL GOVERNANCE, 121–29 (2014).

27   See, e.g., ECHR, supra note 22 art. 1, International Covenant on Civil and Political Rights, GA res. 2200A (XXI), art. 3, U.N. Doc. A/RES/21/2200 (Dec. 19, 1966) Art. 2. See also BENVENISTI, GLOBAL GOVERNANCE, supra note 26, at 132–219.

Hence, when attempting to import international human rights obligations to IOs, two questions emerge, both related to that concept of "jurisdiction." First, can global bodies ever be regarded as having "jurisdiction" over the relevant individuals (those affected by their policies)? And second, if so, what is the spatial scope of those human rights obligations that IOs are accountable for.

When IOs exercise direct control over individuals the answer is clear. This direct control explains for example why the Human Rights Committee found that the UN Mission in Kosovo (UNMIK) was responsible for the human rights situation in Kosovo as long as it administered that territory, despite the fact that UNMIK was not party to the 1966 Covenant on Civil and Political Rights.[28] Similarly, it is obvious that the UN Security Council is responsible to individuals directly subject to its targeted sanctions regime in the counter-terrorism context. The same could easily apply also to employees of IOs who are entitled to expect their employer to respect and ensure their labor rights.[29] But this still leaves out many more types of stakeholders who are indirectly affected by IOs: in what sense are these individuals "subject" to their "jurisdiction"? Does, for example, the World Bank "subject" individuals to its "jurisdiction" when it decides to offer loans to a local government, which then uses the loans to evict those individuals from their homes?[30] And what about private bodies such as the International Olympic Committee which requires athletes to waive their privacy and other rights as a condition for participation in competitions?

Whereas the first question focused on the meaning of "subjection" to the jurisdiction, the second challenge addresses the spatial scope of the IOs' "jurisdiction." Again, it is clear that formal organizations that exercise direct territorial control over territory and people. For example, UN bodies

---

28   Concluding Observations of the Human Rights Committee Kosovo (Republic of Serbia), Hum. Rights Comm., 87th Sess., July 10–28, 2006, ¶ 4, U.N. Doc. CCPR/C/UNK/CO/1 (Aug. 14, 2006), http://docstore.ohchr.org/SelfServices/FilesHandler.ashx?enc=6QkG1d %2fPPRiCAqhKb7yhsq1Qo8bBNdeZ5f8Tz%2bMmes%2f%2bhnnX8dMdT1ka76gby7Q% 2f4D8nzFxqYYyrPwS9%2fLHQzmhdlwFnBgqDGfqdviSRB3loqxQT4I6p9lBbRMmxnQYE (last visited Aug. 11, 2018). This position is based on its general comment No. 26 (1977) on the continuity of obligations. Robert McCorquodale, *International Organisations and International Human Rights Law: One Giant Leap for Humankind, in* INTERNATIONAL LAW AND POWER: PERSPECTIVES ON LEGAL ORDER AND JUSTICE 141, 160 (Kaiyan Homi Kaikobad & Michael Bohlander eds., 2009) (concluding that IOs "can have human rights obligations, at least when exercising sovereign powers" like in Kosovo).

29   Waite and Kennedy v. Germany, App. No. 26083/94, 1999-I Eur. Ct. H.R.

30   *See, e.g.,* Mariarita Circi, *The World Bank Inspection Panel: The Indian Mumbai Urban Transport Project Case, in* GLOBAL ADMINISTRATIVE LAW: THE CASEBOOK, *supra* note 8, at 100.

administering territories, or UNHCR-run refugee centers, will be responsible in the area where they exercise effective control.[31] But these are the exception, and in most cases it remains a question how to translate the concept of "jurisdiction" to the myriad of decision-making bodies that directly and indirectly affect diverse stakeholders across the globe, many of whom are citizens of states whose governments are not parties to the organization. Are, for example, those outside the EU "within the jurisdiction" of the EU when the EU adopts policies that directly or indirectly affect them?[32]

We therefore need a theory that will delimit the substantive and spatial scope of the human rights-based obligations that IOs owe to affected individuals who are not "subject" to their "jurisdiction" in the traditional, state-based sense that is reflected in contemporary international law. Contemporary human rights law does not provide such a theory.

3   The Concept of Trusteeship of Humanity as a Potential Source for Accountability Obligations

3.1   *Trusteeship as the Foundation of Accountability Obligations*

This section explores yet a third ground for IO accountability that is free from the limitations of the first two approaches. This third ground is the concept

---

31   *See* Devika Hovell, *On Trust: The UN as Fiduciary (A Reply to Rosa Freedman)* (LSE Law, Soc'y & Eco. Working Papers, Paper No. 13, 2018); GUGLIELMO VERDIRAME, THE UN AND HUMAN RIGHTS: WHO GUARDS THE GUARDIANS? (2011); RALPH WILDE, INTERNATIONAL TERRITORIAL ADMINISTRATION (2006). *See also* EYAL BENVENISTI, THE INTERNATIONAL LAW OF OCCUPATION, 249–75 (2d ed. 2012).

32   Such foreign stakeholders may seek to rely on recent efforts to interpret the territorial scope of application of human rights conventions as extending beyond the state's "jurisdiction," and extend those arguments further to IOs. But this effort is also undermined by the lack of an accepted theory that could justify the spatial extension of international human rights obligations beyond the jurisdiction of the state parties to the IO. *See* MARKO MILANOVIC, EXTRATERRITORIAL APPLICATION OF HUMAN RIGHTS TREATIES: LAW, PRINCIPLES, AND POLICY 106–17 (2011); MAASTRICHT PRINCIPLES ON EXTRATERRITORIAL OBLIGATIONS OF STATES IN THE AREA OF ECONOMIC, SOCIAL AND CULTURAL RIGHTS (2011), https://www.etoconsortium.org/nc/en/main-navigation/library/maastricht-principles/?tx_drblob_pi1%5BdownloadUid%5D=23 (last visited Aug 11, 2018); MARGOT E. SALOMON, GLOBAL RESPONSIBILITY FOR HUMAN RIGHTS: WORLD POVERTY AND THE DEVELOPMENT OF INTERNATIONAL LAW (2007). Wouter Vandenhole, *Extraterritorial Human Rights Obligations: Taking Stock, Looking Forward*, 2013 EUR. J. HUM. RTS. 804; Yuval Shany, *Taking Universality Seriously: A Functional Approach to Extraterritoriality in International Human Rights Law*, 7 L. & ETHICS HUM. RTS. 47 (2013). *But see* Samantha Besson, *The Extraterritoriality of the European Convention on Human Rights: Why Human Rights Depend on Jurisdiction and What Jurisdiction Amounts to*, 25 LEIDEN J. INT'L L. 857 (2012).

of trusteeship. The concept of trusteeship is no stranger to domestic administrative law.[33] It provided the basis for John Austin's definition of administrative
law long before Dicey's approach gained prominence:

> Administrative law determines the ends and modes to and in which
> the sovereign powers shall be exercised: shall be exercised directly
> by the monarch or sovereign number, or shall be exercised directly by
> the subordinate political superiors to whom portions of those powers are
> delegated or *committed in trust*.[34] (my emphasis)

Austin's view reflected a long-established practice of common-law judges,
who, since the early seventeenth century, invoked and refined the concept of
trust to limit the authority of office holders.[35] This traditional concept also
informed the democratic vision of state authority, derived from the people
and therefore acting as the people's trustee, as exemplified in the writings of
John Locke[36] and James Madison.[37] In the same vein, the Virginia Declaration
of Rights (1776) asserted that "all power is vested in, and consequently derived

---

33   Frank H. Easterbrook & Daniel R. Fischel, *Contract and Fiduciary Duty*, 36 J.L. & ECON.
      425, 425 (1993).

34   JOHN AUSTIN, LECTURES ON JURISPRUDENCE OR THE PHILOSOPHY OF POSITIVE
      LAW 465 (Robert Campbell ed., 5th ed. London, J. Murray 1885).

35   Robert E. Mabry Rogers & Stephen B. Young, *Public Office as a Public Trust: A Suggestion
      that Impeachment for High Crimes and Misdemeanors Implies a Fiduciary Standard*, 63
      GEO. L.J. 1025, 1028–30 (1974) (citing English cases from as early as 1592 which 'embraced
      the private law concept of trust and extended its application even further in regulating
      public offices'). Note that Dicey also emphasized delegation, but from the law: embedded
      in the logic of delegation ('authority given him by the law').

36   JOHN LOCKE, TWO TREATISES OF GOVERNMENT 196–97 (Thomas I. Cook ed., Hafner
      Publishing Co. 1947) (1690):
      "Though in a constituted commonwealth, standing upon its own basis and acting
      according to its own nature, that is, acting for the preservation of the community, there
      can be but one supreme power which is the legislative, to which all the rest are and must
      be subordinate, yet, the legislative being only a fiduciary power to act for certain ends,
      there remains still in the people a supreme power to remove or alter the legislative when
      they find the legislative act contrary to the trust reposed in them; for all power given with
      trust for the attaining an end being limited by that end, whenever that end is manifestly
      neglected or opposed, the trust must necessarily be."
      See also id. at 204 on discretion.

37   James Madison, *The Federalist, 46, in* THE FEDERALIST 315, 315 (Jacob E. Cooke ed.,
      Wesleyan Univ. Press 2008) (1788) ("The Federal and State Governments are in fact but
      different agents and trustees of the people, instituted with different powers, and desig-
      nated for different purposes."); Alexander Hamilton, *The Federalist, 65, in id.* at 439, 440
      ("The delicacy and magnitude of a trust which so deeply concerns the political reputa-
      tion and existence of every man engaged in the administration of public affairs speak for
      themselves.").

from, the people; that magistrates are their trustees and servants and at all times amenable to them."[38] Even monarchic France recognized at the time the concept of trusteeship as limiting the authority of the king.[39]

The trusteeship vision continued to inform the evolution of domestic administrative law in several countries. Conceptualizing the government as a trustee offered courts grounds for extending the scope of administrative law to encompass also activities that are not expressly regulated by statute, such as the management of state owned property. As the Israeli Supreme Court declared in 1962, municipalities must manage property registered under their name as trustees of the public, the true if not formal owner of the property.[40] Appropriately, the concept of trusteeship as the *grundnorm* of administrative law has recently garnered renewed attention from domestic administrative and constitutional law scholars.[41]

3.2   *Trusteeship beyond the State*

In an earlier article, I offered a reading of sovereignty as trusteeship for humanity.[42] I argued that the way to justify the sovereign state and its endowment with exclusive jurisdiction within its boundaries is by regarding it as a trustee on behalf of all humans. This section suggests that IOs are subject to the same discipline of trusteeship that states are bound by, and that the legal discipline that trusteeship offers is a potent source of accountability duties incumbent on IOs. In that article, I submitted that the idea of sovereignty as exclusive authority (and hence trustee of its citizens only) was congruent with democratic notions as long as there was a perfect or almost-perfect fit between

---

38   George Mason & Thomas Ludwell lee, The Virginia Declaration of Rights § 2 (1776).

39   Michel Troper, *Sovereignty and Natural Law in the Legal Discourse of the Ancien Régime*, 16 Theoretical Inquiries L. 315 (2015).

40   HCJ 262/62 Israel Peretz v. The Municipality of Kfar Shmaryahu, 16 PD 2101, 2115 (1962) (Isr.) (Justice Sussman).

41   *See, e.g.*, Evan Fox-Decent, Sovereignty's Promise: The State as Fiduciary (2012); D. Theodore Rave, *Politicians as Fiduciaries*, 126 Harv. L. Rev. 671 (2013). Ethan J. Leib, David L. Ponet & Michael Serota, *A Fiduciary Theory of Judging*, 101 Calif. L. Rev. 699 (2013); Ethan J. Leib & David L. Ponet, *Fiduciary Representation and Deliberative Engagement with Children*, 20 J. Pol. Phil. 178 (2012); David L. Ponet & Ethan J. Leib, *Fiduciary Law's Lessons for Deliberative Democracy*, 91 B.U. L. Rev. 1249 (2011). *See also* Evan J. Criddle, *Fiduciary Administration: Rethinking Popular Representation in Agency Rulemaking*, 88 Tex. L. Rev. 441 (2010); Evan J. Criddle, *Fiduciary Foundations of Administrative Law*, 54 UCLA L. Rev. 117 (2006).

42   Benvenisti, *supra* note 2.

the sovereign and the citizens—those affected by its policies.[43] Such a vision made eminent sense when sovereigns ruled discrete economies, separated from each other by rivers, deserts and other natural barriers, making cross-border externalities, such as pollution, a relatively rare event, to be resolved on the inter-sovereign level, negotiated by emissaries, ambassadors and, later, within international organizations. This solipsistic vision of sovereignty was enhanced by the notion of national self-determination that erected barriers to the demands of non-citizens to weigh in on domestic policy-making processes and shielded the domestic body politic from the obligation to internalize the rights and interests of non-citizens in their policymaking. But today, in our global condominium, the 'technology' of global governance that operates through discrete sovereign entities no longer fits. Sovereigns today cannot be likened to the owners of isolated mansions; they are more analogous to owners of small apartments in one densely packed high-rise in which about two hundred families live. This calls for a more encompassing vision of state sovereignty as embedded in a global order, which is a source not only of powers and rights, but also of obligations that essentially position states—and IOs to which states delegate authority—as trustees of all of humanity. Under this vision, they would be therefore accountable to all those affected by their policies, even if the affected were non-citizens living in faraway lands.[44]

There is obviously a danger associated with invoking the concept of trusteeship in the global context. Cynics will say that the notion of 'trusteeship for humanity' was invented to justify colonialism. Obviously, its underlying rationale was asserted when European powers apportioned African territory among them in the Scramble for Africa,[45] and the League of Nations[46] used

---

43   For such a functional justification of sovereignty, see also HENRY SIDGWICK, THE ELEMENTS OF POLITICS 252 (4th ed. Macmillan and Co., 1919): "the main justification for the appropriation of territory to governments is that the prevention of mutual mischief among the human beings using it cannot otherwise be adequately secured."

44   Benvenisti, *supra* note 2; Eyal Benvenisti, *Legislating For Humanity: May States Compel Foreigners to Promote Global Welfare?*, in INTERNATIONAL LAW-MAKING, ESSAYS IN HONOUR OF JAN KLABBERS 3 (Rain Liivoja & Jarna Petman eds., 2014). *Compare* EVAN CRIDDLE AND EVAN FOX-DECENT, FIDUCIARIES OF HUMANITY (2016) (arguing that states are fiduciaries for their people and, *collectively*, for humanity at large).

45   General Act of the Conference of Berlin, 26 February 1885 ("... concern, as to the means of furthering the moral and material well-being of the native populations.").

46   Antony Anghie, *Colonialism and the Birth of International Institutions: Sovereignty, Economy, and the Mandate System of the League of Nations*, 34 N.Y.U. J. INT'L L. & POL. 513, 604–05 (2002) ("My argument has been that the economic and social policies actively endorsed by the PMC had profoundly damaging consequences for mandate peoples. The Mandate System, however, failed to provide any formal mechanism by which the native could communicate meaningfully with, and represent herself before, the PMC.").

trusteeship to justify a new form of colonialism.[47] The problematic relation-ship between occupier and occupied has also been referred-to as 'grounded in trusteeship'.[48] Exploitative institutions such as the Special Trustee for American Indians[49] existed also under domestic law. But these examples only serve to emphasize the fundamental point that the concept of trustee-ship is not based on actual trust, on confidence in the decision-maker, but to the contrary. As Niklas Luhmann suggested, the emergence of the concept of trusteeship is correlated with peoples' move from their closely-knit communi-ties to the large cities, and their sense of lost confidence in the public actors they had known had had faith in. The concept of trusteeship was designed to offer a legal substitute for the loss of social ties.[50] In other words, trust, as opposed to confidence or faith, 'involves one in a relation where the acts, char-acter, or intentions of the other cannot be confirmed. [...] [O]ne trusts or is forced to trust—perhaps led to trust would be better—when one cannot know, when one has not the capabilities to apprehend or check on the other and so has no choice but to *trust*.'[51] Moreover, and more importantly, the version of trusteeship of humanity advocated here does not justify *more* powers over foreign stakeholders. In fact, it calls for just the opposite. It aims inwardly, as it requires global actors to assume burdens within their own autonomy, rather than endorsing their access to others' resources.[52]

---

47   League of Nations Covenant art. 22 ("the principle that the well-being and development
       of such peoples form a sacred trust of civilisation and that securities for the performance
       of this trust should be embodied in this Covenant.").

48   BENVENISTI, *supra* note 31, at 6; Arnold Wilson, *The Laws of War in Occupied Territory*,
       18 TRANSACTIONS GROTIUS SOC'Y 17, 38 (1933) ("enemy territories in the occupation of
       the armed forces of another country constitute ... a sacred trust."); Adam Roberts, *What
       Is Military Occupation?* 55 BRITISH Y.B. INT'L L. 249, 295 (1985) ("the idea of trusteeship
       is implicit in all occupation law."); GERHARD VON GLAHN, LAW AMONG NATIONS 686
       (5th ed. 1986) (the "occupant ... exercises a temporary right of administration on a sort of
       trusteeship basis.").

49   Cobell v. Salazar, 573 F.3d 808, 809 (D.C. Cir. 2009).

50   NIKLAS LUHMANN, TRUST AND POWER (1979). *See also* Janne Jalava, *From Norms to
       Trust: The Luhmannian Connections between Trust and System*, 6 EUR. J. SOC. THEORY 173
       (2003). According to Adam Seligman, the concept of "trust" was created in "an attempt
       to posit new bonds of general trust in societies where primordial attachments were no
       longer goods to think with." ADAM B. SELIGMAN, THE PROBLEM OF TRUST 15 (1997). I
       thank Neil Walker for elaborating on this point.

51   SELIGMAN, *supra* note 50, at 21. *See also* Virginia Held, *On the Meaning of Trust*, 78 ETHICS
       156, 157 (1968) ("trust is most required exactly when we least know whether a person will
       or will not do an action.").

52   David Luban, *Nationalism, Human Rights, and the Prospects for Peace: An Essay on
       Sovereign Responsibilities* 17 (GlobalTrust Working Paper, Paper No. 02, 2018), ("the model

Invoking the trusteeship to humanity concept revives a venerable tradition in international law concerning the meaning of sovereignty that responds adequately to contemporary challenges. To paraphrase James Madison, IOs are, in fact, but different trustees of all human beings, because the ultimate, inherent authority resides in humanity.[53] It is humanity at large that assigns certain groups of citizens the power to form national governments (and indirectly to form IOs).[54] Stated otherwise, it is possible to reconceptualize Max Huber's famous vision of a global legal order that 'divides between nations the space upon which human activities are employed'[55] and allocates to each the responsibility toward other nations for activities transpiring in its jurisdiction that violate international law, in a relationship of trusteeship. According to Huber's viewpoint, given the precedence of human rights, sovereigns can—and should—be viewed as organs of a global system that allocates competences and responsibilities for promoting the rights of all human beings and their interest in the sustainable utilization of global resources. As trustees of this global system—to paraphrase another statement of Huber's[56]—the competency of contemporary sovereigns to manage public affairs within their respective jurisdictions carries with it a corollary duty to take account of external interests and even to balance internal against external interests. The foreigner remains a foreigner, but she is not a total alien. She has a stake in any public decision, and

---

changes dramatically once we think of sovereigns as trustees not of a colonized people, but of humanity.").

53   As Madison noted in The Federalist Papers, "[t]he federal and State governments are in fact but different agents and trustees of the people [because] the ultimate authority ... resides in the people alone." Madison, *The Federalist, 46, in* THE FEDERALIST, *supra* note 37, at 315, 315.

54   *See also* Hans Kelsen, *Foundations of* Democracy, 66 ETHICS 1, 33–34 (1955). Kelsen prefers the

        "[t]heory according to which the state is not a mysterious substance different from its members, i.e., the human beings forming the state ... This doctrine ... finds this existence in the validity and efficacy of a normative order and consequently in the minds of the human beings who are the subjects of the obligations and rights stipulated by this order.... By demonstrating that absolute sovereignty is not and cannot be an essential quality of the state existing side by side with other states, it removes one of the most stubborn prejudices which prevent political and legal science from recognizing the possibility of an international legal order constituting an international community of which the state is a member, just as corporations are members of the state."

55   Island of Palmas (Netherlands v. US), 2 R.I.A.A. 829, 839 (Perm. Ct. Arb.1928).

56   Huber's statement in the award re. British Claims in the Spanish Zone of Morocco (Gr. Brit. v. Spain), 2 R.I.A.A. 615, 641 (Perm. Ct. Arb. 1925) ("Responsibility is the necessary corollary of rights. All international rights entail international responsibility."). *See* Daniel-Erasmus Khan, *Max Huber as Arbitrator: The Palmas (Miangas) Case and Other Arbitrations*, 18 EUR. J. INT'L L. 145, 156 (2007).

has standing at least to demand to have her interests taken into account and also to demand an account for any policy that directly or indirectly affects her.[57]

Research focused on the trusteeship concept in international law at the GlobalTrust project has identified several areas in which the commitment to 'other-regardingness' or the practice of taking others' interest into account is quite prevalent among states and international tribunals, even this concept is not explicitly articulated.[58] In other words, it is possible to connect all the dots where 'other-regarding' duties have been articulated to a single abstract principle that stipulates a duty of other-regardingness that is embedded in a concept of trusteeship and extended to IOs to require their accountability to those affected by their acts and omissions. Such a duty could very well be included among the "obligations incumbent upon [IOs] under general rules of international law."

As trustees of humanity, then, national decision-makers—and by extension, those to whom they delegate authority, such as IOs—have an obligation to take into account the interests of all who are affected by their acts. Although sovereigns are entitled to prioritize their own citizens' needs and IOs, the citizens of their member states, they must weigh the interests of other stakeholders and consider internalizing them into their balancing calculus. This obligation to foreign stakeholders does not *necessarily* imply an obligation to respond to those interests, and does not even require full legal responsibility for ultimately preferring domestic interests in balancing the opposing claims. Nor does it *necessarily* imply that sovereign discretion should be subject to review by third parties such as foreign or international courts that would replace the sovereign's discretion with their own. What it does imply as a minimum, however, is that sovereigns consider whether the policies they adopt and pursue can be made less detrimental to foreign stakeholders or even improve their condition and otherwise promote global welfare.

This concept of trusteeship applies with even greater force to IOs whose design or intended impact is to shape the behaviour of individuals across

57   Benvenisti, *supra* note 2; BENVENISTI, *supra* note 26, at 145–50.
58   *See, e.g., Eyal Benvenisti & Sivan Shlomo Agon, The Law of Strangers: The Form and Substance of Other-Regarding International Adjudication* (GlobalTrust Working Paper, Paper No. 08, 2017); Alon Jasper, *Participation of Foreigners in Environmental Decision-Making & The Aarhus Convention* (GlobalTrust Working Paper, Paper No. 06, 2017); Marka Peterson, *The Federal Reserve Since the Global Financial Crisis: Do Foreign Interests Matter to the World's Economic Hegemon?* (GlobalTrust Working Paper, Paper No. 03, 2016). *See generally* COMMUNITY INTERESTS ACROSS INTERNATIONAL LAW (Eyal Benvenisti & Georg Nolte eds. 2018).

political boundaries.[59] The implication is that inter-governmental organizations, informal governance bodies coordinated by state executives and other national agencies, as global trustees, need to render account to affected foreign stakeholders and allow them voice in their decision-making processes. The question, then, is not whether administrative law norms would be suitable for IOs and other global governance bodies in their diverse areas of regulation, but rather *which* laws would be fit for purpose. Such rules should be tailored to the various organizations to fit their nature, their functions and their potential impact on individuals. The trusteeship concept provides the starting point for the articulation of accountability obligations.

4   Conclusion

"Power corrupts, and absolute power corrupts absolutely," said Lord Acton, and though in his days the phenomenon of global governance was just making its first appearances, there was no reason to expect that global governance bodies would somehow avoid the pitfalls of every human organization. As the practice over the years demonstrates, there is nothing innate in IOs, public or formally private, that defies this simple logic. The history and theory of administrative law suggest that this law's requirements are not designed *against* the administrative agencies, but just the opposite. The laws that structure the decision-making process assist the agencies, rather than burden them. The question, then, is not whether, but rather *which* administrative law norms would be suitable for IOs in their diverse types and areas of regulation. Such rules should be tailored to fit their nature, their functions, and their potential impact on individuals.

The concept of trusteeship for humanity can sustain the demand for IO accountability. The essence of this obligation is the duty to take account of all those affected by their acts and omissions and to provide account to them. Arguably, this concept is ingrained in international legal practice and is among those general rules of international law incumbent on IOs.

---

59   Particularly in areas under their direct administration: Hovell, *supra* note 31, at 7 (referring to UN territorial administration: "Where the law entrusts irresistible discretionary power over the interests of another party—interests that are vulnerable by virtue of that power—this establishes a relationship premised on a presumption of trust.").

CHAPTER 12

Are International Mass Claims Commissions the Right Mechanism to Provide Redress to Individuals Injured under International Law?

*Chiara Giorgetti**

1 Introduction

I had the good fortune and honor to author a book—*International Claims Commissions: Righting Wrongs After Conflict*—with Lea Brilmayer, together with Lorraine Charlton, which was published in 2017 by Edward Elgar's series Elgar International Law.[1]

I still remember vividly the call I got from Lea on a Saturday morning inviting me to participate in this project—I was watching my son playing soccer on a beautiful spring day in Washington, DC—it was as unexpected as welcomed. Because of my professional experience, I had been thinking about international claims commissions for a while, and I jumped at the opportunity of working with Lea and furthering my exploration of the intricacies and outcomes of a in varied of claims commissions. The process itself of writing the book was a wonderful experience. It was very collaborative and open. We read each other's drafts, freely exchanged ideas and built on each other's thoughts. And in a true mark of Lea's style, it was very enjoyable. I certainly feel that I grew and emerged a better scholar thanks to the collaboration with Lea.

International Claims Commissions provides an extensive review and analysis of the workings and mechanisms of international claims commissions. We examine international claims commissions from multiple viewpoints and we assess their legal framework and establishing instruments, we examined what claims were covered and which claimants were accepted, we studied issues related to costs and the challenges they bring, and we examined issues related to available and acceptable evidence as well as possible remedies and whether decisions of the commissions generated compliance. Principally, the

* I would like to thank Natalie Klein and Harlan Cohen for their helpful comments on this draft. Thank you also to Jason Zarin for his editorial assistance.

1 Lea Brilmayer, Chiara Giorgetti & Lorraine Charlton, International Claims Commissions—Righting Wrongs after Conflict (2017).

© KONINKLIJKE BRILL NV, LEIDEN, 2019 | DOI:10.1163/9789004316539_013

book offers suggestions and best practice for the establishment and management of claims commissions and it endeavors to assist legal advisers and policy
makers in creating the best possible claims commissions for their purpose.

The book focuses mostly on three international claims commissions that
provide the best and most recent examples of claims commissions: the Iran–
US Claims Tribunal (IUSCT), the United Nations Compensation Commission
(UNCC), and the Eritrea-Ethiopia Claims Commission (EECC). These three
commissions represent a variety of different experiences and practices and
enjoyed a diverse degree of success. We thought it was therefore valuable to
examine them together. I had the privilege to work with Lea in some of the
cases related to the EECC, especially on issues of dual nationality, and, in private practice in Geneva, I was part of the team that represented Iraq at the
UNCC in the "F" category (unusually large and complex) of cases.[2]

In a subsequent article published in the *Yale Journal of International Law*,[3]
Lea further explores International Mass Claims Commissions (IMCCs) as
semi-public institutions and she analyzes motivations behind the formation
and function of IMCCs—in particular whether IMCCs are originally created
to provide compensation and/or closure—and connects the reasons behind
the creation of the IMCCs and their treaty terms to their success in providing
effective remedies.

She concludes that, in reading the constitutive instruments of IMCCs, one
can often already foresee the main and preferred assigned functions of IMCCs
and predict their likelihood of success in delivering compensation to injured
individuals. She distinguishes between 'thick' and 'thin' IMCCs, where the
'thick' ones are created by instruments that enable them to provide effective
compensation to a variety of injured claimants, while 'thin' IMCCs may have
been created with the principal aim of providing closure to the parties—and
the international community—after conflict, rather than with the core aim of
ensuring compensation to injured individuals.

My work on the book, and Lea's significant analysis, raised several additional
questions related to the real comparative advantages of claims commissions:
Under what circumstances should parties go to the extensive trouble of

---

2   Claims at the United Nations Claims Commission (UNCC) were divided into several groups,
    identified by a letter. Claims in the A, B, C and D groups were individual claims not in excess
    of $100,000. Claims under the E and F category were considered unusually large and complex
    claims. The UNCC was created in 1991 as a subsidiary organ of the United Nations Security
    Council under Security Council resolution 687 (1991). See generally infra note 8 and relevant
    text in the main body.

3   Lea Brilmayer, *Understanding "IMCCs": Compensation and Closure in the Formation and
    Function of International Mass Claims Commissions*, 43 YALE J. INT'L L. (2018).

creating a completely new, expensive and complex dispute resolution mechanism to address their reciprocal claims? What are the unique features that distinguish IMCCs from other dispute resolution mechanisms that make their creation worth it? How expansive or restricted should the categories of claimants and claims be for the successful operation of a Commission? Several important general questions are also worth further study: How important is a mechanism that ensures the existence of funding for the payment of awards? Is there a role for external actors from the international community to back the implementation of the decisions of the commission? And ultimately, what is a successful IMCC?

In this chapter, I address one specific issue which is of great interest to me: are IMCCs the right mechanism to provide redress to individuals whose rights have been wronged under international law? Indeed, in one aspect IMCCs are truly unique: their ability to provide compensation to individuals for injuries they suffered as a consequence of violations of international law, including obligations deriving from such varied areas as humanitarian law, international investment law and international environmental law. In the continuous quest to find redress for individuals in international forums, are IMCCs the solution? In this contribution, I submit that IMCCs can be especially helpful in redressing meritorious individual claims, and they offer a unique and flexible instrument to fill a significant vacuum in international law.

The analysis in this chapter proceeds as follows: after briefly introducing IMCCs in Part 2, Part 3 explains why separate international instruments that provide access to the individuals to obtain redress are still necessary. In Part 4, I introduce three IMCCs and in Part 5 I examine specifically how they provided access and redress to individuals. In Part 6, I examine particularly IMCC's expansive interpretation of nationality requirements. Part 7 concludes, and also highlights some problems that persist even when IMCCs grant full compensation to individuals.

2   What Distinguishes International Mass Claims Commissions from Other Legal Instruments?

Historically, the end of a war did not generally result in the payment of compensation from each belligerent to the others. Rather, the winning party would request and obtain substantial payments, both monetary and in assets, by the losing party for reparations to the winning State. Conversely, the losing party would have to agree to capitulations or surrenders, which often included significant concessions also in terms of accepting responsibility for the war, restriction on rearmament and harsh reparation costs.[4] Indeed, the terms contained in the treaty of Versailles that ended WWI are at times indicated as one of the causes for the raise of National-Socialism in Germany, the losing party.[5]

Amongst the shortcomings of these historical post-war compensations mechanisms, one stands out: the fact that compensation was mostly awarded to former belligerent States and rarely trickled down to the individuals who suffered war-related injuries. Indeed, it was the State of nationality of the individual which was charged with distributing any compensation received by the defeated State to its injured nationals.[6]

IMCCs adopt a new solution to the compensation problem, as they tend to compensate individuals directly. For this reason, IMCCs can become important international dispute resolution mechanisms in the post-WWII international justice system. Indeed, the legacy of some IMCCs—particularly of the IUSCT and the UNCC—can be transformative for communities and for the international legal system. Yet, the establishment of IMCCs is still a rare occurrence in the aftermath of conflict. IMCCs constitute a niche within the increasingly populated universe of international dispute resolution mechanisms.[7]

So, a question immediately follows: what are IMCCs and what distinguish them from other international dispute resolution mechanisms? An important element to highlight at the outset is that international mass claims commissions vary in form and function—there is no uniform, formal definition of IMCCs. The structure, jurisdiction, procedures and ability to provide remedy of IMCCs vary. And the flexibility that IMCCs have is one of their most attractive features, as IMCCs can be shaped and established to target specific disputes and claims.

IMCCs do, however, share a series of important common features that distinguish them from other international dispute resolution mechanisms and

---

4 On the capitulation agreements that ended WWI, see MAURITS H. VAN DEN BOOGERT, THE CAPITULATIONS AND THE OTTOMAN LEGAL SYSTEM: QADIS, CONSULS, AND BERATHS IN THE 18TH CENTURY (2005).

5 See for example A.J.P. TYLOR, THE ORIGINS OF THE SECOND WORLD WAR (1961), and P.M.H. BELL, THE ORIGINS OF THE SECOND WORLD WAR IN EUROPE (2d ed. 1997).

6 See Bell, supra note 5, at 22. See also RUTH HENIG, VERSAILLES AND AFTER: 1919–1933 (1995).

7 See for example Cesare P.R. Romano, *The Proliferation of International Judicial Bodies: The Pieces of the Puzzle*, 31 N.Y.U. J. INT'L L. & POL. 709, 709 (1999) (arguing that the enormous expansion of the international judiciary will probably be seen in the future as the single most significant post-cold war development in international law) and Benedict Kingsbury, *Foreword: Is the Proliferation of International Courts and Tribunals a Systemic Problem?*, 31 N.Y.U. J. INT'L L. & POL. 679 (1999) (discussing the issue of the rapid proliferation of international courts and tribunals and the increased activity of many of the courts).

transitional justice instruments. Importantly, IMCCs are binding dispute resolution mechanisms that are created to resolve claims after conflict, or more generally after an internationally-relevant upheaval. The UNCC, for example, was created after the invasion of Kuwait by Iraq.[8] The Iran–US Claims Tribunal was established after the Iranian revolution that resulted in the overthrow of the US-friendly Shah.[9] The EECC was part of the Peace Agreement that ended the 1998–2000 war between Eritrea and Ethiopia.[10]

There is also no doubt that IMCCs are international law instruments, created within the international legal system, which they are called to apply and uphold. Importantly, IMCCs engage the responsibility of the State as a sovereign entity and as a subject of international law. Thus, they only engage the responsibility of States for violations of international law. This also means that IMCCs only review claims for damages, loss and injuries to individuals, States and international organizations that result from an international wrongful act of a State, and breaches of an international obligations of the State itself, which are attributable to the State under international law.

Also, IMCCs are structured and act like judicial bodies. They are neutral and impartial bodies, and decisions are taken by independent and impartial adjudicators. In that sense, IMCCs are not akin to truth and reconciliation commissions or other transitional justice instruments whose principal aims are often fostering reconciliation and establishing a historical record of past events.[11] IMCCs follow the principles of due process and incorporate the essence of the principles of fair trial in their proceedings. In some ways, viewed from afar, IMCCs may look like an oversized arbitral tribunal. This is especially true for the EECC, which comprised five members and looked from the outside as other international arbitral tribunals, including—for example—the Eritrea-Ethiopia Boundary Commission, which addressed the related issue of

8   For an introduction to the UNCC, see Timothy J. Feighery, *The United Nations Compensation Commission*, in THE RULES, PRACTICE AND JURISPRUDENCE OF INTERNATIONAL COURTS AND TRIBUNALS (Chiara Giorgetti, ed., 2012) and David Bederman, *The United Nations Compensation Commission and Tradition of International Claims Settlement*, 27 N.Y.U. J. INT'L L. & POL. (1994) 1.

9   For a thorough review, including an excellent historical introduction, see Jeremy Sharpe, *The Iran-United States Claims Tribunal*, in THE RULES, PRACTICE AND JURISPRUDENCE OF INTERNATIONAL COURTS AND TRIBUNALS (Chiara Giorgetti, ed., 2012).

10   *See generally* SEAN D. MURPHY, WON KIDANE AND THOMAS R. SNIDER, LITIGATING WAR: MASS INJURY AND THE ERITREA-ETHIOPIA CLAIMS COMMISSION (2013) (reviewing and assessing all the decisions by the EECC in context).

11   On the form and appropriateness of transitional justice instruments, *see* Yasmin Sooka, *Dealing with the past and transitional justice: building peace through accountability*, 88 INT'L REV. RED CROSS 311 (2006).

the correct location of the boundary arising in the context of the same dispute between the two African countries. The IUSCT is a more complex institution, but it also operates essentially as a three-member arbitral tribunal, whose composition changes depending on the features of underlying dispute. The UNCC stands out and indeed had a more complex structure that required the intervention of a parallel/mirror organ of the UN Security Council. Yet, the Panels of Commissioners that reviewed and decided claims, especially the large and complex ones, were also formed by three-member panels, each reviewing a specific category or sub-category of claims.[12] Fundamentally, therefore, IMCCs are binding dispute resolution mechanisms, whose decisions are binding on all parties.

The most important feature of IMCCs, however, is that they are *ad hoc* instruments, endowed with remarkable flexibility. IMCCs are created *ex post*, after the dispute arises, so that the particular nature and characteristics of the dispute itself can be taken into consideration. How their *ad hoc* nature and flexibility is used to create effective compensatory instruments for individuals is what I seek to analyze in this chapter. Before delving into this, however, it is important to understand why these kinds of instruments are needed.

3 The Persistent Need for International Forums Open to Individuals

IMCCs' remarkable and unique flexibility is drawn from the fact that they are configured as necessary, including as instruments providing direct redress to individuals who suffered injuries under international law. This capacity and purpose are as unique as necessary.

3.1 *Individuals Rarely Have Direct Access to International Forums*

One of the most significant post-WWII developments related to international law is the fact that, increasingly, individuals are recognized holders of international rights and as subjects of international law in their own right. However, they still only rarely possess direct procedural access to international mechanisms to redress their claims. Under human rights norms, individuals enjoy many individual rights enumerated in several international human rights covenants and subsequent specialized treaties. These rights—which include the right to life, the right to a family, the right to privacy, the right to due process

---

12   *See generally* UNCC, *United Nations Compensation Commission*, https://uncc.ch/home (providing background information as well as all primary documents related to the UNCC).

and the right to property—are rights that individuals own vis-à-vis a State. Indeed, the State that exercises control over the territory where the individual resides has an obligation to provide specific, enumerated rights to individuals. In addition to human rights, individuals also enjoy international rights in other areas, including humanitarian law, refugees' law, consular protections, international investment law and others.[13]

Yet, the weak link of this progressive recognition of individuals as full subjects of international law is the lack of access to international adjudicatory forums enabled to hear and decide their claims and award compensation for their injuries. Individuals are generally barred from bringing direct claims to most international courts and tribunals. For example, individuals cannot bring direct claims to the International Court of Justice (ICJ), the Dispute Resolution Mechanism of the Word Trade Organization (WTO), or the International Tribunal for the Law of the Sea (ITLOS). It is true that in some cases they may be able to bring indirect claims through diplomatic representation. For example, claim espousal by the State of nationality of the individual has served to access the ICJ, and its predecessor, the Permanent Court of International Justice (PCIJ). But these efforts are rare and require significant connection and efforts by both the individual and the sponsoring State.

Moreover, diplomatic representation does not guarantee success and thus access to an international forum. The notorious *Nottebohm* case is on point.[14] In this case, Liechtenstein brought a claim against Guatemala asserting that Guatemala had acted in a manner contrary to international law towards Friedrich Nottebohm, a national of Liechtenstein, and thus claimed restitution and compensation from Guatemala on behalf of Mr. Nottebohm. The ICJ, however, found that Mr. Nottebohm did not possess a valid nationality claim for the purpose of accessing the ICJ jurisdiction because his nationality did not express a 'genuine link' between him and Liechtenstein. As a consequence of the ICJ decision, Mr. Nottebohm, who at the time only had Liechtenstenian nationality, was therefore left without an international remedy to claim for compensation for the property he had lost in Guatemala.

It is true that under certain circumstances individuals do have direct access to certain forums. The European Court of Human Rights (ECtHR) is a notable example. Investor State Dispute Settlement (ISDS) also provides forums construed in ways to be directly accessible to both juridical and physical persons.

---

13   *See generally*, Chiara Giorgetti, *Rethinking the Individual in International Law*, 22 LEWIS & CLARK L.R. __ (forthcoming, 2018) (explaining the position of the individual in international law and assessing its shortfalls).

14   *Nottebohm* (*Liechtenstein v. Guatemala*), 2nd Phase Judgment, 1955 I.C.J. 4 (April 6, 1955).

These two forums, however, are the exceptions rather than the norm. And indeed, their existence also serves to highlight the paucity of other similar instruments that are likewise opened to individuals.

Granted, individuals are not the only international legal subjects that are in this predicament. The lack of jurisdiction *ratione personae* of the ICJ in many general matters of international law is notorious and frustratingly common. At the ICJ, for example, declarations recognizing the jurisdiction of the Court as compulsory have not been as successful as the drafters of the ICJ Statute had hoped, and international justice is based on an explicit consent by the State given often ad hoc or by specific treaty.[15] However, the absence of international remedies covering States makes the argument for remedies for individuals even stronger so as to ensure that a panoply of possible international judicial remedies becomes available. Moreover, in the case of individuals, diplomatic representation also adds an extra layer to claims by individuals to access international remedies, making effective access to justice more remote, not closer.

3.2   *The Additional Barrier of States' Jurisdictional Immunities*

In addition to the structural and procedural barriers to entry for individuals in international forums, it is also clear that individuals lack appropriate alternatives in domestic courts. International decisions highlight this problem. The recent ICJ decision in *Jurisdictional Immunities*, for example, demonstrates clearly the concrete and essential need for instruments that grant individuals access to international remedies.[16] In a disappointing 2012 *Jurisdictional Immunities of the State (Germany v. Italy: Greece intervening)* decision, the ICJ confirmed that Germany was entitled to jurisdictional immunity from proceedings in Italian courts under customary international law, even if the allegations against Germany involved violations of *jus cogens* rules and even if the requested redress was of last resort for the injured individuals.

In the case, Germany requested the Court to find that Italy had failed to respect Germany's jurisdictional immunity under international law by allowing, inter alia, civil claims seeking reparation for injuries caused by violations of international humanitarian law committed by the German Reich during WWII to be brought against it in Italian courts. Conversely, Italy argued that Germany's claims were unfounded and submitted a counter-claim for

---

15   *See also* ROBERT KOLB, THE INTERNATIONAL COURT OF JUSTICE (2013).

16   Jurisdictional Immunities of the State (Germany v. Italy: Greece intervening), Judgment, 2012 I.C.J. 99 (Feb. 3, 2012).

reparation owed to Italian victims of grave violations of international humanitarian law by the German Reich.[17]

The ICJ found that while there was no doubt that the acts committed by the German authorities were illegal,[18] it needed to look at whether the proceedings regarding the claims for compensation in Italian courts were properly brought.[19] The Court then regrettably concluded that, under customary international law, States were entitled to immunity in proceedings for torts allegedly committed on the territory of another State by its armed forces and other organs of State in the course of conducting an armed conflict, even when serious violations of human rights law or the law of armed conflict had been committed.[20] Indeed, the conclusion was maintained even though the violations were of *jus cogens* nature.[21] In a somewhat self-serving distinction, the ICJ in fact found that there was no conflict between rules of *jus cogens* and the rules of State immunity as they address different matters: the Court concluded that rules of State immunity are only procedural in nature and do not relate to the question of whether or not the conduct in respect of which the proceedings are brought is lawful or unlawful.[22] The Court was unmoved by Italy's claim that all previous attempts to secure compensation from Germany for various groups of victims involved in the Italian proceedings had failed.[23]

In a more persuasive dissenting opinion, Judge Cançado Trindade explains well the consequences of the decision and highlights the incongruity of the majority's conclusion. He observes that the tension between State immunity and the right of access to justice should have been rightly resolved in favour of the latter, particularly in cases such as the one at issue which related to international crimes. Indeed, he rightly argues that the threshold of the gravity of

---

17   *Id.* at paras. 37–51 (presenting Italy's argument).

18   Acts at the center of the case were perpetrated by German armed forces and other organs of the German Reich. They included three categories: (1) the case of large-scale killing of civilians in occupied territory as part of a policy of reprisals, (for example the massacres of 29 June 1944 in Civitella in Val di Chiana, Cornia and San Pancrazio by members of the "Hermann Göring" division of the German armed forces, involving the killing of 203 civilians taken as hostages after resistance fighters had earlier killed four German soldiers); (2) acts involving members of the civilian population who, like Mr. Luigi Ferrini, were deported from Italy to what was in substance slave labour in Germany; (3) and the fact that members of the Italian armed forces were denied the status of prisoner of war, together with the protections which that status entailed, to which they were entitled, and who were similarly used as forced labourers. *See id.* at paras. 52–6.

19   *Id.* at paras. 62–79.

20   *Id.* at paras. 81–91.

21   *Id.* at paras. 92–97.

22   *Id.* at paras. 92–97.

23   *Id.* at paras. 98–104.

the breaches of human rights and of international humanitarian law should remove any jurisdictional bar, and give priority to reparations to victimized individuals.[24] Importantly, States should not be able to waive rights which are not their own, but which are rather inherent to human beings.[25] In fact, it is individuals who are subjects of international law and are holders of rights that emanate from international law. Indeed, the decision of the majority only served to highlight the fact that the Italian victims of Nazi Germany's grave violations of human rights and of international humanitarian law were left without any form of redress for serious violations of their own rights.[26] The *Jurisdictional Immunities* decision is really a case in point that demonstrates the need to find other remedies that can provide reparation and are accessible directly to individuals, both in international and domestic proceedings.

Moreover, the decision of the ICJ is not in isolation, but follows earlier cases. The existence of sovereign immunities in the context of jurisdiction proceedings involving *jus cogens* violations has also been affirmed by the ECtHR. *Al-Adsani* v. *United Kingdom* addressed the claim of a dual British/ Kuwaiti national against the United Kingdom, where Mr Al-Adsani argued that British courts had failed to protect his right of access to a court, in violation of Articles 6 and 13 of the European Convention on Human Rights (ECHR), by granting State immunity to Kuwait, a State against whose authorities he had brought a civil suit for torture suffered while in detention. In a 2001 judgment, the ECtHR Grand Chamber accepted that the prohibition of torture was a rec- ognised norm of *jus cogens*, but it also held that it could find no basis for the

---

24   D.O. Judge Cançado Trindade Part VI and VII. Argues that all mass atrocities are nowadays to be considered, in his view, in the light of the threshold of gravity, irrespective of who committed them; criminal State policies and the ensuing perpetration of State atrocities are not to be covered up by the shield of State immunity.

25   *Id.* at Part VIII.

26   Part XVII. Judge Cançado Trindade points out that what jeopardizes or destabilizes the international legal order, are the international crimes, and not the individuals' quest for reparation. In case of such crimes or grave violations, Judge Cançado Trindade sustains that the direct access of the individuals concerned to the international jurisdiction is fully justified even against their own State. This is because individuals are the subjects of international law and holder of rights and bearers of duties which emanate directly from international law. Judge Yussuf also lamented the decision and thought that the Court had failed to seize a unique opportunity to clarify the law and to pronounce itself on the effect that the absence of other remedial avenues for reparations could have on immunity before domestic courts. This is an area in which international law is clearly evolving, and the Court, as the principal judicial organ of the United Nations, should have provided guidance on this evolution.

conclusion that a State "no longer enjoys immunity from civil suit in the courts of another State where acts of torture are alleged."[27]

The ECtHR confirmed this conclusion more recently and after the ICJ *Sovereign Immunities* decision. In *Jones and others v United Kingdom* the Court again found that the United Kingdom had not breached Article 6 ECHR by granting immunity from jurisdiction to Saudi Arabia and its officials in respect of civil claims brought against them for alleged acts of torture.[28] The Court reasserted that a generally-recognized rule of public international law did not contain an exception to State immunity in respect of civil claims concerning alleged acts of torture.

In sum, the role of jurisdictional immunities in shielding the State from providing compensation to individuals injured under international law is substantial. It not only shields the State in domestic court, but—importantly—it also deprives the individual of access to justice and reparation. It also seems that this situation will not be corrected any time soon. When discussing the draft of the UN Convention on the Jurisdictional Immunities of States and Their Property, the International Law Commission (ILC) left the specific issue of *jus cogens* unresolved stating it was not yet ripe for codification.[29]

In sum, individuals continue to lack effective remedies in both international and domestic settings for violations of their international rights by another State, including on matters of *jus cogens*. This situation underscores the continued need for international forums accessible to individuals.

Having discussed the unique features of IMCCs above, in the next sections, I examine whether the role IMCCs play in providing access to individuals could

---

27   *Case of Al-Adsani v The United Kingdom App no 35763/97* 2001-XI Eur. Ct. H.R., paras. 59–61. (Finding by majority that there is no general acceptance in international law of the principle that States were not entitled to immunity in respect of civil claims for damages for torture committed in a foreign State. Demonstrating the tensions that exist between different judicial views, note that the decision was taken by nine votes to eight. Judges Rozakis and Calisch joined by Judges Wildhaber, Costa, Cabral Barreto and Vajić appended a joint dissenting opinion arguing that when there is a conflict between a *jus cogens* norm and other rules of international law, norms of *jus cogens* should prevail).

28   *Case of Jones and Others v The United Kingdom* App nos. 34356/06 and 40528/06, 2014-I Eur. Ct. H.R. (ruling that granting immunity from jurisdiction to State officials in civil proceedings with respect to torture was not a violation of Article 6 ECHR granting access to courts).

29   2004 United Nations Convention on Jurisdictional Immunities of States and Their Property, Not yet in force, https://treaties.un.org/doc/Treaties/2004/12/20041202%20 03-50%20PM/CH_III_13p.pdf. See *Jurisdiction Immunities*, para. 89, supra note 16, and generally David P. Stewart, *The UN Convention on Jurisdictional Immunities of States and Their Property*, 99 AM. J. INT'L L. (2005) 194.

be significant and consequential. I begin by describing and assessing the work of three recent IMCCs.

4   Three Recent Examples of International Mass Claims Commissions and How They Granted Access to Individual Claimants

The IUSCT, the UNCC and the EECC are significant examples of post WWII IMCCs that grant, in a variety of ways, access to individuals. They are also very different in terms of mandate, scope, duration, and results. I describe them briefly and generally below first, and will subsequently focus on the different ways in which they grant access to individuals.

4.1   *The Iran-United States Claims Tribunal*

The IUSCT was established in 1981 as part of the peace settlement brokered by Algeria between the United States and Iran, following the overthrowing of the Iranian Shah, a US ally, and the establishment of the Islamic Republic of Iran.[30]

The IUSCT is composed of nine judges: three appointed by each of the parties and the remaining three (including the President) appointed by the party-appointed members or by an appointing authority. Its jurisdiction includes claims between the two sovereigns, as well as private claims of US nationals against Iran and of Iranian nationals against the US arising out of debts, contracts, expropriations or other measures that affected property rights. Claims under $250,000 (about 2,800) were defined as small under the agreement, and were settled by a lump-sum payment by Iran to the US of $105 million, and then distributed to individuals by the US.[31] About 1,000 large claims were filed and decided by 2003. As for sovereign claims, the US has filed 24 cases and Iran has filed 53 cases. Seventy-two of those claims have been decided. The remaining pending cases are all by Iran against the US. Overall, as of 2018, the IUSCT has awarded more than $2.5 billion in awards to US nationals and companies.[32]

The cost of running the Tribunal is split equally between the two parties. Under the Algiers Accord, Iran agreed to place $1 billion in an escrow account as security for payment of IUSCT awards against Iran, and to continue to

---

30   For general information on the IUSCT, see the website of the Tribunal at: https://www.iusct.net/Pages/Public/A-About.aspx. The text of the Algiers Accords, including the General Declaration and the Claims Settlement Declaration, are available here: http://www.iusct.net/General%20Documents/1-General%20Declaration%E2%80%8E.pdf.

31   *See* Sharpe, *The Iran-United Stated Claims Tribunal*, supra n. 9, at 553.

32   See the overview of the tribunal by US State Department, at http://www.state.gov/s/l/3199.htm.

replenish the account to $500 million until all awards against Iran are satisfied. This unique mechanism simplifies the enforcement of awards and makes payments possible.[33]

Despite a challenging mandate and a tense political climate, the IUSCT has successfully resolved over 3,900 claims and is still hearing cases in The Hague. It is the longest-running international commission and enjoyed many successes. Principally, awards have been respected and enforced, even through the slow pace and length of proceedings and the parties' tense relations.[34] Overall, the IUSCT remains an example of a successful IMCC—also as a model for investment tribunals—and sets a useful example for the creation of future IMCCs.

4.2   *The United Nations Compensation Commission*

The UNCC was created as a subsidiary organ of the Security Council (S.C.) by its Resolution 687 to process and pay compensation for a variety of losses resulting from Iraq's invasion of Kuwait in 1990, which caused destruction to property and natural resources, resulted in the death and injury of thousands of civilians and caused the flight of about 300,000 foreign workers from Kuwait. The S.C. Resolution provided the basic framework and jurisdiction of the UNCC and preliminarily established that Iraq was "liable under international law for any direct loss, damage, including environmental damage and the depletion of natural resources, or injury to foreign Governments, nationals and corporations."[35] The Resolution also created a special Fund to be financed by a percentage of the value of Iraq's petroleum and petroleum-products exports. The Fund permitted the payments of all the claims and covered all the cost of the UNCC.[36]

The UNCC jurisdiction included claims for individuals who were forced to leave Iraq or Kuwait as a result of the invasion, individual claims for serious personal injury or death, and individual claims for losses. It also included claims by corporations and other private or public enterprises, claims from governments in the region (including Iran, Saudi Arabia, Syrian, Jordan and Kuwait) and from international organizations. Overall, about 2.7 million claims were filed with the Commission, with an asserted value of $352.5 billion. The Commission concluded the processing of claims in 2005. It awarded

---

33   *See* Sharpe, *The Iran-United States Claims Tribunal*, supra n. 9, at 555–6.

34   *See* Lee Caplan, *Challenges of Arbitrators in the Iran–US Claims Tribunals*, in CHALLENGES AND RECUSALS OF JUDGES AND ARBITRATORS IN INTERNATIONAL COURTS AND TRIBUNALS (Chiara Giorgetti ed. 2015), *see also* Sharpe, *The Iran–US Claims Tribunal*, supra n. 9.

35   UN Security Council Res. 687 (1991) of 8 April 1991, UN Doc. S/Res/687.

36   *See also* Res. 692(1991) for a detailing of the funding procedures.

compensation of about \$52.4 billion to approximately 1.5 million successful claimants.[37]

The structure of the UNCC was more complex than the structure of other smaller IMCCs. The UNCC Commissioners, nominated by the UN Secretary-General, sat in panels of three members to consider and render recommendations on claims in specific categories. The UNCC Secretariat sat in Geneva and supported the work of the UNCC Commissioners as well as the work of the UNCC Governing Council. The UNCC Governing Council, which mirrored the Security Council, reviewed and approved the reports and recommendations of the Commissioners.

In a relatively short time, the UNCC processed a large number of complex claims. It was the first example of a successful mass claims procedure that provided compensation on a priority basis to thousands of foreign workers who had to flee the region. Iraq objected to the creation of the UNCC and saw it as an unreasonable imposition by the international community.[38] Things changed after the fall of Saddam Hussein and the establishment of a new government. This period of greater cooperation coincided with the resolution of larger and more complex claims. Iraq had more extensive access to counsel and decisions were taken after all parties were heard in a setting similar to an arbitration proceeding. Certainly, the processing of claims was facilitated by the creation of the Fund for the payment of awards.

4.3   The Eritrea-Ethiopia Claims Commission

The EECC was created in 2000, and it is the most recent example of an international claims commission. It resolved "all claims for loss, damage or injury by one Government against the other and by nationals (including both natural and judicial persons) of one of the parties against the Government of the other party or entities owned or controlled by the other party" that were related to the conflict and resulting "from violations of international humanitarian law, including the 1949 Geneva Conventions, or other violations of international law."[39]

---

37   For specific awards, see the website of the UNCC at http://www.uncc.ch. The UNCC has so far paid \$47.8 billion in compensation. The remaining amount of \$4.6 billion pertains to a single claim awarded to Kuwait for the production and revenue losses resulting from damages to Kuwait's oil-fields assets.

38   *See* Michael E. Schneider, *The Role of Iraq in the UNCC Process with Special Emphasis on the Environmental Claims*, in WAR REPARATIONS AND THE UN COMPENSATION COMMISSION—DESIGNING COMPENSATION AFTER CONFLICT (Timothy J. Feighery, Christopher S. Gibson, & Trevor M. Rajah eds., 2015).

39   Agreement between the Government of the State of Eritrea and the Government of the Federal Democratic Republic of Ethiopia, 12 December 2000, transmitted to the Secretary

The EECC consisted of five Commissioners: two commissioners appointed by each party and the Presiding Commissioner nominated by the four party-appointed commissioners. The Permanent Court of Arbitration (PCA) in The Hague acted as Registrar and secretary for the EECC. The parties agreed to split the costs of the EECC equally. The Commission was required to finalize proceedings three years after the claims-filing period, though the deadline was extended and the final decision was issued in 2009.

The EECC issued its first decisions on jurisdiction and procedure in 2001, several partial awards on the merits from 2003 to 2005, including on issues of the treatment of prisoners of war, internees and civilians, the legality of certain means and methods of warfare, the treatment of diplomatic premises and personnel, and the looting, seizure and unlawful destruction of private property. Its 2009 final awards on damages ordered the payment of compensation of about $161 million to Eritrea and about $2 million to Eritrean nationals. The EECC awarded about $174 million to Ethiopia.

The EECC was tasked with the assessment of very complex and delicate claims originating from the law of war, which it did carefully and expeditiously. Its work contributed to the maintenance of the peace between Eritrea and Ethiopia. However, the awards have yet to be paid, though neither party has apparently demanded payment. This substantially undermines the very reason that prompted the creation of the Commission.[40]

5   The Three IMCCs Compared—Access by Individuals

Among the many unique features of the three IMCCs described above, the access they each granted to individual claims stands out and demonstrates the innate flexibility of IMCCs compared to existing tribunals. The IUSCT, the UNCC and the EECC provided direct access to individuals to file claims either on their own behalf, or through claims filed by States on their behalf. Indeed, the constitutive instruments of each IMCC identified the kinds of claimants allowed to submit claims for compensation. Each instrument specified individual categories claimants and granted access in unique ways.

The IUSCT accepted claims filed directly by both natural persons and corporations. Individual claimants could submit claims directly to the Tribunal within a given deadline. Large claims, valued at over $250,000, were resolved

---

General of the United Nations and President of the Security Council as UN Doc. A/55/686 and S/2000/1183, Art. 5, https://pcacases.com/web/sendAttach/786.

40   See Lea Brilmayer, Understanding IMCCs, supra n. 3.

directly by the IUSCT in contentious proceedings, smaller claims (under $250,000) were resolved and distributed by the US Foreign Claims Settlement Commission through a lump-sum payment by Iran.[41]

At the UNCC, governments submitted millions of claims on behalf of their nationals. Under the Security Council mandate, compensation to individuals was open to all but Iraqi nationals, which gave the UNCC a unique and expansive jurisdiction. All claims were named claims and they were submitted on behalf of their nationals. Claims were organized in six categories. Category "A" were submitted by individuals who had to leave Iraq or Kuwait because of the Iraq's invasion. Claims were for a small fixed amount of $2,500 per person or $5,000 per family. Category "B" claims were individual claims for serious personal injury or for the death of a close family member, such as a child or spouse, as a consequence of the invasion. These claims were also for a fixed amount of $2,500 per person or $10,000 per family. Category "C" were individual claims for damages of up to $100,000 each. Category "D" claims were individual claims for damages in excess of $100,000.[42] Categories A, B, C, and D claims were filed on behalf of individuals by governments after collecting all the necessary information from individuals. Governments then had a responsibility to deliver any awarded sum to their nationals. This responsibility included the duty of periodically reporting and returning to the UNCC any amounts that could not be so delivered to an awardee. Certain individual claims could also be submitted by international organizations. This was the case for Palestinians' claims, which were submitted by the United Nations Relief and Works Agency for Palestine Refugees in the Near East (UNRWA) and the United Nations High Commissioner for Refugees (UNHCR). The UNCC prioritized small individual claims over other claims and adopted mass claims methodologies to expedite claims review.

Under a Decision agreed by the EECC, claims could be filed in six different categories. Categories 1 to 5 were reserved for individuals, POWs, civilians. Category 6 focused on losses, damages and injury to governments. Eritrea and Ethiopia chose to file all their claims under Category 6. The great majority of claims were filed on behalf of unnamed groups of people. Only six claims were named, all filed by Eritrea. The EECC made it clear, however, that it saw the

---

41   IUSCT, Award on Agreed Terms No. 483-CLTDS/86/B38/B76/B77-FT, filed 22 June 1990.

42   See UNCC, *What Do We Do—The Claims*, http://www.uncc.ch/category. Category "E" were claims from corporations, other private entities and public sectors enterprises. Category "F" were claims from governments.

claims as belonging to individuals and expressed its interest in learning how the parties would distribute damages received to the injured individuals.[43]

While all three IMCCs granted individual access, important procedural and substantive differences among IMCCs exist. At the IUSCT, individuals could file their own claims. Iran and the US could then file claims against each other separately. This approach granted individuals the most independent access. Conversely, in both the UNCC and the EECC, States could bring cases on their own behalf and also on behalf of individuals. A major difference between the UNCC and the EECC existed though: at the UNCC, claims filed on behalf of individuals remained claims of the individuals and required specific claimants to be named and compensated directly. While EECC procedural rules allowed both Eritrea and Ethiopia to follow a similar path and file individual claims on behalf of identified individuals, the parties filed claims relating to large sections of the population on behalf of the governments. Names of individuals were not provided and claims were made on behalf of large groups of victims. Only six claims were filed by Eritrea on behalf of specific individuals.

In terms of hearing sequencing, the Governing Council of the UNCC took the important decision to prioritize small individual claims and rule on those first, so that the millions of individuals who had to flee Kuwait and Iraq during the invasion were compensated expeditiously. Decisions by the EECC were also made expeditiously, but still took longer than envisaged by the Algiers Agreement. Moreover, under the EECC proceedings, the awards were made as lump-sum and not individualized. Under the IUSCT, small claims were resolved in a separate way, by the US Foreign Claims Settlement Commission. Other individual claims were litigated fully through an arbitration process.

Table 12.1 below shows the number of individuals' claims in each IMCC. It also shows the compensation awarded and whether it was paid. The Table vividly shows the different magnitude of each IMCC. The UNCC, by far the largest, addressed and resolved millions of cases. The IUCST, the longest living IMCC, only heard a fraction of the cases, but their magnitude was large. The EECC heard cases on unnamed individuals and awarded a comparatively small amount of compensation. Of the three IMCCs, the EECC is the only one whose awards are still outstanding, neither party having allegedly requested or initiated payments.

How could the UNCC process so many claims in such a short amount of time? The UNCC decided that a detailed individual review was neither warranted nor feasible—also because, as seen above, the legal responsibility of

---

43   For example, in a letter to the parties, the EECC requested information on how the parties would ensure "distribution of damage received to civilian victims." EECC Letter to the Parties of 13 April 2006, cited in EECC Decision Number 8 of 27 July 2007.

TABLE 12.1   Number of individual claims at IUSCT, UNCC and EECC

Type of Claim	No. of claims submitted	No. of claims awarded compensation	Compensation awarded ($)	Outstanding award amount
IUSCT small individual claims	Approx. 3,000	2,884	105,000,000 (lump sum to FCSC)	0
IUSCT large individual claims	Approx. 1,000	960	$2,166,998,515.43 to US $1,014,553,515.03 to Iran and Iranian parties	0
UNCC "A"	923,158	852,499	3,149,692,000	0
UNCC "B"	5,734	3,935	13,435,000	0
UNCC "C"	1,738,237	672,452	5,185,716,912	0
UNCC "D"	11,915	10,343	3,348,902,861	0
EECC claims by governments	N/A	N/A	$161,455,000 to Eritrea $174,036,520 to Ethiopia	$161,455,000 to Eritrea $174,036,520 to Ethiopia
EECC named individuals	6	4 (one person was deceased)	$2,065,865	$2,065,865

SOURCE: DATA ARE AVAILABLE IN THE RESPECTIVE WEBSITES OF THE UNCC, IUSCT, AND
FOR THE ECC ON THE WEBSITE OF THE PCA.

Iraq for damages had already been established. Small urgent claims were therefore reviewed using mass claims processing and computerized methodologies.
Mass claims processing was also available at the EECC, but it was not utilized.

Of note, also, the IUSCT and the EECC are essentially bilateral instruments,
established to resolve a dispute between two distinctive parties—US/Iran for
the former, Eritrea/Ethiopia for the latter. Differently, the UNCC is the only
IMCC to be created to address a multipolar conflict, where on the other side
of Iraq there was a complex web of actors, including individuals from many
Asian and Arab countries, international organizations and several regional
governments. The UNCC was also the only IMCC that was created by the UN
Security Council and whose supervising body mirrored the composition of
the Security Council. In that sense, the UNCC was a real multilateral body,
which was opened to a large class of claimant. The Security Council backing,

and thus the support of the international community, contributed in making
the UNCC a strong IMCC, capable of really innovative contributions and decisions that strengthen access to individual claimants.

As for the payment of awards, applicable rules at the IUSCT and the UNCC
provided specifically, *ad initio* and in the establishing instruments, how compensation would be paid. The UNCC included a financial instrument, which
was highly punishing for Iraq, that provided a steady source of dedicated funds
that diverted parts of the revenue from the Iraqi's sale of petroleum product
to a fund exclusively created for the payment of UNCC awards. The UNCC
established a Compensation Fund to finance both the operations of claims
processing and the payment of awards. The funds for the Compensation Fund
were derived from a percentage of Iraqi petroleum exports, with due consideration given to the needs of the Iraqi people and the Iraqi economy. If Iraq failed
to comply with its funding obligations, the UNCC could take alternative means,
such as freezing assets derived from Iraqi oil sales in particular States. The Oil-
for-Food Program was also later introduced to ensure that Iraq contributed the
necessary payments to the Fund.

Awards by the IUSCT in favor of US parties were paid by an automaticly-
replenishing fund which Iran agreed would never go below $500 million. The
1981 General Declaration that created the Tribunal, provided that Iran was
required to place US$ 1 billion into a security account to ensure payment of
any award rendered by the Tribunal against Iran. Iran was also required to
replenish the account to a minimum balance US$500 million. The establish-
ment and existence of such instruments are essential for the success of an
IMCC. No similar provisions were made for the EECC.

In sum, IMCCs granted access to international remedies that had previously
been generally denied to many individuals through the existence of specific
and unique procedures. Indeed, the establishing instruments and the rules
of procedures of the IUSCT, UNCC and EECC allowed, each on its own terms,
unique, extensive and unusual access to compensation claims for a variety of
categories of individuals who had suffered injuries under international law.

6   IMCCs and Nationality Issues: the Proof in the Pudding?

In addition to the provisions contained in the applicable constitutive and
procedural instruments, several decisions taken by the IMCCs themselves
are also significant in promoting access to compensation for individuals. This
is particularly evident in a series of decisions relating to nationality matters
issued by the three IMCCs separately and individually, which are examined

below. Collectively, these decisions also indicate the proclivity and suitability of IMCCs to grant access to individual claimants more generally.

Traditionally, one of the main obstacles to obtaining international remedy for individuals is the lack of a nationality that would grant them access to an international forum. As the ICJ *Nottenbohm* decision discussed above illustrates, having the 'wrong' nationality might deprive an individual from accessing international remedies.

IMCCs confronted significant issues related to nationality—including claims brought by dual nationals, the understanding of negative requirements of nationality (absence of nationality) and issues related to the deprivation of nationality. Significantly, IMCCs mostly resolved them in ways that generally benefitted individuals' access to the IMCC. This strengthened the conclusion that the flexibility that is innate in IMCCs makes them especially suitable instruments for individuals' access.

At the IUSCT, the Claims Settlement Declaration specified that the IUSCT was created to decide claims of nationals of the US against Iran and claims of nationals of Iran against the United States. The Rules defined who was a national. Article VII of the Claim Settlement Declaration provided that for the purpose of the Agreement: "A "national" of Iran or of the United States, as the case may be, means (a) a natural person who is a citizen of Iran or the United States."[44] Under the IUSCT rules, only a US national could file a case against Iran. But what would happen if that individual also had Iranian nationality? In general, this would bar the individual from filing a claim, and generally move the dispute to the domestic level. Because of the strong historical and

---

44   Article VII, Claims Settlement Declaration, supra n. 30 ("For the purpose of this
      Agreement: 1. A "national" of Iran or of the United States, as the case may be, means
      (a) a natural person who is a citizen of Iran or the United States; and (b) a corporation
      or other legal entity which is organized under the laws of Iran or the United States or
      any of its states or territories, the District of Columbia or the Commonwealth of Puerto
      Rico, if, collectively, natural persons who are citizens of such country hold, directly or
      indirectly, an interest in such corporation or entity equivalent to fifty per cent or more of
      its capital stock. 2. 'Claims of nationals' of Iran or the United States, as the case may be,
      means claims owned continuously, from the date on which the claim arose to the date
      on which this Agreement enters into force, by nationals of that state, including claims
      that are owned indirectly by such nationals through ownership of capital stock or other
      proprietary interests in juridical persons, provided that the ownership interests of such
      nationals, collectively, were sufficient at the time the claim arose to control the corpo-
      ration or other entity, and provided, further, that the corporation or other entity is not
      itself entitled to bring a claim under the terms of this Agreement. Claims referred to the
      arbitration Tribunal shall, as of the date of filing of such claims with the Tribunal, be con-
      sidered excluded from the jurisdiction of the courts of Iran, or of the United States, or of
      any other court.").

economic ties between the US and Iran, this question was not purely theoretical. Would a US individual who also had Iranian nationality be allowed to file a
claim against Iran? Would a dual Iranian/US national be allowed to file a claim
against the US? The IUSCT was confronted by the question when several dual
Iranian-US nationals filed claims against Iran, and Iran objected to them.

The IUSCT took the issue full on and, in a precedent-setting decision in
Case A18, decided that for jurisdictional purposes, a dual US-Iranian national
would be considered a national of his or her "dominant and effective nationality" for the relevant period between the formation of the claim and the date
of the establishment of the Tribunal.[45] The tribunal recalled *Nottebohm*, but
rightly applied it (as it had been done beforehand by other tribunals[46]) to dual
nationals only, and held that to assess the "effective and dominant nationality" the Tribunal would need to review "all relevant factors, including habitual
residence, center of interests, family ties, participation in public life and other
evidence of attachment."[47] Thus, dual Iranian-US nationals would be considered US nationals for the purpose of filing a claim at IUSCT against Iran if their
family ties, residency, center of interest were concentrated in the US.

Case A18 is a particularly important decision, which allowed several dual
nationals access to the IUSCT in a novel and unusual way. Indeed, dual nationals who also possess the nationality of the Respondent State are generally
barred from filing claims. This is, for example, the explicit rule in ICSID proceedings under which numerous investment tribunals are established.[48] The

---

45   *Iran v. United States of America*, Case A18 (Apr. 6, 1984), 5 Iran–US Cl. Trib. Rep. 251 (quot-
      ing at 256 *Nottebohm* Case (*Liechtenstein v. Guatemala*), 1955 ICJ 4, 22 (Judgment of
      Apr. 6)).
46   Indeed, the question of dual nationality was not entirely new in international law, as it
      had been addressed in, for example, in the 1912 Canevaro Claim (Italy v. Peru) in which
      the Tribunal found that Raphael Canvaro who was had Italian and Peruvian nationalities
      could not bring a case against Peru, while his brothers, Napoleon and Carlos who were
      only Italian nationals and the Italian company they had formed had standing for a claim
      against Peru. Canevaro claim (Italy/Peru), PCA Case 1910–01, Award of 3 May 1912 (avail-
      able at https://www.pcacases.com/web/view/80). The subsequent Mergé case specifically
      analyses the issue of dual nationality in light of the dominant nationality principle, how-
      ever though it found it theoretically relevant, it denied its applicability in the specific
      case at issue because Mrs Mergé was effectively an Italian national and thus could not
      bring a case against the Italian government claiming compensation for the loss of a grand
      piano and other personal property as a result of the war. *See* Mergé Case, Italian-United
      States Conciliation Commission, Decision No. 55 of 10 June 1955, XIV RIIA 236 (available
      at http://legal.un.org/riaa/cases/vol_XIV/236-248.pdf).
47   Iran v. United States of America, Case A18, supra n. 45.
48   Article 25 of the ICSID Convention describes the jurisdiction of the Center and provides
      that "(1) The jurisdiction of the Centre shall extend to any legal dispute arising directly out

decision of the IUSCT opened doors to individuals that had been closed before. It is also the correct decision, especially given the historical and economic ties that united Iran and the US prior to the Iranian Revolution, characterized by numerous dual nationals who were hurt by Iran's acts. It would have not made sense for an instrument of IUSCT's novelty and capacity to bar dual nationals from filing claims.

The UNCC was also confronted with an important question related to nationality issues, and resolved it in a way that ensured access to the greatest number of claimants. The issue was also one related to dual nationals, and specifically to individuals who had Iraqi nationality in addition to another relevant nationality. Because of the historical past and economic links between peoples in the Middle East and Arabian Peninsula, some individuals had dual nationalities, including an Iraqi nationality. Under the Security Council mandate, compensation to individuals was open to all individuals with the exception of Iraqi nationals. The question for the UNCC was, therefore, how to ensure that its mandate, which provided access to injured claimants from everywhere but Iraq, was properly implemented. How could Iraqi nationals be excluded from the process without hurting other legitimate claimants? Underlining the importance of the issue for the UNCC, the UNCC Governing Council decided in its first session that "[c]laims will not be considered on behalf of Iraqi nationals who do not have bona fide nationality of any other state."[49] The Governing Council thus emphasized that the necessary requirement for individuals to have access to the UNCC was to possess a bona fide nationality other than Iraqi. The threshold adopted is not high, and favors admission to more individual claims rather than less. The significance of the decision was elaborated by a Category "B" Panel of Commissioners which related to individual claims

---

of an investment, between a Contracting State (or any constituent subdivision or agency of a Contracting State designated to the Centre by that State) and a national of another Contracting State, which the parties to the dispute consent in writing to submit to the Centre" and define national of another Contracting State as "(a) any natural person who had the nationality of a Contracting State *other than the State party to the dispute* on the date on which the parties consented to submit such dispute to conciliation or arbitration as well as on the date on which the request was registered pursuant to paragraph (3) of Article 28 or paragraph (3) of Article 36, but *does not include any person who on either date also had the nationality of the Contracting State party to the dispute*" (emph. added).

49   Governing Council of the United Nations Compensation Commission (S/AC. 26/1991/1), para. 17:1, available at: http://www.uncc.ch/sites/default/files/attachments/documents/dec_01.pdf.

for serious personal injury or death.[50] In its first installment of claims relating
to the eligibility of certain claimants, the Panel concluded:

> Governing Council Decision 1, para. 17 states that: "Claims will not be con-
> sidered on behalf of Iraqi nationals who do not have bona fide national-
> ity of any other State." The first installment contained no claim submitted
> by an Iraqi national. In instances where there was some doubt as to the
> nationality of the claimant, the Panel checked the identity documents
> found in the claim, and took into account the affirmations provided by
> the respective Government.[51]

Therefore, under the UNCC, even Iraqi nationals were allowed to file a claim,
if they possessed a *bona fide* nationality of any other state, regardless of their
dominant and effective nationality. The UNCC was satisfied by identity documents submitted by the claimant and by the statements made by submitting
governments. The simplicity of the decision adopted by the UNCC is in striking
contrast with some decisions made by ICSID tribunals on similar issues.[52]

The breadth of nationalities of individuals who were allowed to file claims
was indeed quite extraordinary. Category "A" claims—submitted by individuals who had fled the region—included claims filed on behalf of their nationals
by Egypt, India, Sri Lanka, Bangladesh, Kuwait, Jordan, Pakistan, Philippines,
Sudan, Syria, Iran, Yemen, Viet Nam, China and more that 41,000 from other
countries.[53] Category "B" claims—submitted by individuals who suffered serious personal injury or whose spouse, child or parent died as a result of Iraq's
invasion—were filed on behalf of their nationals by Kuwait, Jordan, Egypt,
India, UK, Yemen, Bangladesh, Sudan, Israel, Pakistan, Syria, Philippines,
US, Sri Lanka, France and others (including Palestinian claims).[54] In terms of
granting access to individuals the UNCC is unmatched, in both numbers and
breadth.

---

50   Category "B" Panel, First Instalment, A. 2. Eligible claimants/ a (exclusion of claims by
      Iraqi nationals), available at: http://www.uncc.ch/sites/default/files/attachments/docu-
      ments/r1994-01.pdf.
51   Category "B" Panel, Annex II, 14.
52   *See, e.g.*, Soufraki v. The United Arab Emirates, where the arbitral tribunals went to
      considerable extent to review nationality documents submitted by the claimant, and ulti-
      mately disregarded the validity of Italian nationality documents and as a result dismissed
      Mr Soufrakis's claim. *See generally* Anthony C. Sinclair, *ICSID's Nationality Requirements*,
      23 ICSID REV.—FOR INV. L.J. (2008) 57.
53   *See* United Nations Claims Commission, *Category A Claims*, https://uncc.ch/category-a.
54   United Nations Claims Commission, *Category B Claims*, https://uncc.ch/category-b.

The situation at the EECC was more complex. Under Article 5(1), the EECC was tasked with deciding claims of nationals of one party against the government of the other party. Still, Article 5(9) provided that

> In appropriate cases, each party may file claims on behalf of persons of Ethiopian or Eritrean origin who may not be its nationals. Such claims shall be considered by the Commission on the same basis as claims submitted on behalf of that party's nationals.[55]

Thus, the Algiers Agreement allowed Eritrea to file claims against Ethiopia on behalf of a claimant of Eritrean origin who did not possess Eritrean nationality, and allowed Ethiopia to file a claim against Eritrea on behalf of a claimant of Ethiopian origin but not nationality. This is quite extraordinary in a world normally dominated by nationality.

For historical reasons—including the fact that Eritrea had been part of Ethiopia for several decades before obtaining independence—there was a large number of dual Eritrean and Ethiopian nationals. In its filing, the wrongful deprivation of nationality was a core claim made by Eritrea against Ethiopia.

In its Final Award on Damages Claims, the EECC recognized "the continued force of the rule of dominant and effective nationality in many circumstances"[56] but held that

> that application of the rule must be qualified in situations, such as those presented here, involving claims centered on expulsion or deprivation of nationality by the respondent State. It cannot be that, in such situations, international law allows a State wrongfully to expel persons or deprive them of its own nationality, but then deny State responsibility because of the very social connections or bonds of nationality it wrongfully ended.[57]

Citing Article 5(9), the EECC then concluded that the provision was a "compelling indication that the Parties did not view the general rules of diplomatic protection as applying in the unusual circumstances that led to that Agreement."[58] The EECC's pragmatic approach meant that the parties could overcome the usual limitation of diplomatic protection and even the

---

55   Agreement Between Ethiopia and Eritrea, supra n. 39, Art. 5(9).
56   Eritrea-Ethiopia Claims Commission, Final Award: Eritrea's Damages Claims (Perm. Ct. Arb. 2009), https://pcacases.com/web/sendAttach/766 para. 251.
57   Id.
58   Id.

nationality requirement to file a claim on behalf of dual nationals for the deprivation of the other nationality. Thus, the EECC found that Ethiopia was liable for unlawfully depriving four distinct groups of their Ethiopian nationality, and namely:

1.   For erroneously depriving at least some Ethiopians who were not dual nationals of their Ethiopian nationality;
2.   For arbitrarily depriving dual nationals who remained in Ethiopia during the war of their Ethiopian nationality;
3.   For arbitrarily depriving dual nationals who were present in third countries during the war of their Ethiopian nationality;
4.   For arbitrarily depriving dual nationals who were expelled to Eritrea but who were not screened pursuant to Ethiopia's security review procedure of their Ethiopian nationality.[59]

As for compensation, Eritrea claimed $10,000 per injured person for a total of almost $2.4 billion. The Commission decided against awarding compensation for the first two items, the first because it found that Eritrea's claim for compensation for injuries to people holding only Ethiopian nationality did not conform to the requirements of the Algiers Agreement.[60] Similarly, the second head of claim was not compensated for lack of evidence of harm.[61] However, the Commission awarded $50,000 for the "unknown, but apparently small, number of dual nationals who were arbitrarily deprived of their Ethiopian nationality while present in third countries"[62] It also concluded that satisfaction "in the form of the Commission's earlier liability finding" was sufficient reparation for Eritrea's claims for compensation for unlawful deprivation of some dual nationals' Ethiopian nationality.[63] At the end of the day, while the Commission only awarded compensation for claims filed by Eritrea on behalf of dual nationals, still it is remarkable that Eritrea was compensated for the arbitrary deprivation of Ethiopian nationality. Of note, the Commission also awarded $15,000,000 for the wrongful expulsion of an "unknown, but considerable, number of dual nationals by local Ethiopian authorities."[64] The Commission awarded Eritrea compensation of US$11,000,000 for expenses it incurred in receiving, caring for and resettling rural Ethiopian nationals wrongfully expelled from Ethiopia.[65]

---

59   *Id.* para. 252.
60   *Id.* para. 254.
61   *Id.* para. 260.
62   *Id.* para. 267.
63   *Id.* para. 288.
64   *Id.* para. 302 (note that at para. 295, the Commission found the number of dual nationals to be approximately 15,000).
65   *Id.* para. 308.

Issues of nationality are essential to grant access to international remedies to individuals and they go to the very core of the jurisdiction of an IMCC. Each of the IMCCs examined above chose a different approach to the issue, also reflecting the deeply different underlying situations. While the Iran–US Claims Tribunal recognized and applied the rule of the "effective and dominant" nationality as a way to establish which nationality should prevail, the UNCC and the EECC departed from that approach and adapted the issues related to dual nationality they confronted to the specific factual situations at hand. The UNCC allowed claims from bona fide dual nationals so that even Iraqi nationals could file claims, if they also possessed another bona fide nationality. At the EECC, parties were allowed to file claims on behalf of dual nationals and also on behalf of non-nationals. Eritrea filed claims and was awarded compensation on behalf of certain individuals who were deprived of Ethiopian nationality and for the wrongful expulsion of dual nationals.

7   Concluding Remarks

In a universe largely deprived of options for individuals to seek redress for injuries they have suffered under international law, IMCCs offer a welcomed respite. In the paragraphs above, I have explored some of the unique features that characterize individual access to international remedies at the IUSCT, the UNCC and the EECC. These features are both embedded in the applicable rules of procedures of IMCCs, and are also further strengthened by decisions taken by each IMCC, namely on issues related to nationality.

The process of establishing a successful IMCC begins by understanding the unique needs and characteristics of the dispute that the IMCC is meant to resolve and the context that led to its creation. Because IMCCs are ad hoc instruments, they may be created to undertake many different assignments, as the parties have in mind. In the context of granting individuals access to compensation for injury, they have become particularly significant. Certainly, the kind of individual claims an IMCC is geared to hear is strictly linked to the events that resulted in the creation of the IMCC itself and to the types of losses and injury suffered. Thus, claims heard by the IUSCT mostly related to contracts, while claims submitted to the EECC predominately relate to breaches of humanitarian law. This made the work of the EECC extremely difficult from the start. How can compensation for humanitarian law breaches be quantified? The UNCC chose the interesting approach of adopting set amounts of compensation for specific injuries.

This contribution is meant to simply highlight IMCCs as useful mechanisms that may overcome an important problem in international law: granting access to individuals for international law injuries. However, IMCCs are no panacea and are far from being perfect instruments. Importantly, the origin of IMCCs, which is centered in war and violence, can weigh on the commission for its entire duration. Relations between the parties are often antagonistic and sour (note for example, that all UNCCs claims are fully paid, except the one from Kuwait).[66] For this reason, to be successful, it is essential for an IMCC to get buy-in from many constituencies—including support from key constituencies such as international organizations and certain third States. The Parties that created the IMCC do not need to become allies, but they both—or all—need to be convinced that this is the best available instrument to provide compensation to their nationals and to obtain compensation for themselves. Alternatives are few and far between.

The cost and duration of IMCCs is also an important factor to consider. IMCCs can be very expensive and the availability of funds for both running costs and awards is key to their success. The importance of having a mechanism that ensures and oversees payments of claims cannot be overestimated. A commission will and should be judged by how well it is able to compensate those who deserved compensation. Only IMCCs that have available funds will be able to issue payments. The UNCC and the IUSTC, for example, established detailed systems that ensured the funding and facilitation of award payments. That said, it is important to also consider how those funds are obtained. At the UNCC, an example of a successful IMCC, the dedicated funds derived from a highly controversial program—Oil for Food—which some have said have destabilized Iraq and impoverished its people.[67]

When rightly established, IMCCs can be innovative and useful instruments to grant compensation to individuals in a post-war scenario. Whether they are truly helpful depends essentially on how the parties and other involved constituencies use the flexibility that is innate in IMCCs. The proof, as always, is in the pudding.

---

66   UNCC, *Home*, https://uncc.ch/home (stating that "To date, the Commission had paid out about $47.9 billion in compensation awards to successful claimants. There remains only one claim that has not been paid in full, with a balance of about $4.4 billion outstanding. This claim was for production and sales losses as a result of damages to Kuwait's oil-field assets and represents the largest award by the Commission's Governing Council.").

67   For example, see Alain Gresh, *Oil Food: The True Story*, LE MONDE DIPLOMATIQUE, Oct. 2000, available at: https://www.globalpolicy.org/component/content/article/170/42147.html.

CHAPTER 13

Land and Sea: Resolving Contested Land and Disappearing Land Disputes under the UN Convention on the Law of the Sea

*Natalie Klein**

1 Introduction

I was privileged to have the opportunity to write a journal article with Lea Brilmayer, *Land and Sea: Two Sovereignty Regimes in Search of a Common Denominator*,[1] while a doctoral candidate at Yale Law School. The genesis of that article came over a slice of pizza at Yorkside Pizza one evening as we contemplated the reasons why a second round of oral arguments had been requested for the territorial sovereignty phase of the *Eritrea / Yemen* arbitration.[2] After extensive written and oral arguments, the Tribunal had sought further information about oil concession practice by the parties around the disputed islands. Well-familiar with the principle "the land dominates the sea", how could the purported exercise of rights over maritime space contribute to a determination of who owned the land in the first instance? Was this putting the cart before the horse? Should the cart be put before the horse?

In *Land and Sea*, we explored how land and sea regimes were different in international law, why they were different and, importantly, what they had in common. We observed the contrasting histories of each regime, recounting how the allocation of maritime space was predominantly a post-World War II development, occurring at a point in time when developing countries had emerged from decolonization and there was more emphasis on legality

---

*   I acknowledge the support of Macquarie University while writing this chapter. This chapter was written while on sabbatical from Macquarie as a MacCormick Fellow at the University of Edinburgh. My thanks to A/Professor Joanna Mossop for a very useful conversation during the formative stages of this chapter, and thanks also to Professor Alan Boyle and Dr. James Harrison for comments on the arguments presented here. Any errors are of course my own.

1   Lea Brilmayer & Natalie Klein, *Land and Sea: Two Sovereignty Regimes in Search of a Common Denominator*, 33 N.Y.U. J. INT'L L. & POL. 703–768 (2000–2001).

2   Award of the Arbitral Tribunal in the First Stage of the Proceedings (Territorial Sovereignty and Scope of the Dispute), Eritrea / Yemen (Oct. 9, 1998), (1998) XXII RIAA 211.

© KONINKLIJKE BRILL NV, LEIDEN, 2019 | DOI:10.1163/9789004316539_014

and equity.[3] The equitable approach was sustainable in the initial allocation of extended maritime zones, as the areas had not been previously allocated or owned by other States.[4] There was no sense of giving up an exclusive, pre-existing entitlement. The resulting difference is that maritime space has been allocated by operation of law, whereas land was more commonly acquired through physical manifestations of authority.

We had anticipated in *Land and Sea* that the dispute settlement processes for assessing territorial sovereignty and maritime allocations were distinct.[5] The former required State consent whereas the latter would most likely fall within the compulsory dispute settlement system of UNCLOS. This distinction made sense as power over and possession of land would not and could not be readily challenged before a third party.[6] A State in physical occupation of disputed territory would not necessarily be amenable to an international court or tribunal deciding its occupation was illegal. Moreover, that State would have the option to ignore a decision that considered its physical occupation illegal, making rational choices between the potential consequences that would be faced in the event of non-compliance and the benefits of maintaining physical control over the land in question.

By contrast, compulsory, third-party processes were important in the allocation of maritime space, we argued, because of the need to quiet title.[7] States needed internationally marketable title over their maritime space to be able to exploit the resources. Reliance on legal constructs, exclusivity of title, and international recognition all contributed to why international judicial processes made sense.[8]

Consequently, we were able to argue that compliance with maritime judgments is more likely than compliance with land decisions; an illegal possessor will not necessarily vacate disputed land.[9] However, an illegal possessor of maritime space cannot necessarily market to third parties any rights over the marine resources.[10] The key factor, we concluded, was marketable title,

---

3   Hence the continental shelf could not be acquired through occupation. *See* Brilmayer & Klein, *supra* note 1, at 710–712.
4   *Id.* at 713.
5   *Id.* at 740–746.
6   An issue Lea explored further with Adele Faure: Lea Brilmayer & Adele Faure, *Initiating territorial adjudication: the who, how, when, and why of litigating contested sovereignty, in* LITIGATING INTERNATIONAL LAW DISPUTES: WEIGHING THE OPTIONS 192–229 (Natalie Klein ed., 2014).
7   Brilmayer & Klein, *supra* note 1, at 732–734.
8   *Id.* at 734–736.
9   *Id.* at 748.
10   *Id.*

although we also noted this common denominator "is limited to cases in which direct consumption of the particular property or asset in question is not possible".[11] Where marketable title was paramount, and not necessarily tied to direct consumption, the incentives to cheat were all but eliminated and adherence to norms the primary mode of operation. We noted that the land territory jurisprudence was heavily realist in tone; the power dynamics in relation to decision-making and actions over land are crucial. Maritime allocations, with a more egalitarian and equitable emphasis, reflect a norm-based approach to international relations. The normative regimes matter to realism, we argued, when the norms themselves carry value.

Since we wrote *Land and Sea*, developments in the international legal system prompt me to revisit the dynamics we explored in the year 2000. Although the marketability of title remains a relevant consideration for explaining maritime allocations,[12] there is an ongoing need to explain the difference between land and sea in international law. What we are now seeing is that territorial and maritime regimes are increasingly intertwined in different contexts, even in the face of their distinct antecedents and shared purpose of quieting title to allow sovereign enjoyment of the accompanying rights (as discussed in *Land and Sea*). Where this interface emerges most strongly is in relation to maritime allocations and the associated normative framework that are being asserted in the context of the legal regime established under the UN Convention on the Law of the Sea (UNCLOS).[13] Our maritime paradigm is overshadowing the dominant land paradigm in different ways. We therefore see that this dichotomy is now being blurred in different contexts; some of these situations have

---

11   *Id.*, at 750. For example, if the State is very powerful and can use all the resources itself, as might be the case with China, this point is less apt.

12   In recent developments, we can point to the increased number of blocks for oil and gas exploration being offered in coastal States' extended continental shelfs and the slow take up of those offers prior to the conclusion of the work of the Commission on the Limits of the Continental Shelf. *See* Robert Van de Poll and Clive Schofield, *Pushing Beyond the 200 Nautical Mile Limit: Progress and Challenges in Exploration Efforts on the Extended Continental Shelf*, 2017 ABLOS Conference Presentation, Oct. 11, 2017, http://www.ablosconference.com/wp-content/uploads/2017/09/ABLOS9.pdf. Another interesting example, yet to be resolved, is the regulation of marine genetic resources in areas beyond national jurisdiction. These resources do not fit the existing paradigms of sedentary species and consideration is currently being given to whether they are or should be part of the common heritage of humankind or if a sui generis regime is needed for harvesting. *See generally* Joanna Mossop, *The Relationship between the Continental Shelf Regime and a New International Instrument for Protecting Marine Biodiversity in Areas Beyond National Jurisdiction*, ICES J. MAR. SCI., Jul. 5, 2017, fsx111, https://doi.org/10.1093/icesjms/fsx111.

13   United Nations Convention on the Law of the Sea, *opened for signature* Dec. 10, 1982, Art. 7, 1833 U.N.T.S. 397, *reprinted in* 21 ILM 1261 (1982) [hereinafter UNCLOS].

already been borne out in cases resolved under UNCLOS in recent years and others remain as hypothetical uses of the UNCLOS dispute settlement regime.

Is this liberalism with its emphasis on norms in the ascendency? Is our greater reliance on the UNCLOS institutions and principles to address intertwined land and sea concerns evidence of the importance of norms in international relations? Would realists argue that the assertions of these norms are instead continuing to ignore the anarchy and power dimensions that exist in the international system? And in promoting reliance on UNCLOS norms and institutions, do we run the risk of undermining those very institutions and processes on which States might otherwise rely to protect their rights?

This Chapter thus explores the interface between land and sea that has come into sharper relief in recent years. Part 2 briefly describes how different types of land interact with our legal regimes for the allocation of maritime space, especially in relation to islands. From this basis, Part 3 of this Chapter explores how legal processes available under UNCLOS are being prevailed upon, or could be prevailed upon, not only to quiet maritime title but also to resolve territorial sovereignty conflicts persisting over islands. Beyond questions of jurisdiction for courts and tribunals constituted under UNCLOS, we must face challenges to the very nature of land and maritime space and ask how we are to resolve these challenges. To what extent are our processes for allocating maritime entitlements influencing our views on what land is; and what territorial sovereignty entails? What does it tell us about our reliance on norms for quieting title? Are we thwarting the realist paradigm or ignoring it at our peril?

Part 4 of the Chapter examines another area where the interface between land and sea is (literally) blurring: first is the matter of land lost to rising sea levels and second are human-made constructions of "land" and consequent implications for maritime allocations. How well equipped are our existing territorial sovereignty and maritime allocation regimes to deal with these scenarios? Norm reliance comes to the fore, especially when we must address the situation of entire island-States being submerged. But as the international community takes decisions on how to respond to disappearing land, it remains to be seen if the power dynamics more commonly associated with possession of land will come to the fore and displace equitable concerns and deprioritize exclusive maritime allocations. For our appearing land, does marketable title provide an answer to how the legal regimes and power dynamics are responding to State activity in this regard? There are undoubtedly continued economic forces at play in determining State responses to the blurring of land and sea, but power and the rule of law are also critical elements. It is argued that we need to recall that the common denominator between land and sea is a small one and the more we seek to align land and sea regimes, the more we end up reconstructing fundamental conceptions within international law. Whether such a reconceptualization is good or necessary is a debate to continue in the decades to come.

2   Classifying and Connecting Land and Sea

Land remains the central starting point for sovereignty and States' title to both terrestrial and maritime space. The concept of a State encapsulates a territorial entity as well as an organized political and social community.[14] These dual elements may be drawn from the classic definition of statehood in the Montevideo Convention, which looks to the following qualifications: a permanent population; a defined territory; government, and the capacity to enter into relations with other States.[15] The territorial dimension remains a prime feature as "the physical foundation of power and jurisdiction, as well as nationality and, thus the basis upon which peace and security rest".[16]

Maritime title only accrues to States under international law. States have rights over different maritime zones extending from their coasts, with each maritime zone granting the coastal State different rights and requiring different duties to be performed. Within a State's baselines are internal waters, over which a State exercises full sovereignty,[17] and immediately outside a State's baselines is the territorial sea, which is also subject to a State's sovereignty but for a right of innocent passage granted to other States' vessels.[18] A coastal State is also entitled to a contiguous zone for certain policing purposes,[19] and an Exclusive Economic Zone (EEZ), which may extend up to 200 miles from its baselines and in which the coastal State has sovereign rights over the exploration and exploitation of the natural resources and exclusive jurisdiction over matters such as artificial islands, marine scientific research and the marine environment.[20] Other States retain certain high seas rights within

---

14   See Catherine Blanchard, *Evolution or Revolution? Evaluating the Territorial Sate-Based Regime of International law in the Context of Physical Disappearance of Territory Due to Climate Change and Sea-Level Rise*, 53 CAN. YBK INT'L L. 66, 72–73 (2015).

15   Montevideo Convention on the Rights and Duties of States, Dec. 26, 1933, 165 L.N.T.S. 19; 49 Stat 3097, art. 1.

16   Derek Wong, *Sovereignty Sunk? The Position of "Sinking States" at International Law*, 14 MELB. J. INT'L L. 346, 365 (2013).

17   A right of innocent passage through internal waters is granted where a State has enclosed waters by straight baselines. See UNCLOS, *supra* note 12, art. 8(2).

18   *Id.* art. 2, art. 18.

19   *Id.* art. 33.

20   *Id.* art. 56.

the EEZ, the most important being the rights of navigation and overflight.[21] The coastal State also has sovereign rights over its continental shelf, which may extend to 200 miles or beyond depending on the particular seabed configuration and assessment process for the extent of an outer continental shelf.[22] The extent of the coastal State's rights diminish as the distances from the coast increase until the high seas are reached. The high seas remain an area over which no State exercises sovereignty.[23] The Area is the seabed beyond coastal State's national jurisdiction and is subject to a regime of common heritage of humankind.[24]

Although we can commonly draw a clear distinction between what is land and what is sea,[25] it is important to acknowledge that the type of land has implications for what maritime allocations are generated. Islands have particular importance in any land and sea debate, primarily because a State's ownership of an island not only provides the State with more land from which to reap, among other things, economic and social benefits but also the potential to claim rights over the maritime areas surrounding the island. These maritime areas could be much larger than the land area generating these sea allocations. The extent and nature of the maritime rights that might be claimed will vary depending on the geographic location of the island and the island's relationship to the State that exercises sovereignty over that island.

The definition of an island is found in Article 121(1) of UNCLOS. It reads: "An island is a naturally formed area of land, surrounded by water, which is above water at high tide."[26] From that island, a State is then able to determine, consistent with the rules established in UNCLOS, allocations to a territorial sea, contiguous zone, EEZ and continental shelf.[27]

The exception to this grant of authority to States is where the island would be legally classified as a rock under Article 121(3) of UNCLOS. Article 121(3) reads: "Rocks which cannot sustain human habitation or economic life of their own shall have no exclusive economic zone or continental shelf." The negative implication normally drawn from this provision is that an island will still have

---

21   *Id.* art. 58.

22   *Id.* art. 76.

23   *Id.* art. 89.

24   *See id.*, Pt XI and the Agreement relating to the Implementation of Part XI of the United Nations Convention on the Law of the Sea of 10 December 1982 (UNCLOS), July 28, 1994, 1836 U.N.T.S. 3.

25   There are exceptions, of course, if we recall ice-covered areas, extensive deltas and wetlands.

26   UNCLOS, *supra* note 12, art. 121(1).

27   *Id.* art. 121(2).

a territorial sea and a contiguous zone. The legal distinction drawn in UNCLOS between "islands" and "rocks" has been the subject of controversy, which is discussed in more detail in Part 3 below.

In requiring islands (and the less legally-entitled "rocks") to be above water at all times, islands are thus distinguished from low-tide elevations. A low-tide elevation is "a naturally formed area of land which is surrounded by and above water at low tide but submerged at high tide".[28] A low-tide elevation will not generate any maritime zones for a State when it is "wholly situated at a distance exceeding the breadth of the territorial sea from the mainland or an island".[29] However, if it does fall within the breadth of the territorial sea, the low-tide elevation may be used as part of the baseline for measuring the breadth of the territorial sea.[30] Thus, in this limited situation, the low-tide elevation counts as land generating additional maritime entitlements for the State because of its location close to other land that is being used for allocating a territorial sea.

In *Qatar v Bahrain*, the International Court of Justice (ICJ) assessed the difference between low-tide elevations and islands. The Court stated:

> It has never been disputed that islands constitute terra firma, and are subject to the rules and principles of territorial acquisition; the difference in effects which the law of the sea attributes to islands and low-tide elevations is considerable. It is thus not established that in the absence of other rules and legal principles, low-tide elevations can, from the viewpoint of the acquisition of sovereignty, be fully assimilated with islands or other land territory.[31]

On this basis, we can see that certain types of land do not count as land for all legal purposes, but they still have some limited significance for the purposes of maritime allocation.

Islands serve a range of functions for States under international law. Primarily, islands provide the land territory over which the political entity of the State exercises sovereignty. It may be the case that the State is composed of one or more islands. Notable in this regard are the States qualifying as "archipelagic States" under UNCLOS. These States are constituted wholly by one or more archipelagos and may enclose their islands within archipelagic baselines

---

28   *Id.* art. 13(1).
29   *Id.* art. 13(2).
30   *Id.* art. 13(1).
31   Maritime Delimitation and Territorial Questions (Judgment) (Qatar v. Bahrain), 2001 I.C.J. 40 (Mar. 16), para. 206.

if the criteria within UNCLOS are met.[32] There are of course other States, such as New Zealand, that are comprised entirely of islands even if they do not fall within the legal definition of an archipelagic State. For continental territories, islands augment the total land territory for the exercise of the State's sovereignty. This fact remains true irrespective of the location of the island as close to the coast of the continental territory or located some distance from the mainland.

In some circumstances, the location of the island matters. The island may be used as a basepoint for measuring the State's allocations of maritime zones, as allowed under Article 121(2). Where there is a fringe of islands in the immediate vicinity of the coast, a State may be entitled to draw a straight baseline around the outer islands thereby enclosing the waters around those islands as internal waters.[33] The location of an island may affect where a maritime boundary between neighboring States is drawn. In this regard, the effect of the island on the maritime boundary may vary depending on whether it lies close to the continental territory or whether it is mid-sea between the neighboring States.[34] The weight allocated to the island in assessing its relevance for the drawing of the maritime boundary may turn on the size of the island, as well as the population and society conducted on the island in question.[35]

In sum, it is critical to observe that there is a difference between land and sea. How the land might be classified—as island, rock, low-tide elevation, basepoint, archipelagic State—has consequences for the maritime allocation that flows from that land. Land, though, is the starting point. The ICJ has routinely

---

32   UNCLOS, *supra* note 12, art. 47(1) ("An archipelagic State may draw straight archipelagic baselines joining the outermost points of the outermost islands and drying reefs of the archipelago provided that within such baselines are included the main islands and an area in which the ratio of the area of the water to the area of the land, including atolls, is between 1 to 1 and 9 to 1.").

33   *Id.* art. 7(1).

34   A considerable body of jurisprudence has developed assessing the relevance of islands in the delimitation of maritime boundaries. For discussion, *see, e.g.*, Sean D. Murphy, *Chapter VII. Effects of islands on maritime boundary delimitation, in* COLLECTED COURSES OF THE HAGUE ACADEMY OF INTERNATIONAL LAW, The Hague Academy of International Law. Consulted online on 14 November 2017 http://dx.doi.org/10.1163/1875-8096_pplrdc_ej.9789004351332.Co1.cho8; Clive Schofield, *The Trouble With Islands: The Definition And Role Of Islands And Rocks In Maritime Boundary Delimitation, in* MARITIME BOUNDARY DISPUTES, SETTLEMENT PROCESSES, AND THE LAW OF THE SEA 19 (Seoung-Yong Hong & Jon M. van Dyke (eds), 2009).

35   *See, e.g.*, Delimitation of the Maritime Boundary in the Bay of Bengal (Bangladesh / Myanmar) (Case No. 16) 2012 ITLOS Rep. 46, para. 147 (in relation to Saint Martin's Island); Maritime Delimitation and Territorial Questions (Judgment) (Qatar v. Bahrain), *supra* note 31, at 104–109 (in relation to the small island of Qit'at Jaradah).

recognized the principle that land dominates the sea,[36] commenting that it is "clear that maritime rights derive from the coastal State's sovereignty over the land, a principle which can be summarized as 'the land dominates the sea'".[37]

The principle of land dominates the sea is drawn from the connections between land and sovereignty, and with that sovereignty, State power. Max Huber articulated this view in the *Island of Palmas* arbitration when he stated: "International law, the structure of which is not based on any super-State organisation, cannot be presumed to reduce a right such as territorial sovereignty, with which almost all international relations are bound up, to the category of an abstract right, without concrete manifestations."[38] The "concrete manifestations" are typically assumed to be land, but recent developments may make us pause to consider if those manifestations may also be maritime allocations. Is title to maritime space "concrete" enough? This issue will be explored more in Part 4. It is the potential elision of land and sea—the seeming merger of regimes—that also challenges our traditional constructs. Part 3 will explore how this is borne out when a contest over territory and the associated maritime allocation is tested through UNCLOS norms and institutions. In the discussion, we will observe the ascendancy of norms in regulating both land and sea.

3   Resolving Territorial Sovereignty and Maritime Allocation Disputes over Islands

Some of the most polemic and enduring territorial sovereignty disputes concern ownership over islands.[39] Where an island falls within the territorial sea of a State, it is generally presumed that the island is within the sovereignty of that State, unless a superior title is otherwise shown to exist.[40] Sovereignty may be attributed to a State where the island is formed as a matter of natural

---

36   *See, e.g.*, North Sea Continental Shelf (Federal Republic of Germany/Denmark; Federal Republic of Germany/Netherlands), Judgment (1969) I.C.J. 3 (Feb. 20), 51–52; Territorial and Maritime Dispute (Nicaragua v. Colombia), 2012 I.C.J. 624 (Nov. 19), 674; Maritime Delimitation in the Black Sea (Romania v. Ukraine), Judgment (2009) I.C.J. 61 (Feb. 3), 89.

37   North Sea Continental Shelf Cases, *supra* note 36, at 51, para. 96; Aegean Sea Continental Shelf (Greece v. Turkey), 1978 I.C.J. 3 (Dec. 19) at 36, para. 86.

38   Island of Palmas (or Miangas) (US v Netherland) [1928] II R.I.A.A. 829, 839.

39   Disputes over land boundaries also remain a source of considerable international tension and violence, but islands are taken as the focus in this Chapter because of their connections to the sea, as discussed in Part II.

40   Second stage of the proceedings between Eritrea and Yemen (Maritime Delimitation) (Eritrea / Yemen) (Dec. 17, 1999) (2006) XXII R.I.A.A. 335, para. 474.

accretion or through an act of avulsion.[41] Yet where States are closely located together and sovereignty is contested over islands lying between them, it is not legally acceptable for a State to claim ownership over an island by virtue of the fact that each island falls within the territorial sea of another island as those features progress further out to sea away from the State's coast.[42] The *Eritrea / Yemen* arbitral tribunal considered that this "ingenious theory enunciated by Eritrea",[43] referred to as "leapfrogging" of baselines, could not generate sovereignty over the islands so encompassed.[44] Maritime principles could not be used to resolve a territorial sovereignty dispute in this instance.

Where ownership over an island is disputed between neighboring States, there may be particular difficulties in ascertaining where a maritime boundary might be drawn between them. Sovereignty over the island may entitle one of the States to more maritime space in the fixing of the boundary because of the distinct maritime entitlement accorded to the State with sovereignty over the island. This allocation of maritime rights is a key reason why disputes emerge and are not easily resolved between States; each State has an interest not only in the land itself because of its possible relevance to the State but also an interest in the sea surrounding the island. Land and sea both matter to a State in these situations, and potentially for similar reasons: the historic, cultural or social ties that may exist over the land and surrounding water, the defense or strategic importance according to the military concerns of the State, or because of the economic benefits that may derive from the land or sea, or both, of the island. The importance of these interests may vary, making either the land or the sea more valuable to a State. These national perspectives may prove important, if not decisive, in resolving the competing claims over disputed islands or at least in settling a maritime boundary between the States concerned.

In situations where contested sovereignty cannot be readily resolved between the claimant States, additional challenges emerge where there is an acute interest in the associated maritime rights around the islands. In some

---

41   Though additional factors such as relevant treaties, effective occupation and acquiescence may also be relevant in this assessment. *See* VICTOR PRESCOTT & GILLIAN D. TRIGGS, INTERNATIONAL FRONTIERS AND BOUNDARIES: LAW, POLITICS AND GEOGRAPHY 174 (2008).

42   Based on the principle that the territorial sea may extend 12 nautical miles from any island that falls within the territorial sea of the mainland coast, with that island being used as a basepoint. *See* Second stage of the proceedings between Eritrea and Yemen (Maritime Delimitation) (Eritrea / Yemen), *supra* note 40, para. 473.

43   *Id.* para. 473 (I recall describing it as cheeky when Lea explained it to me!).

44   *Id.* para. 474. *See also* Maritime Delimitation and Territorial Questions (Judgment) (Qatar v. Bahrain), *supra* note 31, para. 207 (in relation to pushing the territorial sea boundary out further and further because of the location of low-tide elevations).

instances, States may be able to agree on provisional arrangements pending the resolution of a maritime boundary dispute.[45] Otherwise the efforts to exercise maritime rights around the island may become a source of political, or even military, tension between the claimant States.

In light of the legal difficulties that flow from contested sovereignty over islands and the accompanying maritime rights, the question remains as to what procedures may be available in order to resolve these differences. Negotiations, and possibly mediation, will be the most common method upon which States rely. Obviously, the States concerned may consent to the resolution of their dispute at the ICJ,[46] or through ad hoc arbitration,[47] but, as we highlighted in *Land and Sea*, States may not wish to refer disputes over territory to third-party resolution entailing a binding decision, especially if one of those States is in occupation of the disputed territory in question.[48] In many situations, we have a stalemate between the States concerned—that stalemate either preventing full and proper use of the land and sea in question, or a compromise being reached between the claimant States with reduced rights for each being recognized in the shadow of the overarching dispute.

Faced with this predicament, what has emerged is that some States, judges and commentators have contemplated whether the compulsory dispute settlement regime within UNCLOS could be utilized to resolve the outstanding questions of maritime space and rights either in the face of the contested territory or scooping in the territorial dispute within the jurisdiction of the court or tribunal constituted under UNCLOS. There are different scenarios that might arise under UNCLOS, which will be explored in this Part:

- A State seeks to challenge the territorial sovereignty of a State as a direct claim;
- A State seeks to resolve the territorial sovereignty dispute as part of an overall resolution of its maritime boundary dispute;
- A State challenges the maritime conduct of the other claimant State, and the rights and duties of each State can only be ascertained once the ownership

---

45   As required under Articles 74(3) and 83(3) of UNCLOS.

46   As has occurred on different occasions. *See, e.g.*, Sovereignty over Pedra Branca/Pulau Batu Puteh, Middle Rocks and South Ledge (Malaysia / Singapore) (2008) I.C.J. 14 (May 23); Sovereignty over Pulau Ligitan and Pulau Sipadan (Indonesia / Malaysia) (2002) I.C.J. 625 (Dec. 17).

47   The *Eritrea / Yemen* arbitration being the key example in this regard. See Award of the Arbitral Tribunal in the First Stage of the Proceedings (Territorial Sovereignty and Scope of the Dispute), Eritrea / Yemen, *supra* note 2.

48   Brilmayer & Klein, *supra* note 1, at 748. *See further* Brilmayer & Faure, *supra* note 13.

of the land is ascertained to know which State has rights over the accompanying maritime space; or
– The State seeks a determination of the maritime entitlement of disputed
  land features without attempting to resolve the ownership question.
Each of these scenarios raises questions of legal interpretation as to a court
or tribunal's exercise of jurisdiction under UNCLOS and whether the claim
raised is properly characterized as a dispute "relating to the interpretation or
application" of the Convention.[49] But it also makes us question how the legal
norms and regimes important to the allocation of marketable title are now
being used to resolve territorial disputes that have not previously fallen within
this frame. The very availability of the norms and institutions are encouraging actions that deviate from the political reality that States can occupy and
control what happens on small pieces of land, such as islands. Yet those institutions are being tempted to bring the land and sea regimes into alignment. This
point is seen in relation to the four dispute scenarios set out above, and also
in the judicial classification of land for the purposes of allocating of maritime
space. Does our normative-based approach to international relations trump
the realist construct that otherwise applies in addressing questions of territorial sovereignty in international law? It is appearing so.

3.1   *Direct Challenge to Territorial Sovereignty under UNCLOS*
The first scenario of a direct challenge to territorial sovereignty was raised in an
arbitration instituted by Mauritius against the United Kingdom in relation to the
Chagos Archipelago.[50] Sovereignty was at issue because the United Kingdom
separated out the Chagos Archipelago so as to retain control over the area
when Mauritius gained its independence from the United Kingdom in 1968.[51]
The key motivation for the United Kingdom at the time was to align with the
defense strategy of the United States, which wished to establish a defense facility within the Indian Ocean.[52] An agreement was reached between Mauritius
and the United Kingdom to this effect in September 1965 in what the arbitral
tribunal termed as the "Lancaster House Undertakings".[53] Among the
Undertakings was a commitment that the United Kingdom would use its good
offices with the United States to ensure that Mauritius would still have fishing

---

49   *See* UNCLOS, *supra* note 12, art. 288.
50   Chagos Marine Protected Area Arbitration (Mauritius v United Kingdom), Award of 18
      March 2015, PCA Case No. 2011–03, https://www.pcacases.com/web/view/11.
51   *Id.* para. 69.
52   *Id.* paras. 70–71.
53   *Id.* para. 77.

rights as well as navigational facilities available as far as practicable.[54] Further, "if the need for the facilities of the islands disappeared the islands should be returned to Mauritius".[55] The United Kingdom has maintained that the Chagos Archipelago is British, but Mauritius has challenged the United Kingdom's rights and actions on different occasions, albeit to varying degrees.[56]

For the case instituted under UNCLOS, Mauritius had been particularly concerned with the United Kingdom's declaration of a Marine Protected Area (MPA) throughout the entire EEZ of the Chagos Archipelago. Mauritius claimed that the United Kingdom was not entitled to declare an MPA or other maritime zones because it was not the "coastal State" within the meaning of inter alia Articles 2, 55, 56 and 76 of UNCLOS.[57] Moreover, Mauritius argued it had rights as a "coastal State" within the meaning of *inter alia* Articles 56(1)(b)(iii) and 76(8) of UNCLOS.[58]

The United Kingdom considered that asking the Tribunal whether the United Kingdom was entitled to act as a "coastal State" was to challenge British sovereignty and such questions could not be resolved under UNCLOS.[59] The United Kingdom did not accept that the negotiators of UNCLOS ever contemplated sovereignty disputes being justiciable under UNCLOS dispute settlement procedures,[60] and that reading jurisdiction so broadly risked an abuse of the dispute settlement procedure set out in Part XV of UNCLOS.[61] Mauritius did not agree that such an exception could be read into the grant of jurisdiction under UNCLOS and submitted that an express exclusion was necessary to put the issue outside the Tribunal's jurisdiction when considering the drafting history of UNCLOS.[62] Mauritius considered the circumstances presented to the Tribunal were "unique",[63] and a failure to resolve the issue would weaken the Convention's dispute settlement structure, exacerbating and prolonging the dispute between the States.[64]

---

54   *Id.* (referring to Lancaster House Undertakings, para. 22(vi)).
55   *Id.* (referring to Lancaster House Undertakings, para. 22(vii)).
56   *See id.* paras. 100–125.
57   These provisions concern *inter alia* the rights that the coastal State may exercise over its maritime zones and the requirement to have regard to other international obligations in exercising those rights.
58   Chagos Marine Protected Area Arbitration, *supra* note 50, para. 158.
59   *Id.* para. 170.
60   *Id.* para. 196.
61   *Id.* para. 198.
62   *Id.* para. 179.
63   *Id.* para. 202.
64   *Id.* para. 201.

The Tribunal thus needed to determine whether it had jurisdiction to resolve the sovereignty dispute presented by Mauritius. The Tribunal decided that in resolving whether Mauritius' claims represented a dispute "concerning the interpretation or application" of the Convention, as required for the exercise of jurisdiction, that it first had to consider the nature of the dispute and, second, if it was a matter of territorial sovereignty, to what extent was a tribunal "permit[ted] ... to determine issues of disputed land sovereignty as a necessary precondition to a determination of rights and duties in the adjacent sea".[65] The evidence before the Tribunal clearly answered the first issue, namely that the dispute arising from claims as to which State was the "coastal State" did indeed relate to a question of land sovereignty over the Chagos Archipelago.[66]

More critically, was the dispute concerning land sovereignty within the Tribunal's jurisdiction? Academic commentary has taken different positions on this question. Talmon, for example, has argued: "It is generally acknowledged that the Convention does not deal with questions of sovereignty and other rights over land territory, and that disputes concerning these questions are not subject to the jurisdiction *ratione materiae* of UNCLOS arbitral tribunals."[67] Commentators, including ITLOS judges writing extra-judicially, have taken the opposite view in the context of maritime boundary disputes, which are discussed in the following section.[68]

In assessing the Convention's drafting history, the *Chagos Archipelago* Tribunal considered that it could not be reasonably expected that States would be sensitive enough about maritime boundary delimitations to subject them to optional exclusion whereas land sovereignty claims would be left within the compulsory proceedings entailing binding decisions. It is a common sense conclusion:

> In the Tribunal's view, had the drafters intended that such claims could be presented as disputes "concerning the interpretation or application of the Convention", the Convention would have included an opt-out facility

---

65   *Id.* para. 206.

66   *Id.* para. 212 (addressing the first submission) and para. 229 (addressing the second submission).

67   Stefan Talmon, *The South China Sea Arbitration: Is there a Case to Answer?*, *in* THE SOUTH CHINA SEA ARBITRATION: A CHINESE PERSPECTIVE 19, 31 (Stefan Talmon & Bing Bing Jia (eds), 2014) (and sources cited therein); Alex G. Oude Elferink, *The Islands in the South China Sea: How Does their Presence Limit the Extent of the High Seas and the Area and the Maritime Zones of the Mainland Coasts?* 32 OCEAN DEV'T & INT'L L. 169, 172 (2001); KRIANGSAK KITTICHAISAREE, THE LAW OF THE SEA AND MARITIME BOUNDARY DELIMITATION IN SOUTH-EAST ASIA 140 (1987).

68   *See* below notes 82–89 and accompanying text.

for States not wishing their sovereignty claims to be adjudicated, just as one sees in Article 298(1)(a)(i) in relation to maritime delimitation disputes.[69]

As rightly noted by the Tribunal, the sensitivities over land territory are much greater than those related to maritime territory.[70]

Judges Wolfrum and Kateka dissented on the Tribunal's determination that the sovereignty question lay outside the jurisdiction of the arbitral tribunal. The dissenting judges took issue with the Tribunal's conclusions drawn from the negotiating history of UNCLOS as to whether territorial sovereignty disputes were within jurisdiction. In this regard, they commented: "That the drafters did not foresee the possibility does not in itself justify reading a limitation into the jurisdiction of the international courts and tribunals acting under Part XV of the Convention."[71] Yet it is not so much a question of reading in a new limitation or exception to jurisdiction under UNCLOS,[72] or reading a limitation from Article 298 into Article 288.[73] Nor is it a matter of looking for inherent restrictions.[74] Rather it is a question of deciding whether a dispute is one "concerning the interpretation or application of this Convention" or not. The Tribunal characterized two of the claims of Mauritius as a dispute concerning territorial sovereignty and found that this dispute did not concern the interpretation or application of UNCLOS.

The dissenting judges considered that the arguments of Mauritius were focused more particularly on whether the United Kingdom had competence as the coastal State to establish the MPA, and was not a broader claim to sovereignty as the United Kingdom had argued.[75] As such, they concluded: "The differing views on the coastal State are the dispute before the Tribunal and

---

69   Chagos Marine Protected Area Arbitration, *supra* note 50, para. 217. Guilfoyle has commented to similar effect: "The received wisdom is that it was never intended that disputes as to sovereignty over coastline or maritime features such as islands would fall within the Convention's dispute resolution system. However, if this was the intention of the drafters it was poorly expressed in the final text. At best, the usual wisdom is supported by the argument that the proposition was too obvious to warrant being expressly stated." Douglas Guilfoyle, *Governing the Oceans and Dispute Resolution: An Evolving Legal Order?*, in GLOBAL GOVERNANCE AND REGULATION: ORDER AND DISORDER IN THE 21ST CENTURY 177 (Danielle Ireland-Piper (ed.), 2017).

70   Chagos Marine Protected Area Arbitration, *supra* note 50, para. 219.

71   *Id.* Dissenting and Concurring Opinion, para. 27.

72   *Id.* Dissenting and Concurring Opinion, para. 44.

73   *Id.* Dissenting and Concurring Opinion, para. 39.

74   *Id.* Dissenting and Concurring Opinion, para. 40.

75   *Id.* Dissenting and Concurring Opinion, para. 8–17.

the issue of sovereignty over the Chagos Archipelago is merely an element in the reasoning of Mauritius and not to be decided by the Tribunal".[76] Instead, despite commenting that sovereignty was not to be decided by the Tribunal, the dissenting judges determined that the excision of the Chagos Archipelago violated legal principles of decolonization and/or the principle of self-determination,[77] and that any consent to the detachment of the Archipelago was irrelevant because Mauritius effectively had no choice in the matter.[78]

The majority's decision in *Chagos Archipelago* made sense in its rejection of resolving territorial sovereignty disputes within the framework of UNCLOS dispute settlement. Yet the very challenge of territorial sovereignty by Mauritius before a tribunal constituted under UNCLOS reflects a State perception that land and sea are not, and increasingly cannot be, siloed for dispute resolution purposes. Moreover, as discussed further below, the *Chagos Archipelago* Tribunal did not definitively close the door on territorial sovereignty disputes being resolved through compulsory dispute settlement under UNCLOS. Such a move contradicts the power dynamic that would have more typically prevented a territorial sovereignty dispute from being resolved by a court or tribunal against the wishes of one of the parties.

3.2   *Territorial Sovereignty Disputes as Part of Maritime Boundary Delimitations*

There has been considerable speculation in academic commentary as to whether a court or tribunal constituted under UNCLOS would be able to resolve a territorial sovereignty dispute as part of the process of delimiting a maritime boundary. These so-called "mixed disputes" have been presented by agreement of the parties for resolution at the ICJ.[79]

The issue is more problematic in the context of UNCLOS dispute settlement as the Convention does not specifically deal with rules relating to territorial sovereignty apart from one reference in Article 298. Article 298(1)(a) allows States to exclude disputes concerning maritime delimitation under Articles 15, 74 and 83 (relating to the territorial sea, EEZ and continental shelf, respectively) from the scope of compulsory proceedings entailing binding decisions. If a State party to UNCLOS does make a declaration to this effect, it is still possible for the maritime boundary dispute to be referred to compulsory

---

76   *Id.* Dissenting and Concurring Opinion, para. 17.

77   *Id.* Dissenting and Concurring Opinion, para. 70.

78   *Id.* Dissenting and Concurring Opinion, para. 76.

79   *See, e.g.,* Maritime Delimitation and Territorial Questions (Judgment) (Qatar v. Bahrain), *supra* note 31; Land and Maritime Boundary between Cameroon and Nigeria (Cameroon v Nigeria; Equatorial Guinea intervening), Merits, (2002) I.C.J. 303 (Oct. 10).

conciliation under Annex V of UNCLOS provided various conditions are met. One of the conditions that precludes resort to conciliation is "for any dispute that necessarily involves the concurrent consideration of any unsettled dispute concerning sovereignty or other rights over continental or insular land territory".[80] A court or tribunal constituted under UNCLOS may seek to delimit a boundary to the extent that it is not impacted by a feature with contested sovereignty.[81]

One argument pursued in light of this exception to conciliation is that if territorial sovereignty disputes are to be excluded from compulsory conciliation then that indicates they were otherwise assumed to be with the scope of compulsory arbitration.[82] This *a contrario* reading of the UNCLOS provision is supported on the basis that it enables the full and proper resolution of the dispute before the court or tribunal.[83] In this vein, Rao has argued:

> If a court or tribunal were to refuse to deal with a mixed dispute on the ground that there are no substantive provisions in the Convention on land sovereignty issues, the result would be to denude the provisions of the Convention relating to sea boundary delimitations of their full effect and of every purpose and reduce them to an empty form.[84]

---

80   UNCLOS, *supra* note 12, art. 298(1)(a)(i).

81   Buga has noted, "Article 298(1)(a)(i) does not *preclude* submission of mixed-competence disputes to [UNCLOS] tribunals, but rather only limits their *scope*". Irina Buga, *Territorial Sovereignty Issues in Maritime Disputes: A Jurisdictional Dilemma for Law of the Sea Tribunals* 27 INT'L J. MAR. & COASTAL L. 65, 90 (2012) (emphasis in original).

82   *See, e.g.*, P. Chandrasekhara Rao, *Delimitation Disputes under the United Nations Convention on the Law of the Sea: Settlement Procedures, in* LAW OF THE SEA, ENVIRONMENTAL LAW AND SETTLEMENT OF DISPUTES: LIBER AMICORUM JUDGE THOMAS A. MENSAH 887, 889–890 (Tafsir Malick Ndiaye & Rüdiger Wolfrum (eds), 2007). In this regard, Rao argues: "Taken in its ordinary sense, the exclusionary clause suggests that but for its inclusion in the second proviso in article 298, paragraph (1)(a)(i), the question of a mixed dispute would have remained within the competence of a conciliation commission. As a logical corollary to this, it follows that, since the exclusionary clause does not apply to a compulsory procedure provided for in section 2 of Part XV, a mixed dispute, whether it arose before or after the entry into force of the Convention, falls within the jurisdiction of a compulsory procedure. If the intention of the Convention is to provide that the exclusionary clause in the second proviso made applicable to conciliation should apply with equal vigour to the compulsory procedures in section 2, then it ought to have made this clear in a provision applicable to such compulsory procedures." *Id.*

83   *See, e.g.*, GUDMUNDUR EIRIKSSON, THE INTERNATIONAL TRIBUNAL FOR THE LAW OF THE SEA 113 (2000).

84   Rao, *supra* note 82, at 891.

This approach reflects an effort to strengthen and expand the exercise of jurisdiction under the UNCLOS dispute settlement regime but does not confront the reality that States may not want a territorial sovereignty dispute resolved by a third-party.

From his discussion of the negotiations of UNCLOS, Adede has observed that the view of the President of the Third Conference on the Law of the Sea was that questions of territorial sovereignty were for general international law whereas UNCLOS was to address law of the sea disputes.[85] The exception in Article 298(1)(a) was added to assuage concerns of delegations to this effect.[86] Yet as evident from the opposing views presented by Mauritius and the United Kingdom in *Chagos Archipelago*, the UNCLOS negotiations do not resolve this point definitively. Academic commentary on the review of the negotiations has similarly reflected the differing views. Buga, for example, who has undertaken an excellent review of the literature, has noted as follows:

> It is clear that the prevailing view was that "pure" land territory disputes should not be dealt with directly in the Convention, although it is interesting that some delegates actually proposed their *inclusion*, "arguing that there was no difference between the two kinds of dispute [maritime or territorial] since both deal with areas over which sovereignty or sovereign rights might be exercised". Nevertheless, this leaves undecided the question of *concurrent* territorial issues (although former chairman Professor Sohn argues in his book that "mixed disputes ... will be totally exempt from dispute settlement under the Convention").[87]

Churchill has suggested that the exception should apply beyond compulsory conciliation proceedings.[88] Similarly, Talmon proposes:

> Rather than constructing an argument *a contrario*, it may be argued *a fortiori* that if States are not obliged to submit a dispute to compulsory conciliation if it necessarily involves the concurrent consideration of an unsettled dispute concerning sovereignty or other rights over

---

85   A.O. ADEDE, THE SYSTEM FOR THE SETTLEMENT OF DISPUTES UNDER THE UNITED NATIONS CONVENTION ON THE LAW OF THE SEA 132 (1987).

86   *Id.* at 159.

87   Buga, *supra* note 81, at 70–71 (citations omitted, emphasis in the original).

88   Robin R. Churchill, *The Role of the International Court of Justice in Maritime Boundary Delimitation, in*, OCEANS MANAGEMENT IN THE 21ST CENTURY: INSTITUTIONAL FRAMEWORKS AND RESPONSES 125, n. 51 (Alex G. Oude Elferink & Donald R. Rothwell (eds), 2004).

land territory, this must be true even more so in case of compulsory arbitration.[89]

Talmon's position aligns with the common sense conclusion of the *Chagos Archipelago* Tribunal. However, no court or tribunal constituted under UNCLOS is yet to be presented with this precise question and much may ultimately depend on the particular facts of the dispute and the claims asserted by the parties.[90] Arguably, resolving sovereignty over an island has the advantage of also quieting title over the accompanying maritime zones, but this approach does not surmount the initial importance of determining land sovereignty in accordance with the dispute settlement processes preferred for those questions. As with the direct challenges to sovereignty over UNCLOS, it is highly questionable that UNCLOS courts or tribunals have jurisdiction to resolve "mixed" disputes. States must alternatively consent to the mixed dispute going to arbitration or adjudication or other dispute settlement techniques must be trusted.

3.3 Incidental Resolution of Territorial Sovereignty Disputes under UNCLOS

The third scenario to contemplate concerns a State challenging the conduct of another State in a maritime area over which they both assert rights by dint of their competing claims of sovereignty over a disputed feature. Each claimant State would consider that it could act as the relevant coastal State off the disputed land, resulting in conflicting views as to respective rights and obligations. In that situation, the rights and duties of each State can only be ascertained once the ownership of the land is determined. Knowledge of the State holding territorial sovereignty is critical in ascertaining which State has rights over the accompanying maritime space.[91]

The *Chagos Archipelago* Tribunal concluded that, where a dispute concerns the interpretation or application of UNCLOS, the jurisdiction of a court or tribunal pursuant to Article 288 extends to making such findings of fact or

---

89   Talmon, *supra* note 67, at 47.

90   *See* Tullio Treves, *What have the United Nations Convention and the International Tribunal for the Law of the Sea to offer as regards Maritime Delimitation Disputes?, in* MARITIME DELIMITATION 63, 77 (Rainer Lagoni & Daniel Vignes (eds) 2006).

91   But *see* decision on traditional fishing rights in *South China Sea* where the Tribunal considered that fishers from both China and the Philippines held traditional fishing rights and so the sovereignty over Scarborough Shoal was irrelevant. *See* The South China Sea Arbitration (Philippines v. China), Award of 12 July 2016, PCA Case No. 2013–19, https://www.pcacases.com/web/view/7, para. 812 ("South China Sea (Award)").

ancillary determinations of law as are necessary to resolve the dispute presented to it.[92] Where the "real issues in the case" and the "object of the claim" do not relate to the interpretation or application of the Convention, however, an incidental connection between the dispute and some matter regulated by the Convention is insufficient to bring the dispute, as a whole, within the ambit of Article 288.[93] The Tribunal did not categorically exclude that in some instances a minor issue of territorial sovereignty could indeed be ancillary to a dispute concerning the interpretation or application of the Convention.[94] While it is difficult to envisage a scenario where a State would ever consider a territorial sovereignty dispute as "minor", it is nonetheless notable that the Tribunal sought to delimit the contours of its decision.[95] The Tribunal correctly stated that it did not need to rule on the issue in the *Chagos Archipelago* case.[96]

The views of the Tribunal in this regard reflect a statement of incidental jurisdiction, which is an inherent power existing in international courts and tribunals to decide ancillary matters connected to a dispute over which the court or tribunal has jurisdiction.[97] A key exception to the exercise of incidental jurisdiction is where there is an express provision to the contrary or the law provides otherwise.[98] In this regard, Brown has noted that "there may be a *clause contraire* in the statute or rules of procedure of the international court or tribunal, or the exercise of an inherent power may more generally be inconsistent with the terms of the relevant statute or rules of procedure".[99] The exception was not articulated in the *Chagos Archipelago* award, however.

The ICJ has described incidental jurisdiction in the following terms:

> [I]t is permitted for certain types of claim to be set out as incidental proceedings, that is to say, within the context of a case which is already in

---

92   Chagos Marine Protected Area Arbitration, *supra* note 50, para. 220.

93   *Id.* para. 220.

94   *Id.* para. 221.

95   Tanaka has suggested a low-tide elevation may be considered in this regard. Yoshifumi Tanaka, *Reflections on the Philippines / China Arbitration Award on Jurisdiction and Admissibility*, 15 L. & Practice Int'l Courts & Tribunals 305, 319 (2016).

96   Chagos Marine Protected Area Arbitration, *supra* note 50, para. 221.

97   Bin Cheng, General Principles of Law as Applied by International Courts and Tribunals 266 (1953; *reprinted* 2006).

98   *Id.* at 266–267.

99   Chester Brown, *Inherent Powers in International Adjudication*, *in* The Oxford Handbook of International Adjudication 828, 845 (Cesare Romano, Karen Alter and Yuval Shany (eds), 2014).

progress ... in order to ensure better administration of justice, given the specific nature of the claims in question.[100]

The ICJ had previously discussed its inherent powers in the 1974 *Nuclear Tests* case, where it held:

> [T]he Court possesses an inherent jurisdiction enabling it to take such action as may be required, on the one hand, to ensure that the exercise of its jurisdiction over the merits, if and when established, shall not be frustrated, and on the other, to provide for the orderly settlement of all matters in dispute.[101]

Other international courts and tribunals have affirmed the existence of their inherent powers in order to exercise powers that are not otherwise expressly conferred on them.[102]

Thus while jurisdiction may be set out under the constitutive instrument of the relevant court or tribunal, interpreting the scope of jurisdiction is a matter of implied powers.[103] The approach of a court or tribunal in this regard is similar to the implied powers doctrine that is often followed in assessing the scope of authority of international organizations.[104] Interpreting the scope of jurisdiction aligns with the *non ultra petita* principle, which provides that a tribunal "must not exceed the jurisdiction conferred upon it by the Parties, but it must also exercise that jurisdiction to its fullest extent".[105]

There are examples of law of the sea cases extending jurisdiction to resolve matters closely linked to the core of the dispute. In *Barbados/Trinidad and*

---

100   Application of the Convention on the Prevention and Punishment of the Crime of Genocide (Bosnia and Herzegovina v Yugoslavia) (Counter-Claims) (Order) [1997] I.C.J. 243, 257, para. 30 (Dec. 17).

101   Nuclear Tests (Australia v France) [1974] I.C.J. 253, 259–260 (Dec. 20) (references omitted).

102   These are discussed in Brown, *supra* note 99, 834–835 (referring to the Iran–US Claims Tribunal, an ICSID tribunal and the Appeals Chamber of the Special Tribunal for Lebanon in this regard).

103   Buga, *supra* note 81, at 78.

104   *See* JAN KLABBERS, AN INTRODUCTION TO INTERNATIONAL INSTITUTIONAL LAW 59–64 (2nd ed, 2009). *See also* Reparations for Injuries Suffered in the Service of the United Nations, Advisory Opinion [1949] I.C.J. 174, 182 (Apr. 11) ("Under international law, the Organisation must be deemed to have those powers which, though not expressly provided in the Charter, are conferred upon it by necessary implication as being essential to the performance of its duties.").

105   Continental Shelf (Libya v Malta) (Judgment) [1985] I.C.J. 13, 23, cited in Buga, *supra* note 81, at 78.

Tobago, the tribunal constituted under Annex VII of UNCLOS considered that it had authority to examine the delimitation of the outer continental shelf because it was "sufficiently closely related" to the dispute that had been submitted by the applicant.[106] Although not constituted under UNCLOS, the arbitral tribunal formed to resolve questions of territorial sovereignty and to delimit the maritime boundary between Eritrea and Yemen considered that it could determine the relevant basepoints from straight baselines drawn around fringing islands even though Yemen had not presented its claims on those basepoints.[107]

One difficulty with this aspect of the *Chagos Archipelago* decision is that it refutes the view that questions of territorial sovereignty do not relate to the interpretation or the application of UNCLOS and this conclusion would seem to constitute "the law providing otherwise",[108] so as to prevent the exercise of incidental jurisdiction. If territorial sovereignty is not within jurisdiction, it should not follow that even a "minor issue" of territorial sovereignty can be decided as an ancillary matter. The *Chagos Archipelago* judgment on this point seems to be inconsistent with the established position on incidental jurisdiction and it was wrong to leave open the possibility of any territorial sovereignty dispute falling within a dispute concerning the interpretation or application of UNCLOS.[109]

No specific case has been presented under UNCLOS in this configuration at time of writing. As the current trend in case law under UNCLOS is for jurisdiction to be expanded rather than read restrictively,[110] it must be foreseeable that a dispute of this kind will be presented under the UNCLOS dispute settlement regime. To do so will reflect the increasing reliance—potentially the acceptance—of UNCLOS norms and processes to resolve territorial sovereignty disputes for the purposes of ascertaining the proper allocation of maritime

---

106 In the Matter of An Arbitration between Barbados and the Republic of Trinidad and Tobago, Award of the Arbitral Tribunal, (Barbados / Trinidad & Tobago) (Arbitral Tribunal Constituted Pursuant to Article 287, and in Accordance with Annex VII, of the United Nations Convention on the Law of the Sea) (2006) 45 ILM 800 (2006), para. 213.

107 Second stage of the proceedings between Eritrea and Yemen (Maritime Delimitation) (Eritrea / Yemen), *supra* note 40, para. 146.

108 To use the language of Bin Cheng. *See supra* note 97.

109 Nathan Kensey, *Having Your Jurisdiction and Eating it Too: the* Chagos Archipelago (*Mauritius v the United Kingdom*) *and Incidental Jurisdiction under UNCLOS*, Paper presented at the Joint ANZSIL / KSIL Workshop, December 4, 2015 (paper on file with author).

110 *See* Natalie Klein, *The Vicissitudes of Dispute Settlement under the Law of the Sea Convention*, 32 INT'L J. MAR. & COASTAL L. 332 (2017); Kate Parlett, *Beyond the Four Corners of the Convention: Expanding the Scope of Jurisdiction of Law of the Sea Tribunals*, OCEAN DEV. & INT'L L 1, available at http://dx.doi.org/10.1080/00908320.2017.1327289 (2017).

rights and duties. This approach would align with a stronger notion of public order of the oceans, but compliance may be problematic.

In the hypothetical realm, we can envisage that if the State in occupation of the land and purporting to exercise the relevant maritime rights against the complainant State prevails in the dispute so that its territorial sovereignty and maritime entitlements are confirmed by the international court or tribunal, compliance should not be a problem. However, if the other claimant State, which is not in possession of the territory, is determined to have sovereignty over the land and maritime entitlements, will the other State comply? If it is militarily stronger, the State in possession can continue to exclude physically fishing vessels or oil and gas companies from the maritime area in question even in violation of international law. Yet that same State would potentially have difficulties in exploiting the resources through the grant of fishing licenses or oil concessions if those in the market no longer recognize the legal rights of the occupying State. Alternatively, those in the market may be satisfied that the overall power of the State is sufficient to protect their investment. The national interest (or pride) associated with title to territory may be too strong for a State to give up possession, or its claim in the face of an adverse ruling, even where financial benefits may otherwise be derived from a recognition of maritime entitlement.

3.4 Determining Maritime Allocations When Territorial Sovereignty Is Disputed

The above hypothetical could have potentially played out in the Philippines' case against China in 2013 in relation to the South China Sea. In the South China Sea, China, Taiwan, the Philippines, Viet Nam, Malaysia, and Brunei hold competing claims over different island groups, such as the Paracels and the Spratly islands, as well as over other islands and land features located throughout this semi-enclosed sea.[111] Efforts among the claimant States to exercise rights over fish or hydrocarbon resources have led to military confrontations and strong diplomatic demarches.[112]

The context of the *South China Sea* case concerned in part the disputed sovereignty over various land features in the South China Sea, but the Philippines did not seek to resolve the questions of territorial sovereignty.[113] Instead,

---

111   For a map of the claims, *see* Agora: The South China Sea, 107 AM. J. INT'L L. 95, 96 (2013).
112   *See, e.g.*, M. Taylor Fravel, *China's Strategy in the South China Sea*, 33 CONTEMPORARY SOUTHEAST ASIA 292, 299–307 (2011).
113   *See* The South China Sea Arbitration (Philippines v China), Award on Jurisdiction and Admissibility, Oct. 25, 2015, PCA Case No. 2013–19, https://www.pcacases.com/web/view/7, paras. 152–153.

among the claims asserted against China,[114] the Philippines argued that the maritime entitlements of the different land features could be ascertained as a question of interpretation of Article 121 of UNCLOS and hence was within the jurisdiction of the Tribunal.[115] China opted not to participate in the case,[116] but in a separate policy paper claimed that the case concerned questions of territorial sovereignty and were hence outside jurisdiction,[117] or were inherently related to a maritime boundary dispute and were thereby excluded from the Tribunal's jurisdiction by virtue of China's declaration under Article 298 of UNCLOS.[118]

The Philippines' argument created the curious position of wanting an ascertainment of maritime rights even where it was not known to which State those rights accrued. As I have argued elsewhere,[119] this position appeared to run against the fundamental principle of land dominating the sea because all it looks to is the existence of physical land, without accounting for the importance of a stable political and social community being ascertained to exercise the rights and duties enshrined in the entitlement. A coastal State would normally have both physical land and a stable political and social community by virtue of its statehood. These attributes would normally be essential to obtain and exercise rights over maritime space.

---

114   The Philippines challenged the validity of China's claimed "nine-dash line" in the South China Sea as inconsistent with maritime allocations under the Convention and also claimed violations of UNCLOS in relation to China's conduct in the South China Sea, including in the exercise of fishing rights and the protection and preservation of the marine environment.

115   Article 286(1) of UNCLOS provides: "Subject to section 3, any dispute concerning the interpretation or application of this Convention shall, where no settlement has been reached by recourse to section 1, be submitted at the request of any party to the dispute to the court or tribunal having jurisdiction under this section." UNCLOS, *supra* note 12, art. 286(1).

116   China was entitled to make this decision but in default of the defendant's appearance, the work of the tribunal still continues. *Id.* Annex VII, art. 9. The tribunal may decide the claims provided that it satisfies itself that it has jurisdiction and that the claim is well founded in fact and law. *Id.*

117   Ministry of Foreign Affairs of the People's Republic of China, *Position Paper of the Government of the People's Republic of China on the Matter of Jurisdiction in the South China Sea Arbitration Initiated by the Republic of the Philippines*, Dec. 7. 2014, http://www .fmprc.gov.cn/mfa_eng/zxxx_662805/t1217147.shtml.

118   Article 298 allows States to exclude from compulsory procedures certain specified disputes, including those concerning delimitation under Articles 15, 74 and 83 of UNCLOS. These provisions deal with delimitation of overlapping territorial seas, EEZs and continental shelves, respectively, between States with opposite or adjacent coasts. See further *id.* paras. 57–75.

119   Klein, *supra* note 110, 345–347.

Each of the entitlements to different maritime zones is associated with a "coastal State". To demonstrate briefly:

- Article 2(1) provides: "The sovereignty of *a coastal State* extends, beyond its land territory and internal waters and, in the case of an archipelagic State, its archipelagic waters, to an adjacent belt of sea, described as the territorial sea." [emphasis added]
- Article 55 provides: "The exclusive economic zone is an area beyond and adjacent to the territorial sea, subject to the specific legal regime established in this Part, under which the rights and jurisdiction of *the coastal State* and the rights and freedoms of other States are governed by the relevant provisions of this Convention." [emphasis added]
- Article 76(1) provides: "1. The continental shelf of *a coastal State* comprises the seabed and subsoil of the submarine areas that extend beyond its territorial sea throughout the natural prolongation of its land territory to the outer edge of the continental margin, or to a distance of 200 nautical miles from the baselines from which the breadth of the territorial sea is measured where the outer edge of the continental margin does not extend up to that distance." [emphasis added][120]

In identifying an entitlement without being able to name which State was entitled, the *South China Sea* Tribunal created further difficulties in ascertaining competing claims within those maritime areas. For example, despite the explicit wording of Article 86 that the provisions in Part VII of UNCLOS did not apply in the territorial sea, the Tribunal effectively applied Article 94 in Part VII to the territorial sea. It had to do that because it was not possible to say who was the "coastal State" for the more appropriate application of Article 21 concerning *inter alia* the safety of navigation in the territorial sea.

The *South China Sea* Tribunal ultimately determined that Subi Reef, Gaven Reef (South), Hughes Reef, Mischief Reef and Second Thomas Shoal were low-tide elevations. French has observed that in reaching this conclusion, the Tribunal effectively made a decision on sovereignty. He noted: "By finding that something is a low-tide elevation (the first-order question), incapable of being possessed by means of territoriality, the Tribunal has in essence ruled out the question of sovereignty (a second-order question)."[121]

---

120   *See further id.* 346–347.

121   Duncan French, *In the Matter of the South China Sea Arbitration: Republic of Philippines v People's Republic of China, Arbitral Tribunal Constituted under Annex VII to the 1982 United Nations Law of the Sea Convention, Case No. 2013–19, Award of 12 July 2016*, 19 ENV'L L. REV. 48, 52 (2017). *See also* Murphy, *supra* note 34, at 237 (describing the issue of sovereignty as ancillary to the interpretation or application of the regime established under UNCLOS).

Other features contested by the Philippines, Scarborough Shoal, Gaven Reef (North), McKennan Reef, Johnson Reef, Cuarteron Reef, and Fiery Cross Reef, were ruled to be, in their natural condition, "rocks" within the meaning of Article 121(3). To ensure that there was no possibility of an overlapping Chinese maritime claim that would put the Philippines' claims outside the Tribunal's jurisdiction, the Tribunal further considered the status of other high-tide features in the Spratly Island group. It concluded that none of Itu Aba, Thitu, West York, Spratly Island, South-West Cay, and North-East Cay were capable of sustaining human habitation within the meaning of Article 121(3).[122] Hence, they were also rocks only entitled to a territorial sea and contiguous zone.

The important result of these determinations was that China and the Philippines did not have any overlapping EEZs or continental shelves that would have otherwise occurred if China ultimately did have sovereignty over the land features in question. The fortunate convenience associated with this determination was that the *South China Sea* Tribunal could progress to assess a variety of other claims the Philippines asserted against China, which could not have been determined if there was the specter of needing to resolve a maritime boundary dispute to ascertain the respective rights and duties at issue.

The incongruent position now created is that there are pockets of ocean that have been explicitly earmarked as maritime areas over which sovereignty is to be exercised but it is unknown which State may lawfully assert that sovereignty. Arguably the same was true before the decision in the *South China Sea* arbitration and what has at least been clarified is that there is not a mystery State entitled to claim sovereign rights or exercise exclusive jurisdiction over either an EEZ or continental shelf around these features. As these maritime zones are more extensive,[123] greater practical difficulties may have arisen if it were known that "a" State had exclusive rights within a large expanse of water but we did not know which State. While it worked out neatly in the context of the *South China Sea*, we cannot assume that a comparable result will always be achieved. If there is an EEZ or continental shelf belonging to "a" State around a disputed island, how can any State then proceed to benefit from the economic resources of that maritime allocation? The allocation of maritime space in this setting has done little to advance the marketability of any title.

The situation is not an entirely new one because there is other land that is disputed territory, or occupied, or involves contested government authority

---

122   South China Sea (Award), *supra* note 91, para. 621.

123   Extending up to 200 nautical miles in relation to the EEZ and potentially even further for the continental shelf in line with the process under Article 76 of UNCLOS. *See above* notes 20–22 and accompanying text.

and still has maritime zones allocated. Perhaps what it demonstrates is that UNCLOS dispute settlement procedures cannot solve these problems and efforts to resolve some aspects of a broader dispute through litigation do not ultimately assist. Our norms can only get us so far. At best, the "lawfare" involved is another facet to our larger political, and power-dominated, dispute.

For present purposes, what is interesting in the *South China Sea* decision to proceed to determine maritime "entitlements" is that it focuses on the physical existence of land. Far less relevant was the existence of any organized political or social community that would have the key interest in how rights and duties flowing from the entitlement would be exercised. Associating maritime entitlements with physical land, rather than with land plus an organized community as the essential features of a State, is relevant for our discussion in Part IV on maritime entitlements when land, and potentially the entire territory of States, physically disappear.

3.5   *Assessing Land to Determine Maritime Allocations*

Despite the tidy outcome arguably achieved in the *South China Sea* arbitration in relation to the maritime entitlements of the land features at issue, it remains important to consider *how* the Tribunal reached this result. It concerns the intertwining of land and sea again, as we must ask what the difference is between a rock and an island, since the latter allows for a far greater allocation of maritime space compared to the former. As noted above, the difference is drawn from particular features of an island in accordance with Article 121(3) of UNCLOS. If islands "cannot sustain human habitation or economic life of their own", they are deemed "rocks" that do not have an EEZ or continental shelf.[124] Much then turns on the interpretation and application of "cannot sustain human habitation or economic life of their own" and the *South China Sea* Tribunal has been the first international body to parse these words in detail and offer views on how they should be understood.

The Tribunal undertook a review of the text of Article 121(3), as well as considering the context, object and purpose of UNCLOS and the negotiating history (the *travaux préparatoires*) so as to ascertain the meaning of Article 121(3). In relation to the actual consistency of the feature in question, the Tribunal concluded that what counted was whether it was naturally formed and above water at high tide. It did not matter from what the rock was naturally formed.[125]

In relation to a rock that "cannot" sustain human habitation or an economic life of its own, the Tribunal concluded that an objective determination was

---

124   UNCLOS, *supra* note 12, art. 121(3).
125   South China Sea (Award), *supra* note 91, para. 482.

necessary as to whether the rock had the capacity to sustain human habitation or an economic life, not an assessment of whether the rock actually does
do so.[126] Historical evidence could be considered in this context as indicative
of the rock's capacity.[127]

The Tribunal further indicated that "sustain" had three components: (1) the
"concept of support and provision of essentials"; (2) over a period of time
rather than one-off or short-lived; and (3) a qualitative assessment as to a
minimal standard.[128] These elements all then had to be read in the context
of human habitation or an economic life and what it would mean to "sustain"
either of those elements.

Assessing "human habitation" required the Tribunal to distinguish human
habitation from the mere presence of humans. The latter would not suffice
in assessing the characteristics of a rock, but an indeterminate threshold had
to be reached.[129] In relation to that threshold, the Tribunal considered that a
range of basic requirements would have to be met; these requirements being
those "necessary to provide for the daily subsistence and survival of a number
of people for an indefinite time".[130] The Tribunal further noted that "[a] feature
that is only capable of sustaining habitation through the continued delivery of
supplies from outside does not meet the requirements of Article 121(3)."[131]

For "economic life of their own", like human habitation, this criterion was
assessed as needing more than mere presence; it was not enough for there to
be resources available but that some level of local human activity had to be
involved in the exploitation, development and distribution of those resources.[132]
In anticipating this engagement with human activity, the link between the
concepts of human habitation and economic life was brought into sharper
relief. Moreover, human engagement would be needed so that the economic
life was not simply derived from extractive activities, particularly where those
activities would have no benefit for any local population on the feature itself.[133]
Moreover, the extractive activity had to occur on the land, or be connected

---

126   *Id.* para. 483.
127   *Id.* para. 484.
128   *Id.* para. 487.
129   *Id.* para. 492.
130   *Id.*
131   *Id.* para. 547.
132   *Id.* para. 499.
133   *Id.* paras. 499–500.

with the land, of the feature itself and not merely occur in the waters around the feature.[134]

Taking all of these elements into consideration, it is evident that the Tribunal sought to laden the description of a "fully entitled" island with strong connections to human life and human activity. In terms of "sustain[ing] human habitation or an economic life of its own", the feature must go beyond mere usage as part of the wider activities of a State in the area, but be linked in with a stable community existence. It is a curious emphasis when recalling that this element of organized political and social community was ignored by the Tribunal in considering whether it could proceed to determine maritime entitlements in the absence of knowing who would have authority to regulate the community existence sought.

Having articulated the legal criteria drawn from the words "cannot sustain human habitation or economic life of their own", the *South China Sea* Tribunal sought to apply these standards to each of the features in question. As foreshadowed, the assessment was not always obvious on its face. The Tribunal decided that in such borderline cases, "the most reliable evidence of the capacity of a feature will usually be the historical use to which it has been put".[135] Amid that historical evidence, the human habitation that predated the establishment of EEZs would be considered more significant on the basis that it would be less likely that the activity was designed to enhance maritime claims under UNCLOS.[136] In these circumstances, the Tribunal sought to draw on evidence of mining and fishing activities and the regulation of those activities.[137]

In taking this approach, the Tribunal utilized the type of evidence that would normally be assessed in deciding which State has sovereignty over disputed territory. Courts or tribunals seeking to ascertain territorial sovereignty have often considered what State was in "effective occupation" of the territory in question. Establishing effective occupation necessitates a consideration of whether a State has acted as if sovereign of the territory and whether it has shown its intention to act as sovereign.[138] It essentially requires "the continuous

---

134   *Id.* para. 503. As such, economic life derived from the EEZ or the continental shelf of the feature could not be considered as meeting this criterion. *Id.* para. 502.

135   *Id.* para. 549.

136   *Id.* para. 550.

137   *Id.* paras. 617–619.

138   *See, e.g.*, Legal Status of Eastern Greenland (Denmark v Norway), Judgment, Apr. 5, 1933, PCIJ Ser. A/B, No. 53, 45–46. The "intention" to act as sovereign has received less emphasis in other cases, such as the *Island of Palmas* and *Minquiers and Ecrehos*. See MALCOLM N. SHAW, INTERNATIONAL LAW 513 (2008).

and peaceful display of territorial sovereignty".[139] The evidence that has been used for this purpose includes the adoption and enforcement of legislation or regulations, as well as activities by State officials or activities of private persons regulated by State officials on the territory and around the territory in question.

It should not be any surprise to us that an assessment of the classification of land should in fact address criteria that are typically associated with territorial sovereignty. What was decisive was the quality of the occupation, the extent of human habitation, which became determinative for the extent of the maritime allocations for those areas of land. The predominance of the land over the sea was recognized in this instance.

While normative processes are being brought to bear in these scenarios, they cannot fully disguise the realities of the power dynamics at play. The *South China Sea* Tribunal's characterization of the land features in question ran counter to State practice in varied instances.[140] In emphasizing the interpretation and application of the relevant norms, the Tribunal sought to hold true to what it considered the reasons behind the establishment of the EEZ.[141] In this regard, these maritime areas had to be for the benefit of an actual population rather than for the pure economic benefit of a sovereign State that otherwise has no connection with the land in question in the absence of that human habitation. Yet if States are proceeding to make extended maritime zone claims off small features that may be better classified as "rocks" rather than "islands" in light of the *South China Sea* decision, has the now-incorrect classification of the land in question reduced the marketability of the maritime rights? If there had already been international recognition of the State's claims and, moreover, its exclusive authority over the maritime area was and is generally recognized, irrespective of the *South China Sea* decision, arguably no damage is done to the economic rights in question. However, challenges may now start to emerge against the certainty of maritime allocations on the basis of the *South China Sea* case where States wish to support the rights of its fishing vessels to harvest resources on what may now be perceived as high seas rather than in the EEZ of a coastal State. With the possible undermining of the marketability of title

---

139   Island of Palmas (or Miangas) (US v Netherland) [1928] 11 R.I.A.A. 829, *supra* note 38, 839.

140   *See* Natalie Klein, Agora Contribution, *Rocks and Islands after the* South China Sea *Arbitration*, 34 AUST. Y. BK INT'L L. 21, 28–30 (2016); Alex G. Oude Elferink, *The South China Sea Arbitration's Interpretation of Article 121(3) of the LOSC: A Disquieting First*, JCLOS Blog, (Sept. 7, 2016) available at: https://site.uit.no/jclos/2016/09/07/the-south-china-sea-arbitrations-interpretation-of-article-1213-of-the-losc-a-disquieting-first/ ("At the moment, there is an abyss between the tribunal's approach and the practice of many States.").

141   South China Sea (Award), *supra* note 91, paras. 512–520.

off small marine features, the door has instead been opened to (perhaps only short-term) instability as maritime allocations are recalibrated.

•••

In sum, we have seen in our actual and hypothetical cases under UNCLOS that the maritime dimensions to the dispute have brought norm-reliance to the fore. In these scenarios, the applicant States concerned are depending on a full and proper operation of legal processes to determine and uphold the rights at stake in the maritime areas at issue, even if—or perhaps irrespective of—sovereignty over land being contested. The shift to the normative emphasis and prioritizing of the resolution of maritime disputes is understandable when the power dynamics and limited dispute resolution options exist for settling territory sovereignty disputes. As mentioned previously, the view might be taken that it is better to provide legal answers to some aspects of a dispute when it is not possible to resolve all legal questions that might arise. Yet we can see that in proceeding down this path we are challenging the long-standing principle of the land dominates the sea. How satisfactory are the results of moving away from this approach? Further challenges to our land and sea paradigm are to be considered in the following Part. Part 4 will address other situations that may require a readjustment of maritime allocations and provide further consideration of when maritime rights are marketable.

4 Disappearing and Appearing Land

The connections between land and sea have come into more prominence as greater consideration is accorded to the consequences of sea-level rise on the territorial and maritime rights of States. The two situations that emerge in this regard concern, first, the changing coastlines of States, which has implications for the maritime allocations to which the State is entitled off its land mass, and, second, the potential disappearance of an island State. Scholars and policymakers have already contemplated a variety of responses to these scenarios, and the proposed legal responses are summarized in the sections that follow.

The important question that emerges for our purposes is what do these changes mean for the land and sea sovereignty regimes? Ensuring stability would be important in preserving the value of marketable title over maritime areas. Relying on an equitable distribution of maritime space and international recognition of maritime rights through international processes becomes even more important in the context of maintaining existing rights and expectations

in the use and allocation of maritime space. How well this can be achieved will
depend on the political will of states to act. But the situation prompts a return
to the deeper debate that underlies the law of the sea in relation to the extent
exclusive claims should be recognized in the face of shared, inclusive interests in maritime space (the latter captured by the principle of *mare liberum*)?
If there is an opportunity to release more maritime space to common usage,
should that be preferred or prioritized over ongoing recognition of exclusive
maritime space that no longer accords with the pre-existing constructs of
either the legal regimes allocating maritime zones or the very need for land to
be able to claim those maritime zones?

Connected with responses to sea-level rise, but also distinct activities, are
land reclamation as well as other human efforts to fortify coastlines, and the
construction of artificial islands and other structures at sea. A range of legal
consequences flow from these actions, as was evidenced in the *South China
Sea* arbitration. This "appearance" of land is assessed in this Part, and it is demonstrated that this sort of human effort has reduced import in the assertion
of rights over maritime space. The approach is consistent with the underpin-
nings of the normative regime that prompted the allocation of maritime space
through legal processes and further affirms the ongoing relevance of *mare
liberum*.

4.1   *Changing Coastlines*

It is well accepted that significant sea-level rise is occurring across the globe.[142]
The change in sea levels will fluctuate in different locations because of the
offshore and onshore geographic conditions, and the consequences of that sea
level rise will vary.[143] From a legal perspective, the change in sea levels is relevant in relation to the baselines from which all maritime zones are measured.
The normal baseline is the low-water line along the coast,[144] and is the pre-
dominant baseline used by States.[145] With sea levels rising, the low-water line

---

142   *See generally* Mary-Elena Carr, Madeleine Rubenstein, Alice Graff and Diego Villarreal, *Sea
      Level Rise in a Changing Climate: What do we Know?*, *in* THREATENED ISLAND NATIONS:
      LEGAL IMPLICATIONS OF RISING SEAS AND A CHANGING CLIMATE 15, 25–31 (Michael
      B. Gerrard and Gregory E. Wannier (eds), 2013).

143   Clive Schofield and David Freestone, *Options to Protect Coastlines and Secure Maritime
      Jurisdictional Claims in the Face of Global Sea Level Rise*, *in* THREATENED ISLAND
      NATIONS: LEGAL IMPLICATIONS OF RISING SEAS AND A CHANGING CLIMATE 141,
      142–143 and 145 (Michael B. Gerrard and Gregory E. Wannier (eds), 2013) (also noting that
      some scientists have also suggested that islands or some coastlines may adapt and grow
      rather than inevitably face erosion).

144   UNCLOS, *supra* note 12, art. 5.

145   Schofield and Freestone, *supra* note 143, at 157.

will shift further landward and some basepoints may be completely inundated. With the baselines moving in this direction, the outer-limits of the maritime zones (such as the territorial sea, EEZ and continental shelf) would also recede since the starting point to measure the extent of each zone is drawn from the basepoints or baselines of the coast.[146]

Systems of straight baselines would also be affected by sea-level rise. Straight baselines may be used "[i]n localities where the coastline is deeply indented and cut into, or if there is a fringe of islands along the coast in its immediate vicinity",[147] so long as they follow the general direction of the coast,[148] and meet other conditions set out in Article 7 of UNCLOS. Article 7(2) contemplates that "natural conditions" may render a coastline "highly unstable", allowing for basepoints to be selected "along the furthest seaward extent of the low-water line" and thereby maintained notwithstanding that line receding until the coastal State officially changes the baselines.[149] Although this provision was drafted with the specific situation of Bangladesh under consideration, it could be read as applying to changing coastlines in the light of sea-level rise.[150]

Low-tide elevations will also be affected by sea-level rise, which will have a concomitant effect on a State's maritime zones potentially. As noted in Part 2, under Article 13 of UNCLOS, a low-tide elevation within a State's territorial sea may be used as a basepoint. A fully submerged feature could not be relied upon for the same purpose. Another maritime measurement that could be affected through sea-level rise, including the submersion of particular land features, concerns the calculations for drawing archipelagic baselines.[151] Article 47(1) provides for a ratio of land area to water area that must be met for an archipelagic State to be able to use baselines joining "the outermost points of the outermost islands and drying reefs of the archipelago".[152] The archipelagic State might not only lose land features as a result of sea-level rise, but it may

146   See UNCLOS, supra note 12, art. 4 (addressing the outer limit of the territorial sea); art. 57 (describing the breadth of the EEZ); art. 76 (referring to the definition of the continental shelf).

147   Id. art. 7(1).

148   Id. art. 7(3).

149   Id. art. 7(2).

150   See Schofield and Freestone, supra note 143, at 159; Rosemary Rayfuse, Sea Level Rise and Maritime Zones: Preserving the Maritime Entitlements of "Disappearing States", in THREATENED ISLAND NATIONS: LEGAL IMPLICATIONS OF RISING SEAS AND A CHANGING CLIMATE 167, 181–182 (Michael B. Gerrard and Gregory E. Wannier (eds), 2013) [hereinafter "Rayfuse, Sea Level Rise"].

151   Blanchard, supra note 14, at 82.

152   UNCLOS, supra note 12, art. 47(1).

also lose the right to claim archipelagic waters and hence sovereignty over the waters between its islands.

The prospect of the outer limit of maritime zones shifting is problematic for stability in terms of changing the allocation of rights and duties in different maritime space. States risk losing rights to natural resources as a result. The extent of the impact in this regard may depend on the rate of sea level rise in any particular area and how frequently a State issues large-scale charts marking the State's baselines. One suggestion has been that a State could "freeze" its baselines once published on charts it recognizes and presents to the UN Secretary-General under the requirements of UNCLOS.[153] This approach allows for stability in the outer limits of the State's maritime zones but could create navigational issues with out-of-date information.[154]

In light of the potential for these sorts of ambulatory baselines,[155] proposals have been made to decouple the outer limit of maritime zones from those baselines.[156] Caron proposes freezing the outer limits of maritime allocations as they are at present a reflection of what is considered equitable, and acceptable, as agreed under UNCLOS.[157] A counter-argument would be that if there is an opportunity to return a greater maritime area to designation of high seas or to the Area, more States would ultimately benefit. As noted at the outset of this Part, each approach returns us to the classic Groatian-Selden debate as between open and closed seas. Rayfuse has noted the significance of freezing the outer limits as compared to freezing the baselines. She has observed that once baselines are fixed, a greater maritime area will gradually come under the exclusive sovereignty of the coastal State as coasts recede and a larger area becomes subject to the internal waters regime.[158] Internal waters are the waters

---

153   *Id.* art. 5 and art. 16. *See* discussion in Schofield and Freestone, *supra* note 143, at 162.

154   Schofield and Freestone suggest that two charts could be used: one map that is "recognized by the coastal State" and submitted to the UN, and another that is more accurate and available as a navigational chart. Schofield and Freestone, *supra* note 143, at 162.

155   As discussed in Alfred H.A. Soons, *The Effects of a Rising Sea Level on Maritime Limits and Boundaries*, 37 NETH. INT'L L. REV. 207, 216–218 (1990); David D. Caron, *When Law Makes Climate Change Worse: Rethinking the Law of Baselines in Light of a Rising Sea Level*, 17 ECOLOGY L.Q. 621, 634 (1990); Rayfuse, *Sea Level Rise, supra* note 150, at 171 (drawing on the work of Soons, Caron and others).

156   Schofield and Freestone, *supra* note 143, at 162; Rayfuse, *Sea Level Rise, supra* note 150, at 188.

157   Caron, *supra* note 155, at 640–641.

158   Rosemary Rayfuse, *International Law and Disappearing States: Utilising Maritime Entitlements to Overcome the Statehood Dilemma* (November 7, 2010) [2010] UNSWLRS 52 available at: http://ssrn.com/abstract=1704835, at 6 [hereinafter "Rayfuse, *Disappearing States*"].

that lie on the landward side of baselines, including straight baselines, and over which States have total sovereignty and jurisdictional control.[159] Where the outer limits of an EEZ or continental shelf are fixed, rather than fixing the baselines, there is still a possibility of a State's territorial sea boundary shifting to account for the changing low-water line due to sea-level rise. It would therefore be anticipated that boundaries of each of the maritime zones (territorial sea, contiguous zone, EEZ and continental shelf) would need to be fixed.

If maritime boundaries are to be fixed at a certain point in time (either the baselines or the outer limits), there remains a question as to what point in time should be selected.[160] Hayashi proposes doing so at the date a State publishes its baselines consistent with Article 16 of UNCLOS. A difficulty with the "freezing" approach is that there are instances where States dispute the baselines or maritime allocations that are being claimed by another State. Rayfuse suggests that, similar to Antarctica, the disputed claim is frozen and left to be resolved through "normal processes".[161]

Commentators have remarked upon the possibility that an island entitled to a full complement of maritime zones under Article 121(2) of UNCLOS may lose this status if the island is no longer able to support human habitation or an economic life.[162] The question raised in this setting is whether the State with sovereignty over that island then loses the rights it had accrued in an EEZ or continental shelf around what should now be classed as a rock. Soons has suggested that it may be permissible to maintain an island artificially so that it does not become a rock under Article 121(3).[163]

This conundrum finds some response in the *South China Sea* arbitration. Although not addressing the status of features that had lost land or lost attributes associated with an island, the Tribunal indicated that any assessment has to look at the natural conditions of the feature. If regard must be had to the natural status of the feature, it could be argued that the island was fully entitled to an EEZ and continental shelf and that this entitlement remains even if human-induced climate change has contributed to sea-level rise. The counterargument would be that an assessment of the natural state should take into account changes wrought by nature, such as sea-level rise. The focus would

159   An exception here is that waters enclosed by straight baselines are still subject to the regime of innocent passage. UNCLOS, *supra* note 12, art. 8(2).

160   Rayfuse, *Disappearing States, supra* note 158, at 6 (citing M. Hayashi, "Sea Level Rise and the Law of the Sea: Legal and Policy Options" *Proceedings of International Symposium on Islands and Oceans*, Ocean Policy and Research Foundation (2009) 78, 84).

161   Rayfuse, *Disappearing States, supra* note 158, at 6.

162   Schofield and Freestone, *supra* note 143, at 147.

163   Soons, *supra* note 155, at 223.

then need to be on the point in time that the assessment is made. It could hence be suggested that greater stability is achieved if a feature that had once been recognized as entitled to an EEZ and continental shelf should maintain these entitlements consistent with expectations of the global community.

Could this reasoning still hold if a feature that was an island is reduced to a low-tide elevation eventually? Or disappeared altogether? Arguments in favor of stability would once again have relevance in this regard. In the context of prescription as a mode of territorial acquisition, Shaw has written, "it reflects the need for stability felt within the international system by recognizing the territory in the possession of a state for a long period of time and uncontested cannot be taken away from that state without serious consequences for the international order".[164] This policy could be equally applicable in situations where maritime allocations would change relatively suddenly. This emphasis on stability also comes to the fore, and has been applied in a maritime context, in relation to the doctrine of historical consolidation. Historic consolidation "is founded on proven long use, which reflects a complex of interests and relations resulting in the acquisition of territory (including parts of the sea)".[165] The circumstances are of course not identical so it may not be appropriate to transplant the policy behind these doctrines into another domain. Nonetheless, the importance of stability and continuity resonates with a policy preference to recognize the ongoing rights of States over certain maritime space even in the event of the bases of those claims changing. The *South China Sea* decision to focus on natural conditions preferred an approach that cut against recent changes to land and preferred the earlier status quo.

Maritime boundary delimitation cases have not been amenable to accounting for changing or unstable coastal conditions thus far. For example, in *Bangladesh v India*, the Tribunal stated the:

> ... issue is not whether the coastlines of the Parties will be affected by climate change in the years or centuries to come. It is rather whether the choice of base points located on the coastline and reflecting the general direction of the coast is feasible in the present case and at the present time.[166]

164   MALCOLM N. SHAW, INTERNATIONAL LAW 504 (2008).
165   *Id.* at 507.
166   Bay of Bengal Maritime Boundary Arbitration (Bangladesh v India) Award of July 7, 2014, PCA Case No. 2010–16, http://www.pcacases.com/web/view/18, para. 214.

Similar resistance to accounting for coastal instability is evident in *Nicaragua v Honduras*,[167] and *Romania v Ukraine*.[168]

Nonetheless, one situation where the outer limits of a State's maritime jurisdiction are unlikely to shift despite receding coastlines is in the context of agreed maritime boundaries between neighbouring States. Where the extended maritime zones between opposite or adjacent States overlap, those States will need to reach agreement as to the maritime boundary between them.[169] Once that maritime boundary is fixed by treaty, it would not change because of any shift in the low-water line as such treaties are not subject to change even in the event of "subsequent fundamental change of circumstances".[170] The States concerned may agree to shift the line in a subsequent agreement, particularly if one State is more affected by sea-level rise along its coast than another but it could not be readily expected that once negotiated and agreed, States would be too willing to reconsider a boundary's position. In a similar vein, States that undertake the process for recognition of an outer continental shelf through the Commission for the Limits of the Continental Shelf will be able to establish "permanent" boundaries in accordance with UNCLOS.[171]

Beyond agreed maritime boundaries, or declarations following the outer-continental shelf process under UNCLOS, it remains to be seen what processes may otherwise be put in place to ensure stability in maritime allocations as the land generating those allocations changes. While a new treaty or a protocol to UNCLOS may provide a mechanism for ensuring consistency in approach to this issue and maintaining stability and order in the oceans, the political palatability of such an option is likely low in light of previous difficulties in negotiating treaties responding to climate change.[172] Soons has contemplated

---

167 Territorial and Maritime Dispute between Nicaragua and Honduras in the Caribbean Sea (Nicaragua v Honduras) (2007) I.C.J. 661 (Oct. 8), para. 277.

168 Maritime Delimitation in the Black Sea (Romania v Ukraine) (2009) I.C.J. 62, (Feb. 3), para. 131.

169 In accordance with Articles 74(1) and 83(1) of UNCLOS. See UNCLOS, *supra* note 12, arts. 74(1) and 83(1).

170 Vienna Convention on the Law of Treaties, 23 May 1969, 1155 U.N.T.S. 331, art. 62(2)(a); Aegean Sea Continental Shelf (Greece v. Turkey), 1978 I.C.J. 3 (Dec. 19) at 35–36. *See also* Soons, *supra* note 155, at 222.

171 UNCLOS, *supra* note 12, art. 76(9). See Rayfuse, *Disappearing States, supra* note 158, 5 (citing proposals by M. Hayashi, "Sea Level Rise and the Law of the Sea: Legal and Policy Options" *Proceedings of International Symposium on Islands and Oceans*, Ocean Policy and Research Foundation (2009) 78, 79).

172 Schofield and Freestone, *supra* note 143, at 162–163. The International Law Association established an "International Law and Sea-Level Rise Committee" to develop proposals addressing the impact of sea-level rise under international law, including in relation to maritime zones, territory, statehood, nationality and human rights. A final report is to be

the possibility of customary international law emerging to address the legal effects of sea-level rise on maritime jurisdiction, and considers a rule may be recognized that permits States to maintain territorial sea and EEZ outer limits "at a certain moment in accordance with the general rules in force at that time".[173] While the formation of customary law may be criticized as too slow and impractical,[174] we have seen customary law develop relatively rapidly in the law of the sea following the Truman Proclamation and increasing State claims to continental shelves. A powerful State declaring its outer maritime boundaries to be final and binding *erga omnes* irrespective of changes to its coastline henceforth could similarly catalyze claims by other States in comparable circumstances. It would then be the case that on the back of this State practice, a treaty or protocol, or perhaps a UN General Assembly resolution,[175] could be more readily adopted. The normative importance in allocation of maritime space remains apparent in the scenario of changing coastlines, as does the significance of the marketability of title in adjusting to changing conditions. This emphasis on norms makes sense in this instance as the continued physical presence of land, and sovereignty over that land, persists without disruption to our fundamental precepts of territorial sovereignty and the principle of the land dominates the sea. What may be challenged instead is the ongoing priority accorded to *mare liberum*. The situation changes and all these disruptions emerge when the land disappearing constitutes an entire State, as next addressed.

4.2   *Disappearing States*

While some States may be concerned about losing part of their land territory through coastal erosion and sea-level rise, some small island States face the prospect of being entirely subsumed by the ocean, or otherwise being left with uninhabitable land, because of sea-level rise. For example, Kiribati, the Maldive Islands, the Marshall Islands and Tuvalu may be at risk.[176] Some States

---

submitted in August, 2018. *See* International Law Association International Law and Sea-Level Rise Committee, *Interim Report: 2016*, Johannesburg Conference (2016), http://www.ila-hq.org/index.php/committees (outlining mandate, as well as current discussions and proposals under consideration).

173   Soons, *supra* note 155, at 225.

174   *See* Rayfuse, *Disappearing States, supra* note 158, at 7.

175   Although a UN General Assembly resolution would be non-binding, if it attracted a consensus vote, it could be seen as crystallising the position in customary international law if it aligned with the practice of States.

176   *See* Rayfuse, *Disappearing States, supra* note 158, at 1.

are already acting to remove populations from existing islands,[177] or contemplating what to do with displaced populations from island States that are entirely inundated.[178]

If there is no more land, is there still a State? It requires that we step away from the idea that a State is the physical land mass and embodies a political and social construct.[179] As I argued above, this understanding should have precluded recognizing entitlements to maritime zones when the political and social construct responsible for land could not be identified.

Soons has proposed that alternative territorial structures may be necessary, and suggested acquiring new territory from another State by treaty of cession, or merging with another State (potentially creating a federation).[180] In the former scenario, there may still be scope for claims to new maritime entitlements from the ceded territory, but a merger or union may extinguish the disappearing State's maritime allocation.[181]

Rather than take a position that a State just ceases to exist, Rayfuse has argued that the concept of a deterritorialized State could be recognized. She points to the Knights of Malta and, previously, the Holy See as examples of entities recognized as sovereign international subjects even in the absence of territory in possession.[182] Moreover, a form of "functional" sovereignty has been recognized in relation to supra-national organizations such as the European Union or governments-in-exile.[183] Consequently, "international law already recognizes that sovereignty and nation may be separated from territory".[184] In the context of States disappearing as a result of sea-level rise, the construct would involve a representative authority of the State acting on behalf of the people of

177 Examples cited in this regard include India's decision to move 10,000 people from the island of Lohachara in the Bay of Bengal as a precaution and the relocation of 2,600 inhabitants from the Papua New Guinean Cateret Islands. *See* Schofield and Freestone, *supra* note 143, at 151.
178 *See* Jonathan Adams, *Rising sea levels threaten small Pacific island nations*, NY TIMES, May 3, 2007, http://www.nytimes.com/2007/05/03/world/asia/03iht-pacific.2.5548184.html.
179 Grote Stoutenburg has examined whether such States can continue to function in the international sphere. *See* Jenny Grote Stoutenberg, *When Do States Disappear? Thresholds of Effective Statehood and the Continued Recognition of "Deterritorialized" Island States*, *in* THREATENED ISLAND NATIONS: LEGAL IMPLICATIONS OF RISING SEAS AND A CHANGING CLIMATE 57 (Michael B. Gerrard and Gregory E. Wannier (eds), 2013).
180 Soons, *supra* note 155, at 230. *See also* Caron, *supra* note 155, at 650 (discussing the latter proposal).
181 Blanchard, *supra* note 14, at 96.
182 Rayfuse, *Disappearing States, supra* note 158, at 10.
183 *Id.* at 10–11.
184 *Id.* at 11.

the State within the international system and, most relevant for present purposes, still being able to exercise maritime rights over and benefitting from the pre-existing maritime zones.[185] As Rayfuse recognizes, there are difficulties associated with the concept and, for the management of maritime zones, particularly in the monitoring, control, surveillance and enforcement of resource exploitation, in ensuring that conservation and management requirements are met, and in distributing the income derived from the exploitation of marine resources to the displaced population.[186]

This scenario presents a distinct challenge to our land dominates the sea principle. Without any land, a State seemingly has no more rights to maritime areas. Rayfuse has asserted, "[e]stablishment and maintenance of maritime entitlements is a quintessential hallmark of statehood".[187] However, maritime entitlements are not so much a hallmark of statehood but rather a consequence of statehood in our current international legal order. The deterritorialized State "detaches State and statehood from territory".[188] But can the maritime allocation also be detached from States and statehood?

In the *South China Sea* arbitration, the Tribunal was willing to divorce the political and social construct of the State from the physical landmass for the purpose of ascertaining entitlements. The entitlements to a territorial sea, or potentially to an EEZ or continental shelf, could accrue, under the Tribunal's reasoning, even when there was no knowledge as to who (which State) was entitled. There is a shift occurring in the reasoning. Traditionally, physical land plus community (that is, a State) produced maritime entitlements. Under the *South China Sea* case, physical land, in the absence of a known community, could produce maritime entitlements. Now with deterritorialized States, it is proposed that community, without physical land, can produce maritime entitlements.

Thinking of the State as divorced from land, but seemingly still with sea, is justified when a conceptual shift away from the territorial focus of sovereignty and statehood occurs. Blanchard has presented possible paradigms for exploring this possibility, including diasporas and cosmopolitanism, global governance, and through equity and moral duties.[189] The latter may seem particularly compelling when the fate of people on particular island States is

---

185 *Id. See also* Blanchard, *supra* note 14, at 98; Jörgen Ödalen, *Underwater Self-determination: Sea-level Rise and Deterritorialised Small Island States*, 17 ETHICS, POL'Y & ENV'T 225, 230 (2014).
186 Rayfuse, *Disappearing States, supra* note 158, at 12.
187 *Id.*
188 Blanchard, *supra* note 14, at 102.
189 *Id.* at 108–115.

contemplated. Stoutenburg argues that if the international community cannot act to prevent the disappearance of island States, it should at least acknowledge their entitlement to survive as a legal community.[190]

Alternatively, we can think purely in terms of boundaries rather than the space that falls within the boundaries and avoid classification of that space. In this scenario, we can focus on the stability of boundaries and the fundamental importance attributed to that under international law. "One of the core principles of the international system is the need for stability and finality in boundary questions and much flows from this."[191] If boundaries have been set out in a treaty, the international frontier so defined becomes permanent.[192] Perhaps the outer limits of maritime zones noted in nautical charts submitted to the UN need to be reflected in a multilateral treaty so as to gain this level of notoriety under international law, irrespective of the land or sea space actually involved.

Ultimately, critical to the resolution of legal challenges arising with disappearing coasts and lands is political willingness and endorsement of powerful actors in the international community, which reflects our realist paradigm. Such willingness and endorsement may be forthcoming when it is recalled that those actors' own exclusive rights and maritime jurisdiction may be under challenge, at least in relation to sea-level rise and shifting coastlines. To preserve existing maritime claims and promote stability in the public order of the oceans, all coastal States have an interest in resolving the issue of shifting baselines and boundaries. Devising acceptable normative regimes for this purpose will be critical. In this regard, it could be argued that the self-interest of States and the importance of normative regimes align.

Yet does this interest extend to the continued recognition of maritime zones where a State no longer has the physical land that generated the maritime zones? On the one hand, the rationale of stability in maritime boundaries and rights over maritime space applies equally to disappearing States as it does to disappearing coasts. Consistency could be expected in this regard. On the other hand, to follow this approach requires States to move away from the territorial construct associated with maritime entitlements, and indeed the territorial construct that has been so fundamental to the international legal system for centuries. Moreover, to recognize ongoing maritime zones in the absence

---

190   Grote Stoutenburg, *supra* note 179, at 87. See also Blanchard, *supra* note 14, at 114.

191   SHAW, *supra* note 164, at 522. *See also* Temple of Preah Vihear (Cambodia v. Thailand), Merits, Judgment, (1962) I.C.J. 6, 34 (June 15); Territorial Dispute (Libya v. Chad), Judgment, Merits, (1994) ICJ Rep 6, 37 (Feb. 3); Dubai v. Sharjah Border Arbitration (1981) 91 I.L.R. 543, 578 (Oct. 19).

192   SHAW, *supra* note 164, at 529.

of physical land would disallow the resurgence of *mare liberum* and the ongo-ing importance of the inclusive interests of all States. The policy motivation of the *South China Sea* Tribunal in assessing what features were rocks rather than islands and hence avoiding large claims to exclusive rights over ocean space on the basis of a small physical feature arguably runs counter to maintain-ing exclusive rights over large maritime areas in the absence of any physical feature.

While arguments of equity are important in addressing the rights of those living in territory that becomes uninhabitable because of climate change, another difficult reality of the current international legal regime is that the law of the sea has always prioritized geography as it exists. Consequently, while some consideration is accorded to land-locked States and to geographically-disadvantaged States in the law of the sea, there is a definite skew of advantage for coastal States. International law has done very little to rectify this geographic inequality to date. It raises the question of whether the disappearing States will (or should) instead fall into a category of geographically-disadvantaged States if they are "deterritorialized" and will receive the consideration that is afforded to other States in this category. Perhaps it is the prospect of additional States joining this group that may provide greater impetus for coastal States to take the rights granted to land-locked States and geographically-disadvantaged States more seriously in matters such as the allocation of fish catch surplus and in the impending operation of Article 82, which will require collection and dis-bursement of funds from exploitation of the extended continental shelf.

4.3   *Land Creation*

As part of their responses to sea-level rise, or generally to maintain coastlines in the face of different climatic and other conditions, States have sought to reclaim land or otherwise fortify their coasts. Efforts in this regard include constructing sea walls, wave reduction structures or other "hard engineering options".[193] Schofield and Freestone note that "[i]t is generally accepted that coastal States can, by implementing such measures, stabilize portions of their baselines and thereby preserve their associated maritime zone entitlements".[194] These activities may have, however, a negative environmental impact, poten-tially extending to neighboring States.[195]

A low-tide elevation or fully submerged feature cannot be transformed into an island through human activity, such as reclamation activity or construction

---

193   Schofield and Freestone, *supra* note 143, at 151.
194   *Id.* See also Soons, *supra* note 155, at 222.
195   Schofield and Freestone, *supra* note 143, at 152–154.

of a lighthouse or the like.[196] The feature does not become an island because the legal definition of an island requires it to be "naturally formed" under Article 121(1) of UNCLOS.[197] The International Law Commission had supported this position during its work on the law of the sea prior to the adoption of the 1958 law of the sea conventions.[198] The International Law Commission's commentary on islands noted:

> ... the following are not considered islands and have no territorial sea: (i) Elevations which are above water at low tide only. Even if an installation is built on such an elevation and is itself permanently above water—a lighthouse, for example, the elevation is not an "island" as understood in this article....[199]

An example of such a feature is Ieodo or Socotra Rock, which lies between South Korea and China in the Yellow Sea. It is fully-submerged but Korea has constructed a research facility on it.[200] Both States consider that it falls within their respective EEZs.[201]

---

196   Robert Lavalle, *Not Quite a Sure Thing: The Maritime Area of Rocks and Low-Tide Elevations under the UN Law of the Sea Convention*, 19 INT'L J. MAR. & COASTAL L. 43, 58 (2004); Robert Beckman, "International Law and China's Reclamation Works in the South China Sea" (Paper presented at 2nd Conference on South China Sea, National University of Singapore and Nanjing University, 24–25 April 2015) 7 [Draft paper], https://cil.nus.edu.sg/wp-content/uploads/2015/04/Beckman-Nanjing-Draft-17-April-2015.pdf.

197   The island can consist of any sort of land, including coral, so long as it is naturally formed and above water at high tide. See Territorial and Maritime Dispute (Nicaragua v Colombia) (Judgment) [2012] I.C.J. 624, (Nov. 19) 645, para. 37.

198   Convention on the Continental Shelf, 29 April 1958, 499 U.N.T.S. 311; Convention on the High Seas, 29 April 1958, 450 U.N.T.S. 11; Convention on Fishing and Conservation of the Living Resources of the High Seas, 29 April 1958, 559 U.N.T.S. 285; Convention on the Territorial Sea and the Contiguous Zone, 29 April 1958, 516 U.N.T.S. 205.

199   Report of the International Law Commission Covering the work of its Eighth Session, UNGAOR, U.N. Doc A/3159 (1956); 2 *Yearbook of the International Law Commission* 253, 270 (1956). But see Kwaitkowska and Soons who have argued that a lighthouse or other aid to navigation would give an island an "economic life of its own" because of the value to shipping. See Barbara Kwiatkowska and Alfred H.A. Soons, *Entitlement to Maritime Areas of Rocks Which Cannot Sustain Human Habitation or Economic Life of Their Own*, 21 NETH. YBK INT'L L. 139, 167–168 (1990).

200   *See* Lily Kuo, *Will a Tiny, Submerged Rock Spark a New Crisis in the East China Sea?*, THE ATLANTIC, Dec. 9, 2013, https://www.theatlantic.com/china/archive/2013/12/will-a-tiny-submerged-rock-spark-a-new-crisis-in-the-east-china-sea/282155/.

201   *See* Shannon Tiezzi, *Is China Ready to Solve One of Its Maritime Disputes?*, THE DIPLOMAT, Nov. 7, 2015, https://thediplomat.com/2015/11/is-china-ready-to-solve-one-of-its-maritime-disputes/.

States have nonetheless undertaken an effort to add to small island features, that are naturally formed and above water at high tide, to ensure that their maritime claims extending from those features may be sustained. A prime example in this regard has been Japan's efforts over Okinotorishima. Okinotorishima lies in a 7.8km² coral reef, extending 4.5km from east to west and 1.7km from north to south, with a circumference of 11km.[202] Most of the reef is under water, even at low tide, and there were originally six islets above water level but due to rising tides there remained only two, Eastern Islet and Northern Islet. At high tide, these islets were described as "70 centimeters above water ... [and] the size of two king-size beds".[203] Similarly, it was stated that Eastern Islet was 90cm above water at low tide and 6cm above water at high tide, while Northern Islet was 1m above water at low tide and 16cm above the water at high tide.[204] However, Japan performed extensive construction works upon Okinotorishima, and this work has significantly increased the size of these two islets and established a third islet, the Southern Islet, Minami-Kojima. After concrete encasing was added, each of the islets has a diameter of 60m and there is a 140m platform in the lagoon that has a heliport and large three-story building.[205]

The core of the dispute over Japan's activities in relation to Okinotorishima appears to be whether rocks can be transformed into islands through human intervention.[206] Chinese commentators have argued that the natural characteristics of Okinotorishima demonstrate that it falls within the definition of a rock and submitted that Japan's activities have been undertaken subsequent

---

202   Yann-Huei Song, *Okinotorishima: A "Rock" or an "Island"? Recent Maritime Boundary Controversy between Japan and Taiwan/China*, in MARITIME BOUNDARY DISPUTES, SETTLEMENT PROCESSES, AND THE LAW OF THE SEA 145, 148 (Seoung-Yong Hong and Jon M. Van Dyke (eds), 2009); *Okino-Tori-Shima* (2016) Hawaii eBook Library <http://www.hawaiilibrary.net/articles/okino-tori-shima>.

203   Jon M. Van Dyke, *The* Romania-Ukraine *Decision and Its Effect on East Asian Maritime Delimitations*, in GOVERNING OCEAN RESOURCES: NEW CHALLENGES AND EMERGING REGIMES 43, 58 (Jon M. Van Dyke et al. (eds), 2013).

204   Song, *supra* note 202, at 148.

205   Marika Vilisaar, *Sino-Japanese Maritime Jurisdictional Disputes in the East China Sea*, 4 ACTA SOCIETATIS MARTENSIS 229, 242, 245 (2010).

206   *See, e.g.,* Yann-huei Song, *The Application of Article 121 of the Law of the Sea Convention to the Selected Geographical Features Situated in the Pacific Ocean*, 9 CHINESE J. INT'L L. 663 (2010); Guifang (Julia) Xue, *How Much Can a Rock Get? A Reflection from the Okinotorishima Rocks*, 1 CHINA OCEANS L. REV. 1 (2011); Jun Qui and Wenhua Liu, *Should the Okinotori Reef be entitled to a Continental Shelf? A Comparative Study on Uninhabited Islands in Extended Continental Shelf Submissions*, CHINA OCEANS L. REV. 221, 221 (2009).

to the adoption of UNCLOS with the intent of solidifying Japan's claim to the features as islands entitled to an EEZ and continental shelf.[207]

The difficulty for China with its position on Okinotorishima has been that it cuts against China's activities on features in the South China Sea and its own extensive land reclamation activities. If China is unwilling to recognize Japan's actions as creating islands from rocks then it would not have clean hands in claiming islands based on its own activities transforming the characteristics of what were determined to be either rocks or low-tide elevations in their natural condition.[208] One commentator has suggested that China's interests in undertaking reclamation works on the features in the South China Sea relate more to strategic and military concerns rather than seeking to claim greater access to resources.[209] The *South China Sea* Tribunal confirmed that construction activities on low-tide elevations do not change their status. The land reclamation efforts of China, which have greatly increased the size, habitability and use of different features, could not change the classification of the feature. Instead, the Tribunal had regard to the "earlier, natural condition, prior to the onset of significant human modification".[210]

Under UNCLOS, constructions matter on coastlines or coastal features in different situations. In the context of straight baselines, Article 7(4) allows low-tide elevations to be used as basepoints where "lighthouses or similar installations which are permanently above sea level have been built on them". States using straight baselines therefore may be advantaged against a receding baseline if construction occurs on islands, rocks or low-tide elevations and ensures their possible selection as basepoints from which to measure maritime zones. Even if a feature is fully submerged but has a structure on it, and is in a location that is suitable for the drawing of straight baselines under Article 7 of UNCLOS, its prior recognition may still be sufficient for its continued use.[211]

---

207 *See, e.g.*, Xue, *supra* note 206, at 7–11.

208 The doctrine of "clean hands" is generally intended to prevent a State presenting arguments of wrong-doing when it has also been engaged in comparable wrong-doing. *See* Stephen M. Schwebel, *Principle of Clean Hands*, MAX PLANCK ENCYCLOPEDIA OF INTERNATIONAL LAW (2013).

209 Nong Hong, *Land Reclamation Activities in the South China Sea: Legal Interpretation and Political Implication*, Proceedings of the Workshop on Recent Developments in the South China Sea Arbitration and their Implications, October 6–9, 2015, Taipei, Taiwan, 40, 44 (copy on file with author).

210 South China Sea (Award), *supra* note 91, para. 511.

211 Article 7(4) refers to "instances where the drawing of baselines to and from such elevations [with constructions on them] has received general international recognition". UNCLOS, *supra* note 12, art. 7(4).

For artificial islands, structures and installations outside a coastal State's territorial sea, the legal regime is governed by Article 60 of UNCLOS. Under Article 60, the coastal State shall have the exclusive right to construct and to authorize and regulate the construction, operation and use of artificial islands, as well as installations and structures related to the exercise of the coastal State's economic rights within the EEZ. These constructions are to have no relevance in relation to maritime allocation, as they "do not possess the status of islands"; nor do they have a "territorial sea of their own" and, moreover "their presence does not affect the delimitation of the territorial sea, the [EEZ] or the continental shelf."[212] While UNCLOS thus draws a line between artificial and naturally formed islands, the reality is that the former may blur with the latter due to changing geographic conditions.

Stoutenberg has argued that human construction to protect a natural feature should not transform it into an artificial island or installation on the basis that it "would not try to *generate* maritime entitlements through artificial means, but only aim to *preserve* its already recognized rights".[213] However, what would be the result if the land was ultimately entirely human-made as its natural features are washed away? *Re Duchy of Sealand* tells us that territory must "consist in a natural segment of the earth's surface".[214] Yet under the *South China Sea* ruling, the focus on the natural condition of the feature in question is important and if that is the benchmark, the disappearance of the original feature and replacement with human-made construction may still be acceptable for classification as land that generates maritime entitlements.

However, we must take into account that there is limited recognition under international law, and particularly the law of the sea, of human effort in establishing rights to maritime areas. Maintaining a limited recognition of human constructions on land for the purpose of asserting claims to maritime space would be consonant with *mare liberum* in terms of allowing for greater areas of maritime space available to all States. Other factors at play include the disallowance of more wealthy and technically-advanced States benefitting at the expense of other State's (or States') claims. This approach is consistent with the initial development of the continental shelf, as we discussed in *Land and Sea*, where rights to the continental shelf could not be established by way of occupation. The normative regime would therefore hold sway in scenarios where powerful States create land. It will, however, be tested in the South China Sea in the future, potentially, if China proceeds to assert rights to the maritime

---

212   *Id.* art. 60(8).
213   Grote Stoutenberg, *supra* note 179, at 62 (emphasis in original).
214   *Re Duchy of Sealand* (1989) 80 I.L.R. 683, 685. *See further* Blanchard, *supra* note 14, at 95.

resources around its artificially constructed islands over which it claims sovereignty, despite the findings of the *South China Sea* Tribunal. As China may well be capable of exploiting its resources without engagement of foreign investors, the marketability of the title will not be relevant.[215]

5 Concluding Remarks

This Chapter has demonstrated that there is much that continues to challenge and operationalize the land and sea dichotomy. The dichotomy can still be explained by the contrasting approaches of realism and norm-based theories. Yet in this Chapter, I have identified a number of efforts where the realist paradigm is being confronted, or subverted, through the inclusion of territorial questions into the UNCLOS dispute settlement process. There are legitimate queries to be made as to whether this is consistent with the intended operation of UNCLOS dispute settlement. The continued expansion of UNCLOS jurisdiction may ultimately undermine the success of the UNCLOS regime if that regime is used for purposes beyond the interpretation and application of UNCLOS. States may respond in different ways if they consider that jurisdiction is being exercised in politically inappropriate or arguably unlawful ways under UNCLOS dispute settlement proceedings. For example, China opted not to appear in the *South China Sea* case,[216] arguing that the case was concerned with matters of territorial sovereignty and has since disavowed the validity of the judgment.[217]

This Chapter has also assessed the importance of land in the context of that land changing or disappearing and the implications for maritime entitlements. Our realist construct demands that land generate maritime entitlements, but there are also strong expectations associated with stability and the maintenance of rights once acquired. If maritime entitlements are to be maintained when land decreases or vanishes, reliance on norms again comes to the fore, backed by the self-interested States keen to secure their own power bases and resources. This motivation might be enough when thinking about changing

---

215   As observed above, marketable title is most relevant where a State is not able to consume directly the resources at issue. *See supra* note 11 and accompanying text.

216   China was entitled to take this step, but it did not preclude the tribunal from continuing the arbitration. *See supra* note 116 and accompanying text.

217   *See* Ministry of Foreign Affairs of the People's Republic of China, *Statement of the Ministry of Foreign Affairs of the People's Republic of China on the Award of 12 July 2016 of the Arbitral Tribunal in the South China Sea Arbitration Established at the Request of the Republic of the Philippines,* July 12, 2016, http://www.fmprc.gov.cn/mfa_eng/zxxx_662805/t1379492.shtml.

coastlines, but potentially will not extend for the protection of States that will disappear or become uninhabitable.

These small States are not in the numeric majority and lack political, military or economic power. Their situation can be contrasted to that of the Group of 77 during the UNCLOS negotiations when the New International Economic Order was in the ascent, and common heritage of humankind was established in the relation to the deep seabed.[218] Nor is their situation presently comparable to the time that the continental shelf doctrine was developed prior to the adoption of the 1958 Convention on the Continental Shelf when the principle of self-determination was gaining momentum during the period of decolonization post-World War Two.[219] Upholding and responding to the human rights of the individuals and groups impacted may ultimately be a greater priority than reconceptualizing the territorial primacy that exists within the international legal system.

A reliance on norms would be essential to develop and operationalize the concept of the deterritorialized State, especially if it were to entail ongoing recognition of maritime rights in the absence of land. It is valid to question whether this is consistent with the policy approach of the *South China Sea* Award in denying extended maritime zones to small features. The restrictions that currently exist on recognizing human intervention in the generation of maritime space are consistent with this policy approach. Ultimately, it accords with support for *mare liberum*, which has undergirded the law of the sea for many centuries and persists to this day despite many challenges to its position in the operation of international law.

---

218   *See* Brilmayer & Klein, *supra* note 1, at 712–713.
219   *Id.* at 712.

CHAPTER 14

Professor Lea Brilmayer and the Quest for Evidence from Space

John R. Crook

1 Introduction

> *Eritrea made extensive use of commercially available satellite imagery in establishing the destruction of several buildings in the localities of Serha, Senafe, and Tserona ... Eritrea also made use of satellite imagery in the context of its looting claims... The commission found the satellite imagery to be quite useful in its analysis of the destruction of several structures.*[1]

I came to appreciate Professor Lea Brilmayer's insight and determination through her role as agent for one of the parties before the Eritrea-Ethiopia Claims Commission, on which I was one of five commissioners.

Professor Brilmayer's team somehow located satellite photography showing before and after images of places that figured in important claims. As recorded in its awards, the Commission, assisted by a party-appointed expert familiar with interpretation of satellite images,[2] found this evidence to be very helpful in some situations requiring assessment of the extent of damage and responsibility for causing it.[3] This experience of the Eritrea-Ethiopia Claims Commission thus stands as a useful illustration of how evidence derived from space can contribute to the search for truth, or its approximation, in international legal proceedings, making it a fitting subject for this volume honoring Professor Brilmayer.

Evidence involving earth observation data is increasingly finding its way into domestic and international legal proceedings. Under the leadership of Professor Maureen Williams, the Space Law Committee of the International Law Association (ILA) has worked through the years to promote development

---

1   SEAN D. MURPHY, WON KIDANE & THOMAS R. SNIDER, LITIGATING WAR. ARBITRATION OF CIVIL INJURY BY THE ERITREA-ETHIOPIA CLAIMS COMMISSION 207 (2013) [Hereinafter Murphy].

2   *Id.* at 207.

3   *Id.* at 207–208.

© KONINKLIJKE BRILL NV, LEIDEN, 2019 | DOI:10.1163/9789004316539_015

of standards and procedures to facilitate its use in litigation. British satellite and forensics experts have created Air & Space Evidence,[4] a consulting firm that provides advice and services in national cases involving illegal landfills, logging and dredging of wetlands, and other legal and regulatory matters.[5] Satellite evidence is also playing a significant role in proceedings before international criminal tribunals such as the International Criminal Tribunal for the Former Yugoslavia (ICTY) and the International Criminal Court (ICC).

International court judges have been impressed by the power of such evidence. Writing in 2001—over seventeen years ago—of imagery used in the ICTY, Judge Patricia Wald observed:

> I found most astounding in the Srebrenica case the satellite aerial image photography furnished by the U.S. military intelligence which pinpointed to the minute movements on the grounds of men and transports in remote eastern Bosnian locations. These photographs not only assisted the prosecution in locating the mass grave sites over hundreds of miles of terrain, they were also introduced to validate its witnesses' account of where thousands of civilians were detained and eventually killed.[6]

Nevertheless, the use of such evidence in inter-State and other types of proceeding rooted in international law has been intermittent, and its impact is often difficult to assess. This Chapter considers some of the reasons for this and sketches some techniques that tribunals and parties might utilize to make more effective use of this potentially important source of information.

2   Earth Observation Data—Some Background

Evidence from space is the product of complex processes, the basics of which should be appreciated by decision-makers who need to assess its probative value. It is derived from satellites that use a variety of sensors to capture data from across the electromagnetic spectrum. Some use optical instruments—cameras—to capture images of the Earth's surface from the visible part of the

---

4 space-evidence.net.
5 Paul Marks, *The Detective Watching You From Space*, BBC FUTURE, April 5, 2016, www.bbc. com/future/story/20160404-the-detectives-who-spy-from-space [Space Detectives].
6 Patricia M. Wald, *The International Criminal Tribunal for the Former Yugoslavia Comes of Age: Some Observations on Day-to-Day Dilemmas of an International Court*, 5 WASH. U.J.L. & POL'Y 87, 101 (2001).

spectrum. These images are transmitted to Earth in digital form[7] and are processed to adjust for factors such as the Earth's curvature. Other types of earth observation satellites capture electromagnetic radiation emitted or reflected from the Earth's surface, such as returns of radar transmissions from the satellite. Satellites may carry multiple types of sensors, capturing and transmitting data from different parts of the electromagnetic spectrum.

This raw "earth observation data" is transmitted to ground stations. It is then converted into intelligible formats through various processes; the raw data is not intelligible and must be processed to create "the best possible image or abstraction of the real world as the user understands it."[8] Such processing, inter alia, corrects for geometric or other properties and removes interference. Data may be processed to enhance the appearance of features or characteristics relevant for the purpose at hand.[9] Thus, technology allows for data received from space to be processed in ways that can render it usable—indeed, valuable— for decision-makers. However, processing can also render it less trustworthy.

Potential evidence also can involve geolocation information containing spatial and temporal information that shows the location of persons, ships, aircraft or other physical phenomena on the face of the Earth. Such information is derived from satellite-based systems such as the U.S. Global Positional System (GPS), the Global Orbiting Navigation Satellite System operated by the Russian Federation, and the European Union/European Space Agency's GALILEO system.[10]

There is a great deal of earth observation data potentially available. Over thirty countries now possess significant space industries,[11] and numerous nongovernmental satellite operators and service providers across the globe engage

---

7   In the early days of earth observation satellites, satellites ejected physical canisters of exposed film that were retrieved by aircraft as they descended through the atmosphere on parachutes.

8   Shaida Johnson, *Technical Introduction to Satellite EO, in* EVIDENCE FROM EARTH OBSERVATION SATELLITES. EMERGING LEGAL ISSUES 11, 21 (Ray Purdy & Denise Leung, eds. 2013) [Purdy & Leung].

9   Anna Riddell and Brendan Plant, EVIDENCE BEFORE THE INTERNATIONAL COURT OF JUSTICE 289 (2009) [Riddell & Plant]; International Law Association Space Law Committee, CONFERENCE REPORT BERLIN 12 (2004).

10   Claudia Candelmo & Valentina Nardone, *Satellite Evidence in Human Rights Cases: Merits and Shortcomings*, 1(1) PEACE HUMAN RIGHTS GOVERNANCE 90 (2017) [Candelmo & Nardone].

11   Shaida Johnson, *Technical Introduction to Satellite EO*, in Purdy & Leung *supra* note 8, at 11, 13 n. 3; Fausto Pocar, *An Introduction to the PCA's Optional Rules for Arbitration of Disputes Relating to Outer Space Activities*, 38 J. OF SPACE LAW 171, 175 (2012) [Pocar].

in acquiring earth observation data, either for their own purposes or offering
it for sale.

> [S]pace images have been archived by satellite companies since the
> 1970s—initially in low resolution but gradually improving until in 1999,
> images that could resolve down to less than a metre became available
> outside the military, and much sharper 5cm and 30 cm images are pos-
> sible today.[12]

Drawing on this rich store of earth observation data, Professor Brilmayer and
her team were able to obtain, apparently from commercial sources, imagery
of several legally significant locations in remote areas in Ethiopia and Eritrea
on relevant "before-and-after" dates during the two countries' 1998–2000 war.

In the public sphere, many governments now control observation satellites
of varying kinds and have access to data they generate. However, governments
may be reluctant to fully disclose all information available to them. The potential pitfalls in this regard are illustrated by the U.S. experience in *Oil Platforms*,[13]
where the United States informed the Court that it had not used the best images
available to it as evidence in order to mask the capabilities of U.S. satellites.[14]

The quality of earth observation data, already high, continues to improve.
Indeed,

> [i]n the last two decades alone, satellite imagery data acquisition and
> quality has increased exponentially ... Ground breaking developments
> in the fields of remote sensing, photogrammetry and computer science
> with respect to sensor quality, computer processors and storage capacity
> has enormously increased the quality of satellite imagery....[15]

The characteristics of earth observation data pose challenges in connection
with its use in international litigation:
– This evidence is based on digital data which of itself is likely to be meaning-
  less to the trier of fact.

---

12   Space Detectives, *supra* note 5.
13   Oil Platforms (Iran v. U.S.), 2003 I.C.J 161.
14   Riddell & Plant, *supra* note 9, at 294. *See* Laura Moranchek, *Protecting National Security
     Evidence While Prosecuting War Crimes: Problems and Lessons for International Justice
     from the ICTY*, 31 YALE J. INT'L L. 477 (2006) [Morancheck].
15   Eya David Macauley, *The Use of EO Technologies in Court by the Office of the Prosecutor of
     the International Criminal Court*, in Purdy and Leung, *supra* note 8, at 217 [Macauley].

– The data must be converted into comprehensible forms through some process. It is the processed information or image that will be offered as evidence, not the underlying data. Accordingly, the trier of fact should be sensitive to the possible need to inquire into how, and by whom, data was processed in order to assess its probative value.

– The acquisition, processing, storage, and dissemination of earth observation data are all carried out through electronic processes. This may lead to issues of admissibility and reliability of electronic records.[16]

Given these characteristics, earth observation data generally requires introduction and perhaps explanation by expert witnesses, either offered by the parties or appointed by the tribunal. The experts' tasks may include providing a foundation for a tribunal to assess the reliability and accuracy of material offered as evidence by explaining the system(s) employed and the processes to which the underlying data was subjected.[17]

Decision-makers' confidence in earth observation data and its reliability, is enhanced "when combined with other corroborative evidence, normally 'ground truth' evidence. This ground truth may be aerial or surface observations and samples providing circumstantial evidence, or witness testimony of the relevant event giving direct evidence."[18]

3   Earth Observation Data in National and International Proceedings

Earth observation data is being used for a variety of purposes in national legal systems, has played a role in several international criminal proceedings, and has figured in inter-State boundary disputes before the International Court of Justice (ICJ) and other international tribunals. However, the path to its understanding and acceptance in international proceedings has not always been smooth.

3.1   National Proceedings

Some national legal systems have taken substantial steps in developing standards and procedures facilitating the use of evidence from space in their

---

16   LONDON INSTITUTE OF SPACE POLICY AND LAW, EVIDENCE FROM SPACE 17 (2012) [EVIDENCE FROM SPACE]; American Express Travel Related Services In. v. Vee Vinhee (*In re* Vinhee), 336 B.R. 437 (B.A.P. 9th Cir. 2005) (In a U.S. bankruptcy case, American Express's failure to provide a sufficient foundation to show the integrity of its paperless electronic records led to failure of its claim in a bankruptcy proceeding).

17   EVIDENCE FROM SPACE, *supra* note 16, at 19.

18   *Id.* at 193, § 5.1.

courts and administrative procedures.[19] Such evidence is being used for regulatory and other purposes in numerous countries, including detecting violations of environmental laws[20] (notably detection of marine pollution by ships[21]), monitoring fraudulent claims for agricultural subsidies, detecting unlawful forest clearing,[22] and disputes regarding land title under national law.[23] "In general, there appears to be a broad acceptance of [Earth observation] information" in a number of major European jurisdictions, most frequently to corroborate other evidence.[24] "Before" and "after" images of the village of Dujail, destroyed following an unsuccessful assassination attempt there on Saddam Hussein, were introduced by Iraqi prosecutors in Saddam's subsequent trial.[25]

In the United States, the U.S. Supreme Court articulated standards regulating the admissibility of novel scientific and technical evidence—such as earth observation data—in the leading case of *Daubert v. Merrell Dow Pharmaceuticals*, which emphasizes thorough assessment of the reliability of the techniques involved.[26] Other questions may also arise under, for example, the common law's rule against hearsay evidence. However, such issues should not pose insurmountable difficulties. Common law courts routinely accept x-ray images, also the product of a technological process, as evidence,

19   For reports on the use of earth observation information as evidence in national proceedings in Australia, Belgium, Germany, The Netherlands, United Kingdom and the United States, *see id.* at 297 et seq.

20   Kris Dighe, Todd Mikolop, Raymond W. Mushal & David O'Connell, *The Use of Satellite Imagery in Environmental Crimes Prosecutions in the United States: A Developing Area*, in *id.* at 65 [Dighe et al.].

21   Gérardine Goh Escolar, *The Use of EO Evidence As Evidence in the Courts of Singapore*, in *id.* at 93, 109–110; Sarah Moens, *The Use of Data from Earth Observation Satellites in Criminal Proceedings: Case Study of Illegal Oil Discharges at Sea*, in PROCEEDINGS OF THE INTERNATIONAL INSTITUTE OF SPACE LAW 2012 451, 459 (Corinne M. Jorgenson, ed., 2013), [PROCEEDINGS].

22   Bruce Goulevitch, *Ten Years of Using Earth Observation Data in Support of Queensland's Vegetation Management Framework*, in Purdy & Leung, *supra* note 8, at 113 (utilized in more than 600 investigations).

23   EVIDENCE FROM SPACE, *supra* note 16, at 22.

24   Sa'id Mosteshar, *EO in the European Union: Legal Considerations*, in Purdy & Leung, *supra* note 8, at 147, 175.

25   MICHAEL A. NEWTON & MICHAEL P. SCHARF, ENEMY OF THE STATE: THE TRIAL AND EXECUTION OF SADDAM HUSSEIN 141 (2008).

26   509 U.S. 579 (1993). *See* EVIDENCE FROM SPACE, *supra* note 16, at 122, § 5.2.17; Macauley, *supra* note 15, at 218–219. The U.S. Supreme Court's decision in Daubert authorizes testimony by expert witnesses on matters of "scientific, technical or other specialized knowledge" if the testimony is based on sufficient facts or data, and results from "reliable principles and methods" reliably applied to the facts. 509 U.S. 579, 589.

even though no human eye has perceived what those images represent.[27] In this regard, a U.S. appellate court ruled that a Google Earth Satellite image of an arrest location and a computer generated "tack" showing the GPS coordinates of the arrest, are not barred by the hearsay rule. (Indeed, the court took judicial notice of the fact that the "tack" was computer-generated, verifying this with its own investigation utilizing Google Earth.)[28]

3.2   *International Proceedings*

3.2.1   Early Concerns

Fifteen and more years ago, some space law experts feared that early judicial decisions by the International Court of Justice (ICJ) involving evidence from space showed a problematic lack of awareness of the characteristics and potential value of such evidence, and indeed "entailed a rather gloomy outlook for the future of satellite imagery as evidence in court."[29] The reports of the Space Law Committee of the ILA are replete with such expressions of concern. In retrospect, however, these concerns seem to have been overdrawn; a leading critic of those early decisions has more recently observed that "the situation today seems clearer and possibly less dramatic than in earlier times."[30]

These early skeptical views reflected several concerns. First, some felt that, beginning in its *Burkina Faso/Mali* judgment in 1986 (discussed below), the ICJ assigned too little legal significance to the greater accuracy of representations of the Earth's surface available using space technology. Other concerns stemmed from the fact that digital data from satellites must be processed in order to be usable. This led to fears of an excessive role for technical experts in the presentation of such evidence to courts, coupled with fears that the underlying data might be improperly manipulated in ways that cannot subsequently be detected. These fears led to proposals to develop some type of

---

27   Dighe et al., *supra* note 20, at 83.

28   United States v. Lizarrage-Tirado, No. 13–10530 (9th Cir. 2015). The defendant did not question the authenticity of the Google Earth image introduced at trial. Had he done so, the Court indicated (in dicta) that 'faced with an authentication objection, the proponent of Google-Earth generated evidence would have to establish Google Earth's reliability and accuracy. This burden could be met, for example, with testimony from a Google Earth programmer or witness who frequently works with and relies on the program ... It could also be met through judicial notice of the program's reliability ..." *Id.* at 8.

29   Maureen Williams, *Evidence from Space and Its Validity in Legal Proceedings: Dispute Settlement in Light of the 2011 PCA Procedural Rules on Arbitration* (2011), in PROCEEDINGS, *supra* note 21, at 427, 429.

30   *Id.*

international instrument or standards aimed at assuring the integrity of data and of its processing and presentation in court.[31]

3.2.2   International Criminal Proceedings

However, such concerns have not impeded the use of evidence from space in international proceedings. It has played an increasing role in international criminal proceedings, albeit within the constraints imposed by the more rigorous requirements for proof of criminal guilt. Evidence from space has often served as a guide in identifying the location of terrestrial evidence, often including mass graves. Pioneering work was done in the ICTY, where nationally provided satellite imagery provided leads to identify graves or other physical evidence. ICTY investigators used satellite photography in conjunction with the testimony of survivors and the work of archaeologists, anthropologists, dog teams and other specialized teams and experts to search for evidence of mass executions and mass graves.[32] Thus, the ICTY examined satellite photographs in the *Krstić* case to determine that excavations had occurred around Srebrenica during September/October 1995. These photographs "provided evidence that there had been reburials at that time, to attempt to cover-up the massacres that occurred in the area."[33] Krstić, the first man to be prosecuted for genocide, was convicted in 2001 and sentenced to 46 years with the aid of this evidence from space.[34]

Such evidence has also been used in multiple investigations and prosecutions at the ICC. As a matter of standard procedure, the ICC's Office of the Prosecutor (OTP) "always looks into the applicability and usefulness of [Earth Observation] technologies in all cases being dealt with by the Office."[35] Such technologies "have been used ... to generate evidence or to help with the investigation of nearly all ongoing cases."[36] The OTP obtains relevant imagery both from non-commercial entities with which it has agreements in place, and from commercial providers.[37] OTP's staff includes an in-house specialist who

---

31   *Id.* passim.

32   International Criminal Tribunal for the Former Yugoslavia, *History,* at icty.org.

33   R. Cryer, *Means of Gathering Evidence and Arresting Suspects in Situations of States' Failure to Cooperate,* in OXFORD COMPANION TO INTERNATIONAL JUSTICE (Antonia Cassese, ed.) 201, 204 (2009) (footnotes omitted).

34   EVIDENCE FROM SPACE, *supra* note 16, at 197, § 6.2.3.

35   Macauley, *supra* note 15, at 226.

36   *Id.* at 235.

37   *Id.* at 228.

serves as a conduit between investigating and trial teams and the providers of imagery.[38]

Yet, the use of earth observation data in criminal proceedings, where proof of guilt requires higher standards of proof, poses particular challenges related to authentication, chain of custody and preservation of evidence. In this regard, the ICC has developed protocols to guide the collection, identification and storage and use of digital evidence.[39]

3.2.3   Other Courts and Tribunals
In contrast to such developments in national systems and in international criminal courts, the evidentiary practices of many other international courts and tribunals are not well tailored to assessing and making informed use of evidence from space. In this regard, practices regarding evidence in international adjudication are typically more flexible, and leave greater discretion to decision-makers, than evidence practices in national legal systems. The observations of a former ICJ President regarding the ICJ apply in many other settings as well:

> [T]he rigidity of evidentiary rules found in some municipal legal systems has not been transposed integrally to the international legal order. Quite the contrary, the rule of thumb for evidentiary matters before the [ICJ] is flexibility ... In principle, there are no highly formalized rules of procedure governing the submission and administration of evidence ... nor are there any restrictions about the rules of evidentiary materials that may be produced by parties[40]
>
> ... [T]he Court does not operate on the basis of any preliminary evidentiary filter to weed out inadmissible evidence at the outset; rather the Court possesses a wide margin of appreciation in ascribing weight to different evidentiary materials originating from varied sources.[41]

While beneficial in some ways, this lack of detailed standards and procedures for assessing evidence can lead to difficulty. International courts and tribunals have not always received high marks for their handling of complex technical

---

38   *Id.* at 229.
39   Mark Dillon & David Beresford, *Electronic Courts and the Challenges in Managing Evidence: A View from Inside the International Criminal Court*, 6 INT'L. J. COURT ADMIN. 1 (2014).
40   Peter Tomka & Vincent-Joël Proulx, *The Evidentiary Practice of the World Court*, NUS LAW WORKING PAPER SERIES NO. 2015/010 3 (2015) [Tomka & Proulx].
41   *Id.* at 3.

evidence. Judges Al-Khasawneh and Simma's joint dissenting opinion in the *Pulp Mills* case conveys the discomfort of some distinguished international jurists when confronted with masses of technical evidence on unfamiliar subjects.

> The Court on its own is not in a position adequately to assess and weigh complex scientific evidence of the type presented by the Parties. To refer to only a few instances pertinent for our case, a court of justice cannot assess, without the assistance of experts, claims as to whether two or three-dimensional modelling is the best or even appropriate practice in evaluating the hydrodynamics of a river, or what role an Acoustic Doppler Current Profiler can play in such an evaluation. Nor is the Court, indeed any court save a specialized one, well-placed, without expert assistance, to consider the effects of the breakdown of nonylphenolethoxylates, the binding of sediments to phosphorus, the possible chain of causation which can lead to an algal bloom, or the implications of various substances for the health of various organisms which exist in the River Uruguay.[42]

This view may be unduly pessimistic. Some thoughtful observers view other ICJ cases, such as the Court's 2014 Judgment in *Whaling in the Antarctic*,[43] as showing the ability to deal with complex scientific evidence. Thus, in the view of the Court's former President, *Whaling in the Antarctic*, "constitutes further and incontrovertible proof that the Court can deal with vast amounts of highly technical and scientific evidence in a cogent and methodical fashion...."[44] Nevertheless, it remains true that international courts and tribunals sometimes struggle when confronted with such evidence.

3.3   *A Look at the Cases: Some Unsteady Early Steps*

As a study of earth observation data in domestic legal systems observes, "the presentation of scientific or highly technical evidence in a court or tribunal may result in misunderstanding, conflict or distortion of the process."[45] Such difficulties may be reflected in the uncertain reception of satellite imagery in its early appearances before the ICJ. Indeed, these early cases prompted the ILA

---

42   Case Concerning Pulp Mills on the River Uruguay (Arg. v. Ur.), 2010 I.C.J. 14 (Apr. 20) (Joint Dissenting Opinion of Judges Al-Khasawneh and Simma ¶4).

43   Whaling in the Antarctic (Aus. v. Japan, N.Z. intervening), 2014 I.C.J. 226 (Mar. 31).

44   Tomka & Proulx, *supra* note 40, at 7.

45   EVIDENCE FROM SPACE, *supra* note 16, at 13.

Space Law Committee to warn that "the current situation was running counter to the use of satellite imagery in court, particularly in international boundary disputes where the precision of satellite imagery is essential."[46] "There is still ... a lack of awareness, knowledge and understanding in the legal sector as to what the technology can offer and what are its limitations."[47]

The following survey, while not complete, is indicative. The ICJ seems to have first encountered evidence from satellites in the mid-1980s, in *Frontier Dispute (Burkina Faso/ Republic of Mali*.[48] In this case, decided by a Chamber of five judges, both parties made multiple references to satellite evidence in their oral arguments.[49] Burkina Faso contended that the map evidence in the case convincingly established its *titre cartographique* to the disputed territory, arguing that a substantial body of maps from early colonial times and of more recent vintage confirmed its title. Mali urged that evidence derived from satellite technology showed the gradual shift in the location of a riverbed relevant to the delimitation.

The Court's 1986 judgment rejected the claim that maps, including those rendered more accurate by data from space, could have determinative legal significance:

> Whether in frontier delimitations or in international territorial conflicts, maps merely constitute information which varies in accuracy from case to case: of themselves and by virtue solely of their existence, they cannot constitute a territorial title, that is, a document endowed by international law with intrinsic legal force for the purpose of establishing legal rights.[50]

The Court acknowledged that technological progress, including information from satellites, could improve maps' accuracy, observing that their "technical reliability" has, "considerably increased, owing particularly to the progress achieved by aerial and satellite photography since the 1950s."[51] For the Court, however, these improvements did not give maps any greater legal authority. The ICJ has since reaffirmed that maps cannot of themselves establish territorial rights.[52]

---

46   ILA Space Law Committee, CONFERENCE REPORT—RIO DE JANEIRO 2008 4.

47   *Id.* at 7.

48   Frontier Dispute (Burkina Faso/Rep. of Mali), 1986 I.C.J. 554 (22 Dec.).

49   *Id.* Oral Arguments on the Merits, 16–16 June and December 22, 1986, *passim*.

50   Burkina Faso/Mali, *supra* note 48, at 582, para. 54.

51   *Id.* at 582, para. 55.

52   Case Concerning Kaskili/Sedudu Island (Botswana/Namibia), 1999 I.C.J. 1045, 1098, para. 84 (Dec. 13).

Evidence from space had another seemingly troubled trial run in the preliminary objections stage of *Cameroon/Nigeria*.[53] Nigeria presented a satellite
photograph said to show the location of the village of Tipsan in Nigeria.[54]
Cameroon's counsel disputed Nigeria's interpretation of the image, contending
that it instead showed Tipsan to be in Cameroon.[55] As a result, Nigeria apparently was hoist with its own petard: "this disagreement was a sufficient basis
for the Court to reject Nigeria's preliminary objection, as the Court acknowledged that there was a dispute between the Parties concerning the course of
this segment of the land frontier and sovereignty over Tipsan."[56]

Satellite imagery again figured unevenly in *Kasikili/Sedudu Island* (Botswana/
Namibia),[57] where both parties included satellite images and accompanying
expert reports in their written materials.[58] Botswana argued that the imagery
showed that the northern channel of the Chobe River was its "main channel"
for purposes of establishing its ownership of the disputed island;[59] Namibia
disputed Botswana's analysis of the imagery.[60] While Judge Higgins said that
her decision was influenced by the imagery, Judge Parra Aranguren maintained in dissent that aerial photographs and satellite images were irrelevant,
inter alia, because they were taken after 1914, which he saw as the critical date.[61]

In *Oil Platforms*, the Court again was not impressed by satellite images.
These images, introduced by the United States, were said to show launch sites
of Iranian Scud missiles. The Court was unconvinced.

> The United States contends that the missile was fired from Iranian-held
> territory in the Fao area, and it has offered satellite pictures and expert
> evidence to show that there was, at the time, Iranian missile-firing equip-
> ment present there. Even with the assistance of the expert reports offered
> by both Parties, the Court does not however find the satellite images suf-
> ficiently clear to establish this point.[62]

---

53   Land and Maritime Boundary between Cameroon and Nigeria (Cam. v. Nig.: Eq. Guinea
       intervening), 2002 I.C.J. 303 (Oct. 10).
54   *Id.*, Preliminary Objections, Pleadings, CR 1998/1 30, CR 1998/5 42.
55   *Id.*, CR 1998/6 38.
56   Riddell & Plant, *supra* note 9, at 293.
57   Case Concerning Kaskili/Sedudu Island, *supra* note 52.
58   *Id.* at 1063, para. 29.
59   *Id.* at 1063, para. 29; 1066, para. 33; and 1067, para. 36.
60   *Id.* at 1067, para. 36; Riddell & Plant, *supra* note 9, at 295.
61   Case Concerning Kaskili/Sedudu Island, *supra* note 52 (dissenting opinion of Judge Parra-
       Aranguren) at 1129, para. 78.
62   Oil Platforms, *supra* note 13, at para. 58.

In *Qatar v. Bahrain*,[63] both parties utilized such evidence, again to uncertain effect. One issue concerned whether a natural channel had separated Fasht al Azm from Sitrah Island prior to being filled by construction work.[64] Both parties cited Landsat images taken on different dates in support of their rival contentions.[65] The Court, however, was not persuaded:

> 189. ... Both Parties have submitted reports of experts which come to divergent conclusions as to the existence of such a permanently navigable channel.

> 190. After careful analysis of the various reports, documents and charts submitted by the Parties, the Court has been unable to determine whether a permanent passage ... existed....[66]

The parties also disagreed whether Qit'at Jaradah was a low tide elevation (as Qatar contended) or an island (as claimed by Bahrain). Qatar submitted a satellite image in support of its contention; Bahrain's agent challenged the method by which this image was created, contending that Qatar's expert constructed it using incorrect data.[67] The Court ruled that the feature was an island belonging to Bahrain, but its judgment did not refer to the dispute regarding the satellite image.[68]

3.4   *Growing Confidence in Evidence from Space*

Despite its sometime uncertain beginnings, satellite imagery now appears frequently in international boundary cases, both in the ICJ and in other tribunals, although its impact on outcomes is not always clear. Both parties referred to satellite images to address questions of coast accretion and identification of coast base points in *Territorial and Maritime Dispute* between Nicaragua and Honduras.[69] Honduras used satellite imagery "to show that islands in the river

---

63   Maritime Delimitation and Territorial Questions between Qatar and Bahrain (Qatar v. Bahrain), 2001 I.C.J. 40 (Mar. 16).

64   *Id.* at 98, para. 189.

65   Annette Froehlich, *The Impact of Satellite Data Used by High International Courts Like the ICJ (International Court of Justice) and ITLOS (International Tribunal for the law of the Sea,* in PROCEEDINGS, *supra* note 21, at 471, 476.

66   *Qatar v. Bahrain, supra* note 63, at 98, paras. 189–190.

67   Riddell & Plant, *supra* note 9, at 292.

68   *Qatar v. Bahrain, supra* note 63, at 99, paras. 195–197.

69   Case Concerning Territorial and Maritime Dispute Between Nicaragua and Honduras in the Caribbean Sea (Nica. v. Hond.) 2007 I.C.J. 659 (Oct. 8); *Id.* Pleadings CR 2007/1, paras. 18 & 55; CR 2007/2, para.7; CR 2007/8, paras. 52–59.

mouth of the Rio Coco are formed due to sediment, which assisted in establishing the equidistance line to set the territorial sea of the two countries."[70] In an interesting procedural wrinkle, the Court allowed Nicaragua to introduce a satellite image into the record on the eve of the hearing on the ground that it was "part of a publication readily available" and so could be referred to in the oral proceedings under the Court's rules.[71]

Other ICJ cases involving satellite evidence include, inter alia:

- *Georgia v. Russia* (Preliminary objections):[72] Georgia cited satellite imagery said to show the destruction of certain ethnic villages.[73]
- *Argentina v. Uruguay*: As described by the Court, "Argentina claims that the algal bloom of 4 February 2009 was caused by the Orion (Botnia) mill's emissions of nutrients into the river. To substantiate this claim Argentina points to the presence of effluent products in the blue-green algal bloom and to various satellite images showing the concentration of chlorophyll in the water."[74]
- *Romania v. Ukraine*: Romania referred to several satellite images illustrating features discussed in its oral arguments.[75]

Satellite imagery has not always illuminated the way forward. In *Certain Activities Carried Out by Nicaragua in the Border Area*,[76] Nicaragua introduced a satellite picture from 1961 said to prove the existence of a caño or channel. Costa Rica disputed the clarity of the image, and produced its own image from 2010, said to disprove the existence of the channel. The Court did not find the dueling imagery helpful:

> The Court considers that, given the general lack of clarity of satellite and aerial images and the fact that the channels that may be identified ... do not correspond to the location of the caño dredged in 2010, this evidence is insufficient....[77]

---

70   R. Ridderhof, *Satellite Data in International Law*, peacepalacelibrary.nl.

71   *Nicaragua v. Honduras, supra* note 69, at 665, para. 12.

72   Application of the International Convention on the Elimination of All Forms of Racial Discrimination (Georgia v. Russ. Fed.), 2011 I.C.J. 70 (Apr. 1) (Preliminary Objections).

73   *Id.*, CR 2008/22 at 48, para. 34 (Sept. 8, 2008).

74   Pulp Mills, *supra* note 42, at para. 248 (Apr. 20).

75   Maritime Delimitation in the Black Sea (Rom. v. Uk.), CR 2008/18 at 51, paras. 9–10; CR 2008/19 at p. 53.

76   Certain Activities Carried Out By Nicaragua in the Border Area (Nica. v. Costa Rica), 2015 I.C.J. 665 Judgment (Dec. 16).

77   *Id.* at 701, para. 81. On other issues, the Court found satellite evidence more instructive. *Id.* at 734, para. 206.

Satellite imagery has also figured in the jurisprudence of the International Tribunal for the Law of the Sea. In the 2012 *Bangladesh/Myanmar* case,[78] Bangladesh presented satellite evidence regarding the characteristics of Martin's Island and other maritime features.[79] Evidence from space played an important role in the recent *South China Sea* arbitration, discussed at the end of this Chapter.

Evidence from space is also appearing in proceedings in international human rights courts. In an interesting 2015 European Court of Human Rights case, the Court called for production of satellite imagery relevant to a key issue. In *Sargsyan v. Azerbaijan*[80] the location of the alleged offense, which occurred in a disputed area, was at issue. To resolve the matter:

> [T]he Court requested high-resolution images to ascertain whether there had been a violation or not and, in particular, whether there had been military activity and an indiscriminate destruction of buildings in the relevant area, in the period contested. The images were crucial in ascertaining the situation in the area and in verifying which kind of activity the government of Azerbaijan had been carrying out and if there was a violation of not.[81]

Interestingly, the Court appealed to an outside entity both to provide the images and to assist in their interpretation: "the interpretation was carried out by the American Association for the Advancement of Science—AAAS, from whom the Court had also requested the images."[82] There are also references in the literature[83] to the use of earth observation data evidence in the arbitration between Eritrea and Yemen in the 1990s regarding their respective claims in the Red Sea.[84] However, the awards in the case do not refer to such evidence, and the written and oral proceedings in the case are not available on the PCA website.

---

78   Delimitation of the Maritimes Boundary in the Bay of Bengal (Bangladesh/Myanmar), Judgment, Judgment, 2012 ITLOS REP. 4, 168 (14 Mar.).

79   See, e.g., Bangladesh Counter-Memorial, at 91, 92 (paras. 3.122, 3.124).

80   European Court of Human Rights, Grand Chamber, *Sargsyan v. Azerbaijan*, Application No. 40167/06 (June 16, 2015) (Judgment).

81   Candelmo & Nardone, *supra* note 10, at 87, 102 (2017) (footnote omitted).

82   *Id.*

83   Maureen Williams, *Satellite Evidence in International Institutions*, in Purdy & Leung, *supra* note 8, at 203–204.

84   Eritrea / Yemen—Sovereignty and Maritime Delimitation in the Red Sea, awards of Oct. 9, 1998 and Dec. 17, 1999, *at* www.pca-cpa.org.

4   Making Effective Use of Evidence from Space

4.1   *Are Measures Needed to Assure the Reliability of Evidence from Space?*

Over the years, experts in the ILA's Space Law Committee have urged the development of international standards to validate earth observation data and its interpretation. Proponents of this view contend that the processing and interpretation involved in producing the images placed before courts and tribunals are vulnerable to forgery or misrepresentation. Thus, in their view, it is "imperative to supervise the process of obtaining the image from the moment it is collected as primary data right up to the time it is used in court."[85] Such internationally agreed standards, proponents believe, "would help support the value of satellite imagery when resorted to for different purposes."[86] Indeed, in some supporters' view, there exists a "crisis of confidence" regarding the use of evidence derived from satellites.[87]

Despite such concerns in the ILA's Space Law Committee and elsewhere, it is not clear that there is such a "crisis of confidence," or that there is appreciable support for proposals for international regulation, at least of a mandatory character. Indeed, as described above, national and international courts and tribunals seem to be gaining familiarity with, and confidence in, the use of earth observation data evidence, utilizing existing evidence standards and procedures to assess the reliability of the evidence. Thus, in the United States, for example, "[t]he use of satellite imagery and other remote sensing evidence in all levels of the federal and state court systems in the United States is a rapidly developing area of practice. It has accelerated exponentially...."[88]

That said, there may be room for development of additional voluntary industry standards, either nationally or in international contexts such as the International Organization for Standardization (ISO), regarding such matters as the storage of data derived from space, the recording or certification of associated metadata,[89] or similar matters. These could be akin to existing ISO and

---

85   Williams, in Purdy & Leung, *supra* note 8, at 195, 201–202.
86   *Id.* at 202.
87   *Id.* at 215.
88   Meredith Wright, *The Use of Remote Sensing Evidence at Trial in the United States—One State Court Judge's Observations*, in Purdy & Leung, *supra* note 8, at 313. Judge Wright collects a number of U.S. cases involving use of satellite images.
89   Willibald Croi, Fréderic-Michael Foeteler & Harold Linke, *Introducing Digital Signatures & Time-Stamps in the EO Data Processing Chain*, in Purdy & Leung, *supra* note 8, at 379.

national standards for electronic storage of business and other information.[90] This already seems to be happening with some data from space:

> In the US a certification process has been established to provide confidence to those ordering archived [earth observation] data. Digital data is assigned with unique numbers, which can then be used to verify the validity and authenticity of the 'original image' and be admissible in court for evidentiary purposes. The archives can then certify that the data delivered out of the archive to satisfy an order are the same as the data that was put into the archive originally.[91]

4.2   *Building on Existing Standards and Procedures*

In the absence of international standards addressing the storage and processing of evidence from space, international courts and tribunals can draw upon and refine a body of existing standards and procedures to aid in assessing such evidence.

4.2.1   Guidance from the ICJ

The ICJ has articulated some potentially relevant standards. In *Armed Activities*,[92] the Court identified several considerations to be weighed in assessing evidence, notably that the Court "will treat with caution evidentiary materials specially prepared for this case and also materials emanating from a single source."[93] In *Bosnian Genocide*,[94] the ICJ referred with approval to the standards articulated in *Armed Activities*, observing along similar lines that the probative value of reports submitted by official bodies depends on factors such as the origin of the evidence (that is, whether it is from a partisan or neutral source), the process by which it was generated, and the character of the evidence.[95] These judicial observations may be a caution to litigating states intending to utilize their national assets to acquire and process earth observation data.

---

90   Alan Shipman, *Authentication of Images*, in Purdy & Leung, *supra* note 8, at 359, 364–69.

91   Ray Purdy, *Pulling the Threads Together and Moving Forward*, in Purdy & Leung, supra note 8, at 399, 411–412.

92   Armed Activities on the Territory of the Congo (D.R. of Congo v. Uganda), 2005 I.C.J. 168 (Dec. 19).

93   *Id.* at 201, para. 61.

94   Application of the Convention on the Prevention and Punishment of the Crime of Genocide (Bos. & Herz. v. Serb. & Mont.) 2007 I.C.J. 43, 131, para. 213 (26 Feb. 2007).

95   *Id.* at 135, para. 227.

Another potential peril of state parties' reliance on their own satellite imagery was noted above in connection with the *Oil Platforms* case. Particularly as some states' satellite imagery has reportedly acquired resolution of just a few centimeters, states may be reluctant to use the best available imagery in litigation, or may elect to degrade existing imagery, for fear of compromising their intelligence gathering capabilities. While the author knows of no state party in the ICJ using imagery from its own satellites in a manner comparable to the U.S. experience in *Oil Platforms*, that case stands as a caution to states concerned about using evidence that may disclose classified capabilities.[96]

The ICJ has also taken a modest step to counter any temptation for parties to incorporate earth observation data images not previously of record in a case into their oral presentations.[97] A Practice Direction adopted in April 2013 is aimed at improving the process for identifying and regulating admission and use of visual exhibits, such as images derived from space data.[98] It requires:

> [A]ny party wishing to present audio-visual or photographic material at the hearings which was not previously included in the case file of the written proceedings shall submit a request to that effect sufficiently in advance of the date on which that party wishes to present that material to permit the Court to take its decision after having obtained the views of the other party.[99]

Nevertheless, international judges or arbitrators faced with earth observation data evidence may still face unfamiliar challenges in assessing that evidence. In the first instance: what is it? Is it an image derived from radar returns or a photographic image derived from reflected light? What is the source of the underlying data? What processes have been used to transform it into the image now before the tribunal? What assurances can the tribunal have that the visual image is a trustworthy and informative portrayal of what it is said to represent? And, ultimately, what does it mean?

---

96   The PCA's Optional Outer Space Rules include Article 17(8), authorizing appointment of a "confidentiality adviser" to review and report to a tribunal regarding an issue on the basis of confidential information that is not shared with the tribunal or the other party. *See* Pocar, *supra* note 11, at 183. It is not clear whether governments will be willing to rely on this procedure to protect sensitive intelligence gathering methods.

97   *See, e.g.*, Territorial and Maritime Dispute (Nic. v. Col.), 2012 I.C.J. 624, 632 (para. 13) (Nov. 19) (production of documents in judges' folders not previously of record not allowed).

98   ICJ Press Release, "The Court adopts Practice Direction IX*quater* for Use by States," April 11, 2013.

99   ICJ Practice Direction IX*quater*. at icj-cij.org.

With Professor Brilmayer's team's use of photographic imagery in the Eritrea-Ethiopia proceedings more than a decade ago, the relatively low-resolution imagery involved was still sufficient to show the location of military vehicles, trench lines, and the effects of hostilities on towns and major buildings. Opposing counsel did not dispute the images' authenticity, and the Commission did not face disagreements in this regard. Placed in the context of other evidence available to the Tribunal, these images made useful contributions to the Tribunal's appreciations of some situations. Nevertheless, Tribunal members were sometimes left to wonder or speculate about the import of particular images.

4.2.2   Expert Decision Makers

One potential solution to such challenges is to seek decision-makers with relevant technical expertise. The Permanent Court of Arbitration included an option in this regard in its 2011 Optional Rules for Arbitration of Disputes Relating to Outer Space Activities.[100] These rules seek in varying ways to "tackle the potential technical and scientific complexity of disputes relating to outer space."[101] Inter alia, they empower parties to choose technically astute decision-makers, and "to enhance this advantage, Article 10(4) of the Outer Space Rules assists parties in their choice of arbitrators by mandating the Secretary-General of the PCA to compile a standing list of arbitrators with an expertise in space-related matters."[102]

A significant recent case involving difficult and disputed technical questions illustrates the potential value of technically sophisticated decision-makers. The arbitration between India and Pakistan addressing Pakistan's claims under the Indus River Treaty[103] posed challenging technical questions regarding the design and operation of dams and associated works in the Indus River Basin. In designing the treaty's dispute settlement procedures, the parties took the usual step of requiring that any future arbitral panel should include an engineering expert. The Secretary-General of the Permanent Court of Arbitration applauded the result:

> The Indus Waters Treaty's requirement that there be at least one engineer who was not only an expert but also a full voting Member of the

---

100   Permanent Court of Arbitration, Optional Rules of Arbitration of Disputes Relating to Outer Space Activities (Dec. 6, 2011), pca.cpa.org.

101   Pocar, *supra* note 11, at 171, 182 (2012).

102   *Id.*

103   Indus Waters Arbitration (Pak. v. Ind.), Partial Award (Feb. 18, 2013), Final Award (May 20, 2013), pca-cpa.org.

Court of Arbitration is another feature rarely seen in arbitration clauses and agreements governing inter-State cases. Having an expert hydrologist raise questions to the Parties as well as participate fully in the deliberations doubtlessly aided in the resolution of the complex technical matters presented in this case.[104]

Thus,

While an outside observer cannot know, it seems very likely that the presence on the panel of a distinguished engineer and hydrologist significantly enhanced both its ability to assess such technical issues and the clarity and persuasiveness of the awards' treatments of them.[105]

4.2.3   Making Effective Use of Party-Appointed Experts

The ICJ in *Pulp Mills* made clear its unhappiness with an occurrence in that case: experts appearing as counsel in effect offered testimony on highly technical matters, testimony that was not subject to cross-examination or questioning by the Court.[106] Judges Simma and Al-Khasawneh underscored this concern in their joint dissenting opinion.[107] Such blurring of roles has indeed occurred in some past cases involving earth observation data; counsel have sometimes made unchallenged assertions regarding the factual import of satellite images. Courts and tribunals must be mindful of possible risks in this regard, even if opposing counsel do not contest such arguments.

In international litigation settings, parties wishing to rely upon scientific or technical evidence usually introduce the evidence by means of experts' reports and testimony. The opposing party may then introduce its own experts' reports and testimony in rebuttal. Both are then subject to examination at the hearing. Thus, international investment disputes are often marked by dueling expert reports and testimony on complex issues, particularly where large economic interests are involved. These encounters between experts can veer off into debates regarding refined points of finance theory, debates that may not assist decision-makers very much.

To date, such debates regarding interpretation of evidence from space have not been frequent. There was such a disagreement in *Nigeria v. Cameroon*,

---

104   Hugo Siblesz, *Foreword, in* THE INDUS WATERS KISHENGANGA ARBITRATION (PAKISTAN V. INDIA), RECORD OF PROCEEDINGS (2010–2013) xii (2014).
105   John R. Crook, *Introduction*, in *id.* at 16–17.
106   Pulp Mills, *supra* note 43, at para. 167.
107   Joint Dissenting Opinion, in Pulp Mills *supra* note 42, at para. 68.

Bahrain and Qatar debated the correctness of images of Qit'at Jaradah, and Iran and the United States disagreed regarding interpretation of the U.S. images in *Oil Platforms*.[108] As evidence from space becomes more common in international litigation, such debates between party-appointed experts also may become more frequent.

However, techniques have been developed in investment arbitration that aim to render dueling experts' contributions more helpful to tribunals. Experts are sometimes asked to meet prior to a hearing to define and then prepare a joint report on their areas of agreement and disagreement.[109] Some tribunals have taken a further step of "witness conferencing," in which expert witnesses instructed by the two parties appear before the tribunal as a panel, and in effect carry on a directed discussion of issues in response to the tribunal's questions. Advocates contend that such practices can significantly aid in clarifying and narrowing the technical issues concerned.[110]

4.2.4   Refer Disputed Matters to the Parties

If the parties to a disagreement involving assessment of evidence from space nevertheless have a positive relationship that allows them to cooperate, a tribunal might consider referring a disputed issue back to them for joint assessment. In the *Iron Rhine* arbitration,[111] the Tribunal recommended that the parties establish a committee of independent experts following the award to determine several facts, including the costs of reactivating the Iron Rhine Railway, the costs of alternative autonomous development by the Netherlands, and the quantifiable benefits that could accrue to the Netherlands by reason of the reactivation.[112]

4.2.5   Court- or Tribunal-Appointed Experts

Perhaps the most important option, urged by Judges Simma and Al-Khasawneh in their joint dissenting opinion in *Pulp Mills*, is for courts and tribunals to make more substantial and effective use of their authority to appoint their own experts. While this sometimes may be beneficial to decision-makers, such

---

108   Riddell & Plant, *supra* note 9, at 294.
109   MARGARET MOSES, THE PRINCIPLES AND PRACTICE OF INTERNATIONAL COMMERCIAL ARBITRATION 198 (3rd ed. 2017).
110   Hilmar Raeschke-Kessler, *Witness Conferencing*, in THE LEADING ARBITRATORS' GUIDE TO INTERNATIONAL ARBITRATION 415 (Lawrence W. Newman & Richard D. Hill, eds.) (2d ed. 2008); Dana H. Freyer, *Assessing Expert Evidence*, in *id.* at 429, 439–440.
111   Arbitration Regarding the Iron Rhine Railway (Belgium v. Netherlands), Award, 24 May 2005, pca-cpa.org.
112   *Id.* at para. 235.

assistance may also come at a cost. Court- or tribunal-appointed experts can add significant delays and financial costs to a proceeding. Moreover, parties' counsel may resist such appointments, as they fear a reduction of their control over the proceedings.

The procedural rules of international courts and tribunals regularly offer the option of court- or tribunal-appointed experts to assist decision-makers. For example, Article 29 of the UNCITRAL Arbitration Rules (2010), which are widely used in different dispute settlement settings, establishes a detailed regime in this regard. Under Article 29(1):

> After consultation with the parties, the arbitral tribunal may appoint one or more independent experts to report to it, in writing, on specific issues to be determined by the arbitral tribunal. A copy of the expert's terms of reference, established by the arbitral tribunal, shall be communicated to the parties.

Tribunal-appointed experts have been rare in investment arbitration, perhaps reflecting their associated costs and delays, as well as the possible reluctance of parties' counsel to yield control over important issues. (One notable exception occurred in the Iran-United States Claims Tribunal, when a chamber of the tribunal appointed an independent expert to assess the value of the allegedly expropriated property at issue.)[113]

Tribunals' power to utilize experts is much more developed in the World Trade Organization (WTO), where Article 13 of the WTO Dispute Settlement Understanding "grants panels the authority to appoint individual experts or set up expert review groups."[114] Indeed, in cases under the WTO Agreement on Sanitary and Phytosanitary Measures, Article 11.2 of that agreement directs that "a panel should seek advice from experts."[115] It provides:

> In a dispute under this Agreement involving scientific or technical issues, a panel should seek advice from experts chosen by the panel in consultation with the parties to the dispute. To this end, the panel may, when it deems it appropriate, establish an advisory technical experts group, or

---

113   Starrett Housing Corp. v. Iran, Award No. 314–14–1, 16 Iran-U.S. C.T.R. 112 (Aug. 14, 1987).
114   Michelle Grando, EVIDENCE, PROOF AND FACT-FINDING IN WTO DISPUTE SETTLEMENT 55 (2009).
115   *Id.*

consult the relevant international organizations, at the request of either party to the dispute or on its own initiative.[116]

Article 50 of the ICJ Statute, while less detailed, empowers the Court at any time to, "entrust any individual, body, bureau, commission or other organization that it may select, with the task of carrying out an enquiry or giving an expert opinion."[117] The ICJ used this power to good effect in *Corfu Channel*, its first contested case, where it appointed a group of experienced naval officers to advise it on naval matters, and another expert to provide advice on ship repair costs.[118] Since that time however, "the Court has not made much use of this arguably important tool for elucidating facts, and indeed, members of the Court themselves have ... occasionally criticized the collegiate failure to order an expert opinion or enquiry."[119] Instead of transparent expert proceedings notified to the parties and subject to their comments, the Court seems occasionally to have consulted experts on cartography and perhaps other matters in camera.[120]

However, change may be in the air. In June 2016, the Court resuscitated Article 50, appointing experts to address four questions bearing on the location of the starting-point of a maritime boundary disputed between Costa Rica and Nicaragua.[121] The experts conducted two intensive site visits that included physical investigations conducted with the support of personnel from both parties and Registry staff. The experts' detailed report frequently utilizes satellite images as evidence and as the basis for maps illustrating their analysis.[122] Hearings in the case concluded in July 2017. At the time of writing, it is not known what role the report may play in the Court's eventual decision.

In another significant recent example, the tribunal constituted to hear the Philippines' claims regarding China's actions in the South China Sea relied extensively upon the reports of its appointed experts, including on matters

---

116   WTO Agreement on the Application of Sanitary and Phytosanitary Measures (SPS Agreement), Art. 11.2.

117   Statute of the International Court of Justice, Art. 50.

118   Corfu Channel case (U.K. v. Alb.), 1947–48 I.C.J. 124 (Order Dec. 17 1948); *Id.* (Order of 19 November 1949) (Assessment of the amount of compensation due from the People's Republic of Albania: Appointment of Expert).

119   Riddell & Plant, *supra* note 9, at 333.

120   *Id.* at 336–337.

121   Maritime Delimitation in the Caribbean Sea and the Pacific Ocean (Costa Rica v. Nicaragua), Order (June 16, 2016).

122   Maritime Delimitation in the Caribbean Sea and the Pacific Ocean (Costa Rica v. Nicaragua), Report of the Court-Appointed Experts (April 30, 2017).

involving evidence derived from space. The tribunal's July 2016 concluding press release describes its approach:

> China has repeatedly stated that "it will neither accept nor participate in the arbitration unilaterally initiated by the Philippines." Annex VII [of the UN Convention on the Law of the Sea] however, provides that the "[a]bsence of a party or failure of a party to defend its case shall not constitute a bar to the proceedings." Annex VII also provides that, in the event that a party does not participate in the proceedings, a tribunal "must satisfy itself not only that it has jurisdiction over the dispute but also that the claim is well founded in fact and law." Accordingly, throughout these proceedings, the Tribunal has taken steps to test the accuracy of the Philippines' claims, including ... by appointing independent experts to report to the Tribunal on technical matters....[123]

Thus, for example, the tribunal appointed a team of experts in coral reef ecology to assess the impact of China's activities.

> [I]n light of China's non-participation, the Tribunal decided to appoint coral reef ecology experts to provide their independent opinion on the impact of Chinese construction activities on the coral reef systems in the Spratly Islands. A team composed of Dr. Sebastian Ferse, Professor Peter Mumby, and Dr. Selina Ward prepared a report (the "Ferse Report"), on which both sides were invited to comment.[124]

The tribunal's 501-page award frequently cites the Ferse Report in support of factual assessments, referencing its conclusions regarding such matters as Chinese fishermen's damage to coral reefs,[125] the impact of coral harvesting,[126] harvesting of giant clams,[127] destructive fishing methods,[128] and the environmental harm caused by construction activities.[129]

---

123   Press Release, *The South China Sea Arbitration* (*The Republic of the Philippines v. The People's Republic of China*), July 12, 2016, at www.pca-cpa.org.
124   South China Sea Arbitration (Phils. v. China), PCA No. 2013–19, Award (July 12, 2016) paras. 136 & 821 [South China Sea Award].
125   *Id.* at para. 848.
126   *Id.* at para. 955.
127   *Id.* at para. 957.
128   *Id.* at para. 970.
129   *Id.* at para. 977.

The Tribunal also appointed an expert to assess technical evidence (discussed below) as well as an expert on questions of navigational safety.[130]

4.2.6   Tribunal Experts as Assessors of Parties' Technical Evidence
The role of court- or tribunal-appointed experts can be adapted as required to meet the needs of particular cases. Thus, court-appointed experts have sometimes served as checks on technical evidence adduced by the parties. The ICTY thus utilized its own expert to assess and confirm the reliability of some unusual prosecution evidence:

> [S]ome of the individuals called before the Tribunal to identify voices or corroborate intelligence may have been working as covert assets within Serbia, and thus could not testify without exposing themselves and their methods. In December 2003 the Tribunal preliminarily accepted into evidence en masse 245 intercepts, based on testimony of a single witness known as B-1793 who testified in closed session as to their authenticity; these were later fully admitted into evidence after the court hired its own expert to spot-check fifteen of them for accuracy and tampering.[131]

For its part, the *South China Sea* tribunal appointed an independent expert to assess and advise it regarding technical evidence, including the reliability and weight of such evidence presented by the Philippines. As the tribunal's award explains:

> [I]n accordance with Article 24 of the Rules of Procedure, and after seeking the views of the Parties, the Tribunal retained an independent technical expert—Mr. Grant Boyes—to assist it in "reviewing and analysing geographic and hydrographic information, photographs, satellite imagery and other technical data in order to enable the Arbitral Tribunal to assess the status (as a submerged feature, low-tide elevation, or island)" of the features named in the Philippines' Submissions or any other such feature determined to be relevant during the course of the reference. While the appointment of hydrographic experts is common practice in Annex VII arbitrations, in light of China's non-participation, Mr. Boyes was also tasked with assisting with a "critical assessment of relevant expert advice and opinions submitted by the Philippines."[132]

---

130   *Id.* at para. 138.
131   Moranchek, *supra* note 14, at 494.
132   South China Sea Award, para. 133 (footnotes omitted).

5   A Significant Recent Experience and Some Concluding Thoughts

The handling of evidence from space in the recent *South China Sea* case offers a fitting conclusion for this Chapter. The tribunal's award offers excellent illustrations of some of the techniques and procedures sketched above in making effective use of evidence from space.

5.1   *The South China Sea Arbitration*

The PCA's website describes the case's background in characteristically careful prose:

> On 22 January 2013, the Republic of the Philippines instituted arbitral proceedings against the People's Republic of China under Annex VII to the United Nations Convention on the Law of the Sea (the "Convention"). The arbitration concerned the role of historic rights and the source of maritime entitlements in the South China Sea, the status of certain maritime features in the South China Sea, and the lawfulness of certain actions by China in the South China Sea that the Philippines alleged to be in violation of the Convention. China adopted a position of non-acceptance and non-participation in the proceedings. The Permanent Court of Arbitration served as Registry in this arbitration.[133]

The tribunal made extensive use of satellite evidence adduced by the Philippines in order to see and assess the great physical changes to reefs and atolls resulting from China's extensive construction there. The award includes multiple satellite images illustrating the extent of these activities.

While the tribunal thus made heavy use of evidence from space, it was also sensitive to its limitations. In terms indicating a sophisticated and technically astute panel, the tribunal offered thoughtful—and sometimes critical—assessments of the satellite evidence it received.[134] For example, it questioned the utility of some imagery in identifying the characteristics of small maritime features:

> [T]he Tribunal considers that satellite imagery may be able to disprove the existence of large sand cays or features where the area in question clearly covers with water across a series of images. Additionally, the more far-reaching conclusions advanced by the Philippines regarding the

---

133   The South China Sea Arbitration (Phil. v. China), at pca-cpa.org.
134   *Id.* at paras. 322–325.

(non-) existence of small sand cays or rocks could perhaps be established with very high-resolution stereoscopic imagery, taken at or near high tide, with in-person observations of tidal conditions taken at a nearby location. Absent such information, however, the Tribunal does not believe that the majority of the conclusions it has been asked to reach concerning the status of features as above or below water at high tide can be drawn on the basis of satellite evidence alone.[135]

Thus, the tribunal carried out what appears to be a technically informed and sometimes critical assessment of the satellite evidence in the record. The following excerpt from the award, while lengthy, nicely demonstrates the ability of an astute and well-advised tribunal to assess the probative power—and limitations—of evidence from space:

[T]he Philippines has placed heavy reliance on remote sensing through satellite imagery. The Tribunal agrees with the general point that satellite imagery may be a very useful tool, but cannot accept the degree of accuracy or certainty that the Philippines would give to such imagery. The Philippines has, for instance, relied upon a spectral analysis of imagery derived from the Landsat 4, 5, 7 and 8 satellites. According to the Philippines, such a comparison of images will establish whether any portion of a reef is above water at high tide, as the ability of different wavelengths of light to penetrate water differs ... Landsat 4 and 5, however, are satellites with a 30-metre ground resolution, meaning that each pixel of the image is equal to a square on the ground of 30 metres on each side. Landsat 7 and 8 include a panchromatic (black and white) band with a ground resolution of 15 metres, but otherwise have the same 30-metre ground resolution for the spectral bands as the earlier Landsat 4 and 5. In the course of the hearing, the Tribunal asked the Philippines' expert to clarify whether the imagery analysed included the use of the panchromatic band (sensitive to all wavelengths of visible light and thus black and white in appearance), which would represent a commonly used process known as pansharpening, in which a higher resolution panchromatic image is used to increase the resolution of a colour image. The Philippines' expert indicated that this had not been done. Whether or not this is the case, however, the maximum resolution that could possibly be derived from the satellite imagery used by the Philippines for this purpose is 15 metres. Small rocks or coral boulders on a reef platform may be

---

135   *Id.* at para. 326.

a metre or less across and still reach above water at high tide. The resolution of the satellite imagery being used here is insufficient to establish the presence or absence of such features.[136]

Thus, the tribunal clearly acknowledges the utility of satellite imagery. However, it also casts a technically informed eye on the satellite evidence presented by the Philippines to support its claims regarding certain small maritime features. Based on its assessment of the resolution of the imagery used, and of the techniques used to analyze that imagery, the tribunal finds that, in this instance at least, evidence from space is not sufficiently precise to sustain the claim.

5.2   *Concluding Thoughts*
As imagery from space improves and becomes more readily available at reasonable cost, it will likely play an increasing role in international cases where decision-makers need to understand places or events on the surface of the physical world. This process is well underway, supported by the adaptation or evolution of legal rules and procedures to meet new requirements.

In this process, as in many others, Lea Brilmayer has made her innovative and distinctive contribution.

---

136   *Id.* at para. 322 (footnotes omitted).

CHAPTER 15

The Eritrea-Ethiopia Claims Commission's Partial Awards on Eritrea's and Ethiopia's Diplomatic Claims

Robert G. Volterra *

1   Introduction

It is a great pleasure to contribute to this book in honour of Professor Lea Brilmayer. I knew Lea as a member of the legal teams that she led in the context of the various international law litigations in which Eritrea found itself embroiled following its independence from Ethiopia. Lea was passionate about the rule of law, passionate about helping the young lawyers working with her to learn and to grow professionally, and most of all passionate about helping the people of Eritrea. That passion, combined with seemingly limitless energy and a brilliant focus on facts and law, enabled her to accomplish prodigious feats of advocacy in furthering the interests of the people of Eritrea. Those accomplishments are part of her lasting legacy reflecting, in no small part, her significant contributions to the theory and practice of international law. Lea also has a wicked sense of humour, which helped keep us all sane.

Eritrea regained its independence from Ethiopia in May 1993, following the alliance between the Eritrean People's Liberation Front and the Tigray People's Liberation Front and the fall of the dictatorship of Mengistu Haile Mariam in 1991.[1] Before that, Eritrea had been incorporated into Ethiopia by 1952 UN General Assembly Resolution 390. Historically, Eritrea had been an independent territory, from 1890 an Italian colony and, from 1941 until the 1952 Resolution, a unit of territory under British administration. Despite the initially strong ties between the two leaders of the liberation fronts, who became leaders of their respective States following the fall of Mengistu, tensions soon arose between the two States about the question of sovereignty over the Badme region. These tensions eventually resulted in armed conflict that broke out in May 1998.

---

*   Professor, Faculty of Law, University College London; partner, Volterra Fietta.
1   This event marked Eritrea's *de facto* independence from Ethiopia.

© KONINKLIJKE BRILL NV, LEIDEN, 2019 | DOI:10.1163/9789004316539_016

The provincial town of Badme, in the Yirga Triangle, had been part of the Italian colony of Eritrea that existed between 1890 and 1941.[2] It was included in the British administration of Eritrea from 1941 to 1952. It then became, as Eritrean territory, a part of the federation created between Eritrea and Ethiopia by the 1952 Resolution 390 of the United Nations General Assembly. In 1962, the Government of Ethiopia unilaterally dissolved Resolution 390 and turned Eritrea from one of two component parts of a federation into an Ethiopian province. Badme was part of the province of Eritrea that was administered by Ethiopia until May 1998.[3]

The first armed hostilities started in May 1998, at the border between the two States.[4] The armed conflict escalated quickly. Badme became the focus of military activities between the States that eventually spread to other locations along their border. There were air strikes, armed incursions, human suffering and physical damage. Many thousands of civilians were killed and displaced.[5] Military casualties were significant.[6] The rupture between the two previously integrated States negatively affected many forms of personal, cultural, business and other relationships and activities on both sides of the border.

On 18 June 2000, an Agreement on Cessation of Hostilities was signed by Eritrea and Ethiopia.[7] It called for a Peacekeeping Mission to separate the two armed forces. On 12 December 2000, the States concluded an Agreement (the "Algiers Agreement")[8] for the permanent termination of military hostilities between them.[9] To facilitate this, the Algiers Agreement called for the creation of three bodies. The first was an independent body created under the Organisation of African Unity (the "OAU") to investigate the origins of the

---

2   As set out by the colonial treaties in 1897, 1900 and 1902 between Italy and the Ethiopian emperor Menelik II.

3   *See* 1998 U.N.Y.B. 52, Sales No. E.01.I.1, at 146–147. Lantera Anebo, *The Fallacy of Virtual Demarcation as a Primary Scheme of International Land Boundary Setting: Why the Eritrea/Ethiopia Boundary Conflict Remains Unresolvable*, 24 WILLAMETTE J. INT'L L. & DIS. RES. 257, 274 (2017).

4   *See* Christine Gray, *The Eritrea/Ethiopia Claims Commission Oversteps Its Boundaries: A Partial Award?*, 17 EJIL 699, 701 (2006).

5   *See* 1999 U.N.Y.B, 130–138; Jan Abbink, *Briefing: The Eritren-Ethiopian Border Dispute*, 97 Afr. Aff. 551, 552 (1998).

6   Bethany Lacina & Nils P. Gleditsch, *Monitoring Trends in Global Combat: A New Dataset of Battle Deaths*, 21 EUR. J. POPUL. 145, 155 (2005).

7   Agreement on Cessation of Hostilities between the Government of the Federal democratic Republic of Ethiopia and the Government of the State of Eritrea, June 18, 2000, 2138 U.N.T.S. 85.

8   Agreement between the Government of the State of Eritrea and the Government of the Federal Democratic Republic of Ethiopia, Eritrea v. Ethiopia, Dec. 12, 2000, 2138 U.N.T.S. 93, 40 I.L.M. 260 (2001).

9   Algiers Agreement, Art. 1(1).

conflict. It was never created and the investigation was never undertaken.[10] The second was the Eritrea-Ethiopia Boundary Commission (the "Boundary Commission"), which was in charge of demarcating the border between the two countries.[11] The Boundary Commission, presided over by Professor Sir Elihu Lauterpacht, issued its decision of 13 April 2002 holding that Badme was Eritrean territory.[12] Until June 2018, Ethiopia refused to accept that outcome. Then, finally, Ethiopia announced that it would accept the 2002 award of the Boundary Commission to delimit the two States' boundary.[13]

The third body that the Algiers Agreement called for was the Eritrea-Ethiopia Claims Commission (the "EECC").[14] The mandate of the EECC was to rule through binding arbitration on "all claims for loss, damage or injury [...] related to the conflict". It was to do so by applying the "relevant rules of international law."[15]

The EECC was composed of Professor Hans van Houtte (President), Judge George Aldrich (appointed by Ethiopia), John Crook (appointed by Eritrea), Dean James Paul (appointed by Ethiopia) and Lucy Reed (appointed by Eritrea). In total, the EECC issued thirteen partial awards, four final awards and eight decisions.[16] These dealt with, amongst other things, the consequences of the violation of the *jus ad bellum*,[17] the economic losses, unlawful killings,

---

10 An OAU mission of ambassadors from Burkina Faso, Zimbabwe, Rwanda and Djibouti attempted to investigate on the origins of the conflict but its peace plan was not implemented. Article 3 of the Algiers Agreement provides for the creation of an independent and impartial body "to determine the origins of the conflict, an investigation will be carried out on the incidents of 6 May 1998 and on any other incident prior to the date which could have contributed to a misunderstanding between the parties regarding their common border, including the incidents of July and August 1997."

11 Algiers Agreement, Art. 4 provides: "The parties agree that a neutral Boundary Commission composed of five members shall be established with a mandate to delimit and demarcate the colonial treaty border based on pertinent colonial treaties (1900, 1902 and 1908) and applicable international law."

12 *Decision on delimitation of the Border between Eritrea and Ethiopia (Eritrea v Ethiopia)*, 25 R.I.I.A. 83, ¶ 8.1 (EEC 2002 13).

13 See *Ethiopia 'accepts peace deal' to end Eritrea border war*, BBC, June 5, 2018, available at https://www.bbc.co.uk/news/world-africa-44376298; Aaron Maasho, *Ethiopia says will 'accept, implement 2000 deal with Eritrea*, Reuters, June 5, 2018, available at https://uk.reuters.com/article/uk-ethiopia-eritrea-agreement/ethiopia-says-will-fully-accept-implement-2000-deal-with-eritrea-idUKKCN1J12ID.

14 Algiers Agreement, Art. 5 (1).

15 Algiers Agreement Art. 5 (13). These rules are listed in Article 19(2) of the Commission's Rules of procedure, which reflects Article 38 of the Statute of the International Court of Justice.

16 While awards ruled on issues of fact or law, decisions reflected the policy stance of the EECC on questions of procedure or competence unrelated to specific claims.

17 *Jus Ad Bellum—Ethiopia's Claims 1–8 (Eritrea v Ethiopia)*, Partial award, 26 R.I.I.A. 457 (EECC 2005).

beating and abduction of civilians, looting, forced labour, failure to take effective measures to prevent the rape of women,[18] unlawful requisition of property,[19] destruction of private and public buildings and violations of diplomatic law.[20]

This chapter considers and examines the two partial awards issued by the EECC on the claims brought by each of Eritrea and Ethiopia for the violations of diplomatic immunities and privileges allegedly committed by the other State. A particular focus of the EECC's examination of this subject was related to allegations about the breach of diplomatic inviolability. These two partial awards are disappointingly Spartan in terms of their legal analysis. They are open to criticism on a number of other grounds, as well. Amongst others, the partial awards appear to have been based on a number of incorrect factual premises. The EECC also adopted an unorthodox interpretation of the international law of diplomatic immunities and privileges. In the result, and sadly for international law scholars and practitioners, the EECC's partial awards on Eritrea's and Ethiopia's diplomatic claims contribute in only a limited way to an understanding of this important area of international law.

This chapter first briefly examines the relevant rules of diplomatic law, in particular the regime governing diplomatic inviolability (Section 2). It then describes the partial awards issued by the EECC on Eritrea's and Ethiopia's diplomatic claims (Section 3). Finally, it analyses the reasoning of the EECC in the partial awards and their effect on the underlying border dispute between Eritrea and Ethiopia (Section 4).

2   The Legal Principles Governing Diplomatic Inviolability

Diplomatic inviolability is an absolute principle that States must respect and protect. These norms of international law will be examined briefly in turn.

2.1   *The Absolute Principle of Diplomatic Inviolability*
Although diplomatic inviolability is not expressly defined in an international instrument, its broad scope of application is justified by the necessity to ensure the good functioning of diplomatic relations between equal sovereign States.

---

18   *Western and Eastern Fronts—Ethiopia's Claims 1 & 3 (Eritrea v Ethiopia)*, Partial Award, 26 R.I.I.A 351 (EECC 2005).

19   *Loss of Property in Ethiopia Owned by Non-Residents—Eritrea's Claim 24 (Eritrea v Ethiopia)*, Partial Award, 26 R.I.I.A. 429 (EECC 2005).

20   *Western Front, Aerial Bombardment and Related Claims—Eritrea's Claims 1, 3, 5, 9–13, 14, 21, 25 & 26 (Eritrea v Ethiopia)*, Partial Award, 26 R.I. I. A 291, (EECC 2005).

2.1.1   An Unclear Notion Resulting in an Unqualified Duty of Protection
Among diplomatic immunities and privileges, the diplomatic mission enjoys
complete inviolability.[21] This is one of the clearest, oldest and most uncontroversial
norms of international law. The notion of diplomatic and consular inviolability
has been developed extensively in customary international law over the centuries.
It is codified today in the Vienna Convention on Diplomatic Relations (the "1961
Vienna Convention"),[22] the 1963 Vienna Convention on Consular Relations (the
"1963 Vienna Convention"),[23] the 1969 Convention on Special Missions[24] and
the 1973 Convention on the Prevention and Punishment of Crimes against
Internationally Protected Persons, including Diplomatic Agents.[25]

Significantly, the concept of inviolability is not defined in those instruments.
It has been described as the duty "to protect, by unusually severe penalties,
from all offence, injury, or violence on the part of the inhabitants of the
country"[26] or "the right to absolute and complete security, it is freedom without
restrictions."[27] Diplomatic inviolability is a concept that envisages a broad
scope of protection, *ratione personae, ratione materiae* and *ratione temporis.*

Diplomatic agents,[28] diplomatic staff,[29] heads of states[30] and ministers
for foreign affairs are all protected by diplomatic inviolability. Not only does
it concern their physical integrity but also the premises of their mission,[31]
their archives, documents[32] and their correspondence.[33] It applies during
the course of the usual conduct of a diplomatic mission. It is one of those
international law norms that also applies in full in situations of disagreement,

---

21   *See* EILEEN DENZA, DIPLOMATIC LAW—COMMENTARY ON THE VIENNA
        CONVENTION ON DIPLOMATIC RELATIONS, 110–148 (4th ed. 2015).
22   Vienna Convention on Diplomatic Relations, Apr. 18, 1961, 500 U.N.T.S. 95, 23 U.S.T. 3227.
        There are 191 States party to the 1961 Vienna Convention.
23   Vienna Convention on Consular Relations, Apr. 24, 1963, 596 U.N.T.S. 261, 21 U.S.T. 77.
24   Convention on Special Missions, Dec. 8, 1969, 1400 U.N.T.S, 231.
25   Convention on the Prevention and Punishment of Crimes against Internationally
        Protected Persons, including Diplomatic Agents, Dec.14, 1973, 1035 U.N.T.S., 167.
26   Regulations on Diplomatic Immunities adopted by the Institute of International Law at
        the Session of 13 August 1895, Resolutions of the Institute of International Law Dealing
        with the Law of the Nations 119, Art. 3 (James Brown Scott ed., 1916).
27   Pietri definition as quoted by Franciszek Przetacznik, *Notion of Personal Inviolability of
        Diplomatic Agents in the Doctrine of International Law,* 1968–1969 POLISH Y.B. INT'L L.
        156, 158.
28   *See* 1961 Vienna Convention Art. 29.
29   *See* 1961 Vienna Convention Art. 37.
30   *See* Certain Questions of Mutual Assistance in Criminal Matters (Djib. v. Fr.), Judgment,
        2008 I.C.J. Rep. 177, ¶ 174, (June 4).
31   *See* 1961 Vienna Convention Art. 22.
32   *See* 1961 Vienna Convention Art. 24.
33   *See* 1961 Vienna Convention Art. 27.

hostility and "even in case of armed conflict."[34] The language in the Vienna conventions is absolute and without exception. Thus, in the terms of the 1961 Vienna Convention, archives and documents shall be inviolable "at any time."[35]

The International Court of Justice (the "ICJ") has identified that the concept of diplomatic inviolability is a deeply rooted principle in all legal and cultural traditions.[36] In her commentary, Eileen Denza observed that diplomatic inviolability has been universally recognised as a "custom or religion invariably accorded a special protection"[37] to ambassadors. She noted:

> Among the City States of ancient Greece, the peoples of the Mediterranean before the establishment of the Roman Empire, among the States of India, the person of the herald in time of war and of the diplomatic envoy in time of peace were universally held sacrosanct.[38]

It is a necessary corollary to the concept of the formal establishment of diplomatic relations, which manifested itself in the sixteenth century in the earliest treaties on diplomatic law. As such, under international law, when the protection of diplomatic inviolability is at stake, it is recognised to take precedence over legal rights such as freedom of speech and assembly,[39] the enforcement of one's contractual or property rights[40] or service of process.[41]

---

34   1961 Vienna Convention Art. 45.

35   1961 Vienna Convention Art. 24.

36   United States Diplomatic and Consular Staff in Tehran (U. S. v. Iran), Judgment, 1980 I.C.J. Rep. 3, ¶ 86 (May 24). The ICJ held that the principle of inviolability has a "long-established regime, to the evolution of which the traditions of Islam made a substantial contribution." Islamic Siyar recognises diplomatic inviolability as did the Old Testament in Samuel 10:2–4.

37   Denza, *supra* note 21, at 213.

38   *Id* at 213.

39   Frend et al v. United States, 100 F.2d 691 (D.C. 1938); Minister for Foreign Affairs & Trade & others v. Magno, G. & others, [1992] 7 FCR 298 (Austl.).

40   Company Limited v. Republic of X (1999) 2 Lloyd's Rep 520 (U.K.); 87 ILR 412; Bundesverfassungsgericht [BVerfGE][Federal Constitution Court] December 13, 1977 46 BVerfGE 342 (Germany). The latter case concerned a judgment from a German court against the Republic of the Philippines for payment of its debts arising out of a rental contract between the creditor and the State. The contract concerned a house used as an office for the embassy in Germany. The seizure of the embassy's account was objected to by the Philippines.

41   App. Turin, Foà v. Boselli, 21 October 1921, 1 I.L.R. 305 (It.); Re Thomas v. Sargent, 2 I.L.R. 307 (Chile Sup Ct. 1923); Engelke v. Musmann, [1928] AC 433 (U.K.); Hellenic Lines Ltd v. Moore, 345 F.2d 978 (D.C. 1965); Swezey v. Merrill Lynch, 87 AD3d 119 (N.Y. 2011); Arrest Warrant of 11 April 2000 (Dem. Rep. Congo v. Belgium), Judgment, 2002 I.C.J. Rep. 3, ¶ 54.

2.1.2   Diplomatic Inviolability Is Only Very Exceptionally Limited

Diplomatic inviolability is an unqualified right, guaranteed by international law. It is, in almost all circumstances, not susceptible to exception, even in case of suspicion of torture,[42] war crimes or crimes against humanity.[43]

The absolute character of the inviolability of a diplomatic mission arises particularly in the context of hostilities and conflict. It can come into sharp focus in situations where a State claims self-defence from attack. Self-defence is a fundamental principle of customary international law that is enshrined in Article 51 of the United Nations Charter. Following the terms of Article 21 of the International Law Commission (the "ILC") Draft Articles on Responsibility of States for Internationally Wrongful Acts (the "ILC Draft Articles on State Responsibility"), it can preclude the otherwise wrongfulness of an act of a State.[44]

Claims of self-defence have been used historically to justify a limitation on the notion of diplomatic inviolability.[45] This latitude has been restrictively interpreted since the implementation of the 1961 Vienna Convention.[46] One example confirming this restrictive interpretation occurred in 1984, when a British police officer who had been protecting the premises of the diplomatic mission of the People's Libyan Arab Jamahiriya in London was fatally shot, apparently from the mission premises. The Libyan government refused to permit an investigation by British police within the premises. The British government complied with the inviolability principle codified in Article 22 of the 1961 Vienna Convention: it first severed diplomatic relations with Libya and

---

42   Armed Activities on the Territory of the Congo (Dem. Rep. Congo v. Uganda), Judgment, 2005 I.C.J. Rep. 168, ¶ ¶ 337–340. The ICJ held that Uganda's "grave violation of the prohibition on the use of force" expressed in Article 2(4) of the United Nations Charter did not preclude Congo from breaching diplomatic inviolability.

43   See Arrest Warrant of 11 April 2000, 2002 I.C.J. Rep. at ¶ 70.

44   Article 21 of the ILC Draft Articles on State Responsibility provides: "the wrongfulness of an act of a State is precluded if the act constitutes a lawful measure of self-defence taken in conformity with the Charter of the United Nations." See also United States v. Brenner, 24 Fed. Cas. 1084 (C.C.E.D.Pa. 1830) (No. 14,568) and Costa Rica v. Acuna Araya, 4 ILR 359 (Costa Rica Cass. 1927).

45   In 1717, Gyllenburg, a Swedish ambassador, was arrested for conspiracy to invade England and dethrone the King. The justification satisfied most of the ambassadors informed.

46   China and Switzerland requested the admission of exceptions of "self-defence or, in exceptional circumstances, measures to prevent the diplomatic agent from committing crimes or offences" to moderate the principle of personal inviolability. The ILC included them in its Report covering the Work of its Ninth session (23 April–28 June 1957). See I.L.C., Observations of Governments on the draft articles concerning diplomatic intercourse and Immunities adopted by the International Law Commission at its ninth session in 1957, Doc. A/CN.4/114 and Add.1–6, II Y.B. Int'l L. Comm'n, 1958.

then searched the premises of the mission after Libya's withdrawal. Despite the provocation and public outcry, the British House of Commons Foreign Affairs Committee determined that the United Kingdom was required to comply with international law. It thus held that the concept of self-defence could not have provided a lawful basis for the forcible entry of the Bureau premises.[47] Only consent could justify it.[48]

Similarly, the obligation to respect diplomatic inviolability restricts the scope of possible countermeasures. Countermeasures are measures taken by a State against another State responsible for an internationally wrongful act to induce the latter to comply with its obligation.[49] Under no circumstances can countermeasures affect fundamental human rights or peremptory norms of general international law.[50] Nor does their imposition (or a State's wish to impose them) relieve a State of its obligation to respect the inviolability of diplomatic or consular agents.[51] The ILC recalled that this limitation was justified "not so much [by] the substantive character of the obligation but [by] its function in relation to the resolution of the dispute."[52] This is consistent with the premise that diplomatic inviolability is a functionally critical aspect of basic inter-State relations.

2.1.3 The Functional Justification of Diplomatic Inviolability

The legal concept of diplomatic inviolability has evolved over time. Arguably, it once was an absolute concept justified only by its very existence as a legal

---

47   UK Parliament House of Commons Foreign Affairs Committee, First Report Of The Foreign Affairs Committee Of The House Of Commons, H.C. 127 (1984), ¶¶ 88–95. *See* also Iain Cameron, *First Report of the Foreign Affairs Committee of the House of Commons*, 34 Int'l Comp. L.Q., 610, (1985).

48   *Report of the International Law Commission covering the Work of its Ninth session, 23 April - 28 June 1957*, U.N. Doc. A/3623, Doc. A/CN.4/110 II Y.B. Int'l L. Comm'n, 1957, at 136. At the tenth session of the ILC, the United States agreed that only consent could justify the entry into diplomatic premises, however such consent was presumed "when immediate entry is necessary to protect life and property, as in the case of fire endangering adjacent buildings." ILC, *Diplomatic Intercourse and Immunities—Summary of observations received from Governments and conclusions of the Special Rapporteur, Mr. A. Emil F. Sandström*, Doc. A/CN.4/116, at 37. *See also* the Diplomatic and Consular Premises Act, 1987 (U.K.), which provides that if a State ceases to use land for the purposes of its mission or exclusively for the purposes of a consular post, the land not be regarded as a diplomatic or consular premises.

49   ILC Draft Articles on State Responsibility Article 50.

50   ILC Draft Articles on State Responsibility Article 50 (1) (a) and (c).

51   ILC Draft Articles on State Responsibility Article 50 (2) (b).

52   Article 50 Commentary of the ILC Draft Articles on State Responsibility.

norm.[53] Over time, it has become justified by reference to and conditioned by the effective exercise of the diplomatic function.[54] This consists *inter alia* in promoting friendly relations between the sending State and the receiving State and in protecting the sending State's interests in the host country.[55]

The concept of effective performance of diplomatic functions as justifying and giving scope and effect to the idea of diplomatic inviolability has been used in municipal and international law before and after the implementation of the 1961 Vienna Convention.[56] This is, in part, reflected in the descending scales of protection afforded to different categories of diplomatic staff.[57] Thus, as with all State immunities, diplomatic privileges are interpreted more restrictively the more the State's activities in question shift from *jure imperii* toward *jure gentium*.[58] This is particularly the case when diplomatic privileges confront rights such as freedom of speech,[59] service of process[60] or the right to have one's claim heard.[61]

---

53   Kenyan Diplomatic Residence, 128 I.L.R. 632 (Ger. Sup. Ct. 2003); In Re Chayet, 6 I.L.R. 329 (Sup. Ct. Chile 1932).

54   As reminded in the Preamble of the 1961 Vienna Convention. See also Certain Questions of Mutual Assistance in Criminal Matters (Djib. v. Fr.), Judgment, 2008 I.C.J. Rep. 177, ¶ 173, (June 4). The ICJ held that the formal defects in the summons addressed to the Djiboutian Head of State by Judge Clement "do not in themselves constitute a violation by France of its international obligations regarding the immunity from criminal jurisdiction and the inviolability of foreign Heads of State."

55   *See* 1961 Vienna Convention Art. 3.

56   Petrocochino v. Swedish State, 5 ILR 306 (Fr. Civ. Trib. 1929); *See* In Re Chayet, 6 I.L.R. 329; Tietz et al v. Bulgaria, 28 I.L.R. 369, (Berlin Sup. Rest. Ct for Berlin 1959); Weinmann v. Latvia, 28 I.L.R. 385 (Berlin Sup. Rest. Ct. 1959); Hellenic Lines Ltd v. Moore, 345 F.2d 978 (D.C. 1965); Ministère Public and Republic of Mali v. Keita, 77 I.L.R. 410 (Brussels App. Ct. 14 1977); Philippine Embassy Bank Account Case, 65 I.L.R. 146 (Ger. Fed. Const. Ct. 1977); Arrest Warrant of 11 April 2000 (Dem. Rep. Congo v. Belgium), Judgment, 2002 I.C.J. Rep. 3. *See* Kenyan Diplomatic Residence, 128 I.L.R. 632.

57   *See* 1961 Vienna Convention Article 37(3).

58   *See* Hazel Fox and Philippa Webb, THE LAW OF STATE IMMUNITY, 331–332 (3rd Edition 2013). They assert that this same functional criteria justified the existence of the concept of State immunity developed coherently with the development of diplomatic inviolability.

59   *See* Boos v. Barry, 485 U.S. 1988 (Sup. Ct. 1988); Aziz v. Aziz and others and Sultan of Brunei [2007] EWCA Civ. 712.

60   *See* Certain Questions of Mutual Assistance in Criminal Matters (Djib. v. Fr.), Judgment, 2008 I.C.J. Rep. 177, ¶ 174, (June 4). Although the ICJ broadly interpreted inviolability by creating an obligation to protect the "honour and dignity" of heads of States, it refused to admit a violation of this inviolability by the sole submissions of a summons *in specie*.

61   Reyes v. Al-Malki and another, [2017] UKSC 61 (U.K.). The Supreme Court held that a former diplomat and his wife did not enjoy immunity from a claim brought against them by their former domestic worker.

Of course, inviolability does not mean impunity. The legal protection accorded to a diplomat comes with a duty to comply with the obligations and scope of the mission, within the time-limit of the mission, if any, being loyal to the sending State[62] and not interfering in the internal affairs of the receiving State.[63]

2.2   *The Protection of Diplomatic Inviolability*
States are under an obligation to take appropriate steps to ensure the effective protection of diplomatic inviolability, as required by the 1961 Vienna Convention.

2.2.1   The Extent of the Protection of Diplomatic Inviolability
Defining the extent of the duty of States to ensure diplomatic inviolability is not an easy task. Certain States have held that the duty is discretionary in nature.[64] On the other hand, it is also common practice for States to compensate each other in case of attacks on their diplomatic premises.[65]

Ensuring diplomatic inviolability entails a two-pronged obligation for the receiving State.[66] Not only is it bound to prevent its agents from entering the premises, but it is also under a special duty to take all "appropriate steps to protect the premises from any invasion or damage, and to prevent any disturbance of the peace of the mission or detraction from its dignity."[67] The

---

62   Rex v. Rose, 13 I.L.R. 161 Court of King's Bench of Quebec, 28 May 1946.
63   1961 Vienna Convention Article 41.
64   Ignatiev v. United States, 238 F.3d 464 (D.C. Cir. 2001).
65   This was the case in 2003 when President Karzai of Afghanistan apologized and compensated Pakistan for the damage done by protesters at the embassy of Pakistan in Afghanistan. Similarly, the United States paid the Chinese government USD 28 million after bombing the Chinese embassy in Belgrade during the NATO campaign in 1999 against Serbia for the liberation of Kosovo. Equally, Libya apologized and offered to pay compensation for damage caused by the attacks on the embassies of Venezuela and Russia and UN Security Council member States in April 1992 who voted to impose sanctions on Libya. Jean d'Aspremont, *Premises of Diplomatic Missions*, MAX PLANCK ENCYCLOPEDIA OF PUBLIC INTERNATIONAL LAW (2009), ¶ 30; Rosanne van Alebeek, *Diplomatic Immunity*, MAX PLANCK ENCYCLOPEDIA OF PUBLIC INTERNATIONAL LAW (2009), ¶ 10.
66   The ICJ held that Article 29 of the 1961 Vienna Convention contained a positive obligation for the receiving State as regards the actions of its own authorities, and obligations of prevention as regards possible acts by individuals. *See Certain Questions of Mutual Assistance in Criminal Matters (Djibouti v. France)*, Judgment, 2008 I.C.J. Rep. 177, ¶ 174, (June 4).
67   ILC, *Report of the International Law Commission covering the Work of its Ninth session, 23 April–28 June 1957*, U.N. Doc. A/3623, Doc. A/CN.4/110 II Y.B. Int'l L *See* I.L.C., *Observations of Governments on the draft articles concerning diplomatic intercourse and Immunities*

receiving State must, in order to fulfil this obligation, take special measures—over and above those it takes to discharge its general duty to ensure order.[68]

The practice of compensation is perceived as a way to preserve diplomatic ties and reinforce the functional role of the norm in international law. However, this does not preclude a State from taking appropriate steps to ensure the effectiveness of diplomatic inviolability.

The notion of "appropriate steps" has been incrementally developed by case law before municipal and international courts. Courts and tribunals regularly take into account the receiving State's knowledge of any special danger faced by the protected person or premises,[69] the degree of the threat, and the proportionality of the intervention that would have been required to prevent the violation. For the most serious attacks against diplomatic inviolability, the 1973 Convention on the Prevention and Punishment of Crimes against Internationally Protected Persons, including Diplomatic Agents sets out a threshold. The 180 parties to that Convention have undertaken to criminalise in their municipal legal system the murder, kidnapping and assaults upon diplomats and other persons entitled to special protection[70] and to establish their jurisdiction over them.[71] Nevertheless, this obligation does not free States from the duty to "take all appropriate measures to prevent other attacks on the person, freedom or dignity of an internationally protected person."[72]

2.2.2 The Failure to Protect Diplomatic Inviolability Sanctioned by the "Self-Contained Regime" of the 1961 Vienna Convention

The 1961 Vienna Convention contains its own rules and sanctions in case of violation of any of the obligations that it sets out. It gives the power to a State

---

adopted by the International Law Commission at its ninth session in 1957, Doc. A/CN.4/114 and Add.1–6, II Y.B. Int'l L. Comm'n, 1958.

68   See, Report of the International Law Commission covering the Work of its Ninth session supra note 67. See Observations of Governments on the draft articles concerning diplomatic intercourse and Immunities adopted by the International Law Commission at its ninth session in 1957.

69   For the application to the consuls See Francisco Mallén (United Mexican States) v. U.S.A, 4 R.I.I.A. 173, ¶ 6 (Gen. Cl. Comm'n, 1927); William E. Chapman (USA) v. United Mexican States, 4 R.I.I.A. 632, 638 (Gen. Cl. Comm'n, 1930).

70   1973 Convention on the Prevention and Punishment of Crimes against Internationally Protected Persons, including Diplomatic Agents Article 2(2).

71   1973 Convention on the Prevention and Punishment of Crimes against Internationally Protected Persons, including Diplomatic Agents Article 3.

72   1973 Convention on the Prevention and Punishment of Crimes against Internationally Protected Persons, including Diplomatic Agents Article 2(3). This convention was applied in Duff, John William v. The Queen Case, [1979] FCA 133, ¶ 104.

to declare a diplomat *persona non grata*,[73] to reduce the size of the diplomatic mission,[74] to terminate or suspend diplomatic relations[75] and to recall their own ambassadors. It could be argued that this set of rules establishes the regime of diplomatic protection as a self-contained system; that is, a system that comprises not only primary rules laying down rights and duties but also secondary rules on remedies to sanction the misapplication of the former.

The Optional Protocol to the 1961 Vienna Convention concerning the compulsory settlement of disputes establishes the jurisdiction of the ICJ, "unless some other form of settlement has been agreed upon by the parties within a reasonable period."[76]

That was the case for Eritrea and Ethiopia, each of which consented to the EECC having jurisdiction to rule on their diplomatic claims.[77] It is worth noting that, on 16 February 1999 Eritrea had attempted to bring the dispute to the ICJ,[78] although it noted in its application that Ethiopia had not yet given its consent to the jurisdiction of the Court over the dispute and invited Ethiopia to do so.[79]

3   Summary of the Partial Awards on Eritrea's and Ethiopia's Diplomatic Claims Issued by the EECC on 19 December 2005

On 19 December 2005, the EECC issued two partial awards on the diplomatic claims brought by Eritrea against Ethiopia and by Ethiopia against Eritrea, respectively. Each of the States had alleged that a number of breaches of international diplomatic law had been committed by the other State during the armed conflict between them during the period 1998 and 2000.[80]

---

73   1961 Vienna Convention Art. 9.
74   1961 Vienna Convention Art. 11.
75   1961 Vienna Convention Art. 9.
76   Optional Protocol to the Vienna Convention on diplomatic relations concerning the Compulsory Settlement of Disputes, preamble, 500 U.N.T.S. 241.There are 70 State parties to the latter.
77   Algiers Agreement Art. 5.
78   *See* ICJ, *Basis of the Court's jurisdiction*, available at https://www.icj-cij.org/en/basis-of-jurisdiction.
79   *See* ICJ, *Eritrea Applies to International Court of Justice in Diplomatic Dispute with Ethiopia*, Press Release (ICJ/563) available at https://www.un.org/press/en/1999/19990216.icj563 .html. The author was counsel and advocate of Eritrea in the ICJ Application.
80   *Diplomatic Claim—Eritrea's Claim 20, (Eritrea v Ethiopia)* Partial Award, 26 R.I.I.A 381 (EECC 2005); *Diplomatic Claim—Ethiopia's Claim 8, (Eritrea v Ethiopia)* (Partial Award, 26 R.I.I.A. 407 (EECC 2005).

Eritrea filed its claims on 12 December 2001, pursuant to Article 5 of the Algiers Agreement. In its submissions, Eritrea requested monetary compensation and additional remedies for the alleged violations of international law. It alleged that:

> Ethiopia is liable for loss, damage and injury suffered by Eritrea from the injuries sustained by the Eritrean diplomatic mission and consular posts and personnel in Ethiopia including its accredited representative to the Addis Ababa based headquarters of the Organisation of African Unity ("OAU") and the United Nations Economic Commission for Africa ("UNECA"), as a result of the [Ethiopia's] alleged violations of the international law of diplomatic and consular relations.[81]

At the same time, Ethiopia filed its claims, pursuant to Article 5 of the Algiers Agreement, requesting monetary compensation for alleged violations of international law by Eritrea. It requested the EECC to find that Eritrea was:

> liable for loss, damage and injury suffered by Ethiopia from the injuries sustained by the Ethiopian diplomatic mission and consular post and personnel in Eritrea as a result of [Eritrea's] alleged violations of the international law of diplomatic and consular relations.[82]

The findings and analysis of the EECC in the two partial awards will be considered in turn.

3.1   *The EECC's Partial Award on Eritrea's Diplomatic Claim*
3.1.1   The EECC's Jurisdiction
In its Partial Award on Eritrea's Diplomatic Claim, after recounting the terms of its mandate pursuant to Article 5(1) of the Algiers Agreement, the EECC first analysed Ethiopia's jurisdictional challenge over certain claims brought by Eritrea. In a previous decision, the EECC had declined jurisdiction over claims regarding the interpretation or implementation of the Algiers Agreement.[83] Strictly interpreting its mandate, the EECC limited itself to hearing claims

---

81   See *Diplomatic Claim—Eritrea's Claim 20*, at ¶ 1.
82   See *Diplomatic Claim—Ethiopia's Claim 8*, at ¶ 1.
83   *Eritrea-Ethiopia Claims Commission—Preliminary Decisions-Commission's Mandate/ Temporal Scope of Jurisdiction*, Decision No. 1, 26 R.I.I.A. 1, 3 (EECC 2001). It explicitly departs from the supervisory jurisdiction of the Iran-United States Claims Tribunal.

relating to the conflict that were filed before 12 December 2001.[84] Accordingly, it rejected certain of Eritrea's claims, including the claims brought in relation to the Eritrean Consulates in Mekelle and Ayasa'ita and the restrictions imposed by Ethiopia on Eritrea's embassy in Addis Ababa that were founded on the 1963 Vienna Convention, on the basis that they were extinguished by the terms of Article 5(8) of the Algiers Agreement.[85] On the other hand, the EECC found itself competent to hear Eritrea's claim that Ethiopia should have enabled Eritrea's ambassador to remain in Addis Ababa to "perform his responsibilities in relation to [the OAU]" as well as all other claims asserted by Eritrea.[86]

3.1.2   Applicable Law

The EECC noted that both Parties relied on the 1961 Vienna Convention. In particular, both relied on the principles of inviolability of diplomatic envoys and premises, as guaranteed by Article 22 and Article 29 of the Convention. However, the Parties took different positions in relation to the effect that the state of war had on the application of international diplomatic law. Ethiopia took the position that a state of war must modify the application of international diplomatic law, whereas Eritrea argued for the strict application of the standards in the 1961 Vienna Convention.[87] The EECC noted that the ICJ had affirmed, in the *Case concerning United States Diplomatic and Consular Staff in Tehran*, that the principles set out in the 1961 Vienna Convention applied even in the case of armed conflicts.[88] The EECC thus rejected Ethiopia's position.[89]

Noting that there was little jurisprudence on this issue, the EECC held that Eritrea and Ethiopia were both bound by their fundamental obligations under the 1961 Vienna Convention. The EECC reasoned that either State had been free at all times to relieve themselves of the obligations arising under the 1961 Vienna Convention by terminating their diplomatic relations with the other but that neither had chosen to do so.[90] In light of the circumstances, the EECC determined that a critical standard when applying the 1961 Vienna Convention must be "the impact of the events complained about on the functioning of

---

84   Algiers Agreement Article 5(8) provides that "all claims submitted to the Commission shall be filed no later than one year from the effective date" of the Agreement.

85   *See Diplomatic Claim—Eritrea's Claim 20*, at ¶ 11. However, the Commission held obiter that the 1963 Vienna Convention "codifies largely consular law."

86   *Id.* at ¶ 12.

87   *Id.* at ¶ 17.

88   *Id.* at ¶ 16.

89   *Id.* at ¶ 17.

90   *Id.* at ¶ 20.

the diplomatic mission."[91] The EECC noted that other sources of applicable law in Eritrea's Diplomatic Claim include the primary documents of the OAU and the UNEC, including the OAU Charter, the OAU Headquarters Agreement, the UNECA Headquarters Agreement, and the OAU Privileges and Immunities Convention.

3.1.3   Eritrea's Claims and the EECC's Decision

Eritrea organised its claims into four categories, or heads of claim. These were: a) the alleged illegal expulsion of diplomats and staff; b) the alleged seizure of the embassy residence and detention of personnel; c) the interference with embassy and consulate operations; and d) the interference with Eritrea's participation in the OAU and UNECA. The findings of the EECC in relation to each category are summarised below.

3.1.3.1   *Expulsion of Diplomats and Staff*

Under the first head of claim, Eritrea advanced three main complaints. These were: first, the short length of time allowed by Ethiopia for the departure of Eritrean diplomats and staff; second, Ethiopia's treatment of the Eritrean personnel during their departure; and third, the size and makeup of the Eritrean mission following their departure.

In relation to the first complaint, Eritrea argued that the time period given by Ethiopia for Eritrean diplomatic staff to depart the country was unreasonably short. Eritrean diplomatic staff were given 48 hours to depart the country and the Eritrean Ambassador was ordered to leave Ethiopia within 24 hours (later extended to 25 hours).

The EECC decided that, given the circumstances of the armed conflict, there was no violation of international diplomatic law by reason of the limited time periods for the Ambassador and other diplomatic staff to leave Ethiopia. It held that the available evidence revealed that the diplomatic staff had been able to gather family members and transportable belongings within the time allotted. The EECC noted that Eritrea itself had allowed Ethiopian diplomatic staff a similar time period to depart from Eritrea.

In relation to the second complaint, Eritrea argued that the treatment of its personnel when departing Ethiopia violated the 1961 Vienna Convention. The EECC found blatant breaches by Ethiopia of the inviolability of Eritrea's diplomatic staff. The EECC held that Eritrea provided detailed and corroborated evidence which showed that Ethiopian security agents searched diplomatic baggage and hand luggage, confiscated papers and attempted searches of the

---

91   *Id.* at ¶ 22.

diplomatic personnel during their departure. The EECC held that diplomatic personnel who are declared *persona non grata* enjoy privileges and immunities until they are recalled and until they have left the country. As a result, the EECC concluded that Ethiopia was liable for breaching Articles 29 and 36 of the 1961 Vienna Convention.

In relation to the third complaint, Eritrea claimed that the restrictions on the size of its mission in Ethiopia violated Article 11 of the 1961 Vienna Convention.[92] Eritrea alleged that the skeletal diplomatic and service staff allowed by Ethiopia was unreasonable, particularly given the increased consular, negotiation and press responsibilities faced by the mission during the armed conflict. The EECC rejected this argument. It held that under Article 9 of the 1961 Vienna Convention Ethiopia had absolute discretion to declare diplomatic agents *persona non grata*. The EECC noted that during wartime a receiving State must have a legitimate interest in limiting the presence of the sending State diplomats in its territory.[93] As a consequence, the EECC found that Ethiopia had reasonably exercised its discretion granted by Article 11 of the 1961 Vienna Convention.

3.1.3.2 *Seizure of the Embassy Residence and the Detention of Personnel*

Under the second head of claim, Eritrea alleged that Ethiopia had entered and seized the embassy residence and took diplomatic property shortly after the Eritrean Ambassador's departure, in breach of the inviolability of mission premises. Ethiopia admitted "sealing off" the residence from Eritrean use. However, Ethiopia argued that its acts did not violate international law. Ethiopia's defence was that its own security reports indicated that the residence was used for illegal purposes, specifically to stockpile weapons and to counterfeit money for its war effort.[94]

The EECC held that the residence was inviolable under Article 22 of the 1961 Vienna Convention. It further held that Ethiopia's alleged suspicions did not justify any violation of the 1961 Vienna Convention. It held that in the face of allegedly illegal Eritrean activity at its mission, Ethiopia at all times could have, pursuant to Article 43 of the 1961 Vienna Convention, terminated diplomatic relations with Eritrea and closed the mission. Ethiopia had not done this and thus Ethiopia was not permitted to unilaterally take possession of and "seal off" the Eritrean mission.

---

92   *Id.* at ¶ 39.
93   *Id.* at ¶ 41.
94   *Id.* at ¶ 44.

On the other hand, in relation to the alleged detention and torture of locally employed Eritrean diplomatic staff, the EECC did not find a violation of international diplomatic law. It so concluded because it determined that those individuals were not part of the essential functioning of the Eritrean mission.[95]

3.1.3.3   *Interference with Embassy Operations*

Under the third head of claim, Eritrea alleged that Ethiopia monitored, harassed and intimidated embassy staff and visitors and interfered with embassy communications. The EECC recognised that the activities of Ethiopian security forces in targeting the Eritrean embassy and communications was "sometimes intrusive and even perhaps abusive". However, it concluded on balance and "in light of the seriousness of other claims competing for attention"[96] that Ethiopia's security measures did not compromise the basic functioning of the diplomatic mission in violation of international diplomatic law.[97] The EECC also dismissed Eritrea's claims of unlawful interference with free embassy communications for failure of proof.

3.1.3.4   *Interference with OAU and UNECA Participation*

Under the fourth head of claim, Eritrea alleged that Ethiopia's expulsion of Eritrea's Ambassador interfered with Eritrea's full participation in the OAU and the UNECA, which were both hosted by Ethiopia at the time. Eritrea alleged that by refusing to permit Eritrea's nominated representative to attend the OAU and UNECA Ethiopia had violated its international law obligations, including its obligations as host State under the relevant international agreements.[98]

The EECC decided that nothing in the relevant OAU and UNECA agreements gave Eritrea absolute discretion in its choice of representative to the OAU and UNECA.[99] Therefore, it decided that there was no international law basis for Eritrea's allegation that Ethiopia had affirmative obligations vis-à-vis Eritrea's selection of its particular representatives to the OAU and UNECA and the EECC dismissed the claim. The EECC also concluded that Eritrea had failed to prove as a matter of fact that Ethiopia's interference impaired Eritrea's ability to participate fully in the OAU and UNECA.

---

95   *Id.* at ¶ 49.
96   *Id.* at ¶ 55.
97   *Id.* at ¶ 55.
98   *Id.* at ¶ 59.
99   *Id.* at ¶ 61.

3.2   *The EECC's Partial Award on Ethiopia's Diplomatic Claim*

3.2.1   The EECC's Jurisdiction

In its Partial Award on Ethiopia's Diplomatic Claim, the EECC considered Eritrea's jurisdictional challenge over certain claims brought by Ethiopia. Eritrea asserted that 17 of the claims advanced by Ethiopia were extinguished because they were not filed before 12 December 2001 and because they were outside the scope of the temporal jurisdiction of the EECC (i.e., May 1998 to December 2000) in accordance with the terms of the Algiers Agreement.[100] The EECC upheld almost all of Eritrea's challenge. It held that it did not have jurisdiction over 16 of Ethiopia's claims, although it did have jurisdiction over all other claims asserted by Ethiopia.[101]

3.2.2   Applicable Law

In the Partial Award on Ethiopia's Diplomatic Claim, the EECC adopted the same analysis it used in determining the applicable law in the Partial Award on Eritrea's Diplomatic Claim. The EECC noted that both States relied on the 1961 Vienna Convention but took different positions in relation to the effect that the state of war had on the application of international diplomatic law. For its part, the EECC determined that a critical standard when applying the 1961 Vienna Convention must be "the impact of the events complained about on the functioning of the diplomatic mission."[102]

3.2.3   Ethiopia's Claims and the EECC's Decision

Ethiopia organised its claims into six categories or heads of claim. These were: a) the alleged arrest, detention and interrogation of the Chargé d'Affaires; b) the alleged harassment of Embassy personnel; c) the alleged seizure of Embassy documents; d) the alleged interference with Embassy access; e) the alleged failure to protect the security of the Embassy and its personnel; and f) the alleged failure to facilitate the repatriation of staff of the consulate in Assab and their families, as well as the restriction of their freedoms of movement and communication. The EECC did not address the merits of the final category because it had determined that the claim was not timely filed and was extinguished. The findings of the EECC in relation to each of the other five categories are summarised below.

---

100   *Diplomatic Claim—Ethiopia's Claim 8, (Eritrea v Ethiopia)*, Partial Award, 26 R.I.I.A. 407, ¶¶ 8–16 (EECC 2005). Algiers Agreement Article 5(8) provides that "all claims submitted to the Commission shall be filed no later than one year from the effective date" of the Agreement.

101   *Id.* at ¶ 16.

102   *Id.* at ¶ 26.

3.2.3.1   *Arrest, Detention and Interrogation of the Chargé d'Affaires*

Under the first head of claim, Ethiopia alleged that Eritrea violated Articles 26, 29 and 31 of the 1961 Vienna Convention when it arrested, detained and interrogated the Chargé d'Affaires. The EECC found that Ethiopia presented clear and convincing evidence that Eritrean guards twice arrested, detained and interrogated the Chargé in September 1998 and October 1999. On this basis, it held that Eritrea was liable for violating Article 29 of the 1961 Vienna Convention by arresting and detaining the Chargé without regard to his diplomatic immunity.[103]

The EECC also held that the circumstances did not give rise to violations of Articles 26 and 31 of the 1961 Vienna Convention. The EECC was not convinced that Eritrean officials' questioning of the Chargé for less than one hour constituted interrogation in the context of compulsion of evidence, nor did the arrests and detentions inhibit his freedom to perform his consular functions for Ethiopian nationals. Therefore, the EECC dismissed these claims.[104]

3.2.3.2   *Harassment of Embassy Personnel*

Under the second head of claim, Ethiopia alleged that Eritrean agents "consistently engaged in harassment, intimidation, abusive search, interrogation, arrest and detention" of non-diplomatic Embassy staff who were Ethiopian nationals.[105] The EECC determined that there was no clear and convincing evidence that the treatment of permanent resident service staff compromised the essential functioning of the Ethiopian mission. It concluded that the evidence in the record indicated, instead, that the Ethiopian Embassy stayed open and continued to provide services throughout the war. As a result, the EECC dismissed this claim for failure of proof.[106]

The EECC also dismissed for lack of proof a separate claim advanced by Ethiopia that Eritrean officials mistreated a group of Ethiopian diplomats in the course of their departure from Eritrea in violation of Articles 29 and 44 of the 1961 Vienna Convention.[107]

3.2.3.3   *Seizure of Embassy Documents*

Under the third head of claim, Ethiopia alleged that Eritrean Customs officials at the Asmara airport had intercepted and retained a diplomatic bag sent

---

103   *Id.* at ¶ 33.
104   *Id.* at ¶ 36.
105   *Id.* at ¶ 37.
106   *Id.* at ¶ 39.
107   *Id.* at ¶ 41.

from the Ethiopian Consulate in Jeddah to the Embassy, which contained 100 blank passports, invoices and receipts, in violation of Articles 24, 27 and 29 of the 1961 Vienna Convention. The EECC found that the bag was not labelled in any fashion to indicate its character as a diplomatic bag and hence Ethiopia did not establish a violation of Article 27 of the 1961 Vienna Convention. However, the EECC found that Eritrea refused to release the bag to Ethiopia for more than five years despite being under an obligation promptly to transfer the box and its contents to the Ethiopian mission after its official character became apparent. The EECC therefore found Eritrea liable for violating official Ethiopian diplomatic correspondence and interfering with the functioning of the mission in breach of Articles 24 and 29 of the Convention.[108]

3.2.3.4   Interference with Embassy Access

Under the fourth head of claim, Ethiopia alleged that Eritrean security personnel increased monitoring of the Ethiopian Embassy after the outbreak of the war and harassed and intimidated Ethiopian diplomatic staff and Embassy visitors. The EECC found that following the outbreak of war both Eritrea and Ethiopia increased its monitoring of the other's Embassy and its scrutiny of both staff and visitors to the Embassy. It held that once the Parties decided to keep their Embassies open during the war, the increase in monitoring was neither surprising nor contrary to international law. The EECC also noted that, given the tension in both capitals, it was in no doubt that there was some level of harassment and intimidation of Embassy staff and visitors.

The EECC found that, on balance "and particularly in light of the seriousness of other claims competing for its attention",[109] Eritrea's security measures involving the Ethiopian Embassy, while sometimes intrusive and even perhaps abusive, did not compromise the basic functioning of the Ethiopian mission. Therefore, it found that there was no violation of the applicable international diplomatic law.[110] The EECC also dismissed Ethiopia's claims of unlawful interference with free embassy communications for failure of proof.

Under the fifth head of claim, Ethiopia alleged that Eritrea violated Article 22 of the 1961 Vienna Convention for failing to protect the Ethiopian Embassy and it personnel. The claim concerns two intrusions into the Embassy by individuals who jumped over the Embassy fence. The EECC found that Eritrea presented clear and convincing evidence that it took action consistent with

---

108   *Id.* at ¶ 44.
109   *Id.* at ¶ 50.
110   *Id.* at ¶ 50.

its obligations under the 1961 Vienna Convention. In both instances Eritrean police arrested the intruders.

4 Analysis of the EECC's Partial Awards on Eritrea's and Ethiopia's Diplomatic Claims

The EECC's partial awards on Eritrea's and Ethiopia's diplomatic claims are Spartan in terms of their legal analysis. They are also open to criticism on a number of other grounds. Amongst others, they appear to have been based on a mistake on the part of the EECC about its mandate. They also adopted an unorthodox interpretation of the international law of diplomatic immunities. For this reason, and sadly for international law scholars and practitioners, the EECC's partial awards on Eritrea's and Ethiopia's diplomatic claims provide only a very limited contribution to an understanding of this important area of international law.

4.1 *The Partial Awards Show a Misconception on the Part of the EECC About Its Mandate and of the Applicable Principles of International Diplomatic Law*

4.1.1 The EECC Overstepped Its Mandate

In its partial awards, the EECC emphasised the importance of a strict interpretation of its mandate. However, it clearly overstepped its mandate in many respects.

As noted above, the Algiers Agreement provided that an independent and impartial body would carry out an investigation on the origins of the conflict. That body was never established.[111] The EECC only had jurisdiction to rule on the consequences of the armed conflict, not to determine its origin. The concept of what constitutes armed conflict is well-developed in international law and thus there was no need for it to do so, functionally.[112] Nonetheless, the EECC, in its Decision No.1, stated that the conflict between Eritrea and Ethiopia dated from May 1998 had been started by Eritrea and that any events prior to

---

111   Algiers Agreement Art. 3 provides: "In order to determine the origins of the conflict, an investigation will be carried out on the incidents of 6 May 1998 and on any other incident prior to that date which could have contributed to a misunderstanding between the parties regarding their common border, including the incidents of July and August 1997."

112   For example, *see* Prosecutor v. Tadić, Case No. IT-94-1-I, Decision on Defence Motion for Interlocutory Appeal on Jurisdiction, ¶ 70 (Int'l Crim. Trib. for the Former Yugoslavia Oct. 2, 1995), which held that an armed conflict exists "whenever there is a resort to armed force between the States."

this date were not "related to the conflict."[113] Curiously, the EECC, presumably aware that it did not have a mandate to make such determinations, stated in another partial award:

> Determination of the origins of the conflict and the nature of any misunderstandings about the border, had they been made by the impartial body anticipated by Article 3, could have been helpful in promoting reconciliation and border delimitation, but they certainly would not have answered the question of the legality of Eritrea's resort to force.[114]

This statement, made rather incongruously, fails to address the reality that the jurisdiction to conduct any such inquiry had been allocated to another body under the Algiers Agreement. The EECC failed to establish its own jurisdiction to make the findings that it did on this point.

The EECC further misinterpreted and misapplied its mandate. It did so in ways that significantly altered the scope of its jurisdiction *ratione temporis*, compared to what was in the Algiers Accords. Thus, the EECC inexplicably reduced the scope of its jurisdiction by preventing the Parties from bringing claims relating to events before May 1998 (when it deemed the conflict to have started) and, at the same time, it inexplicably expanded the scope of its jurisdiction by allowing the Parties to bring claims relating to events after the conflict had ended.[115]

Against the express terms of the Algiers Agreement, establishing the existence and cause of the armed conflict between Eritrea and Ethiopia became the foundation of the EECC's various awards. The EECC's findings triggered the application of international humanitarian law and affected, among other things, the application of the international law regime of diplomatic protection. Yet, while the EECC proclaimed itself competent to fix the dates and cause of the war, it did not draw from those findings coherent legal consequences, in relation to the issues of international diplomatic law.

---

113   *Eritrea-Ethiopia Claims Commission—Preliminary Decisions-Commission's Mandate/Temporal Scope of Jurisdiction*, Decision No. 1, 26 R.I.I.A. 1 (EECC 2001).
114   See *Jus Ad Bellum—Ethiopia's Claims 1–8, (Eritrea v Ethiopia)*, Partial award, 26 R.I.I.A. 457 (EECC 2005).
115   Provided that they were the result of the armed conflict. Thus, the EECC refused to rule on Eritrea's Claims 15, 16, 23, 27–32 alleging the expulsion of 772 people in July 2001, because it failed to prove this was linked to the disengagement of armed forces.

4.1.2   The Partial Awards Reveal a Questionable Application of the
         International Law of Diplomatic Immunities

The essential function of diplomatic agents sent between States is peaceful communications and the furtherance of international relations.[116] This mission becomes frustrated during an armed conflict between those States. Therefore, the usual practice of States is to sever diplomatic relations with each other during wartime. When suspending or terminating diplomatic relations, the common practice of States is to entrust any residual diplomatic and consular functions to representatives of neutral States.[117] As noted above, unusually, Eritrea and Ethiopia maintained diplomatic relations throughout their armed conflict. The EECC expressly recognized that it was thereby faced with an "unusual challenge for the application of diplomatic law".[118] Unfortunately, despite recognizing that it had an opportunity to bring clarity to this area of law, the EECC failed to do so.

The EECC followed the ICJ's rulings in the *Tehran Hostages* Case[119] by asserting the strict application of the principle of diplomatic inviolability in case of armed conflicts.[120] It thus rejected Ethiopia's argument that a state of war must modify the standard of application of international diplomatic law.[121] Instead, the EECC held that the Parties were bound by their fundamental obligations under the 1961 Vienna Convention, especially since each was free at all times to relieve itself of such obligations by unilaterally terminating its diplomatic relations with the other.[122] Accordingly, as explained in Section 3, the EECC found, on the facts, both Ethiopia and Eritrea to have been in breach of the principle of diplomatic inviolability.

Additionally, the EECC used the notion of "reciprocity" as a guide to measure the extent of the Parties' obligations under the 1961 Vienna Convention. The EECC referred to the notion of reciprocity as a "helpful indicator"[123] that enabled it to interpret the 1961 Vienna Convention's obligations flexibly. The EECC assessed the reasonableness of the deadlines set by one Party for the

---

116   Franciszek Przetacznik, *Les Pouvoirs Découlant Pour L'Etat Accréditaire de L'Inviolabilité Personnelle de L'Agent Diplomatique*, 17 MCGILL L.J. 360, 404 (1971).

117   *See* Hazel Fox and Philippa Webb, THE LAW OF STATE IMMUNITY, 331–332 (3rd Edition 2013).

118   *Diplomatic Claim—Eritrea's Claim 20 (Eritrea v Ethiopia)*, Partial Award, 26 R.I.I.A 381, ¶ 6 (EECC 2005).

119   *United States Diplomatic and Consular Staff in Tehran (United States v. Iran)*, Judgment, 1980 I.C.J. Rep. 3, ¶ 86 (May 24).

120   *Id.* at ¶ 20.

121   *Id.* at ¶ 17.

122   *Id.* at ¶ 20.

123   *Id.* at ¶ 21.

departure of the other's diplomats[124] or the reduction of the size of the other's mission[125] by referring to how the other Party dealt with the same actions.

This use of reciprocity as a measure of the reasonableness of each Party's actions is understandable, when applied to evaluate a State's exercise of its discretionary powers. However, the EECC also used this evaluative tool almost as a legal standard, in a manner that fundamentally altered the absolute character of diplomatic inviolability.[126] Thus, referencing reciprocity, the EECC declined to find that the Parties' breach of the absolute inviolability of diplomatic communications, guaranteed under Article 27 of the 1961 Vienna Convention, constituted a breach of the 1961 Vienna Convention.[127] This was a shocking error on the part of the EECC and one that could have negative consequences for international law and international relations, were it to gain currency. The obligation under Article 27 is absolute and unqualified, and with good reason. There is no legitimate basis on which to conclude that it should be susceptible of alteration by reference to the reciprocally wrongful conduct of another State and none was offered by the EECC. In misapplying the obligation, using the reference point of reciprocity, the EECC effectively redrafted the 1961 Vienna Convention. It was perhaps convenient for the EECC to avoid a hard decision by referencing the reciprocal acts of the Parties. But there is no basis in international law or policy that would justify the EECC washing its hands of the issue on the basis that both Parties were breaching the Convention.

The EECC stated that the existence of an armed conflict can justify a State's decision to "monitor and even limit activities of the diplomatic mission of an enemy."[128] This bald statement did not benefit from additional reasoning or reference to customary international law.[129] Indeed, there have been historic examples of restrictions on freedom of diplomatic communications during armed conflicts.[130] Instead of substantiating its conclusion, the EECC merely emptied Article 27 of meaning with no explanation.

---

124   *Id.* at ¶ 33.
125   *Id.* at ¶ 41.
126   *Id.* at ¶ 37.
127   *Id.* at ¶ 21.
128   *Id.* at ¶ 21.
129   In line with the preamble of the 1961 Vienna Convention that provides: "the rules of customary international law should continue to govern questions not expressly regulated by the provisions of the present Convention."
130   This was the case during the siege of Paris by the Germans in 1870 when Bismarck permitted envoys in Paris to send couriers to their sending States only if their dispatches were open. The UK prohibited missions in London from dispatching telegrams in cipher for a brief period of time during the First World War. Israel restricted secret diplomatic

It appears that the EECC held to the view that international diplomatic law is a self-contained regime, hermetically sealed from any external set of legal norms. The EECC thereby missed an opportunity to contribute to the development of international law related to the effect of armed conflict on the law of diplomatic inviolability.

4.2   *The Limited Impact of the Partial Awards of the EECC*

The partial awards of the EECC on diplomatic law have had limited effect on the subject of diplomatic immunities during wartime. This illustrates more broadly the inconclusive contribution of the EECC to resolving the crisis between Eritrea and Ethiopia.

4.2.1   The Limited Legal Impact of the EECC's Awards
4.2.1.1   *The Limited Contribution of the EECC's Partial Awards to the Unresolved Question of the Impact of Armed Conflict on Diplomatic Inviolability*

The partial awards on Eritrea's and Ethiopia's diplomatic claims presented the EECC with an opportunity to clarify and develop this area of international law. As the EECC noted itself, the answers to the challenges presented within the Parties' claims lay largely in the "uncharted legal waters"[131] of the application of the relevant treaties during wartime. Nonetheless, the EECC failed to provide reasoning for its conclusions on this point. The lack of reasoning of the EECC on this point stands in contrast with the reasoning contained in its final award on the *Pensions* claims (issued on the same date as the partial awards on the diplomatic claims) that "the 1998–2000 conflict resulted at the least in the suspension of pension-related treaty obligations during the period of the conflict and its immediate aftermath."[132]

There is no explicit guidance on the issue in the text of the Vienna Convention on the Law of Treaties.[133] At the time of the partial awards, the question of the effect of armed conflict on treaties was not subject to any general consensus.[134]

___

communications during the hostilities in 1948–1949. South Vietnam refused the transmission of diplomatic messages in code for a few days in 1963.

131   *See Diplomatic Claim—Eritrea's Claim 20 (Eritrea v Ethiopia)*, at ¶ 20.

132   *Final Award: Pensions-Eritrea's Claims 15, 19 & 23 (Eritrea v Ethiopia)*, Final Award, 26 R.I.I.A. 471 (EECC 2005).

133   The Vienna Convention on the Law of Treaties provides that the Convention shall not prejudge questions that may arise from the outbreak of hostilities between States.

134   As noted by Ian Brownlie, Special Rapporteur to the ILC, *Report of the international Law Commission on the work of its fifty-seventh session* [2005], 2 Y.B. Int'l L. Comm'n 1, U.N. Doc. no. A/60/10 27. Two main approaches have developed concerning the effect of armed conflict on treaties. The "intention school" adopts a subjective test to establish

Indeed, the International Law Commission had only recently been mandated by the General Assembly to consider the question of the effect of war on the law of treaties in 2000.[135]

The maintenance of diplomatic relations and the existence of a state of war between two countries is *a priori* antithetical.[136] Historically, customary international law considered that most treaties did not survive armed conflict.[137] This was especially so for treaties "the object of which 'is to promote relations of harmony between nation and nation', generally regarded as belonging to the class of treaty stipulations that are absolutely annulled by war."[138]

However, by the early twentieth century, a view had emerged under customary international law to the effect that armed conflicts did not *ipso facto* terminate the application of a treaty. By the early twenty-first century, the ICJ recognised in the *Case on Legal Consequences of the Construction of a Wall in the Occupied Palestinian Territory* that the protections offered by human rights conventions do not cease during armed conflicts, save certain specific provisions.[139] In 2011, the ILC adopted this view in its Draft Articles on the effects of armed conflicts on treaties. In relation to diplomatic and consular relations, Article 7 of the Draft Articles creates a rebuttable presumption for the continuance "in whole or in part, during armed conflict" of treaties concerning diplomatic and consular relations.[140] Interestingly, at the date of publication of the Draft Articles, the EECC was the only international tribunal to have pronounced itself on this question directly. Notably, the ILC Draft Articles make no mention of the EECC's partial awards or its utterances on these issues.[141]

---

whether the signatories intended the treaty to remain despite the existence of hostilities. The "compatibility doctrine" adopts an objective test that was adopted by the Permanent Court of International Justice in its *S.S. Wimbledon* case, Judgment, 17 August 1923.

135   The ILC was mandated by G.A. Res. 55/152 (Dec. 12, 2000) and G.A. Res. 56/82 (Dec. 12, 2001).

136   *Armed Activities on the Territory of the Congo (Dem. Rep. Congo v. Uganda)*, Judgment, 2005 I.C.J. Rep. 168.

137   In the *"The Louis" Case*, 3 Brit. Int'l. L. Cas. (Brit. High. Ct. Admiralty 1817), the court held that treaties "are perishable things and their obligations are dissipated by the first hostility."

138   Karnuth v. United States, 279 U.S. 231 (U.S. Sup. Court 1929).

139   Legal Consequences of the Construction of a Wall in the Occupied Palestinian Territory, Advisory Opinion, 2004 I.C.J. Rep. 136 (July 2004).

140   In this respect, it follows the stance adopted by the 1961 Vienna Convention. Although the convention does not contain any clear indication on its application in wartimes, the few occurrences relating to armed conflict promote a continuous protection of diplomats.

141   The ILC referred however as authority to *United States Diplomatic and Consular Staff in Tehran* (U. S. v. Iran), Judgment, 1980 I.C.J. Rep. 3, ¶ 86 (May 24) in which the ICJ held

4.2.1.2   *The Partial Awards of the EECC Were Issued in Blatant Contradiction of the Decision of the Boundary Commission*

The Eritrea-Ethiopia Boundary Commission was formally constituted on 20 February 2001. It issued its decision on 13 April 2002.[142] The Boundary Commission applied the *uti possidetis* doctrine, as argued by Eritrea, which provides that decolonisation involving a change of sovereignty does not affect colonial-era boundaries.[143] The Boundary Commission thus concluded that Badme was Eritrean territory.[144]

Three years later, the EECC contradicted the Boundary Commission's findings in its controversial partial award on *jus ad bellum*. In so doing, the EECC acted *ultra vires*, outside its jurisdiction, and undermined the Boundary Commission's decision.[145] Regrettably, the EECC thereby implicitly encouraged Ethiopia's refusal to comply with the decision[146] and delayed for more than a decade and a half the demarcation and return of the territories to Eritrea.[147]

4.2.2   The Limited Practical Impact of the EECC's Awards

4.2.2.1   *The EECC's Awards on Damages*

On 17 August 2009, the EECC submitted two final awards for damages. In them, it awarded Eritrea USD 161,455,000 for its State claims and USD 2,065,865 regarding its individual claims. Ethiopia was awarded USD 174,036,520. The EECC stated that it took into account the payment capacity of the two countries in determining its awards. It noted that both Eritrea and Ethiopia were parties

---

inviolability of diplomatic envoys and service staff applied even in the case of armed conflict. *In specie*, no armed conflict actually existed between the United States and Iran, unlike the situation brought before the EECC.

142 *Decision on delimitation of the Border between Eritrea and Ethiopia* (*Eritrea v Ethiopia*), 25 R.I.I.A. 83, ¶ 8.1 (EEC 2002). Its decision was finally accepted by Ethiopia in 2018. Statement of Ethiopian People's Revolutionary Democratic Front Executive Committee, Ethiopian Broadcasting Corporation, 5 June 2018 available at http://www.ebc.et/web/news-en/-/ethiopia-decides-to-fully-accept-algiers-agreement.

143 That doctrine was applied by the ICJ in the *Frontier Dispute* (Burkina Faso v. Republic of Mali), Judgement, 1986 I.C.J. 554, ¶ 25. The ICJ recognised though the tension that existed between the doctrine and the right to self-determination.

144 Bilateral negotiations between States are normally the standard measure to resolve boundary disputes, as was the case for the Ethiopia-Kenya alignment in the Treaty between Kenya and Ethiopia Respecting the Boundary between the Two Countries. Eritrea and Ethiopia however resorted to adjudication.

145 Christine Gray, *The Eritrea/Ethiopia Claims Commission Oversteps Its Boundaries: A Partial Award?*, 17 EJIL 699, 710 (2006).

146 *Id.* at 710.

147 The Algiers Agreement provided that the demarcation of the border should be accomplished six months after the Boundary Commission's Decision.

to the International Covenant on Economic, Social and Cultural Rights and the International Covenant on Civil and Political Rights, which both provide that "[i]n no case may a people be deprived of its own means of subsistence."[148]

Critics have argued that this resulted in an outcome that was "far from [...] fair compensation for the parties' wrongful actions".[149] Dissatisfaction of both sides rendered the EECC's awards ineffective and unimplemented.

4.2.2.2   A Peace Process Still Incomplete

The peace process between the two States has been largely stalled for a decade and more. Ethiopia resisted accepting and implementing the Boundary Commission's decision until 2018. Ethiopia has explicitly and publicly expressed its dissatisfaction on the EECC's decisions while Eritrea expressed reservations about the amounts granted in its Final Awards on damages.[150] Tensions still exist today between the two States. It is yet to be seen if the apparent détente that began at the start of 2018 will continue.

5   Conclusion

This chapter has examined the partial awards issued by the EECC on Eritrea's and Ethiopia's diplomatic claims in light of international diplomatic and consular law. It has analysed the reasoning of the EECC and the effect of its decisions on the underlying disputes between Eritrea and Ethiopia. It is probably not controversial to conclude that the work of the EECC does not appear to have had a cathartic effect on the Parties or on their relationship, to date.

The EECC overstepped its mandate. It reduced and expanded its jurisdiction *ratione temporis*. It gratuitously undertook part of the mandate of another body envisaged in the Algiers Agreement. It *ultra vires* contradicted the *intra vires* decision of yet another body created under the Algiers Agreement. More significantly for the topic of this chapter, the EECC missed a unique opportunity to make a contribution to the development and clarification of the international law of diplomatic privileges and immunities.

---

148   International Covenant on Economic, Social and Cultural Rights, Art. 1(2) December 16, 1966, 993 U.N.T.S. 3; International Covenant on Civil and Political Rights, Art. 1(2), December 16, 1966, 999 U.N.T.S. 171.

149   Ari Dybnis, *Was the Eritrea-Ethiopia Claims Commission Merely a Zero-Sum Game: Exposing the Limits of Arbitration in Resolving Violent Transnational Conflict*, 33 LOY. L.A. INT'L AND COMP. L. REV. 268 and 272 (2011).

150   *Id.* at 274.

CHAPTER 16

The Misinterpretation and Misapplication of the Minimum Standard of International Law

Stephen M. Schwebel

Aware of Lea's academic attainments, I encountered her as Eritrea's counsel in two fraught boundary arbitrations—the first with Yemen over sovereignty over islands in the Red Sea, the second with Ethiopia—following hostilities between them. She is as outstanding an international litigator as she is a professor.

In this contribution to her Festschrift, I focus on the topic of misinterpretation and misapplication of the Minimum Standard of Treatment (MST) in the context of international arbitration within the scope of the North Atlantic Free Trade Agreement (NAFTA), a multilateral treaty whose parties include Canada, Mexico and the United States.

The enquiry relies on the analysis contained in a heretofore unpublished, enlightening, opinion of the late Sir Robert Jennings, former judge and president of the International Court of Justice, and on a close reading of the several conflicting international arbitral awards that analyze the issues in question. My own views appear at the end of this essay.

I initially reproduce the text of NAFTA Article 1105(1) and the meaning that the NAFTA Parties have officially attached to it. In my view, the NAFTA Parties have, for defensive reasons, interpreted—indeed, misinterpreted—Article 1105(1) to lessen their exposure to suits against them. I shall set out and comment upon the principal pertinent arbitral awards, which are in conflict over the rectitude of the NAFTA Parties interpretation of Article 1105(1). I conclude with a statement of my own views.

1   The Scope of NAFTA Article 1105(1)

Article 1105(1) of NAFTA, entitled "Minimum Standard of Treatment", provides:

> Each Party shall accord to investments of another Party treatment in accordance with international law, including fair and equitable treatment and full protection and security.[1]

---

1 North American Free Trade Agreement, Dec. 17, 1992, 32 I.L.M. 289 & 605 (1993).

© KONINKLIJKE BRILL NV, LEIDEN, 2019 | DOI:10.1163/9789004316539_017

In July 2001, a rare pronouncement of NAFTA's Free Trade Commission ("FTC"), composed of cabinet-level representatives of the three Parties, interpreted Article 1105(1) in part as follows: "Article 1105(1) prescribes the customary international law minimum standard of treatment of aliens as the minimum standard of treatment to be afforded to investments of another Party."[2]

NAFTA Article 1131: "Governing Law" provides:

1. A Tribunal established under this Section shall decide the issues in dispute in accordance with this Agreement and applicable rules of international law.

2. An interpretation by the Commission of a provision of this agreement shall be binding on a Tribunal established under this Section.[3]

Article 1131(2) is consonant with the Vienna Convention on the Law of Treaties. Article 31(3) of the Vienna Convention provides that, in the interpretation of treaties, "There shall be taken into account, together with the context: (a) any subsequent agreement between the parties regarding the interpretation of the treaty or the application of its provisions". It follows therefore that the FTC interpretation of Article 1105(1) is binding upon NAFTA Tribunals called to interpret and apply it.

And indeed, NAFTA Tribunals have treated the FTC interpretation as binding.

Of note, the FTC interpretation was issued during the pendency of litigation in *Pope & Talbot v. Canada*.[4] The question of the content of the interpretation, and whether it was more and in actuality an amendment to NAFTA than an interpretation of it, was controverted by the parties. The controversy was substantial. In response to inquiries from the claimant, the three NAFTA Parties maintained that no records were kept of the negotiation of NAFTA. Nevertheless, the claimant eventually managed to elicit from the Canadian Government extensive records of the negotiating texts of provisions of NAFTA. More than

---

2 NAFTA Free Trade Commission, Notes of Interpretation of Certain Chapter 11 Provisions, July 31, 2001 (and further stating that "[t]he concepts of 'fair and equitable treatment' and 'full protection and security' do not require treatment in addition to or beyond that which is required by the customary international law minimum standard of treatment of aliens" and that a "determination that there is a breach of another provision of the NAFTA, or of a separate international agreement, does not establish that there has been a breach of Article 1105(1)").

3 North American Free Trade Agreement, Dec. 17, 1992, 32 I.L.M. 289 & 605 (1993). It should be noted that paragraph 1 of Article 1131 specifies "applicable rules of international law", not "applicable rules of customary international law.

4 *See Pope & Talbot Inc. v. The Government of Canada*, UNCITRAL, Award on Damages, May 31, 2002, at 15–19 (describing the process of extracting the *travaux* of NAFTA Article 1105 from Canada).

forty versions of what became Article 1105(1) were provided. All of them referred to the applicable rules of international law; none of them contained the specification of "customary" international law or referred to "aliens".[5] An important article by Meg Kinnear, then a very senior Canadian official, that closely analyzes the *travaux* as well as the case law confirms that in the drafting of Article 1105(1), only "international law" and never "customary international law" appeared.[6] But in their later versions of their model bilateral investment treaties ("BITS"), both Canada and the United States substituted "customary international law" for "international law".[7]

The claimant in *Pope & Talbot* filed four expert opinions of Sir Robert Jennings, former Judge and President of the International Court of Justice. The Fourth Opinion, signed and dated 6 September 2001, read in part as follows:

> The intervention of the Free Trade Commission is expressed in three prop-ositions.... proposition number '1' reads: '1. Article 1105(1) prescribes the customary international law minimum standard of treatment of aliens as the minimum standard of treatment to be afforded to investments of investors of another Party.' The trouble with this proposition is just that Article 1105(1) in fact provides nothing of the sort. The Article nowhere mentions 'aliens'; nor indeed does any other article of Chapter 11 of the NAFTA Agreement. Article 1105 is not about aliens but about 'investments of investors of another Party' (see also Article 1101 on 'Scope and Cover-age'). Nor does it use the word 'customary'; not even in the heading of the Article 'Minimum Standard of Treatment'.
>
> This attempt to 'interpret' the paragraph only after first materially changing the text of the paragraph does, however, betray the aim of this so-called interpretation, which is to replace the plainly stated require-ments for the treatment of 'investors of another Party', by the former cus-tomary international law minimum standard for the treatment of <u>*aliens.*</u>
>
> That so-called 'minimum' standard for the treatment of 'aliens' was the product of the European and North American States wishing to demand a standard for the treatment of their nationals in foreign coun-tries, which they called 'minimum', but was nevertheless thought to be

---

5 *See* Government of Canada Global Affairs, NAFTA Chapter 11—Trilateral Negotiating Draft Texts, *available at* http://www.international.gc.ca/trade-agreements-accords-commerciaux/ topics-domaines/disp-diff/trilateral_neg.aspx?lang=eng (last visited July 15, 2016).

6 Meg Kinnear, *Article 1105—Minimum Standard of Treatment, in* INVESTMENT DISPUTES UNDER NAFTA: AN ANNOTATED GUIDE TO CHAPTER 11, at 1105–57 (Andrea K. Bjorklund, et al., eds., March 2008 Supp. 1).

7 *Id.*

higher than the local *national* standard in some defendant countries....
One of these older cases, the *Neer* case, is cited by the United States
Rejoinder as *seminal*.... That was the case where the tribunal rejected a
United States claim that the Mexican State was liable to make reparation
for its failure to find and punish the bandit who had murdered Mr. Neer
in up-country Mexico; and held that in order to amount to 'an international delinquency', the Respondent's failure 'to act should amount to an
outrage, to bad faith, to willful neglect of duty, or to an insufficiency of
governmental action so far short of international standards that every
reasonable man would readily recognize its insufficiency'. These are the
familiar words that strongly attract the United States as a classical statement of a minimum standard for the treatment of aliens, which standard
it asks the Tribunal to apply in the present case. But quite apart from the
rather startling anachronism of trying to apply to investors and investments in 2001 the standards for the protection against bandits in 1924,
the *Neer* case was not a parallel case to the present one even in 1926. The
present claim is not a claim based upon a customary law 'international
delinquency', but a claim based upon the express terms of the NAFTA
Agreement. And it is not a case complaining of an insufficiency of a
State's response to actions that were not actions of the State or its agents
and so were not directly attributable to the State in international law, but
of 'measures adopted or maintained by the United States' (NAFTA Article
1101), which measures are believed to be in breach of the NAFTA Agreement. Thus, the relevance of *Neer* is very doubtful.

[...] the very existence of a so-called minimum standard for the treatment of aliens was vigorously contested by Latin American and other
defendant States. But that once famous international legal controversy is
now forgotten, and in contemporary law concerning the treatment of
aliens, the position has changed much with the advent of an international law of human rights which are irrespective of nationality or of
alienage. It is interesting to note that the International Law Commission's
latest draft codifying the existing international law of State Responsibility has found no need to mention a minimum standard for the treatment
of aliens in any one of its draft 59 articles.

As to the heading of Article 1105, 'Minimum Standard of Treatment',
one might with reason suppose that this heading was intended to refer to
the minimum standard required by the NAFTA Agreement for the treatment of 'investments of investors of another Party,' which standard is
indeed, in conformity with that meaning of the heading, defined by that
Article.

Finally, on this first proposition of the Free Trade Commission, it is an ingenious diversion inviting examination of the complicated area of the general international law concerning the treatment of aliens. But this is not what Article 1105 is about. It is about the minimum treatment of the investments of an investor of another Party to the NAFTA Agreement. Article 1105 does not anywhere mention either the term 'customary' or the term 'alien'. The first proposition of the Free Trade Commission, far from interpreting Article 1105(1), simply tries to substitute for the express terms of Article 1105 an altogether different standard [...]

What matters, for the purposes of interpretation, is that these 10 words '... including fair and equitable treatment and full protection and security'—are textually part of Article 1105(1) and define obligations of the Parties and must be applied [...]

There can be no mystery about why these concepts were included in the Article. They are provisions that have been included in virtually all investment treaties, including not scores but hundreds of BITs. And this being a question not about the sources of international law nor even about the nature of customary law, but about the correct interpretation of a given text, it is surely obvious that the interpretation must take into account that great volume of general law that employs these concepts. The Parties when they concluded the NAFTA Agreement may or may not have thought about the ambiguity of the word 'including' in the English language; but what they did clearly wish to say was that the required treatment must in either case include 'fair and equitable treatment and full protection and security'. They certainly did not expect that this treatment would be diminished by a pretense that it is included in the customary international law about the treatment of aliens. For if that were the net result of Article 1105(1), what was the point of drafting a treaty undertaking which did no more than require what the general law already required anyway?

The issue in a nutshell, is this: if the three governments are suggesting that NAFTA (and the hundreds of BITs) does *not* require a State to provide fair and equitable treatment, the suggestion is preposterous. It cannot be reconciled with the text of Article 1105(1), nor with any canon of interpretation of international law. If that is indeed the position of the three governments, then the Tribunal should treat the 'interpretation' as an attempted amendment that has no binding effect.[8]

---

8   *Pope & Talbot Inc. v. The Government of Canada*, UNCITRAL, Fourth Opinion by Sir Robert Jennings, dated 6 September 2001.

In my view, Judge Jennings' analysis is as sound as it is incisive. While NAFTA Tribunals are bound to treat the FTC interpretation as binding, by no means are they bound by the argumentation of any of the three NAFTA Parties in *Pope & Talbot*, in subsequent NAFTA cases addressing extrapolations of that interpretation, or by holdings of the NAFTA tribunals that have followed that case which accept that argumentation (as several of the awards summarized below do not). NAFTA Tribunals furthermore are free to weigh the import of the preparatory work of NAFTA, which reveals that the more-than-forty drafts of what came to be Article 1105(1), nowhere include the words 'customary' and 'alien'.[9]

The main question to be addressed is: What is the customary international law minimum standard of treatment ("MST") that Article 1105 prescribes, having regard to the interpretation of the FTC? To answer this question, I shall discuss the relevant sources for determining the MST, and then address the content of the MST. In so doing, I shall, as noted, take account of leading arbitration awards that have dealt with these matters.

2   Relevant Sources for Determining the Minimum Standard of Treatment

State practice and *opinio juris* are the primary sources for determining a rule of customary international law. As the International Court of Justice stated in *Continental Shelf (Libyan Arab Jamahiriya/Malta)*, "the material of customary international law is to be looked for primarily in the actual practice and *opinio juris* of States, even though multilateral conventions may have an important role to play in recording and defining rules deriving from custom, or indeed in developing them".[10]

As examples of *opinio juris* bearing on the minimum standard of treatment, the U.S. President or Secretary of State made the following statements in letters transmitting bilateral investment treaties to the U.S. Senate for its advice and consent:

---

9   For the widespread, actual reliance upon preparatory work by States and counsel, see Stephen M. Schwebel, *May Preparatory Work Be Used to Correct Rather than Confirm the 'Clear' Meaning of a Treaty Provision?*, in THEORY OF INTERNATIONAL LAW AT THE THRESHOLD OF THE 21ST CENTURY: ESSAYS IN HONOUR OF KRZYSZOF SKUBISZEWSKI (Makarczyk ed., 1996), *reprinted in* STEPHEN M. SCHWEBEL, JUSTICE IN INTERNATIONAL LAW, FURTHER SELECTED WRITINGS (2011).

10   Continental Shelf (Libyan Arab Jamahiriya/Malta) 1985 I.C.J. at 13–30.

Paragraph 3 [of Article II of the U.S.-Estonia BIT] guarantees that investment shall be granted 'fair and equitable treatment'. It also prohibits
Parties from impairing, through arbitrary or discriminatory means, the
management, operation, maintenance, use, enjoyment, acquisition,
expansion or disposal of investment. This paragraph sets out a minimum
standard of treatment based on customary international law.[11]

Paragraph 3 [of Article II of the U.S.-Honduras BIT] sets out minimum
standard of treatment based on standards found in customary international law. The obligations to accord 'fair and equitable treatment' and
'full protection and security' are explicitly cited, as is each Party's obligation not to impair, through unreasonable and discriminatory means,
the management, conduct, operation, and sale of covered investments. The
general reference to international law also implicitly incorporates other
fundamental rules of customary international law regarding the treatment of foreign investment....[12]

Thus, the United States has "accepted as law"[13] the proposition that the MST
includes not only fair and equitable treatment but also the prohibition of
impairment of an investment "through arbitrary or discriminatory means" or
"through unreasonable and discriminatory means."

Sources for determining the minimum standard of treatment include the
treaty practice of States, the decisions of international courts and tribunals,
and the general principles of law. These sources are discussed in the sections
that follow.

2.1   States' Treaty Practice

The treaty practice of States may contribute to the establishment of a rule of
customary international law. Comment (i) to the *Restatement (Third) of the
Foreign Relations Law of the United States* provides: "A wide network of similar
bilateral arrangements on a subject may constitute practice and also result in
customary law."[14]

---

11   Letter of Transmittal of the U.S.-Estonia BIT, September 27, 1994.
12   Letter of Transmittal for the U.S.-Honduras BIT, May 23, 2000. Identical language appears
      in the letters of transmittal for the U.S. BITs with Jordan, Bolivia and Bahrain.
13   See the ICJ Statute at Article 38(b) referring to "international custom, as evidence of a
      general practice accepted as law".
14   RESTATEMENT OF THE LAW (THIRD) OF THE FOREIGN RELATIONS LAW OF THE
      UNITED STATES § 102(i), cmt i (1987).

In the famous case of *The Paquete Habana*, the U.S. Supreme Court heavily relied on a range of treaties to establish a rule of customary international law.[15]

As the U.N. International Law Commission put it: "An international convention admittedly establishes rules binding the contracting States only, and based on reciprocity; but it must be remembered that these rules become generalized through the conclusion of other similar conventions containing identical or similar provisions."[16]

In my view, the more than 2,000 BITs in force and some 3,000 signed are the contemporary exemplar of the process by which treaty practice may influence the content of customary international law.[17] This "wide network of similar bilateral arrangements" constitutes remarkably consistent state practice with respect to the duty of States to provide 'fair and equitable treatment'.[18]

As the Tribunal in *Mondev International v. United States of America* stated:

> In their post-hearing submissions, all three NAFTA Parties challenged holdings of the Tribunal in *Pope & Talbot* which find that the content of contemporary international law reflects the concordant provisions of many hundreds of bilateral investment treaties. In particular, attention was drawn to what those three States saw as a failure of the *Pope & Talbot* Tribunal to consider a necessary element of the establishment of a rule of customary international law, namely *opinio juris*. These States appear to question whether the parties to the very large numbers of bilateral investment treaties have acted out of a sense of legal obligation when they include provisions in those treaties such as that for 'fair and equitable' treatment of foreign investment.
>
> The question is entirely legitimate. It is often difficult in international practice to establish at what point obligations accepted in treaties, multilateral or bilateral, come to condition the content of a rule of customary international law binding on States not party to those treaties. Yet the United States itself provides an answer to this question, in contending that, when adopting provisions for fair and equitable treatment and full

---

15   *See generally* The Paquete Habana, 175 U.S. 677 (1900). For example, the case relied on the French treaty of 1900, at 680, the Pakistan treaty of 1932, at 690, etc.

16   Report of the International Law Commission covering the work of the twelfth session, *Yearbook of the International Law Commission* 2 (1960), 145, UN Doc. A/4425.

17   Stephen M. Schwebel, *The Influence of Bilateral Investment Treaties on Customary International Law*, PROC. OF THE 98TH ANN. MEETING OF THE AM. SOC'Y OF INT'L L. (2004).

18   RESTATEMENT OF THE LAW (THIRD) OF THE FOREIGN RELATIONS LAW OF THE UNITED STATES § 102(i), cmt i (1987).

protection and security in NAFTA (as well as in other BITs), the intention was to incorporate principles of customary international law. Whether or not explanations given by a signatory government to its own legislature in the course of ratification or implementation of a treaty can constitute part of the *travaux préparatoires* of the treaty for the purposes of its interpretation, they can certainly shed light on the purposes and approaches taken to the treaty, and thus can evidence *opinio juris*....[19]

Thus, the question is not that of a failure to show *opinio juris* or to amass sufficient evidence demonstrating it. The question rather is: what is the content of customary international law providing for fair and equitable treatment and full protection.

2.2   *Decisions of International Courts and Tribunals*

International tribunals, and counsel pleading before them, regularly refer to and rely upon the prior decisions of other tribunals to establish or confirm a rule of customary international law. For example, in the *ELSI* case before a Chamber of the International Court of Justice, the United States cited multiple awards—as well as highly qualified publicists—to support the proposition that "th[e] international minimum standard" prohibited "arbitrary and unjust treatment".[20] It should be noted that the United States spoke of "arbitrary" treatment being prohibited by the minimum standard—not outrageous treatment in the vein of *Neer.*

According to Amerasinghe, international decisions play "an especially important role in the determination of State practice," because "[t]he processes of juristic reflection in one sense render intelligible the concept of State practices".[21]

2.3   *Other Sources of International Law May Influence the Content of Customary International Law*

As observed in the *Restatement (Third) of the Foreign Relations of the United States:* "Much of international law, whether customary or constituted by agreement, reflects principles analogous to those found in the major legal systems

---

19   *Mondev International Ltd. v. United State of America*, ICSID Case No. ARB(AF)/99/2, Award, October 11, 2002, ¶¶ 110–113 (footnotes omitted).

20   Elettronica Sicula S.p.A. (ELSI) (U.S. v. Italy), Memorial of the United States, 1987 I.C.J. (May 15), at 93.

21   C.F. AMERASINGHE, STATE RESPONSIBILITY FOR INJURIES TO ALIENS 32–33 (1967).

of the world ...".[22] As was stated by the NAFTA tribunal in *ADF Group Inc. and United States of America*, it is "not necessary to assume that the customary international law on treatment of aliens and their property, including investments, is bereft of more general principles or requirements, with normative consequences, in respect of investments, derived from—in the language of *Mondev*—'established sources of international law'."[23]

In its Memorial in *Methanex Corporation and the United States of America*, the United States quoted approvingly the following statement from ¶ 165(2) of the Restatement (Second) of the Foreign Relations of the United States:

> The international standard of justice is the standard required for the treatment of aliens by (a) the applicable principles of international law as established by international custom, judicial and arbitral decisions, and other recognized sources or, in the absence of such applicable principles (b) analogous principles of justice generally recognized by states that have reasonably developed legal systems.[24]

Here too the United States treats judicial and arbitral decisions as a recognized source of international law, in contrast to the line of argument it has mounted since 2001.

3   The Content of the Minimum Standard of Treatment

The content of the MST has been heavily litigated in NAFTA cases, in which each of the factors set out above have been mentioned. NAFTA tribunals have been divided in their understanding and evaluation of the MST. I shall now set out pertinent passages of the leading cases.

3.1   *Mondev v. US*

I was a member of the Tribunal in *Mondev*. My colleagues were exceptionally distinguished jurists: President, Sir Ninian Stephen (former member of the High Court of Australia, former Governor-General of Australia) and James Crawford (another Australian, then Whewell Professor of International Law at

---

22   RESTATEMENT OF THE LAW (THIRD) OF THE FOREIGN RELATIONS LAW OF THE UNITED STATES § 102(l), cmt l (1987).

23   At ¶ 185.

24   *Methanex v. United States*, Memorial of the United States, at 43–44 (quoting RESTATEMENT OF THE LAW (SECOND) OF THE FOREIGN RELATIONS LAW OF THE UNITED STATES § 165(2), cmt l (1987)).

the University of Cambridge, now a Judge of the International Court of Justice) It treated the questions addressed in this opinion at length and in depth. Paragraphs 110–113 of the Award have been reproduced above. Paragraphs 117–125 and paragraph 127 further pertinently provide:

> Thirdly, the vast number of bilateral and regional investment treaties (more than 2000) almost uniformly provide for fair and equitable treatment of foreign investments, and largely provide for full security and protection of investments. Investment treaties run between North and South, and East and West, and between States in these spheres *inter se*. On a remarkably widespread basis, States have repeatedly obliged themselves to accord foreign investment such treatment. In the Tribunal's view, such a body of concordant practice will necessarily have influenced the content of rules governing the treatment of foreign investment in current international law. It would be surprising if this practice and the vast number of provisions it reflects were to be interpreted as meaning no more than the *Neer* Tribunal (in a very different context) meant in 1927.[25]

Thus, the *Mondev* Tribunal cut *Neer* down to size. It continues:

> When a tribunal is faced with the claim by a foreign investor that the investment has been unfairly or inequitably treated or not accorded full protection and security, it is bound to pass upon that claim on the facts and by application of any governing treaty provisions. A judgment of what is fair and equitable cannot be reached in the abstract; it must depend on the facts of the particular case. It is part of the essential business of courts and tribunals to make judgments such as these. In doing so, the general principles referred to in Article 1105(1) and similar provisions must inevitably be interpreted and applied to the particular facts.
>
> That having been said, for the purposes of the present case the Tribunal does not need to resolve all the issues raised in argument and in the written submissions concerning the FTC's interpretation. The United States itself accepted that Article 1105(1) is intended to provide a real measure of protection of investments, and that having regard to its general language and to the evolutionary character of international law, it has evolutionary potential.... At the same time, Article 1105(1) did not give a NAFTA tribunal an unfettered discretion to decide for itself, on a subjective basis, what was 'fair' or 'equitable' in the circumstances of each

---

25   Mondev, supra n. 19.

particular case. While possessing a power of appreciation, the United States stressed, the Tribunal is bound by the minimum standard as established in State practice and in the jurisprudence of arbitral tribunals. It may not simply adopt its own idiosyncratic standard of what is 'fair' or 'equitable' without reference to established sources of law.

The Tribunal has no difficulty in accepting that an arbitral tribunal may not apply its own idiosyncratic standard in lieu of the standard laid down in Article 1105 (1). In light of the FTC's interpretation, and in any event, it is clear that Article 1105 was intended to put to rest for NAFTA purposes a long-standing and divisive debate about whether any such thing as a minimum standard of treatment of investment in international law actually exists. Article 1105 resolves this issue in the affirmative for NAFTA Parties. It also makes it clear that the standard of treatment, including fair and equitable treatment and full protection and security, is to be found by reference to international law, i.e., by reference to the normal sources of international law determining the minimum standard of treatment of foreign investors.[26]

In referring to "the normal sources of international law", the *Mondev* Tribunal thus rejected the contention of the NAFTA Parties that state practice is the sole relevant source.

To this the FTC has added two clarifications which are relevant for present purposes. First, it makes it clear that Article 1105(1) refers to a standard existing under customary international law, and not to standards established by other treaties of the three NAFTA Parties. There is no difficulty in accepting this as an interpretation of the phrase 'in accordance with international law'. Other treaties potentially concerned have their own systems of implementation. Chapter 11 arbitration does not even extend to claims concerning all breaches of NAFTA itself, being limited to breaches of Section A of Chapter 11 and Articles 1503(2) and 1502(3)(a). If there had been an intention to incorporate by reference extraneous treaty standards in Article 1105 and to make Chapter 11 arbitration applicable to them, some clear indication of this would have been expected. Moreover, the phrase 'Minimum standard of treatment' has historically been understood as a reference to a minimum standard under customary international law, whatever controversies there may have been over the content of that standard.

---

26   *Id.*

Secondly, the FTC interpretation makes it clear that in Article 1105(1) the terms "fair and equitable treatment" and "full protection and security" are, in the view of the NAFTA Parties, references to *existing* elements of the customary international law standard and are not intended to add novel elements to that standard. The word 'including'" in paragraph (1) supports that conclusion. To say that these elements are included in the standard of treatment under international law suggests that Article 1105 does not intend to supplement or add to that standard. But it does not follow that the phrase "including fair and equitable treatment and full protection and security" adds nothing to the meaning of Article 1105(1), nor did the FTC seek to read those words out of the article, a process which *would* have involved amendment rather than interpretation. The minimum standard of treatment as applied by tribunals and in State practice in the period prior to 1994 did precisely focus on elements calculated to ensure the treatment described in Article 1105(1).

A reasonable evolutionary interpretation of Article 1105(1) is consistent both with the *travaux*, with normal principles of interpretation and with the fact that, as the Respondent accepted in argument, the terms 'fair and equitable treatment' and 'full protection and security' had their origin in bilateral treaties in the post-war period. In these circumstances the content of the minimum standard today cannot be limited to the content of customary international law as recognised in arbitral decisions in the 1920s.[27]

Again, Mondev inferentially rejects reliance by the NAFTA Parties on *Neer.*

The Respondent noted that there was some common ground between the parties to the present arbitration in respect of the FCT's interpretations, namely, "that the standard adopted in Article 1105 was that as it existed in 1994, the international standard of treatment, as it had developed to that time.... like all customary international law, the international minimum standard has evolved and can evolve.... the sets of standards which make up the international law minimum standard, including principles of full protection and security, apply to investments." Moreover, in their written submissions, both Canada and Mexico expressly accepted this point.

The Tribunal agrees. For the purposes of this Award, the Tribunal need not pass upon all the issues debated before it as to the FTC's interpretations of 31 July 2001. But in its view, there can be no doubt that, by

---

27   *Id.*

interpreting Article 1105(1) to prescribe the customary international law minimum standard of treatment of aliens as the minimum standard of treatment to be afforded to investments of investors of another Party under NAFTA, the term "customary international law" refers to customary international law as it stood no earlier than the time at which NAFTA came into force. It is not limited to the international law of the 19th century or even of the first half of the 20th century, although decisions from that period remain relevant. In holding that Article 1105(1) refers to customary international law, the FTC interpretations incorporate current international law, whose content is shaped by the conclusion of more than two thousand bilateral investment treaties and many treaties of friendship and commerce. Those treaties largely and concordantly provide for 'fair and equitable' treatment of, and for 'full protection and security' for, the foreign investor and his investments. Correspondingly the investments of investors under NAFTA are entitled, under the customary international law which NAFTA Parties interpret Article 1105(1) to comprehend, to fair and equitable treatment and to full protection and security...."[28]

Thus, *Mondev* rejects argumentation of the NAFTA Parties to the effect that BITs do not influence the content of customary international law.

In the *ELSI* case, a Chamber of the Court described as arbitrary conduct that which displays "a willful disregard of due process of law, ... which shocks, or at least surprises, a sense of judicial propriety". It is true that the question there was whether certain administrative conduct was 'arbitrary', contrary to the provisions of an FCN treaty. Nonetheless (and without otherwise commenting on the soundness of the decision itself) the Tribunal regards the Chamber's criterion as useful also in the context of denial of justice, and it has been applied in that context, as the Claimant pointed out. The Tribunal would stress that the word "surprises" does not occur in isolation. The test is not whether a particular result is surprising, but whether the shock or surprise occasioned to an impartial tribunal leads, on reflection, to justified concerns as to the judicial propriety of the outcome, bearing in mind on the one hand that international tribunals are not courts of appeal, and on the other hand that Chapter 11 of NAFTA (like other treaties for the protection of investments) is intended to provide a real measure of protection. In the end the question is whether, at

---

28   *Id.*

an international level and having regard to generally accepted standards of the administration of justice, a tribunal can conclude in the light of all the available facts that the impugned decision was clearly improper and discreditable, with the result that the investment has been subjected to unfair and inequitable treatment. This is admittedly a somewhat open-ended standard, but it may be that in practice no more precise formula can be offered to cover the range of possibilities."[29]

3.2   *ADF Group v. US*

The *ADF* Tribunal in its Award of 2003 quoted and accepted much of the exposition and analysis of the *Mondev* Award in respect of the binding character of the FTC interpretation, the content of the minimum standard, and the irrelevance of *Neer.* Customary international law was to be taken as it stood when NAFTA came into force, not as it may have been in the 1920s. It did not find it necessary to take a position on whether the Claimant was required to show that the Respondent was in breach of specific rules of customary international law.[30]

3.3   *Waste Management II v. Mexico*

In 2004, based on its survey of the prior NAFTA decisions, the *Waste Management v. Mexico II* Tribunal, of which then Professor James Crawford was president, provided this synopsis: "Taken together, the *S.D. Myers, Mondev, ADF* and *Loewen* cases suggest that the minimum standard of treatment of fair and equitable treatment is infringed by conduct attributable to the State and harmful to the claimant if the conduct is arbitrary, grossly unfair, unjust or idiosyncratic, is discriminatory and exposes the claimant to sectional or racial prejudice, or involves a lack of due process leading to an outcome which offends judicial propriety—as might be the case with a manifest failure of natural justice in judicial proceedings or a complete lack of transparency and candour in an administrative process. In applying this standard it is relevant that the treatment is in breach of representations made by the host State which were reasonably relied on by the claimant."[31] As the *Waste Management v. Mexico II* Tribunal further noted: "Both the *Mondev* and *ADF* Tribunals

---

29   *Mondev International Ltd. v. United State of America,* ICSID Case No. ARB(AF)/99/2, Award, October 11, 2002, ¶¶ 117–125 and 127 (footnotes omitted).

30   *ADF Group Inc. and the United States of America,* Award of January 9, 2003. See in particular ¶¶ 193–198.

31   *Waste Management Inc. v. United Mexican States,* Award of April 30, 2004, ¶ 98.

rejected any suggestion that the standard of treatment of a foreign investment set by NAFTA is confined to the kind of outrageous treatment referred to in the *Neer* case...."[32]

It is to be noted that if the conduct is "arbitrary"—simply arbitrary, not "manifestly" arbitrary etc.—it suffices to infringe the minimum standard of treatment.

3.4   *Cargill v. Mexico*

Cargill Corporation v. United Mexican States (2009) embraced an analysis supporting the positions espoused by the NAFTA Parties, in emphatic and extensive terms. Professor David D. Caron was a member of the *Cargill* Tribunal as well as of the *Glamis Gold* Tribunal. The Award in *Glamis Gold* repeats and elaborates the analysis of *Cargill*, frequently using the very same words. Accordingly, quotations of *Cargill* largely subsumed by *Glamis Gold* are omitted in the interest of brevity.

3.5   *Mobil*

The Decision on Liability in *Mobil Investments Canada Inc. & Murphy Oil Corporation v. Canada* (2012) is notable in reverting to the *Neer* approach:

> The fundamentals of the *Neer* standard thus still apply today: to violate the customary international law minimum standard of treatment codified in Article 1105 of the NAFTA, an act must be sufficiently egregious and shocking—a gross denial of justice, manifest arbitrariness, blatant unfairness, a complete lack of due process, evident discrimination, or a manifest lack of reasons—so as to fall below accepted international standards and constitute a breach of Article 1105(1). (...) The standard for finding a breach of the customary international law minimum standard of treatment therefore remains as stringent as it was under *Neer*; it is entirely possible, however that, as an international community, we may be shocked by State actions now that did not offend us previously.[33]

Citing *International Thunderbird*, the tribunal added:

> legitimate expectations relate to an examination under Article 1105(1) in such situations 'where a Contracting Party's conduct creates reasonable

---

32   *Waste Management Inc. v. United Mexican States*, Award of April 30, 2004, ¶ 93.

33   *Mobil Investments Canada Inc. & Murphy Oil Corporation v. Canada ICSID Case No. ARB(AF)*, Decision on Liability and on Principles of Quantum, ¶¶ 135–39, 107.

and justifiable expectations on the part of an investor (or investment) to act in reliance on said conduct....' In this way, a State may be tied to the objective expectations that it creates *in order to induce* investment.[34]

3.6   *Glamis Gold v.* US

The Award in *Glamis Gold, Ltd. and the United States of America* (2009) is fully supportive of the position and analysis maintained by the United States, Canada and Mexico since the 2001 FTC interpretation. It is a sophisticated analysis but, for the reasons stated in respect of the opinion of Judge Jennings as well as my contentions at the end of this essay, it is—however smoothly written—unconvincing.

> There is no disagreement among the State Parties to the NAFTA, nor the Parties to this arbitration, that the requirement of fair and equitable treatment in Article 1105 is to be understood by reference to the customary international law minimum standard of treatment of aliens. Indeed, the Free Trade Commission ("FTC") clearly states, in its binding Notes of Interpretation on July 31, 2001, that "Article 1105(1) prescribes the customary international law minimum standard of treatment of aliens as the minimum standard of treatment to be afforded to investments of investors of another Party."
>
> The question thus becomes: what does this customary international law minimum standard of treatment require of a State Party vis-à-vis investors of another State Party? Is it the same as that established in 1926 in *Neer v. Mexico*? Or has Claimant proven that the standard has "evolved"? If it has evolved, what evidence of custom has Claimant provided to the Tribunal to determine its current scope?
>
> As a threshold issue, the Tribunal notes that it is Claimant's burden to sufficiently answer each of these questions. The State Parties to the NAFTA (at least Canada and Mexico) agree that "the test in *Neer* does continue to apply," though Mexico "also agrees that the standard is relative and that conduct which may not have violated international law [in] the 1920s might very well be seen to offend internationally accepted principles today."
>
> The Tribunal acknowledges that it is difficult to establish a change in customary international law. As Respondent explains, establishment of a rule of customary international law requires: (1) "a concordant practice of a number of States acquiesced in by others," and (2) "a conception that

---

34   *Id.* at 67 (emph. in the original).

the practice is required by or consistent with the prevailing law (*opinio juris*)."

The evidence of such "concordant practice" undertaken out of a sense of legal obligation is exhibited in very few authoritative sources: treaty ratification language, statements of governments, treaty practice (e.g., Model BITs), and sometimes pleadings. Although one can readily identify the practice of States, it is usually very difficult to determine the intent behind those actions. Looking to a claimant to ascertain custom requires it to ascertain such intent, a complicated and particularly difficult task. In the context of arbitration, however, it is necessarily Claimant's place to establish a change in custom.

The Tribunal notes that, although an examination of custom is indeed necessary to determine the scope and bounds of current customary international law, this requirement—repeatedly argued by various State Parties—because of the difficulty in proving a change in custom, effectively freezes the protections provided for in this provision at the 1926 conception of egregiousness."

(In the author's view, this holding of the *Glamis Gold* Tribunal is fundamentally erroneous. The *Neer* Award of 1926, far from establishing customary international law in respect of the treatment of foreign investment, had nothing to do with foreign investment. As Judge Jennings is quoted as observing at the outset of this essay, it rather dealt with the question of whether Mexico was guilty of a denial of justice in its investigation of the circumstances of the murder of an alien.)

Claimant did provide numerous arbitral decisions in support of its conclusion that fair and equitable treatment encompasses a universe of "fundamental" principles common throughout the world that include "the duty to act in good faith, due process, transparency and candor, and fairness and protection from arbitrariness." Arbitral awards, Respondent rightly notes, do not constitute State practice and thus cannot create or prove customary international law. They can however, serve as illustrations of customary international law if they involve an examination of customary international law, as opposed to a treaty-based, or autonomous, interpretation.

This brings the Tribunal to its first task: ascertaining which of the sources argued by Claimant are properly available to instruct the Tribunal on the bounds of "fair and equitable treatment." As briefly mentioned above, the Tribunal notes that it finds two categories of arbitral awards that examine a fair and equitable treatment standard: those that look to define customary international law and those that examine the autonomous language and nuances of the underlying treaty language.

Fundamental to this divide is the treaty underlying the dispute: those treaties and free trade agreements, like the NAFTA, that are to be understood by reference to the customary international law minimum standard of treatment necessarily lead their tribunals to analyze custom; while those treaties with fair and equitable treatment clauses that expand upon, or move beyond, customary international law, lead their reviewing tribunals into an analysis of the treaty language and its meaning, as guided by Article 31(1) of the Vienna Convention.

Ascertaining custom is necessarily a factual inquiry, looking to the actions of States and the motives for and consistency of these actions. By applying an autonomous standard, on the other hand, a tribunal may focus solely on the language and nuances of the treaty language itself and, applying the rules of treaty interpretation, require no party proof of State action of *opinio juris*. This latter practice fails to assist in the ascertainment of custom.

As Article 1105's fair and equitable treatment standard is, as Respondent phrases it, simply "a shorthand reference to customary international law," the Tribunal finds that arbitral decisions that apply an autonomous standard provide no guidance inasmuch as the entire method of reasoning does not bear on an inquiry into custom. The various BITs cited by Claimant may or may not illuminate customary international law; they will prove helpful to this Tribunal's analysis when they seek to provide the same base floor of conduct as the minimum standard of treatment under customary international law; but they will not be of assistance if they include different protections than those provided for in customary international law.

Claimant has agreed with the distinction between customary international law and autonomous treaty standards but argues that, with respect to this particular standard, BIT jurisprudence has "converged with customary international law in this area." The Tribunal finds this to be an over-statement. Certainly, it is possible that some BITs converge with the requirements established by customary international law; there are however, numerous BITs that have been interpreted as going beyond customary international law, and thereby requiring more than that to which the NAFTA State Parties have agreed. It is thus necessary to look to the underlying fair and equitable treatment clause of each treaty, and the reviewing tribunal's analysis of that treaty, to determine whether or not they are drafted with an intent to refer to customary international law.

.... The Tribunal therefore holds that it may look solely to arbitral awards—including BIT awards—that seek to be understood by reference to the customary international law minimum standard of treatment, as opposed to any autonomous standard. The Tribunal thus turns to its second task: determining the scope of the current customary international law minimum standard of treatment, as proven by Claimant.

It appears to this Tribunal that the NAFTA State Parties agree that, at a minimum, the fair and equitable treatment standard is that as articulated in *Neer*:... Whether this standard has evolved since 1926, however, has not been definitively agreed upon. The Tribunal considers two possible types of evolution: (1) that what the international community views as "outrageous" may change over time; and (2) that the minimum standard of treatment has moved beyond what it was in 1926.

The Tribunal finds apparent agreement that the fair and equitable treatment standard is subject to the first type of evolution: a change in the international view of what is shocking and outrageous.

As the *Mondev* tribunal held:

Neer and like arbitral awards were decided in the 1920s, when the status of the individual in international law, and the international protection of foreign investments, were far less developed than they have since come to be. In particular, both the substantive and procedural rights of the individual in international law have undergone considerable development. In light of these developments it is unconvincing to confine the meaning of 'fair and equitable treatment' and 'full protection and security' of foreign investments to what those terms—had they been current at the time—might have meant in the 1920s when applied to the physical security of an alien. To the modern eye, what is unfair or inequitable need not equate with the outrageous or the egregious. In particular, a State may treat foreign investment unfairly and inequitably without necessarily acting in bad faith.

Similarly, this Tribunal holds that the *Neer* standard, when applied with current sentiments and to modern situations, may find shocking and egregious events not considered to reach this level in the past.

As regards the second form of evolution—the proposition that customary international law has moved beyond the minimum standard of treatment of aliens as defined in *Neer*—the Tribunal finds that the evidence provided by Claimant does not establish such evolution. This is evident in the abundant and continued use of adjective modifiers throughout arbitral awards, evidencing a strict standard. *International Thunderbird* used the terms "*gross* denial of justice" and "*manifest* arbitrariness" to describe the acts that it viewed would breach the minimum standard of treatment. *S.D. Myers* would find a breach of Article 1105 when an investor was treated "in *such an unjust or arbitrary* manner." The

Mondev tribunal held: "The test is not whether a particular result is surprising, but whether the *shock or surprise* occasioned to an impartial tribunal leads, on reflection, to justified concerns as to the judicial propriety of the outcome...."

The customary international law minimum standard of treatment is just that, a minimum standard. It is meant to serve as a floor, an absolute bottom, below which conduct is not accepted by the international community. Although the circumstances of the case are of course relevant, the standard is not meant to vary from state to state or investor to investor. The protection afforded by Article 1105 must be distinguished from that provided for in Article 1102 on National Treatment. Article 1102(1) states: "Each Party shall accord to investors of another Party treatment no less favorable than that it accords, in like circumstances, to its own investors...." The treatment of investors under Article 1102 is compared to the treatment the State's own investors receive and thus can vary greatly depending on each State and its practices. The fair and equitable treatment promised by Article 1105 is not dynamic; it cannot vary between nations as thus the protection afforded would have no minimum.

It therefore appears that, although situations may be more varied and complicated today than in the 1920s, the level of scrutiny is the same. The fundamentals of the *Neer* standard thus still apply today: to violate the customary international law minimum standard of treatment codified in Article 1105 of the NAFTA, an act must be sufficiently egregious and shocking—a gross denial of justice, manifest arbitrariness, blatant unfairness, a complete lack of due process, evident discrimination, or a manifest lack of reasons—so as to fall below accepted international standards and constitute a breach of Article 1105(1). The Tribunal notes that one aspect of evolution from *Neer* that is generally agreed upon is that bad faith is not required to find a violation of the fair and equitable treatment standard, but its presence is conclusive evidence of such. Thus, an act that is egregious or shocking may also evidence bad faith, but such bad faith is not necessary for the finding of a violation. The standard for finding a breach of the customary international law minimum standard of treatment therefore remains as stringent as it was under *Neer*; it is entirely possible, however that, as an international community, we may be shocked by State actions now that did not offend us previously.

Respondent argues below that, in reviewing State agency or departmental decisions and actions, international tribunals as well as domestic judiciaries favor deference to the agency so as not to second guess the primary decision-makers or become "science courts." The Tribunal disagrees that domestic deference in national court systems is necessarily applicable to international tribunals. In the present case, the Tribunal finds the standard of deference to already be present in the standard as stated, rather than being additive to that standard. The idea of deference is found in the modifiers "manifest" and "gross" that make this standard a stringent one; it is found in the idea that a breach requires something greater than mere arbitrariness, something that is surprising, shocking, or exhibits a manifest lack of reasoning.

With this thought in mind, the Tribunal turns to the duties that Claimant argues are part of the requirements of a host State per Article 1105: (1) an obligation to protect legitimate expectations through establishment of a transparent and predictable business and legal framework, and (2) an obligation to provide protection from arbitrary measures. As the United States explained in its 1128 submission in *Pope & Talbot*, and as Mexico adopted in its 1128 submission to the *ADF* tribunal: "'fair and equitable treatment' and 'full protection and security' are provided as examples of the customary international law standards incorporated into Article 1105(1) ... The international law minimum standard [of treatment] is an umbrella concept incorporating a set of rules that has crystallized over the centuries into customary international law in specific contexts." The Tribunal therefore finds it appropriate to address, in turn, each of the State obligations Claimant asserts are potential parts of the protection afforded by fair and equitable treatment.

As explained above, the minimum standard of treatment of aliens established by customary international law, and by reference to which the fair and equitable treatment standard of Article 1105(1) is to be understood, is an absolute minimum, a floor below which the international community will not condone conduct. To maintain fair and equitable treatment as an absolute floor, a breach must be based upon objective criteria that apply equally among States and between investors.

The Tribunal notes Respondent's argument that even those expectations that manifest in a contract are insufficient to provide a basis for a breach of the minimum standard of treatment. The Tribunal agrees that mere contract breach, without something further such as denial of justice or discrimination, normally will not suffice to establish a breach of Article 1105. Merely not living up to expectations cannot be sufficient to find a breach of Article 1105 of the NAFTA. Instead, Article 1105(1) requires the evaluation of whether the State made any specific assurance or commitment to the investor so as to induce its expectations.

The Tribunal therefore agrees with *International Thunderbird* that legitimate expectations relate to an examination under Article 1105(1) in such situations "where a Contracting Party's conduct creates reasonable and justifiable expectations on the part of an investor (or investment) to act in reliance on said conduct ..." In this way, a State may be tied to the objective expectations that it creates *in order to induce* investment.

As the Tribunal determines below that no specific assurances were made to induce Claimant's "reasonable and justifiable expectations," the Tribunal need not determine the level, or characteristics, of state action in contradiction of those expectations that would be necessary to constitute a violation of Article 1105.

With respect to the asserted duty to protect investors from arbitrariness, the Tribunal notes Claimant's citations to several NAFTA arbitrations that have found a violation of Article 1105 in arbitrary state action. Claimant cites to *S.D. Myers* for its holding that "a breach of Article 1105 occurs only when it is shown that an investor has been treated in such an unjust and arbitrary manner that the treatment rises to the level that is unacceptable from the international perspective." Similarly, it quotes *International Thunderbird*'s holding that "manifest arbitrariness falling below acceptable international standards" is prohibited under Article 1105.

The Tribunal also notes, however, Respondent's argument that no Chapter 11 tribunal has found that decision-making that appears arbitrary to some parties is sufficient to constitute an Article 1105 violation. In *Mondev*, for instance, the tribunal held: "the test is not whether a particular result is surprising, but whether the shock or surprise occasioned to an impartial tribunal leads, on reflection, to justified concerns as to the judicial propriety of the outcome...." Respondent understands this to be the case because tribunals consistently afford administrative decision-making a high level of deference. Respondent quotes *S.D. Myers* to illustrate this deference: "determination [that Article 1105 has been breached] must be made in light of the high measure of deference that international law generally extends to the right of domestic authorities to regulate matters within their own borders." This, Respondent argues, leads to the result that merely imperfect legislation or regulation does not give rise to State responsibility under customary international law.

The Tribunal finds that, in this situation, both Parties are correct. Previous tribunals have indeed found a certain level of arbitrariness to violate the obligations of a State under the fair and equitable treatment standard. Indeed, arbitrariness that contravenes *the* rule of law, rather than *a* rule of law, would occasion surprise not only from investors, but also from tribunals. This is not a mere appearance of arbitrariness, however—a tribunal's determination that an agency acted in a way with which the tribunal disagrees or that a state passed legislation that the tribunal does not find curative of all of the ills presented; rather, this is a level of arbitrariness that, as *International Thunderbird* put it, amounts to a "gross denial of justice or manifest arbitrariness falling below acceptable international standards."

The Tribunal therefore holds that there is an obligation of each of the NAFTA State Parties inherent in the fair and equitable treatment standard of Article 1105 that they do not treat investors of another State in a *manifestly* arbitrary manner. The Tribunal thus determines that Claimant has sufficiently substantiated its arguments that a duty to protect investors from arbitrary measures exists in the customary international law minimum standard of treatment of aliens; though Claimant has not sufficiently rebutted Respondent's assertions that a finding of arbitrariness requires a determination of some act far beyond the measure's mere illegality, an act so manifestly arbitrary, so unjust and surprising as to be unacceptable from the international perspective.

The Tribunal holds that Claimant has not met its burden of proving that something other than the fundamentals of the *Neer* standard apply today. The Tribunal therefore holds that a violation of the customary international law minimum standard of treatment, as codified in Article 1105 of the NAFTA, requires an act that is sufficiently egregious and shocking—a gross denial of justice, manifest arbitrariness, blatant unfairness, a complete lack of due process, evident discrimination, or a manifest lack of reasons—so as to fall below accepted international standards and constitute a breach of Article 1105. Such a breach may be exhibited by a "gross denial of justice or manifest arbitrariness falling below acceptable international standards;" or the creation by the State of objective expectations *in order to induce* investment and the subsequent repudiation of those expectations. The Tribunal emphasizes that, although bad faith may often be present in such a determination and its presence certainly will be determinative of a violation, a finding of bad faith is not a requirement for a breach of Article 1105 (1).[35]

3.7   *Merrill & Ring v. Canada*

Merrill & Ring Forestry L.P. and the Government of Canada (2010), a NAFTA case administered by ICSID, was adjudicated by a Tribunal composed of Professor

---

35   *Glamis Gold, Ltd. v. United States of America*, UNCITRAL, Award, June 8, 2009, ¶¶ 598–627 (footnotes omitted).

Francisco Orrego Vicuna, President, Professor Kenneth W. Dam (former U.S. Deputy Secretary of State), and J. William Rowley. It sharply differs from *Cargill, Mobil* and *Glamis*, rejects *Neer* and its progeny, and holds that customary international law has evolved to produce a standard that "protects against all such acts and behavior that might infringe a sense of fairness, equity and reasonableness".[36] It merits extended quotation:

> The most complex and difficult question brought to the Tribunal in this case is that concerning fair and equitable treatment. This is so because there is still a broad and unsettled discussion about the proper law applicable to this standard, which ranges from the understanding that it is a free-standing obligation under international law to the belief that the standard is subsumed in customary international law. NAFTA and investment treaty tribunals have had the occasion to discuss this question under different legal frameworks. Under either view, the difficulties associated to this question are further compounded because of the need to determine the specific content of the standard. In addition, in this case there is a particular difficulty in assessing the facts and how they are related or unrelated to the governing law.
>
> The Tribunal first notes that Article 1105(1) provides for the treatment of another Party's investors "in accordance with international law". It goes on to indicate that such treatment includes fair and equitable treatment and full protection and security. Under the methods of interpretation generally accepted under international law, in particular Article 31 of the Vienna Convention on the Law of Treaties, a treaty "shall be interpreted in good faith in accordance with the ordinary meaning to be given to the terms of the treaty in their context and in the light of its object and purpose". Consistent with this use of terms, NAFTA Article 1131(1) directs NAFTA tribunals to decide the issues in dispute in accordance with "this Agreement and applicable rules of international law".
>
> The meaning of international law can only be understood today with reference to Article 38(1) of the Statute of the International Court of Justice, where the sources of international law are identified as international conventions, international custom, general principles of law, and judicial decisions and the teachings of the most highly qualified publicists as a subsidiary means for the determination of the rules of law. The Investor's

---

36   *Merrill & Ring Forestry L.P. and the Government of Canada*, ICSID Case No. UNCT/07/1, Award, March 31, 2010, at ¶ 210.

understanding of the role of Article 38(1) of such Statute in the context of this particular discussion is correct. In fact, the reference that Articles 1105(1) and 1131(1) make to "international law" must be understood as a reference to the sources of this legal order as a whole, not just one of them.

Had a more limited meaning been intended it would have had to be specifically identified in the terms of the Agreement, which was not the case. The Max Planck Encyclopedia of Public International Law has concluded in discussing the minimum treatment standard that its development "has been through customary international law, judicial and arbitration decisions, and treaties".

To the extent relevant, it is thus possible for this Tribunal to examine various sources of international law in the effort to identify the precise content of this standard. Treaties and international conventions, however, are not of great help to this end, as for the most part, they also contain rather general references to fair and equitable treatment and full protection and security without further elaboration. This is the case with most bilateral investment treaties and multilateral instruments. More important, besides the NAFTA Agreement itself, there does not appear to be in this matter relevant treaties to which all three NAFTA members are parties, which is where the standard could have been spelled out in greater detail. This leaves customary international law as the other principal source to be applied.

The Tribunal must note that general principles of law also have a role to play in this discussion. Even if the Tribunal were to accept Canada's argument to the effect that good faith, the prohibition of arbitrariness, discrimination and other questions raised in this case are not standalone obligations under Article 1105(1) or international law, and might not be a part of customary law either, these concepts are to a large extent the expression of general principles of law and hence also a part of international law. Each question will have to be addressed on its own merits, as some might be closely related to such principles while other issues are not. Good faith and the prohibition of arbitrariness are no doubt an expression of such general principles and no tribunal today could be asked to ignore these basic obligations of international law. The availability of a secure legal environment has a close connection too to such principles and transparency, while more recent, appears to be fast approaching that standard.

The same holds true for the role of the subsidiary sources indicated above. Judicial decisions, while not a source of the law in themselves, are a fundamental tool for the interpretation of the law and have contributed to its clarification and development. The teaching of highly qualified publicists has a similar role. The fact that both parties have made extensive use of the jurisprudence and the views of writers in their pleadings is sufficient evidence to demonstrate this role. Here again, cases and writers have to be considered on their own merits, as some might be related to different legal frameworks and applicable law. Yet, on the whole, they all contribute one way or the other to the same end of identifying the content of customary law and other sources.

The jurisprudence of NAFTA tribunals has dealt directly and indirectly with the question whether fair and equitable treatment is linked to a particular source of international law, notably customary law, or is a concept that can be applied in some autonomous manner. In linking fair and equitable treatment with the requirement of transparency under international law, but not identifying a specific source of this requirement, the *Metalclad* tribunal appears to have relied on some kind of autonomous role of fair and equitable treatment, a view that was not shared by the reviewing court. This also appears to have been the case of *S.D. Myers* in emphasizing the relationship between fair and equitable treatment and international law generally. These interpretations prompted the Free Trade Commission Notes of Interpretation of July 31, 2001, noted above, to the effect of linking fair and equitable treatment with customary law only and to the effect of de-linking it from breaches of other NAFTA articles or separate treaties.

While NAFTA tribunals have thereafter followed the FTC Interpretation in the light of its binding character, as provided for in Article 1131(2), the first major question as to the meaning of customary international law in this matter, is whether the customary international law minimum standard of treatment of aliens has been frozen in time since the 1920s or has evolved accordingly with current international law. *Mondev* and *ADF*, while accepting that fair and equitable treatment had to be understood within customary international law, favored a dynamic interpretation of the content of this source, the first in conjunction with the role of investment treaties and the second, it appears, more generally on state practice, judicial and arbitral case law or other sources of customary or general international law. This evolutionary approach was also endorsed by *Waste Management II* and *Gami*.

The second major question which the Tribunal requires to address is the meaning of customary international law regarding fair and equitable treatment and full protection and security. And as to this, the Tribunal is mindful of the FTC Interpretation referred to above, as well as Canada's *Statement of Implementation*, which understood Article 1105 as a minimum standard of treatment under customary law.

However, the binding character of the FTC Interpretation does not mean that that interpretation necessarily reflects the present state of customary and international law. As the Investor has argued, the FTC Interpretation seems in some respect to be closer to an amendment of the treaty, than a strict interpretation. In any event, the Tribunal is mindful of the evolutionary nature of customary international law, as discussed below, which provides scope for the interpretation of Article 1105(1), even in the light of the Free Trade Commission's 2001 interpretation.

In spite of arguments to the contrary, there appears to be a shared view that customary international law has not been frozen in time and that it continues to evolve in accordance with the realities of the international community. No legal system could endure in stagnation. The issue is then to establish in which direction customary law has evolved. State practice and *opinio juris* will be the guiding beacons of this evolution.

Canada has maintained that, to the extent that an evolution might have taken place, it must be proven that it has occurred since 2001, when the FTC Interpretation was issued, and this almost certainly has not happened. Such a view is unconvincing. The FTC Interpretation itself does not refer to the specific content of customary law at a given moment and it is not an interpretative note of such content. Accordingly, the matter needs to be examined in the light of the evolution of customary law over time.

The concept of a minimum standard of treatment of aliens was born over a century ago. After 1840, about sixty claims tribunals were established to resolve claims by foreign citizens. The concept became paramount in the context of the work of international claims commissions, particularly as a result of the work of the Mexico-United States Claims Commission. This is how it came to be identified with the oft-cited *Neer* case, which has been paramount in Canada's pleadings in other NAFTA cases. The Tribunal notes, however, that that decision has not been invoked by Canada in the instant case, perhaps because of its contention that arbitral awards do not form part of customary international law.

The Commission in the *Neer* case referred to a breach of the minimum standard of treatment of aliens as requiring treatment that amounts "to bad faith, to willful neglect of duty, or to an insufficiency of governmental action so far short of international standards that every reasonable and impartial man would readily recognize its insufficiency". A few other historical cases applied that or a similarly worded standard in connection with treatment to aliens.

The Tribunal notes, however, that all such cases were dealing with situations concerning due process of law, denial of justice and physical mistreatment, and only marginally with matters relating to business, trade or investments. This was also the case of the International Court of Justice decision in *ELSI*. This oft-cited decision also set a high threshold requiring "wilful disregard of due process of law, an act which shocks, or at least surprises, a sense of judicial propriety".

In the NAFTA context, a number of tribunals have adopted that demanding standard. *Pope & Talbot*, in particular, applied the *Neer* standard to conduct that would "shock and outrage every reasonable citizen in Canada". The same holds true of the more recent *Loewen* case, where a NAFTA tribunal identified the minimum standard with "manifest injustice in the sense of lack of due process leading to an outcome which offends a sense of justice ...". Similarly, the *Thunderbird* tribunal required a finding of conduct that amounts "to gross denial of justice or manifest arbitrariness falling below acceptable international standards" for there to be a breach of the standard.

Waste Management also identified unfair and inequitable treatment with conduct that is arbitrary, grossly unfair, unjust or idiosyncratic which, in so far as it also encompasses questions of due process, leads to an outcome which "offends judicial propriety". Even before the FTC Notes of Interpretation the *S.D. Myers* tribunal required unjust or arbitrary treatment unacceptable from the international perspective.

It is also quite evident that NAFTA jurisprudence has stiffened since the FTC Interpretation. For example, the recent *Glamis Gold* decision relied on the *Neer* Standard requiring an act which is "egregious" and "shocking".

The approach of the *Neer Commission* and of other tribunals which dealt with due process may best be described as the first track of the evolution of the so-called minimum standard of treatment. In fact, as international law matured and began to focus on the rights of individuals, the minimum standard became a part of the international law of human rights, applicable to aliens and nationals alike. This evolution led to major international conventions on human rights as well as to the development of rules of customary law in this field. A second track, which shall be discussed below, is also discernable insofar as it concerns business, trade and investment.

The early work of the International Law Commission on the principles of international law governing state responsibility was well aware of the evolution that characterized customary law in this matter, gradually evidenced by the increasing obsolescence of the traditional (first track) standard of minimum treatment in the light of different and more recent standards. Similarly, the Asian African Legal Consultative Committee concluded in 1961 that the "minimum standard of treatment" had become outmoded and that, in the context of human rights, what mattered was "fair treatment" to nationals and foreigners alike.

The work of highly qualified writers and associated codification efforts also patently reflected the evolution that was taking place. Although issues concerning the minimum standard of treatment (particularly regarding questions of due process) were prominent in the first decades of last century, particularly in Borchard, the early approach was subject to criticism in the work of the International Law Commission on State Responsibility in the late 1950s and early 1960s. Thereafter it has been scarcely mentioned in the principal works concerning the codification of the law of state responsibility, particularly the draft articles prepared by Baxter and Sohn and, more recently, the Commentary on the Articles on State Responsibility approved by the United Nations General Assembly on the basis of the draft of the International Law Commission.

This development was indicative of the fact that state practice was increasingly seen as being inconsistent with the first track concept of an "international minimum standard." State practice was even less supportive of the standard referred to in the *Neer* case. And in the absence of a widespread and consistent state practice in support of a rule of customary international law there is no *opinio juris* either. No general rule of customary international law can thus be found which applies the *Neer* standard, beyond the strict confines of personal safety, denial of justice and due process.

As foreshadowed above, just as there was a first track concerning the evolution of the minimum standard of treatment of aliens in the limited context indicated, there was also a second track that concerned specifically the treatment of aliens in relation to business, trade and investments. This other standard, which was much more liberal, is evidenced by the tendency of states to support the claims of their citizens in the ambit of diplomatic protection with an open mind, and without requiring a showing of "outrageous" treatment before doing so. Parallel to the development of this second track, diplomatic protection gradually gave way to specialized regimes for the protection of foreign investments and other matters.

The digest of cases concerning state responsibility in respect of acts of legislative, administrative and other state organs, published by the United Nations Secretariat in 1964 unequivocally illustrates a new liberal

approach. Indeed, a host of successful claims were made without conceptual restrictions dealing with interference with and annulment of private rights, the breach of concession contracts by the state, acquired
rights under the law in force at the time of the investment, the entitlement to money wrongfully withheld, the entitlement to the value of
money orders, and the refusal to grant an export permit. In many
instances, it was the commissions, courts or tribunals that had to make a
determination on the applicable legal principles. This is another good
reason why judicial decisions, as a subsidiary means for the determination of the rules of law, are not lightly to be dismissed.

The trend towards liberalization of the standard applicable to the
treatment of business, trade and investments continued unabated over
several decades and has yet not stopped. The examination of claims
brought by many governments for settlement by agreement is also illus-
trative of such open-minded standards, including all kinds of property,
rights and interests. The Iran-United States Claims Tribunal has also significantly contributed to this trend.

Conduct which is unjust, arbitrary, unfair, discriminatory or in violation of due process has also been noted by NAFTA tribunals as constituting a breach of fair and equitable treatment, even in the absence of bad
faith or malicious intention on the part of the state. Transparency as
noted was unsuccessfully linked to this concept and legitimate expecta-
tion has been discussed in several cases, although not endorsed on
questions of fact and evidence.

State practice with respect to the standard for the treatment of aliens
in relation to business, trade and investments, while varied and sometimes erratic, has shown greater consistency than in respect of the first
track, as it has generally endorsed an open and non-restricted approach
to the applicable standard to the treatment of aliens under international
law. At the same time, it shows that the restrictive *Neer* standard has not
been endorsed or has been much qualified. The parties have extensively
discussed whether the customary law standard might have converged
with the fair and equitable treatment standard, but convergence is not
really the issue. The situation is rather one in which the customary law
standard has led to and resulted in establishing the fair and equitable
treatment standard as different stages of the same evolutionary process.

A requirement that aliens be treated fairly and equitably in relation to
business, trade and investment is the outcome of this changing reality
and as such it has become sufficiently part of widespread and consistent
practice so as to demonstrate that it is reflected today in customary

international law as *opinio juris*. In the end, the name assigned to the standard does not really matter. What matters is that the standard protects against all such acts or behavior that might infringe a sense of fairness, equity and reasonableness. Of course, the concepts of fairness, equitableness and reasonableness cannot be defined precisely: they require to be applied to the facts of each case. In fact, the concept of fair and equitable treatment has emerged to make possible the consideration of inappropriate behavior of a sort, which while difficult to define, may still be regarded as unfair, inequitable or unreasonable.

In the context of the FTC Interpretation, the Tribunal accepts that it cannot be said that fair and equitable treatment is a free-standing obligation under international law and, as concluded in *Loewen*, its application will be related to a finding that the obligation is part of customary law. As to this latter point, Canada has argued that the existence of the rule must be proven. But against the backdrop of the evolution of the minimum standard of treatment discussed above, the Tribunal is satisfied that fair and equitable treatment has become a part of customary law.

The Tribunal also notes that if the FTC Interpretation was construed so as to narrow the protection against unfair and inequitable treatment to an international minimum standard requiring outrageous conduct of some kind, then consistency would demand that the same standard be followed in respect of such claims made by the NAFTA States in respect of the conduct of other countries affecting business, trade or investments interests of their citizens abroad. Yet, this is not the case under current international practice. Customary international law cannot be tailor made to fit different claimants in different ways. To do so would be to countenance an unacceptable double standard.

In conclusion, the Tribunal finds that the applicable minimum standard of treatment of investors is found in customary international law and that, except for cases of safety and due process, today's minimum standard is broader than that defined in the *Neer* case and its progeny. Specifically, this standard provides for the fair and equitable treatment of alien investors within the confines of reasonableness. The protection does not go beyond that required by customary law, as the FTC has emphasized. Nor, however, should protected treatment fall short of the customary law standard."[37]

---

37   *Id.* ¶¶ 182–213 (footnotes omitted).

3.8   *Bilcon v. Canada*

William R. Clayton et al. & Bilcon Corporation of Delaware v. The Government of Canada (2015), a NAFTA case administered by the Permanent Court of Arbitration, ("Bilcon"), under the presidency of Bruno Simma, former Judge of the International Court of Justice, also declined to interpret customary international law to reflect *Neer.* It took a view of the content of contemporary customary international law closer to that of *Merrill & Ring.*

> NAFTA Article 1105 has by now been the subject of considerable analysis and interpretation by numerous arbitral tribunals. The Tribunal in the present case is guided by these earlier cases, particularly the formulation of the international minimum standard by the *Waste Management* Tribunal.
>
> The disputants in the present case both agree that the FTC Notes [of Interpretation on Article 1105] are binding, although they disagree on their interpretation. Their disagreement concerns the relationship between the minimum standard of international law and the concepts of "fair and equitable treatment" and "full protection and security", particularly the question whether the Tribunal can look at other sources of international law beyond the FTC Notes to shed light on the meaning of Article 1105.
>
> According to the Investors, the FTC Notes are only one element that the Tribunal should use, whereas Canada took the view that the Tribunal was limited to the authentic interpretation of the fair and equitable treatment standard provided by the FTC. The Tribunal agrees with Canada on this point. In light of the FTC Notes and in the specific context of NAFTA Chapter Eleven in which this Tribunal operates, "fair and equitable treatment" and "full protection and security" cannot be regarded as "autonomous" treaty norms that impose additional requirements above and beyond what the minimum standard requires.
>
> NAFTA Article 1105 is, then, identical to the minimum international standard. The crucial question—on which the Parties diverge—is what is the content of the contemporary international minimum standard that the tribunal is bound to apply. NAFTA awards make it clear that the international minimum standard is not limited to conduct by host states that is outrageous. The contemporary minimum international standard involves a more significant measure of protection.
>
> Many tribunals have reviewed the historical development of the international minimum standard, so that the present Tribunal can focus on the aspects that are particularly important for the present case. The starting point is generally the *Neer* case....

The NAFTA tribunal in *Glamis* considered that the *Neer* articulation is still the standard, although notions may have changed about what in the circumstances constitutes outrageous conduct.

NAFTA tribunals have, however, tended to move away from the position more recently expressed in *Glamis*, and rather move towards the view that the international minimum standard has evolved over the years towards greater protection for investors. Thus, the NAFTA tribunal in *ADF Group* in 2003 held that the customary international law referred to in Article 1105(1) is not "frozen in time" and that the minimum standard of treatment does evolve. The tribunal in *Merrill & Ring*, in 2010, referred to practice, decisions and commentary within both NAFTA and in the wider world....

At the same time, the international minimum standard exists and has evolved in the direction of increased investor protection precisely because sovereign states—the same ones constrained by the standard— have chosen to accept it. States have concluded that the standard protects their own nationals in other countries and encourages the inflow of visitors and investment.

Three additional considerations are relevant in applying the international minimum standard. First, third-party adjudicators must, in applying the international minimum standard, take into account that domestic authorities may have more familiarity with the factual and domestic legal complexities of a situation. Secondly, domestic authorities may also enjoy distinctive kinds of legitimacy, such as being elected or accountable to elected authorities. Thirdly, the NAFTA parties have expressly chosen not only to provide a third-party dispute settlement machinery, but to make it directly accessible to investors. Third-party adjudicators may have their own advantages including independence and detachment from domestic pressures....

In order to strike an appropriate balance and taking into account the FTC Notes, a number of NAFTA tribunals have attempted to identify a "threshold of seriousness" that an alleged breach of equity, fairness or law must attain before constituting a breach of the international minimum standard. Many NAFTA tribunals have shared the emerging consensus that the *Neer* standard of indisputably outrageous misconduct is no longer applicable, but there is no consensus yet on a formulation that best suits the modern evolution of the standard. For example, the *S.D. Myers* tribunal found that the investor must have been treated in "such an unjust or arbitrary manner that the treatment rises to the level that is unacceptable from the international perspective". It also noted that a determination of a breach "must be made in light of the high measure of deference that international law generally extends to the right of domestic authorities to regulate matters within their own borders".

The Tribunal in the present case agrees that there is indeed a high threshold for Article 1105 to apply. The language of Article 1105 itself is the necessary reference point in interpreting the international minimum standard. The search is to determine whether there has been a denial of "fair and equitable treatment" and "full protection and security". According to the FTC Notes, NAFTA tribunals are bound to interpret and apply the standard in accordance with customary international law. In interpreting the international minimum standard, the Tribunal also drew guidance from earlier NAFTA Chapter Eleven decisions.

The formulation of the "general standard for Article 1105" by the *Waste Management* Tribunal is particularly influential, and a number of other tribunals have applied its formulation of the international minimum standard based on its reading of NAFTA authorities: ...

While no single arbitral formulation can definitively and exhaustively capture the meaning of Article 1105, the Tribunal finds this quote from *Waste Management* to be a particularly apt one. Acts or omissions constituting a breach must be of a serious nature. The *Waste Management* formulation applies intensifying adjectives to certain items—but by no means all of them—in its list of categories of potentially nonconforming conduct. The formulation includes "grossly" unfair, "manifest" failure of natural justice and "complete" lack of transparency.

The list conveys that there is a high threshold for the conduct of a host state to rise to the level of a NAFTA Article 1105 breach, but that there is no requirement in all cases that the challenged conduct reaches the level of shocking or outrageous behaviour. The formulation also recognises the requirement for tribunals to be sensitive to the facts of each case, the potential relevance of reasonably relied-on representations by a host state, and a recognition that injustice in either procedures or outcomes can constitute a breach.[38]

Once again, a leading arbitration tribunal rejected the *Neer* criterion of "shocking or outrageous" conduct. The Tribunal continues

On the facts, the *Waste Management* tribunal concluded that Mexico had not breached Article 1105. In setting out its persuasive test for breach

---

38   *William Ralph Clayton, William Richard Clayton, Douglas Clayton, Daniel Clayton and Bilcon of Delaware, INC. v. Canada*, UNCITRAL, Award, March 17, 2015, at ¶¶ 427–456, 577–603 (footnotes omitted).

of the international minimum standard, the tribunal noted *obiter* that the breach of reasonably relied-on expectations could be a relevant factor—but concluded that no such representations had been made by the Mexican authorities. The tribunal's qualifier that the investor needs to have 'reasonably relied' on the representations is important. The *Glamis* tribunal refers to 'objective expectations *in order to induce* investment and the subsequent repudiation of those expectations'. The *ADF* tribunal suggests that only representations made by authorized officials qualify for consideration in this context.

In the reasons that follow, the Tribunal will review the various aspects of the Investors' claim that there has been a breach of the international minimum standard. Even though the Tribunal by no means sustained all of these contentions, it finds that Canada breached Article 1105. This finding rests on the following factual and legal determinations.

First, the Investors understood that they would only obtain environmental permission if the project satisfied the requirements of the laws of federal Canada and Nova Scotia. They expected, however, that absent any change in the federal or provincial law, the project site was not effectively zoned against development, and that their project would be assessed on the merits of its environmental soundness in accordance with the same legal standards applied to applicants generally.

Secondly, the Investors reasonably relied on specific encouragements at the political and technical level to pursue the project not only in Nova Scotia but in the specific site they chose.

Thirdly, these encouragements contributed to the Investors' decision to not only proceed with their business plans, but to invest very substantive corporate resources—including several millions of dollars—in good faith to obtain and present an Environmental Impact Statement.

Fourthly, the JRP, by its own acknowledgment, adopted an unprecedented approach. This approach was inimical to the proponents having any real chance of success based on an assessment of their individual project on its merits in accordance with the laws in force at the time.

Fifthly, this "community core values" approach of the JRP was open to at least four possible interpretations. On any plausible interpretation, it was highly problematic in light of the applicable law and facts of the case. The Investors were given no reasonable notice that the JRP was going to adopt this unique approach and therefore had no opportunity to seek to clarify or contest it.

Sixthly, the "community core values" approach of the JRP was the decisive and overriding consideration. The JRP did not carry out its mandate to conduct a "likely significant effects after mitigation" analysis to the whole range of potential project effects, as required by the *CEAA*. The JRP thus arrived at its conclusions under both the laws of federal Canada and Nova Scotia without having fully discharged a crucial dimension of its mandated task. The ultimate decision makers in the governments of federal Canada and Nova Scotia were not provided with all the information that could have provided a proper foundation from which to arrive at their own final conclusions.

In the result, the Investors were encouraged to engage in a regulatory approval process—costing millions of dollars and other corporate resources—that was in retrospect unwinnable from the outset, even though the Investors were specifically encouraged by government officials and the laws of federal Canada to believe that they could succeed on the basis of the individual merits of their case.

The approach by the JRP that constitutes a breach of Article 1105 is not merely a matter of disputed judgments interpreting grey areas of the law, weighing contested points of evidence, or exercising scientific judgment. In the end, the JRP's decision was effectively to impose a moratorium on projects of the category involved here—a kind of zoning decision.

The reasonable expectations of the investor are a factor to be taken into account in assessing whether the host state breached the international minimum standard of fair treatment under Article 1105 of NAFTA. In this context, the Tribunal will review what the Investors could reasonably expect in their interactions with officials of federal Canada and Nova Scotia (and the legal and policy framework that existed at the time), in light of the general and specific encouragements Bilcon received to invest....

The official public policy of Nova Scotia has been to welcome investment in mining. This official welcome has extended to foreign investors, to tidewater developments (projects on or near the coastline taking advantage of Nova Scotia's access to markets through ocean transport) and to the extraction of aggregate for construction purposes.

...

As both Parties agree, it was ultimately a set of decisions taken by the Governments of federal Canada and Nova Scotia—not the JRP Report itself—that led to the rejection of the Investors' project. The Tribunal shall accordingly deal with two related issues discussed by the Parties— the relationship of the decisions at both levels of Government and the level of independent scrutiny that these Governments were required to exercise in reviewing the JRP's recommendations.

Could the other part of the JRP's mandate, under the laws of Nova Scotia, justify or render moot conduct that would ordinarily be contrary to federal Canada law?

.... The Tribunal has already identified many problems with the adoption of the "community core values" approach, including lack of fair notice in this particular case, that extend to its adoption under the laws of Nova Scotia as well as federal Canada. Let it be supposed, however, for the sake of argument, that the JRP would and could still have recommended against the project under Nova Scotia law pursuant to a "community core values" approach supposedly permitted under Nova Scotia law. The fact would remain that the JRP might still have concluded that the project, at least with mitigation measures recommended by the JRP, passed muster under the federal Canada environmental law framework. With the benefit of a report compliant with the CEAA requirements, and a positive recommendation from the JRP on the federal Canada track, Nova Scotia decision-makers might have ultimately exercised their own discretion in favor of approving the project. Federal Canada officials might have concurred with the proponent in trying to persuade Nova Scotia officials of the merits of approving the project, even in the face of a negative recommendation from the JRP based on "community core values"....

A positive decision on the federal Canada track could have simplified and reduced Bilcon's challenges in other ways.... At each level, decision-makers could in the alternative have determined that the broad public interest in all the circumstances warranted proceeding—even if some significant adverse effects would likely still occur, even if all conditions concerning mitigation were observed....

[...]

The Tribunal has referred to the *Waste Management* epitome of the minimum standard and will now specifically apply it to the facts of this case.

The *Waste Management* standard calls for a consideration of representations made by the host state which an investor relied on to its detriment. What is needed are specific representations, rather than abstract references to the general legal framework in relation to an investment or general statements about the attractiveness of an investment destination. In the present case, they were very clear, repeated encouragements by authorities of Nova Scotia that Bilcon was welcome to pursue its coastal quarry and marine terminal project, including at the specific Whites Point location. All the relevant encouragement was in the context of Bilcon being required to present a project that would comply with federal and provincial laws concerning the environment. There was no indication in either the encouragements from government or in the laws themselves that the Whites Point area was a "no go" zone for projects of the kind Bilcon was pursuing, regardless of their individual environmental merits, carefully and methodically assessed.

The *Waste Management* standard calls for a consideration of procedural ands well as substantive fairness. Bilcon was denied a fair opportunity to know the case it had to meet. It had no reason to expect, under the law or any notice provided by the JRP, that "community core values" would be an overriding factor; that this factor would pre-empt a thorough "likely significant adverse effects after mitigation" analysis of the whole range of project effects; and that this factor would contain elements that would effectively preclude any real possibility that an application could succeed, even if Bilcon showed in each and every respect mentioned in the EIS Guidelines that the project would, after mitigation, likely have no significant adverse effects on environmental, social and economic conditions. Bilcon in fact submitted extensive expert evidence to address the issues raised in the EIS Guidelines, including social effects. Bilcon could not be faulted for failing in its initial submissions to anticipate the unprecedented approach that the JRP articulated in its final report. As for the JRP hearings themselves, the Tribunal has noted the relative lack of interest displayed by the JRP in hearing from the experts Bilcon had assembled—devoting to Bilcon's experts only 90 minutes out of 90 hours of the hearing (less than 2 percent of the total hearing time).

The *Waste Management* test mentions arbitrariness. The Tribunal finds that the conduct of the joint review was arbitrary. The JRP effectively created, without legal authority or fair notice to Bilcon, a new standard of assessment rather than fully carrying out the mandate defined by the applicable law, including the requirement under the *CEAA* to carry out a thorough "likely significant adverse effects after mitigation" analysis.

Viewing the actions of Canada as a whole, it was unjust for officials to encourage coastal mining projects in general and specifically encourage the pursuit of the project at the Whites Point site, and then, after a massive expenditure of effort and resources by Bilcon on that basis, have other officials effectively determine that the area was a "no go" zone for this kind of development rather than carrying out the lawfully prescribed evaluation of its individual environmental merits.

Canada is one entity for the purposes of NAFTA responsibility. There is a saying that sometimes "the left hand does not know what the right hand is doing". For the purposes of state responsibility, the combined impact of its left hand and right hand can be determinative even if the actions of either in isolation do not rise to the level of a breach. In this case there were opportunities for federal Canada to harmonize its deliberations. Federal Canada as well as Nova Scotia were able to provide input to the JRP. Both had the later opportunity to address its problematic aspects of the JRP Report.

The *Waste Management* standard involves a high threshold before conduct will be considered as rising to the level of international responsibility under NAFTA. From the Tribunal's perspective, mere error in legal or factual analysis, is by no means sufficient to rise to that threshold. However, the Tribunal considers the breach here to rise to that threshold, in light of: the Investors' reasonable expectations and major consequent investment of resources and reputation in a process that is the most rigorous, public and extensive kind provided under the laws of Canada; the fact that the JRP's distinctive approach in adopting the concept of community core values was not proceeded by reasonable notice; and the fact that the approach of the JRP departed in fundamental ways from the standard of evaluation required by the laws of Canada rather than merely being controversial in matters of detailed application.

The Tribunal notes that this case involves environmental regulation, and that there is substantial concern among the public and state authorities that investor-state treaty provisions not be used as obstacles to the maintenance and implementation of high standards of protection of environmental integrity. The Tribunal therefore wishes to make several points very clear.

The Tribunal notes the statement in the Preamble of NAFTA according to which the Parties are resolved to "ensure a predictable commercial framework for business planning and investment,", but the same Preamble also refers to a resolve to "strengthen the development and enforcement of environmental law.". NAFTA places no inherent limits on how demanding the standards of a domestic statute may be. The concepts of promoting both economic development and environmental integrity are integrated into the Preamble's endorsement of the principle of sustainable development.

Environmental regulations, including assessments, will inevitably be of great relevance for many kinds of major investments in modern times. The mere fact that environmental regulation is involved does not make investor protection inapplicable. Were such an approach to be adopted— and States Parties could have chosen to do so—there would be a very major gap in the scope of the protection given to investors. The Laws of Canada and Nova Scotia, as well as the NAFTA itself, expressly acknowledge that economic development and environmental integrity can not only be reconciled, but can be mutually reinforcing.

In arriving at its conclusion in this case, the Tribunal is not suggesting that there is the slightest issue with the level of protection for the environment provided in the laws of Canada and Nova Scotia. Each is free under NAFTA to adopt laws that are as demanding as they choose in exercising their sovereign authority. Canada and Nova Scotia have both adopted high standards. There can be absolutely no issue with that under Chapter Eleven of NAFTA. The Tribunal's concern is actually that the rigorous and comprehensive evaluation defined and prescribed by the laws of Canada was not in fact carried out.

It was open under NAFTA for legislatures to adopt different environmental assessment standards and processes than they had in place at the time of the Bilcon Project. Nova Scotia lawmakers could, for example, have provided that local governments must approve the project or that it could not proceed without support in a local referendum. Federal Canada could by legislation have relaxed its requirement that to be assessable, an effect must have a biophysical pathway.

The problem in this case is whether the Investors' application was assessed in a manner that complied with the laws that Canada and Nova Scotia actually chose to adopt. The Tribunal has considered all the evidence from participants and experts on both sides, and concluded—, based on the reports of two highly experienced and respected experts in Canadian environmental law—that there was in fact a fundamental departure from the methodology required by Canadian and Nova Scotia law.

The Tribunal would further reiterate that under the laws of Canada and Nova Scotia, social impacts can be within the scope of a valid assessment. Furthermore, the value placed by members of a community on distinctive components of an ecosystem can be taken into account in an assessment under the laws of Canada and Nova Scotia. The Tribunal has respectfully taken issue with only the distinct, unprecedented and unexpected approach taken by the JRP to "community core values" in this particular case.

This Tribunal also wishes to be very clear that it has not purported in these reasons to conduct its own environmental assessment, in substitution for that of the JRP. The Tribunal at this stage simply holds that the applicant was not treated in a manner consistent with Canada's own laws, including the core evaluative standard under the CEAA and the standards of fair notice required by Canadian public administrative law. The Tribunal is not here deciding what the actual outcome should have been, including what mitigation measures should have been prescribed if the JRP had carried out the mandate contained in applicable laws.

The Investors' position is that, properly considered, their application would have led to a project that would have promoted the economic and social vitality of a local community; that would have helped to diversify the economy at a time when some traditional industries were suffering; and that it was designed to be carried out in a manner that would not be deleterious in areas such as human safety, the protection of animal and plant life, the continuation of traditional economic activities and the aesthetics of the area. The basis of liability under Chapter Eleven is that, after all the specific encouragement the Investors and their investment had received from government to pursue the project, and after all the resources placed in preparing and presenting their environmental assessment case, the Investors and their investment were not afforded a fair *opportunity* to have the specifics of that case considered, assessed and decided in accordance with applicable laws.[39]

3.9   *Mesa Power v. Canada*

Mesa Power v. Canada (2016), a NAFTA proceeding administered by the PCA and chaired by Gabrielle Kaufmann-Kohler, concluded that "arbitrariness" or "arbitrary" measures by a State breach Article 1105 (it did not speak of "manifestly arbitrary measures"); it discounted the modern pertinence of the *Neer* "outrageous" standard; it endorsed *Waste Management's* synopsis; but in some other respects it inclines in favor of the thrust of views of the NAFTA Parties. It held:

> The Claimant acknowledges that on 31 July 2001, the NAFTA Free Trade Commission issued the FTC note, which addressed (*inter alia*) Article 1105. However, it argues that the FTC Note is not the exclusive source of interpretation for Article 1105: "the Tribunal should consider itself at liberty to interpret the meaning of 'fair and equitable treatment.' as contained in NAFTA Article 1105 as an autonomous standard in accordance with all the normal and well-accepted sources of international law—not just customary international law." Further, the Claimant argues that the FTC Note is not a *bona fide* interpretation of Article 1105 and amounts to an

---

39   *Id.* at ¶¶ 427–456, 577–603 (footnotes omitted).

amendment of the NAFTA with the result that the FTC Note "has no legal force or effect." Should the Tribunal consider itself bound by the FTC Note, the Claimant stresses that such instrument itself states that it is merely one of the sources of interpretation of the customary international law standard of treatment.

By contrast, the Respondent considers that the FTC Note constitutes the only source of interpretation for Article 1105. According to it, had the NAFTA Parties intended that Article 1105 be interpreted in accordance with the customary international law rules of treaty interpretation, they would not have issued the FTC Note. The fact that they did issue the note "leaves no space for the application of the customary international law rules of treaty interpretation."

The Respondent further opposes the Claimant's argument that the FTC Note is not binding on the Tribunal. It points to the wording of Article 1131(2), from which it is clear that the Tribunal cannot question the validity of the FTC Note. Moreover, it submits that the FTC Note would bind the Tribunal even in the absence of Article 1131(2), as it merely emphasizes that Article 1105 prescribes the customary international law minimum standard of treatment of aliens, an interpretation that the NAFTA Parties have always given to Article 1105....

Having established that Article 1105 must be interpreted in accordance with the FTC Note, which is binding upon it, the Tribunal will now proceed to determine the scope and content of Article 1105.

In the Claimant's view, Article 1105 obliges the Respondent to provide investments of foreign investors treatment that accords with the rules and principles established by the four sources of international law as enumerated in Article 38 of the ICJ Statute. It submits that the standard set out in Article 1105 at least includes a requirement that Canada follow customary international law. For Mesa, Article 1105 consists of several components including the duty to act in good faith; fairness and reasonableness; treatment free from arbitrary conduct; transparency; protection against abuse of rights; procedural fairness; legitimate expectations; treatment free from political motivation; and treatment free from discriminatory conduct. Further, the Claimant contends that the "full protection and security" requirement in Article 1105 "requires a host country to exercise reasonable care to protect investments against injury by private parties.

...

The Parties diverge on the content of the customary international law minimum standard of treatment found in Article 1105. Mesa submits that such standard has evolved and now has the same content and meaning as the so-called "autonomous" FET standard of modern BITs, while the Respondent holds the contrary view.

An analysis of the content of the customary international law minimum standard of treatment usually starts with a reference to the U.S.-Mexico Claims Commission's decision in *Neer*. There the Claims Commission defined the standard....

A number of Chapter 11 tribunals have since set out the content of the customary international law minimum standard of treatment in Article 1105. Broadly, two lines of decisions can be discerned: decisions questioning the relevance and applicability of the *Neer* standard, and decisions applying it with a number of important qualifications.

Tribunals following the first approach emphasize that *Neer* did not deal with investment protection, but concerned Mexico's alleged failure to carry out an effective investigation of the killing of a US citizen by armed men who were not even alleged to be acting under Mexico's control or direction. According to the *Mondev* tribunal, due to this dissimilarity in circumstances, "there is insufficient cause for assuming that provisions of bilateral investment treaties, and of NAFTA [...] are confined to the *Neer* standard of outrageous treatment [...]." Similarly, for the *ADF* tribunal "there appear[ed] no logical necessity and no concordant state practice to support the view that the *Neer* formulation is automatically extendible to the contemporary context of foreign investors and their investments by a host or recipient State." More recently, the *Bilcon* tribunal noted that the NAFTA protection was not restricted to the *Neer* requirement of outrageous conduct:

"NAFTA awards make it clear that the international minimum standard is not limited to conduct by host states that is outrageous. The contemporary minimum international standard involves a more significant measure of protection."

Tribunals adopting the second approach apply the stringent requirements of *Neer* for purposes of breaches of Article 1105. However, even under this approach, they consider that the principles of customary international law are not understood to be "frozen in amber at the time of the *Neer* decision." They observe that the *Neer* test of severity is easier to satisfy now than it was at the time of the *Neer* decision. Canada itself does not rely on the *Neer* decision; it rather invokes the articulation of the minimum standard as it was set out in *Glamis, Cargill* and *Mobil*.

In practice, these two approaches have much in common. Most importantly, they both accept that the minimum standard of treatment is an evolutionary notion, which offers greater protection to investors than that contemplated in the *Neer* decision.

Having considered the Parties' positions and the authorities cited by them, the Tribunal is of the opinion that the decision in *Waste Management II* correctly identifies the content of the customary international law minimum standard of treatment found in Article 1105. This decision was cited with approval in the Claimant's submissions. It was also quoted in the recent *Bilcon* decision, with which the Claimant agrees, in the following terms:

"The formulation of the 'general standard for Article 1105' by the *Waste Management* Tribunal is particularly influential, and a number of other tribunals have applied its formulation of the international minimum standard based on its reading of NAFTA authorities: ....

443. While no single arbitral formulation can definitively and exhaustively capture the meaning of Article 1105, the Tribunal finds this quote from *Waste Management* to be a particularly apt one. Acts or omissions constituting a breach must be of a serious nature. The *Waste Management* formulation applies intensifying adjectives to certain items—but by no means all of them—in its list of categories of potentially nonconforming conduct. The formulation includes 'grossly' unfair, 'manifest' failure of natural justice and 'complete' lack of transparency.

444. The list conveys that there is a high threshold for the conduct of a host state to rise to the level of a NAFTA Article 1105 breach, but that there is no requirement in all cases that the challenged conduct reaches the level of shocking or outrageous behaviour. The formulation also recognises the requirement for tribunals to be sensitive to the facts of each case, the potential relevance of reasonably relied-on representations by a host state, and a recognition that injustice in either procedures or outcomes can constitute a breach."

On this basis, the Tribunal considers that the following components can be said to form part of Article 1105: arbitrariness; "gross" unfairness; discrimination; "complete" lack of transparency and candor in an administrative process; lack of due process "leading to an outcome which offends judicial propriety"; and "manifest failure" of natural justice in judicial proceedings. Further, the Tribunal shares the view held by a majority of NAFTA tribunals that the failure to respect an investor's legitimate expectations in and of itself does not constitute a breach of Article 1105, but is an element to take into account when assessing whether other components of the standard are breached.

The Tribunal disagrees with the Claimant's submissions that the "autonomous" fair and equitable treatment provisions in other treaties impose additional requirements on Canada beyond those deriving from the minimum standard. As was already discussed above, the FTC Note is clear that the Tribunal must apply the customary international law standard of the international minimum standard of treatment, and nothing else. There is thus no scope for autonomous standards to impose additional requirements on the NAFTA Parties. This was the conclusion in *Bilcon* as well.

The threshold for a breach of Article 1105 is also relevant to the Tribunal's analysis. The Claimant does not appear to dispute—and rightly so—that the threshold for Article 1105 is high. Indeed, the three NAFTA Parties concur on this issue and other Chapter 11 tribunals have come to the same conclusion.

Finally, when defining the content of Article 1105 one should further take into consideration that international law requires tribunals to give a good level of deference to the manner in which a state regulates its internal affairs....

In reviewing this alleged breach, the Tribunal must bear in mind the deference which NAFTA Chapter 11 tribunals owe a state when it comes to assessing how to regulate and manage its affairs. This deference notably applies to the decision to enter into investment agreements. As noted by the *S.D. Myers* tribunal, "[w]hen interpreting and applying the 'minimum standard', a Chapter Eleven tribunal does not have an open-ended mandate to second-guess government decision-making." The tribunal in *Bilcon*, a case which the Claimant has cited with approval, also held that "[t]he imprudent exercise of discretion or even outright mistakes do not, as a rule, lead to a breach of the international minimum standard."[40]

4 The NAFTA Parties Have Acted Defensively—and Dubiously—to Narrow the Scope and to Constrain the Meaning of Article 1105(1)

In my view, the 2001 interpretation placed on Article 1105(1) by the FTC is open not only open to question, but to questions. The three NAFTA Parties—having belatedly perceived that a trilateral treaty runs more than one way and that each might be sued, and offended by the terms and tenor of the Award in *Pope & Talbot*—acted defensively in 2001 to narrow the scope and to constrain

---

40 *Mesa Power Group LLC v. Canada*, PCA Case No. 2012–17, Award, March 24, 2016, at ¶¶ 468–484, 495–506, 553 (footnotes omitted).

the meaning of Article 1105(1). Their action gives rise to the following challenging points.

Not only the text of Article 1105(1), but the whole of the extensive, detailed, extraordinarily complex text of NAFTA, does not contain the words "customary international law" or "alien" but does provide, more than once, for the application of "international law".

Since the adoption of the Statute of the Permanent Court of International Justice in 1920, it has been universally accepted that its specification of the sources of international law is authoritative: international conventions recognized by the contesting States; international custom, as evidence of a general practice accepted as law; the general principles of law; and as subsidiary means for determination of the rules of law, judicial decisions and the teachings of the most highly qualified publicists of the various nations. A reference to "international law" is not understood to equate with or be confined to only one of its four sources, customary international law.

The *travaux préparatoires* of NAFTA, insofar as ultimately produced by Canada, and set out and analyzed by its then senior related official, Meg Kinnear, show that none of the more-than-forty renderings of what became Article 1105(1) referred to "customary" international law; they uniformly referred rather to "international law". Under Article 32 of the Vienna Convention on the Law of Treaties, recourse in this case to NAFTA's *travaux* may be had because the meaning of Article 1105(1) is "ambiguous". Were Article 1105(1) not ambiguous, there would have been little scope or reason for the issuance of the 2001 interpretation. Nor would the diverse interpretations of the 2001 interpretation have ensued.

If the NAFTA Parties meant Article 1105(1) to be interpreted to mean not what it expressly provides, "international law", but one element of international law, namely, "customary international law," they would have so specified, as they did not in the text of NAFTA or any of its 40-odd preparatory versions but only subsequently in the 2001 interpretation and otherwise. The failure in more than forty renditions of Article 1105(1) to speak of "customary international law" rather than "international law" indeed belies the verity of the 2001 "interpretation".

The implausibility of the 2001 interpretation is deepened by the espousal by each of the NAFTA Parties of the *Neer* Award as the key to the minimum standard for the treatment of aliens and hence to the standard for the interpretation of Article 1105(1). Objectively viewed, *Neer* teaches nothing for the contemporaneous interpretation of NAFTA. *Neer* does not concern "fair and equitable" treatment of investors or investment; it rather addressed a claim for denial of justice by the Mexican judiciary for its inadequate investigation of the murder of a U.S. national. It made the two abbreviated holdings for which it is well known: first, that the propriety of governmental acts should be put to the test of international standards; second, that the treatment of "an alien" should amount to an "outrage" etc. These holdings referred to no State practice whatsoever nor to other sources of international law apart from a few academic works. The first of these holdings was fundamental and valid, though hardly seminal (it was a central premise of the earlier *Norwegian Shipowners Award*); the second is a dated distraction exhumed by the NAFTA Parties because it suits their defensive purposes.

The NAFTA Parties contend that the awards of arbitral tribunals interpreting bilateral investments treaties are not a source of State practice—but that the *Neer* Award is an authority that today governs the interpretation of Article 1105(1). This contention spawns its inherent refutation. If indeed arbitral awards cannot be weighed in finding customary international law, why is it that the *Neer* Award is not only weighed but determined to outweigh a cascade of subsequent arbitral awards? *Neer* could not and did not interpret NAFTA. It did not concern the treatment of foreign investors or investment. As aptly recognized in *Mondev*, *Neer* was adopted in 1926, when the standing of the individual (and corporation) in international law were, procedurally and substantively, far less developed than they have today become to be. *Neer* is argued to be key to the meaning of the minimum standard of treatment of aliens, but the very concept of the minimum standard in the treatment of aliens and their property is hardly found in contemporary international law. It does not appear in the draft Articles on State Responsibility of the International Law Commission produced after two decades of learned and searching work. It is perplexing that the Tribunal in *Glamis Gold* swallowed whole the argumentation of the United States, going so far as to state that, "because of the difficulty in proving a change in custom, [*Neer*] effectively freezes the protections provided for in this provision at the 1926 conception of egregiousness".[41] *Glamis Gold* holds that: "The fundamentals of the *Neer* standard thus still apply today: to violate the customary international law minimum standard of treatment codified in Article 1105 of the NAFTA, an act must be sufficiently egregious and shocking—a gross denial of justice, manifest arbitrariness, blatant unfairness, a complete lack of due process, evident discrimination, or a manifest lack of reasons—so as to fall below accepted international standards and constitute a breach of Article 1105(1).... The standard for finding a breach of the customary

---

41   *Glamis Gold*, supra n. 35, ¶ 604.

international law minimum standard of treatment therefore remains as stringent as it was under *Neer*....[42]

In my view, the foregoing holdings of *Glamis Gold* are profoundly unconvincing for the reasons set out in *Mondev, ADF, Merrill & Ring*, and *Bilcon*, as well as in the quoted opinion of Judge Sir Robert Jennings. While the 2001 interpretation binds a NAFTA Tribunal, the baggage of the NAFTA Parties that has been collected by them in support of that interpretation does not bind a NAFTA Tribunal. That baggage is not part of the interpretation; it has no inherent standing, and so much of that baggage, and the awards that sustain it, is inapposite and unpersuasive. A NAFTA Tribunal—not to speak of an objective analyst—is free to put *Neer* back in its dated, obsolete, irrelevant box. It is free to discount the arbitral awards that sustain the thrust of *Neer* and rather to follow the arbitral awards—notably, *Mondev, ADF, Waste Management II, Merrill & Ring*, and *Bilcon*—that accept and espouse a modern, enlightened perspective.

Because the premise of the NAFTA Parties' extrapolations from *Neer*, and the holdings in respect of it by *Cargill, Glamis Gold* and allied awards, are unsound—because *Neer* is irrelevant—the structure that the NAFTA Parties have erected on the foundation of *Neer* collapses. There is no persuasive reason to take *Neer* as the interpretive key to the meaning of customary international law in respect of the treatment of foreign investors and investment. There is no burden on investors to prove that customary international law has changed since *Neer* by pleading multiple and successive incidents of State practice. It is quite enough to show the modern development of State practice through citations of the official statements of States, as above; through the provisions of two to three thousand bilateral investment treaties that prescribe fair and equitable treatment; through the acknowledgement of the United States in its pleadings that NAFTA is meant to provide a real level of protection of the foreign investor and investment; and through the analyses and holdings of arbitral awards, most notably, *Mondev, Merrill & Ring*, and *Bilcon*.

A State's "arbitrary" measures that infringe a sense of "reasonableness, fairness and equity" suffice to violate Article 1105(1). Those measures need not be "manifestly" arbitrary. "Manifestly" means "obviously", that which is "evident, clear, plain".[43] If an arbitral tribunal, on analyzing the facts and the law of the case, concludes that the measures of a State as applied to an investor or

---

42   *Id.*, ¶ 616. See also, Jan Paulsson & Georgios Petrochilos, *Neer-Ly Misled*, 22 FOREIGN INV. L.J. 242 (2007) and Judge Stephen M. Schwebel, *Is Neer Far from Fair and Equitable?*, 27 ARB. INT'L 555 (2011).

43   WEBSTER'S NEW UNABRIDGED DICTIONARY 1095.

investment are "arbitrary", why is that insufficient to violate international law including Article 1105(1)? Is not the adjective "manifestly" hyperbole in the vein of *Neer* designed to shield States that transgress international law?

CHAPTER 17

Conflict of Laws: a Recipe for Transformative Contributions

Erin O'Hara O'Connor

Lea Brilmayer has been an incredibly prolific and influential scholar in the area of Conflict of Laws, and her contributions will long endure. To be sure, Lea didn't invent an approach to resolving Conflicts matters that was widely adopted in any particular jurisdiction. Nor has she yet served as a Reporter to any of the Restatement projects on the subject. When it comes to the area of legal reform, other law professors take center stage.

However, when viewed as a matter of foreseeing and contributing to an intellectual understanding of the role of Conflict of Laws, its inherent tensions, and the contributions of other fields to this understanding, no scholar's work is as broad reaching as Lea Brilmayer's. Equally important, Lea has an uncommon understanding of the practical effects of competing treatments of conflict of laws. This blending of theoretic contribution to conceptual understanding with the practical consequences of resolutions forces other scholars to follow Lea's work and to take it very seriously. In the process, that work has transformed the way conflicts scholars think about their subject. Moreover, her dedication to the field and to furthering its understanding creates enormous value for all students of the conflict of laws.[1]

This essay discusses just a few of Lea's many contributions in the area with the hope of convincing the non-conflicts reader of Lea's very substantial talents. Section 1 briefly describes Lea's recognition of the importance of interdisciplinary tools to understanding the subject. Section 2 outlines Lea's use of legal reasoning to further our conceptual understanding of conflicts doctrine and to critique popular conflicts proposals. Section 3 focuses on Lea's ultimate commitment to finding pragmatic solutions to conflicts problems.

---

1 Lea's casebook in the area, developed originally by James Martin but under Lea's able leadership for more than two decades, is the best-seller. BRILMAYER, GOLDSMITH & O'HARA O'CONNOR, CONFLICT OF LAWS: CASES AND MATERIALS (7th ed. 2015).

© KONINKLIJKE BRILL NV, LEIDEN, 2019 | DOI:10.1163/9789004316539_018

1   The Importance of Interdisciplinary Tools

Lea's work has been very important to the conceptual understanding of conflict of laws. Recognizing that the area had been woefully undertheorized, Lea undertook to provide it interdisciplinary grounding. Several other conflicts scholars also have contributed to this endeavor, but none have undertaken to ground conflicts principles on such a broad range of philosophical, political, economic and game theoretic principles. This combination lends considerable strength to Lea's work.

    Lea understood very early that Conflict of Laws primarily engaged itself with the allocation of sovereign authority. As a conceptual matter, she understood that any justification of sovereign authority must ultimately contend with both philosophical and political theory principles. Consider, for example, the insights from democratic theory that she brought to bear in her critique of interest analysis as well as the constitutional treatment of both intrastate and interstate discrimination more broadly.[2] Other scholars of democratic theory both inside and outside legal scholarship had focused on the right to vote as a justification for the assertion of coercive state authority over the individual. Lea showed the shortcomings of that rationale; it assumes that duties extend from the right to vote rather than observing that the right to vote is an important procedural right that extends from the state's general duty to govern fairly. Citizens have rights to participate in the shaping of the laws and the values they reflect, while outsiders do not. But when it comes to sharing in the benefits of those laws once created, democratic theory can justify that sharing even for nonresidents based on the same general duty to govern fairly. In the case of nonresidents, Lea relies on a quid pro quo theory of having undertaken the responsibilities or burdens of state law while within the borders. The problem with interest analysis, Lea points out, is that it forces nonresidents to bear the burdens of state law while denying the corresponding benefits. The sharing and shaping framework can be used to help sort permissible from impermissible forms of state discrimination. Ever more important, was Lea's ability to identify the connection between conflict of laws and political theory.[3]

    In *Justifying International Acts*,[4] Lea explored insights from Rawls, Nozick, H.L.A. Hart, and numerous other philosophers in an attempt to develop a

---

2   Lea Brilmayer, *Carolene, Conflicts, and the Fate of the "Insider-Outsider"*, 134 U. PA. L. REV. 1291 (1986); Lea Brilmayer, *Shaping and Sharing in Democratic Theory: Toward a Political Philosophy of Interstate Equality*, 15 FLA. ST. L. REV. 389 (1987).
3   *See* Brilmayer, *Shaping and Sharing, supra* at 391 ("[i]n short, the law of interstate relations can be recast as a question of political theory").
4   LEA BRILMAYER, JUSTIFYING INTERNATIONAL ACTS (1989).

coherent normative account of at least the limits of the exercise of sovereign authority across national borders. Those insights were then tailored to apply to the problem of choice of law across both state and national boundaries in *Rights, Fairness, and Choice of Law*.[5] This exploration led Lea to conclude that modern conflicts were too quick to reject deontological approaches to choice of law, and that their rejection of individual rights led to unjustifiable choice-of-law results. She has developed a negative-rights-based approach to creating constraints on choice-of-law outcomes that focuses on the burdens rather than benefits of state laws. In the process, she showed how interest analysis and intuitive notions of fairness can conflict.

In *Liberalism, Community, and State Borders*,[6] Lea identified an interesting parallel between the exercise of jurisdiction and debates within political philosophy. Specifically, the debate in political philosophy involves whether state coercive authority is justified according to communitarian principles, which focus on the inculcation of collective and shared norms and desired ends, or instead by liberal principles, which honor personal autonomy and thus justify state coercion only to prevent harm to others. Principles of general jurisdiction, or the application of state law whenever a party is a member of the community, strengthen communitarianism. In contrast, principles of specific jurisdiction, or of the law of the place of the harm, fit more in line with liberal principles. Lea attempted to use these parallels to argue that perhaps in practice communitarianism and liberalism can coexist peacefully.[7]

Because the allocation of sovereign authority is often left to the sovereigns themselves, Lea has drawn many connections between positive political theory and conflict of laws. She uses the work of Alfred Hirschman[8] to draw parallels between forward vs. backward looking choice-of law methodologies and differing political devices used to influence legal rules.[9] And she draws on political economy to evaluate the institutions that could promulgate choice-of-law principles, including courts, legislatures, and restatements.[10]

---

5   Lea Brilmayer, *Rights, Fairness, and Choice of Law*, 98 YALE L.J. 1277 (1989); *see also* LEA
        BRILMAYER, CONFLICT OF LAWS: FOUNDATIONS AND FUTURE DIRECTIONS, Ch. 5
        (2d ed. 1995).

6   Lea Brilmayer, *Liberalism, Community, and State Borders*, 41 DUKE L.J. 1 (1991).

7   *Id.* at 3. Although these connections illustrate Lea's amazing ability to draw connections
        between interstate procedure and political theory, both her analogy and her hope for
        peaceful coexistence are difficult to establish when explored vigorously, as illustrated by
        the tentative language used in the article.

8   ALFRED HIRSCHMAN, EXIT, VOICE AND LOYALTY (1970).

9   BRILMAYER, CONFLICT OF LAWS, *supra* note 5, at 251–52.

10   *Id.*, ch. 4.

In order to work well, choice-of-law methodologies must not only seem fair to individuals, but they must also appeal to the interests of sovereigns generally, otherwise sovereign assent and coordination to the principles would not be possible. Because choice of law entails a coordination game, Lea has used game theory, especially as developed in the field of international relations, to help identify potential gains from coordination as well as possible coordination mechanisms.[11] In that analysis, she recognizes the important but far too often overlooked connection between choice-of-law principles and their effects on primary behavior.[12] Calling on basic principles of law and economics, Lea proposes a cost-benefit analysis of the extent to which any particular choice-of-law rule might effectuate states' potentially competing policy goals.

Lea Brilmayer also understands that precisely because choice of law appeared to be a dry and boring procedural question, a prevailing approach to resolving these problems could easily imbed substantive and political biases. She astutely intuited that interest analysis would create systemic biases in favor of residents, forum law, and recovery,[13] all of which subsequently were shown to be empirically present.[14]

2   Lea's Signature Gift: Conceptual Legal Reasoning

Although Lea has supported and substantially contributed to the infusion of other fields into conflict of laws, she is perhaps even better known for using the tools of legal reasoning to add conceptual rigor to how we think about the field. In making these conceptual legal arguments, Lea uses her strength to draw parallels across subject matter. In the interdisciplinary context, those parallels are drawn between non-legal and legal principles. When conducting conceptual methodology, her parallels are drawn between two legal principles. Examples of this technique and the important insights they have produced are far too numerous to exhaustively explore here. Instead, a small number of illustrations are described. In critiquing traditional interest analysis, for example, Lea has drawn a critical distinction between objective and subjective

---

11   *Id.*

12   *Id.* at 199–205.

13   Lea Brilmayer, *Interest Analysis and the Myth of Legislative Intent*, 78 MICH. L. REV. 392 (1980).

14   Michael Solimine, *An Economic and Empirical Analysis of Choice of Law*, GA. L. REV. 49 (1989); Patrick Borchers, *The Choice-of-Law Revolution: An Empirical Study*, 49 WASH. & LEE L. REV. 357 (1992); Stuart Thiel, *Choice of Law and the Home-Court Advantage: Evidence*, 2 AM. L. & ECON. Rev. 291 (2000).

determinations of state interests and argued compellingly that using an objective test to determine the interests of another state constitutes a misuse of judicial authority,[15] whereas subjective tests, although more defensible, deny private parties the benefits of predictability.[16] In the area of international conflicts, she has used these tools to equally compellingly argue that at least conceptually, there should be constitutional constraints on the extraterritorial application of U.S. federal law.[17]

Another conceptual strength of Lea's is her ability to dissemble a theory or approach by taking it very seriously on its own grounds. In *Interest Analysis and the Myth of Legislative Intent*,[18] for example, she shows that interest analysts' claim that their approach to choice of law reflects legislative intent is false and that the approach is ultimately grounded in metaphysical assumptions. The irony in this conclusion, Lea explains, is that Currie used the metaphysical assumptions grounding the First Restatement as a primary argument for jettisoning it.[19] Along the way, she demonstrates the ultimate logical impossibility of interest analysts' defenses of interest analysis. In a separate article, she showes that Currie's assertions that interest analysis was essentially a method of gleaning legislative intent could not be squared with his assertion that courts should never look to the choice-of-law principles of other states when resolving conflicts problems.[20]

In this and other articles, Lea exposes the folly of claiming that the Supreme Court's use of state interests on constitutional scrutiny of choice of law is equivalent to interest analysis, for multiple reasons.[21] First, this equivalence would functionally disable the courts from ever scrutinizing interest analysis decisions, because the test for constitutionality would then turn on whatever interest the state produced to justify application of forum law. Indeed, if the question was ultimately answered by reference to a state court's interpretation of the reach of state law, no federal question would present itself for review by the Supreme Court. Second, the end result would be contrary to common

---

15   Lea Brilmayer, *The Other State's Interests*, 24 CORNELL INT'L L.J. 233 (1991).

16   BRILMAYER, CONFLICT OF LAWS, *supra* note 5, at 123.

17   Lea Brilmayer, *The Extraterritorial Application of American Law: A Methodological and Constitutional Appraisal*, 50 Law and Contemp. Probs. 11 (Summer 1987); Lea Brilmayer & Charles Norchi, *Federal Extraterritoriality and Fifth Amendment Due Process*, 105 HARV. L. REV. 1217 (1992).

18   *Supra* note 13.

19   *Id.* at 392.

20   Lea Brilmayer, *Methods and Objectives in the Conflict of Laws: A Challenge*, 35 MERCER L. REV. 555 (1984).

21   *See also* Lea Brilmayer, *Governmental Interest Analysis: A House Without Foundations*, 46 OHIO ST. L.J. 459 (1985).

understandings of the role of constitutional law. Specifically, the equivalence constitutionalizes a choice-of-law approach that relies on parochial self-interest to the exclusion of party claims of unfair surprise or sister-state pleas for comity. After establishing that the state interest component of the constitutional test could not sensibly be equivalent to the state interests embedded in interest analysis, Lea offers her own resolution of the state interest dilemma by proposing that states must be able to demonstrate substantive regulatory interests that implicate a contact with the state in order to constitutionally apply forum law.[22] In defending this proposal, Lea returns to her exceptional skill of drawing parallels between the choice-of-law test and the constitutional tests for personal jurisdiction, judgment recognition as well as for commerce, property and contracts clause issues. By weaving together Court and commentator reasoning from each of these areas, Lea convinces the reader that her proposal fits quite naturally into the existing jurisprudential landscape.

3   An Ultimate Commitment to the Pragmatic

Lea is undoubtedly brilliant at identifying fascinating intellectual puzzles and seeming incongruities in the law, and she quite ably identifies the theoretical literatures that can inform our understanding of conflict of laws. But it is important to note that she is equally motivated by a desire to resolve actual problems and legal issues. For example, in one of her articles on shaping and sharing, Lea explains:

> interstate relations is a fertile field for applied political philosophy. The subject is not only philosophically interesting, it also presents a rare opportunity to put basic philosophical insights to good practical use.[23]

Lea's writings suggest that the fundamental purpose of theoretical and conceptual exploration is to ensure that the on-the-ground decisions are as sound as possible. In the process of dismantling the foundations of interest analysis for example, she states:

> ... most importantly, perhaps, there is a *need* for a theoretical foundation in novel or controversial cases if one is to think intelligently about what

---

22   Lea Brilmayer, *Legitimate Interests in Multistate Problems: As Between State and Federal Law*, 79 MICH. L. REV. 1315 (1981).

23   Brilmayer, *Shaping and Sharing, supra* note 2, at 393.

one wishes to do.... It just does not seem that one can really apply a choice of law analysis sensibly without knowing the underlying reasoning.[24]

Moreover, in offering a solution to the question of state interests that satisfy constitutional scrutiny of state choice-of-law decisions, Lea devises a solution that can prove satisfactory on both conceptual and pragmatic grounds. Specifically, by insisting that states justify application of forum law by reference to substantive domestic policies that are tied to domestic contacts, Lea's proposed test hinders states' abilities to invent interests for the purposes of justifying overreaching into other states. Thus, she demonstrates a profound understanding of the potential gamesmanship embedded in essentially self-regulating choice-of-law policies. As an added bonus, her test avoids the unrealistic formality of requiring states to document policy goals in their legislative history or otherwise.[25]

Indeed, Lea's more recent scholarship increasingly focuses on the pragmatic resolution of the choice-of-law problem. Conceptual and theoretical exploration are furthered by paring down the problem to one or a small number of factors. But over time, Lea has come to see that single-factored approaches to choice-of-law inevitably lead to seemingly arbitrary, unjust, or simply nonsensical results. As a result, she increasingly embraces multifactored approaches to choice of law that enable a full consideration of potentially competing factors.[26]

This pragmatic approach does not indicate that Lea has turned her back on the power of conceptual perspective as the means to fundamentally understanding this subject area. Rather, it illustrates her ultimate ends—to aid in the production of sound and coherent choices for producing sensible results. Lea's enormous influence in conflict of laws results from both her means and her ends. She doesn't carry a toolbag just to show off her clever offerings; she actually uses them to illuminate and to offer solutions to solving or at least improving a very complex set of issues. Although Lea's scholarly influence spans multiple subject areas, all conflicts scholars hope she will continue to help guide the way we conceive and navigate this curious and confounding field.

---

24   See Brilmayer, *supra* note 13, at 461.

25   *Supra* note 22, at 1340–41.

26   Lea Brilmayer, *Hard Cases, Single Factor Theories, and a Second Look at the Restatement 2D of Conflicts*, 2015 U. ILL. L. REV. 1969; Lea Brilmayer & Rachael Anglin, *Choice of Law Theory and the Metaphysics of the Stand-Alone Trigger*, 95 IOWA L. REV. 1125 (2010); Lea Brilmayer, *What I Like Most About the Restatement (Second) of Conflicts, and Why It Should Not Be Thrown Out With the Bathwater*, 110 AJIL UNBOUND 144 (2016).

Index

Printed in the United States
By Bookmasters